D0094955

Portals to Hell

Portals to Hell

Military Prisons
of the Civil War

Lonnie R. Speer

STACKPOLE
BOOKS

Copyright © 1997 by Stackpole Books

Published by
STACKPOLE BOOKS
5067 Ritter Road
Mechanicsburg, PA 17055

Printed in the United States of America

First Edition

10   9   8   7   6   5   4   3   2   1

Library of Congress Cataloging-in-Publication Data

Speer, Lonnie R.
    Portals to hell : military prisons of the Civil War / Lonnie R. Speer.
        p.   cm.
    Includes bibliographical references (p.   ) and index.
    ISBN 0-8117-0334-7
    1. United States—History—Civil War, 1861–1865—Prisoners and prisons.   2. Prisoners
of war—United States—History—19th century.   3. Prisoners of war—Confederate
States of America—History.   I. Title.

E615.S65   1997
973.7'71—dc21   97-2719
                                                                                                            CIP

To Mark, Lori, and Andy,
who suffered through the frustrations
of getting this accomplished more than anyone else,
and
to Lloyd Rex,
who couldn't wait for it to become a reality.

CONTENTS

ACKNOWLEDGMENTS

I t has become a cliché, but no less true, that the writing of a book such as this could not be accomplished without the help, interest, and encouragement of others. I am greatly indebted to a lot of people who, without even knowing me except through a letter, a phone call, or a brief meeting over a library counter, went out of their way to assist me. They located rare books, old magazine articles, photos, long-forgotten information I had once heard about or found a brief reference to. Or they "knew someone who knew someone" who could provide me with the information. Many times, I was left in awe over their ability and eagerness to help.

My many humble thanks go out to the courteous and helpful staff of the Library of Congress, especially Fred Bauman and John R. Sellers, who seemed to enjoy being able to show me unusual and seldom used resource material and rare contemporary sketch books in the library's holdings; the staff of the National Archives, who showed great interest in directing me to many previously neglected sources they possessed; the Manuscripts, Rare Book and Photo Department staff of the Wilson Library at the University of North Carolina at Chapel Hill; the staff of the Pack Memorial Library in Asheville, North Carolina, Stephen E. Massengill of the North Carolina Division of Archives and History, for his immense help and interest in locating some hard-to-find photos; Karen Podzamsky of the Filger Library in Minonk, Illinois, for her diligent efforts and interest in locating some rare historical information for me; Rose Huffman of the Kansas City Public Library, for her special efforts in locating some very old and little known information; Charles E. Brown of the St. Louis Mercantile Library Association, the oldest private library west of the Mississippi, which has a vast holding of contemporary Civil War POW books; Frank Jewell of the Chicago Historical Society; Mrs. Bleecker Harrison of the St. Mary's County,

Maryland, Historical Society; Norma Grivich, formerly of Texas, for information she and her friends provided; Randy W. Hackenburg of the U.S. Army
Military History Institute, for meticulously going through the files there to locate
some very good and seldom used photos; Scott S. Sheads of the National Park
Service; Andy Kraushaar, Reference Archivist and Visual Materials Archivist of
the State Historical Society of Wisconsin, who searched their files for some rare
and seldom-seen material; Daniel T. Whiteman, Director of the Rock Island
Arsenal Museum; Nelson Morgan of the Hargrett Rare Book and Manuscript
Library at the University of Georgia; Randy L. Goss, Archivist Supervisor of the
Delaware State Archives; Angela S. Anthony, Assistant Curator of the Prints
and Photographs Division of the Maryland Historical Society; and Chris Steele,
Curator of Photographs of the Massachusetts Historical Society; Virginia
Buchanan, Archivist of the Smith County, Texas, Historical Society; Cynthia
Mathews of the Chicago Historical Society; Pat Maurer, Librarian of the
Bostonian Society; Martha L. Bennett of the Fort Delaware Society; Martha
Utterback at the Daughters' of the Republic of Texas Library; John Anderson
in the Archives Division of the Texas State Library, for going out of his way to
locate a number of sources for me; Mr. James I. Robertson, Jr., for his advice
and guidance; and a big thanks to Sylvia Frank for her help in the beginning
and her interest and encouragement ever since.

My thanks also go out to the following for the information they provided
and/or for giving me complete access to their very precious family letters and
historical papers: Niles Schuh of Florida; Dorothy E. Kelly of Knoxville; the late
Buford Gotto of Brentwood, Tennessee; Lee and LeEleanor Tomberlain of Nashville; Larose A. Wynne of Memphis; Joel Jackson of Jackson, Tennessee; Dom
Tedford of Huntingdon, Pennsylvania; David and Beebee Watson; John and
Debby Birchfield; Danny and Pam Slagle; Bob Milner; Earl Waldrep Jr.; Hugh
Furan; Dr. Robert and Pat Fulbright; Evalee Fulbright; and the late Flora Mae
Fulbright Ward. In addition, my appreciation goes to the following for their
interest and constant encouragement throughout this ordeal, which kept me
going: Randy and Merlinda S., Glen and Betty S., John and Debby, David and
Beebee, Danny and Pam, Hugh and Jeanette, Charles and Fran Dewberry,
Len and Carol Amato, Evelyn Frizzell, Bob and Pat, Mandi S., Liz Schlotte,
Ralph and Alice Schiefelbein, Charlene, Josh and Greg Larrabee, John Pavone,
Amy Saunooke, Jennifer Nye, Steve and Lenna Bucy, Pansy Hooper, Brenda
Cartwright, Doug Grimm and Cindy Pickelsimer, Greg Goodman, Tommy
Bright, Kris Hargis, Mike Burnette, Jerry Fuller, Chris Ryan, David Revis, Jim
Neff, Helen Haynes, Ginny Wells, June Rogers, Sue Mac, Betty Budd, Al Ellis,
Phillip McCloud, Geoff Morrison, Dave and Kathy DeGonia, Tom and Linda
Jones, Jim Kempf, Gary and Kay Quint, Rich Wheeler, Rich Franz, and especially
Melba Avenido, for her endearing praise, gentle encouragement, and continued
interest.

I also owe a great debt of gratitude to my editors William C. Davis and Michelle Myers for their patience and guidance during this long, tedious process and for being able to recognize merit in my original manuscript. Without their help and that of all the others mentioned, this could never have been accomplished. I extend my most sincere thanks to you all.

INTRODUCTION

P ossession of the Cumberland Gap in the southeast corner of Kentucky exchanged hands as many as three times during the American Civil War. It was a strategic location because it provided a natural passageway through the rugged, mountainous region where Kentucky, Tennessee, and Virginia meet.

In August 1863, it was again under Confederate control and occupied on the Tennessee side by, among others, the 62nd North Carolina Regiment. While stationed there, thirty-three-year-old Sergeant Solomon F. Cook, Company G, took time to write to his wife, Martha, back home.

"We are well fortified here," he reported, "and can defend ourselves [against] far superior forces. If they come here you will hear of them getting hurt."[1]

No doubt Cook was serious when he wrote those words on August 23, but several days later, on September 9, he probably wasn't quite so confident when he found himself crouched behind some breastworks as a loud Yankee cheer went up. Cannons of both sides were pounding the air with a deep, thunderous roar and shot, shell, and cannister seemed to be hurling from every direction. As dirt rained down around him, Cook peered over the breastworks just in time to see the enemy rushing his position. Frantically, he stood up and began firing and loading as quickly as he could, but the enemy stormed over the works and began hand-to-hand combat. Cook repeatedly fended off the Union forces but he was finally overpowered. Reluctantly, he gave up to become a prisoner of war.[2]

After being marched behind the lines and then to the nearest railhead, Cook, among a group of other prisoners, was placed on a train bound for the Camp Douglas Military Prison in Chicago. There, he was confined for over a year.[3]

Solomon Cook, a strong, able-bodied soldier who had survived more than a year of war fighting bravely and fiercely on the battlefield, was unable to survive one of the Civil War's military prisons. He died at Camp Douglas December 11, 1864.[4]

Cook was just one of the more than 674,000 soldiers taken captive during the Civil War. It amounted to nearly 16 percent of the total enlistments; more than in any other war, before or since.[5]

In the beginning of the war, most of the captives were released on parole in the field but, later, nearly 410,000 were held in over 150 different compounds throughout the country for periods ranging anywhere from a few days to several years. These institutions were established all along the East Coast as far north as Boston, as far south as Dry Tortugas Island off Key West, Florida, and as far west as Fort Riley, Kansas, and Fort Craig, New Mexico. They began as prisons or holding facilities but, with few exceptions, quickly became nothing more than American concentration camps. Prisoners were crammed into them with complete disregard of capacity limits, hygiene, nutrition, or sanitation needs. Within a short time neither government could cope with the problems created by such a high concentration of people in such small areas or the lack of coordination within the prison system. In the end, more than 56,000 prisoners of war died in confinement, and many more were in poor or failing health when finally released.[6]

Neither side was more at fault than the other. The number of deaths in Confederate prisons totaled 30,218, or a little more than 15 percent of those incarcerated. In Federal prisons, there were 25,796 deaths, or slightly more than 12 percent. Although propaganda during and after the war convinced many people that the Confederate prisons were much worse than those maintained by the Union, a close examination reveals there were few differences. If Union soldiers were stricken with fear upon entering the gates of Andersonville Prison, Confederates were shocked upon learning that they were headed for Fort Delaware or Elmira prisons.[7]

The death rate in all the prisons amounted to nearly 13 percent of the total confined. In comparison, those who remained on the battlefield fared much better; based on available figures there, only 5 percent of the total enlistments of both sides were killed.[8]

When the remaining prisoners were finally released at the end of the war, they were convinced they had suffered through a conscious government effort to reduce their ranks by starvation and disease. At the same time, the public accused both sides of having used the prisoners as pawns to be sacrificed.

In reality, though, the high mortality rate in the prisons was never intended by either side. There was never any organized effort by one government or the other to eliminate its enemy through concentration camps. The closest either of the two came was when the Union instituted retaliation measures against its prisoners by reducing rations. The Confederate government, on the other hand, did quite the opposite. Early in the war the Confederate Congress passed an act specifying that rations furnished for prisoners of war would be the same in quantity and quality as those furnished for enlisted men in the Confederate army. Unfortunately, the Confederacy began having problems providing food even for its own troops soon afterward.[9]

Many modern-day historians attribute what happened to the POWs to the ignorance of the times, including the indifference of many of the prison commandants and the public's general lack of knowledge at the time regarding nutritional needs, proper sanitary requirements, and proper medical care. Those problems were then compounded by shortages of food, shelter, and medical supplies, as well as delays in their delivery when they were obtained.

Granted, these were major factors, but there is ample evidence to suggest additional reasons for the prisons taking such a fearful toll. The lack of proper preparation for war played a major part. History had proven time and again that it is inevitable some portion of those involved in an armed conflict will eventually fall captive to their opponent. And it was apparent to both sides that the events of the winter of 1860–61 were slowly leading to war. After all, because of the growing differences between the agricultural South and the industrialized North, a number of Southern politicians had argued for secession as early as 1848, while Lincoln made no secret of the fact he was determined to preserve the Union at all costs. Both North and South remained earnest in their beliefs. When South Carolina finally seceded from the Union and the other southern states quickly followed, one of the initial steps after uniting among themselves and organizing the Confederacy was to begin raising an army. By all appearances, they realized that the next step was war. Jefferson Davis even mentioned it himself soon after his election. The Federal government realized it too, and it reluctantly began moving its already-established army to occupy various strategic points in and around the South and along its coast, but cautioned commanders to do nothing that would ignite the conflict.[10]

Still, neither side made any preparations for taking or confining prisoners. There were no efforts to organize a system until the situation was so far out of control that catch-up measures had to be initiated. By then, it was too late: The lack of centralized control and the congested conditions had produced such nightmarish problems of feeding, housing, and medical care that they would never be overcome.

The failure to plan ahead often condemned thousands of POWs to suffering. Treatment of Civil War prisoners proved to be no different from any previous war. The sick and wounded were treated appallingly during the Crimean War, and English prisoners suffered severely in the Black Hole of Calcutta. During the Napoleonic wars, English prisoners languished in an internment camp at Verdun, while Napoleon's soldiers suffered just as badly at Liverpool Gaol and Norman Cross.

Until the Civil War, the American Revolution caused the most controversy in this country. Eventually, both wars paralleled one another in many ways: Both were fought for independence, both included cases of brother fighting against brother and father against son, and both created bitter controversy regarding the treatment of POWs held by each side.

In the Revolution, the British confined their POWs in the hulls of ships anchored offshore. One such prisoner, held on the prison ship *Jersey*, wrote in August 1781 that up to eleven prisoners died each day on the ship while two hundred more sick and dying remained confined. The Colonists held their prisoners in such places as the Newgate Prison in Connecticut, which was nothing more than an old abandoned copper mine with a perpendicular fifty-foot-deep shaft as its main entrance. There, English prisoners were confined in dark, dripping, noxious underground galleries. Before long, Newgate became infamous to the British, but other holding facilities used by the Colonists were just as bad. The Continental government used whatever structures were available in addition to their jails during the war. Some of them included the Old Sugar House on Liberty Street in New York City, along with several of the city's churches. Another notorious hellhole used during this war was Waxhaws Prison in South Carolina. Like Andersonville of the Civil War, Waxhaws was well known for its brutal conditions during the Revolutionary War. These places often resulted in thousands of prisoners on both sides suffering through the same type of poor food, crowded conditions, and vermin as those who had suffered during the world's previous wars. In the end, many hundreds on both sides died of disease, starvation, and cold.[11]

The Civil War, however, was unique in two aspects: All POWs held by both sides were Americans, and the number held at any one time was higher than in any other war. The overwhelming number held, in itself, would be responsible for much suffering and death.

But if it was simple overcrowding, the lack of planning, and the ignorance of the times, we could reasonably expect conditions in POW camps to improve in post-Civil War conflicts. Yet, over half a century later, Americans would be horrified at the stories of the Turks' treatment of prisoners during World War I and the Japanese treatment of them in World War II. Ingolstadt would become a notorious German prisoner of war camp in World War I as would Colditz in World War II. Stalag-Luft III became as infamous to American soldiers in Europe and to their families back home as Newgate had been to the English during the American Revolution. The poor conditions of the prisons and the poor treatment of the prisoners would continue through the last half of the twentieth century in the Korean and Vietnam conflicts. With all those years of increased knowledge and technology, why would atrocities continue and conditions remain barbaric?[12]

The truth is, the care and feeding of prisoners is, and always has been, the last concern—the least of any government's worries—at the beginning of any war.

In the Civil War, the situation was worsened by the general contention, of both sides, that it would be of short duration and permanent facilities for POWs would not be necessary. When the combatants discovered they needed places to keep prisoners, whatever facilities were available were quickly pressed into use.

Probably the first to advocate preparation for POWs at all during the Civil War was the Confederate president, Jefferson Davis, who was previously a secretary of war in the Pierce Administration. "At the request of the President," wrote Leroy P. Walker, secretary of war for the Confederacy, in a dispatch to North Carolina's governor dated June 8, 1861, "I write to inquire whether the [state] could not furnish a suitable place for the safe-keeping of our prisoners of war . . . where large buildings [are] located and where the prisoners might be supported at moderate cost."[13]

Except for a brief engagement at Fort Sumter, minor skirmishes in Virginia, and activities taking place in Texas and in parts of Missouri, the South had no prisoners to speak of at that time. Most had been released on parole, and no commander would be assigned to oversee prisoners in the Richmond area for another two weeks. Yet, despite Davis's foresight, the South never formally assigned a commander over their prisons until 1864, and even then the position was severely limited.

U.S. Quartermaster General Montgomery C. Meigs, on the other hand, was probably the first in the North to advocate that something be done to prepare for the eventual accumulation of prisoners. He wrote to Simon Cameron, the U.S. secretary of war, on July 12, 1861, more than a week before the First Battle of Bull Run, and encouraged him to prepare for the inevitable. "[I]t is to be expected," wrote Meigs, "that the United States will have to take care of large numbers of prisoners of war. I respectfully call your attention to the propriety of making some arrangements in time."[14]

Apparently, Meigs's suggestion was temporarily ignored. An administrator in charge of prisons was not named until the following October and very little was done about organizing the prison system until then.

The indifference displayed by both sides, however, was typical. At the beginning of any war, the main emphasis has always been on the difficult tasks of organizing and equipping a fighting force and planning strategy. As the war progresses, developing strategy and keeping the force equipped and supplied remains the prime concern of the authorities, while the welfare of POWs remains a low priority.

For the South, keeping its army supplied and equipped was an overwhelming obstacle from the very beginning of the conflict. Within months, the Confederacy had trouble providing for its troops. As early as October 29, 1861, letters from soldiers revealed problems with supply: "What we had to dine upon tonight," wrote Matthew M. Rogers of the 25th North Carolina Regiment, "consisted of a little boiled beef and rice." He went on to complain members of his regiment hadn't had enough to eat in quite some time. Prisoners of war would fare no better.[15]

Another fate that POWs often suffer is a certain amount of individual or collective retaliation that is used against those captured. During the American Revolution, the Continental Congress declared that Newgate Prison was to be used for "the reception of British prisoners of war and for the purpose of retaliation." Even George Washington, highly regarded today for his ideals, was known to have referred to Newgate as a fitting place for such "flagrant and atrocious villains."[16]

Forms of mental abuse and several degrees of physical abuse were used to obtain information, to recruit prisoners for military service, or to sign an oath of allegiance. Throughout the Civil War, military authorities from both sides scouted their prison camps in an effort to recruit troops or to eliminate potential manpower for the enemy. The prisoners' refusal to join or to take an oath of allegiance often led to reprisals against them. Sometimes rations were withheld, or sometimes severe physical and mental abuse resulted.[17]

To their captors, confined troops were the embodiment of the opposing army—a group that frustrations and anger could be vented against on a personal level. The anger might result from the death of a friend or loved one from the war, a certain lost battle, or frustration over the war in general. These hostilities were acted out by a wide variety of groups, including prison commandants and guards—many of whom were unqualified for their task during the Civil War—as well as the press, the public and, sometimes, even the government holding them.

On several occasions during the Civil War, a combination of these groups became involved. The *New York Times* accused the Federal government of treating prisoners of war better than its own troops. The paper noted that prisoners were lounging around and getting fat while Union prisoners held in the South were starving. Before long, other newspapers carried the campaign, publishing articles and editorials that aroused and inflamed the public's anger. Soldiers' relatives and politicians quickly became involved, which resulted in retaliatory measures being instituted against Confederate prisoners. As the newspapers continued to complain about poor treatment of those held in Southern prisons, food rations to Confederate prisoners were cut in half and harsher treatment ensued.[18]

Similarly in the South, the Richmond *Daily Dispatch* accused the Confederate government of coddling prisoners. When the newspaper learned that as many as thirty cattle were being butchered each day to feed prisoners while the people of Richmond were doing without, it published editorials that caused enraged citizens to lobby for elimination of such a program.[19] In effect, then, the perceived treatment of prisoners could cause just as much misery for the POWs as the actual inability to provide.

It was also near this time in 1863 that the North stopped exchanging prisoners with the South. Federal authorities recognized that the success or failure of the Union's war effort hinged on its supremacy in numbers. Federal authorities decided to stop further exchanges of prisoners in order to prevent Confederates from being released and reentered into the army. Although the government would never acknowledge its policy, Union prisoners held in the South were "sacrificed" to make further gains. General Ulysses S. Grant came closest to admitting it when he said, "It is hard on our men held in Southern prisons not to exchange them, but it is humanity to those left in the ranks to fight our battles."[20]

Meanwhile, Union troops under Generals William T. Sherman and Philip H. Sheridan marched through the South, burning and destroying everything in sight. Cities, farms, crops, and railroad lines were leveled or laid to waste. The destruction of crops and the facilities for processing and transporting food and other necessities quickly began to affect the entire South, including Union prisoners held there. The more the Union army destroyed, the more the prisoners suffered.

What magnified the atrocities in the Civil War and made them even more appalling was the fact it was Americans mistreating Americans. There were even a number of cases where a prisoner recognized one of his own guards as a distant relative or an old friend. One of the most abusive prison commandants in the South was David H. Todd, brother-in-law to President Lincoln.[21]

The whole purpose of taking prisoners of war is to allow them to live while depriving the opposing force of their service. For many in the Civil War's prisons, though, to have been killed on the battlefield might have been more humane. Those who were captured found that their most intense battle was simply to survive until the end of the war. For over one-eighth of the total fighting force, it became the cruelest struggle of the entire conflict.

Chapter 1

OVERVIEW ON TRAGEDY

Man is not the creature of circumstances. Circumstances are the creature of men.

Benjamin Disraeli

The first prisoners taken in the Civil War were part of a work detail at Castle Pinckney in South Carolina's Charleston Harbor. The taking of this fort is considered by some historians as the first overt act of the Civil War.

Within a week of South Carolina's secession, Major Robert A. Anderson, in command of all Federal forts in Charleston Harbor, moved his entire force from Fort Moultrie to the nearby, larger and more defensible, Fort Sumter. Before leaving Fort Moultrie, however, his forces spiked the guns and left the carriages in flames to prevent them from being captured by the state forces. In retaliation, Governor Francis W. Pickens of South Carolina ordered the taking of Castle Pinckney on the pretext of preventing further destruction of public property. At the time, a repair party composed of Lieutenant Richard K. Meade, four mechanics, thirty laborers, and an ordnance sergeant and his family occupied the fort. The sergeant lived there as caretaker of the property.

On the afternoon of December 27, 1860, Colonel James J. Pettigrew, by order of the governor, took an assault force of about 150 men across the short stretch of harbor toward the castle.

When he saw them approaching, Meade ordered the fort's gates closed. Undaunted by the maneuver, the state troops quickly threw scaling ladders up on all sides of the fort and scrambled over the walls unchallenged. Pettigrew announced that he was taking the works and demanded the surrender of those inside. Meade protested but admitted he had no means of resistance. He declined any receipts for the public property, refused to take a pledge for parole—an oath promising not to take up arms if released—and continued to protest that the governor had no authority over such matters. Finally, after being assured of considerate treatment, Meade and the others were allowed to leave for Fort Sumter.

Six days later, state troops seized the inactive Fort Johnson in Charleston Harbor, and the following day Georgia troops took over Fort Pulaski along the Savannah River. Neither fort was occupied, so there was no resistance and no prisoners were taken. On January 20, 1861, Mississippi troops seized Fort Massachusetts on Ship Island in the Gulf. It, too, was unoccupied.

Meanwhile, in Texas, Brevet General David E. Twiggs was in command of U.S. troops there when the state's secession convention assembled. On February 1, 1861, an ordinance of secession was passed and a committee of public safety was elected. The committee appointed four commissioners to meet with Twiggs to discuss the surrender of the U.S. government property under his control. Twiggs immediately contacted headquarters for advice, but upon receiving no reply, he reluctantly appointed a military commission to negotiate with the state commissioners to determine the terms and details of a surrender.

The War Department in Washington strongly disapproved of Twiggs's action, and soon removed him from command. Colonel Carlos W. Waite was ordered to relieve him. The change in command was interpreted by the state to mean that the arrangements with General Twiggs were unacceptable and that his successor had no intention of carrying them out. Action was taken immediately to seize the government property by force before Waite could arrive and Twiggs could leave. State troops were sent to various points to demand the evacuation of all U.S. troops and the surrender of all government property. The first such action took place under the direction of Colonel Ben McCulloch at Twiggs's headquarters in San Antonio.

At four o'clock in the morning on February 16, 1861, McCulloch marched into San Antonio with about nine hundred volunteers and militia. At the approach of the Texas force, the Federal guards on the Alamo withdrew, and McCulloch posted men around the historic building to take a commanding position. The commissioners of public safety then made their demands to General Twiggs. Reluctantly, he agreed to surrender the property on the condition that his troops be permitted to keep their sidearms and allowed to leave the state unmolested. The commissioners agreed but stipulated that they had to go by way of the coast, which was to prevent the troops from passing through the free soil of New Mexico with the possibility of them becoming the nucleus of the Union army if they entered Kansas.

After arrangements for the surrender were completed, the officers and men of Company A, 8th Infantry and Company I, 1st Infantry marched out of San Antonio to set up camp about a mile southeast of town. There they awaited transportation to the coast.

"The headquarters of the post and the 8th Infantry along with the band of the 8th remained in town," reported Lieutenant Colonel William Hoffman, who was being held there as a prisoner of war. They were later confined in the San Antonio barracks.[1]

Upon learning of Twiggs's surrender, Colonel Waite, with a small cavalry escort, immediately left Camp Verde, Texas, and headed for San Antonio. He arrived shortly after the final negotiations were completed and realized that there was nothing he could do. On February 19, Twiggs officially transferred the command of the Department of Texas to Colonel Waite and left for New Orleans.

Colonel Waite began to fear that an outbreak of hostilities might result in his troops being prevented from leaving the state or being seized as prisoners of war. He began concentrating his forces at Green Lake, the largest body of fresh water near the coast that could support a large encampment, until ships could arrive to transport them out of Texas. This concentration of troops, still armed, began to worry Confederate authorities. It was quickly becoming a well-fortified military threat rather than a temporary way station. In addition, Confederate leaders believed that the troop concentration prevented enlistment of some of the troops into Southern ranks. The South needed some of these experienced men and feared the assistance they could give to the North. When this was brought to the attention of Confederate authorities in the east, Colonel Earl Van Dorn was sent to Texas to deal with the situation.

In the meantime, an official act of war erupted at Fort Sumter on the South Carolina coast. Anxiety among the Texans increased, and many began to call for the capture of the remaining Federal troops to prevent their use by the Union. Confederate officials decided that the authority of the state's committee of public safety had expired when the Confederate government assumed military responsibility for Texas. In addition, it was said, a state of war had not existed between Colonel Twiggs and the public safety committee. Now that it did, the Confederacy no longer felt obligated to the agreement. Van Dorn was given orders to either enlist the Federal troops into Confederate service or to take them as prisoners of war. Some of the commissioned officers and about 15 percent of the regular troops were persuaded to join the Confederacy. Those who refused were seized as prisoners.[2]

By the second week of April there were still sixteen uncaptured U.S. companies in Texas—nine in the Green Lake area and seven en route to that point. Since Van Dorn's instructions were to prevent their escape, one of his next moves was to capture the *Star of the West* off the coast of Indianola. The *Star of the West*, the same sidewheel steamer that had attempted to reinforce the Fort Sumter garrison in January, was now loaded with the next contingent of evacuating Federal troops from Texas as Van Dorn approached it by surprise with a commandeered vessel full of Confederate volunteers. The Confederates boarded the ship and captured the troops, thus reducing the chances of escape for the remaining troops at, or nearing, Green Lake.[3]

Back in South Carolina, the bombardment of Fort Sumter resulted in more prisoners being taken by the Confederacy. Major Anderson and his command of 127 men hoisted the white flag of surrender but were given permission to fire a hundred-gun salute to the American flag the following day before hauling it down and evacuating the fort.

A stiff breeze blew from the sea toward the guns as the salute began the following morning. Upon firing the fiftieth gun, Private Daniel Hough quickly rammed another cartridge into it. Apparently, sparks from a previous round had not been properly swabbed out. The new charge prematurely ignited and a terrific explosion resulted, killing Hough instantly. Smouldering debris blew back into a pile of cartridges near the weapon, and a second explosion killed another gunner and wounded four others.

The salute was stopped abruptly at fifty guns. After necessary arrangements were made for the wounded and dead, the Fort Sumter prisoners were marched out and loaded onto a steamer. The next day they were taken North on parole.[4]

In effect, Hough died as a prisoner of war—one in a long succession. However, he was not the first. The first POW death had occurred on March 20, 1861, during the process of transporting troops to the Texas coast for evacuation. First Lieutenant James B. Witherell, who was nearsighted, fell overboard and drowned as he was being transferred from the steamboat *Mustang* to the coastal steamer *Arizona* while they were anchored at the mouth of the Rio Grande.[5]

Although the evacuation of Texas continued throughout the spring, no other deaths occurred. Between April 23 and May 13, Confederate troops continued to cut off various Union detachments enroute to the coast and force them to surrender. During that time, Confederate steamers sailed into the channel and blocked the exit from Indianola. Colonel Waite and his officers protested the action, but they later signed paroles that allowed the officers to return north. A number of enlisted men, on the other hand, were confined to the limits of Bexar County, Texas, until exchanged.[6]

The system of parole and exchange was an old European tradition that operated on the good faith of the governments involved. Captured soldiers who were released often went home to wait for orders to rejoin their units, which came after a corresponding number of prisoners were captured and "exchanged," on paper, by the opposing side. During the Civil War, any prisoner not exchanged within ten days of being captured was usually released upon signing a pledge that he would not take up arms against his enemy until notified he had been exchanged for an enemy captive.

Texas authorities, however, became the first in this war to modify the policy and hold prisoners of war until the exchange. General Van Dorn, recently promoted, was assigned responsibility for them and thus became the first general to deal with the care and feeding of a large number of confined prisoners. In all, 2,648 officers and enlistees were captured in Texas. Eventually, nearly 2,350 were released on parole before Confederate authorities decided to confine 300 of the captives in a Texas prison camp until they could be formally released.[7]

The first such camp was called, appropriately enough, Camp Van Dorn. It was a temporary POW camp seven miles east of San Antonio, along the Salado River. Those originally held in the San Antonio barracks were also later moved to this location. "It [was]," reported prisoner Stephen Schwartz, "situated on a bluff in the prairie. Three hundred yards off [was] a small creek, but nearly dried up with the exception of a few pools. A half mile farther on the east side [was] a Chapparel grove. Only a few houses were visible and the site was desolate in general."[8]

The camp was run by a Captain Graham, a former U.S. Army officer, along with his Confederate cavalry as guards. Security was lax, to say the least, in this first Civil War prison camp. Those being held "captive" were allowed to roam within a one-mile radius of the site. They were also allowed twenty-four- or forty-eight-hour passes to visit San Antonio or other nearby towns.

But it wasn't long before conditions deteriorated. Local newspapers in the San Antonio area began to complain about the prisoners' preferential treatment.[9]

"Those damnable prisoners are a great nuisance," complained one newspaper editorial, "and an injury to the Confederacy; their privileges should and must be taken away from them; lying in camp, and allowing those vagabonds of a Yankee mob to visit our cities and towns, stirring up all the imaginary evils, etc., among our citizens and soldiers, and those prisoners are also the cause of the desertion of one of our best officers, Captain Graham . . . Their everlasting troublesomeness drove him away . . . treat those prisoners as they deserve. Curses on them and confinement in a deep dark dungeon is too good for them, and far better than they actually deserve."[10]

Afterward, the prisoners were confined to the limits of the camp, which soon proved to be inadequate. The prison population continued to increase as more and more POWs were gathered up throughout the area. Finally, in mid-September 1861, the prisoners were divided into six groups and distributed among the state's northwestern forts. Camp Verde, sixty-five miles northwest of San Antonio, eventually received the majority.

Camp Verde was a former U.S. military post established in 1856 on the northern bank of Verde Creek near Bandera Pass. Within a year, it was nicknamed "Little Egypt" because it became headquarters for the famous Camel Corps established by Jefferson Davis while he was U.S. secretary of war. Camp

Verde's prison camp was established four to five hundred yards west of the post.[11]

"The first thing we did after arriving in camp was to pitch tents," reported prisoner Schwartz, "and no sooner done than we were ordered to strike tents for the purpose of having them turned in to the Quartermaster at Camp Verde." When the prisoners inquired about shelter they were told their tents would be issued to soldiers of the Confederate army and that they would have to do without or make their own. Provided with spades and axes, they went to work constructing their own shelter out of logs and mud. "In four or five days our huts were finished," continued Schwartz, "and 'Prisontown' stood defiant with her streets laid out beautifully, situated on a small hill opposite Camp Verde."[12]

More than 330 prisoners were held at Camp Verde. In addition, ten women married to prisoners were allowed to accompany their husbands. These women took the responsibility as laundresses for the entire prison.[13]

At first, visitors were allowed into the camp to "see what Yankees looked like," but the possibilities of escape later ended the practice. When escapes did occur and escapees crossed the border into Mexico, they were often robbed and killed by Mexican highwaymen. Those who got through usually headed for the American consul in Tampico, Mexico, where they received food, clothing, and shelter until a U.S. ship could convey them back to the United States.[14]

In the three months that the prison existed, though, no more than twelve men escaped. The prison was under the strict discipline of a Captain Holmes, who was as intensely hated by the prisoners as the eighty enlisted men who acted as his guards. "His men, who lacked discipline, were allowed to do as they pleased," complained one prisoner. "We were insulted daily and maltreated with violence by them throwing stones, brickbats, etc., [when] any of us were passing near."[15]

In time, Holmes reduced food rations, issued orders which forbade band-member prisoners from playing their instruments or organizing dances, and had a picket fence erected around "Prisontown" using prison labor.[16]

When the site was abandoned the following December, the prisoners were moved back to a place within six miles of San Antonio called San Antonio Springs. There, the POWs were kept under close guard in an open field. They had no tents or shelter and their rations were reduced yet again. Sentries were posted around them and no one was permitted to go beyond the guardline. Prisoners gathered brush and dead wood within the camp perimeter to build their own lean-to's and similar structures. Many others simply burrowed into the ground.[17]

The following month the prisoners moved to within four miles of San Antonio where a prison camp was set up at San Pedro Springs. "We were halted on the worst spot that could have been selected," recalled Schwartz, "right in the thickest part of the brushwood." Again, they dug holes and cut wood and brush to use as shelter.

The prison commandant at San Pedro Springs was a Major Taylor who had four battalions of troops to guard the prisoners. Taylor, too, was disliked by the prisoners. "In reference to the daily treatment," wrote Schwartz, "it went from bad to worse." Nor did the food situation get better. "From one ration day to another," Schwartz continued, "our usual allowance of provisions was diminished in quantity and likewise in quality." Toward the end of 1862, the prisoners were moved again. "We were marched in a column of twos," wrote another prisoner, "one company of Taylor's battalion took the lead, acting as advance guard, and another the rear, acting as rear guard . . . and a few troops on the left and right flank for the purpose of keeping the prisoners from scattering along the road."[18]

By this time the prisoners' clothing was tattered and torn and many had no shoes. Yet, hungry and weak, they were forced to march in the heat of the Texas sun to their new location.

"[We] only rested twice, five minutes each time," one of the prisoners complained years later.[19]

The procession came to a halt thirty-five miles later. Here, prisoners were told to build their own shelters, as they would remain there until their parole. After three days, the 350 prisoners, by this time, had constructed 90 to 100 huts, which they named "Prisontown in the Woods." On the fourth day, however, the prisoners were ordered back to San Pedro Springs, and this new site was left abandoned.[20]

Arriving back in San Pedro Springs, the prisoners found their old huts completely destroyed. Reluctantly, they proceeded to build shelter for themselves. They remained at this location for another month.

"[These] troops," Major General Nathaniel Banks wrote sometime later, "[were] separated from their officers, divided into squads, and removed to different posts on the frontiers of Texas . . . they were subjected to degrading labors, supplied with scanty food and clothing, and sometimes chained to the ground or made to suffer other severe military punishments."[21]

On January 2, 1863, the prisoners were marched out of Texas to Shreveport, Louisiana, and loaded onto steamers bound for Baton Rouge. Finally, on February 25, 1863, this first group of POWs confined during the Civil War, was released on exchange after twenty-two months of captivity.

On April 20, 1861, pioneer balloonist Thaddeus S. C. Lowe took flight from Cincinnati, Ohio, to prove that upper wind currents move from west to east. Being correct, he came down nine hours and nine hundred miles later at Unionville, South Carolina, and was promptly arrested as a Yankee spy. After being confined for a few days, he was sent back North. From that day until his death, Lowe mistakenly boasted that he was the first prisoner taken in the Civil War. He was, however, definitely the first American *aviator* ever taken prisoner during a war.

In St. Louis, Missouri, Brigadier General Daniel M. Frost surrendered his 669 men when Captain Nathaniel Lyon seized the arsenal at Camp Jackson on May 10, 1861. These prisoners were released on parole after taking oaths not to bear arms against the United States during the conflict.

On June 3, the small schooner *Savannah* was captured along with her crew of twenty men. The first privateers captured by the North, they were taken to New York City and incarcerated at the Tombs prison.

On July 11, Major General George B. McClellan took several hundred Confederate prisoners at Rich Mountain, Virginia. These were all paroled except for two who had previously served in the U.S. Army. Under orders from the War Department, those two were retained and sent to Fort Lafayette prison in New York City for confinement.

But even before uniformed soldiers or sailors were captured as POWs, people were taken into custody and incarcerated in provost prisons in many parts of the nation. These included deserters, stragglers, and citizens whose loyalty to the government had become questionable.

In an attempt to crush secession sentiment in the North, President Lincoln claimed the right to suspend the writ of habeas corpus as part of the war powers granted by the Constitution. A number of citizens were arrested on suspicion without warrants, imprisoned without charges, and incarcerated for months or years without trials.

Such arbitrary arrests were less frequent in the South but they did occur. President Davis did not assume the same privileges as Lincoln but the Confederate Congress granted them for limited periods.

Government authorities of both sides appointed a provost marshal for each of their military districts to suppress insurrection, preserve order, and maintain discipline. Although highly controversial, searches, seizures, and arrests were made in many communities across the nation under their authority. In Baltimore, newspaper editor Francis K. Howard was arrested and incarcerated for daring to criticize the government in print. About the same time, a number of Maryland's state legislators and the Baltimore police chief were arrested and placed in jail. In fact, many citizens throughout the North found themselves incarcerated for various periods for making critical comments or offhanded remarks about the government. And still more people—such as Charles C. Spencer of Memphis, Tennessee, who was arrested, his trading boat confiscated, and all of his property disposed of by Union soldiers while he and his son were incarcerated in St. Louis—were accused of disloyalty for doing business with the wrong people, without any formal charges or investigation, and were later exonerated when the proper authorities finally looked into the matter.[22]

The number of citizens arrested and imprisoned in this manner during the course of the war has never been determined because accurate records were never kept. According to one report, 13,535 citizens were arrested and confined on various charges between February 1862 and April 1865 in the North alone. According to that same source, a comparable number of arrests would have occurred in the South, and many more were probably made by military commanders or provost marshals that went unreported.[23]

Each major city, North and South, had its own holding facility for such "prisoners of state" or political prisoners. Local jails were often used, such as in Baltimore, but other facilities—such as Fort McHenry in Baltimore, Lynch's Slave Pen in St. Louis, Castle Thunder in Richmond, Fort Lafayette in New York, Fort Warren in Boston, and Old Capitol Prison in Washington City— began as provost prisons and later evolved into POW facilities.

Eventually more than 150 military prisons came into existence. Of that number, only two—Fort Warren in the North and Raleigh Barracks in the South—were considered tolerable. All others varied only in the degree of filth, disease, illness, and death.

Those 150 prisons can be grouped into seven classes:

Existing Jails and Prisons. The first to come into use, these ranged in size from small city jails—such as those at Selma, Alabama; Savannah, Georgia; the Tombs prison in New York; and Castle Godwin in Richmond—to medium-sized county jails such as the Parish Prison in New Orleans and the Henrico County Jail in Richmond to large state prisons such as those used in Virginia; Huntsville, Texas; Columbus, Ohio; and Western Penitentiary in Allegheny City, Pennsylvania.

Coastal Fortifications. Second to be pressed into use, mostly in the North, were forts along the Atlantic. Prime examples of these included Fort McHenry at Baltimore, Fort Warren in Boston, Fort Lafayette, Columbus and Castle Williams in New York, and Fort Delaware below Philadelphia. The South did, however, have one facility of this type—Castle Pinckney in Charleston Harbor.

Old Buildings Converted into Prisons. This type, used primarily in the South, included the Ligon and Libby Prisons in Richmond; Castle Thunder (II) at Petersburg, Virginia; and the six tobacco warehouses at Danville, Virginia. The North used a few of this type also, most notably Gratiot Street Prison and Myrtle Street Prison in St. Louis.

Barracks Enclosed by High Fences. These were groups of wooden buildings on a large plot of land previously used as basic-training camps or rendezvous points for recruits. High fences were later built around the camps to enclose and confine POWs. This type of prison existed mostly in the North:

Camp Chase in Columbus, Ohio; Camp Douglas at Chicago, Illinois; Camp Morton in Indianapolis, Indiana; and Elmira in New York. A number of these were originally fairgrounds before becoming troop rendezvous points. In the South, only two of this type were well-known—Raleigh, North Carolina, and Macon, Georgia. Johnson's Island Military Prison near Sandusky, Ohio, fits this category, but unlike the other facilities, it was built with the full intention of housing prisoners.

Clusters of Tents Enclosed by High Fences. This was one of the cheapest methods to confine prisoners, and it existed in both the North and the South. Examples included Point Lookout in Maryland and Belle Isle in Virginia.

Barren Stockades. By far the cheapest and worst of the seven types constructed, this was used exclusively in the South. These stockades were constructed around a number of acres that included no shelter except what individual prisoners could construct for themselves. Prime examples included Camp Asylum and Florence in South Carolina, Camp Sumter (Andersonville) in Georgia, Salisbury in North Carolina, Camp Ford in Texas, and Cahaba in Alabama.

Barren Ground. This last type was nothing more than the gathering of prisoners on barren land, surrounded with a guardline. The outer limits of the camp were often marked by crossed sticks, branches, or several batteries of cannon directed at the gathering. Outside these markers, a line of sentries stood or patrolled back and forth. Mostly used by the South late in the war, this method was utilized by the North on some occasions after a major battle. Examples of this type included Camp Sorghum in South Carolina, Charlotte in North Carolina, and, on several different occasions, East Point outside Atlanta, Georgia.

The North and the South both began with a hodgepodge of facilities for holding their prisoners of war because the already established jails and prisons were quickly filled beyond capacity. It wasn't at all uncommon for some of the first POWs to be incarcerated along with the local thieves and murderers.[24] The provost prisons were utilized next. These, too, quickly filled. Pressed for both time and space, the North began converting forts into POW facilities. Out west, the Union army confiscated two buildings in St. Louis: a former slave auction house in May of 1861, and a medical college in December. When these became overcrowded, an old abandoned state prison in nearby Alton, Illinois, was pressed into use.

Meanwhile, the Confederate government confiscated tobacco factories and warehouses in and around Richmond to convert into prisons. At the time, such buildings seemed well-suited for the purpose: they were usually constructed of

brick and were sturdy; they were usually rectangular and entirely without orna-
ment, making them easily guarded; they were usually two or three stories high;
they possessed good light and ventilation; they contained very little machinery;
their floors were usually constructed of heavy planks; and quite often, the entire
floor area of each story was one large room or several large rooms divided by
partitions.

The scattered system of prisons that evolved in the North soon became
unsatisfactory from a military standpoint. There was no centralized control or
coordination among the institutions, nor was there a centralized system of
supply. The Atlantic forts being used were not well-suited for holding a large
number of men in confinement and quickly became crowded and insufficient.
Hoping to develop a more organized military prison system, Quartermaster
General Meigs contacted Secretary of War Cameron and recommended that
a commissary general of prisons be appointed and a special camp for the confinement of prisoners of war be created. Meigs suggested a secure site, far from
the seat of war, such as an island in Lake Erie.[25]

The Confederacy, on the other hand, although trying to develop a centralized prison system within the Richmond area, simply did not have the
resources to feed, clothe, and shelter the large number of prisoners they quickly
acquired. Consequently, conditions in the Southern military prison system
began to deteriorate rapidly.

The North finally established some order in its chaotic prison system in
October 1861. Lieutenant Colonel William H. Hoffman, who had been part
of the 8th U.S. Infantry—the regiment that had surrendered in Texas and was
released after taking the oath not to take up arms against the Confederacy—
was appointed commissary general of prisoners. He was soon promoted to
colonel and he set to work on the structure of the prison system. Hoffman was
a methodical, budget-conscious administrator, and insisted that money be spent
only on absolute necessities. "So long as a prisoner has clothing upon him, however much torn," he maintained, "issue nothing to him."[26]

Hoffman centralized the system so that all correspondence regarding prisoners of war passed through his hands. He also established rules to guide the
prison commandants and developed an elaborate system of inspections and
reports.[27] Next, he began searching for an ideal site to establish a new prison
for captured Confederates. Concentrating his efforts in the Lake Erie area,
Hoffman finally chose Johnson's Island.

Johnson's Island seemed perfect for its purpose. Surrounded by water to
prevent escapes, it was free of inhabitants, was economical to lease, had a convenient site already cleared, and was only a mile off the mainland, making it
accessible by railroad at Sandusky.

Under Hoffman's direction, the buildings of this new prison were constructed as cheaply as possible. The compound was originally intended to hold one thousand prisoners at a time, but within two weeks of the prison's completion, Fort Donelson, Tennessee, fell. Nearly 15,000 more POWs were in Union hands.

The Donelson prisoners were shipped by steamboats to St. Louis. Both St. Louis prisons soon became crammed beyond capacity. The overflow was sent to Alton, which was already at capacity. Looking around for some alternative, Colonel Hoffman sent several thousand to Camp Morton, the former troop training camp in Indiana. The governor there complained that he had no facilities to handle such responsibilities. Hoffman told him to do the best he could and sent along the same instructions to such places as Terre Haute, Ft. Wayne, Lafayette and Richmond, Indiana.[28]

Hoffman and his staff saw that the use of the old training camps was an easy solution to their dilemma. Since these camps had been created to train Union volunteers, they were usually located in state capitals or principal cities with good railroad connections and some form of barracks for shelter. In fact, many were former fairgrounds with buildings already converted over for military use or ample space for additional barracks or rows of tents. These sites were often sitting idle and could be easily acquired. With the addition of highboard fences and walkways for guards, the training camps could easily become prisons.

So, quite quickly, prisons were temporarily created at Camp Butler near Springfield, Illinois, and at Camp Randall at Madison, Wisconsin. Permanent prisons appeared at Camp Morton, at Camp Douglas in Chicago, and at Camp Chase in Columbus.

The South continued to centralize its prisons by using confiscated buildings in and around Richmond. Due to continued overcrowding, the nearby resort area of Belle Isle was pressed into use in June 1862. It, too, had been originally used as a muster site for new recruits but lacked any buildings.[29] Tents were erected to shelter the POWs and guards, and artillery was positioned around the cluster of tents. The Confederacy was now resorting to the use of such barren-ground or stockade-type prisons, and would do so until the end of the war. Unfortunately, the mortality rate would prove to be higher in these facilities because they offered no shelter comparable to the old buildings in use at other locations.

The Confederacy had only a few prisons in use outside of Richmond in the early years of the war. Besides Castle Pinckney in South Carolina, there was Salisbury Prison in North Carolina. Salisbury was originally used for holding prisoners of state and Confederate soldiers who had committed military offenses, but, later Salisbury began receiving the overflow of prisoners from Richmond. In a continuing effort to ease overcrowding and dwindling supplies, a number of POWs were also temporarily moved to such places as Tuscaloosa, Alabama; the

Charleston city jail in South Carolina; Danville and Petersburg, Virginia; and the Raleigh barracks in North Carolina.

Because the early POW facilities were mostly centralized in Richmond, the provost marshal of the city, John H. Winder, was placed in charge of them. As prisoners were shipped out to other points, Winder continued to exercise control over them. Winder had originally come to Richmond from Maryland. He was a West Point graduate who had served in the U.S. Army as an artillery major. When the war broke out, he resigned his commission and accepted a brigadier general's commission in the Confederate service. Being an old friend of Jefferson Davis and having his trust, Winder was assigned provost marshal of Richmond. He was a rigid disciplinarian and took his job seriously. While carrying out his duties, Winder often won the praise of his superiors and the scorn of the public. His methods were considered high-handed and antagonistic by many of the citizens of Richmond, and they resented his harsh and strict rule. At one point Winder even employed citizen-detectives to inform on others and to help enforce his regulations.[30]

The buildup of prisoners on both sides came to a temporary end in July 1862 with the signing of a cartel, or agreement, regulating how exchanges could take place. The prison populations slowly began to shrink and many of the makeshift camps were emptied. The Union closed down a number of prisons and began concentrating its POWs at Johnson's Island, Camp Chase, Alton in the west, and Fort Delaware in the east. Gratiot Street Prison remained the distribution point in the west and Old Capitol Prison in the east. The Confederacy concentrated its POWs at Danville and Salisbury, with Libby as the distribution point.

With the collapse of the cartel in 1863, POWs again began accumulating in the facilities at an alarming rate. The Union reacted by reactivating several of the closed camps and building additional barracks at others. By late 1863, it established two new facilities: a fenced group of barracks at Rock Island, Illinois, and a tented camp at Point Lookout, Maryland. Before long, Point Lookout became the most populated Union prison, at one time holding twenty thousand captives, because it was close to the eastern battlefields.

For better control, Hoffman expanded previous attempts to segregate Confederate officers from enlisted men held captive. For the most part, officers were held at Johnson's Island or in separate facilities at Fort Delaware in the east and Gratiot Street in the west. Those requiring special security were sent to Fort Warren or, in some cases, regular state penitentiaries were utilized. This was the case with the Ohio State Penitentiary in Columbus, Ohio, and Western Penitentiary in Allegheny City, Pennsylvania.

The South built several stockade prisons in Texas to handle the large number of prisoners obtained during the Red River Campaign. Attempts to negotiate exchanges continued because the South needed the manpower held captive in the North. By this time, adequate food, clothing, and medication was nearly depleted and the South could no longer afford to keep its captives. As food shortages and unrest developed in Richmond, Confederate authorities began looking for alternatives to holding the increasing number of prisoners. They had ignored the problems that had been developing in their prison system for some time, hoping that exchange negotiations would resume and the problems would go away. They had neither the desire nor the resources to provide for longterm incarceration of enemy soldiers but, under the circumstances, had no choice.

Meanwhile, Union captives languished. Many were no longer able to digest the rough cornbread, which was all the South could provide by this time. Dysentery and diarrhea began killing the prisoners and became the cause of more deaths between 1863 and 1865 than the actual absence of food.[31]

Southern authorities finally decided to move most of the prisoners to areas with more abundant supplies. Winder sent two relatives from his staff to locate a site in south Georgia for a prison. Outside of Andersonville they erected a stockade of timber. Several more of these stockades, such as Blackshear and Millen, were later built. Like Belle Isle, these were nothing more than corrals for human beings.

As the South proceeded with an uncoordinated enlargement of its prison system, the North continued with a more planned expansion. In addition to ordering the construction of new barracks at existing posts, in 1864, Hoffman had a fence erected around a camp originally used for Union recruits in Elmira, New York. In 1865 he briefly opened a similar facility at Hart's Island, New York. Thus, with the development of Andersonville in the South and Elmira in the North, the period of the concentration camps began. By August 1864, the South held 50,000 prisoners of war while the North held 67,500.[32]

Facing a rigid economy and needing a budget increase to maintain such huge numbers of prisoners, Hoffman authorized a plan to withhold part of the regular rations at each prison and place the savings in a prison fund, which was intended to be used for the purchase of fruits and vegetables for the prisoners. In some prisons this fund grew to staggering amounts, but authorization to use it was never obtained. At the end of the war Hoffman proudly returned over $1.8 million to the government, representing what he had saved from his budget and accumulated in the prison funds by reducing prisoner rations.[33] In other prisons this accumulation of money often led to graft and corruption among prison officials.

As Union authorities received reports of hunger and suffering among their men in Confederate hands, they instituted a policy of retaliation. From mid-1864 to 1865, Hoffman, backed by Meigs and Edwin M. Stanton, intended to treat Confederate prisoners of war as they believed the Confederate government was treating Union captives. Hoffman ordered a further reduction of rations, restricted sutlers' access to the prisoners, and eliminated the prisoners' receipt of food packages from home. The result was an increase in disease from malnutrition, as well as starvation.

Concerned about Sherman's invading force, the South began searching for safer holding areas for prisoners in the Georgia pens. These prisoners, they still believed, were their only hope in obtaining Confederate soldiers held in Federal prisons. Late in the summer of 1864, the Confederates began to remove the enlisted men from Andersonville and the officers from Macon. For a time, some were held at a temporary camp in Savannah and Millen, while others were sent to Charleston, South Carolina.

Union forces soon discovered that prisoners were being housed at the old Roper Hospital in Charleston, which was in the range of Union seige guns. Although most of the city was within the range of the seige guns, Union authorities believed that the Confederates had deliberately put prisoners under fire, and retaliated by taking six hundred Rebel officer prisoners held at Fort Delaware and placing them in a stockade erected on Morris Island near Charleston, under Confederate artillery fire. The Confederates soon moved the Charleston prisoners inland to camps at Columbia and Florence, South Carolina.

During this disruption and movement of prisoners held in the deep South, captives continued to accumulate at Richmond, mainly on Belle Isle. Still ill-prepared and inadequately organized to handle the number of POWs brought into the city, the Confederate government sent a few to Danville and decided to transfer others to Salisbury, North Carolina. In October 1864, almost without warning and with a complete lack of forethought, Richmond authorities dropped nearly 7,500 men off at Salisbury Prison, more than doubling its population.[34]

Finally recognizing the chaotic condition of their prison system, Confederate officials created a central authority in November 1864 by naming Winder to the post commissary general of prisoners, responsible for all prison facilities east of the Mississippi River. Winder spent the rest of his life in that capacity, attempting to cope with Sherman's advance and seeking prison locations that would be safe from attack. While at the Florence prison in February 1865, Winder collapsed and died.

At about this time negotiations resumed to arrange an exchange of prisoners. Several thousand sick prisoners had been exchanged the previous fall and public pressure was mounting to free the rest. With the end of the war in sight, Union officials agreed to a general exchange. Thousands were sent across the lines at City Point, Virginia, and Wilmington, North Carolina, as fighting continued nearby. With the collapse and surrender of the Confederacy the following April, the remaining prisoners of both sides were released over the next several months.

When the war was finally over, it was determined that more than 56,000 men had died as prisoners of war.[35]

Twenty, or about ten on each side, of the 150 military prisons that came into existence during the Civil War attained major notoriety. It would be these twenty prisons that would furnish nearly the entire total of 56,000 deaths later compiled in the official records. By nearly all accounts, those twenty prisons became, as one prisoner put it, "the closest existence to a hell on earth."[36]

1861

Chapter 2

MAKESHIFT PRISONS

As the evening closed, and we lay upon the floor,—a few upon straw mattresses,—we but faintly realized that henceforth we were prisoners of war.

Lt. William C. Harris

A lthough research shows that the Civil War's POW facilities were created haphazardly and were ill-planned and ill-conceived from the start, each seems to have been established quite innocently. Authorities on both sides honestly believed that each facility or site they established as a military prison was perfect at the time for its intended use. By all evidence, neither government nor the individuals responsible for establishing these prison sites ever intended any of the facilities to become lethal to those confined. Yet, the inevitability of overcrowding soon led to just such situations.

RICHMOND

By July of 1861, Richmond, with a population of thirty-eight thousand, served as the seat of four different governments: the city, the county, the state of Virginia, and the Confederacy. Founded nearly two hundred years before Washington, Richmond had many buildings and monuments that identified strongly with the history and growth of the United States. But when the Civil War erupted locals were quick to point out that no conflict of interest existed because the city's famous equestrian statue of George Washington in Richmond's Capitol Square had always faced south with its rear end pointed to the North, anyway.[1]

After Virginia seceded from the Union, local citizens suspected of disloyalty to the Confederacy were incarcerated in the "Negro Jail" on Lumpkin Alley, at the lower end of town. Before long, the Lumpkin jail became known as Castle Godwin, after Archibald C. Godwin, assistant provost marshal of the city.

19

Within two weeks of the declaration of martial law, Castle Godwin held twenty-eight men and two women accused of disloyalty. Within five months it held 250.[2]

Other facilities within the city, such as the city jail at 15th and Marshall streets and the Henrico County Jail at 22nd and Main, quickly filled with political prisoners, army deserters, and disorderly Confederate soldiers. The Virginia State Penitentiary on the west end of town was filled to capacity with criminals.

As an important industrial and railroad center of the South, Richmond was intended to serve as the distribution point for all prisoners of war. For a few months, it worked. The taking of prisoners across the nation had been sporadic and wide-ranged up to July but the number that resulted from the first major battle caught the Confederates completely by surprise.

On July 21, 1861, Bull Run, or Manassas, brought nearly thirteen hundred Federal prisoners into the city. Since all available jails were already filled beyond capacity, Brigadier General Winder quickly converted the John L. Ligon and Sons Tobacco Factory for prison use.[3]

A three-story brick structure containing rooms of 75 by 30 feet and located on the southwest corner of 25th and Main streets, the building became known as Ligon's Military Prison and was the first nonjail confiscated by Richmond authorities to hold prisoners of war. Federal officers were quartered on the ground floor, but rows of tobacco presses occupied about half of the floor space. In the beginning, Confederate guards were quartered on the second floor and Federal enlisted men were held only on the third. Later, as prisoners from the battle of Ball's Bluff arrived, enlisted men were also confined on the second floor and the Confederate guards moved to other quarters nearby.

When General Winder inspected the building, he saw immediately that it was overcrowded and realized that the officers, along with several civilian prisoners who had been caught as spectators fleeing the fringes of the Manassas battlefield, needed to be separated from the enlisted men. He appropriated the adjoining Howard's Factory for confining the civilians and officers and, within days, took over nearby Ross's Factory to hold the ever-increasing number of soldiers.

Among the first guards of these facilities was Lieutenant David H. Todd, brother of Mary Todd Lincoln. Within a short time, Todd was in charge of Richmond's 25th Street prison facilities, which by then also included Mayo's Factory at 25th and Cary streets and Taylor's Factory. Although one Richmond newspaper reporter described Lieutenant Todd as "a gallant and meritorious gentleman," he was thoroughly hated by the prisoners. Among other things, he reportedly shot at a prisoner for sticking his head out of a window shortly after the POWs were first incarcerated; he also struck another prisoner with the back side of his sword for not moving fast enough to line up for roll call.

The *New York Times* later reported: "From all sides come stories of the acts of this sneaking, savage, cowardly scoundrel who seems fitted by nature for the position of a plantation overseer—that is if these attributes would fit him for such a post. Todd wants no better amusement than to come into the prison on a forenoon and to kick the helpless, crippled and wounded prisoners."[4]

A number of prisoners agreed. "Drunk during nearly the entire period of his authority at the prison," insisted prisoner William Harris, "and seething with malignity and bitterness, he made the life of the Federal officers one of daily indignity and hardship. Foul and scurrilous abuse was heaped upon them at his every visit: sentinels were charged to bayonet them at the slightest infringement of prison-rules; men were shot down at prison windows by his orders; and, as if nature had centered the essence of evil in his foul heart, on one occasion he thrust his sword into the midst of a crowd of Federal privates in the warehouse. . . . Fortunately, it passed through a man's leg and not his body."[5]

By October 1861, a total of 2,685 captives had been brought to Richmond. Because Confederate authorities had never expected such a large population, longterm preparations were nonexistent. Additional buildings were confiscated one by one as the need arose, with the hope that each would be the last.[6]

These buildings contained nothing except tobacco presses. There were some toilet facilities and gaslights, but little else. The captives slept on the floor on blankets, if they had them, or sometimes on loose straw if they didn't. "For weeks they slept upon the floor," remembered one of the earliest Richmond prisoners, "without blankets or overcoats, with blocks of wood—and not enough even of those—for pillows. It was not until three months had elapsed that the Confederate authorities furnished straw and cotton coverlets."[7]

They ate their rations with their fingers. In the beginning these rations consisted primarily of brown bread, small amounts of beef, and water, with rice soup occasionally substituted for the meat. In the officers' prison building, rations were given out three times a day: at nine, one, and five. Those who had successfully concealed money and other barter items were allowed to purchase additional articles such as vegetables, butter, and coffee. Black cooks and attendants were available for those who could afford it. These servants entered and exited the prison buildings quite freely—cooking, taking orders, and making deliveries. Lieutenant Todd, however, quickly put an end to this practice. As the months passed, many of these earlier privileges were eliminated.[8]

Enlisted men received different treatment. "Each floor containing privates is placed under the charge of one of their number, who is called the 'sergeant of the floor,'" noted one prisoner. According to another prisoner, rations were issued once a day and were devoured in one sitting. Normally, however, prison accounts agree that the regular policy in Richmond's prison buildings was to issue rations twice a day, in the morning and in the afternoon. It was only on occasions, and only at some prisons, that rations were issued once a day. A Confederate guard would enter the room and announce "Sergeant of the floor; Four men and four blankets!" The sergeant would then send four prisoners with four blankets downstairs to get the day's rations. The other prisoners would eagerly gather around the windows or doorway to await the arrival of the rations being carried back in the blankets. On the days soup was issued, it was brought back in buckets and distributed to the other prisoners in whatever containers they could assemble.[9]

The sergeant of the floor in the privates' quarters was allowed out on parole to visit Richmond stores to make purchases for the enlisted men. This privilege, too, was suspended under Lieutenant Todd. Despite Todd's tougher policies, the first prisoners still experienced little difficulty sneaking out at night to roam the streets. Within months, escapes were nearly commonplace and became a great source of irritation to the Confederate public.

"Eleven more Federal prisoners confined in the tobacco factories escaped on Friday and have not since been heard from," complained the *Charleston Daily Courier,* referring to the situation in Richmond on September 14. "At least twenty Yankees have taken leave since the Manassas battle."[10]

"It is impossible to keep liquor away from the guard," Captain George C. Gibbs, commander of the prison detail, offered in his report. "I can account for the escape of the prisoners only by supposing that some particular sentry was drunk on post."[11]

A number of prisoners reached Union lines in safety and provided Northern newspapers with some of the first accounts of Confederate imprisonment. Within a short time, two books appeared in print. *Prison-Life in the Tobacco Warehouse at Richmond by a Ball's Bluff Prisoner* was published in Philadelphia by William Charles Harris in 1862. Harris, confined in Ligon's, wrote it "to lessen the tedium of a lengthy imprisonment." He had smuggled his manuscript out "sewn securely in the lining of an overcoat." The second account provided to the North was *Five Months in Rebeldom; or, Notes from the Diary of a Bull Run Prisoner at Richmond,* written by William Howard Merrell, 27th New York Infantry, and published in Rochester, New York, in 1862. Both of these books created a stir among the public over the condition of prisons and the treatment of prisoners in the South.[12]

The authorities in Richmond had plenty to contend with besides bad publicity. Although prisoners did escape, more and more arrived almost daily on one of the five railroad lines that entered the city. Additional buildings soon were confiscated and converted into prisons, including Harwood's Tobacco Factory at Main and 26th streets, Gwathmey's Tobacco Warehouse on Cary Street near 25th, the Crew and Pemberton Warehouse, Barrett's Tobacco

Factory, Palmer's Factory, Grant's Factory, Scott's Factory, and Smith's Factory. By the end of the war, nearly one-fourth of the city's tobacco warehouses and factories would be converted into POW facilities or prison hospitals.[13]

Main Street was the busiest thoroughfare of the city—the hub of the business district. It ran in a northwest-to-southeast direction into a suburb called Rocketts. Most of the hotels, banks, stores, and newspaper offices were located on or near Main Street. In the early months of the war, most of the makeshift prisons were established on Main where it crossed 25th Street about six or seven blocks northwest of Rocketts. Later, Cary Street, running parallel but a block south of Main, became the primary prison area, especially between 18th and 19th streets, which relieved some of the congestion.

Still, there were problems. "On Sundays," reported the *New York Times,* "there is always a great crowd gathered in front of the tobacco houses . . . looking up, hour after hour at the windows."[14]

"[T]he square was for weeks packed with Rebels," agreed one of the prisoners, "[and] whenever they caught a glimpse of a Federal officer, [they] hooted at and insulted him . . . men, women, and even little children scarcely old enough to walk, united in heaping scurrilous abuse upon them."[15]

For the South, POWs were trophies—symbols that the Confederacy could protect itself as a nation. And, at least two of the prisoners gained celebrity status within the city. The first was U.S. Congressman Alfred Ely of New York, who had been a spectator at the battle of Bull Run when the Union retreat overran his position and he was unable to drive his carriage off the sidelines quickly enough to flee the area. Captured along with the Federal troops and incarcerated at Ligon's, he drew large crowds of curious citizens.

Colonel Michael Corcoran of the 69th New York Militia was also apprehended at Bull Run. His capture created great excitement among the Confederates because he was well known for his fiery temper and his incendiary statements against the South long before the war began. He had become colonel of the Irish Regiment in 1859 but lost his commission the following year for refusing to parade his regiment before the Prince of Wales, who was visiting New York City. He escaped court-martial only because war broke out with the South soon afterward. Corcoran became a disciplinary problem as soon as he reached Richmond. In September 1861, he was transferred to Charleston, South Carolina, for incarceration, but because he was one of the South's highest-ranking Federal prisoners, he was later chosen for retaliatory action to prevent the crew of the *Enchantress,* held by Federal authorities in New York on piracy charges, from being executed. Corcoran remained in the Charleston City Jail until the fate of those men was determined.[16]

Even without such celebrities, the crowds of curiosity-seekers continued to turn out to see the Yankees. In addition to standing in front of the buildings, they often were escorted inside, or they gathered at the train depots and along the streets leading to the prisons to catch a glimpse of the new arrivals. They called the captives "Blue Bellies," "Lincolnites," "Lincoln Hirelings," and a host of other names. Prisoners were teased, ridiculed, yelled at, spit upon, and cursed as they were force-marched from the depot to the prisons.[17]

Later, the Spotswood Hotel and many stores along Main Street began to capitalize on Richmond's status as a prison center. Window displays were often used to attract curious shoppers passing by. "In the shop windows of Richmond," declared one prisoner, "pieces of cord are exhibited, announced to have been taken from knapsacks of prisoners captured."[18]

But the burden of caring for the prisoners was already overwhelming the city and eroding its lifestyle and economy. The military and civilian populations were already suffering. Food and medical supplies were scarce as inflation increased. "When the first prisoners taken from the enemy arrived after the Battle of Bethel," admitted one Confederate, "a certain amount of pity prevailed . . . [which] soon disappeared after the murderous Battle of Manassas, when they were brought in in large numbers."[19]

In the meantime, suffering within the prisons gradually became worse. Prisoners' clothing was now worn, ragged, and louse infested. Filth and debris were accumulating in and around the buildings. Within only three months of First Manassas, the captive population had increased the city's population nearly 12 percent and the strain was having an effect. "[We] are served with two-third army rations," complained one prisoner by late December 1861. "[We sleep] on bare boards and are now very ragged and many are without shoes."[20]

In the early months of confinement, prisoners were allowed to exercise for half an hour twice a day on the grounds outside their facility. They also took turns cleaning and sweeping out their rooms. As the facilities became more crowded, both activities ceased, resulting in a dramatic increase of unhealthy conditions. "In one particular I am sure," wrote Colonel William R. Lee, 12th Massachusetts Regiment, comparing the Henrico County Jail where he was confined, to other places in Richmond, "they cannot vie with us in the number, variety, and size of vermin that infest our cell!"[21]

At Smith Prison, toilet facilities consisted of no more than a space in one corner of each floor, about six or eight feet long and several feet wide, which extended down into the basement. The basement was slowly becoming full of excrement. Enclosed on only three sides, it constantly emitted a permeating stench. Some prisons, however, had latrines outside. In those cases, when crowding and a lack of guards became a problem, buckets, which often overflowed before they were emptied, were placed in the corners of the rooms. Conditions became so crowded at some locations that prisoners simply defecated where they ate and slept.[22]

Still, prisoners attempted to bring some regularity and order to their chaotic lives. "Out of the loose tobacco leaves and scraps," wrote prisoner James Gillette, New York 71st Regiment, "we manufacture cigars, cigarettes, and even chewing tobacco by aid of the presses we taught ourselves to use. Pieces of sheet-iron, tin and nails afford material for cooking utensils . . . a little burnt crust and water makes excellent coffee when boiled."[23]

Other prisoners whittled, played cards and board games, or read. Partly for amusement and partly to police themselves, they formed the Richmond Prison Association and developed an "official seal," consisting of a ring of lice chasing each other around a circle with the motto "Bite and be damned" inscribed within it. The organization held court with mock trials for prisoners accused of theft or other wrongdoing, and established debates and other forms of entertainment for the inmate population. Congressman Ely was elected the society's first president.[24]

CHARLESTON

Confederate authorities gradually increased efforts to find locations outside Virginia for the mounting number of POWs. Attempts to plan ahead had been made as early as June of 1861, when the governor of North Carolina was requested to help find a location in his state for holding civilians and Confederate soldiers awaiting courts-martial. He located an old cotton factory in Salisbury, North Carolina, but negotiations were soon dropped. By October, Confederate officials were desperate. Negotiations resumed in North Carolina, and the governors of Alabama and Georgia were advised to find additional facilities. South Carolina, on the other hand, had been accepting POWs since September.[25]

During the first week of that month, Charleston officials were notified to prepare Castle Pinckney for the incarceration of prisoners of war. On September 10, 154 prisoners were shipped from Richmond to Charleston by train. Most of these men had been held in Ligon's Prison and, according to the *Charleston Mercury*, the prisoners were selected by Richmond officials "chiefly from among those who had evidenced the most insolent and insubordinate dispositions." These prisoners mostly were from the 11th New York Zouaves, the 79th New York Regiment, the 69th New York Regiment, including Colonel Michael Corcoran, and members of the 8th Michigan Infantry. They arrived at 5:45 on September 13 and were received by the Charleston Zouave Cadets, under the command of Captain C. E. Chichester.[26]

"[The Cadets formed] into two ranks," reported the *Mercury*, "at intervals of two paces—faced inwards—giving a width of twelve paces. On the right of the Zouaves the first platoon of the Louisiana Volunteers were posted—on the left, the second platoon—leaving an opening for the prisoners to march into the Square." From the Square another line of soldiers formed by the Carolina Light Dragoon led the prisoners through the streets as the German Hussans took up the rear.[27]

The prisoners were escorted to the Charleston City Jail, a three-story structure temporarily under the command of Captain Theodore G. Boag, where the 34 Union officers were placed in three rooms on the second floor. The 120 Union enlisted men were secured in twelve rooms on the uppermost floor. They were held there until September 18, when a renovation of Castle Pinckney was completed and these first prisoners were moved in.[28]

Castle Pinckney, located on the southern tip of a small island called Shute's Folly in Charleston Harbor, was a masonry fort with thick walls sixty feet high. It had been built in 1809 to replace a log fort that had been destroyed by a hurricane in September 1804. The island lies near the conjunction of the Cooper and Ashley rivers less than a mile off the coast of Charleston, and approximately 3½ miles northwest of forts Moultrie and Sumter. It was named for Ambassador Charles Cotesworth Pinckney, a Revolutionary War hero and the American diplomat involved in the XYZ Affair—a late-eighteenth-century scandal involving three French agents known only as X, Y, and Z, who demanded money from the American envoy headed by Pinckney before peace negotiations would be allowed to begin with the French government. Pinckney refused their demands and openly defied European powers with his famous statement, "Millions for defense but not one cent for tribute."[29]

The horseshoe shaped fort was officially described as an elliptical form built of brick, with two tiers of guns, having a good magazine and sufficient quarters to house two hundred men and officers. From the time the small fort was built, however, it was considered a prime example of bad engineering. The fort sat on a marsh, making the lower batteries worthless. An exposed rampart provided the only point of effective defensive operations, and ten 24-pounder smoothbore cannon were mounted there. A lower tier contained some fifteen smaller pieces, some of which were casemated.

While the fort's semicircular face was presented to the south, a line of ramparts formed the eastern and western faces. The diameter of the fort was 170 feet, with the entrance on the northern side. The officers' and privates' quarters, including a mess room, were located on either side of the entrance. In the center of the fort was a furnace for heating shot, but the lower portions of the fort were poorly ventilated and of little use.

By 1826 the fort had become of secondary importance to the U.S. War Department and remained so until it was renovated in 1831. That year, a new seawall was also constructed, and by January 1832, the fort was regarrisoned by the 2nd U.S. Artillery. Within a few years, though, the fort again fell into disuse and disrepair and was virtually abandoned until South Carolina seceded from the Union nearly twenty-five years later. After state troops took possession of the structure, it was garrisoned and maintained as an armed Confederate fort until requested as a POW facility. By that time, the North had already resorted to using a number of its coastal fortifications for the same purpose.

The Charleston Zouave Cadets were assigned to sentry duty at the new prison. Consisting of about forty young men, the group was probably one of the most professional regiments organized in the city. A contemporary Zouave recruiting poster declared, "Any person of moral character and gentlemanly deportment, and who is 17 years old and measures 5 feet 4 inches . . . may become a subscribing member on the payment of $5 a year. These are privileged to use the bowling alley and gymnasium at all times excepting on Tuesday and Friday evenings." It went on to promise a uniform of the French army type and warned the young men they would not be allowed to violate the "Golden Rules: No drinking in uniform, no patronage of saloons or houses of ill-fame and no gambling." These young Zouaves never got their fancy scarlet and blue uniforms but did have complete Confederate uniforms of gray with red trimming when they began guard duty at the Castle.[30]

Prison renovations at the fort consisted of bricking in the casemate openings to form individual rooms with heavy wooden door entrances. Three-tiered bunks lined the walls inside. The prisoners were locked into these casemate dungeons at night but were allowed to wander in and out during the daytime, being restricted to the fort's interior parade grounds.

Although these prisoners had been a discipline problem in Richmond, they were well behaved here. This might have been due to the conditions they found at Castle Pinckney, which were not as crowded as they had been at Richmond. The men had more freedom of movement and were not confined continually in one small room; they received coffee and sugar in their daily rations until the blockade made it impossible; and they were treated more professionally by their guards.

In fact, at Castle Pinckney, a camaraderie developed between the prisoners and their young overseers. They indulged in good-natured banter with one another and morale was outstanding. Each group of prisoners hung humorous signs over the entrances of their individual casemate prison rooms and several groups even constructed verandas over them. Since captives and guards shared the same rations, the prisoners took the time to teach the cadets the army method of softening hardtack so it would be easier for them to eat.[31]

The prisoners willingly policed their own quarters and kept their casemates in excellent condition. They also formed the Castle Pinckney Brotherhood, modeled after the Richmond Prison Association, to establish rules for prisoners to live by, including rules for cleanliness, and to provide organized forms of entertainment. The Charleston Zouaves often helped with the Brotherhood's activities.[32]

Captain Chichester acted as the prison commandant and even commissioned a photographer, at his own expense, to take photos inside the prison of the cadets and the prisoners. The number of photographs of the fort as a POW facility gives the impression that it remained a prison during the entire conflict. All, however, were taken within a six week period and were the result of Captain Chichester's interest in making a photographic record for posterity.

To the chagrin of the Confederacy, within a matter of weeks, the Castle was found entirely too small and too inadequate as a permanent POW facility. What had been intended as a permanent place of confinement proved to be nothing more than a wayside stop for a handful of prisoners. The extensive renovations had been a waste of time. On October 31, 1861, the prisoners were removed from Castle Pinckney and held, again, in the Charleston City Jail. By this time there were nearly two hundred additional prisoners there. The Castle Pinckney prisoners remained in these crowded conditions throughout the following six weeks until the great fire of Charleston occurred on December 11.[33]

The jail was located in the southeast part of town. It was a strange-looking, octagon-shaped, stuccoed masonry building officially described as having three stories. A forty-foot tower loomed over the structure, giving it a somewhat fortress-like appearance.

As more POWs were brought into the city during the incarceration of those at Castle Pinckney, the Union officer prisoners originally confined on the second floor and the enlisted men held on the uppermost floor continued to be crowded together more and more until additional large rooms on additional floors were used. Finally, overcrowding became so bad that the enlisted men were moved to the Charleston Race Course for confinement.

As late as December 1861, Federal POWs were still being confined with the local criminals. "There are under the same roof with us," reported Lieutenant John W. Dempsey, 2nd Regiment, New York State Militia, "murderers, thieves, mail robbers, colored, and even the abandoned wretches of easy virtue!" Other sources indicate that these conditions continued through 1864. Prisoners sentenced to death, as Colonel Corcoran was, were confined in one of seven condemned cells in the tower.[34]

Letter-writing and newspapers were prohibited at the jail, with "every channel of communication being cut off," complained a prisoner. Nor was furniture allowed. In addition, as another prisoner noted, "There [was] no means of heating the cells except by a stove situated in the cellar, the pipe of which ran up through the roof." The stove was usually heated by coal but, as one prisoner learned, "I am told there is none to be had at present."[35]

By December of 1861, the Guard House on the southeast corner of Broad and Meeting streets was also being used to confine prisoners of war. Built in 1838, the building was a remarkable display of Greek Revival architecture in heavy stonework. It originally had a portico of six Doric columns along Broad Street and a colonnade along Meeting Street. The colonnade, however, was removed in 1856 to allow the widening of the roadway. The windows of this two-story structure were covered by wrought-iron grills of a sword design. Inside, two tiers of cells were built around a large, vacant square court in the center. Up until the war, recalcitrant slaves had been held here. Both the city jail and the Guard House, within a week after they were opened, held their capacity of three hundred prisoners each, including those originally held at Castle Pinckney.[36]

On the night of December 11, a fire broke out in the Russell and Company Sash and Blind Factory at the foot of Hasell Street. A stiff breeze quickly drove the flames to Broad Street, engulfing the theater, Institute Hall, and a number of other public buildings. The Guard House and the city jail lay in the fire's path, endangering the Federal prisoners. "Nearly all that part of the city," reported the *New York Times*, "from Broad Street on the Southeast Bay on the east and King Street on the west, is said to be destroyed. . . . Half of the city is in ashes including the heart of the city. . . . Thousands have been left homeless."[37]

"When the fire broke out, nearly all the prisoners were in a large upper room," reported prisoner Samuel D. Hurd, 2nd Regiment, Maine Volunteers, who was confined in the city jail. "The windows were barred and closed with iron shutters, except for one small window overlooking a very narrow street in the rear of the building." The fire spread rapidly and soon the jail roof was ablaze. "No movement was made to let the prisoners out," declared Hurd. "The guards, usually stationed around the building, were away and no soldiers were visible."[38]

The guards had left to assist the firemen. According to the *Charleston Mercury*, even "the regiments from the Race Course came down at doublequick to assist."[39]

The fire steadily advanced southwest across the city and increased in intensity, creating a storm with a backdraft of tremendous proportions. The resulting wind, according to the *Mercury*, "swept the dust and smoke and sparks hither and thither in blinding clouds [as] great flaming bits of wood were borne in dense showers for a distance of nearly a mile . . . and the whole city was brightly lit up by the dreadful and widening glare."[40]

"The fire seems making straight towards the Jail," the report continued. "Companies of the Reserves have been ordered out to repress any possible disturbance among the prisoners confined in the building."[41]

But it was too late. As the heat increased and the flames spread across the roof, the prisoners panicked. Finally, they decided to make an attempt to squeeze through the small window and drop to the street.

"Colonel Corcoran was the first one to leap through the window," reported Hurd, who went next. When he fell to the pavement, a half dozen others tumbled down upon him. Within moments, the entire room was emptied of its inmates. [42]

They spent the rest of the night in the vicinity of the fires, keeping together the best they could. Many had been hurt in their jump to safety and were unable to travel far. During the night, several men ran off to search abandoned homes for food. Nothing could be found except a few bottles of liquor, which were brought back to the rest of the group. By ten o'clock the next morning, guards arrived to take charge of the prisoners. "They treated them with great brutality," reported the *New York Times*, "striking with their guns those of them who did not move quickly enough."[43]

Hurd agreed: "The treatment of the prisoners [was] brutal and infamous."[44]

Narrowly escaping the conflagration, the prisoners were rounded up and, at about two o'clock in the afternoon, transported to Castle Pinckney. With more than twice as many prisoners as before, guards left most of these POWs in the open courtyard of the fort with no shelter, no blankets, and no change of clothing. The entire squad of more than three hundred prisoners was held here under these conditions for over a week, during which time ten prisoners took the oath of allegiance promising not to take up arms against the Confederacy and were transported to Fortress Monroe, Virginia, on parole for exchange. Eventually, the others were transferred out. By the first of the following year, Castle Pinckney had been converted into a defensive fortification.[45]

The cause of the Charleston fire was never determined. Some blamed "Yankee spies," while others blamed former slaves in the area. Whatever the cause, it destroyed a quarter of the city and left the citizens with staggering losses. They were unable to rebuild in the midst of siege, and the path of the fire remained a scar across the city throughout the remainder of the war.

Most of the buildings consumed in the stricken area had been old, closely built, and surrounded by small outbuildings. The jail and Guard House, for the most part, survived. After some efforts to clean up the debris, both buildings confined prisoners again by late January 1862.

In addition to Charleston, Richmond sent groups of POWs to Columbia, South Carolina, where nearly 200 were held in the city jail, the fairgrounds, and various town jails. Other contingents ranging anywhere from 150 to 200 were sent to such places as Atlanta, Georgia, where they were held in the Fulton County jail; Macon, Georgia, where they were held downtown in the Davis Smith Slave Mart building; New Orleans, Louisiana, where they were held in the Orleans Parish prison; and Montgomery, Alabama.[46]

Those held at Montgomery were originally destined for Tuscaloosa but an old abandoned paper mill purchased by the Confederacy there was found to be too dilapidated to use. Attempts were made to lease the old legislative buildings, abandoned since 1846 when the capital was moved to Montgomery, and the lunatic asylum in Tuscaloosa, but authorities finally had to settle on leasing a number of old downtown hotels, including the well known Drish building, and confining the POWs on the upper floors. The Montgomery prisoners were moved to Tuscaloosa on December 14, 1861.

SALISBURY

During the previous month, the Confederate government's purchase of the old Salisbury, North Carolina, cotton factory was finalized. The building was originally intended to confine only Confederate soldiers who had committed military offenses, and in that first month, many were moved there. But in the continuing effort to reduce the number of POWs in Richmond, the first Federal prisoners arrived at the facility on December 12. This group consisted of 120 Union soldiers captured at First Manassas. Their arrival, according to one report, "caused great excitement among the Salisburians because few had ever seen a 'live Yankee soldier.'" On December 26, a group of 176 more Union prisoners arrived.[47]

The property, consisting of a large four-story brick building and six small cottages on sixteen acres heavily shaded by oak trees, had been built in 1845 by local resident Maxwell Chambers. He had gone out of business in 1853 and had sold the property for use as a school. The site, however, had been sitting dormant for a number of years.[48]

Authorities estimated that the buildings at the site would have a capacity of 1,500 to 2,000 men, and with the addition of a highboard fence, bars for the windows, and other changes, the cost of renovation would probably be no more than $2,000 over the purchase price of $15,000. The owner was willing to take Confederate bonds in payment. In addition, there was $500 worth of machinery on the site that could be sold. Authorities believed that the property would easily sell for $30,000 to $50,000 after the war.[49]

What made the property even more attractive was that Salisbury sat at the crossroads of North Carolina's major railroad lines in an area rich in produce. Fruit and vegetables were abundant, and the commissary general of the state could contract with local farmers to feed the captives at half the cost of regular army rations.

The site sounded too good to be true. The purchase was overwhelmingly approved and the governor was assured that if he could enlist a guard unit for the prison, the Confederate government would assume the cost.

But when the first Union captives arrived, the prison was not ready. Renovations being done by the Confederate prisoners awaiting courts-martial were incomplete, and a local unit of guards was not available. Out of desperation, the Confederate government procured the services of a company made up of students from nearby Trinity College, commanded by Reverend Braxton Craven, the school president. Craven was named commandant of the prison, but the arrangement with the Trinity guards lasted only a few weeks. Colonel George C. Gibbs soon arrived from Richmond to take command of the prison.[50]

The completed prison was enclosed with a fence eight feet high with a parapet about four feet high running along the outside for guards to patrol along and have an unobstructed view of the prison's interior. The main entrance was on what is now Bank Street. Two cannon guarded the entrance and others were positioned along portholes in the fence, with a full sweep of the inside of the compound. The Confederate headquarters was outside, on the north side of the entrance gate. The main factory building was located toward the southeast corner of the enclosure. The cottages were located in groups of three at right angles a short distance from that building, toward the center of the compound, and a blacksmith shop toward the front gate later served as the "deadhouse." Unnoticed until after the first prisoners arrived, the one well that existed on the property usually was dry by noon. Water had to be carried by prison details sent outside under heavy guard to a nearby creek or to public wells in town.

Union officers included in the first arrivals of POWs were quartered in the upper story of the four-story factory building and were allowed passes into town on some occasions. Enlisted men, who didn't have that privilege, were quartered on the lower floors of the main factory building as well as in the smaller cottages.[51]

After a few months, Colonel Gibbs finished forming his regiment made up of guards and left for the seat of war. He was replaced by Captain A. C. Godwin of Richmond. Like Gibbs, Godwin showed some compassion for the prisoners and became well-liked by them. When Godwin was later captured in the field and sent to a Northern prison, he was "sought out and favored by those he had once held or by their relatives and friends."[52]

In the beginning, the Salisbury prisoners enjoyed adequate space and shelter, reasonable rations, and decent water and sanitation. Women from town were allowed to visit and volunteer help inside the stockade, and they often brought home-cooked meals to the prisoners. There were Sunday afternoon dress parades for the visitors, and some of the earliest baseball games were played here. In fact, the townsfolk often turned out in force to watch the prisoners playing baseball, and one of the earliest pictures of a ball game in progress was drawn by a Salisbury inmate, Major Otto Boetticher.[53]

"For months Salisbury was the most endurable prison I had seen," agreed prisoner Albert D. Richardson, who was also news correspondent for the

New York *Tribune*. "There were 600 prisoners, they were exercised in the open air, comparatively well fed and kindly treated."[54]

The prison population continued to fluctuate drastically during its first few months. By spring of 1862, the inmate population would reach seventeen hundred and would include Union POWs, Confederate military convicts, and prisoners of state.

While Richmond was trying to get out of the POW business, New York City was inadvertently becoming the prison center of the North. It possessed the major railroads and seaports of the North and, for lack of a better place, Confederates captured by Union forces often were brought into the city. Within four years, more than thirteen different locations in the metropolitan area would be used for confinement. Like Richmond, none of these facilities had a very high capacity. In fact, most averaged from fifty to several hundred, but within a short time, as in Richmond, more prisoners than had ever been anticipated would be crammed into each of these structures, causing them to become just as overcrowded and horrifying as those established in the Confederate capitol.

THE TOMBS

New York City's first POWs arrived on June 15, 1861. They were the twenty-man crew of the Confederate privateer *Savannah* that was captured outside Charleston Harbor on June 3. Considered pirates at the time, they were taken to the nearest Federal court which, in this case, was in the city of New York. The ship was escorted to New York Harbor and anchored at the Battery. The crew, being the first privateers captured by the North and the first Confederate prisoners brought into the city, were ceremoniously paraded through the streets in shackles on their way to the Tombs prison on Center Street. "The captain, the executive officer, and the purser were linked together," reported one newspaper, "the others followed in couples."[55]

The procession was led by city policemen and flanked by deputy marshals. Crowds of curious spectators gathered along the streets and crowded the windows along the route, taunting and insulting the captives. Mothers even held up their children to give them a better look at the "Johnny Rebs."

Upon arriving at the multicolumned portico entrance of the Tombs prison, the prisoners were led in, one shackled pair at a time, and placed into cells usually reserved for civilian prisoners among the city's most violent criminal element. Reluctantly, the new prisoners became acquainted with their surroundings, described as "foul," and "awful smelling," under the watchful and brutish stares of a ragged and dirty population of convicts. Even the police department physician, Doctor A. S. Jones, had to admit that a "more miserable, unhealthy, and horrible dungeon cannot well be conceived of."[56]

Unfortunately, it was the only secure place in the city at that time to hold prisoners for trial.

"When we first came here and were put into this cell, the very appearance of it was enough to sicken a man," wrote prisoner Thomas H. Baker, former captain of the *Savannah*, "but after being annoyed by bugs, lice, and roaches, etc. for five days, we obtained permission to have our own bedding brought— so we had the place scrubbed and whitewashed, everything moved out, and procured a couple of camp cots that we can stow in a corner in daytime, a little out of the way."[57]

"[We] have got rid of the vermin and are just as comfortable as we can be in this infernal place," agreed First Lieutenant John M. Harleston. "This close confinement is bad. I am afraid when I get out—if I ever do—that I won't be able to walk."[58]

"Our cell is quite small," Baker wrote, "less than eight feet long by five and a half wide, so we have no room at all for exercise."[59]

Confined in the new prison section of the building, the *Savannah* officers had the "luxury" of barred windows overlooking Center Street. Most of the captives, however, sat idly on the edge of their cots throughout the day listening to the hollow clang of cell doors echoing up and down the halls. After 6:00 P.M., the corridors were lit by kerosene instead of gas, which added to the eerie, dungeon-like nature of their quarters. By the spring of the next year there would be about three hundred prisoners of war and common criminals mixed together within these walls.[60]

The Tombs was a combination of a city jail and criminal courts building, covering two blocks between Center and Lafayette streets. Its official title when built in 1838 was The Halls of Justice, but because the building resembled an Egyptian mausoleum, New Yorkers quickly began referring to it simply as "the Tombs."[61]

"The perceptibly sloping walls and the crowning cornices are familiar in other structures," reported the *New York Times* some years later, "but the dark and frowning portico, with the low, wide steps and the heavy columns filling up the deep entrance [give] it a peculiarly forbidding aspect, as suggestive of hopeless imprisonment as of perpetual burial."[62]

Constructed of huge granite blocks, the four-story building was in the form of a parallelogram. The jail section contained 150 cells arranged in four tiers facing inward and overlooking a courtyard where a gallows often stood in plain view of all the inmates. The first tier cells contained "lunatics" and prisoners under sentence. The second tier held those charged with more serious crimes such as murder. The third tier was for those charged with burglary, grand larceny, and similar offenses, while the fourth tier held the less serious offenders.[63]

By the time of the Civil War, the prison had become well-known for being damp, unsanitary, and frequently overcrowded. According to a survey conducted around 1860, the Tombs was considered "one of the four worst prisons in the country."[64]

The cells, according to a *New York Times* correspondent during the Civil War, "are what in darker ages would have been the dungeons but now-a-days a long line of cells [with] narrow and unyielding masonry, [and] one tiny slip near the ceiling admitting the light."[65]

Three stages of security guarded this area: a heavy wooden door, an iron barred door covered by closely latticed wire, and a group of civilian, or police, guards. "The inner, wooden, door is left open during the daytime," reported the correspondent, "but the iron one is closely secured." After 6:00 P.M. both doors were closed and locked until daylight the following morning. "In [the] lower corridor are placed three enormous stoves which diffuse ample warmth throughout the building."[66]

While the officers of the *Savannah*, along with a few other privateers captured soon afterward, were held in the upper, new prison area of the Tombs with larger cells and windows, the crewmen were all held in the smaller, dimly lit cells of the lower section. There they remained until turned over to the War Department and transferred to Fort Lafayette on February 3, 1862. After that date, the Tombs was no longer used for military prisoners.

FORT LAFAYETTE

Fort Lafayette had served as a U.S. military prison since July 15, 1861, when Edward D. Townsend, assistant adjutant general, ordered Major General Nathaniel P. Banks to take prisoners captured by General McClellan in West Virginia. Townsend then advised, "A permanent guard will be ordered to the fort in time to receive the prisoners." The first POWs arrived July 22. Prior to this, the fort had served as one of the first Northern coastal fortifications to hold Federal political prisoners.[67]

The fort was built on a small rock island lying in the Narrows between the lower end of Staten Island and Long Island, opposite Fort Hamilton. All POWs enroute to Fort Lafayette arrived at Fort Hamilton first, where they were searched, had their names recorded, and were placed on a boat for the quarter-mile trip to the offshore island prison. Erected in 1822 and originally named Fort Diamond, Fort Lafayette was an octagonal structure with the four principal sides much larger than the others, making the building appear somewhat round from the outside and square from the inside.

The fort's walls were 25 to 30 feet high, with batteries commanding a view of the channel in two of its longer and two of its shorter sides. Two tiers of heavy guns were on each of these sides, with lighter barbette guns above them under a temporary wooden roof. The two other principal sides were occupied by two stories of small casemates, ten on each story. The open area within the fort was 120 feet across with a pavement 25 feet wide running around the inside, leaving a patch of ground 70 feet square in the center.

Long before the Civil War this fortress was renamed Fort Lafayette, in honor of the Marquis de Lafayette, the young French general who had aided the American cause in the Revolutionary War. By the second year of the Civil War, however, it would be hatefully referred to, by many, simply as "that American Bastille."

Francis K. Howard, a prisoner at Fort Lafayette, wrote: "A gloomier looking place than Fort LaFayette, both within and without, would be hard to find in the whole state of New York, or indeed, (hard to find) anywhere." Prisoner John I. Shaver, a citizen of Canada arrested in Detroit for aiding the Confederacy, was confined in a dark and unventilated casemate with forty-eight other prisoners and, according to the *Montreal Advertiser,* "in an atmosphere rendered pestiferous by the want of the common decencies of life."[68]

The prisoners were confined in the fort's two principal gun batteries and in four casemates of the lower story that had all been converted into prison rooms by bricking up the open entrances.

"Each of these batteries was paved with brick," reported Howard, "and was about 60 feet long and 24 feet wide . . . [but] there were five large 32-pounders in this room about eight feet apart on carriages which occupied a great deal of space."[69]

The enclosures were lighted by five embrasures measuring, about 2½ by 2 feet, which were covered with iron gratings. Five large doorways, 7 or 8 feet high, opened upon the enclosure from within the walls but were covered by solid folding doors. "We were only allowed to keep two of these doors, at one end of the battery, open," complained Howard, "and at that end only could we usually see to read or write. The lower half of the battery was in a state of perpetual twilight."[70]

The four casemates were nothing more than vaulted cells measuring 8 feet at the highest point and 24-by-14 feet wide. Each was lighted by two small loopholes in the outer wall and one on an inner wall. Large wooden doors of the casemates were shut and locked at 9:00 P.M. and remained so until daylight. Although these rooms remained dark and damp most of the time, they did have fireplaces, which the batteries lacked. Later, stoves had to be installed in the battery rooms to combat the cold.

Neither location had furniture except for a few beds. "Beds, where used," reported Howard, "were positioned between the guns and nearly touched one another." Those not given iron beds were provided bags of straw but many of those in the lower casemates had no beds, bags of straw, or blankets. "Their condition," wrote one prisoner, "could hardly be worse if they were in a slave-ship." Howard noted, "Our imprisonment [was] exactly like that of those who used to be held in the Bastille."[71]

Fort Lafayette's commandant was Colonel Martin Burke, commander of nearby Fort Hamilton. General Winfield Scott once remarked that he was "famous for his unquestioning obedience to orders. He was with me in Mexico, and if I told him at any time to take one of my aides-de-camp and shoot him before breakfast, the aide's execution would have been duly reported."[72]

In immediate command over the Fort Lafayette prisoners was Lieutenant Charles O. Wood, who was described as "brutal" by many of the prisoners. He had been a baggage handler on the Ohio and Mississippi Railroad before the war and had received his commission, it was said, from President Lincoln as a reward for successfully smuggling Lincoln's baggage through Baltimore prior to his inauguration.[73]

When originally converted to a prison, the fort was believed capable of holding up to fifty POWs. From the very beginning, however, twenty were held in each battery while nine to ten were held in each casemate. Before long there were often thirty-five to a battery and up to thirty in a casemate. "The fort could not be made to accommodate twenty people decently besides the garrison," Howard wrote, "nevertheless, there were always over a hundred crowded into it and at one time there was as many as 135."[74]

When the prisoners arrived at Fort Lafayette, they were escorted to the office of Lieutenant Wood where, again, they were searched and had their names recorded. All their money was confiscated; they were given a receipt and then shown to their quarters.

Some of the first inmates included those who had done nothing more than express sympathy for the South: members of the Maryland legislature; Baltimore's police commissioners; James W. Ball, a New Jersey Democrat who was later elected to the U.S. Senate; and Francis K. Howard, editor of a Baltimore newspaper and grandson of Francis Scott Key. In addition, all officers who had resigned commissions in the U.S. Army to accept Confederate commands were, if captured, automatically sent there.

Although the privateers transferred from the Tombs were originally kept in shackles and confined both day and night in the lower casemates of the fort, the regular prisoners of war and political prisoners were allowed to exercise in the open area of the compound two times each day—from six to seven in the morning and from five to six in the evening. The exercise usually consisted of individuals simply walking along the pavement around the inside of the fort several times. As the prison became more crowded, these walks were limited to one half hour twice a day and then, finally, eliminated altogether. At dark the prisoners were confined to their rooms and all candles were extinguished at nine. Later, candles were also eliminated and, according to one prisoner's account, "the night to us now is nearly 15 hours, counting from lock-up time to the opening of the cell in the morning."[75]

According to the *New York Times*, at daybreak, doors were unlocked and the prisoners would "amuse themselves . . . by exchanging visits from casemate to casemate, playing whist, chess, or backgammon, or simply smoking cigars."[76]

Rations distributed at Fort Lafayette were described by one prisoner as "tough beef, dry bread, beans, and bad coffee." The kitchen facilities were so bad, though, that meals were often served only half-cooked. For those who could afford it, there was also a mess under control of the fort's ordnance sergeant and his family. For these meals, prisoners were charged one dollar per day, credited against what the prisoners had turned over to Lieutenant Wood when they arrived at the fort. They were denied the use of their own funds to make food purchases from a sutler outside the fort or to receive food sent by friends, thereby eliminating all competition with the ordnance sergeant's service.[77]

"Dinners," complained one prisoner, "consisted of fat pork and beans, a cup of thin soup and bread, or of boiled beef, potatoes and bread on alternate days. . . . The coffee was a muddy liquid in which the taste of coffee was barely perceptible, the predominating flavor being a combination of burnt beans and foul water."[78]

The fort's water was indeed foul. The prisoners often complained that the fluid provided by a cistern, contained dirt and "animalcules." There were also several periods during which prisoners had to go without water altogether.

While records and memoirs indicate that conditions in the Confederate prisons remained generally healthy throughout 1861, the question of health among prisoners in Union hands during the same period has remained a matter of controversy. Although official records show that only two deaths occurred at Fort Lafayette during its use as a prison, there was no requirement by the War Department prior to July 7, 1862, to keep records or report such matters. Contemporary sources present a picture different from official records. Newspapers reported that a typhoid fever epidemic at the fort in late 1861 caused prisoners to die so rapidly "as to arouse public attention and produce an outcry of indignation."[79]

GOVERNORS ISLAND

At the same time, POWs held at other New York prison locations were suffering just as horribly. "Our men are now suffering very greatly from disease," wrote prisoner Andrew Norman, 7th Regiment, North Carolina Volunteers on September 30, 1861, while being held at Castle Williams on Governors Island.

"Today 115 of the 630 are confined by disease which threatens to prostrate us all. Four of our men have died within the past five days and many others are dangerously ill."[80]

Dr. William J. Sloan, medical director of the Federal army, reported that the prisoners "are crowded into an ill-ventilated building which has always been an unhealthy one when occupied by large bodies of men. There are no conveniences for cooking except in the open air, no means of heating the lower tier of gun rooms and no privies within the area. As the winter approaches I cannot see how these 630 men can be taken care of under the above circumstances. . . . There are now upwards of eighty cases of measles amongst them, a number of cases of typhoid fever, pneumonia, intermittent fever, etc. . . . Every building upon the island being crowded with troops, with a large number in tents, I know not how the condition of these prisoners can be improved except by a change of location. . . . If 100 are removed to Bedloe's Island as contemplated and including a large portion of the sick, there will be better facilities for improving the condition of those remaining [at Castle Williams]."[81]

Authorities took Doctor Sloan's advice and began transferring prisoners to Bedloe's Island in mid-October. Here they were confined at Fort Wood, a star-shaped rampart built in 1811 on the east side of the twelve-acre, egg-shaped isle.

But conditions for the prisoners confined in all of New York's harbor facilities continued to worsen as illness and deaths increased. Finally, on October 30, all prisoners confined at Fort Lafayette, Governors Island, and Fort Wood were evacuated and transferred by steamer to newly converted Fort Warren in Boston Harbor. Within a few months, though, as additional captives continued to be brought into the city, authorities ignored the previous recommendations, and again began filling the harbor facilities beyond capacity.[82]

Fort Wood and Governors Island, consisting of Castle Williams and Fort Columbus, were situated in the Upper Bay area. Governors Island, 170 acres and 500 yards off the southern tip of Manhattan where the East and Hudson Rivers converge into the bay, was originally called Nutten, or Nut, Island because of the massive grove of nut trees growing there. Wouter van Twiller, second governor of then New Netherland, purchased the island in 1637, and in 1698, the New York Assembly set the land aside for the "benefit and accommodation of His Majesty's governors," hence its present name.[83]

At the dock on the northwest tip of the island, two roads branched out in different directions. One led to Castle Williams on the southern side of the island, and the other led to Fort Columbus on the northern end of the isle. Both forts were built originally as a defense against the British.

Fort Columbus dominated the island from a knoll. It was a red-brick, star-shaped structure built in 1794 with the name Fort Jay, in honor of John

Jay, diplomat and the first Chief Justice of the U.S. Supreme Court. Its four bastions of masonry once held one hundred guns and a drawbridge approach over a dry moat to a sally port. During the Civil War, a quadrangle of officers' dwellings within the fort served to confine captured Confederate officers. Although the combined capacity of Fort Columbus and Castle Williams was estimated at five hundred, more than that number were incarcerated there most of the time.

"The fort itself furnishes no room for prisoners," admitted Colonel William Hoffman, after he became commissary general of prisoners, in a letter to Secretary Stanton, "but in Castle Williams an outbreak of two tiers of guns in casemates and one of 15-inch guns in barbettes, the third floor of which consists of arched rooms for the garrison, some 500 prisoners may be accommodated." Eventually, he would allow as many as 713 to be crammed into these quarters.[84]

Many prisoners, complained a shocked Colonel James V. Bomford, 8th U.S. Infantry, when he took over as prison commandant, "are entirely destitute of bedding, and in a great measure, of the necessary clothing to insure cleanliness and comfort."[85]

Castle Williams was a circular fort, and because of its shape, was often referred to as "the cheese box." It was named in honor of Lieutenant Colonel Jonathan Williams, who designed the structure. The fort was two hundred feet in diameter with walls of red sandstone forty feet high and eight feet thick. Construction had begun in 1807 but wasn't completed until 1811.

Castle Williams was used to hold Confederate enlisted men. These men were confined to their quarters at all times, while the officers at Fort Columbus were given the privilege of roaming about the west and south sides of the island. At times, the prisoner population of Castle Williams included deserters from the U.S. army, but generally it served as a POW facility.[86]

The only other New York facility that came into use during 1861 was the Ludlow Street Jail, which primarily held prisoners of state before Fort Lafayette came into use.

WASHINGTON

Regarding prisoners of war, probably the second most important city to the Union was Washington, D.C., or Washington City, as it was commonly referred to then. A number of facilities were used there, and gradually the city developed into the Union's eastern depot prison center.

The first city building pressed into use was the Washington County Jail on Judiciary Square. It had been built in 1830 to house up to 100 prisoners, but with the arrival of the Civil War, as many as 240 prisoners were held there, with up to 10 men crammed into an eight-by-ten-foot cell. This crowding, along with the absence of restrooms and a jailyard covered with stagnant water, caused the secretary of the interior to once remark that it was "little better than the Black Hole of Calcutta."[87]

Next to be used was the federal penitentiary on Arsenal Point. Constructed in 1827, this building, too, quickly became overcrowded and obsolete.

Finally, in August 1861, authorities confiscated a dilapidated three-story brick building at the corner of First and A streets for prison use. It had been erected in 1800 as a tavern and boarding house, but because of bad management, it closed before the War of 1812. The structure was then purchased for government use after British troops entered Washington and burned the Capitol, along with other buildings, in August of 1814. Its interior was completely renovated and both Houses of Congress used the site for many years. When the new Capitol was completed, this structure was abandoned, but city residents continued to refer to it as "the Old Capitol building."

During the following years it had several different uses. For a while it became a boarding house again, and sometime later, it was used as a school. By 1861, when the city's provost marshal commandeered the structure, its only occupant was an old German cobbler. Its walls were decaying, the doors and stairways creaked, and wooden slats covered the windows. Eventually, the wooden slats were replaced with iron bars, a highboard fence enclosed the open areas between the building and nearby structures, and extensions were built upon the back and sides that included mess halls and additional quarters.

The first inmates to be moved into this facility were mostly political prisoners, but POWs were incarcerated as early as August 8. They included men from the 4th Alabama, the 1st, 5th, and 27th Virginia, and the 8th Georgia regiments, all captured at Bull Run; and of the 2nd South Carolina and 6th Alabama taken at Fairfax Courthouse. By October 1861, Old Capitol Prison was full.[88]

FORT WARREN

Fort Warren Military Prison came into existence with the arrival of New York City's harbor POWs. This fort eventually became the North's most tolerable facility, yet it too had its problems.

A two-story pentagon-shaped fortress of heavy granite built on Georges Island, it was situated at the entrance of Boston Harbor, about seven miles out from the city. The island on which it was built originally consisted of forty-three acres, nearly all of which were covered by various fortifications, but Fort Warren itself enclosed only six acres on the upper end of the island. A large lighthouse occupied a small isle off the lower end, opposite the fort.

Construction on the fort began in 1834 and it was named in honor of Joseph Warren, a hero of Bunker Hill. Its five sides, each measuring 600-to-666 feet long and 8 feet thick, were not completed until 1845, and even by 1860, some of its interior quarters and gun emplacements were still under construction.

At the beginning of hostilities, Fort Warren served as a training camp for a number of Massachusetts regiments, including the 2nd and 14th, but the structure quickly proved inadequate to house and maintain large groups. In fact, its overall capacity for prisoners was later estimated at 175.

According to Dr. Samuel G. Howe, who inspected the quarters soon after the first state troops arrived, each soldier should be allowed 600 cubic feet of air in his barrack but, at Fort Warren, there was less than 145 feet. And, according to the Boston *Evening Transcript*, there was still dissatisfaction among the troops with their quarters nearly a year into the war, and it apparently continued to the end. When army surgeon Charles T. Alexander inspected the fort two years later, he noted that the quarters occupied by the troops and prisoners were still "too crowded for comfort" and "deficient both in neatness and order." He went on to call attention to the hospital privy, which was "a close, offensive place, without drainage, unsupplied with water."[89]

Regardless of the conditions in the fort, in October 1861, the U.S. War Department requested that John A. Andrew, governor of Massachusetts, provide a contingent of guards for duty at Fort Warren. It also requested that the quartermaster in Boston prepare rations for one hundred POWs for a thirty-day period. Colonel Justin E. Dimick, the commanding officer at Fortress Monroe, then transferred to Boston to assume command of the new prison. Dimick, a professional soldier who had graduated from West Point in 1814, had served in the war against the Florida Indians as well as in the Mexican War, and received promotions for gallant and meritorious conduct in both. Dimick maintained discipline through kindness, a trait he carried with him as he took command of the Fort Warren Military Prison.

"[His] demeanor towards us was, on all occasions, that of a gentleman," one prisoner later wrote. "I have formed a very high opinion of him as a gentleman and Christian; all the prisoners, without exception, speak well of him," wrote another. In fact, his kindness was more than his adjutant general, Lorenzo Thomas, could apparently handle. Thomas later chastised Dimick for making his guards empty the night buckets of the Confederate prisoners each morning: "Let it be done by the prisoners under a guard!" Thomas ordered.[90]

When Colonel Dimick went to the dock to greet the first set of prisoners, he was horrified and dismayed. Aboard the steamer were 755 prisoners, consisting of 155 political prisoners and 600 prisoners of war, 60 of whom were suffering from typhoid fever.

"On reaching the wharf, Colonel Dimick came on board and informed us that he had not been notified by the Government of our intended removal," wrote prisoner Lawrence Sangston, "except that he had received orders, in general terms, to prepare quarters for one hundred political prisoners from Fort Lafayette, and had no accommodations for a larger number." Dimick went on to explain he had only arrived the day before and that there was no furniture of any kind on the island nor anything to eat.[91]

Dimick told the officer in charge that the captives would have to remain on the ship overnight. The ship's captain protested, saying the ship was overcrowded. After much argument, nearly four hundred prisoners, mostly North Carolinians captured at Hatteras Inlet, were allowed ashore, while the others remained on the ship.

The following day, the remaining prisoners were marched to the fort, where they were held in two of the fort's five sides that were divided into deep casemates opening onto the parade grounds. Additional prisoners were placed on an opposite side that contained ten smaller rooms originally serving as the fort's officers' quarters. These, too, opened upon the parade ground.

Political prisoners were held in smaller, inner rooms behind those of the POWs and in twenty small rooms beneath them, below ground level. A pump in this basement area furnished the water for all the prisoners.

"The front rooms above ground are well lighted with large windows," declared one prisoner, "the back rooms are dark, being lighted with narrow slits in the wall, six inches wide, and the light and view [are] shut off . . . the lower rooms of course are still darker, being ten feet below the level of the parade ground, and receiving their light from a narrow area—all the rooms are however dry—the lower ones have stone floors, the upper ones plank floors."[92]

The most notorious quarters at Fort Warren were the larger rooms where up to 160 men were crammed into a space of 17-by-50 feet. One such room became known as "Room number forty-five."

"The atmosphere of number forty-five was almost unendurable," reported Sangston, "[having] that peculiar sickening smell known as a 'Poor House smell.'"[93]

Except for stoves, none of the rooms had furniture. The prisoners simply sat or slept on the cold stone or wood floors. "At times," complained one prisoner, "the wind would whistle through the casemate windows equal to the shrill whistle of a locomotive engine."[94]

With many more prisoners than expected, many captives missed as many as five meals in their first two days at the fort. "Two raw hams and a barrel of soda crackers was all the food that 700 people had during the whole [first] day and part of the next," reported Sangston. "During the [second] day a sharp

Yankee came down from Boston and proposed to draw our rations," reported another prisoner, "and furnish us with two meals a day in good style for one dollar per day."[95]

Such offers were accepted by a few of the political prisoners. Others made arrangements to acquire supplies delivered by a government boat that made regular runs between the fort and Boston.

Political prisoners were kept separated from the POWs and, in some cases, were treated more severely. They were allotted a small exercise area measuring 150 by 30 feet outside their rooms but within the fort, unlike the Confederate enlisted men, who were allowed the fresh air of the parade grounds. Confederate officers were given a limited parole of the entire island, as long as they stayed away from the wharves and other barracks.

Gradually, conditions at the prison began to improve. At the end of the first week, bunks were acquired and each prisoner was furnished with a cotton sack and twelve pounds of straw for a mattress along with a blanket.

At first, boilers were placed outside the doors of the POW quarters for cooking rations but were not supplied to the political prisoners. "Exposed to the weather," Sangston later noted, "I have often noticed them, thinly clad, cooking their rations in a driving rain or snowstorm."[96]

Cooking stoves were provided eventually for the others, and food rations were acquired in ample quantity.

"[We] had a regular Yankee breakfast," boasted Sangston on November 5, 1861, "codfish and potatoes, baked beans and pumkin 'sass.'" Still later he wrote, "Had an extra dinner at the mess today, being Sunday, roast turkies, roast and boiled mutton, roast beef and lobster salad, and dessert of nuts of several kinds, fresh peaches in cans, honey and coffee."[97]

As time went on, the fort's rations became more routine and consisted of beef with potatoes three times a week, and salt beef, pork, or ham on the other days, along with baked beans on Sundays. Fort Warren became unique among all prisons because tea or coffee and several ounces of bread were provided with each meal.

A large amount of clothing, shoes, and other necessities were distributed among the prisoners as a result of local newspapers in Boston urging citizens to donate such items. This campaign was further endorsed by Joseph W. Wightman, Boston's mayor, and Colonel Dimick.

This citizen aid, more than anything else, was the reason Fort Warren became the Union's most tolerable military prison. Unfortunately, Mayor Wightman probably later regretted his participation, because it quickly became a reelection issue. Within a month of his efforts, he was publicly ridiculed for aiding "the traitors at Fort Warren" by some of the same newspapers and citizens who had initiated the campaign to help them.[98]

FORT McHENRY

The Fort McHenry Military Prison was also considered tolerable for a short time. It too was one of the Union's first fortifications to hold political prisoners. Ross Winans, a member of Maryland's House of Delegates, is believed to have been the first on May 15, 1861. Additional members were confined there as the weeks passed, along with members of the Baltimore police board, the mayor of the city, and a congressman, before they were transferred out to other prisons. The first POWs arrived at McHenry in July, after being captured by General Nathaniel P. Banks in the Shenandoah Valley.[99]

The fort is located on Whetstone Point overlooking the northwest and middle branches of the Patapsco River, three miles from the original downtown area of Baltimore, Maryland. It was named in honor of Colonel James McHenry, a Baltimore native who had been an aide to General Washington during the American Revolution and secretary of war from 1796 to 1800.

Fort Mac, as it was sometimes called, was an old structure that had been built over a fourteen-year period between 1798 and 1812. It consisted of five main buildings surrounded by massive bastions that formed a star. The fort's walls were constructed of brick, twenty feet high. Outside the sally port was a detached bastion with a drawbridge on each side protecting the approach.

The fort's five interior buildings were designated A through E. Building A was the commanding officers' quarters, building B was a powder magazine with walls ten feet thick, building C was the junior officers' quarters, and buildings D and E were the enlisted men's barracks, later used by guards.

The prisoners held at Fort McHenry consisted of three classes: Union soldier prisoners charged with offenses punishable by military law, political prisoners, and prisoners of war.

POWs were held in two brick buildings measuring 120 by 30 feet. Prisoners still suffering from wounds were held on the upper floor of one building while the other POWs, both officers and enlisted men, occupied the upper floor of the other building.

Political prisoners were held in two of the fort's interior rooms, measuring 60 by 30 feet. They were allowed to go out onto a balcony for sun and air, into the prison yard or parade grounds, for water, roll call, and to the sutler to purchase allowable items. All prisoners had been allowed the freedom of the entire grounds until ten escaped. Dungeons beneath each side of the sally port, as well as the guard houses, where cells were entered through narrow wooden doors battened with iron supports, were used for Union soldiers and others who violated prison rules. Eventually Union prisoners were also held in one of the stable buildings.

"[I] visited the building in which rebel and other prisoners [were] confined . . . it [was] filthy in the extreme and a disgrace both to humanity and the service," reported Surgeon George Suckley of the U.S. Volunteers. Another prison official, referring to the stables converted into prison barracks, wrote that "the only alteration[s] being made since its use as a prison have been in throwing up some board partitions; even the old stalls still remain, [and] at the outside it ought not to receive more than 300 prisoners."[100]

Fort McHenry had a capacity of about 100 prisoners with 500 more accommodated in the stables and their surrounding enclosure. For a long time, however, the facility held an average of 400 Federal prisoners and 250 POWs, including 30 political prisoners.[101]

FORT DELAWARE

Just up the coast from Fort McHenry stood another Union fort quickly converted to prison use in early 1861. Built by General George B. McClellan while he was a member of the Corps of Engineers in the 1850s, Fort Delaware was relatively new. It was a huge pentagon-shaped structure of solid granite, with walls up to thirty feet thick and thirty-two feet high. Enclosed within these walls were two three-story Georgian brick buildings, in which troops were garrisoned, and a two-acre parade ground. Massive brick arches supported three tiers of gun emplacements and a drawbridge was used over the wide moat that surrounded the entire structure.[102]

The fort was situated on the southeast corner of Pea Patch Island, a mud shoal in the middle of Delaware Bay. This island, a narrow and marshy strip of land, was 178 acres, but nearly 128 of those were useless bogs. It was formed in the 1700s when a vessel loaded with peas floundered on a sandbar. The peas sprouted, caught drifting debris and sediment, and as the years passed, became an island.[103]

Around 1814, a small fort was built on the site to protect the cities of Wilmington and Philadelphia but it burned down in 1831. In 1849, work began on this fortress. Numerous pilings were sunk but disappeared in the muck. Finally, in 1859, the fort was finished at a cost of twice the amount originally appropriated.

As tensions grew in 1860, the War Department ordered Captain Augustus A. Gibson to the newly built fort with a small garrison to ensure that it remain in Union possession. It held prisoners of state as early as February 1861.

The fort's service as a POW facility began in late July 1861, when eight Confederate soldiers captured near Harper's Ferry and Martinsburg were sent to the fort and kept in the guard house until they were exchanged in the fall. It remained a political prisoner facility until the following spring.[104]

CAMP CHASE

Out west, Camp Chase, named in honor of Salmon P. Chase, a prominent abolitionist, then-current treasury secretary under President Lincoln, and former governor of Ohio, became a holding facility for political prisoners of Ohio, Kentucky, and Western Virginia as early as August 7, 1861. By all appearances, anyone from these border states who even mentioned the word "secession" became a prime candidate for confinement. "[T]here have been from six to seven hundred political prisoners at Camp Chase at a time," marvelled one prisoner. "There are unquestionably," noted Captain Henry M. Lazelle, 8th Infantry, U.S. Army, "a large number of prisoners amounting to perhaps 200 confined here whose cases I think [are] of unjust confinement . . . [t]here are among the prisoners two idiots, two insane and several so maimed as to be utterly harmless in any community."[105]

The camp, originally a training site for Ohio troops, was situated four miles west of Columbus on an extension of Broad Street. From its beginning as a prison facility, it was a source of irritation between the state and Federal governments. There was little doubt who had authority over the facility when it held political prisoners from Ohio, but once Federal authorities brought in those from other states and then started moving prisoners of war to the site the following year, control over the camp became a constant issue.

GRATIOT STREET

St. Louis, Missouri, gradually developed into the Union's westernmost depot prison center. Its principal facility was Gratiot Street Prison. Originally known as McDowell's Medical College, it was a strange-looking graystone building that consisted of a three-story octagonal tower and two wings. It stood at the northwest corner of Eighth and Gratiot streets and was erected in 1847 to house the highly successful medical college established in 1840 by Dr. Joseph N. McDowell of Tennessee.

McDowell was a tall and imposing man who had been active in politics for a number of years. Somewhat eccentric, he was known as a staunch pro-slavery advocate and a bitter secessionist. He designed his building to have a fortresslike appearance and during the political troubles of the 1850s, he purchased a number of muskets and small cannon from the U.S. Arsenal. The arms were stored in the building's cupola until the outbreak of the Civil War. Passersby often claimed that they could see the muzzles of the cannon sticking out from the portholes around the top of the college's tower.[106]

On May 10, 1861, shortly after the attack on Camp Jackson in St. Louis, a small detachment of home guards stormed the medical college and began a search for the arms. None were found. McDowell had shipped everything to Memphis upon realizing Union forces were closing in on him and fled with his two sons to that city.[107]

Because of McDowell's allegiance to the South, Provost Marshal George E. Leighton seized the building. For a while it was used as headquarters for the recruiting department of St. Louis. Later, since General John Fremont's head-quarters of the Western Department was nearby, the building was used as a barracks. On December 21, 1861, the McDowell building was converted into a military prison to relieve overcrowding of a much smaller facility at Fifth and Myrtle streets.[108]

That facility, previously known as Lynch's Slave Pen, was a brick building confiscated by military authorities on September 3. It had originally been a slave auction house, but with the outbreak of war, "traffic in human beings suddenly ceased" and its owner, Bernard M. Lynch, fled from the city. After military authorities took possession of the building, it became known as Myrtle Street Prison. During the first week of September the first prisoners, twenty-seven in number, were moved into the facility. Among those first was Max McDowell, son of Joseph McDowell. Young Max had been captured after returning to St. Louis to gather recruits for Major General Sterling Price's army.[109]

The maximum number of prisoners that could be incarcerated in Myrtle Street Prison was 100. Already 150 were confined there when word was received that nearly 2,000 more would soon arrive from the battlefields of southwest Missouri. A Major Butterworth was assigned the task of converting the medical college into a prison. Fifteen slaves, temporarily held at Myrtle Street as contraband confiscated from rebels, were removed from confinement and detailed for the work. Bunks and cooking stoves were installed and the medical college's dissecting room was transformed into a mess hall. General Henry W. Halleck, commanding the Department of the West by December 1861, placed Colonel James M. Tuttle in charge of the prison's internal operations.

The first POWs arrived on December 22. On that day a large crowd of curious spectators gathered at the depot. Before the train pulled into the station, the crowd became unruly, causing the 2nd Iowa and the 25th Indiana regiments to be dispatched to the scene to maintain order. As the train stopped, the Indiana regiment formed two single files from the cars to the prison. The U.S. Band quickly assembled along the tracks and "welcomed" the prisoners with strains of "Yankee Doodle." After the captives were lined up and given the order to march, the band began playing "Hail, Columbia" and the prisoners were forced to move off in step toward the prison.[110]

The people who stood along the streets and harassed the captives that day were shocked at their first view of the Confederates. Many of these first western POWs had no uniforms, and what clothing they did have was already tattered and torn. Privates were wearing mostly blankets, coverlets, quilts, and buffalo robes. Their shoes were torn and ragged. Officers' clothing was in better shape but nothing extraordinary.[111]

Colonel Ebenezer Magoffin, the highest ranking officer in this first group of captives and brother to Beriah Magoffin, governor of Kentucky, was wearing a high felt hat, a blue blanket coat, and other attire "denoting a well-to-do farmer." Magoffin was a tall, dark-complected, stoop-shouldered man of forty-five, and according to the newspapers was "the boldest, most reckless and un-scrupulous of the [captured] rebel officers."[112]

Magoffin and the other thirteen hundred Confederates who had arrived on this first train had been captured by General John Pope at Blackwater, Missouri. The group included nearly two hundred of General Price's regulars who had fought in all the battles in Missouri.

Similar to the military prisons established elsewhere, Gratiot Street Prison was hastily acquired and prepared. The building's capacity was only one-third of the number that arrived that first day; its holding areas were badly ventilated and not suited to incarcerating large numbers of people; and planned sanitary procedures quickly became useless.

Waste buckets placed in each room were entirely insufficient, as was a small trench latrine in the fenced-in yard area. Colonel Tuttle had planned to divide the prisoners into squads of twenty, separating the officers from the enlisted men, and make them responsible for the cleanliness of their quarters. They were to sweep the rooms every morning and scrub them every two weeks. Overcrowding made these tasks impossible. When scrubbing details were enforced, water sloshed around in the rooms and seeped into the lower-level rooms, making conditions even worse.[113]

The facility differed from most other prisons in existence only in that, here, prisoners of all types were incarcerated in the same rooms. Held within its walls were not only Confederate prisoners of war but also Southern sympathizers and political prisoners, bushwhackers, spies, mail runners, Union deserters, bounty jumpers, Union soldiers arrested for criminal activity and, separated from the main population but sometimes confined in the very next room, women accused of sympathizing with the South.[114]

Discipline in the prison was said to be severe from the beginning. Guards were, in fact, ordered to shoot any person who put his or her head or any body part out the window and refused to immediately withdraw upon command. As in Richmond, the guards were often accused of showing no hesitancy to shoot. There were even complaints that they often took potshots at the prisoners just to "stay in practice."[115]

One prisoner, Captain Griffin Frost, Company A, Missouri (CSA) State Guards, captured in Arkansas, noted in his journal, "The officers of the regiment now guarding us are perfect devils—there is nothing too low, mean, or insulting for them to say and do. . . . We are surrounded by bayonets and artillery, guarded by soldiers who curse, swear and fire among us when they please, and resort to balls, chains, and dungeons for the slightest offense."[116]

"One night," wrote prisoner Henry M. Cheavens, Company E, 6th (CSA) Missouri, captured after the Battle of Wilson's Creek, "the guards shot at one [prisoner] because he refused to put out the light."[117]

Frost and Cheavens were referring to the 2nd Iowa Infantry, Gratiot Street's first guards. Although they apparently failed to impress the inmates, they thoroughly impressed the citizens of St. Louis. The *Daily Missouri Democrat* reported on December 31, 1861, "The 2nd Iowa Infantry, Lieut. Col. Baker commanding, has established an enviable reputation for drill and discipline. . . . They have turned out in fine style and have done excellent service."[118]

The 2nd Iowa guarded all approaches to the prison quite heavily for a distance of a half-block. During the first three years of the prison's existence, no visitors or parcels of any kind were permitted; in fact, in the first month of operation, even the provost-marshal general was sternly repulsed and prevented from entering the area until the military commandant came to his rescue.[119]

As if the outside, with its fortresslike appearance and strict security, wasn't forbidding enough, the inside had a medieval, dungeonlike appearance. Upon his arrival at Gratiot Street, Captain Frost was escorted to quarters in the prison's "round room" which he found to be "a very dark, gloomy place, and very filthy besides." The round room was the middle level of the octagonal portion of the building. It was sixty feet in diameter, with 250 men crammed into its space. Although crowded, the round room was much better ventilated than what was referred to as the "square room." The square room was seventy by sixty by fifteen feet, with 250 men also crammed into its space, and was said to be in "utter disregard to the rules of hygiene." It would be this room that the commandant of the prison later referred to in his response when the question was asked where all the sick were coming from: "From this room, sir, all from this room!"

Frost was later moved to officers' quarters, which were "cleaner and not as crowded." These were rooms sixteen feet square, with eight men confined to a room. Here, the prisoners slept on bunks instead of the floor and they were allowed to walk in the halls and look out the windows into the street.

In these quarters the officers began to regain a more pleasant outlook, and their place of confinement began to appeal to their sense of humor. The inmates began referring to one another as "student" and they talked of their "college life." Those who were transferred to another prison or exchanged were said to have "graduated from medical school."[120]

But the reality of their circumstances was never far away. The noise from the lower rooms echoed through the building. "All through the night can be heard coughing, swearing, singing and praying," wrote Frost, "sometimes drowned out by almost unearthly noises, issuing from uproarious gangs, laughing, shouting, stamping and howling, making night hideous with their unnatural clang. It is surely a hell on earth."[121]

Nearly all of the prisoners' quarters were reconditioned classrooms. One wing of the building was occupied by Federal officers and attendants, with the upper story reserved for Confederate officer prisoners. The north wing contained a divided basement, having one large room to confine prisoners. The middle floor was also divided, with one large room for prisoners. The lower floor of the tower was originally a cool room but later was fitted to accommodate captives. An upper amphitheater was later converted into two stories—one as a convalescent hospital and the other as a dungeon. Female prisoners were generally held on a floor in between.

The large rooms were fitted with three-tier double bunks with one and two rows to a room. As overcrowding continued, though, prisoners with no beds slept on the floor. The rooms were very cold during the winter and nearly impossible to keep warm. There were only two stoves in each room to warm more than two hundred men.

The dining room was located on the middle floor of the north wing. The cook room, located in the walk out basement area below, was fitted with brick furnaces with sheet-iron boilers for boiling coffee, meat, and so on. Both the dining room squad and the cook room squad were chosen from among the prisoners. "The fare," wrote Frost, "is so rough, it seems an excellent place to starve."[122]

Above the dining room and extending the entire length of the north wing's upper floor was the prison hospital. It occupied the former site of the college museum. The loft was used as a deadroom and a rubbish room. The convalescent room, in the tower portion of the building, was located just off the south end of the hospital.

The hospital contained seventy-six bunks arranged in eight lines or four wards. To every half ward, two nurses or attendants were assigned and stayed all day; one was always present. At first, most of the sick were cared for in buildings adjoining the medical college, where they were under the care of Confederate surgeons taken prisoners of war. The surgeons volunteered for the duty and served under the direction of a Federal medical officer. This arrangement was practiced in nearly all the Federal prisons until February of 1862, when contract physicians took their place. Hospital attendants, though, continued to be detailed from among the prisoners.

Henry Cheavens was among those in that detail. He later wrote that smallpox occurred in epidemic proportions while he was there and he became quite familiar with the disease. He also saw outbreaks of measles, pneumonia, chronic diarrhea, erysipelas, and vermin infestation.

Throughout the first couple of months of the prison's existence, the hospital population remained around one-seventh of the total confined. But within only four weeks of the prison's establishment, the St. Louis *Republican* reported that it was filthy and unhealthy and that orders had been issued to clean up the rooms, alleviate overcrowding, and provide the doctor-inmates with medicine to treat the sick. In an effort to comply, Union officials began looking for another facility.[123]

As 1861 drew to a close, the Federal government had captured approximately 3,000 men and the Confederates had taken nearly 6,000. Already both sides had accumulated more prisoners of war than they had anticipated, and were attempting to release them on parole as quickly as possible. The strain was already beginning to show.[124]

Chapter 3

LIFE AS A PRISONER OF WAR

*The tramp of time was noiseless, leaving the clatter of no event to echo
down the corridors of time; We slept, ate and yawned; Yawned, ate
and slept.*

Griffin Frost, *Camp & Prison Journal*

Upon capture, prisoners underwent a cursory search and were then marched to the rear. Once behind the lines, they were lined up and searched again. "[W]e were halted and formed in one long column four abreast, with a row of guards upon each side," recalled Julius F. Ramsdell, Company K, 39th Massachusetts Regiment, who was incarcerated at Belle Isle. "An officer passed from man to man and took [everything] he could find, knapsacks, shelter tents."[1]

"They took possession of overcoats, blankets, and the contents of our pockets," reported George Putnam, 176th New York State Volunteers, who was held at Libby Prison. "They also took what under the circumstances was the most serious loss for men who had a long march before them, our shoes."[2] Money, canteens, eating utensils, and pocketknives also were appropriated.

"I was subjected to the grossest and most inhuman treatment," complained Brigadier General Thomas J. Churchill, (CSA), 1st Arkansas Mounted Rifles. "[M]y person insulted, the clothing torn from my back, my baggage robbed of all it contained, my overcoat and gloves taken and . . . [m]y spurs were taken from my feet, my sash from my waist, my combs, brushes, and all such necessary articles of comfort were ruthlessly taken."[3]

In many contemporary accounts, prisoners complained that they were "robbed" of everything by the time they arrived at the prison gates. Many were indeed subjected to as many as four or five searches by the time they reached prison. Records, however, indicate that they continued to make purchases with their own money and often possessed knives and other such personal items while incarcerated at the various prison institutions.

Prisoners folded and hid money in their socks, hats, inside their brass buttons, and many other places. "One man," reported Sam Boggs, 21st Illinois Infantry, who was held at Belle Isle prison, "put several bills in some tobacco leaves and was chewing it; when they searched him he dropped the tobacco into his hand until the examination was over."[4]

Pocketknives were often considered a necessity and therefore, not confiscated. Prisoner James J. Williamson reported that before he was placed in Old Capitol Prison, he was simply asked if he had anything he shouldn't have. When he handed over a pocketknife, the guard merely looked it over and handed it back.

Confederates searching Union prisoners became notorious for taking blankets and shoes because, they themselves, were badly in need of them. Union soldiers often took buckles or cut the brass buttons off their Confederate prisoners' uniforms as valued souvenirs.

After an appropriate number of prisoners were gathered behind the lines, they were usually marched to the nearest community that possessed a large jail. For instance, following the battle of Wilson's Creek in southwest Missouri, prisoners were held at nearby Springfield in the county jail, the upper floors of the courthouse, and in a row of dilapidated sheds. After the battle of Cedar Mountain in Virginia, prisoners were temporarily confined on the upper floor of the Culpeper Court House. And during the Red River Campaign, Federal prisoners were held in the city hall at Mansfield, Louisiana.[5]

When enough prisoners were accumulated at these locations, arrangements were made to take them to the nearest military prison. This often involved another forced march, sometimes covering a long distance, to the nearest railhead or boat landing.

Gratiot Street prisoner Henry M. Cheavens recalled being marched from Springfield to the railhead at Rolla, Missouri, covering 150 miles in six days through rain, mud, and snow before boarding a train bound for St. Louis. Several prisoners died from exposure along the way. Sergeant Charles W. Rivenbark, Company C, 1st North Carolina Regiment, captured at Gettysburg, told of being marched to Baltimore, a distance of some fifty miles, while still fatigued from battle. He and the other prisoners were held at Fort McHenry and underwent "three days of speech-making, promises, threats and persuasion" to take an oath of allegiance. Afterward, they boarded a steamer toward Fort Delaware Prison.[6]

Travel by ship or train, however, could be as difficult as the forced marches. Prisoners often were crammed into the transports with no regard for comfort or limitations. Colonel R. F. Webb, 6th North Carolina Regiment, reported that he was on "a train of dirty box cars into which we were packed like fish in a barrel." A. R. Calhoun, later transported to Libby, noted that "[we were] transferred to prison in open box cars. . . . All were packed closely. Men with diarrhea had no accommodations and had to perform the operations of nature in the cars."[7]

One prisoner reported a bit of ingenuity that developed during these times. As the guards walked along the train loading groups of prisoners into box cars, he and the others pushed and crowded around the doorway of the car to give the impression that there was no more room. When the train began moving, they spread out and had enough space to sit.[8]

Still, there were other problems. "The car that I was in had been used as a lime car," reported Sam Boggs. "Any moving around would stir up the dust. Our lips and tongues seemed parched and cracked. Two died in our car on the trip."[9]

Many prisoners complained that they were packed so tight that those who died couldn't even fall to the floor until the train was unloaded. They also claimed that the cattle cars were seldom cleaned before prisoners were loaded into them, forcing them to stand in manure during the entire trip.[10]

The Confederates often used flatcars to haul prisoners, who were crowded into the middle of the car as guards were seated around the outside. "There was but a single track," complained one prisoner, "and our train switched frequently to allow of the passing of passenger trains and supply trains, so that our progress to Richmond was slow." In some cases these trains pulled onto a side track for the night and the prisoners were allowed to sleep along the roadbed under heavy guard until morning.[11]

Ship travel could be just as bad, with prisoners confined in poorly ventilated holds. Rough bunks, four tiers high, were lined up from stem to stern, and prisoners were crammed into these areas shoulder to shoulder. "Only one hatch was left open," wrote Captain Walter G. MacRae, Company G, 7th North Carolina Regiment, who was transported to Morris Island on such a ship. "The hold was fairly dark, crowded, and stifling hot." Because of the heat and seasickness, the floors were usually covered with vomit by the time the ships arrived at their destination, prompting several prisoners to compare conditions to those of slave ships.[12]

Food rations were seldom issued on these trips, either because they were unavailable or because they took too long to distribute. For the same reasons, water was seldom dispensed, nor were prisoners allowed to empty the single latrine bucket haphazardly provided on each car or ship.

If the prison was located in a rural area, such as Andersonville in the South or Camp Butler in the North, the transports usually arrived there at night, which allowed more control over the disoriented prisoners. The walkways between the railroad tracks and the prison gates, a distance of no more than

100 to 500 yards, were lined with torches for light and guards for security. All along the route, the new arrivals were herded like cattle, being prodded and struck from behind. The darkness, the shout of orders, and the frequent hail of blows from the guards continued the disoriented feeling and created meek souls out of men who were once strong, independent soldiers.[13]

If the prison was located within a large city, the arrivals were usually scheduled for daylight hours when large crowds could gather to jeer and throw things, creating the same submissive effect upon the captives. "Everybody was out to see the Yankees," recalled one prisoner. "[The] street through which we had to pass was literally walled, on either side, with old men, women, and children."[14]

Confederate prisoners were objects of curiosity and anger as they passed through northern cities. Nearly everywhere in the North, large crowds gathered along the routes to stare, yell, or scream at the captured Rebels.

Sometimes, however, the jostling along the lines was not an effort to harm or ridicule the prisoners. "It was very hot and we were all terribly thirsty not having had a drink of good water since we [became] prisoners," Julius Ramsdell noted in his diary after being marched through Richmond. "[T]hey came out to the gates of the houses with pails of good cold water and tried every means in their power to get it to us. But the guards prevented it in almost every instance."[15]

"A negro woman came out of one of the houses," recalled a POW as the group was marched through another town, "and had some chicken and corn- bread upon a plate which she managed to give to one of our men." Reported another prisoner, "[T]hey were not allowed to approach us, [but] occasionally some daring one would rush to us with tobacco, water or some other little gift of luxury, but always at the risk of arrest."[16]

In Baltimore, prisoner arrivals were scheduled for daylight hours strictly for security reasons. Daylight afforded a safer environment for the heavy guard required to escort the prisoners through the city streets because the city had a large faction of intensely prosouthern sympathizers.[17]

Prisoners were usually taken to depot prisons first. They were searched again, their names and units were recorded, and they were reassigned to another prison. Transfer usually took place within a few days or several weeks. Gratiot Street Prison was the Union's depot for its Midwest prisons while the Old Capitol Prison and Fort Lafayette served as depots in the east. Libby Prison served as the Confederacy's only depot prison.

When the prisoners arrived at their final destination, they were again searched and enrolled. This process could last several hours, depending on the number of POWs, in all kinds of weather. The prisoners were then led into the prison one, two, or a few at a time.

"Immediately after the big gate slammed," wrote prisoner John V. Hadley, "someone inside shouted at the top of his voice, 'F-R-E-S-H FISH! F-R-E-S-H FISH!' which was caught up all over the pen and re-echoed by perhaps five hundred men." The cry was raised whenever there was a new arrival. Everyone ran to see who it was, what regiment he was from, and to hear the latest news or learn the latest developments about the war. As many as possible would crowd around the "fresh fish" and bombard him with questions.[18]

"I have often seen men gather," Hadley later wrote, "rushing and shoving . . . and many times getting the object of their interest under foot, and sometimes hurt. This [became] known among us as a 'raid.'" Later, as prison conditions worsened, "fresh fish" were immediately rushed by mobs of prisoners who often robbed them of anything usable, including haversacks, shoes, and clothing.[19]

It was often said that as new arrivals entered Andersonville, they vomited at the sight of the other prisoners and the odor of the compound. The same, however, was true at Elmira and many other locations, including many prison buildings, where the stench of dirty, ragged, sweating men filled the air.[20]

"It is impossible to have any idea of the state of the skin covering bodies," reported Surgeon William S. Ely, executive officer of the Union General Hospital at Annapolis. "In many cases I have observed, the dirt encrustration has been so thick as to require months of constant ablution to recover the normal condition and function . . . patients repeatedly stated that they had been unable to wash their bodies once in six months."[21]

As overcrowding continued, the accumulated filth reached overwhelming proportions. Garbage, trash, and debris were everywhere. Amid the chaos, prisoners became apathetic about sanitary standards. Few bothered to use the slit-trench latrines and most failed to cover their feces when they did. Many simply resorted to urinating or defecating outside their quarters. As William W. Wilcox of the 124th Ohio Volunteers noted of Danville Prison, "[There was] a great deal of human excrement on the floor every morning." Some of this was also the result of prisoners, often suffering from acute diarrhea, not being allowed to use the latrines at night.[22]

Floors were often crudded over to the extent that they resembled earthen floors. Walls, whether they were of brick, stone, or wood, were covered with scribble and graffiti. Prisoner George Putnam recalled that years after the war he was contacted by a Richmond resident who offered to sell him a brick on which Putnam had scratched his name while confined at Libby.[23]

The graffiti and scribble were, in turn, covered with smashed bugs, dried mucus, and spittle. Floors and walls were "so covered with slime and filth that we could neither sit nor lie down without getting besmeared," reported one prisoner.[24]

Not wanting to sit in the filth, new arrivals usually ventured no farther than the entrance, and remained in a standing position for as long as possible. "We stood as long as we could," reported one prisoner. "We stood until our legs swelled," said another. Eventually, they had no choice but to join in.[25]

When they finally proceeded farther into the compound, the jockeying for space began. Colonel R. F. Webb after being sent to Johnson's Island Prison, noted that "we were very unceremoniously thrown in among twenty-five hundred men and left, as the old story goes, 'to root hog or die!'"[26]

Some prisoners bought a spot to live. "For a consideration of money or some usable item," wrote another prisoner, "old prisoners would move or scatter to other spots."[27]

In open stockades as well as in buildings, bedbugs and lice infested the facilities in epidemic proportions. "We brush them off our pillows by the dozens," reported one prisoner, "and all night long groaning and swearing may be heard from prisoners suffering under their attack. They were everywhere—bedbugs on the walls, in our blankets, our boots, and sometimes even in our [food]."[28]

Many prisoners became covered with sores from head to foot. "In some cases," testified one doctor, "they were so badly eaten by lice as to resemble a case of scabbing from smallpox."[29]

Besides lice, fleas, and bedbugs, prisoners were also pestered by flies, gnats, rats, and mice. In the open stockades of the South, they also had problems with scorpions, lizards, and snakes. "We grow used to both vermin and reptiles," confided A. J. H. Duganne, who was held at Camp Ford, Texas. "At one time a hollow log was pitched into a fireplace whereupon a large bullsnake slithered out of the fire."[30]

"The scorpion, or stinging lizard as we called it, is another of our insect enemies," declared one prisoner. "Its quick dart from beneath a slab of wood, with curving tail erect, became quite familiar to us." Duganne added, "The horrible spider, the tarantula, is an especial object of hostility. . . . When our prisoners first began to build their log huts at Camp Ford, they suddenly lost a comrade by some strange wound which he discovered on his neck . . . the neck swelled tumorously and the poor man died . . . a short time later diggers found an old tarantula [and deduced] that their unfortunate comrade has been bitten by it."[31]

Some vermin became so prevalent that many starving prisoners resorted to catching and eating rats and reptiles in addition to any dogs or cats that chanced to wander into their compound.[32]

These conditions were often worse for enlisted men, who were separated from their officers. Officers were held in separate quarters within the same prison, as was done at Gratiot Street and Salisbury (when they were first opened), or they were assigned to a prison reserved strictly for officers, as was done at Libby or Danville in the South and Fort Warren and Johnson's Island in the North.

The rationale is often given that such arrangements kept the large number of enlisted men prisoners in a leaderless, helpless mass, thereby preventing mass escapes or insurrections. Research reveals, though, that escapes still occurred, and it wasn't at all unusual for an organizational structure to evolve among prisoners despite the absence of officers. The truth is, in any group there is always a particular person who is skilled or charismatic enough to become the leader. For reasons such as respect, admiration, or fear, others follow. Such was the case in many military prisons, including those for enlisted men as well as those for officers.

The original reason for separating the two classes was most likely out of the belief that officers, because of rank, were entitled to, or deserved, better quarters, increased privileges, and preferential treatment over that of the enlisted men. Thus, the prison used at Houston confined Union enlisted men captured at Galveston while the officers enjoyed parole and liberty to walk the streets. Confederate officers held at Camp Chase were allowed to roam the streets of Columbus, register at fine hotels, and attend sessions of the state senate. Union officers held near San Antonio were given passes to visit town, and those on Governors Island were allowed to walk the beach. Officers held at Gratiot Street were confined on the upper floors, which were less crowded and contained furniture, in addition to being allowed to walk the halls for exercise and peer out the windows, while enlisted men confined in the large, more crowded lower floor rooms were denied exercise and were shot if they came too close to the windows. In fact, officers in nearly every prison enjoyed special privileges up until the elimination of prisoner exchanges.[33]

The daily routine in all the prisons was mostly the same, and life was extremely monotonous. Prisoners found that most of their time was spent standing in line. They stood in line for morning roll call. They stood in line for morning rations. They stood in line to use the latrine and to get water. They stood in line for afternoon rations. They stood in line for evening roll call.

"Long before daybreak the camp begins to stir," wrote one prisoner, "tatterdemalions roll out of burrowing places, creep up from caverns, and emerge from hut openings. Hatless, bootless, shirtless. They swarm out upon the [paths], flow into crossways, jostle one another at cooking fires; pass and repass; Laden with fuel, rations, water-vessels. Another day begins."[34]

Water was scarce in most camps, so men began lining up with some kind of receptacle as soon as possible to secure their day's supply. After roll call, breakfast came, usually somewhere between 8:00 and 11:00 A.M. Afterward, a squad policed the camp, or individual inmates would clean their quarters. In cases where tents or dugouts were used, the prisoners might pick up around them, but in the latter part of confinement most inmates no longer bothered.

The only "activity" for those not assigned to special details was to wait for dinner, which usually came sometime in the afternoon, generally between 3:00 and 5:00 P.M.

Idleness, accompanied with homesickness and depression, was one of the most distressing aspects of prison life. Thousands of men lapsed into helpless and hopeless apathy, caring for nothing and thinking of nothing except their homes and the friends and family they had left behind.

Abner Small of the 16th Maine recalled that many of his fellow prisoners at Danville seemed to lose all interest in life. They sat in the same position for hours, staring at the wall or floor. Others recalled that many would sleep through the day out of boredom or depression. According to one prisoner, "It not infrequently happens that a man dies in his bunk and the fact is not discovered for several hours."[35]

It was common for surgeons in these places to list nostalgia, meaning homesickness, as a cause of death. The prisoners' will to live diminished and they slowly deteriorated both in mind and in health.[36]

There were others who recalled fighting off suicidal thoughts. One minute they would wish for "the calm of death" and the next they would have a sudden urge to live. For some, fighting off depression and suicide became a constant, desperate struggle. Prisoner Francis Walker wrote of "a period of nervous horror such as I had never before and have never since experienced. . . . I remember watching the bars of my window and wondering whether I should hang myself from them."[37]

Unfortunately, some prisoners found it easier and quicker simply to step over the prison deadline in an invitation for guards to kill them. The guards, more often than not, usually seemed more than willing to oblige. Sergeant Sam Boggs claims to have witnessed one such incident. "One prisoner from the 38th Illinois stepped over the dead-line," professed Boggs. "The guard leveled his gun and ordered him to get back. The prisoner straightened up, pulled his shirt open and told the guard to shoot. The guard fired, the buck-shot and ball tearing away the lower jaw and entered the lower part of the neck." The prisoner died later that day.[38]

The amount of a prisoner's education played a vital role in just how well he was able to adapt to his new circumstances. Prisoners who were more educated developed greater resources within themselves, enabling them to devise some means of occupying their time. Intellectual stimulation often helped a prisoner keep some distance between himself and the reality of his surroundings.

It also became important to be part of a unit of friends who could support one another as the days passed. These units often consisted of acquaintances from one's hometown, members of the same company or regiment, or soldiers from the same city or state. Group members shared living quarters and stayed together as a "family." Such cooperative relationships provided moral support for each member of the group and, as the friendships intensified, they became essential. The caring and camaraderie of the group encouraged the individual to continue his struggle to survive.

Oftentimes if one member of a "family" was assigned to a prison work detail, he would obtain other positions for family members or get them special privileges, which might include sneaking extra bread back home if he worked in the bakery, an extra stick or two of wood if he was in a gathering detail, or a clothing item if he worked in the burial detail.

Within the prison camps, longtime prisoners often enjoyed better status by the simple virtue of their own survival. They were looked upon by the others with a certain amount of respect because they had learned the ways of the camp and how to exploit them.

One such exploitation was "ration flanking." A prisoner would stand in one group and be counted as rations were issued and then sneak over to be counted in another group, thereby receiving double rations. But it was dangerous; if he was caught, severe punishment resulted.

Many prisoners became engaged in free enterprise within the prison. For an item of barter or extra food, a prisoner might fashion a needle from bone and offer to sew clothing. Others advertised to wash clothes, using water when it was available or sand when it wasn't. Prisoners who had successfully concealed their pocketknives during the numerous searches offered to cut hair. Some sold freshly dug roots, while others sold soup made from roots or from portions of their rations. Many prisoners engaged in making trinkets out of trash and jewelry-making became a favorite pastime. POWs at a number of prisons hung signs over their dugouts or huts and set up jewelry businesses. They became ingenious at using whatever was available. Gutta-percha buttons, beef bones, brass buttons, and coins were most often used. Other arts and handicrafts evolved and became elaborate and meticulously done. Chess sets, checkers, paper cutters, letter openers, pen holders, broaches, bracelets, necklaces, and busts carved or fashioned from bone, wood, brick, and other material soon became valuable for barter or exchange. Many were sold to guards, sutlers, or other inmates. As time went on, they were sold to civilians outside the prison by using guards or sutlers as middlemen.

Those who were neither business-minded nor artistically inclined passed the long hours in other pursuits. Debating societies, as well as French, German, Spanish, and religion classes were formed. In some prisons the inmates, like those at Richmond and Castle Pinckney, devised their own form of government. Entertainment such as dancing and music performances were organized.

Other prisoners organized ball games, pitched stones, rolled dice, or played marbles.

Backgammon, checkers, and chess games were popular and vast tournaments were held. At Libby Prison the chess games became so intense that players sometimes fainted. Malnutrition probably played a part, though the excitement was certainly high.[39]

Passion for gambling was as strong in the prisons as in any place. In the absence of money, captives were known to stake their food, clothing, blankets, or other precious belongings on such games. It was said that the cards were used long after the corners had disintegrated and the markings had become so faded that card value became uncertain. Games sometimes continued for days at a time and sometimes large-scale fights erupted over the results.

Surprisingly, several prisons allowed inmates to publish a prison news-paper. Usually handwritten, the papers were also hand-delivered. Thus, a number of prisoners were kept busy on the publishing and delivery end of the business while others acted as roving reporters to gather the news.

Journal-keeping was another activity that occupied the time. Because paper was often hard to come by and ink was scarce, journalists used whatever scraps they could find and often wrote with ink made from a mixture of water and rust or soot. Some prisoners, though, were able to find additional pencils among their fellow inmates. John Ransom of the 9th Michigan Cavalry, who was held at Andersonville, often bartered for pencil stubs as he did for any-thing else of value. These journals often served, for those who survived, as the basis of a book after the war.

Some prisoners were content to spend their otherwise dark existence with long walks around the prison camp. They would often trace over paths they had walked hundreds of times.

Reading passed the time for many, but books or newspapers from the out-side were rare. According to prisoner John McElroy, Company L, 16th Illinois Cavalry, the only book he could obtain at Andersonville besides the Bible was *Gray's Anatomy.* At other prisons, such as Camp Douglas in the North and Cahaba in the South, prisoners or nearby residents accumulated enough books to set up a library system, loaning out a wide range of publications to inmates. Books and periodicals were also sometimes distributed by religious leaders or relief agencies. Prisoners read and reread these until they fell apart. Many POWs later wrote that they eventually memorized entire books while those who had retained their own Bibles had read through them several times, memorizing them in the process.

Rules prohibiting the possession of local newspapers varied from prison to prison and even from time to time within individual prisons. When prohibited, possession of such an item was punishable by several days, and sometimes weeks, in solitary confinement. At other times, guards gave or sold newspapers to the prisoners.

In some prisons, inmates were permitted to correspond with families and friends, but their letters often were limited to thirty-two lines or one page and were subject to strict censorship. "I found all letters had to go first to the Provost-Marshal's office for inspection," wrote an inmate in Old Capitol Prison, "and then it was doubtful when they would reach their destination, if at all. . . . A young man wrote a letter to his father, who was residing in Washington City and nine days passed before it was delivered."[40]

"I found it impossible," wrote one Northern prison commandant, "to permit [the prisoners] to write to everybody as they pleased. . . . They found out the names of notorious rebel sympathizers, to whom hundreds of letters were directed asking for assistance."[41]

Although both sides had their complaints, within a short period of incarceration, few letters were written from prison. As with local newspapers, at certain intervals and at certain prisons, mail and packages continued to be distributed to the inmates but that, too, created problems. Before long, the practice was eliminated. If by chance a relative learned of a family member being incarcerated and sent a parcel of food or clothing, it was frequently pilfered by the guards or prison authorities to prevent, among other things, the contents from becoming valuable barter items within the prison or for use in bribing guards.

Another pastime enjoyed by inmates was to gather into groups for conversation. "[The] meeting of old friends and comrades, and the making of new acquaintances," wrote one prisoner, "is a source of great pleasure to us and a relief from the monotony of what could otherwise be a dull routine of prison life."[42]

"I have probably fifty acquaintances here," wrote John Ransom, speaking of Andersonville, "that visit us each day to talk the situation over."

They told stories, talked about home, good food, survival, the possibility of exchange, the possibility of the war's end, or the possibility of escape. Some passed the time by planning escapes in great detail. Others passed the time digging tunnels in the hope of making escape a reality.[43]

All of these activities continued until the prisoners were lined up for evening roll call and the issuing of rations.

After meals, many of these activities resumed until lights out—usually around 9:00 P.M.—or in the case of stockade prisons, until dusk. Around nine o'clock taps was sounded. Pitch-pine torches were fired up around the stockade or oil lamps were lit in the halls of buildings.

Prisoners began to retire as guards began to cry out from their posts: "Post number one, nine o'clock and all is well." The cry was taken up by each post in succession and repeated all around the prison every hour throughout the night. Later in the war, additional guards armed with revolvers patrolled the crowded maze of tents and dugouts.[44]

Many prisoners found it difficult to sleep. Confederate prisoners suffered in the cold while Union prisoners suffered in the heat. Tents, dugouts, barracks, and buildings occupied by the POWs were often damp and cold in the winter and stifling hot in the summer. Hunger gnawed at the men from the inside while rats, flies, and lice gnawed at them on the outside. Furthermore, the noise from the guards along with the moaning, groaning, and crying of other prisoners made sleep nearly impossible.

1862

Chapter 4

PRISON CREATION

> *Our prison experience [will] never be forgotten. Sometimes I wonder*
> *if the young men of this day and generation could endure such ordeals.*
> Colonel George H. Moffett

As the Civil War continued into its second year and more captives arrived at the already overcrowded prisons, Union and Confederate authorities began to search for new sites to deposit their prisoners of war.

ALTON PRISON

In an effort to relieve overcrowding at Gratiot Street Prison, Major General Henry W. Halleck, commanding the Department of the Missouri, asked Adjutant General Lorenzo Thomas for authority to take over an abandoned penitentiary at nearby Alton, Illinois, provided he could obtain the consent of the state governor, Richard Yates. Thomas gave permission and Yates gave consent. At the end of January 1862, Halleck sent an agent to build fires in the penitentiary building to dry out the walls. By February 9, the first prisoners arrived, transferred from Gratiot Street, and in the following days POWs continued to arrive. By February 12, Alton Prison was overcrowded.[1]

This facility, built in 1830–31 on the north side of Alton at Broadway and Williams streets, was the first state prison built in Illinois. By the 1850s, Dorothea Dix, a reformer and leader in the movement to improve conditions for prisoners, the insane, and the mentally ill, had led a crusade to prevent the prison from being used because it was "badly situated too near the river, undrained and ungraded and, generally, unsanitary." This led to a heated controversy that eventually ended in a legislative investigation and the construction of a new facility at Joliet, Illinois. The Illinois convicts were transferred from the "unsanitary" facility, and Alton sat abandoned until it came to Halleck's attention.[2] Under the present situation, it passed the military's inspection.

"Drainage—very good," reported Augustus M. Clark, medical inspector of prisoners of war, "drains in good order, lead into main sewer emptying into river."[3]

The prison had a main, three-story penitentiary building containing 256 cells. Each of these measured about 4 feet by 7 feet. There were also five large rooms divided by partitions, providing two enclosures each. One measured about 7 by 4 feet and the other 20 by 4 feet. There were several buildings in the yard, enclosed by a large stone wall. One was a two-story wood-frame building measuring 46 by 97 feet on the first floor and 46 square feet on the second, and an old two-story stable measuring 29 by 49 feet on each floor. Two other buildings in the yard were used for confining Union troops held under court martial and civilian prisoners. These buildings measured, respectively, 50 by 103 feet and 50 by 36 feet.[4]

The maximum capacity of this institution was estimated at 800. Throughout most of the war, however, it held between 1,000 and 1,500 and sometimes more. By the last year of the war it held nearly 1,900 prisoners.[5]

The prison's first commandant was Lieutenant Colonel Sidney Burbank, 13th U.S. Infantry, an 1829 West Point graduate and a veteran infantryman.

In March, one of the first POWs transferred in was Colonel Ebenezer Magoffin, a Missouri Confederate who had become a discipline problem for prison officials at Gratiot Street. He had led insurrections among the inmates and was involved in several arsons inside the prison. He was moved to Alton after being sentenced to death.

Magoffin was placed in a small room on an upper floor behind a pad-locked door, with a guard stationed in front. Other Confederate officers, however, were allowed on parole to roam within the city limits of Alton during the daytime.[6]

Most of the other prisoners remained in their cells and had limited access to the prison yard. Those confined in the buildings of the yard were allowed certain periods for outside recreation. "Thirty-two of us occupied a room about 18 feet square," recalled one prisoner, "some have bunks, others take the floor."[7]

The prison had no water supply. A well was located on the grounds, but as soon as POWs were transferred in, officials discovered the water wasn't potable. They remedied the situation by hauling water in casts from the river. Later, a six-mule-team wagon hauled barrels of water up to the prison and, when the prison became even more crowded, two such wagon teams were used.

"Imagine," wrote Sergeant Jacob Teeple, Company H, 10th Missouri (CSA) Infantry, who was in one of the first groups transferred from St. Louis, "twelve hundred men shut up in prison in three rooms . . . with only Mississippi water direct from the river! . . . [T]welve hundred of us in that cold stone prison had four little bell stoves. There was heavy snow on the outside, and very few of us had coats or blankets."[8]

Heat was supplied by wood-burning stoves set up in the corridors. The yard buildings had stoves in the rooms. In those buildings coal-oil lamps were used for light, while "modern" gaslights were placed throughout the prison.

"In this prison more than any other," reported Augustus Clark during another inspection, "regard seems to be paid to the comfort as well as security of the prisoners. The military discipline maintained is not as strict as should be, yet every precaution seems to be taken to prevent escapes."[9]

But Clark would be proved wrong in his assessment. During the early morning hours of July 25, 1862, sentries along the back wall of the prison heard noises and found a herd of cattle in the area. At dawn the sentries discovered a hole in the ground about eighteen inches in circumference where the cows had been. Further investigation uncovered a tunnel entrance in the washhouse in the prison yard. A roll call revealed 36 prisoners missing—including Colonel Magoffin and his two sons, who were also POWs. The guard outside Magoffin's door had wandered off during the night, and he must have picked the lock.[10]

"I have sent out several parties to scour the country," Major Franklin F. Flint, 16th U.S. Regiment, commanding the guard, offered in a dispatch fired off to Colonel William Hoffman. "Many have undoubtedly crossed the river at this place, as several skiffs are missing." Only eight of the escapees were recaptured. By August 9, General Halleck was calling for a court of inquiry into the escape. Secretary Stanton soon agreed and one was ordered by President Lincoln.[11]

Colonel Burbank and the 13th Regiment were transferred to the front on September 4, after the court of inquiry obtained their sworn statements. The 16th transferred out soon afterward. The 77th Ohio Volunteer Regiment took over guard duties at the prison and Colonel Jesse Hildebrand was assigned as commandant.

The findings of the court of inquiry determined that the escape was "due to dereliction of duty, but to whom the court is unable to say from the evidence before them." The tunnel, eighteen inches in diameter for its entire length, ran a distance of fifty feet, only three feet below the ground surface, to the stone wall that surrounded the prison yard. "They then cut through a solid limestone wall under ground," according to the testimony, "and awaiting a dark and cloudy night made their escape one by one."[12]

Colonel Hildebrand hadn't even settled into his new assignment before another escape occurred. At the same time, he was having trouble getting organized, figuring out what his duties were, and delegating authority.

"The commanding officer has not given as much of his personal attention to the prison as [is] required," Hoffman was advised in a report the following November. "He has attempted to take the entire charge of his regiment, of the prisoners, the duties of the adjutant and of the provost-marshal of the prison. . . . He has had but little experience, and in taking upon himself the entire charge, he has undertaken more than he [is] able to perform. . . . The colonel, while he endeavors satisfactorily to perform his duties, has but little system or organization in his office and there is a culpable want of discipline in his command."[13]

About 11:00 P.M. on Sunday, November 16, a fire broke out in the straw storage room north of the prison hospital. Similar to previous fires at Gratiot Street in February, the fire was most likely the result of arson. The Alton fire department was summoned and soon extinguished the blaze. At 6:00 A.M. the following morning, the same room burst into flames again, and again, the fire was quickly extinguished. As dawn brought light into the prison yard, guards noticed a ladder against the south wall of the prison, just west of the big gate entrance. The guards discovered a braided bedclothes cord tied off at the top of the ladder and dangling down the other side of the wall. Roll call soon afterward revealed four prisoners missing.[14]

"There are stationed here," blasted the next day's Alton *Telegraph,* "not less than 1,300 U.S. troops as guards . . . there is gross negligence somewhere; for prisoners to have or get ladders and climb over prison walls within ten steps of a sentinel certainly argues a laxity of discipline which demands instant reform."[15]

An exasperated Colonel Hoffman fired off a letter to Secretary Stanton. "I have urged on General Curtis," wrote Hoffman, "to detail a more competent officer for the command than Colonel Hildebrand . . . but he informs me that he has no better available. . . . I therefore respectfully recommend that Capt. H. W. Freedley, Third Infantry, be placed in command."[16]

Freedley arrived on November 27 and soon notified Hoffman of his cursory examination of Alton Prison. "Inexcusable neglect," he reported. "So incomplete and incorrect were the rolls that at this time there [are] [f]our names found on the rolls who were not found in the prison, and three persons were found in the prison whose names were not found on the rolls. . . . Many of the prisoners here are sadly destitute of clothing. . . . I have found the guard . . . duties were performed in a loose and careless manner, arising from a relaxation of discipline. . . ."[17]

Hoffman, in turn, notified General Samuel R. Curtis, by then the commander of the Department of the Missouri, that Alton Prison was "in such an utter state of confusion and disorder" that he had applied to the secretary of war to place Freedley in command. "Colonel Hildebrand," Hoffman reported to Curtis, "means well but he is wanting in many things essential to such a command."[18]

CAMP DOUGLAS

Upon the establishment of the prison in Alton, Gratiot Street became the Union's westernmost depot, or receiving, prison. Much like at Richmond, however, authorities at St. Louis found that there was no control over the number of captives coming into the city. As quickly as groups of POWs were dispersed to other prisons more would arrive, and the overcrowding continued.

Prison officials then received notification that forts Henry and Donelson had been captured in Tennessee, which would add another 15,000 Confederate prisoners to the Union's rolls. Frantically, Colonel Hoffman looked around for anyplace with room to distribute the overwhelming number of captives.

On February 20, 1862, the first steamboats arrived in St. Louis with many of those prisoners. Most of the new arrivals were in poor physical condition and 250 sick men were immediately placed into the hospital, filling that facility beyond capacity. During the following days more boats arrived and continued to arrive in a seemingly never-ending procession.[19]

Hoffman ordered that contingents of five hundred to several thousand each be trained out to sites around Illinois and Indiana, after ordering a number of former training camps to be converted over for prison use immediately.

The first group, consisting of thirty-two hundred Confederate captives, arrived in Chicago on February 21. After disembarking the trains, they were marched into Camp Douglas, searched, and shown to their quarters in a compound prepared for their arrival.[20]

Camp Douglas was originally created as a rendezvous point to train and quarter regiments raised in the Chicago area at the beginning of the war. It was established on the south side of the city on grounds originally occupied by the 7th Annual Fair of the United States Agricultural Society, held in 1859. The camp was named in honor of Illinois statesman Stephen A. Douglas, whose residence was nearby. In fact, this site occupied a portion of Oakenwald, the Douglas estate.[21]

The camp enclosed about sixty acres, which were further divided by interior partitions to create compounds of various sizes. Each of these compounds, or squares, was named according to its purpose.

Garrison Square, which contained about twenty acres, was lined on all four sides by the quarters of the officers and men, and it had a flat and level parade ground in the center. Hospital Square contained ten acres and served as its name implied. Whiteoak Square, which contained ten acres, originally served as the post's prison. When orders were received to prepare the camp for the arrival of a large number of POWs, Whiteoak was merged with parts of the other squares, creating Prison Square, a compound of twenty acres, along the west and south sides of Garrison Square.

Prison Square contained 64 barracks sitting side by side. Each building was 24 by 90 feet, with 20 feet partitioned off as a kitchen. The remaining 70 feet held tiers of bunks along its walls. The top capacity of this prison was established at 6,000, or an average of 95 men to a barrack. Eventually, each barrack would have to hold an average of 189 men.[22]

Within a few days of this first group of POWs, a second group of 1,259 arrived. A few weeks later, 2,000 more. At first, though, the prison was able to accommodate them fairly easily.

"When Camp Douglas was first established," reported prisoner Thomas A. Head, 16th Tennessee Volunteer Regiment, "the prisoners had kitchens supplied with stoves and cooking utensils, and were supplied with more provisions than they were able to consume. They were also allowed as much clothing as they pleased." R. T. Bean, Company I, 8th Kentucky Cavalry, exclaimed that "a good sutler's store was running in full blast and we could buy many luxuries that Uncle Sam failed to furnish."[23]

The people of Chicago were curious about the POWs, and before long, one of the more enterprising entrepreneurs of the city developed a unique method for their exploitation. "An observatory was erected just outside the gate of our prison," recalled M. J. Bradley, Company G, 10th Kentucky Infantry, "and spectators were permitted, for the sum of ten cents, to ascend to an elevated platform, where, with the aid of spy or field glasses furnished by the proprietors, they could look down upon, and inspect us as objects of curiosity."[24]

"The rebels in camp," reported I. N. Haynie, adjutant general of Illinois, "occupied their time in a variety of ways . . . [some] revived the games of childhood, and could be seen busily engaged in playing leap frog or marbles. . . . In another portion of the square was seen a faro bank in full operation, on which the 'banker' had amassed the fortune of some $150,000 in Confederate currency."[25]

The Union victories at Pittsburg Landing, Tennessee, and Island No. 10 the following April brought nearly 1,500 more POWs into Prison Square. By the late summer of 1862, the compound held nearly 9,000 captives, and conditions deteriorated. Reverend Henry Bellows of the U.S. Sanitary Commission found the barracks and grounds in general disorder during his inspection in mid-1862, with large amounts of standing water, foul sinks, and the soil around the barracks "reeking with miasmatic accretions, of rotten bones and the emptying of camp kettles."[26]

Camp Douglas was indeed established on low ground, and it flooded with every rain. During most of the winter months, when it wasn't frozen, the compound was a sea of mud. "Our prison pen was like a cattle-yard," complained Henry Morton Stanley, Company E, 6th Arkansas, who would later become a journalist and utter the famous phrase 'Doctor Livingstone, I presume' on his search through Africa. "We were soon in a fair state of rotting while yet alive."[27]

"Nothing but fire can cleanse [it]," exclaimed Reverend Bellows when he urged Union authorities to abandon the site as soon as possible. But Union officials had no intentions of abandoning Camp Douglas. Steadily, illness and death began to increase. In those first few groups to arrive, the rate of illness rose from 167 to 373 in three months, and deaths rose from 34 to 123.[28]

In July 1862, there were 146 deaths. The Sanitary Commission argued that a proper sewage system was needed immediately. It pointed out that the prison hospital was in poor condition; that the sick lay on cots without mattresses, sheets, or any other kind of bedding; that many sick prisoners remained in the barracks; that inmates had no change of clothing; that they were covered with vermin and without proper beds; and that the death rate was rapidly mounting. Colonel Hoffman proposed to Quartermaster General Meigs the construction of a proper sewer system as soon as possible. Meigs replied that such an undertaking would be much too "extravagant."[29]

CAMP BUTLER

Nearly two hundred miles southwest of Camp Douglas, Camp Butler was experiencing its own problems. Located in a rural setting 5½ miles east of Springfield, Illinois, it was another state military instruction camp converted for prison use under Hoffman's orders.

The camp, named for William Butler, Illinois state treasurer, became a POW facility one day after Camp Douglas, when trains carrying another two thousand of the Tennessee captives arrived from Chicago on February 22. Like Camp Douglas, Camp Butler also consisted of three separate compounds, totaling forty acres, used for troop training. An adjacent fifteen-acre site on the west side of the parade grounds was set aside to confine a portion of the prisoners from forts Henry and Donelson.

The POWs were quartered in twenty-one wood-frame buildings similar to those at Camp Douglas and other such facilities, these measuring 24 by 100 feet each and meant to house up to one hundred men. Suffering among the Camp Butler POWs began almost from the day the first contingent arrived. Within a short time, three of the prisoner barracks had to be used as hospitals, causing further crowding in the remaining structures.[30]

Those first POWs were escorted to the camp by four hundred troops of the 54th Illinois Infantry, who remained there as guards. Due to the lack of a wall around the compound, the 12th Illinois Cavalry, from Camp Douglas, was rushed to the site to assist. These prisoners, too, were a novelty to the area.

Carriages and buggies and people on foot arrived from Springfield and the surrounding countryside to look them over. "Not withstanding the unfavorable weather," reported the (Springfield) *Illinois State Register,* "streams of visitors poured in."[31]

The prison commandant was Colonel Pitcairn Morrison, originally a recruiter in Springfield. He was described as a kindly old gentleman with forty-one years of military service.[32]

Within four days of the captives' arrival, one of the first burials of a Camp Butler POW took place. "No solemn requiem was there sung," reported the *Illinois State Journal,* the community's other newspaper, "no funeral dirge was chanted. The whistling of the night wind and the grating [noise] of the grave diggers' picks and shovels was the only [sound]."[33]

A group of 1,013 more POWs arrived two months later with the capture of Island No. 10 in Missouri. They had to be quartered in tents set up west of the prisoner barracks, adding to the intolerable conditions of the camp.[34]

"The sickness among the prisoners," reported the *Register,* "has almost assumed the features of an epidemic. We learn that on the afternoon of Friday no less than nine deaths occurred, and in the previous days the daily average of mortality was three or four." In a later edition, "On Saturday some fifteen deaths had occurred among them."[35]

At Camp Butler, the POWs mostly suffered from the weather. Over and over it either rained or snowed during a five week period in February and March. "[S]harp winds, cold rains," reported the *Journal,* "for the two weeks past, have produced colds, coughs and sore throats innumerable."[36]

By the end of March 1862, 148 prisoners had been buried in a nearby, newly established Confederate cemetery. All of the deaths, according to the prison physician, were caused by pneumonia. "The change of climate was about the worst thing for us," agreed prisoner L. V. Caraway, 24th Texas Regiment, "from mild to frigid. When we got off the cars, after eleven hours without a spark of fire, we were all nearly dead." The incessant rain, freezing drizzle, and snows didn't help.[37]

By mid-March, even Morrison, prison commandant, suffered from "a violent attack of pneumonia," but he was alarmed, not over the prisoners' health, but over the high cost of coffins for the camp. Purchase of the coffins from Springfield was costing $6.50 each, so Morrison quickly made arrangements with a camp carpenter to produce them for $5.[38]

Escapes were also a big problem at Camp Butler. At 7:00 A.M. and 6:00 P.M. each day, the prisoners were lined up two deep in front of their barracks and tents for roll call and counting. Invariably, a prisoner or two would be missing. Escapes became so frequent and the authorities so confused that they would often enter the date of the escape as "unknown" on their reports and seldom pursued the escapees.[39]

On March 24, according to one newspaper, six prisoners escaped by bribing a guard. Since the facility had continued as an instruction camp, many of the guards were members of various Illinois regiments either just arriving or soon departing. As a consequence, few felt a responsibility for maintaining tight security. Visitors allowed in the camp often encouraged escapes and, sometimes, even provided help.[40]

Finally, in May 1862, a twelve-foot-high plank fence was erected around the camp to discourage escapes. Three large gates, located on the north, south, and east sides, provided limited access to the compound.

On June 22, Colonel Morrison returned to recruit duties in Springfield and turned the command of Camp Butler over to Major John G. Fonda of the 12th Illinois Cavalry. Upon his review of the records, Fonda was amazed at the number of escapes. He immediately ordered more intensive roll calls, canceled visitation privileges, and enforced more stringent sentry duties.[41]

CAMP MORTON

Other Fort Henry and Fort Donelson prisoners fared little better when they were distributed to various compounds hastily arranged around the state of Indiana. Contingents of five hundred each were sent to Terre Haute, Evansville, New Albany, Lafayette, Richmond, and Fort Wayne, and three thousand were sent to Indianapolis. These sites, too, were nothing more than training camps converted to prisons under Hoffman's orders. Only one, the largest at Indianapolis, called Camp Morton, became well-known.[42]

As a POW facility, Camp Morton was no different from the others except that its prison buildings were unique in appearance. The setting of this camp was the Indiana State Fairgrounds, and the Victorian architecture of its prominent structures at the entrance, complete with gingerbread trim, gave the camp, in the beginning at least, a somewhat cheerful appearance.

The fairground, established in 1852 on thirty-six acres of the old Henderson farm, was often the scene of Methodist camp meetings during the off-season. In late 1861, Oliver P. Morton, governor of Indiana, converted the site into a recruitment and instruction camp for state volunteers. It quickly, but never formally, became known as Camp Morton.[43]

The five-acre confinement area was a gently rolling plain with maple trees to provide plenty of shade. A deep runoff creek, later jokingly referred to by the inmates as "the Potomac," ran through the middle of the camp but seldom contained much water except after a heavy rain. Water for the compound was provided by five wells on the property.[44]

The first POWs arrived by train on February 24 and were marched through the city, arriving about a mile north of town at the fairgrounds.[45]

Quarters for the prisoners consisted of five large wood-frame fair buildings toward the center of the prison area. Four of the structures housed prisoners, and one served as the hospital. These structures were nothing more than exhibition halls, stables, and barns. The stables and barns, of course, had dirt floors covered with straw. The prisoners occupied and slept in the stalls and wherever else they could find space.

The confinement area was surrounded by a poorly constructed wide-board fence, and at some locations the backs of other exhibition halls served as part of the enclosure. An elevated platform along the outside of the fence served as a walkway for the sentries. The ornate buildings at the entrance to the fairgrounds were used as post headquarters and as housing for the guard.

Camp Morton's commandant when the POWs arrived was Colonel Richard D. Owen, 60th Indiana Regiment, of whom the Indianapolis *Journal* described as a "patriotic, energetic, and painstaking officer." His regiment served as guard, though many of the troops were ill and a number had died since the regiment was first assigned to the post.[46]

The capacity of the prison was originally estimated at two thousand, though three thousand were crammed into the facility with the first arrivals. As the weeks passed, more arrived. By April, over forty-two hundred were confined.[47]

Colonel Owen complained in a dispatch to Colonel Hoffman, "that two regiments are guarding about 1,000 prisoners [elsewhere]; and here a minimum regiment, assisted by 207 from another, is guarding over 4,000 and furnishing details for several hospitals. . . . We have 130 on the sick-list in our regiment."[48] But Hoffman would not authorize any additional manpower.

Realizing he was shorthanded, Colonel Owen possibly attempted to manage the prison with extraordinary compassion in the hope of gaining cooperation from the prisoners. Instead of having a sutler selling items like tobacco and stationery, the chaplain distributed such supplies on Wednesdays and Saturdays at 2:00 P.M., and although visitors were not allowed in the camp by order of the governor, Colonel Owen allowed some prisoners to go into Indianapolis accompanied by a guard to purchase other articles.[49]

Before long, an Indianapolis *Journal* editorial complained that the POWs were frequenting the taverns of the city. "That I committed an error," Owen apologized in a letter to the editor, "in trusting some officers to take a few prisoners down on two different days to make purchases, with the promise that the privilege should be used for no other purpose, I now see . . . the promise was violated by permitting some of them to enter a saloon. The order as soon as the violation was known [has been] promptly [rescinded]."[50]

Although Colonel Owen did all he could to relieve the discomfort of the POWs, he found his resources and possibilities limited. Even the newspapers he provided to the prisoners from the camp fund were ordered stopped by Colonel Hoffman as soon as he learned of the practice.

"[T]he adjustment of small grievances and difficulties all make a great draft on the time and patience of those connected with the charge," Owen wrote of his disappointment in how the prison was operated. "Indeed our officers and men, particularly the latter, are overworked . . . duties have been performed without complaining, but we signified to Governor Morton our gratitude in advance should he relieve us from a position in which any want of success was certain to bring censure and the best management unlikely to gain us the slightest credit."[51]

Conditions for the prisoners continued to decline. The buildings had been constructed cheaply for the display of livestock in the warmer months, and after ten years, the dried planks and wide cracks offered little protection against rain, wind, or cold. In the hospital building, sick prisoners found it necessary to use their only blanket to cover the wall next to their cots as protection against the weather.

From the day Camp Morton was established, the latrines were large open pits near the center of the camp. As the compound became more and more crowded, the latrines were filled and reestablished elsewhere in various parts of the enclosure until the ground became filled with poisonous matter. Within a short time, hundreds became ill, and not too long after, they began to die.

Those who remained healthy tried desperately to escape. On July 14, fifty POWs rushed the dilapidated wall. Although five did escape, some were killed, some were wounded, and some were recaptured. As at Alton Prison, such attempts would plague this prison throughout its existence.

JOHNSON'S ISLAND

With the prisoners from Tennessee distributed to every conceivable Midwest location, Hoffman elected to send a remaining six hundred to his newly completed Johnson's Island Military Prison near Sandusky, Ohio. The facility, completed just days before forts Henry and Donelson were captured, wasn't expected to start housing prisoners until April, but this first contingent arrived the same day as those at Camp Morton, February 24.

Johnson's Island, so named because it was owned by L. B. Johnson of Sandusky, was the Union's first effort to construct a facility solely for the internment of prisoners of war. During Colonel Hoffman's original search for a suitable site in the area, he had rejected a number of other available islands— one because it was unsafe, being too near Canada, another because of the exorbitant rent demanded by its owner, and yet another because it provided too much of an enticement for prison guards by being too close to a brandy establishment on the mainland.[52]

Hoffman found Johnson's Island the most suitable in the area. It was situated one mile from the mainland, 2½ miles north of Sandusky, which was serviced by good railroad lines, and covered three hundred uninhabited acres. The site was also heavily wooded, providing good building and fuel supplies. With a forty-acre clearing along the waterfront, Hoffman reasoned, half the island could be leased by the government at only $500 a year, with complete control over the remainder. The site lay not far out in Lake Erie, in the protected waters of Sandusky Bay. The mile of water separating the site from the mainland provided security against escape and its proximity to the city provided an availability of guards and enhanced security against an uprising by the POWs.

Construction began in November 1861. The total cost of the compound was estimated at around $30,000, including a blockhouse with a howitzer and a guardboat positioned offshore. Union authorities believed that, once completed, the facility could accommodate up to 1,000 POWs.[53]

The compound was built on an already cleared area of approximately fifteen acres on the southeast end of the island. Stockade planks fourteen feet high were erected around the site with the gate facing, and about twenty yards from, the shoreline. A platform, or parapet, was constructed along the top around the outside of the wall for the sentinels to patrol along. At the two corners fronting the lake, blockhouses were constructed to house light artillery. At the main entrance, another blockhouse was built, which could cover, from any direction, the approach to the gate. Additional artillery would be aimed at the interior of the compound from a small rise called Fort Hill overlooking the prison from a short distance away.

Within the stockade, thirteen two-story barracks, referred to as blocks, were constructed. Twelve housed prisoners and one was to be used as a hospital. The barracks were arranged in two rows with a 150-foot-wide street between them. Another street ran behind the row of barracks, inside a series of stakes that served as a deadline (the boundary line that prisoners were forbidden to cross). Later, additional pathways would be worn in the ground radiating outward from the barracks area toward three shallow wells near the front of the stockade. Along the front or lakeside walls of the fence, the deadline extended out anywhere from forty to fifty yards from the wall. With the buildings and wide deadlines, the fifteen acre range the prisoners had access to was actually only eight acres, although this space would be increased somewhat with a reduction of the deadline area later in the war as the prison became more crowded.

The barracks, or blocks, were built on a temporary basis in the original belief that the prison's existence would be brief. The buildings lacked foundations and were constructed as cheaply as possible out of knotty green lumber nailed to upright beams. The boards warped within a short time. There were no interior walls or ceilings to prevent the outside air from entering.

The interiors of four prisoner barracks were partitioned off into twenty-two rooms, eleven on each floor, while the other eight barracks were divided into six large rooms, three on each floor. Originally, authorities planned to incarcerate both enlisted men and officers at the island, and the blocks with the smaller rooms were intended for the officers. There were two kitchens to each block, built as additions to the main building. Stairs led to the upper floors from the outside.

Beyond the stockade, about two hundred yards away, barracks for the guards and houses for the families of the Union officers were built. The officer housing was on the west side, facing the prison. Guard barracks were situated on the south and north sides. Colonel Hoffman regarded Johnson's Island as the model military prison and had all the buildings and the stockade brightly whitewashed just before the first prisoners arrived.

Colonel Hoffman recommended William S. Pierson, a Yale graduate and mayor of Sandusky, as commandant of the prison. Pierson took over the new assignment on January 1, 1862, before the prison was completed. He had no prior military experience, but was given the commission of major and, later, lieutenant colonel, in order to command a battalion of guards to be raised. When construction was completed the following month, Secretary Stanton authorized Ohio's governor, David Tod, to "raise for the service of the United States a select company of volunteers for duty as a guard."[54]

Four hundred men were recruited, trained, and organized into four companies. Eventually this group was referred to as the "Hoffman Battalion." It would go on to serve as the guard until January 1864, when six more companies would be added and the regiment would be designated the 128th Ohio Volunteer Infantry.[55]

As the prison began operation, its population varied greatly from month to month. The number of inmates fluctuated anywhere from six hundred to two thousand and even dropped down to three hundred in one short period. The facility received prisoners of all types, including officers, enlisted men, and even civilian political prisoners until June 1862, when the secretary of war ordered all Confederate officers held as POWs to be sent to Johnson's Island. From then on, the Johnson's Island Military Prison was officially designated as a prison for Confederate officers, although any number of enlisted men and political prisoners could be found confined there.[56]

CAMP CHASE

Just over a hundred miles south of Johnson's Island, Camp Chase received its first contingent of POWs during the second week of April 1862, complicating the issue of who was to assume control of the camp—federal officials or the state of Ohio, which used the facility for political prisoners.

Governor Tod, who insisted on signing all his correspondence "Governor and Commander in Chief," made no claim to Johnson's Island, but continued his fight with Federal authorities for complete control of Camp Chase. Tod named Colonel Granville Moody, a former minister and commander of the 12th Ohio Regiment, prison commandant. Meanwhile, the lax security under the governor's and Moody's command irritated Federal authorities.

Captain Henry Lazelle bitterly complained: "Camp Chase is made the place of rendezvous for all furloughed and paroled or disabled soldiers in the State. . . . [The governor] gives to the commanding officer such orders as he pleases. . . . He is utterly ignorant of the most common requirements of the Army regulations. . . . [H]e regards this as a camp of instruction of the State of Ohio for its recruits. . . . that he controls the soldiers and you [the Federal government] care for the prisoners together with him. . . . He paroles prisoners within the limits of the town and he gives instruction to the commanding officer relating to their control and discipline. He grants permits to visit them . . . [and] has no knowledge of the importance of discipline and of the effect upon it of citizens lounging in great numbers about the camp."[57]

Captain Lazelle blasted Colonel Moody as well: "The commanding officer of the camp is uncertain and in constant doubt as to whom he should go to for instructions, which together with his ignorance of his duties quite overpowers him."[58]

Prisoners at Camp Chase were allowed the privilege of receiving gifts of food and money and purchasing whatever they wanted from the sutler. Upon a simple oath not to escape, Confederate officer prisoners were allowed to wander the streets of Columbus, register to stay in its hotels, and attend sessions of the state senate. At the same time, for a small admission fee, the public was allowed to tour the prison. It became one of the most popular tourist attractions around. "It is pleasing to [Moody]," grumbled Lazelle, "to talk and guide and explain to [the tourists] all curious points of interest."[59]

Before long, complaints over lax discipline and the camp's state administrators provoked anger, even among the Ohio residents.

N. A. Reed, pastor of the Market Street Baptist Church in Zanesville, Ohio, griped in a letter to President Lincoln dated April 26, 1862, "Having sons in the Third and Thirteenth Ohio Regiments, the matter has become too much . . . to be endured. . . . [t]o have our sons toil in the Army and be subjected to trials and the most severe deprivations, and then to have these rebel officers actually at their ease in our streets speaking treason openly and boldly is almost too much for human endurance."[60]

Somewhat sensitive to the complaints, Governor Tod transferred Moody and his regiment to the seat of war and appointed Colonel Charles W. B. Allison prison commandant. Allison, a lawyer and son-in-law to Ohio's lieutenant governor, proved no better, probably because he, too, was unfamiliar with military procedure and remained under Tod's control.

"Colonel Allison," howled an exasperated Lazelle, "is not in any degree a soldier, he is entirely without experience and utterly ignorant of his duties."[61]

While the state and Federal governments quibbled over control of the prison, the guards took charge. "I knew nothing of prison rules," declared J. Coleman Alderson, Company A, 36th Battalion, Virginia Cavalry. "(But) within one hour after entering the prison I was walking within a few feet of the wall, when on hearing a 'click, click' I looked up and saw the guard on top of the parapet with his gun leveled at me." Camp Chase prisoners quickly learned that although state administrators were lax, state troops used as sentries were not. "Shots were fired into the barracks at night," Alderson continued, "often without cause. . . . On one occasion the moon was shining through a back window in barracks No. 2, on the opposite side from the guard who called 'lights out,' and as the moon did not go out, he (shot and) killed two men sleeping together in their cold, narrow bunks."[62]

"A fresh prisoner," wrote prisoner George Moffett, "[who was] ignorant of the rule relating to the extinguishment of fires and lights, was turned into the prison one cold morning and, having a match in his pocket, struck it with the intention of kindling a fire in the stove. The sentinel on the parapet, who saw the light through the window, fired immediately and killed the poor fellow."[63]

"I fired at the light to shoot it out according to my instructions," insisted John W. White, Company D, 15th Regiment Invalid Corps, one of the many guards involved in shooting prisoners at Camp Chase. "I did not leave my post, and never saw the prisoner that was shot."[64]

"[C]ases have occurred," declared Colonel Hoffman in a letter to the prison commandant, "of the wounding of prisoners at night by the guard when they neither were sent to the hospital nor received medical treatment until the next morning. Such treatment of prisoners, whatever may be the necessity for wounding them, is barbarous and without possible excuse."[65]

Many prisoners died in such cases because even their mess mates were unable to help them. "It was some time before I could get permission from the sentinel to light a candle to dress the wound," noted J. G. Nance, Company I, 10th Kentucky Cavalry, on his attempt to aid a fellow prisoner who had been shot.[66]

There were other complaints that prisoners were often shot when they misunderstood and stepped out of line during roll call, failed to quickly follow demands yelled down to them from the guards on the parapet, or gathered into large groups.

Another incident involved an order prohibiting the wasting of water. "One of the unfortunates," declared John H. King, Company H, 40th Georgia

Infantry, "not aware of the order, washed out his tin cup at the pump and threw out the water on the ground before filling the cup with water to drink. A guard seeing him throw the water on the ground, at once fired at him and missing his aim severely wounded an unlucky prisoner standing some distance beyond."[67]

Various regiments performed sentinel duty at different times at Camp Chase. Those involved in a majority of the shootings belonged to the 12th Ohio Volunteer Cavalry, the 88th Ohio Volunteer Infantry, and the 15th Regiment Invalid Corps.

By the end of September, Colonel Allison's term of service had expired. Tod quickly replaced him with Major Peter Zinn of the Governor's Guard.

OLD CAPITOL PRISON

By mid-1862, Old Capitol Prison in Washington City had also gained a reputation for strict discipline. The facility's original prison building had an estimated capacity of five hundred, but a row of houses on the adjoining block, known as Duff Green's Row, was added in May, bringing the total capacity to fifteen hundred. This annex became known as Carroll Prison.

Old Capitol Prison began to play an important part in the Federal Secret Service system by its second year. In addition to holding political prisoners and Confederate prisoners of war, a number of suspected Confederate spies were held there. These included people such as Rose O'Neal Greenhow, who took her eight-year-old daughter to jail with her and continued espionage work using the young girl as a courier, and nineteen-year-old Belle Boyd, who continually taunted the guards and sang Confederate songs at her window. William P. Wood, the prison commandant, acted as a special agent for the War Department and frequently interrogated the inmates. When critical information was obtained, he forwarded it directly to Secretary Stanton.[68]

Forty-one years old and a native of Alexandria, Virginia, Wood had enlisted in the Mounted Rifles during the Mexican War and served under Sam H. Walker, the noted Texas Ranger. After serving out his enlistment, Wood returned to private life in Washington City and married a Maryland debutante.[69]

When Stanton became secretary of war in January 1862, he appointed Wood as superintendent of the military prisons of the District of Columbia, and concentrated the "state prisoners" and all others suspected of disloyalty in Old Capitol Prison, where Wood, and ultimately Stanton, would have complete control over their destiny.

Eventually, the prison would become identified with the Confederate spies it held and as the location where the Lincoln conspirators were held after his assassination, but to the inmates confined there, the prison was most notable for its strict discipline and its incredible infestation of bedbugs.

"Night after night I suffered from the onslaughts of those bugs," complained prisoner Miles O. Sherrill, 12th North Carolina Regiment. "As soon as it was light enough to see I would sit upon my humble couch and commence a war of revenge."[70]

"I could see them by the hundreds," grumbled prisoner James N. Bosang of the 4th Virginia, "all over me [and] all over my bed." Captain Bosang came up with an ingenious scheme to combat the critters. Realizing they could reach him only by climbing up the legs of the bed, he placed cups under the legs and filled them with water. "I found but very few that even attempted to swim, and they were drowned."[71]

While bedbugs made conditions uncomfortable inside the prison, guards made conditions downright deadly from the outside. According to prisoner James J. Williamson and many others there was often "punishment inflicted upon some poor wretch for a violation of some unwritten rule." Unlike many other prison buildings in the North or South, prisoners at Old Capitol were allowed to look out the windows as long as they didn't touch the bars. The guards, however, would often order them away from the window, whether they were touching the bars or not, depending upon their mood.[72]

Jesse W. Wharton, a young prisoner about twenty-six years old and son of Dr. Wharton, a professor of agricultural chemistry in Prince Georges County, Maryland, was shot by guard Harrison Baker of the 91st Pennsylvania Regiment for standing too close to the cell window. Wharton had been warned several times to get away from the window. Believing he was not infringing on any of the rules, he ignored the guard's demands and continued looking out the window with his arms folded across his chest. The guard leveled his musket and fired. The ball struck Wharton in the left hand, passed through his right arm, broke the bone at the elbow, continued into his right side and exited at the spine. Wharton died eight hours later.[73]

Another case involved prisoner Harry Stewart, the twenty-three-year-old son of Dr. Frederick Stewart of Baltimore. A guard, this one a member of the 86th New York Volunteers, agreed to allow Stewart to escape upon a bribe of $50. Stewart waited for the appointed night and hour and began lowering himself from his window to the pavement below. After being lowered just a few feet, the guard yelled out "Halt!" and fired. The ball shattered Stewart's right knee cap. He was quickly hoisted back into his cell by his roommates and a physician was summoned. The mangled leg was amputated, but the shock was too great and Stewart died. In his pocket, authorities found the bribery note incriminating the guard who shot him, but disciplinary action was never taken.[74]

In yet another case of guard abuse, a sentry entered a cell room and accused the inmates of spitting out the window at him. It was after a brief rain, and the prisoners pointed out that water drops accumulated on the windowsill had apparently dripped down on him as he stood on the pavement below. Even after witnessing the rain continuing to drip from that location, the guard ordered the window sealed. "We are now forced to remain in a closed room," bemoaned one of the prisoners involved, "with no ventilation and the breaths of 37 men poisoning the air."[75]

Standing at the windows not only jeopardized the prisoners' own welfare, it was often hazardous to those passing by on the street below. "No persons [were] allowed to show any signs of recognition," recalled Williamson. "If a person [was] seen loitering in passing the prison, or walking at a pace not considered satisfactory by the guard, he soon received a peremptory command to 'pass on,' or 'hurry up, there,' and if this warning [was] not heeded the offending person, whether male or female, [was] arrested and detained."[76]

The brutality at Old Capitol Prison wasn't necessarily limited to Confederate or political prisoners. Several cases involved Union soldiers held there. A lieutenant entered the guardhouse where a sentry was incarcerated for being drunk and noisy and proceeded to slap and kick him several times. In another case, when a Union prisoner knocked down a portion of the guardhouse wall, he was taken out and hung from a tree by his wrists.[77]

Unknowingly, the guards at this prison also struck terror among the inmates by the way they handled their weapons. Unlike most other prisons, the sentries here remained on constant patrol throughout the interior of the prison as well as the exterior. "[We] heard the steady tramp of the sentry up and down the halls all night," reported one prisoner, "clanking of arms, challenging of the guards and the calls of the relief."[78]

It wasn't at all unusual for these prisoners to hear the report of a musket and to have a bullet come whizzing through the floor or the wall as the guards clumsily passed up and down the stairways. "The floors and ceilings of some of the rooms bore unmistakable evidence, in the shape of bullet-holes," noted one prisoner, "that there was sufficient cause for the apprehensions of the prisoners."[79]

One such occurrence was documented at 2:40 P.M. on October 22, 1862. A prisoner in room No. 16 was in his bunk, talking to his roommates, when a sharp report was heard from the room below. At the same time a ball passed through the headboard area of the bed, narrowly missing the prisoner, and lodged in the ceiling. A guard, who had accidentally discharged his musket, was found to be responsible. "The force with which the ball was shot," read the affidavit, "will be understood from the fact that, after passing through the ceiling and floor underneath room No. 16, it went through one of the slats of the bed, through two bedticks, and through a blanket of twelve thicknesses rolled up as a pillow, and through a feather pillow, and then penetrated the ceiling overhead of room No. 16."[80]

During that same month, a guard patrolling the front of the prison accidentally shot himself in the head.[81]

Normally, the daily routine at Old Capitol began with the doors to the prisoners' rooms being thrown open, one at a time, to announce breakfast. Breakfast began at daybreak and continued with one or two rooms at a time until all were served.

About nine in the morning, the doors were thrown open again and a voice from the hall shouted out "sick call!" Then all who had need of medicine or treatment proceeded under guard to the hospital, located in a two-story building attached to the main building and reached by a flight of stairs leading up from the prison yard. During the remainder of the morning, the prisoners busied themselves with their various pursuits.

"Next to poker," reported D. A. Mahony, "the favorite game was muggins or as it was called in prison, 'Old Capitol.'" Another prisoner added, "Some devote much of their time to smoking, others to relating stories of adventure, with an occasional song and dance." Prisoner Gus Williams related: "When Belle Boyd was here, I was on the same floor. She would sing that song ["Maryland, My Maryland"] as if her very soul was in every word she uttered. It use to bring a lump up in my throat every time I heard it. . . . I've seen men, when she was singing, walk off to one side and pull out their handkerchiefs and wipe their eyes, for fear some one would see them doing the baby act."[82]

Prisoner James Williamson also called attention to the fact that liquor remained accessible at Old Capitol Prison late into the war. "It is an easy matter to get whiskey here," he wrote in his diary. "A bright young contraband . . . comes into our room every morning to remove ashes [from the stove] and refuse. For a trifling sum Charlie will bring in two flasks of whiskey in the breast pockets of his coat, and afterward take back the empty flasks. Many of the prison guards are ready to do the same when asked."[83]

Still, the prisoners had to be careful. At Old Capitol Prison they couldn't trust everyone they met. "Persons are often put in the rooms with the prisoners, who, while posing as prisoners themselves, are really spies or detectives in the employ of the officials."[84]

The next main event of the prisoners' day was the dinner call. At Old Capitol the inmates had the choice of using this half hour for either dinner or exercising in the yard. The yard was about one hundred feet square and partly paved with bricks or cobblestones. Executions at the prison took place here.

On the side of this yard, extending from the wooden building occupied by the sutler's shop, mess room, and hospital, and running back to a gate, was a one-story stone building that served as the cookhouse, guardhouse, and washhouse. Prisoners had access to sinks in back of this building.

These sinks, or latrines, were wide trenches with a long wooden rail along the front, similar to those used in the camps. However, these were never covered after use. "The presence of these sinks, used for months by several hundred men," complained a prisoner, "did not contribute to the beauty of the scenery or add sweetness to the tainted air!"[85]

According to many accounts, attending dinner was not necessarily a good choice either. The mess room was described as a "dirty, dismal room," having long tables "of what material were constructed was impossible to determine on account of the accumulation of dirt." "Here, grouped around a big stove," reported one prisoner, "was a gang of Negroes, one of whom, at the Lieutenant's command, brought out a chunk of beef, a slice of bread over an inch thick, and a cup of coffee."[86]

The meals were served on dented, old tin plates and, according to many prisoners, "[t]here being neither knife, fork, nor spoon given out with it, the only way to eat was with hands."[87]

"The waiter," Williamson reported, "stood at the head of the long board table with a handful of tin cups filled with a liquid, by courtesy called coffee, [and] with a dextrous twist of the wrist, sent them spinning along down the table, leaving each man to catch one of the flying cups before it slid past. . . . No more than half of each cup spilled out."[88]

There was little variation from one meal to the next or from one day to the next. Generally each breakfast at Old Capitol consisted of unbuttered bread, beef, and coffee. Dinner was often the same but sometimes included boiled beans and pork with molasses, and supper was nothing more than bread and coffee. The prison was, however, one of the few to provide three meals a day.

Those who could afford to do so "clubbed" together and, with permission, purchased additional items from the prison sutler. "His stock is neither choice nor varied," complained one prisoner, "chiefly tobacco, cigars, cakes, candy, pies, etc.—all of which he furnishes at prices far beyond their market value." In addition, inmates of this prison could purchase passes from the sutler, which allowed them the privilege of using the cleaner, enclosed sinks of the prison officials.[89]

Unlike at most other prison buildings, Old Capitol prisoners remained locked in their rooms between meals. Roll call didn't take place but once a day, after supper, and it consisted of the inmates lining up in their respective rooms and answering as their names were called from the hallway. This usually took a couple of hours each night.

Each day ended with the guards marching through the hallways and calling out at the doors of the room: "Lights out!" At this announcement, every light was immediately extinguished. The prisoners were then compelled to crawl into their bunks or sit in the dark.

By mid-1862, Fort Delaware became a full-fledged POW facility with the arrival of 250 men of Thomas J. "Stonewall" Jackson's brigade, captured at the Battle of Kernstown. Upon their arrival in April, Commandant Gibson moved his troops to the third floor of the fort's quarters and confined 200 of the POWs on the second floor over the sally port, while the remaining 50 were placed in the fort's dungeons, or lower quarters.

Afterward, the fort's prisoner population fluctuated greatly. By June 15, there were 600 POWs, and two weeks later there were 3,434.

By midsummer Captain Gibson had thoroughly irritated Secretary Stanton for allowing a political prisoner to have visitors; he subsequently was transferred out. Major Henry S. Burton, 3rd U.S. Artillery, was then assigned command of the fort. At the time, it held 1,260 POWs but the population would drop as low as 482, only to climb to 2,582 by the end of the year. By then Burton had also angered Stanton by releasing a number of political prisoners; he too, was quickly relieved of command and replaced by Lieutenant Colonel Delavan D. Perkins.[90]

Conditions for prisoners remained about the same at the other forts. Fort McHenry remained overcrowded, while Fort Warren continued to decrease its population. Most of the Hatteras Inlet captives were exchanged or released by February 1862, but before they left they formally praised Colonel Justin Dimick, the fort's commander, and presented the head of the prison guards, Lieutenant James S. Casey, with a gold-headed cane. Prisoners continued to arrive and depart Fort Warren during the following months, and the population fluctuated from 100 to 250 through July. By August, however, nearly all of the POWs had been transferred out and the fort reverted to being a troop facility.[91]

A general exchange of prisoners took place for those at Camp Morton before the end of 1862. Beginning in September, by the following month, Camp Morton had returned to being a full-time training facility.[92]

The Camp Morton prisoners had been unique in several aspects. There, a fad developed, with the POWs wearing their blankets, or whatever they had left of them, fashioned into capes or cloaks, which they tied around their necks and draped down their backs as they walked around the facility during the daytime. The fad had evolved out of the realization that failure to hold on to their blankets usually meant immediate loss of them to someone else before nightfall.[93]

Colonel Richard Owen, the prison commandant, who was from New Harmony, Indiana, and had been a science teacher at the Nashville Military Academy in Tennessee before the war, became thoroughly disgusted with the prison system and resigned from military service to accept a professorship at the University of Indiana. Years after the war, many of his former prisoners would commission a memorial bust of him to pay tribute to his acts of courtesy, caring, and kindness while they had been confined at Camp Morton.[94]

By late September, the population of Camp Douglas was down to just over 7,000 POWs, on its way to being emptied of prisoners on exchange by the end of the year. In its nine-month history as a POW facility, more than 300 died, more than 50 escaped, and nearly 1,000 were released upon taking the Oath of Allegiance.[95]

More than 3,000 POWs had been confined at Camp Butler by September. During that month, 300 were escorted to the nearby tracks of the Great Western Railroad and sent on their way to Vicksburg for exchange. A few days later, 1,793 more were loaded up and sent off, leaving 23 in the hospital who were too weak to travel. By October 6, these, too, were gone.[96]

Training continued at Camp Butler, and no more prisoners arrived. In its nine-month period as a POW camp, 470 prisoners had died, 202 had escaped, and 278 had been released upon taking the Oath of Allegiance.[97]

In St. Louis, because conditions at Myrtle Street Prison had become deplorable, the facility was ordered closed in May. Its 150 inmates were moved to Gratiot Street, where conditions continued to worsen.

By November 5, the population of Gratiot Street stood at 1,100 men and women. Sanitary conditions and food rations declined further, and disease swept through the facility. Additional prisoners were transferred to nearby Alton Prison to bring the population down to 800, but that number still severely taxed the facility. At the same time, a smallpox epidemic broke out at Alton.

Colonel Thomas Gantt took possession of the old Myrtle Street facility that month and put it back into condition for receiving prisoners again. Within days of its being renovated, Lieutenant Colonel Franklin A. Dick became provost marshal general and ordered 150 prisoners to Myrtle Street. Its capacity was still only 100, but the influx of prisoners at Gratiot Street made the action necessary.[98]

The relief, however, was only temporary. Within a few weeks the population of Gratiot Street soared back to over 1,100. By the middle of the month, sickness began to increase at an alarming rate, with 235 cases of illness breaking out in one week. Unable to gain admission to the hospital, many more sick and dying lay on the floors of the prison. Before long, the dawn of each day revealed from one to four dead inmates on the prison floors.[99]

"The prisoners," wrote inmate Griffin Frost, "were poorly fed, worse bedded, and nearly suffocated in the impure air. It is said there have been as many as 1,700 men at one time in these lower quarters. That number could scarcely find standing room; sleeping would be out of the question; of course they must suffer, sicken, and die."[100]

In December, the Alton prison was overcrowded but excess from Gratiot Street was sent anyway. The population of Gratiot was finally reduced to 471, Myrtle to 145, and Alton to 800.[101]

Throughout the year the Confederacy struggled with its POW situation as well. Colonel George C. Gibbs had succeeded Lieutenant David Todd as commandant of Richmond's prisons in the fall of the previous year, but by January 1862, Gibbs was promoted to major and transferred to Salisbury as commandant of that prison. Lieutenant J. T. W. Hairston of the 11th Mississippi took over duties as the Richmond commandant for a short time, but by the end of February, recently promoted Major A. C. Godwin was placed in overall command. "He, too, is stern," reported the *New York Times*, "but a gentleman." Godwin went on to become well-liked by the prisoners.[102]

The changes in leadership were the result of General Winder's attempt to bring some semblance of order into Richmond. To relieve some of the economic strain, he began transferring 150 to 250 prisoners out every two or three weeks on exchange or to other prison locations. He revamped his entire prison system by having Ligon's warehouse and the Crew-Pemberton, Taylor, and Mayo factories converted into hospitals while he began a search for a larger, more convenient warehouse somewhere in the city. Eventually his eyes settled on the Libby & Son warehouse on the southeast corner of 19th and Cary streets.

LIBBY PRISON

The Libby building, the only one in the area having running water, was considered ideal by Confederate authorities because it was somewhat isolated and could be easily guarded. It was situated in a Richmond neighborhood that consisted of several warehouses, a number of shanties, an old meeting house, several stables, and numerous vacant lots. It was accessible by both railroad and water transportation and was away from the congestion of Main Street.

The building, three stories high at the front along Cary and four stories high in the rear where the street sloped toward the canal, was about 135 feet wide and extended 90 feet back to Canal Street. Its interior was divided into three sections by thick walls that extended up from the basement to the roof, giving the appearance from the back that the building was made up of three smaller buildings constructed side by side. Each story was divided into three low, oblong rooms, 45 by 90 feet, with exposed beams.

The history of the building went back to 1845, when Luther Libby moved from Maine to Richmond and went into partnership with a Richmonder in the ship chandling business. Their proprietorship near the riverfront in the Rocketts section of town quickly prospered. Around 1860, Libby saw an opportunity to expand to a site one mile closer to the center of town. When his partner refused, their partnership was dissolved. Libby went off on his own to build a new brick warehouse on Cary, established a business of ship chandler, grocer, and commission merchant, and named the business "Libby & Son." It had just begun to flourish when Confederate officials, under the command of Winder, confiscated the building for government use. The Libbys were told they had forty-eight hours to vacate the building, which they did without even taking time to remove the new signs attached to the front of the building.[103]

General Winder arranged for flat-iron bars to be installed over the windows and makeshift water closets to be constructed on each floor. Tents for guards were pitched on the nearby vacant lots of Cary and 20th.

Prisoners were to occupy the two upper floors, or six upper rooms. "Four small-sized windows at each end of these rooms admit a limited amount of light for about 25 feet," according to one prisoner, "leaving about 40 feet in the center of each where print cannot be read in the daytime."[104]

The middle room on the first floor was to be used for cooking. This kitchen was the only place in the building to which the prisoners could have free access. The fireplaces were not utilized, but in front of each were three stoves, the pipes of which went into the chimney flues, running upward above the fireplaces. The east room on the first floor would be used as a hospital. The west room was the office where prison officials would be quartered, and the basement beneath was divided into dungeons for the confinement and punishment of unruly prisoners. All doors and windows of the prison were barred.

Lieutenant Thomas Pratt Turner of White Post, Virginia, was placed in charge of the new prison. Turner had attended the Virginia Military Institute as a member of the class of 1862, but had left after only one year to obtain a commission in the 1st Virginia Battalion. He was twenty-one years old, with a thin build. He was always clean-shaven and had close-cut dark hair, gray eyes, and a deep voice. A strict disciplinarian, he would eventually be deeply despised by his prisoners. He walked with a stiff gait and always wore a full-dress Confederate uniform of gray cap, coat, and pants.[105]

Second in command, with more direct control over the prisoners, was Richard R. Turner, who had attended West Point for six months before being dismissed on a conviction of forgery. Better known as Dick Turner, he was twenty-three years old, with dark hair and blue eyes. Dick was built much larger than the commandant and had been a plantation overseer in eastern Henrico County, Virginia, before the war. He quickly attracted the hatred of the Libby prisoners because of his haste in using physical punishment. He once threatened to hang a prisoner who refused to get twelve volunteers to sweep the street in front of the prison, and he chained four others in the dungeons for refusing to clean his stables. He was known to kick dying prisoners for no apparent reason when he found them lying on the prison floor.[106]

Third in command was a Baltimore man named George Emack who later received a lieutenant commission. Lieutenant Emack was apparently as ruthless as Dick Turner and was equally hated by the POWs. He once held a gun to the head of a sick prisoner and threatened to blow his head off if he didn't get up. He was twenty-five years old, six feet tall, and had short light hair, a slight moustache, a fair complexion, and blue eyes. He always wore a snappy uniform of a sky-blue cap, gray coat, light blue pants with black stripes, and a sword with steel scabbard.[107]

Erasmus Ross rounded out the quartet as prison clerk. Ross was twenty-one and had a large, heavy-set frame. He recorded the prisoners names upon their arrival at the facility and conducted the daily roll calls. Whenever he entered the prison rooms he was accompanied by two armed guards, and he himself wore a pair of prominently displayed revolvers and a large Bowie knife. His continual taunts of the prisoners, as well as his apparent fear of them, made Ross another target of the prisoners' hatred at Libby Prison.[108]

The first prisoners were moved in on March 26, 1862, when more than five hundred POWs from Richmond's various prisons were mustered into the streets and marched to the new facility. Once there, they stood in formation for several hours in front of the building as prisoners were led one at a time into the office. The first inmate registered on Libby's rolls was Philander A. Streator of Massachusetts.[109]

"[A]fter registering our names, rank and regiment," recalled one prisoner, "we were relieved of the few valuables we chanced to have left. We were then conducted to the floor above and put through a door which was immediately closed and bolted on the outside."[110]

The prisoners soon discovered that Libby Prison was no different than the other prison buildings in Richmond. The rooms contained no furniture, ventilation was poor, and the lighting was gloomy. Although this building had running water, it was drawn straight from the James River and was of extremely poor quality.

The inmates also learned that, just like at the other prisons, they were not allowed to go within three feet of the windows. Libby was guarded by two companies of soldiers totaling sixty men, and half that number were on duty at all times. These guards, according to many prisoners, patrolled with their guns cocked and endlessly watched the windows for a chance to shoot, often referred to as "Sporting for Yankees."[111]

According to the prisoners, the only good aspect about the new prison was that it was not as crowded as the others, although more than 100 men were confined in each of the 45-by-90-foot rooms.

For a while, a reasonable attempt was made to keep the prison clean. Black prisoners were brought in to sweep the floors daily and to scrub the floors weekly, and the walls were frequently whitewashed. Within a short time, however, conditions at Libby became just as bad as at the other places.

Three days after the prison opened, the population had grown to 700. Nearly 600 political prisoners were added a few days later. Due to extreme overcrowding, political prisoners were moved out and confined elsewhere.

BELLE ISLE

In full view of Libby's southwest windows was a small island in the James River named Belle Isle, which seemed perfect for holding POWs. It would be a refreshing change of environment, officials reasoned; it was abundant in wildlife and had gentle slopes that rose from the water's edge to a low hill. This beautiful green island had been a favorite resort area for Richmonders since 1815, when part of the eighty-acre site had supported an iron ore company with a little village for its employees. It had also been a muster and training site for new recruits at the beginning of hostilities.[112]

The site was beyond the congestion of the city; it was located near a fall line in the river where swift currents discouraged escape attempts. The bridge that linked the island to the mainland could be easily guarded yet connected the site to the nearby Richmond and Danville Railroad depot for easy transfer of supplies and prisoners.

In mid-June, authorities began removing all Federal noncommissioned officers and privates from Richmond's prison buildings and transferring them to the newly acquired site.

"The place occupied by the prisoners," noted Howard Leedom, 52nd New York Regiment, "[was] about six acres enclosed by an earthwork three feet in height." The earthworks served as the deadline. There were no trees at this location and the site was exposed to the intense heat of summer and the bitter cold of winter.[113]

A maze of tents was pitched on the site for housing, but authorities were not able to obtain enough. The site was believed capable of accommodating 3,000 POWs; capacity was reached within two weeks.[114]

The prison's first commandant was Captain Norris Montgomery, who became well-liked by the prisoners because he offered them many privileges with minimal restraints. The POWs were allowed to bathe in the river— seventy-five prisoners per day in squads of five or six escorted under heavy guard—and to purchase additional foodstuffs from sutlers. "[Many] prisoners who had money," recalled one prisoner, "often bought little extras such as sweet potatoes or bread."[115]

These privileges, however, were abolished by order of Captain Henry Wirz, Madison Infantry, Louisiana Volunteers, when he was placed in command of Richmond's prisons in August.[116]

By mid-July there were 5,000 POWs on Belle Isle and a total of 8,000 throughout Richmond as a result of the Seven Days Battles. About this time, Confederate authorities confiscated the newly built Warwick and Barksdale Mill, believing it could hold another four thousand prisoners, but conversion plans never materialized because Union and Confederate officials made an agreement to begin exchanging prisoners soon afterward.[117]

Hundreds of captives were shipped out of Richmond under this agreement. Belle Isle prisoners were processed through Libby Prison until the island was nearly vacant. By September 23, Belle Isle ceased to exist as a POW facility.[118]

CASTLE THUNDER

Another infamous Richmond prison came into existence the month before Belle Isle went out of business.

On March 19, homes of many Richmond citizens were raided in a crackdown on contraband liquor. Accused of being disloyal, eighty-nine citizens were arrested and taken to Castle Godwin for confinement, but the addition of these prisoners into Godwin's already overcrowded thirteen rooms made survival of any of the prisoners nearly impossible. To reduce the congestion, a number of these political prisoners were moved to Libby, but when this proved to be a mistake as well, they were transferred back while the authorities searched for another solution.

Within a short time, Gleanor's Tobacco Factory, a large brick building on Cary at 18th Street, was seized for government use, along with two smaller brick buildings, Palmer's Factory and Whitlock's Warehouse. Although three separate buildings, they were attached by a highboard fence. By August Castle Godwin was closed, and its six hundred inmates were moved to the new site.

The prisoners were separated upon their arrival. Confederate deserters and political prisoners were placed into the Gleanor's building, which had an estimated capacity of 650. Blacks and women prisoners were confined in Whitlock's Warehouse, with an estimated capacity of 350. Federal deserters and, later, Federal POWs were placed in Palmer's, which had an estimated capacity of 400, for a total of 1,400 prisoners in the three-building complex. As with other facilities in Richmond, the estimated capacity was quickly reached and surpassed.[119]

The prisoners themselves applied the officious title of "Castle Thunder" to their new institution, evidently as a sardonic reference to having evoked the thunder of the gods. Even the Richmond *Daily Enquirer* thought the name entirely appropriate, and reported that it was "indicative of Olympian vengeance upon offenders [of] her laws."[120]

Indeed, in the following months, vengeance was practiced quite regularly within the walls of Castle Thunder. The prison quickly acquired a reputation for unnecessary brutality, and by the spring of 1863, the Confederate House of Representatives would order an investigation of the prison.

The "thunder" of the castle came in the human form of George W. Alexander. "[A]s a prison commandant," reported one source, "he was harsh, inhuman, tyrannical, and dishonest in every possible way."[121]

Alexander, a native of Washington, Georgia, had served in the U.S. Navy for nearly thirteen years before resigning his position and enlisting as a lieutenant in the Confederate States Army. While serving in Maryland in July 1861, Alexander was captured, found guilty of treason, and sentenced to death at Fort McHenry. While awaiting execution, he escaped and after hiding out in Baltimore for several days, fled to Richmond.[122]

Alexander joined General Winder's force on June 12, 1862, and by October was commissioned a captain. During that time he was assigned as commandant of Castle Godwin and moved with the prisoners to their new facility. By November, he was given full control of Castle Thunder.

As commandant of the prison, the thirty-two-year-old Captain had a bizarre appearance, with "his tight-fitting suit of black trousers, buckled at the knees, his black stockings and black loose shirt relieved only by a white collar, with his long, black whiskers flowing in the wind, riding at full gallop on his black horse . . . with his large, magnificent black dog Nero following at his heels."[123]

Nero became one of the most formidable guards at the prison. A huge Bavarian boar hound, the dog was originally imported as a pup to be trained to fight bears. The dog did later fight three battles with full-grown bears and won each time. On one occasion, $12,000 rode on the outcome of the fight. For three years, Alexander used his dog as a guard at the prison. "This hound," insisted George Putnam, one of the Federal prisoners who still had most of his uniform while confined at the prison, "had been taught to go for anybody wearing blue cloth!"[124]

Security at Castle Thunder was intense under Alexander's rule. "Nearly every week some new restriction is imposed," complained one prisoner. "Southerners on sentry duty made nothing of watching for an excuse to pop off one of the 'Yanks' at the windows," reported another. Security became so tight that in at least one instance, a guard shot and killed another guard who had entered an upper-story prison room and peered out the window.[125]

The three buildings that formed Castle Thunder resembled a parallelogram. The main building was in the front, or middle, with the two smaller buildings, or wings, on either side. Although board fences connected them across the front, a long brick wall connected the two wings at the rear, providing a small enclosed yard. Sentry boxes lined the top of the walls looking into the yard. This common area behind the three structures served as a place of exercise and as the location of the latrines. As the prison became more crowded, though, exercise was eliminated and, aside from using the latrines, activity in the yard became limited to executions by firing squads along the back wall or at the gallows erected along a side ledge. Barred windows along the backs of the buildings overlooked the yard, giving the other prisoners a full view of each execution.

Gaslights were used inside and water was available with the guards' approval. Due to poor air circulation, the odor of prisoners became exceedingly foul. Most prisoners slept on ragged blankets or piles of straw. The second floor of the main building contained a number of cells about fifteen feet square with boarded-up windows. A long hallway led to a large whitewashed room with four barred windows. This was known as the "prison parlor," where civilian prisoners could "stroll without interference." The third floor was divided into two rooms: a large room for POWs and a smaller room partitioned off with cells for Confederate prisoners awaiting courts-martial.

The first floor contained what became known as the infamous "inner room," full of balls and chains and including two "condemned cells" that were completely dark. The doorless latrine in the center of the room emitted a sour, putrid smell. The floors were sticky with crud and filth. A door led straight out of the first floor into the execution yard.[126]

No other prisons were established in Richmond after August. At mid-year, 8,000 captives were still housed throughout the city. The number was slowly reduced as Belle Isle was abandoned. Libby Prison briefly served as a hospital facility during the summer, but by the end of the year more inmates were moved in, bringing the population up to an overwhelming 1,350.[127]

During this time, conditions remained fairly stable at Salisbury Prison in North Carolina. From the day of its opening to April 21, there were 403 cases of illness among its inmates and only three deaths, which was apparently normal, because the guards fared about the same, with 509 cases of sickness and three deaths.[128]

The Salisbury commandant, Captain A. C. Godwin, made his prison guard unit the nucleus of a full regiment, was promoted to colonel and left for the seat of war. His regiment became the 57th North Carolina. Captain Henry McCoy, who had been quartermaster of the post and was a relative of General Winder, took over as commandant.

By the fall, POWs were moved out of Salisbury under the cartel agreement, leaving about 800 Confederate convicts, deserters, and political prisoners in the stockade by the end of 1862.[129]

Although many of Charleston's first prisoners were eventually transferred to Salisbury, the city remained one of the South's principal prison locations from the day the first POWs arrived for incarceration in Castle Pinckney. Once those prisoners were moved into the fort, a week after they arrived in Charleston, the city jail continued to be used, confining several hundred POWs at a time. As additional prisoners were transferred there, the enclosed jail yard of the facility came into use.

With the cartel agreement, many of Charleston's prisoners were exchanged, leaving only a few hundred convicts, black prisoners, and Confederate deserters in the city's military prisons by the end of the year. The Tuscaloosa, Alabama, facilities also came into disuse when the POWs there were paroled in December.

During 1862, only two additional locations of any significance were established by the Confederates for holding POWs. One was at Memphis, Tennessee, where Confederate authorities confiscated the Botanico-Medical College on Beale Street and converted it for prison use. The other was at Lynchburg, Virginia, where the jail, fairgrounds, and a number of converted buildings were used during the period of Richmond's peak POW population until the exchange cartel came about.

Unfortunately, many of the sites that were closed down when the exchange cartel was agreed upon would have to be reopened, in both the North and the South, when the cartel collapsed.

Chapter 5

PRISONER EXCHANGE

The usages of civilized warfare require that the commanding generals on each side should agree on a cartel of exchange.

Judah P. Benjamin, Secretary of War (CSA)

The process of prisoner exchange in the Civil War developed slowly and with great difficulty, and was extremely fragile from the beginning. On July 22, 1862, newspapers of both the Union and the Confederacy announced that an exchange cartel had been agreed upon. To the delight of families, politicians, and POWs on both sides, many prisoners were exchanged during the following months. Within 307 days, however, the agreement came to a bitter end.

POWs have held a precarious position throughout history. In ancient times, the victors killed or enslaved their captives. The Crusaders held them for ransom. Through the ages, the principle of prisoner exchange slowly evolved. As time—and armed conflicts—continued, the custom of exchanging captives grade for grade and man for man slowly developed. By the American Revolution it had become universally accepted, and by the War of 1812 it was actively practiced.

Looking to the American Revolution for a precedent on prisoner exchange, it appears that history was doomed to repeat itself in many ways during the Civil War. The rebellion against Great Britain presented some of the same problems later faced by the Federal and Confederate governments. The British feared that a general exchange of prisoners would give official recognition to the Colonies as a sovereign power. At the same time, unofficial exchanges took place between commanders in the field quite often. But the British government refused to negotiate on the basis of "nation against nation at war." To them, the conflict was simply an insurrection.[1]

In that conflict, the first official complaint and threat of retaliation over the treatment of prisoners came in 1775. In a letter dated December 18, General

Washington demanded an explanation from British General William Howe
for the severe treatment of Colonel Ethan Allen. Allen had been taken prisoner
by the British near Montreal, and it was later learned he had been taken aboard
the *Gaspee,* a schooner of war, and confined, "hands and feet in irons." Washington
threatened Howe that "whatever treatment Colonel Allen received [would] be
retaliated upon Brigadier-General Prescott" who was in American hands.
Washington ended the letter by proposing that "an exchange of prisoners was
proper; citizens for citizens, officers for officers of equal rank, and soldier for
soldier."[2]

Howe replied only to defend his actions and made no mention of the proposed exchange. By the end of 1776, the British held 4,845 American prisoners
and the colonies held 2,860 British.[3]

Finally, exchange commissioners were appointed on both sides, but repeated
attempts at a general exchange failed because "official" obstacles continued to
get in the way. As the war continued, several more exchanges took place in the
field, but they were never sanctioned by the British government. An official
exchange never took place during the war. On April 11, 1783, Congress issued
a proclamation for the suspension of hostilities, and on April 15, a resolution
was passed providing for the liberation of all prisoners. By that time, the American colonies held over 6,000 British prisoners of war.[4]

Eighty-six years after General Washington sent his letter to General
Howe, President Davis fired off a similar dispatch to President Lincoln,
threatening retaliation upon POWs held by the Confederacy in response to
the treatment received by the *Savannah* crew being held at the Tombs prison
in New York.[5]

Like the British during the American Revolution, the Federal government
regarded this conflict as only an insurrection, instead of an all-out war and,
therefore, believed that the rules of conflict and the issue of what to do about
prisoners did not apply. Captured sailors were to be considered pirates and
captured soldiers would be tried for treason; both would be hanged if found
guilty. Because of this official stance, the exchange of prisoners quickly became
a matter of principle. The Union feared that a general exchange would officially
recognize the Confederate government as a legitimate, sovereign power and,
therefore, no general exchanges could be permitted.

"In regard to the exchange of prisoners," Brigadier General U. S. Grant flatly
responded on October 14, 1861, when a Confederate General made such an
offer, "I recognize no Southern Confederacy."[6]

"To exchange prisoners," declared Brigadier General Charles F. Smith
a month later to an offer by another Confederate general, "would imply that
the United States government admitted the existing war to be one between
independent nations. This I cannot admit."[7]

Meanwhile, as in the Revolutionary War, other commanders *were* making such exchanges on the battlefield, albeit unofficially. "In the exchange of prisoners with General Price," Assistant Adjutant General John C. Kelton reasoned regarding one such exchange, "it was understood that General Price did not claim to be in the Confederate service but a general of Missouri Militia."[8]

It soon became widely known, however, that a precedent had already been set that would eventually force the Federal government, under pressure from the public, to make an official agreement to a general exchange of prisoners. On August 30, 1861, Colonel William H. L. Wallace, commanding Union forces at Bird's Point, Missouri, agreed, under a flag of truce, to exchange a number of prisoners with Brigadier General Gideon J. Pillow.

"[This] involves a question which has not been settled between the contending parties in this war," cautioned Wallace, "but waiving such question for the present case and protesting that this case shall not in any sense be regarded as a precedent, it has been determined . . . to exchange prisoners with you, man for man of equal rank."[9]

"A board of officers shall determine the character of those offered as prisoners and make the exchange," commanded Wallace. "This board shall consist of a colonel, major and captain of cavalry or infantry from each army, to be associated with a member of General Pillow's staff and one from [my staff]. . . . The prisoners to be accompanied by an armed escort of thirty mounted men each. The mounted escort and prisoners to be conducted within 100 paces of each other and there await the orders of the colonel of each party."[10]

Pillow readily agreed. Four days later, on September 3, in what is believed to have been the first formal, but officially unsanctioned, exchange of Civil War POWs, four officers of Pillow's command along with their escort and prisoners met four of Wallace's command, along with their escort and prisoners, on the outskirts of Charleston, Missouri, and exchanged three privates that were held by one side for three held by the other.[11]

Of course, Wallace's fear of setting a precedent was soon realized. "I have in my camp," Major General Leonidas Polk, CSA, wrote to the commander of U.S. forces in Cairo, Illinois, "a number of prisoners of the Federal Army. . . . I propose an exchange of these prisoners . . . [t]he principles recognized in the exchange of prisoners effected on the 3d of September between Brigadier-General Pillow, of the Confederate army, and Colonel Wallace, of the U.S. Army, are those I propose as the basis of that now contemplated."[12]

"The chances of the present unhappy war having left in my hands a number of prisoners who have been detained at this post for some time past," responded Brigadier General John A. McClernand, U.S.A., "I have for special reasons as well as in obedience to the dictates of humanity determined unconditionally to release."[13]

General McClernand gave specific directions to Colonel Napoleon B. Buford, 27th Regiment Illinois Volunteers, to accompany the prisoners: "In your conversation with the commandant," he ordered, "you will avoid all discussion upon the rights of belligerents and place my action herein simply upon the ground of humanity." McClernand released three POWs to General Polk who, in turn, released sixteen prisoners; the principle of "man for man and rank for rank" was disregarded.[14]

During the following months, exchanges continued in the field, although haphazardly and unofficially, as the Federal government continued to avoid official recognition of the Confederate government.

As early as mid-July 1861, though, the Federal government had realized that eventually exchanges would have to take place, as evidenced by U.S. Quartermaster General Montgomery C. Meigs's letter to the U.S. Secretary of War, Simon Cameron, encouraging him to appoint a commissary of prisoners. In that letter, Meigs noted that one of the commissioner's duties would be to "negotiate exchanges" and that "[t]he negotiation of exchange of prisoners is important."[15]

At the time, the Union had only about 800 POWs, compared to the Confederate government's 2,000. The general public in the north, many of whom had friends and relatives in southern prisons, began to demand that something be done. Newspapers got into the act too.[16]

"The course pursued by our Government now is precisely that pursued by the British Government then," argued a New York Times editorial in comparing the American Revolution with the American Civil War. "Yet, exchanges of prisoners were of constant occurrence between them. Why may not the same course be pursued now? Why should any exchange of prisoners now involve a recognition of the South . . . any more than a similar exchange during the Revolution involved such a concession to the revolted Colonies?"[17]

The controversy continued, and even the prisoners became involved in the debate. "We have been anxiously awaiting some action on the part of our Government for our release," Captain J. T. Drew, Company G, 2nd Vermont Regiment, complained in a letter to one northern newspaper while being held in Richmond. "There are 53 officers here and nearly 1,500 men. They are willing to suffer for the good of their country, but cannot see . . . laying in prison indefinitely."[18]

"We are," wrote another POW held in Richmond, "entitled to protection under the Government to which we have given proof of our loyalty. . . . [W]e do not see how the public good is to be increased by retaining us in our present condition. . . . [I]n the name of humanity, we call upon the Government . . . to make measures to procure for us a speedy and honorable release."[19]

Meanwhile, special exchanges took place between Brigadier General Benjamin Huger, commanding Confederate forces at Norfolk, Virginia, and Major General John E. Wool, commanding Union forces at Fortress Monroe.[20]

"In the barracks and jails of Richmond, several hundred Northern prisoners captured at Bull Run are confined," declared another *New York Times* editorial. "In the forts about our harbor, a still larger number of rebels are entertained at a very serious cost to the Government; and these men are the coin with which, without the slightest difficulty, we can buy back our imprisoned soldiers. Heretofore the objections urged against an exchange have been that we had no prisoners to offer in trade, and that any exchange would operate as an acknowledgment that the rebels possess belligerent rights. The first point has been disposed of by the success at Hatteras Inlet. The second never deserved the slightest attention; and if it did, the act of [Colonel Wallace] has certainly set it at rest. The first flag of truce displayed by any portion of our Army was an acknowledgment of the enemy's character as a belligerent. Maj. Anderson made such an acknowledgment at Fort Sumter. . . . After these transactions, nothing can be more idle than to contest the belligerent rights of the rebellion . . . [and] reinforced by the precedent now supplied us by [Colonel Wallace], there no longer remains a semblance of reason why measures should not be taken to terminate the imprisonment of the Richmond prisoners."[21]

Washington officials began to yield. On December 3, 1861, General Halleck wrote in agreement that exchanges should take place, adding that "it is simply a convention and the fact they [have] been exchanged [does] not prevent their being tried for treason, if desired, after the war."[22]

The government slowly moved into action. In January 1862, several negotiations for prisoners took place. The opening exchange came on January 3, 1862, when 240 Richmond prisoners were put aboard the steamer *Northampton* and shipped down the James River. Nine miles northwest of Newport News, according to a previous arrangement, the Union steamboat *George Washington* was met and the prisoners were exchanged under a flag of truce.

"They stepped on board under the protection of the national flag as the roll of their names was called," reported one northern newspaper, "and such happy-looking men are seldom seen. Cheer after cheer arose from each boat as they approached." Another observed, "It is affirmed that the Government will at last yield to the pressure brought to bear against it by public opinion . . . and will make proposals for the exchange of prisoners."

The Confederacy released an additional 150 prisoners two weeks later. On February 13, 1862, Major General Wool announced that he had been permitted to arrange a general exchange. Confederate officials, already aware of their dwindling resources, welcomed the news. Wool met with Confederate

Brigadier General Howell Cobb on February 23, and a tentative agreement was reached for the delivery of all prisoners. It was further agreed that prisoners in excess of the number held by the other side would be released on parole. Within days at another meeting, Wool announced that his instructions had been changed; the trade of prisoners would be on a man for man basis only. At this, Cobb refused, charging that the only reason for the change from the original agreement was the recent capture of Confederate forts Henry and Donelson. "The Federal Government," Cobb charged, "[has] an excess of prisoners it [is] unwilling to release on parole!" Further negotiations for the exchange of prisoners remained stalled during the following months.[23]

In June, Union General George B. McClellan, under pressure from influential friends and relatives of certain prisoners, wrote a letter to Confederate Secretary of War George W. Randolph to propose some individual exchanges. "No arrangement of any sort has been made," Randolph responded on June 14, "and individual exchanges are declined. We will exchange generally or according to some principle, but not by arbitrary selections."[24]

Unknown to Randolph, though, an unofficial courtesy exchange had just taken place on June 6, a week after the Battle of Seven Pines. A general order had been issued from Washington stating that surgeons should be considered noncombatants and not sent to prison. Confederate General Robert E. Lee accepted the order on June 17, and by July 9, proposed to release General McClellan's wounded on parole as well. McClellan quickly accepted the offer.[25]

The reluctance to officially sanction prisoner exchanges continued as Secretary Stanton announced the appointment of John A. Dix as a commissioner to begin negotiations for the United States. Privately, Stanton cautioned Dix to avoid any official recognition of the Confederate government. The next day, General Lee announced his appointment of Daniel H. Hill as commissioner for the Confederate government, and negotiations began.

Finally, on July 22, 1862, a cartel was reached for an immediate and general exchange of prisoners based on the cartel adopted between Great Britain and the United States during the War of 1812. In that agreement, signed on May 12, 1813, POWs were exchanged on a basis of man for man and rank for rank with a scale of equivalents if lower ranks were exchanged for high ranks. One commanding general, for instance, could be exchanged for sixty privates, one lieutenant general for forty, one major general for thirty, one brigadier general for twenty, one colonel for fifteen, one lieutenant colonel for ten, one major for eight, one captain for six, one first lieutenant for four, one second lieutenant for three, and one noncommissioned officer for two men.[26]

"The principle of exchange has now been accepted by our Government," declared the *New York Times*. "A similar announcement has been made several times before; but there have been delays, postponements, difficulties, and obstructions of various kinds in carrying it out, and in the meantime the Union prisoners have lingered month after month. . . . [Now] there is no reason, if the rebels are willing, as they seem to be, that there should be any delay in carrying it out."[27]

By this time there were about 20,000 Confederate prisoners in Union prisons and somewhere between 9,000 to 12,000 Union captives in Confederate facilities. Per the arrangements, all prisoners held in the east were to be exchanged at Aiken's Landing on the James River in Virginia. The POWs were brought from Richmond or Fortress Monroe by boats bearing white flags. Upon arrival, the two commissioners would meet, exchange rolls, and work out their exchanges. Within weeks, the exchange location was moved to City Point, Virginia. Prisoners held in the west were exchanged under the same procedures at Vicksburg, Mississippi. In addition, prisoners were sometimes transferred to other locations to be "declared exchanged."[28]

Each government appointed two exchange agents to carry out the stipulations of the agreement. U.S. Adjutant General Lorenzo Thomas was temporarily assigned to act as agent in the east, while Colonel Robert Ould was appointed to represent the Confederate government. They, along with the help of General Dix, proceeded to make the exchanges. The first exchanges in the west were conducted under the supervision of Union Captain Henry M. Lazelle and Confederate Major N. G. Watts. Once the exchanges were under way, Thomas returned to Washington while Lieutenant Colonel William H. Ludlow took over as agent and General Ethan Allen Hitchcock was appointed commissioner for exchange and established his headquarters in Washington. As exchanges continued in the west, Union Colonel Charles C. Dwight was assigned as agent there.

Difficulties developed almost immediately. Secretary of War Stanton issued orders allowing his military leaders in Virginia to confiscate and use any property necessary to supply their commands. He ordered that they keep records so that compensation could be made in "proper cases." "This was simply a system of plunder," declared Confederate President Jefferson Davis, "for no compensation would be made to any person unless he could prove his fidelity to the Government of the United States."[29]

Major General John Pope, commanding Union forces in Virginia, then issued orders to his commissioned officers to immediately begin arresting all disloyal male citizens within their lines.[30]

Furthermore, Commandant Dimick at the Fort Warren Prison interpreted the calculated value of Confederate officer prisoners he was holding, in anticipation of exchanging his North Carolina POWs for the U.S. troops held in Texas, to be "480 privates for a brigadier general and thirty privates for a captain."[31]

Such orders and miscalculations severely stressed the relationship between the two governments. Sputtering through some tense periods, the exchanges slowly continued until many of the prison forts, compounds, and buildings were virtually emptied.

In the cases of excess numbers, paroled Union soldiers from the eastern prisons were sent to Camp Parole at Annapolis, Maryland. In the west they were sent to Camp Chase. The prisoners stayed at these locations until they were officially exchanged on paper for a prisoner of equal rank or based on the higher-rank calculations of the cartel.

Parole was the European tradition originally relied upon during the numerous scattered exchanges of POWs in parts of Texas, Missouri, and Virginia, during the initial outbreak of hostilities when there was a lack of holding facilities. Under the parole system, the captives signed an oath not to take up arms against their captors until they were formally exchanged for an enemy captive of equal rank. Such exchanges were to take place within ten days of capture, but they often took up to thirty days or more. At first, many of the early parolees were sent home to await notice of their exchange or waited it out near their commands. The Confederate government continued to operate in this manner during implementation of the cartel. Once officially exchanged, Confederate soldiers released from Union prisons returned to service in far greater numbers than did Union soldiers released from the South. Upon realizing that, and believing some troops were actually allowing themselves to be captured in order to go home or to get out of the service, Federal officials established the detention, or parole, camps.

With the cartel in full progress and bringing such a large number of parolees into the camps, the paperwork, provisions, and the care for these parolees became overwhelming. Individual names, places of internment, exchange information, and ranks had to be kept and calculations made based on the complex scale included in the cartel. Before long, implementing the system led to a mountain of paperwork and extremely long delays. Again, the government found itself unprepared, disorganized, and unable to adequately cope with the system it had created. When Colonel William Wallace arrived to take over command of Camp Chase, he found over 3,000 parolees lounging around the post. He was disgusted with the entire process and described the parolees as lazy, ragged, dirty, louse-infected, and demoralized.[32]

While the Union tried to cope with the chaos, frequent violations and bickering developed between the governments and individual exchange agents. The South was accused of violating the use of paroled soldiers in battle. The North was accused of murdering unarmed civilians in New Orleans. Then an insurmountable stalemate developed between the governments over the exchange of the black Union soldiers, inducted into the lines in late 1862.

The Confederate government refused to exchange them, insisting they were runaway slaves who didn't figure in the man-for-man exchange for white soldiers and they had to be returned to their owners instead. The Union demanded they be considered in the same manner as POWs and exchanged accordingly. When President Lincoln issued his preliminary proclamation of emancipation, President Davis retaliated by issuing a decree that any white officer captured while leading black soldiers into battle could be charged with inciting a slave insurrection and, if punished according to the laws of the Confederacy, could be put to death. Secretary Stanton reacted by suspending the exchange of all commissioned officers on December 28, 1862.[33]

The exchange cartel was left to stumble along. The exchange of enlisted men continued, but the relationship between the two governments and their agents became stressed to the breaking point. Finally, when the Confederate Congress seemed to back President Davis's proclamation about white officers leading black troops, the exchange cartel collapsed. On May 25, 1863, less than a year after the exchanges began, General Halleck ordered them halted immediately.[34]

Almost as soon as the cartel collapsed, Union forces captured Vicksburg, Mississippi, and Port Hudson, Louisiana. Disagreement immediately broke out over declarations of exchange and parole and who actually had authority over such matters. A series of angry dispatches shot back and forth between Colonel Ould and a number of Union generals, resolving nothing. Although a number of incidents and various arbitrary orders contributed to the collapse, the threat against black soldiers and their white commanding officers was, no doubt, the most devestating factor.

Chapter 6

BLACK SOLDIERS AND POWS

They were ineligible for promotion; they were not to be treated as prisoners of war. Nothing was definite except that they could be shot and hanged as soldiers.

Colonel Norwood P. Hallowell,
55th Massachusetts Volunteer Regiment

Nearly 3,000 blacks served in both segregated and integrated units of the Continental army, representing each of the thirteen colonies, during the Revolutionary War, and another 1,000 served with the British. During the War of 1812, several hundred blacks served with Andrew Jackson at New Orleans. As POWs in these wars, they seem to have been treated little different than whites. By the Mexican war of 1842, however, African-American soldiers were specifically excluded from service by U.S. army regulations.

As early as 1860, some Northern politicians advocated the arming of blacks if war broke out. When it did, a number of free blacks rushed to enlist in the Confederate Army as well as the Union only to learn their services were unwanted.[1]

By August of 1862, Major General Benjamin F. Butler, who had acquired a reputation as an astute politician and strategist, and was intensely hated by the South because he often referred to slaves as property to be confiscated for use as military labor—began to recruit free blacks to defend New Orleans after General John C. Breckenridge's assault on Baton Rouge.

Within weeks, the Civil War's first regiment of blacks was recruited and designated as the 1st Louisiana Native Guard. Many were said to be descendants of those who were led by Jackson during the war of 1812. On September 27, 1862, this unit became the first black regiment mustered into Federal service. In October and November, the 2nd and 3rd Louisiana Native Guard Regiments were mustered into service. These units later became known as the 1st, 2nd, and 3rd Corps d'Afrique under General Banks and, still later, as the 73rd, 74th, and 75th U.S. Colored Infantry.[2]

Although they were the first to be organized and drilled, the Louisiana regiments were not the first to engage the enemy. After Lincoln's emancipation decree, a number of states began to recruit blacks for military service. The first to issue such a call to arms was Rhode Island, followed by Massachusetts and Kansas. By October, nearly 500 men had been enrolled in eastern Kansas and designated the 1st Kansas Volunteer Colored Infantry (later to be mustered into Federal service as the new 79th U.S. Colored Infantry). While bivouacked near Island Mound outside Butler, Missouri, on October 28, 1862, they were attacked by Confederate forces led by Colonel Francis M. Cockrell. They stood their ground and drove off the enemy in what is believed the first engagement of black troops in the Civil War. The casualties suffered by the 1st Kansas that day amounted to ten killed and twelve wounded but none were captured. Their next engagement was an entirely different experience that would become all too common for black POWs during the Civil War.

While in Jasper County, Missouri, they, along with members of the 2nd Kansas Battery, were attacked by a Confederate force led by Major Tom R. Livingston. The Union force was defeated with a loss of sixteen killed and five taken prisoner, two of whom were from the black regiment. The three white troops from the 2nd Kansas were soon exchanged by Livingston for three that had been captured by the blacks, but he refused to exchange the two from the 1st Kansas, claiming he had to hold them until further orders came from the Confederate War Department. Days later it was learned that the two remaining POWs had been executed.[3]

The same was true at Poison Springs, Arkansas. "Many wounded men belonging to the 1st Kansas Colored fell into the hands of the enemy," reported Colonel James M. Williams, regiment commander, "and I have the most positive assurance from eyewitnesses that they were murdered on the spot."[4]

There is ample evidence that the Confederacy dealt with black prisoners of war, in many cases, quite differently than they did whites. In fact, even the official records reflected that a U.S. Colored Troops member captured by the Confederate army, had less chance than a white soldier of surviving imprisonment—providing he survived to be taken prisoner in the first place.

Statistics indicate that nearly 800 black POWs were taken during the Civil War. Of those, 284—or 35 percent—died in captivity. But upon closer examination, the official records also show that hundreds more who were captured in various engagements apparently never made it to the prisons.[5]

"The Yankees are not going to send their Negro troops into the field," an early Richmond *Enquirer* editorial warned. "Should they be sent to the field, and be put in battle, none will be taken prisoners. Our troops understand what to do in such cases." Major General George E. Pickett, CSA, once boasted, "[H]ad I caught any negro, who had killed either officer, soldier, or citizen of the Confederate States, I should have caused him to be immediately executed."[6]

"They cannot be recognized in any way as soldiers subject to the rules of war and to trial by military courts," Confederate Secretary of War Seddon declared after conferring with President Davis.[7]

These men were not alone in their sentiments. When the U.S. Colored Troops were organized, they were subjected to prejudices and indignities from all sides. There was the hatred espoused by Southern officials, civilians, military personnel, and the Confederate Congress. White Union officers often threatened to resign, enlisted men threatened to desert, the Northern press condemned the idea, civilians were beside themselves, and some members of the U.S. Congress were outraged. Yet, in view of all this opposition, and the likelihood that it was placing black troops into unnecessary danger, the Federal government proceeded with plans to recruit, train, and place blacks into combat. Apparently, it was a matter of principle, because there was no manpower shortage in the North.

There was no doubt in the mind of Joseph T. Wilson, a black officer who served in the 2nd Louisiana Native Guard and, later, in the 54th Massachusetts Volunteer Infantry, what the Union was putting black soldiers up against. "The confederates were no cowards; braver men never bit cartridge or fired a gun," he wrote, "and when they were to meet 'their slaves,' as they believed, in revolt, why, of course, honor forbade them to ask or give quarter. This fact was known to all, for, as yet, though hundreds had been captured, none had been found on parole, or among the exchanged prisoners."[8]

The threat of Confederate vengeance or retaliation became so great that there were even cases of white Union soldiers bayoneting blacks in the back during battle in the hope that the southern troops would not fight with such ferocity.[9]

When more than 550 black prisoners were taken at the Battle of Milliken's Bend, Confederate Lieutenant General E. Kirby Smith later chastised his subordinates for their actions. "I have been unofficially informed that some of your troops have captured negroes in arms," he declared in a dispatch addressed to Major General Richard Taylor. "I hope this may not be so, and that your subordinates who may have been in command of capturing parties may have recognized the propriety of giving no quarter to armed negroes and their officers. In this way we may be relieved from a disagreeable dilemma."[10]

Confederate deserters later testified that they saw captured blacks hanged three days after the battle. A month later, when Smith's original statement became public, the Confederate War Department felt obliged to issue Smith a reprimand. The practice, however, apparently continued.[11]

Hangings behind the lines were not uncommon. Many black prisoners, though, were simply shot on the spot. Warren Lee Goss, a white Massachusetts artilleryman captured at Plymouth, North Carolina, reported that black captives "were drawn up in line, and shot down like dogs," and Union Brigadier General George L. Andrews, commander of the Corps d'Afrique, later gathered sworn statements from local whites who witnessed a Confederate officer kill a wounded black prisoner. He also reported seeing other bodies of blacks piled along the road and concluded that many blacks were often deliberately executed after capture. Brigadier General James S. Brisbin also reported seeing papers that had been placed on the dead bodies of captured troops from the 6th U.S. Colored Cavalry threatening death to all black troops.[12]

The most notorious act is probably the one that occurred at Fort Pillow, Tennessee. Confederate cavalry Brigadier General James R. Chalmers, commanding 1,500 men of Major General Nathan Bedford Forrest's Cavalry Corps, attacked Fort Pillow at 5:30 A.M. on April 12, 1864. When Forrest arrived at 10 A.M., he took command of the Confederates and ordered a general assault that took the Federal barracks on the fort's south side. Sometime after 3:30 P.M. the Rebels demanded the surrender of the fort's garrison, comprised of 295 white troops of the 13th Tennessee and 262 blacks of the 11th U.S. Colored Troops and Battery F, 4th U.S. Colored Light Artillery. At first, the Federals stalled and then refused, whereupon the Confederates stormed the earthworks, resulting in 231 Federals killed and 100 wounded. The Confederates, who lost only 14 men, took 226 prisoners, of which only 58 were black. The remaining 204 had been killed, reportedly during combat.[13]

The battle has remained controversial to this day. Federal soldiers claimed afterward that Confederates scaled the earthworks and screamed racial epithets as they killed black troops who had thrown down arms in surrender. They also claimed Forrest's men killed wounded blacks where they lay. Confederates, on the other hand, claimed that many blacks had retrieved their weapons after surrender and merely suffered the consequences.[14]

The U.S. Congress's committee on the conduct of the war investigated the incident and gathered testimony from some of the survivors. The Confederate government moved slowly in responding to the accusations, and Forrest's battle report supposedly became stalled in transit and was not made public for nearly four months after the engagement.[15]

Massacres of surrendering blacks also reportedly occurred at Petersburg and Saltville, Virginia.

In the latter incident, Union Brigadier General Stephen G. Burbridge, with a force of 3,600 troops, including 400 of the 5th U.S. Colored Cavalry, attacked a Confederate force of 2,800 at Saltville. Repeated attacks failed to capture the town and by sundown, Burbridge withdrew his troops, leaving nearly 350 Union casualties on the battlefield. The next morning, Confederates under the direction of Brigadier General Felix H. Robertson and Captain Champ Ferguson roamed among the wounded and executed helpless blacks where they lay. The exact number was never determined, but it was well over a hundred. Although no charges were brought against Robertson, Champ Ferguson was apprehended, arraigned for murder, and hanged after the war.[16]

It should be no wonder, then, that Sergeant Samuel Johnson, Company D, 2nd U.S. Colored Cavalry, immediately stripped off his uniform and pretended to be a local slave when his unit surrendered at Plymouth, North Carolina. "I pulled off my uniform and found a suit of citizen's clothes, which I put on," related Johnson. "Upon the capture of Plymouth by rebel forces all the negroes found in blue uniform, or with any outward marks of a Union soldier upon him, was killed. I saw some taken into the woods and hung. Others I saw stripped of all their clothing and then stood upon the bank of the river with their faces riverward and there they were shot. Still others were killed by having their brains beaten out by the butt end of the muskets in the hands of the rebels. All were not killed the day of the capture. Those that were not were placed in a room with their officers, they having previously been dragged through the town with ropes around their necks, where they were kept confined until the following morning, when the remainder of the black soldiers were killed."[17]

Provided a black POW survived capture, there was still a variety of other fates he might suffer. "Every person of color who ever was a slave in any of the eleven Confederate States," maintained the official Confederate position, "shall not be treated as a prisoner of war, but when captured are to be deemed to be slaves, and may be turned over to their masters as such by the Confederate Government." In such cases, any white man could claim a captive as his former slave. The only proof needed was the claimant's word. "Some were claimed as slaves by men who had never known them," advised an officer of the 7th U.S. Colored Troops when a hundred blacks in his regiment were captured.[18]

Later in the war, commandants of several Confederate POW facilities allowed local planters to inspect the black prisoners to claim any as their own. In at least one documented case, when a black prisoner was claimed, although white soldiers insisted they knew him as a free man who had been born in New England, the black captive was enslaved anyway.[19]

If unclaimed, black POWs were often sold. "As negroes without free papers when not claimed by the owners," announced Secretary Seddon, "[then] they will be . . . sold as slaves." In one documented case, two free blacks captured at Galveston, Texas, in April 1863, who were from a prominent Massachusetts family, were sold at a Houston slave market. The following year, a Confederate colonel admitted he obtained his general's permission to sell their black captives and divide the proceeds among the troops.[20]

During the Atlanta campaign, the 44th U.S. Colored Infantry surrendered to Lieutenant General John Bell Hood at Dalton, Georgia. The terms set forth by Hood stipulated that white troops would be paroled, while the blacks would be enslaved. A Union officer later filed a report to complain that Major General William B. Bate, one of Hood's subordinates, "had my colored soldiers robbed of their shoes and sent them down to the railroad and made them tear up the track. . . . One of my soldiers, who refused . . . was shot on the spot, as were also five others shortly after the surrender. . . . A number of my soldiers were returned to their masters. . . . I tried to get the free servants and soldiers in the regiment belonging to the free states [Ohio and Indiana] released, but to no avail."[21]

The third method of enslavement the Confederates used sometimes involved the more complicated policy of turning black prisoners over to the state governments. South Carolina Governor Milledge L. Bonham requested that the Confederate army turn over all black troops captured after the Union attack on Fort Wagner so they could be tried under his state's law, which stipulated that any black person who assisted a slave insurrection was "guilty of treason against the state and must suffer death."[22]

In effect, then, if a black soldier survived a battle, wasn't killed when he surrendered or when he was captured, wasn't forced into slavery or sold into it, and didn't get tried by a state government and sentenced to death, the ordeal he faced was survival in a military prison.

It wouldn't be until February 1865 that the Confederate government would officially recognize black captives as prisoners of war, yet slave and free blacks had been confined in their military prisons from the day the first numbers were captured in 1863. In those prisons they were usually confined separately from whites. In cases where prison officials wanted to show contempt for white soldiers, though, blacks were placed in the same room or cell with them. In a case at Libby prison, white officers received "special" punishment by being confined with four black prisoners. First Lieutenant Asa B. Isham, Company F, 7th Michigan Volunteer Cavalry, witnessed just such an incident. "An open tub was placed in the room for the reception of their excrement," he related, "where it was permitted to remain for days before removal." Isham went on to explain that the small cell was overcrowded with no light and that the prisoners had no eating utensils and no medical care for five months. Under these conditions, the blacks suffered along with the whites, who were supposed to be the ones actually being punished.[23]

Because of their color, black soldiers had to endure additional mistreatment or more severe punishments than whites. As a result, many quickly became discouraged. "All ambition to live seems to have died out in them," observed Sergeant Benjamin Booth, a white prisoner at Salisbury. "They become so despondent that they will tumble down almost anywhere, give up the struggle, and die." "The negro soldiers suffered the most," admitted Homer Sprague, a white prisoner confined at Danville. "There were sixty-four of them living in prison when we reached Danville, October 20, 1864. Fifty-seven of them were dead by the 12th of February, '65."[24]

One reason so many perished in prison was the lack of medical care. Many witnesses claimed that some Confederate doctors refused to treat wounded blacks. "There were, in the pen, about 200 colored soldiers of the 8th U.S. Rangers captured at Olustee, Florida; a number of them wounded," advised a white prisoner held at Andersonville. "One fellow had a hand shot off and some deranged brutes had cut off his ears and nose. The doctors refused to dress his wounds or even amputate his shattered arm; he was naked in the prison and finally died from his numerous wounds."[25]

Another reason for the high mortality rate among black prisoners might have been their contact with dead bodies. In nearly every prison where blacks were held, they were detailed to carry off the dead for burial. Due to their mental and physical condition after confinement for any period, their resistance to disease was, no doubt, diminished.

Black prisoners were often put to hard labor in the southern prisons. As early as April 1863, the Confederate War Department had approved the use of captured blacks for labor and often used them as military laborers. Many of the earthworks and other defenses and fortifications thrown up around southern cities, especially around Richmond, Mobile, and Vicksburg, and all of the Confederate stockade prisons were built by black laborers.

While confined within those prison walls, blacks were also the labor force used for details around the compound. "The negroes were put into a squad by themselves," advised one white prisoner, "and a white Union sergeant [was] appointed over them. They were taken outside and made to work. The sergeant was later murdered by a guard of the 55th Georgia who walked up and shot him because he was so friendly with the blacks."[26]

Private Joseph Howard of Company F, 110th U.S. Colored Infantry, tried to sum it up calmly when he said, "The rebels robbed us of everything we had . . . We were kept at hard labor and inhumanely treated. . . . If we lagged or faltered or misunderstood an order we were whipped and abused. . . . For the slightest causes we were subjected to the lash [and] we were very poorly provided for with food."[27]

"For the most trifling offense," recalled another white prisoner, "they were [whipped] on the bare back from thirty to forty lashes, with a horsewhip or cat-of-nine tails."[28]

There are no reliable records to indicate the number of African-American soldiers taken prisoner during the Civil War. As the conflict progressed, at least nine different southern prisons are known to have held black prisoners, far outnumbering the official report compiled by the U.S. House of Representatives in 1869. In that particular treatise—once regarded as authoritative and often cited—a total of 776 blacks were reported to have been captured during the war, with only 79 prison deaths. Yet Andersonville Prison had 200 black POWs in March 1864 alone, all captured from one battle; Salisbury Prison had a total of 120 confined just in the month of January 1865; and Danville Prison had nearly 200 during the summer of 1864. Over 600 were taken at Athens and Sulphur Branch Trestle, Alabama, in September 1864, and were immediately placed on work-detail in the defense of Mobile, without ever going into a prison camp. Blacks were also known to have been confined at Florence, Charleston, Libby, Castle Thunder, Cahaba, and Huntsville, Texas.[29]

Official battle records exceed these allegedly official figures as well. At least 58 black prisoners were taken at Fort Pillow, and the 54th Massachusetts Colored Regiment reported between 50 to 100 taken in the battle of Fort Wagner, in addition to the previously mentioned 600 taken in Alabama.

Nor should the later-revised number of 284 prison deaths be believed. A walk through the Andersonville cemetery reveals 111 marked graves of black prisoners. Many other graves, both marked and unmarked, surely exist near the other prison sites known to have confined blacks.

The lack of Confederate records on black captives was originally designed to keep statistics unknown. In April 1864, General Braxton Bragg, chief military adviser to President Davis, directed North Carolina's governor to "take the necessary steps to have the matter kept out of the newspapers . . . and in every available way to shun its obtaining any publicity." In June 1863, the agent for prisoner exchange advised Secretary Seddon he had "no especial desire to find" records of captured blacks. No one did and, because of that, no one has been able to since. Because of the lack of Confederate records and because few black prisoners left memoirs, we will probably never know the true extent of what they suffered during the war.[30]

The Federal government demonstrated no "especial desire" either. After unabashedly putting blacks up against the Confederates, Union authorities, led by Stanton and Grant, used the results as the basis for stopping all exchanges. The North's motives, however, were apparently twofold, for they also realized by this time that further exchanges merely served to reinforce the Confederate ranks and prolong the war.

"I have seen from Southern papers that a system of retaliation is going on in the South which they keep from us and which we should stop in some way," declared Grant. "On the subject of exchange. . . . every man we hold, when released on parole or otherwise, becomes an active soldier against us at once either directly or indirectly. If we commence a system of exchange which liberates all prisoners taken, we will have to fight on until the whole South is exterminated. If we hold those caught they amount to no more than dead men."[31]

For the next twenty months, from May 1863 until nearly the end of the war, general exchanges became nonexistent. The prison populations would grow to overwhelming numbers, the battles would continue, and more captives would arrive.

1863

Chapter 7

PRISON EXPANSION

The extinction of the last hope of an exchange . . . has had the effect of depressing our spirits to an extent truly deplorable.

Lieutenant Colonel Frederic F. Cavada,
114th Pennsylvania Volunteers

B ecause of the prisoner exchange agreement, neither side had established any major holding facilities after February 1862. Hundreds of captives were shipped out of the cities daily, with the sick and wounded receiving first priority. But when the entire process came to a grinding halt, prison populations began to grow to unprecedented numbers. The gradual buildup of accumulated POWs in both the North and the South necessitated the expansion of established prison sites and the reopening of others.

BELLE ISLE

On January 17, 1863, Belle Isle was reactivated for a short time, emptied out and closed down, and then reopened again in May. Belle Isle's original earthworks were increased to five feet high, with ditches running along both sides, and guards were stationed at forty-foot intervals along the top. The interior of the compound was marked off with sixty streets radiating from a central avenue. The streets were lined with Sibley tents and the prisoners were separated into squads of fifty and assigned to specific rows.

"About 14 to 15 men sleep in a Sibley tent," reported prisoner Jackson O. Broshers. "[Most] contained up to 10 men or more crowded together," reported another prisoner. If this was the case, and because records indicate that only enough tents to serve the original estimate of 3,000 inmates were ever provided, then Belle Isle prison undoubtedly began with less than 300 tents. Once the population grew to more than 3,000, which happened quite quickly, the remaining prisoners were on their own. "The men would dig holes in the ground to lie in at night," wrote one prisoner, "to protect them[selves] from the air." Another reported, "We would pile up in bunches, as you have seen hogs do . . . to keep off the cold and rain."[1]

Even prisoners fortunate enough to be in a tent at Belle Isle were not that well off. "I was protected from the weather by a tent," reported Alfred P. Jones of the 1st Massachusetts Cavalry, "[but] it was full of holes." According to most prisoners, all the tents at Belle Isle were old, rotten, and full of holes from the very beginning.[2]

The Confederate officers' and guards' quarters, also tents, were located outside the compound, as were five hospital tents and a cookhouse constructed of wood. A graveyard was established just north of the hospital.

Segments of the river along the island were marked off into sections for specified purposes. The upper segment extending down the island for approximately ten feet was reserved for drinking water. Following this was a 30-foot stretch reserved for bathing. Below this was a 150-foot stretch reserved as the latrine. In addition, eight wells were located throughout the prison grounds.

During this period, Lieutenant Virginius Bossieux was the prison commandant. A native of France who had become a Virginian, he acted and talked more like a Creole. "[He was] a rather young and gallant looking sort of fellow," recalled prisoner John Ransom, "talking so much like a negro that you would think he was one if you could hear him talk and not see him." Another prisoner observed, "He did not seem to be extremely cruel, but he went leisurely about and showed a criminal indifference for the comfort and welfare of those in his care."[3]

In one case in particular, a prisoner on a work detail momentarily stepped upon the earthworks surrounding the camp, which served as the deadline, and was mistakenly shot dead by one of the guards. According to a witness, Lieutenant Bossieux arrived on the scene and told the guard he "ought to be more careful than to shoot those who were on parole and doing fatigue duty," then calmly ordered that the body be taken to the deadhouse and walked away.[4]

His callous unconcern possibly developed while he and his brother, Cyrus, were assigned to duty at Castle Thunder soon after that prison was established, or maybe at Libby, where Virginius had temporary command in December 1862 while Thomas Turner was away from Richmond. In any event, the Belle Isle prisoners were convinced that Commandant Bossieux easily ignored their plight.

"He has two rebel sergeants to act as his assistants," Ransom continued, "Sergt. Hyatt and Sergt. Marks. These two men are very cruel."

Another prisoner noted that the sergeants were "the dread and terror of the prisoners . . . [They] tied men up by their thumbs, bucked and gagged others, and made some carry a heavy sack of sand until they were unable to stand under the burden." Sergeant Hyatt, a large Baltimore pugilist who seemed to enjoy threatening and harassing the prisoners, was in charge of roll call and issuing the rations.[5]

Belle Isle prisoners passed much of their time in the same manner as those in the other prisons. Games of chess, checkers, and cards were common, as was jewelry-making and other crafts.

"Chuck-a-luck is a favorite game," noted Ransom. "You lay your ration of bread down on a figure on a board, and a fellow with a dice box shakes it up a little, throws out the dice, and your bread is gone. Don't understand the game myself. That's all I ever saw of the game. Lay down the bread and it's gone."[6]

By November, cold weather had arrived and Belle Isle held 6,300 POWs. Additional tents were distributed but there still weren't enough, and they were in worse condition than those already in use. Authorities distributed straw and boards for cover, but the prisoners burned them in their attempts to stay warm. "About half of the six thousand prisoners here have tents," agreed Ransom, "the rest sleep and live out of doors."[7]

This particular winter would prove to be one of the coldest and most brutal all across the nation, and POWs in many camps on both sides suffered as a result. At Belle Isle, many cold nights were spent without wood.

Some prisoners attempted to construct lean-tos or wedge tents out of their ragged blankets while others simply huddled together on the ground. "We lay in rows," reported one prisoner, "and take turns who has the outside of the row." By morning the rows were plainly marked by the bodies that didn't wake, such as the morning of November 23 when five men were found frozen to death. According to the U.S. Sanitary Commission, as many as fourteen prisoners froze to death in one night; one prisoner's memoirs claimed as many as thirty were carried out dead in a single day from the effects of the cold.[8]

"Many have no pants, many have no shirts [or] shoes," related John Hussey, inspector for the U.S. Christian Commission when he visited the site that month, "and almost every individual lacks some essential article of clothing. They are on half rations, have no fuel of any kind, no soap is issued to them. . . . They are consequently very filthy . . . [and] are dying at the rate of eight to ten daily now."[9]

The frigid cold continued unabated into December. The night of December 20 went into the record books as one of the coldest in Richmond's history, nearly causing the James River to freeze over completely. "There are hundreds with frozen feet, ears, and hands," Ransom noted in his journal, "and laying all over the prison—the suffering is terrible."[10]

"I saw a number of men who suffered from frozen feet at Belle Isle," Private William D. Foote later testified. "[T]hey first took off the toes . . . then the foot, [and] in a few days they died from the amputations."[11]

By this time, the island, which was never intended to hold more than 3,000 POWs, confined more than twice that number. Libby Prison, which had only 1,447 in January, now held 4,221 and 3,000 more were crammed into the Castle Thunder complex.[12]

In the midst of this renewed congestion, an influx of disease began to take its toll. Diarrhea, dysentery, typhoid, pneumonia, and smallpox passed through the Richmond prisons at an alarming rate.

"In the three hospitals for Union soldiers in Richmond," reported U.S. Volunteer Surgeon Daniel Meeker in a letter to the *Army and Navy Journal* in December 1863, "deaths average 40 per day and by reliable testimony about deaths in the tobacco factories and upon the island, total mortality is averaging [another] 50 per day or 1,500 a month. . . . A thousand are already under treatment at the 3 hospitals with another 500 throughout the city who need hospital treatment. . . . Rations issued at this time include nothing more than corn bread and sweet potatoes."[13]

LIBBY PRISON

The POWs in Richmond's prison buildings suffered from the intense cold almost as much as those outside on Belle Isle. Windows that had been broken out of the buildings for relief from the summer heat now allowed bone-chilling winds and cold to enter. Sufficient amounts of wood or coal remained unavailable here, too, so by mid-December sleeping became nearly impossible. It wasn't at all unusual to see prisoners at any time, day or night, running in place in an effort to relieve their agony. Still, many died from the effects of the cold.

Conditions had become so bad that by the autumn of 1863 many of the city's former prison buildings now served as prison hospitals. For the most part, the majority of Richmond's POW population was now concentrated in three locations: Belle Isle, Libby, and Castle Thunder. Libby, serving as head-quarters for the Confederate States Military Prisons since the first of the year, was the depot prison to which all POWs were brought before being trans-ferred to other facilities in or outside the city. Each day brought more POWs to the facility than could be shipped out, and the numbers confined within the building at any one time continued to increase. After the short lull during the exchange agreement, the prison's population quickly climbed to over 4,000 and was never less than 1,200 on each floor, or an average of 400 to each room, thereafter.[14]

By then the prison was filthy beyond description. The floors were crudded over to a depth of inches and the walls were covered with graffiti. According to prisoner A. R. Calhoun, the prison was so dirty that "clothing and blankets became covered with vermin" within moments of a new arrival entering one of the prison rooms. Prisoner James M. Wells of the 8th Michigan Cavalry recalled seeing "pencil and pen sketches drawn on whatever even surface might be found," covering every wall and beam throughout the building, while other POWs recalled that many prisoners had scratched their names into the bricks of Libby's walls.[15]

The rooms eventually became so crowded that prisoners had to sleep spoon-fashion, head to foot in alternating rows along the floor, "wormed and dove-tailed together like fish in a basket," according to prisoner Robert H. Kellogg. The prisoners were packed in so tightly when they slept that it became the responsibility of the highest-ranking prisoner in each room to call out "spoon over!" throughout the night to enable everyone to roll over in unison.[16]

Among the many activities that the Libby POWs engaged in during the daytime, most notable were their chess tournaments. The prisoners also formed a debating club called the Lyceum, humorously referred to by members as "Lice, I see 'em," while others formed religious groups or foreign language clubs. The inmates also established self-rule by organizing the Prisoners' Club, and a number of foreign-born prisoners formed the "Libbyan Society."[17]

Another unique aspect of life at Libby was that the possession of a toothbrush became a status symbol worn on the clothing. "There were not more than a dozen or so among [the inmates]," recalled George Putnam. "Those who did have them carried them in the button-hole of their shirt partly because there was no other safe or convenient storage place and . . . to emphasize a sense of aristocratic opulence."[18]

By mid-1863, Thomas Turner, who had been promoted to captain and placed in charge of Richmond's entire prison system under General Winder, had the outside walls of Libby whitewashed to the height of the second story as a security measure. At the top of the stairs leading from the commandant's office to the prison rooms he hung a sign that declared "Abandon hope all who enter!"[19]

By this time, the names of Libby's prison rooms had evolved into "upper and lower Milroy's," for the highest-ranking prisoner, Brigadier General Robert H. Milroy of the 9th Indiana, being held there; "upper and lower Streight's room," for Colonel Abel D. Streight of the 51st Indiana Volunteers, being held in that section, and the "Gettysburg Room," the "Chickamauga Room," and other similar names for the battles in which a majority of the inmates of a particular room had been captured.

In late 1863, Libby became one of a number of prisons to have its own newspaper. Called the *Libby Prison Chronicle*, it was edited by Louis N. Beaudry, a chaplain of a New York regiment, who collected weekly contributions from the inmates, prepared a single handwritten copy, and read it to the prison population each Friday at 10:00 A.M. According to one prisoner, "there was soon organized an extensive corps of able correspondents, local reporters, poets, punsters, and witty paragraphers, that gave the chronicle a pronounced success."[20]

These newspaper reports served only to take the inmates' minds off prison life, for it wasn't news that prison conditions were getting worse. By 1863, daily rations at Libby had been reduced to a couple of ounces of meat, half a pound of bread, and a small cup of beans or rice.

Efforts had been made since early 1863 to hold Libby's population down by sending the overflow to Castle Thunder. By fall, however, even the Castle's three buildings were filled beyond capacity.

CASTLE THUNDER

Life in Castle Thunder seems to have been more barbarous than at the other institutions. Complaints by new arrivals of being beaten and robbed of their valuables became common; prison officials often gave 50 to 100 lashes to newly arriving Confederate deserters just on principle. Before long, even the Richmond newspapers noted that Castle Thunder was a "high risk" institution. One correspondent wrote in amazement that inmates of the prison became so hardened they would laugh whenever one of their fellow prisoners died and would merely yell to the guard, "There's a fellow here got his discharge and wants to get out."[21]

Richmond citizens heard that the brick wall in the rear yard was chipped and scarred as a result of numerous executions by firing squads; that a dark room in the center of the main building housed fifty pairs of balls and chains, each with leg-irons and handcuffs attached; that Commandant George Alexander was an eccentric and strict disciplinarian. The gossip finally reached such proportions that, on April 4, 1863, a special committee was appointed by the Confederate House to investigate the matter. During the following month, officials heard hair-raising testimony of the cruelty of jailers, of inmates against other inmates, and of Captain Alexander in particular.

The public learned that prisoners were severely punished for insulting prison officials, for trying to bribe guards, for fighting, for stealing, and for attempting to escape. They learned that some of the forms of punishment included suspending prisoners by their thumbs or handcuffing them high on a post and leaving them dangling for hours on end, flogging them with up to one hundred lashes at a time, bucking and gagging them for long periods, securing them in balls and chains or bolting them to the walls or floors, and even branding them.[22]

It was further revealed that in November 1862, several prisoners had amassed a sizable charge of gunpowder from numerous cartridges and placed it all into a stove. The disturbance caused by the explosion resulted in several inmates being interrogated intensely by General Winder and Captain Alexander. When no one confessed to the deed, they were all placed in outdoor pens to endure the cold and heavy rains for several days. A number of inmates, although unhurt by the small explosion, died as a result of the punishment.[23]

Though many testified against Captain Alexander, many came to his defense. Ironically, that he gave Castle Thunder's milk rations to Richmond's needy, that he allegedly established Richmond's Angel of Mercy Hospital with his own funds, and that he placed his wife in charge of the hospital, weighed heavily in his favor. Alexander even testified in his own defense that, although some prisoners were indeed branded, it was done under the supervision of a physician. The committee decided that the charges against Alexander were unsubstantiated and the matter was dropped.[24]

During the prison's existence, an estimated 100 women were confined there. Most were held as spies or political prisoners, although a few were captured in uniform. Women prisoners spent an average of six months within the prison's walls before being released. The most notable of these was probably Dr. Mary Walker, the first woman surgeon in the Union army. Mary Lee, a prisoner held for unspecified disloyalties in 1863, became equally well-known for having a baby during her confinement. She named the girl, Castellina Thunder Lee and often visited the prison after her release to show off the baby.[25]

As at Libby, smallpox and diseases were increasing dramatically. "Little or no pains are taken by the officers of the prison to prevent the disease from spreading," reported one prisoner. "Persons upon whom the disorder has broken out are allowed to remain a whole day and night among other prisoners before being removed to the hospital."[26]

Some Castle Thunder prisoners found they could get into the hospital by smearing their bodies with yellowish-brown croton oil and claiming to have smallpox. Once there, they thought they had a better chance to escape, but few were successful. In one instance, fifteen prisoners tried to dig their way out of the Palmer's Factory building, which had been converted into a prison hospital by that time, but word of the escape apparently leaked out. As the first prisoner crawled out of the tunnel toward freedom, he was confronted by Captain Alexander pointing a gun at him. Alexander quietly ordered the man out of the hole, and captured the men one by one.[27]

The scarcity of food by this time also became a big problem at the prison as its population increased. "Our only fare consists of scanty rations of bread and meat," insisted one prisoner, "and generally we get nothing but horse meat and mule meat. [It's] always after a cavalry fight of any magnitude that our rations are more liberal!" This same prisoner maintained that several attempts were made to smuggle bones out to prove to Union authorities prisoners were being fed horse meat but, "samples of these bones were detected in [a released prisoner's] carpetbag and Captain Alexander vowed he would give him another bone to pick, and sent him back to his cell, charged with attempting to carry contraband information to the enemy."[28]

DANVILLE

Because of the continued supply problems and overcrowding of the city's prisons, General Robert E. Lee suggested the use of Danville, Virginia, as another place to hold POWs. It had good railroad connections, availability of wood, cheaper abundance of provisions, was a safe distance from enemy attack, and a short distance to City Point.

"The Federal Government seems to have made permanent arrangements to keep their prisoners during the war," Lee advised Secretary Seddon on October 28. "I think that [a] like disposition on our part would manifest our indifference on the subject and would bring them to terms of exchange sooner than anything else we could do." Seddon responded within a few days: "I commenced immediately instituting inquiries, with a view to the selection of an appropriate place, convenient, yet secure, in which the prisoners might be retained for an indefinite period. Arrangements are being made to send a considerable portion to Danville."[29]

The town of Danville, located at the extreme south-central part of the state, 143 miles southwest of Richmond and 4 miles north of the North Carolina border, was symbolic of antebellum southern culture. Situated in the heart of rich tobacco country and thus far spared the ravages of military actions, it possessed homes of some of the finest examples of Victorian and Edwardian residential architecture in the South. Its economy revolved around the textile and tobacco industries, and the small community had grown into one of the largest tobacco auction centers in the nation.

By November 11, General Winder ordered Captain Turner to arrange for the transportation of a number of prisoners to Atlanta and Columbus, Georgia, and 4,000 to Danville. On November 17, Captain Turner, a contingent of guards, and the POWs arrived at the new facilities in Danville.

The prison consisted of six vacant brick buildings, mostly tobacco and cotton warehouses in the heart of downtown Danville. One, a three-story structure with an estimated capacity of 700, had an attached bakehouse and cooking range with the capability to prepare rations for 3,000. Opposite this building was a large frame house with a large room to be used as the commandant's headquarters, as well as workshops for garrison use. Three other warehouses, all within a hundred yards of one another, had a combined estimated capacity of 2,300 prisoners. Two additional buildings, not far away and both located within the town's business district, also came into use. The combined capacity of these two was about 1,300.[30]

For the most part, these buildings, overlooking the Dan River that ran through the center of town, were similar to the warehouses used at Richmond. They were three stories with attics, bare of furniture, with rows of large wooden support posts running down the middle. Each floor was a wide-open area of about 2,400 square feet. Prisoners were confined only on the upper two floors, while the lower floor was heavily patrolled by the sentry. Wooden staircases along the inside walls connected the floors.

"The lower floor," according to prisoner George Putnam, "was used merely as a thoroughfare to the yard and for the water parties who were permitted once or twice a day to bring water from the river."[31]

The buildings were designated as Prisons No. 1 through No. 6. Prisons No. 1 through No. 4 were located near the intersection of Spring and Union streets. No. 1 was the largest, and included the bakehouse addition. Prisons No. 2 through No. 4 were warehouses owned by J. W. and C. G. Holland. Prison No. 5 was situated at Floyd and High streets, a few blocks away; the Dibrell Brothers Tobacco Warehouse, a large portentous structure at the corner of Lynn and Loyal streets, with two ornamental turrets on the front, was designated Prison No. 6.

Although Danville became known as a prison for Federal officers, enlisted men were also included initially, and Prison No. 6 was used for the confinement of black POWs. Major Mason Morfit, formerly prison quartermaster in Richmond, was transferred to the facility and placed in charge. Within weeks of being established, the Danville prison was overcrowded; an average of 650 prisoners were confined on each floor of each building.[32]

"At the outset," noted Putnam, "the men were arranged in two rows with their heads to the wall and two rows with their heads to the centre." Major Abner R. Small continued, "We lay in long rows, leaving narrow aisles between the rows of feet. The wall spaces were preferred because a man could brace his back there and sit out the long day or the longer night. There was a row of posts down the center of the room, but these were too few and too narrow to give much help; I know, because I had a place by one of them."[33]

The space allotted to each POW amounted to about four square feet, just enough to lie down in, according to some prisoners. At each end of each floor was an old-fashioned stove fitted out for burning wood, which was brought in from a woodpile in the yard by prisoners under heavy guard. The supply of wood was scant, according to one prisoner, and "there were long hours when the fires were out [and] permission to bring in more wood received no attention."[34]

As the weather grew colder, sleeping positions near the stoves increased in value. While some men tried to pull rank, the trade of valuable possessions was finally settled upon as the fair method. Pieces of blankets, dilapidated boots or shoes, and pocketknives became the most common articles traded.[35]

Cold penetrated the building through the broken windows and drafty walls. Blankets were scarce, overcoats and shoes had often been confiscated, and vermin were a constant irritation. As one prisoner noticed, "the vermin grew bigger as we grew smaller."[36]

It eventually became the custom at Danville, as the prisoners lay down "sardine style" for the night and all became quiet across the floor, for two or three prisoners to somberly break into a song and the rest to join in. Some of the most frequently sung tunes were "Home Sweet Home," "Tenting on the Old Camp Ground," and "Mother, Will You Miss Me?" The singing usually continued until the senior officer on the floor called out "Taps!" and then the room became quiet as everyone tried to sleep.[37]

The Danville POWs experienced firsthand how the average southerner coped by using food substitutes because of the Union blockade. From the beginning, prison rations included black bread made from ground sorghum cane and coffee made from burnt rye. "[We got] a piece of beef with it, about two ounces," recalled prisoner William M. Smith, "[and] a little beef soup, with red peas in it, and rice."[38]

Eventually, there was nothing more available and the daily rations at Danville consisted of nothing but a pound and a half of cornbread per man. Prisoners there often carved slivers off the rafters to boil for "coffee." According to one prisoner, the rafters above the top floor of most of the warehouses had been whittled to near the breaking point by late 1864.[39]

Even water became scarce at Danville. Originally, for something to do, the men often drew lots for the opportunity to make the water run. The water parties usually consisted of six to eight POWs guarded by two or three sentinels. Each prisoner on the detail was expected to carry a pail full of water, but as time went on and the men became weaker, a full pail or even a half-full pail became difficult to manage. Eventually, it required two men to carry one half-full pail of water back to the prison.[40]

Death from disease was increasing rapidly. Smallpox broke out in the Richmond prisons shortly before the transfer of prisoners and apparently was carried to Danville. By November 30, 12 POWs had died, 4 from smallpox. By the end of December 1863, 111 POWs had died, including 58 from smallpox. By the end of the following month, another 139 died, 91 from smallpox, and the increasing death rate continued month after month. The disease continued to spread throughout the prison buildings, among the guard, and into town.[41]

HUNTSVILLE

In Texas, a number of Union POWs in jails in Houston and Galveston were transferred to the state penitentiary at Huntsville. In Houston and Galveston, the officers had been permitted to roam the downtown area on parole during the day, while the enlisted men remained imprisoned in their cells. At the Texas State "Pen" in Huntsville, everyone was confined in cells. "The cells of this state prison," observed one prisoner, "were not inviting dormitories, being over-run with cockroaches and over-brooded by mosquitoes."[42]

By the 1860s, the prison, built in 1848, was simply referred to locally as "the Walls," and its grim gray towers dominated 12th Street, three blocks east of the Walker County Courthouse. The barred windows of its upper floors provided a view of the desolate, red sandy hills in the distance. Prisoners were held in nine-by-six-foot cells. During the daytime the POWs mingled with the general prison population in the two-hundred-square-foot prison yard. A few weeks later, the Union prisoners were moved out of the cells and into a large eighteen-by-twenty-five-foot upper room containing cots with mattresses. Thomas Carothers, the prison superintendent, was placed in charge of the POWs. He put them to work alongside the general prison population in the state-run prison textile mill manufacturing cotton and woolen cloth. Such prison labor at Huntsville generally produced over a million and a half yards a year, which were then provided to the Confederate army, the soldiers' families, and regular consumers.[43]

CAMP GROCE

By mid-1863, governor of Texas, Francis R. Lubbock began to worry that the presence of Yankee POWs at Huntsville might attract a Federal expedition to the area. Under his orders, a prison camp was established on land offered by Leonard W. Groce of the Liendo Plantation, two and a half miles northeast of Hempstead, Texas. This site, one of the earliest cotton plantations in Texas, had been used as a training center for Confederate troops when hostilities first broke out in the state.[44]

The first group of 132 prisoners was loaded onto the Navasota Railroad and transported to Camp Groce during the last week of June. A group of about 100 was moved from Huntsville the first week of August.[45]

The barracks at Camp Groce were apparently a great improvement over the cells at Huntsville and the conditions previously experienced at Houston and Galveston. "We are pleasantly situated in camp barracks," agreed Colonel Charles Nott, 176th New York Volunteers. "Our quarters at Camp Groce," explained prisoner A. J. H. Duganne, "were upon the railroad line, removed about 200 yards from the road. The 'camp' consisted of four stacks of barracks looking from three sides into a rhombus area. Beyond these buildings a tract of wild country, wood, swamp, and prairie, stretched for miles around."[46]

The camp sat at the top of a gentle two-hundred-yard slope above the railroad grade. The distance included a thin line of timber and rough ground covered with scrubbrush. Off in the opposite direction, about a quarter mile away, a small, sluggish brook meandered through the property.

"Another line of barracks running nearly parallel to ours, at a distance of one hundred yards or more," Duganne continued, "was occupied by the guard, a company of 60 to 80 militiamen under the command of a fat officer known as Captain Buster."[47]

The guards at this camp were strict and energetic in their duties, but apparently not too proficient. "[W]hile playing ball," recalled a prisoner, in one example, "a young prisoner ran after a runaway ball to the guard line and was shot at by the guards. They continued firing and missing as the lad ran for the barracks."[48]

Water at the camp was provided by two deep wells several hundred yards from the POW barracks. Rations were provided in small quantities. Prisoners augmented their allowances with food purchases from, according to some POWs, "the local negroes and hucksters" who were allowed into the camp to sell them overpriced provisions. "Java coffee at $10 the pound in Confederate currency," exclaimed one prisoner, "soda at $5, tea at $20 the pound, molasses at $5 the gallon, and vinegar at fifty cents." The prisoners at Camp Groce soon learned to make corn coffee, which they referred to as "Lincoln coffee," by blackening corn kernels in a pot over an open fire and allowing them to steep in water afterward. They also had the opportunity to buy sweet potatoes, eggs, butter, milk, and poultry from the locals.[49]

During the hot months, POWs were allowed to bathe under heavy guard in the nearby brook and to go out and gather brush to make verandas on the outside of their barracks for shade to sit in. As winter approached, they were permitted into the woods to gather fuel, although the barracks had no stoves for heat. "We have dug two fire places below our flooring, at either wing," declared one prisoner, "and pierced some apertures in the wooden roof to serve as smokeholes."[50]

While the POWs were adjusting to life at Camp Groce, the exchange cartel was in the process of nearly emptying most of the midwestern and eastern prisons. It seemed that those held captive way out in Texas were all but forgotten. "The attention of the Government is earnestly called to the condition of the prisoners captured at Galveston on the 1st day of January, and now in Texas with some other prisoners subsequently captured at different places," pleaded Major General Banks, commander of the Department of the Gulf in October 1863. "These prisoners are at Camp Groce. . . . They have suffered greatly from confinement, and think they have been neglected by the Government, which, they say, should have made provision for their exchange." Exchange commissioner Hitchcock, in an obviously ill-informed reply, declared that "the prisoners in Texas probably suffer less than those in Richmond, on account of the mildness of the climate and the greater abundance of provisions."[51]

Several months passed and nothing much was done. As the cartel came to a halt, the POWs in Texas were left stranded. "It is useless after so long a confinement to describe our present condition," complained Colonel Issac S. Burrell, 42nd Massachusetts Volunteer Regiment. "We were all nearly destitute of money when captured. Two officers have died of my command and many are sick and prostrate from acclimating fevers and other diseases incidental to the climate and long tedious confinement with no hope held out for release. We are informed here that it is the fault of our own Government that we have not been exchanged. . . . It is now over a year since my officers left their homes, during which time they nor their families have received any pay what-ever from their Government, while others who have been recently captured, we see by the public papers, have been promptly exchanged."[52]

Burrell was correct; a large number of POWs in the midwest and east had been exchanged after only a few weeks or months in captivity during the full operation of the cartel. He was not exaggerating about the health of his fellow inmates. Illness, indeed, had quickly spred across Camp Groce. By mid-August, only two weeks after the prison was established, 15 of the 35 POW officers were sick. By the first week of October, 129 of the camp's prisoners had become ill.[53]

The prevailing illness at Camp Groce was typhus flux, a serious contagious disease transmitted through body lice, and accompanied by a high fever; cerebral disorders, such as a stupor, delirium, and/or intense headaches; the eruption of a dark red rash over the body; and acute or chronic diarrhea.[54]

Camp Groce prisoners were also often confronted with copperheads, rattle-snakes, and "hooded vipers" that wandered into the compound, as well as myriad flies and other insects.

Although these conditions, along with the heat of summer, made the camp uncomfortable, Camp Groce didn't become intolerable until September 1863, when another 271 captives arrived, which more than doubled the original prison population. Doubling up in the bunks soon became necessary. Other POWs built shacks of their own around the camp. A company of conscripts who escorted the new prisoners to the site took over guard duty, and Captain Buster and his regi-ment left for new duties at Camp Lubbock near Houston. A Colonel Bates took over as camp commandant.[55]

About November, black laborers were put to work erecting a stockade around the site. That same month, a Lieutenant Colonel Barnes relieved Colonel Bates of command. POWs continued to be brought to the facility and the overcrowd-ing continued.

CAMP FORD

As conditions worsened at Camp Groce, groups of prisoners were transferred out in December and January to a larger POW facility established at Tyler, Texas, nearly 160 miles away. That facility, Camp Ford, was named in honor of Colonel John S. "Rip" Ford, one-time Texas Ranger, state senator, newspaper editor, and commander of Confederate forces in Texas. Originally established as a camp of instruction for east Texas after hostilities broke out, in July 1863 it became a POW facility for the region, and would eventually grow to become the largest military prison west of the Mississippi River.[56]

As the first contingent of POWs arrived from Camp Groce, there were only sixty-five Federal prisoners there, although the population had reached five hundred the previous month. Major Thomas F. Tucker was prison commandant, having relieved Captain S. M. Warner, Camp Ford's first commander, in October. A company of forty-five men guarded the prisoners. For the most part, Camp Ford was still a desirable location to be confined, if confinement was unavoidable. "I have never been in better health since I have been here," wrote Captain William P. Coe, Company B, 176th New York Volunteers, on Christmas Eve in 1863. "It is a very healthy location and our diet is simple and nourishing—corn bread and beef. We are as comfortable and as well treated as prisoners can expect, much more so than I expected to be when captured."[57]

Camp Ford was located four miles northwest of Tyler, and was originally, for the POWs, just an open area surrounded by guards. In November black laborers erected a stockade around the camp.

"It is situated on high table lands covered with pine and oak," advised Chaplain M. H. Hare, 36th Iowa Regiment. "There are about eight acres in the stockade. A spring in the south-west corner of the lot furnishes a good supply of water, impregnated with sulphur."[58]

"The area outside of Camp Ford's stockade consisted of prairies interspersed with timbered hills," added prisoner Duganne, who was transferred here when Camp Groce was abandoned. "The north gate of the prison yard or 'corral' opens up an open plain where sheep and hogs are herded. On the east are woods and cultivated lands. [The] west is hilly, crowned with scrubby oaks and ash [with] a rebel camp of cavalry and the huts of conscripts hide behind these. Upon the south a hill abruptly rises with a streamlet at its base which flows within the stockade [called] 'the spring.' The rebel commandant's headquarters, two or three log houses, look down upon the corral from that hill."[59]

The stockade consisted of split pine timbers submerged three to four feet in the ground and extending eight feet above. No shelter was provided; prisoners were placed into the open pen and left to construct their own. Under heavy guard, POWs were allowed out to cut logs and gather material to build their own huts, cabins, and shanties. Some prisoners were content to burrow into the ground for shelter, while others constructed elaborate huts complete with stacked clay chimneys. Still others, like Duganne, found prisoners who were experienced in such matters and paid them to build their housing.

The first prisoners confined at Camp Ford on July 30 were 360 Union navy POWs. The following October they were joined by 11 officers and 203 enlisted men of the 19th Iowa Regiment, captured in an engagement at Sterling Farm near the Atchafalaya River.[60]

About December 1863, all but 65 of those POWs were marched out of Camp Ford to Shreveport, Louisiana, nearly one hundred miles away, for exchange. The prisoner exchange, however, never took place. As the new arrivals from Camp Groce settled into the abandoned huts and shanties of Camp Ford, the former prisoners spent the winter in Shreveport before they were force-marched back to the prison in the spring.

During this time, conditions at the Texas prison remained somewhat comfortable. Prisoners busied themselves with such cottage industries as basket weaving using ashwood peelings, building chairs from grapevines, making table mats and drinking cups, and carving a wide variety of chess pieces. A Lieutenant Mars became well-known in camp for his expertly turned-out banjos from ash and hickory wood. Other prisoners engaged in soap-making or turning out pottery bowls, plates, coffee cups, and smoking pipes from the red clay of the area. As at all the other prisons they often sold or traded these items to the guards or to the local farm families who visited the site to sell or trade their produce and dairy products.[61]

Conditions continued to decline in the prisons of the North as the buildup of prisoners continued with the collapse of the exchange cartel.

GRATIOT STREET

In St. Louis's Gratiot Street Prison, the lack of space, shortages of food, and shortages of medical supplies continued to create chaos. By March smallpox had broken out in epidemic proportions. At the same time, the polluted conditions in the lower rooms declined further. Vermin infested the prisoners, their bedding, and everything else.

"Every disease under heaven," wrote prisoner Griffin Frost, "break[s] out in the lower quarters; half starved and crowded together as they are in their dirt and rags."[62]

In April, the Sanitary Commission appointed two physicians to look into the situation at Gratiot Street. Among other things, they found that bunks, designed for two people and three tiers high, were placed so close together that there was hardly space to pass between them. A lack of bedding in the hospital left only ragged blankets and bits of carpet for the prisoners to keep themselves warm. The floors were so encrusted with dirt that they resembled earthen floors. The report concluded by saying, "It is difficult to conceive how human beings can continue to live in such an atmosphere."[63]

Unfortunately, many couldn't. Prisoners began dying at an alarming rate—sometimes as many as four a day. Eventually, between August 1863 and April

1864, the monthly death rate at Gratiot Street Prison would average more than 10 percent of the total sick in the prison hospital and in some months up to 15 percent. The mortality rate reached over 50 percent of the total sick from October 1864 through January 1865, with most deaths attributed to smallpox and typhoid fever.[64]

On July 30, 1863, there were 206 sick out of the total prison population of around 700. During the first week of August, steamboats arrived with POWs from the Vicksburg vicinity, which brought the prison population to nearly 1,100 again. Many were dead on arrival, and many more died soon after. The Gratiot Street, Myrtle Street, and Alton prisons were all over capacity, so 387 of the Vicksburg POWs were immediately transferred to Camp Morton. This still left 707 prisoners at Gratiot Street, and by August 5, a total of 218 of these were listed as sick and one to three were dying each day.[65]

Finally, the authorities worked out a plan to maintain an average of 140 prisoners at Myrtle Street and 650 at Gratiot Street, while the average daily population of the prison hospital remained at 150.

ALTON PRISON

A smallpox epidemic erupted at Alton in August and September, apparently transferred in with new arrivals from Gratiot Street, causing these prisoners to die at a rate of six to ten a week. Over the course of several months, more than fifty died when the average population was around fifteen hundred. The prevailing diseases at Alton also included malaria, pneumonia, dysentery, erysipelas, and chronic diarrhea.[66]

At the insistence of local citizens, who feared that the disease might spread into town, the smallpox-infected prisoners were moved to a dilapidated summer cottage on the north end of McPike's Island, a small uninhabited isle in the Mississippi River directly across from the prison. The small, abandoned dwelling was converted into a hospital pest house—a ward to quarantine those having highly contagious diseases—but as it became overcrowded, sick prisoners had to remain at the prison hospital in the prison yard until there was a vacancy on the island. This procedure continued the spread of disease among inmates.

The prison hospital originally began as a room in the main prison building. As illnesses increased, first one and then two converted workshops in the yard were used. The prison deadhouse was simply a shed in the yard where bodies were kept until they could be buried.

In the beginning, the prison burials were done at the Alton cemetery near Rosier and State streets in the north part of town. Records fail to indicate if any of the prisoners taken to "smallpox island," as it came to be referred to by the townsfolk, ever recovered and were returned to the prison. It is believed, however, that between August 1863 and March 1864, several hundred POWs were simply buried on the island because of the great number, while some were buried closer to the prison building.[67] "[They] died by the hundreds," professed prisoner Jacob Teeple, who was also incarcerated at Alton with his sixty-year-old father and a cousin. "My father died in [Alton] prison, and they would not let me see him buried, nor do I know whether he was buried or not."[68]

CAMP DOUGLAS

By early 1863, the mortality rate at Camp Douglas had climbed to 10 percent a month, more than would be reached by any other Civil War prison in any one-month period. In February, 387 of the facility's 3,800 prisoners died. Between January 27 and February 18, 260 died. The Sanitary Commission pointed out that at that rate, the prison would be emptied out within 320 days.[69]

"Of the whole number," Adjutant Haynie claimed in his report on the prison at the end of the war, "[the prisoners] died of contagious diseases brought with them, or from the results of long standing affections." The claim, of course, was untrue. The southerners found the Chicago fall and winter extremely wet, cold, and windy. The majority of deaths here was from typhoid fever and pneumonia—a result of the filth, the bad weather, and a lack of heat and clothing.[70]

An inspection of Camp Douglas in October revealed nearly 6,100 POWs, of which 325 were in a hospital, with a capacity for only 120, 150 sick in the barracks. Renovation of the chapel was underway to handle an additional 60 patients.[71]

"[A]ll of the prisoners' barracks are greatly in need of repair," the inspection report noted. "There is not a door and hardly a window among them; a large proportion of the bunks are so mutilated as to be useless; much of the flooring and siding is removed and the open fire places in the cook houses are in a dilapidated condition; the roofs of all require repairs."[72]

Worst of all was the lack of stoves in the barracks. "[T]he guard barracks are kept too warm," it said, "there being two stoves in each, while but very few—I noticed but one or two—of the prisoners' barracks have any."[73]

The report also pointed out that only three hydrants were provided to supply water for the entire camp and that stagnant water stood at various parts of the prisoner compound. The report concluded: "[T]he camp is simply filthy in its condition, [and] many of the prisoners are miserably clad and already suffer much from the cold."[74]

Although typhoid fever and pneumonia were the top two killers in this prison, its other prevalent diseases included measles, mumps, "epidemic" catarrh, and chronic diarrhea.

"The [camp] is low and flat, rendering drainage imperfect," admitted Surgeon Edward D. Kittoe, U.S. Volunteers, "[I]ts proximity to Lake Michigan, and consequent exposure to the cold, damp winds from off this large body of water, with the flat, marshy character of the soil, must of necessity create a tendency to disease. . . . At [times] the ground is covered with snow and the frost is severe. When the frost gives way and fogs and usual dampness of spring succeed, in conjunction with the surroundings of large cattle yards, slaughter-houses, and other offensive matter usual to the suburbs of large cities . . . disease will assume a low or typhoid type and, per consequence, the rate of mortality increased."[75]

As a result of continued pressure by the Sanitary Commission, Meigs finally relented and authorized the construction of a sewer system for Camp Douglas in June 1863.

CAMP BUTLER

Conditions were just as bad at Camp Butler, which was reestablished as a prison camp at the beginning of 1863. In January, the new commandant, Colonel William F. Lynch, 58th Illinois Volunteers, was ordered to prepare for the arrival of more prisoners. On January 31, a group of 1,665 POWs captured at Arkansas Post and Murfreesboro arrived by train, under escort of the 113th Illinois Infantry. A total of 500 more arrived over the next two months.

Before long, these prisoners found conditions at Camp Butler just as bad as those the year before. "[I]t had rained almost daily for some weeks," reported Captain Freedley on March 21, during an inspection of the camp. "The camp [has] never been dry since the prisoners arrived." Because of the muddy roads, wagons from Springfield were unable to reach the camp to deliver supplies and it became difficult to obtain wood for heating the barracks.[76]

"The barracks occupied by the prisoners are sadly in need of repairs," continued Freedley. "New bunks should be constructed . . . repairs in floor and roof are required . . . [and] the prisoners' barracks, [are] internally and without, exceedingly filthy."[77]

Colonel Lynch had been a POW in the South early in the war. Whether he harbored ill feelings or not is unknown, but his only concern at Camp Butler was the suppressive confinement of his captives. "They [are] closely confined within limits," admonished Freedley in his report, "and no regard [is] paid to their wants or comforts . . . [and many] are destitute of proper clothing."[78]

Lynch had made no effort to have badly needed heating stoves installed or straw bedding replaced. "[T]he rebel prisoners of war confined at Camp Butler have suffered severely from the severity of the weather," Major General Horatio G. Wright chastised Lynch from headquarters in Cincinnati in a dispatch dated

February 7, 1863. General Wright ordered Lynch to provide prisoners with stoves for their barracks, fresh straw for bedding, one blanket each, and adequate clothing.[79]

Despite the order, it was a week before the stoves arrived. Lynch interpreted the provisions for blankets and clothing as meaning only for prisoners in absolute need; and he didn't enforce the order for repair of the barracks and for straw until March 24, when the worst weather was over. In the meantime, 345 prisoners had died from pneumonia, and over 200 were in the hospital.[80]

Pneumonia was the primary killer at Camp Butler, but other ailments flourished. Erysipelas, remittent fevers, and chronic diarrhea were prevalent, and in March 1863, smallpox briefly broke out there as well.

On April 7, 600 prisoners were escorted on trains to City Point, Virginia, in one of the last exchanges of the cartel. Three days later, another 1,700 were transported out. Fire broke out in several of the barracks soon after their departure, destroying many of the prisoner quarters.[81]

There were only 134 POWs left at Camp Butler by the end of April—most of them had been in the hospital and were too weak to travel when the exchanges took place. Of those, 51 died. The others rioted on April 27, damaging the stockade before the uprising was quelled. On May 19, 1863, these last Confederate prisoners left Camp Butler and the facility ceased to be a military prison for the remainder of the war. During Camp Butler's thirteen-month existence as a POW facility, a total of 203 prisoners escaped, 339 were released upon an oath of allegiance, and 866 died.[82]

CAMP CHASE

In Ohio, Camp Chase and Johnson's Island had gone into full operation as POW facilities by early 1863. At Camp Chase, Major Zinn hadn't served as commandant for long before he was replaced by Brigadier General John S. Mason of the U.S. Volunteers. He, too, was an Ohioan, but he was also a professional military man who had graduated from West Point. With his arrival in April, the Federal government assumed increased control over Camp Chase and was finally able to keep Ohio Governor Tod from asserting state control of the prison.

Mason immediately exercised military control over the compound and tightened security. All prisoners were restricted to the camp. By mid-1863, Mason transferred all officers and political prisoners to Johnson's Island. At the same time, tourists and visitors were prohibited and all mail was censored, the quality of food rations was improved with a change in suppliers and closer inspection, and prisoner trade with the sutler was restricted.

Camp Chase was an enclosed barracks prison. It consisted of 160 acres divided into three sections by plank walls sixteen feet high. The divided sections

were designated Prisons No. 1, No. 2, and No. 3. There were double outside
walls, with a sentry's parapet along the outside about three feet from the top.
Outlooks or guardhouses were located at each corner. Housing and barracks for
the Federal officers and guards were located outside the prison walls. In violation
of POW regulations, prison labor was often used to rebuild barracks inside
the prison or to construct larger or stronger fence sections around the camp.[83]

Prison No. 1 enclosed about an acre and could hold approximately 200
prisoners. Prisons No. 2 and No. 3 contained about five acres each and sometimes
held as many as 4,000 in each. The original capacity of the camp was estimated
at 3,500 to 4,000 but as many as 5,000 to 6,000 were often held there. By January of 1865, the population would reach an all-time high of more than 9,000.[84]

Prisoners were assigned to quarters in small houses or shanties measuring
sixteen-by-twenty feet. "It was without ceiling," noted prisoner John H. King,
Company H, 40th Georgia, of one such shanty, "and the floors of green lumber,
with cracks between the planks wide enough to let the cold wind freely circulate."
Twelve to fifteen POWs occupied each little shed, with double or triple bunks
arranged along each wall. At one end of the shanty, a room was partitioned off
as a kitchen. A small opening in the partition was just large enough for a plate
or cup to be passed through.[85]

The living quarters within the three prison sections were generally arranged
in clusters of six, with the buildings of each cluster about five feet apart. Narrow
streets or pathways separated the clusters. "The spaces between the clusters of
quarters are heaped with the vilest accumulations of filth," reported one government inspector. "All the refuse of the prisoners' food, clothing and the general
dirt of the camp is gathered here."[86]

The streets, drains, and gutters of the camp were in the same condition, and
the latrines were nothing more than open excavations. The stench that permeated
the air of the camp was described as "horrible, nauseating and disgusting."[87]

The prison grounds were unlevel, soft clayish soil with poor drainage. After
a mild rain, stands of deep mud and water would remain for days. Since none
of the living quarters were shingled, the roofs leaked. "The buildings are set
directly on the ground," complained the inspector, "with the floors in very many
instances in contact with it. The drainage is so incomplete that water falling
accumulates under the buildings and remains there constantly."[88]

"We had never experienced such intensely cold weather," as one prisoner
recalled the winters. In December and January the temperatures often went
from ten to twenty degrees below zero. "When the chilling winds and the frost
and ice of this bleak region came," agreed King, "with our bodies wasted by
starvation, without fires sufficient to warm our emaciated forms, there came
a season of real suffering, of real pain, that ended only in the death of many a
helpless victim."[89]

JOHNSON'S ISLAND

The POWs confined at Johnson's Island found the Ohio winter even worse. The prison's population had declined to 72 prisoners toward the end of the exchange cartel, but immediately climbed to more than 2,000 when the cartel collapsed. From then on the average population remained around 2,500 for some time before gradually increasing to over 3,200 the following year.

In nearly every prison memoir about Johnson's Island there are complaints about suffering from the cold. The winter of 1862–63 had been unusually mild for the area, but those that followed were unusually intense. "(It) was just the place to convert visitors to the theological belief of the Norwegians that Hell has torments of cold instead of heat," complained prisoner Henry K. Douglas.[90]

Each room in the barracks was outfitted with a woodburning stove. "I was confined in one room with 70 other Confederates," argued one prisoner. "The room was provided with one antiquated stove. Fuel given us was frequently insufficient . . . [and] in our desperation we burned every available chair, box, and even parts of our bunks. . . . Some of us maintained life by forming a circle and dancing with the energy of despair."[91]

December and January of 1863–64 were especially brutal. The temperature stood at twenty-two degrees below zero and remained there for several days. The prisoners suffered intensely from frostbite and several died. "Water froze in our canteens under our heads," exclaimed prisoner R. F. Webb, who, along with many others, often used his as a pillow. "I was afraid to walk from one end of the enclosure to the other for fear my blood would congeal and I would freeze to death."[92]

Lake Erie was just a few yards from the other side of the prison gate. In the dead of winter, when the well pumps froze, the guards opened the big, heavy gates and fifty prisoners at a time were allowed to the lake's edge to fill their canteens. It soon became a daily routine, with set times of 10 A.M. to noon and 2 to 4 P.M., but due to the cold, the ice often had to be broken up each time to get to the water.

"I once saw 1500 Federal troops march in perfect security from Sandusky to Johnson's Island across the firmly frozen harbor," recalled prisoner Henry E. Shepherd.[93]

It wasn't long before the POWs realized the extreme cold of the region could be used in their favor. "There was but a single hope of escape, and that was by means of the dense ice which enveloped the island during the greater part of winter." When the bay was free of ice, the *Michigan,* a sloop of war, lay constantly off the island with her guns trained upon the prisoner barracks. During the dead of winter, it was no longer there. The sentry patrol along the shore, likewise, was missing. Winter was the only period Johnson's Island was not secured against escapes.[94]

"Repeated efforts were made," recalled Colonel Thomas S. Kenan, Company A, 43rd North Carolina, "but their plans were [usually] discovered by the guards." First Lieutenant J. F. Cross, Company B, 5th North Carolina boasted, "I secured a Federal uniform from one of the guards, and made the attempt, but was detected and returned to prison and punished."[95]

"Lieutenants William T. Williamson of Benton, Florida, and J. B. Murphy of Columbia, Tennessee escaped into Canada." Lieutenant Archibald McFadyen, Company A, 63rd North Carolina noted.[96]

There were only twelve successful escapes from the island during its existence as a military prison. The first didn't occur until the prison was nearly two years old, on the last day of December 1863. It became one of the most daring, and involved Lieutenant Colonel John R. Winston of the 45th North Carolina Regiment and two others.

"They had been engaged for some time," reported Kenan, "in making preparations for escape in securing additional clothing, ladders, etc." On the intensely cold night of 31 December, 1863, when the thermometer was several degrees below zero and the sentinels on the walls were in consequence forced to remain in their boxes for protection, they saw their opportunity and took advantage of it. "They scaled the wall without being seen by the guards, and walked on the ice to the opposite shore."[97]

The three made their way toward Canada on New Year's Day in the frigid, near-record, cold. Winston was the only one to succeed. "The others," continued Kenan, "were recaptured, with hands and feet frozen."[98]

The cold winter of the region also brought a special form of recreation to the prisoners of Johnson's Island. With the abundance of snow, the prisoners often engaged in great snowball battles. "They divided themselves into two teams," declared Captain Decimus U. Barziza, 4th Texas Infantry, "and further separated into companies and battalions."[99]

In one particular skirmish, prisoner Isaac Trimble, a major general who lost a leg in Pickett's charge at Gettysburg, commanded his "army" against the "army" of prisoner M. Jeff Thompson, the "Swamp Fox of the Confederacy." The pitched battle carried on for three or four hours until the participants' hands became numb.

CAMP MORTON

Conditions were similar at Camp Morton in Indiana but they weren't having as much fun. By December 1863, the number of captives confined within the stockade had grown to over 3,300. During a thirty day period of sub-zero weather there, 263 prisoners perished.[100]

Camp Morton had been emptied of POWs in September 1862, but Union authorities reactivated the site in February 1863 due to the growing need for space.

"I find it much dilapidated and sadly in need of repairs," reported Captain Freedley during his initial inspection when Camp Morton was reopened. Weeks later, however, Freedley advised Colonel Hoffman, "I have directed no improvements at Camp Morton excepting such as could be made without additional expense to the Government. Captain [James A.] Ekin has furnished a carpenter and had some bunks constructed, additional windows, glazing and window sash supplied and other general repairs made."[101]

By this time, the deep ravine containing the creek that ran through the camp had become the receptacle for the camp's trash and debris, and the wells had become saturated with seepage from the surrounding terrain. "The limestone causes diarrhea with the newcomers," explained one of the camp's medical inspectors.[102]

Freedley assigned a detail to clean up the banks along the creek, had the prison pen enlarged somewhat, and arranged for additional barracks to be moved to the site.

Within a short time, three barracks were dismantled and moved from Camp Carrington, on the other side of Indianapolis, and erected at Camp Morton. Two served as housing for the prisoners and one was an additional hospital building. "They are temporary frame barracks," reported Freedley, "16 by 100 feet, divided into four rooms and capable of accommodating 100 troops each."[103]

Throughout February and March, the population of the prison remained around 652. These were all sick or wounded POWs belonging to various Kentucky, Tennessee, and Alabama regiments. The original intent for reestablishing Camp Morton as a POW facility was to hold only sick or wounded prisoners. However, as the prison populations increased elsewhere, POWs of every classification were, again, sent there for confinement.[104]

The new commandant was Colonel James Biddle of the 71st Indiana Volunteers. Of the 738 men in his regiment, 504 were on parole, having been captured in Kentucky, and were unable to perform guard duty. Two companies of the 63rd Indiana Regiment were assigned to the post to assist in that detail.

"The accommodations for prisoners at Camp Morton are not good," admitted Colonel Hoffman in June 1863, "but they are about as good as at other camps, and as altogether they will not hold more than 12,000 to 15,000, it will hardly be possible to dispense with Camp Morton."[105]

As at Camp Chase, control of Camp Morton had been allowed to fall under the control of the state governor during its first year of operation. With its reestablishment, however, Colonel Hoffman and the Federal government took over completely. More prisoners were moved into the facility as the weeks passed. By October, there were 2,362 confined there, including seven Confederate officers and 30 civilian political prisoners.[106]

"The camp is a disgrace to the name of military prison," reported Union medical inspector Augustus Clark. "It is filthy in ever respect. The vicinity of the sinks is obvious for many yards around . . . cleanliness of men and clothing [is] foul; bathing and laundry facilities [are] entirely insufficient." He noted of the two hospital buildings: "One [is] dilapidated and utterly unfit for use; the other—a former guardhouse—[is] in good condition, but much overcrowded."[107]

On October 22, 1863, Colonel Ambrose A. Stevens, 5th Regiment Invalid Corps, took over as prison commandant. He found more than 200 prisoners in the hospital and another 125 sick in the barracks. Tents were being used for the overflow from the hospital buildings. "I found the barracks in a bad condition," admitted Stevens, "wanting extensive repairs in order to render them fit for occupancy during the winter."[108]

In addition, Stevens found the stockade fence in need of repair, and the guards, by this time the 51st and 73rd Indiana Volunteer Regiments, with low morale and incompetent in their duties. For the most part, the guards were in an apathetic state. They, too, had been former prisoners, recently exchanged, and their officers were still confined at Richmond.

In the two months prior to his arrival, there had been thirty escapes and nearly sixty deaths in the camp. Those who weren't sick or dying seemed to be constantly scaling the fence. In fact, many found it easy, using crude ladders or board planks pulled from the barracks and fleeing into the night.[109]

FORT McHENRY

Conditions had become worse at the Union's fort prisons as well. When prisoner exchanges were suspended and the captive population continued to increase everywhere, 120 POWs were moved back into Fort Warren near Boston. Worse yet was Fort McHenry near Baltimore. Although prison officials were required to file monthly returns for their facilities as of mid-1862, none were filed for Fort McHenry until March 1863. At that time, the prison's population stood at 726. By May and June, there were 1,500 there, while its official capacity remained at around 600, assuming the stockaded enclosed stables were used.

According to most sources today, the fort held a total of 5,325 POWs, 33 of whom died, during its eventual fifty-two months of existence. Conservatively, the total held was probably closer to 10,000. While the political prisoners and POWs were being transferred out to such places as Fort Lafayette and Fort Delaware, more were arriving every month, and in July 1863 alone, Fort McHenry held nearly 7,000 captives.[110]

During this same time, a number of hospitals in Baltimore held wounded captives, most notably West Hospital, and many POWs were held in the city jail. "Some 700 rebel prisoners are confined in the city jail here," reported James L. Donaldson, U.S. quartermaster in Baltimore. "[T]here being no room for them at Fort McHenry or Fort Delaware, I have made a contract with the warden of the jail to feed and lodge them at 20-cents a day."[111]

Additional prisoners were held at other locations throughout the city, including the yard of Hope Slater's jail for blacks. "I know this place well," remembered R. F. Webb, who was held there prior to being transferred to Johnson's Island. "It is about 50 by 30 feet square, with very high walls. We were all thrust into this miserable den and kept there until morning. It was quite cold and chilly, and we could neither walk, stand or sit."[112]

Sergeant Warren D. Reid, 11th Mississippi Volunteers, had a similar experience at Fort McHenry after he was wounded and captured at Gettysburg and placed in a corral near the battlefield. That night, July 3, and the next day were spent marching to Westminster, Maryland, where he and nearly 1,500 others were placed onto a train bound for Baltimore. Upon their arrival, they were marched from the depot to Fort McHenry and then held in a corral surrounding what was once the fort's stables. "It rained all night," declared Reid, "and we stood huddled out in the open slush, unable to lie or sit down."[113]

Major William W. Morris, 4th U.S. Artillery, Fort McHenry's commandant since May 1861, began to plead with Colonel Hoffman to erect temporary barracks at the fort to relieve overcrowding throughout Baltimore. "A large portion of the prisoners of war," wrote Morris, "are, while here, entirely without shelter!"[114]

The unmerciful overcrowding ended in August 1863, when a new Maryland prison was established. The total at Fort McHenry ranged between 300 and 400 every month thereafter.

FORT DELAWARE

By mid-1863, however, none of the Union's facilities were any worse than Fort Delaware. "It happened to be my good fortune," wrote prisoner Decimus Barziza, after his confinement at Johnson's Island, "not to go to Fort Delaware during my involuntary stay in the North. But this place is spoken of by all who have been confined there as a perfect hell on earth."[115]

No other northern prison was as dreaded by the South. By 1863 Fort Delaware had gained a reputation among Confederate soldiers as a place of cruelty. It was often referred to as "that 'lowermost Hell' of human hells" and, because it had engendered one of the highest mortality rates of any Civil War prison, its inmates called it "The Fort Delaware Death Pen." The news of being sent there often caused "faces to grow white" and "hands to clench" in fear.[116]

Although the prison was already considered intolerable for various reasons, the commandants up to that time apparently had treated the POWs fairly and had attempted to make the prison as efficient as possible. Colonel Perkins was replaced by Colonel Robert C. Buchanan, 4th U.S. Infantry, in March 1863. He immediately worked on plans to build additional barracks and to enlarge the existing hospital, but he was transferred by Colonel Hoffman under the direction of Secretary Stanton within a mere thirty days of taking command. Albin Francisco Schoepf took over command and served in this capacity until the end of the war. Schoepf allowed his subordinates unrestrained control inside the compound, and it eventually evolved into the most brutal POW institution in America.[117]

Between the mess hall and the kitchen was a sally port, about twelve feet wide, through which the wind from the bay blew constantly. There, prisoners were tortured at the malicious whim of the prison authorities. They were bucked and gagged and hung by the thumbs for the slightest infractions. "This was a daily occurrence," insisted prisoner George Moffett, "and I have seen six or eight 'thumb hangers' suspended at a time . . . a guard stood by to shoot anyone who interfered."[118]

Many contemporary and official accounts agree that this form of torture was used on an almost daily basis at Fort Delaware. Prisoners were hung by the thumbs, with their toes barely touching the ground, slowly swinging in the sea breeze anywhere from a few hours to a few days. As prisoner John P. Hickman wrote, "In many instances they were left there until their thumbs burst." According to Moffett, there were numerous instances of dislocated shoulders and joints and thumbs were often cut to the bone by the tight cords. "In some cases," he said, "mortification would set in and the thumbs would have to be amputated."[119]

"Another method of punishment," reported prisoner Calvin Dearing, "was to require the victim to stand on the top edges of a barrel with the head knocked out and to hold a log so heavy that it took two men to hand it up to him. He was made to hold it for three hours. If he dropped it, he was shot."[120]

In addition to inhumane treatment, forced labor—also officially prohibited for prisoners of war—was commonly practiced at Fort Delaware. According to official records, "men were compelled to labor in unloading Federal vessels and in putting up buildings for Federal officers, and if they refused were driven to the work with clubs."[121]

As in all the prisons, sentry duty at Fort Delaware was handled by different regiments at various times. These included the Commonwealth Artillery of Pennsylvania, the 5th Delaware, the 5th Maryland and Purnell Legion of Maryland, the 6th and 7th Massachusetts, and the 157th Ohio National Guard. The Ohio regiment became the most hated by the prisoners.[122]

Four lines of security were utilized at Fort Delaware. One guardline was stationed along the dikes that surrounded the entire island, while another patrolled along the parapets surrounding the barracks built outside the fort's walls in the summer of 1862. A third line patrolled around the enclosure, and a fourth patrolled inside the prison.

Besides carrying out wanton acts of torture and brutality as directed by the prison authorities, the sentries sometimes initiated their own acts of violence. "A young man merely threw a cup of water from a window," recalled one prisoner, "when a guard on the outside fired upon him, the ball passing through his neck, killing him instantly."[123]

In another incident, guard Bill Douglas of the 157th Ohio National Guard, shot and killed prisoner Edward P. Jones of Virginia for not returning from the sinks fast enough. Jones was unable to run, as Douglas had ordered, because he was lame from a war wound. Douglas not only escaped punishment for the act but, instead, was promoted to sergeant soon afterward.[124]

Other conditions were also insufferable. At six feet below water level and protected by a surrounding dike, drainage of the island was poor. Muddy canals without outlets traversed the island, according to the POWs, and for a time supplied the only water. The island surface was black, loamy, porous soil, which, after the slightest rain, turned into a quagmire. "The whole place was a bed of mud and filth," remarked one Confederate prisoner, "our men actually went bare-footed, their pants rolled up, when walking in the yard."[125]

A regulation at Fort Delaware forbade more than a few prisoners at a time to go to the latrines (sinks) after dark. "I have seen as many as 500 men in a row waiting their turn," claimed one witness. "The consequence was that they were obliged to use the places where they were." Eventually, the sludge mingled with the water they drank from the canals, resulting in aggravated cases of disease.[126]

Despite a surgeon general's and, later, a military tribunal's declaration early in the war that the fort was unsuitable for large numbers of prisoners, Colonel Hoffman continued to insist that it was "an excellent place to hold prisoners of war," and he ordered construction of additional barracks there on three different occasions. For the first arrivals, barracks were hastily erected on the parade grounds within the fort. Within a month, these POWs, and all later arrivals, were confined in fence-enclosed barracks newly erected outside the fort on the north end of the island. Shortly thereafter, additional barracks were built within this enclosure. From then on, only the fort's lower quarters, often referred to as dungeons by the POWs, were used, and only in times of punishment.[127]

The enclosed prison pen, 400 to 500 yards northwest of the fort, was formed by enclosing some eight acres within a continuous line of crudely built T-shaped barracks. The enclosure, or courtyard, was then divided into two prison yards by a double line of high plank fences. A parapet was constructed across the top of this for guards to walk along and have a complete view of the prisoners in each square. Confederate officers occupied the smaller pen nearest the fort, while privates were incarcerated in the other, larger pen. "An alley ten feet [wide] separated the two fences," reported prisoner Randolph Shotwell, "preventing any intercourse between the two pens [and] giving access to gates opening into each."[128]

Each pen contained up to ten rows of barracks, more aptly referred to as "cowsheds" by the inmates, which were under one continuous roof. Each shed was then divided into rooms, numbered from one to forty, called "divisions." Measuring nineteen by sixty feet, with bunks in three tiers on either side and a narrow passage between, each division confined anywhere from 400 to 900 prisoners. "Each division was named after the state from which the occupants hailed," prisoner George Moffett reported. "For instance, there were four Virginia divisions, a Louisiana division, two Tennessee divisions, etc."[129]

"The buildings," reported Shotwell, "were mere shells, constructed of long planks (of rough pineboard) standing on end." They offered little protection. After enduring the summer's stifling heat, flies, mosquitoes, bedbugs, lice, and rats, prisoners suffered from the cold of winter in these barracks as well. The icy wind came through the walls almost unobstructed, and snow often blew in between the cracks to pile onto the bunks and floors. Finding prisoners frozen to death in their bunks became a common occurrence.

The "one blanket to each man rule" was strictly enforced at Fort Delaware. "No matter how many blankets a man may have brought with him or purchased from the sutler with his own money," wrote Shotwell, "he is stripped of all but one single one!" In addition, a rule at this prison allowed only one blanket or one overcoat—but not both.[130]

With several hundred men in each barracks starving and therefore producing very little body heat, fighting for position near a stove became a kind of winter sport. "Those who crowded around the stove continually were dubbed 'stove rats,'" reported prisoner W. H. Moon of Alabama. "On very cold days those who spent most of their time on their bunks trying to keep warm would get down in the passageway between the bunks, form in a column of one or two with as many in the rear as wished to participate, and charge the 'stove rats.' The hindmost would push those in front until the stove was cleared. The rear ones would then take possession of the stove until another column would form and make a counter charge. . . . These charges and counter charges would sometimes continue for several hours."[131]

Fresh water was hard to come by at Fort Delaware. As the prison population continued to increase and the canals built within the stockade became visibly polluted, two wooden barrels placed in the corners of the barracks to catch rainwater from the roofs provided the total water supply. "When the rains were frequent [the water was] kept tolerably pure," reported one prisoner, "but when several weeks elapsed without showers, they became putrid [and] the contents would appear to be fairly swarming with wiggletails and white worms."[132]

Other attempts to provide enough water included shipping it across the Delaware River from nearby Brandywine Creek on tugs, and installing a new patented water purifier to process water pumped from the bay into holding tanks.

After the Battle of Gettysburg, when all the Confederate officers held at Union prisons were moved to Johnson's Island, the population of Fort Delaware dropped from around 12,600 to about 9,000, while the prison's sick population remained at around 300. Before long, the fort's hospital population averaged 600, as many of the wounded from the recent Pennsylvania battle arrived. Eventually, the fort's hospital became a major holding site for wounded and sick Confederate prisoners in the East. Other major locations by then included Pittsburgh Penitentiary Hospital and General Hospital in Chester, Pennsylvania, West's Hospital in Baltimore, and David's Island in New York City.

DAVID'S ISLAND

Until the Gettysburg battle, David's Island had served as a medical facility for only Union troops. Being a previously established and equipped facility surrounded by water, Union authorities saw it as an excellent place to hold extremely ill prisoners or those who were still suffering from battle wounds.

Located in Long Island Sound just off the coast of what is today the New York suburb of New Rochelle, this eighty-acre site would eventually hold more than 2,500 Confederate prisoners at a time. The isle was a long, narrow stretch of land that contained twenty-two temporary structures extending nearly the entire length of the island. Each building was divided into four wards that contained up to twenty cots each. A doctor's office was located in the front of each building and a toilet was at the rear. Mess halls were located between every two buildings. Whenever the population increased to more than 1,800 prisoners, tents were used for the overflow.

"Upon our arrival," reported prisoner Samuel Hankins of Gulfport, Mississippi, "we were at once divested of all wearing apparel, which was burned, and each one given a bath. Then a hospital suit was provided . . . I was consigned to Pavilion 4, Ward 1. Irish women were employed to scrub the floors daily. . . . There was a large steam laundry kept going constantly for the use of all. In one large general kitchen food was prepared and sent to mess rooms . . . the whole island was at our disposal. When the tide went out, we gathered clams for bait and fished. . . . Many sympathizers from New York visited us every day and brought things."[133]

Hankins was fortunate to be confined in one of the buildings while he was there. The population at that time was up to 2,500 and many were housed in tents. When U.S. Surgeon Charles Crane inspected David's Island the following August, the population was at 2,538, but a total of 84 had died over the previous four-week period. According to *Frank Leslie's Illustrated News-paper,* the population rose to nearly 3,000 soon afterward.[134]

Conditions were similar at New York's other prison locations. The facilities were gradually growing more crowded and accommodations eroded further. Not wanting to bury deceased POWs on Governors Island, Federal authorities leased Deer Island in Boston Harbor, nearly two hundred miles away, to use as a burial site.[135]

OHIO PENITENTIARY

As prison populations steadily increased after the Battle of Gettysburg, it became apparent to Federal officials that the combination of original and reactivated prison facilities was unable to hold the number of captives coming into Union hands. Since no major facilities had been established since the February 1862, capture of Forts Henry and Donelson, Quartermaster General Meigs directed Brigadier General Daniel H. Rucker, chief quartermaster, to establish a holding facility at Point Lookout, Maryland, which could confine up to ten thousand captives. At the same time, Meigs ordered Captain Charles A. Reynolds, assistant quartermaster, to establish a prison for POWs on Rock Island in the Mississippi River to help relieve overcrowding in the western facilities.[136]

In the meantime, a number of eastern state penitentiaries were pressed into use. These places seemed ideal for a number of reasons: they were close to a recent battlefield, they had the additional space available, and in some cases, they had the additional security that was necessary.

Some of the major locations used were the Allegheny Penitentiary at Pitts-burgh, Pennsylvania; Moyamensing Penitentiary at Philadelphia; the Albany Penitentiary in New York; and the Ohio State Penitentiary at Columbus. Of these locations, the Ohio facility became the most well-known to the general public because of the notoriety of one of the POWs confined there.

On July 30, Governor Tod notified Nathaniel Merion, the warden of the Ohio Penitentiary, of the impending arrival of Confederate Brigadier General John Hunt Morgan and thirty of his men, who were recently captured near New Lisbon, Ohio. The additional security of the prison was believed necessary over the use of Camp Chase for their confinement. Characteristically, when Tod notified Union commanders that there might be room for thirty POWs, sixty-eight were sent.

The Ohio State Penitentiary was located near the river in downtown Colum-bus. It occupied three blocks bounded by Maple on the north, Dennison on the west, West Street on the east, and Spring Street on the south. It was the state's largest penal institution, built in the 1830s, with its first prisoners confined in the facility in 1834. Even before the POWs arrived, the building was considered seriously overcrowded and antiquated.[137]

Built of hammered limestone, the three-story prison was divided into five-tier cell blocks, with thirty-five cells per tier. Each block was 100 feet long, 20 feet wide, and 40 feet high. The cells, 3½ feet wide, 7 feet long, and 7 feet high, were constructed of a latticework of heavy two-inch flat-iron bars on the front, with three interior walls of brick. The outside of the prison was surrounded by a four-foot-thick, twenty-five-foot-high stone wall surmounted by sentry turrets, which adjoined the administration building and cell blocks to enclose a large prison yard.

When the POWs arrived they were searched, stripped, and bathed by two convicts wielding bars of soap and horsehair brushes. Then each new prisoner was escorted to the barber's room, where his beard and mustache were trimmed and his hair cut. "They were not shaved and dressed in convict clothes as alleged," reported Brigadier General William W. Orme during a later inspection, "but [instead] wore their own dress and were confined in a part of the building to themselves." Generally, the sanitary procedures at this prison required that all new prisoners be scrubbed clean and have their head and face completely shaved when they first entered. Although Morgan and his officers were incensed over someone trimming their beards and cutting their hair, they were spared the more severe treatment.[138]

"Morgan had no 'belt filled with gold, greenbacks and Confederate notes,'" advised prison chaplain J. L. Grover in an attempt to dispel the popular rumor at the time. "His valuables amounted to twenty-three dollars and a butternut breast-pin."[139]

The POWs were then individually confined in cells on the first and second floors of the east wing, which had no windows. Each cell was furnished with a metal bed attached to the wall, a spittoon, and a night bucket. To keep them separated from the hardened criminals, a board partition was constructed across the open space in front of the south end of the cell block on the ground floor. During the day, the POWs were allowed the freedom to walk and talk in this open space or hall that was created in front of the cells. Another privilege they were allowed was the use of candles for one additional hour after the prison gaslights were turned out at 8 P.M. They took their meals as a group in the prison dining hall, but at a different time than the convicts, and received the addition of coffee with sugar in their prison fare.

Their days at the prison quickly became routine. At 7:30 A.M. and 3:00 P.M. they were marched to the dining hall for meals. At 4:45 P.M. they were locked in their cells and required to remain silent. At 8 P.M. the gaslights were turned off. Once their candles were extinguished, the cell became pitch-black. The darkness remained total except when the guard shuffled by and held a lantern near the cell's grating to check the bed.

From the beginning, and possibly through some influence of Governor Tod, Federal officials found it difficult to deal with Warden Merion. In charge of the prison, he considered himself in charge of anyone in it, especially the new Federal POWs. "I was refused admission by the warden," complained Augustus Clark to Colonel Hoffman when he attempted to inspect the facility under Hoffman's orders, "and was referred to General Mason, commanding the district, for the required order. . . . [This] I declined doing, and consequently was unable to inspect the quarters of the prisoners there confined."[140]

Adding to the chagrin of Union officials, Merion complained of the expense in keeping the Federal prisoners, refused to file monthly reports, and subjected the POWs to prison discipline by placing them in solitary confinement in the dark holds of the prison basement, restricted to bread and water, for any violation of prison rules. Morgan wrote a letter to Governor Tod complaining of the treatment and reminded him it was a violation of the rules governing confinement of prisoners of war. When Tod visited the facility later, some of those rules were relaxed.[141]

Security, however, remained tight. The POW cells were inspected daily by the prison guard, and a guard remained in the hall area and checked the cells at certain intervals throughout the night. A military guard of twenty-five men was assigned to the prison and placed at the warden's disposal. During the day, when the POWs were allowed out of their cells, military sentinels were placed at each end of the hall while the balance of the guard was stationed on call outside the prison. During mealtimes, additional sentries were brought in and stationed throughout the dining hall.

In a subsequent meeting between General Mason and Warden Merion, the Federal government assumed immediate control over the POWs and assigned their own surgeon and steward to watch over them in conjunction with the regular military guard assigned to the prison. They took over their duties on November 4, and although no one thought about it at the time, the Federal authorities failed to do a daily search of the cells, and the state prison guards no longer considered it their responsibility.[142]

On the morning of November 28, the guards were shocked to find seven cells with crudely fashioned dummies beneath the covers of the beds, and Morgan and six others gone. It was later determined that the POWs had chipped away at the stone floor with knives stolen during mealtime, worked their way into an air shaft and then tunneled out of the prison. It was also determined the work had begun November 4, the day the Federal government took over the watch, and had continued for three hours each day until its completion on November 26. Not only had Federal guards failed to notice the missing knives at mealtime, they had been completely oblivious to all the hard labor put forth by the POWs throughout the cell block every day for over three weeks.[143]

A house-by-house search was conducted throughout Columbus at once. A reward of $1,000 for Morgan's capture was immediately offered and quickly increased to $5,000. Federal authorities rushed to the pen to conduct an investigation. Days and then weeks passed without a sighting of Morgan.

By December, the investigations into Morgan's escape continued and the POW population of the prison had increased to seventy-nine. On December 5, two captains who had escaped with Morgan were captured in Louisville, Kentucky, and returned to the prison. Rumors that Morgan was in Canada circulated throughout the country but were never confirmed. On December 23, Morgan surfaced in Franklin, Tennessee, completely out of the Union's reach.

As a result of the escape, a number of changes took place at the Ohio and Allegheny Penitentiaries, where another 112 of Morgan's men were being held. All POWs were moved to the third floor for confinement, four military guards were assigned to watch and attend to them day and night, and they were fed in their cells instead of in the dining hall.[144]

POINT LOOKOUT

Point Lookout Military Prison opened in 1863 and was well on its way to becoming the largest Union POW facility in existence. A long, low, sandy peninsula formed at the junction of the Potomac River and the Chesapeake Bay, it had been a resort area with hotels, boarding houses, cottages, and commercial establishments before the war. The site was leased to the government in June 1862, and quickly became a major government installation.

"The hotel buildings and 'cottages by the sea,'" the *New York Times* proudly informed its readers, "are now occupied by United States troops as officer's quarters."[145]

Although situated opposite Virginia on the other side of the Potomac, the site was comparatively isolated and easily protected. At the extreme end of the peninsula, near the point's lighthouse, the government built a 1,400-bed hospital complex with twenty buildings arranged in a circle like spokes of a wheel, a large, wide wharf to receive supplies and the wounded that came in from nearby battlefields; a number of storehouses and stables; laundry and dining facilities; and additional quarters for officers, doctors, surgeons, and troops. In a short time, the hospital, named Hammond General Hospital in honor of Surgeon General William A. Hammond, grew into one of the largest and busiest medical facilities in the Union's service.

General Halleck ordered Brigadier General Gilman Marston, U.S. Volunteers, to Point Lookout at the beginning of its construction to organize the prison camp and take command. A forty-acre site about a half mile northeast of the hospital and military complex was selected, and work began on enclosing the area with a fifteen-foot-high board fence with a gallery along the top for the sentry. The fence also divided the camp into two sections, one of thirty acres and one of ten, to keep the troops and officers separated. The inside of the compound was a flat stretch of sand devoid of any trees or shrubs. All POWs were to be sheltered in tents.

On July 25, 1863, before construction was completed, 136 POWs from the Gettysburg battlefield were brought in and immediately put to work helping in the construction of the camp. More POWs arrived a few days later, and by mid-August, Hoffman had sent 800 from Baltimore and transferred 500 from Old Capitol Prison to relieve overcrowding there. By the end of the month, nearly 1,700 were confined at Point Lookout.[146]

Officially, the prison's name was Camp Hoffman but the name was seldom used. Nearly all of the official records simply refer to the facility as Point Lookout, although that name actually applied to the entire military complex on the point. The site's original name is said to derive from the fact that the narrow, sandy peninsula gradually comes to a point in the bay with a slight curvature at the end, which always interfered with normal navigation down the river. As vessels neared the site they had to "look out" and steer out around the point.[147]

The first guard detail assigned to the prison was from the 2nd and 12th New Hampshire regiments. When the first prisoners arrived, part of the construction not yet completed was the stockade fence surrounding the camp. The open sections had to be guarded by the New Hampshire troops with bayonets fixed and rifles at the ready. Five escapes occurred during this period, and several attempts cost POWs their lives.[148]

Throughout the following weeks, large contingents of prisoners continued to arrive. By September, the captive population had grown to nearly 4,000, and climbed to more than 9,000 by December. Eventually the prison would hold up to 20,000 prisoners on several different occasions.

"The first thing that struck me as peculiarly prominent within the fence," exclaimed Anthony M. Keiley, Company E, 12th Virginia Infantry, "was a row of eight or ten wooden buildings jutting out from the western face of the pen." Among all the POW tents, the cook and mess halls in the northwest corner of each compound did indeed stick out prominently. The small enclosure held one, while the larger enclosure held seven, with the addition of an eighth used as the commissary store. Each of these wooden buildings was 160 feet long and about 20 feet wide, with 20 feet at the end of each building partitioned off as a cookhouse. Four long tables ran down the center of each mess hall and Farmers' boilers, or cauldrons, were installed in the "kitchens" to cook rations.[149]

"A street, twenty feet in width, ran along the front of these houses," continued Keiley, "and at right angles to this street were long rows of tents of all imaginable patterns, and of no pattern at all, to within twenty or thirty feet of the opposite face of the enclosure."[150]

Old tents of every type—including French bell, round, or Sibley; wedge or A-tents; shelter or pup tents; wall, hospital, hospital fly, and wall-tent fly—

were pitched throughout the compound laid out in nine parallel "streets" running east and west. These thoroughfares would eventually become hard and smooth with constant use. The main path through the center of the camp would become known to the prisoners as "Pennsylvania Avenue." Each row of tents was referred to as a "division" and housed one thousand or more prisoners. A majority of the tents used at Point Lookout were the A-tents which, out of necessity, housed at least five prisoners, Sibleys housed thirteen to fourteen, hospital tents from fifteen to eighteen, wall tents ten to twelve, hospital flys ten to thirteen, wall-tent flys three to eight, and shelter tents three.[151]

As winter approached, both Marston and Hoffman recommended that wooden barracks be erected for the prisoners, but Secretary Stanton turned down the recommendation. The tents, 980 the first winter, intended to house 9,000 POWs, were old, worn, and far too crowded. Sixteen prisoners were often assigned to the bell tents and five to the shelter tents. Many of the bells had stoves, but prisoners in other tents had to get by with outside campfires. "They were allowed only one blanket to several men," noted one prisoner, "and their sufferings from the cold were intense."[152]

Weekly inspections took place, and the inmates were required to stand in formation outside their tents while the guards searched for and confiscated contraband, which often included what the guard considered to be too many blankets.

"Many of these men are without the necessary clothing even to hide their nakedness," complained Dr. Montrose A. Pallen, a Canadian advocate for the POWs, "more than half of the 9,000 and more there confined have not even a single blanket for covering or bedding and sleep on the bare ground."[153]

"During all this season," noted Keiley, "the ration of wood allowed to each man was an arm-full for five days." Prisoner J. B. Traywick agreed, "Almost no wood was furnished."[154]

The small wood ration, lack of heat, and penetrating northeastern cold seemed to have been mentioned in nearly every Point Lookout prisoner memoir. There is no doubt that the situation was devastating and that there was little exaggeration in most of the POW accounts. According to official records, between November 1863, and February 1864, more than 540 southern men confined at Point Lookout perished from their new environment.

Even clear and sunny days often brought no relief from the suffering. The combination of the sun's glare on the sand, the white canvas of the tents, and the water surrounding the site sometimes produced a temporary blindness in the prisoners for a part of each day. They would sometimes lose their sight and not regain it until the following morning, needing to be led around the camp by friends during such times.[155]

Flooding of the pen also occurred quite often, soaking the men, their tents, and what clothing they had. "The tide is higher on the Chesapeake than I ever saw it," Charles Warren Hutt, Company K, 40th Virginia Volunteers, noted in his diary. "Our camp is very muddy, so much so that the streets are nearly impossible . . . the whole camp is overflowed—in some houses knee deep." Keiley added, "[I]n the winter, a high tide and an easterly gale would flood the whole surface of the pen, and freeze as it flooded."[156]

ROCK ISLAND

In November 1863, Colonel Hoffman inspected the newly completed, but still empty, prison at Rock Island, Illinois. He then notified Secretary Stanton that construction of the prison was finished and that he intended to transfer one thousand POWs from Camp Douglas, which had suffered a recent barracks fire.

At the same time, a large group of POWs who had been recently captured at Lookout Mountain and Missionary Ridge, Tennessee, were being held in a Louisville, Kentucky, prison. Eventually, they would be transferred to Rock Island about two weeks before those from Chicago, making them the first prisoners incarcerated at the new facility.

Rock Island was a government-owned island in the Mississippi River between Davenport, Iowa, and Rock Island and Moline, Illinois. It was about three miles long and a half mile wide, with a solid foundation of limestone rock, from which it got its name. The island had been appropriated by the U.S. government back in 1804 but had remained unoccupied until 1812, when war broke out with Great Britain. By 1816 a fort named Fort Armstrong in honor of the then-current Secretary of War was established on the west end of the island. It remained garrisoned by troops until May 1836. In 1840 the government established an ordnance depot there but moved the stores to the St. Louis Arsenal in 1845. In 1862 the island was converted into an arsenal for the Union. At that time, it was connected to the Iowa side of the river by a 1,550-foot, government-owned bridge and to the Illinois side by two bridges, one to the town of Rock Island and the other to the town of Moline.

Colonel Hoffman had furnished the plans for the prison, which called for eighty-four barracks surrounded by a rough board fence. Each barrack was to be one hundred feet long, twenty-two feet wide, and twelve feet high with twelve windows, two doors, and two roof ventilators. At the west end of each building was a kitchen or cookhouse eighteen feet long. The remaining eighty-two feet would be living and sleeping quarters for the prisoners. Sixty double bunks had been moved into each building so that each barrack could house 120 POWs, setting the planned capacity at 10,080.[157]

A site at the center of the north side of the island, facing the Iowa side of the river, had been chosen, and construction began at the end of August. At that time, Meigs informed the builder that the barracks "should be put up in the roughest and cheapest manner, mere shanties, with no fine work about them." The barracks, six rows of fourteen buildings each, were erected thirty feet apart facing 100-foot-wide streets, except the fourth row, which fronted a 130-foot-wide avenue, one of two that bisected the prison. The stockade fence enclosing the site was twelve feet high with a board walkway along the outside, four feet from the top, with sentry boxes every one hundred feet. Double-gate sally ports were constructed on the east and west ends of the prison and were the only openings into the facility. Guardhouses were built outside the fence at each gate.[158]

On December 3, 1863, the first prisoners—5,592 in all—arrived at the new facility. On the day of their arrival, the temperature stood at thirty-two degrees below zero and two feet of snow lay on the ground. Worse, it was discovered that ninety-four of those prisoners had smallpox. Hoffman had neglected to include any construction plans for a hospital at his new prison camp. Consequently, the sick had to be left in the barracks among the healthy. By the end of the month, 245 were sick, from smallpox and pneumonia, and 94 had died. Before long, there would be an average of more than 250 deaths a month in the prison's first four months of operation.[159]

A number of depot prisons of minor importance also came into existence in 1863. In addition to the training-camp barracks used in Louisville, Union authorities used McLean Barracks on West Third Street in Cincinnati; the Athenaeum building in Wheeling, West Virginia; an old carriage factory at the corner of Fifth and Buttonwood Streets in Philadelphia; and Fort Mifflin, seven miles below Philadelphia.

Mifflin was a small fort on Mud Island in the middle of the Delaware River. Like all the other forts used by the Union, Mifflin had no actual accommodations for prisoners. Those held there were confined in three poorly ventilated bombproofs, underground structures used as safe haven from enemy shelling. Seventy-five Union soldiers being held for criminal violations were confined in one, fifty-eight political prisoners were held in another, and eighty-three Confederate POWs were imprisoned in the third.

Federal authorities occasionally used the Louisiana State House in Baton Rouge to hold prisoners until it was gutted by fire, and a number of Confederate naval officers were held in a small enclosure on Mare Island in San Francisco Bay in California.

The Kansas-Missouri area also possessed an insignificant makeshift prison that held a handful of prisoners for a very short time, but what happened there propelled the facility into national significance.

In a frustrated effort to curb guerrilla activity in western Missouri and eastern Kansas, Brigadier General Thomas Ewing, Jr., commanding the District of the

Border, issued the now-infamous General Order No. 11 on August 25, 1863: "First: All persons living in Cass, Jackson, and Bates Counties, Missouri, and in that part of Vernon County, included in this district, are hereby ordered to move from their present places of residence within 15 days from [now]. Those who within that time establish their loyalty to the satisfaction of the commanding officer . . . will receive from him certificates stating that facts of their loyalty and the names by whom it can be shown."[160]

In effect, the order demanded that all inhabitants of the Missouri counties that bordered Kansas pack up and get out if they were in any way related to any member of William C. Quantrill's band or any other Southern-sympathizing band roaming the area, or if they had at any time aided any member in any way, such as providing them shelter, horses, or food.

The intent of the decree was to eventually transfer known relatives and Southern sympathizers in this part of Missouri to the Confederate state of Arkansas in the hope that the guerrillas and bushwhackers would follow.

The order continued: "Second: all grain or hay in the fields or under shelter in the district from which the inhabitants are required to move . . . will be taken to [local military] stations and turned over to the proper officers there. . . . All grain and hay found in such district after the ninth day of September next, not moved . . . will be destroyed."[161]

Ewing's demand was backed by President Lincoln. Under threat of execution, hundreds of families abandoned their property and fled south. After September 9, Ewing's troops rode across the countryside, destroying all that was abandoned and ordered those who lingered to leave. "I have the honor to report," boasted Ewing, "orders of banishment against sixty-four persons, many of them heads of families, living in Kansas City and its vicinity and Independence and its vicinity. . . . A large number have been placed upon a suspected list and orders will be given the detective force to keep them under close surveillance until additional evidence is obtained."[162]

"Tell them to prepare their clothing and baggage for a journey southward," declared one Union officer. "They shall be sent to the people and region they hurrah for."[163]

Up to this point, Union soldiers had been scouring the countryside and taking women into custody from the farms and towns in Bates, Cass, Jackson, and Lafayette counties, charging them with such crimes as sheltering guerrillas or buying percussion caps or men's clothing with stolen money. The women were taken to Kansas City, Missouri, and confined to rooms in the Union Hotel with military guards stationed outside their doors.[164]

On July 29, nearly a month before the official order was ever issued, the Kansas City *Daily Journal* reported that guards had arrived in the city on July 28 with seven females "of the bushwhacking persuasion" to be held until they could be sent out of the country. "The squad which brought them in," the article continued, "was fired upon from the bush."[165]

As the hotel rooms set aside for these prisoners became more and more crowded, General Ewing left for St. Louis to confer with military authorities there. When he returned on August 9, permission was granted for General Order No. 11.[166]

Within days, the Order was officially issued. "They were banished and robbed by the same order," exclaimed John McCorkle, who rode in Quantrill's band. "Their horses, mules and cattle had already been stolen and taken to Kansas, along with their buggies, carriages and wagons. . . . They did not have very much left to move." The mass exodus from the region continued as Union troops swept over the land, burning houses, barns, outbuildings, and crops. The destruction was so complete that years after the war the area continued to be known as the "burnt district."[167]

In Kansas City, however, the Union Hotel had become overcrowded before the order was ever issued. So eleven female prisoners, or "the guerrillas' women," as they were referred to at the time, were moved to a large three-story brick building at 1409 Grand Avenue. These particular prisoners had high-profile names associated with Quantrill's band. Among them were Mary, Josephine, and Jenny Anderson, sisters of Bill Anderson, who would later acquire the nickname "Bloody Bill;" Susan Vandiver and Armenia Gilvey, cousins of Cole Younger; Charity Kerr, sister of John McCorkle; Nannie Harris McCorkle, John's sister-in-law; Mollie Grindstaff, Martha Munday, Susan Munday Womacks, and Lou Munday Gray, whose brothers, husbands, and cousins all rode with Quantrill.

"My [sister and sister-in-law] went to Kansas City in a wagon," declared John McCorkle, "driving a yoke of oxen, with a load of wheat to exchange it for flour, the women having all the buying to do. When they were ready to start home . . . [a neighbor] reported to the authorities that these two women were rebels and were buying flour to feed the bushwhackers. They were immediately arrested and placed in jail with some other girls, who had been arrested and sentenced to be banished."[168]

The majority of these women were less than twenty-one years old. The youngest, Jenny Anderson, was ten. Still, even while confined in the building, they were all required to wear an iron ball attached to one leg.[169]

The building was situated along a ravine in what was part of the Metropolitan Block of McGee's Addition, between 14th and 15th streets, in the heart of the middle-class neighborhood where most of the city's German population lived. The building had been built by E. M. "Milton" McGee, a wealthy influential political leader in the city, but it was owned by Mrs. George C. Bingham.[170]

When originally built in 1857, the building appeared strong and stable, but its foundation was poorly constructed. By the time the Civil War broke out, its floors had begun to sag and had to be reinforced with wooden supports. Very little maintenance or upkeep had been done since.

The first story of the building contained a grocer and liquor shop. The third story was vacant. The "guerrillas' women" were confined in somewhat dilapidated, unkempt, rooms on the second floor. The women were guarded by sentries assigned from Ewing's Kansas troops.

Sometime between August 10 and 13, Joshua Thorne, the Kansas City post surgeon, supposedly inspected the prison and advised General Ewing that the structure was unsafe and the women should be moved as soon as possible. Nothing was done.

On the afternoon of August 13, some of the women incarcerated on the second floor became alarmed when the building began to creak and groan. When the south portion of the structure seemed to settle, plaster cracked and fell from the ceiling and walls in several places. The women became more alarmed when they heard people on the floor below frantically running around in the store and saw the grocer moving his stock out into the street.[171]

As a guard accompanied Nannie Harris McCorkle and Mary Anderson out into the hall to get a pail of water, he noticed the building sway. Immediately, as the women in another room began screaming about the roof, the guard grabbed both women and raced down the stairway. At the same time, ten-year-old Jenny Anderson, in another room, tried to climb out a nearby window, but found it impossible with a 12-pound ball chained to her ankle. Suddenly, the building collapsed.[172]

Scared off at first by the sudden rumble, passersby began to return and gather around the site. There they saw crushed and mangled bodies in the rubble. Groans and screams of pain were heard. Someone in the ruins cried out for help in moving the bricks off her head. After a while, her cries became faint and stopped.[173]

As the initial shock of the catastrophe faded, members of the gathering crowd began trying to help. They jerked on, pulled at, and finally moved the heavy debris from the immense pile of rubble, locating the victims one by one.

Susan Vandiver, Armenia Gilvey, Charity Kerr, and thirteen-year-old Josephine Anderson were found dead. Martha Munday was hurt badly and later died. Sixteen-year-old Mary Anderson was severely injured and would remain crippled for the rest of her life. Nan Harris McCorkle was injured but not seriously, as was the guard who carried her and Mary down the stairs as the building came tumbling down. Jenny Anderson was pulled out of the rubble with two broken legs, the ball and chain still attached to one. Susan Munday Womacks, Lou Munday Gray, and Mollie Grindstaff were also hurt, but would survive.[174]

Very little was mentioned in the next day's local newspaper—ten lines on column four of page three. "The large three story brick building, occupied for the last two weeks as a guard house, fell in yesterday afternoon carrying with it the adjoining building south. There were in the building at the time, nine women prisoners, two children and one man. Four women were killed; the balance escaped without fatal injuries."[175]

Several days later the incident was mentioned in the St. Louis papers and in the *New York Times* with very little detail.

Rumors persisted for many years afterward that Union soldiers, at the direction of General Ewing, deliberately undermined the building to cause it to collapse. The building's owners later sued the Federal government for damages, but the only thing Ewing was really guilty of was failing to move the prisoners when warned the building was in a dangerous condition.[176]

By the end of 1863, prison officials all across the nation were coping with death and disaster in all forms. Prisoners suffered from overcrowding and the unusually cold winter as far south as Salisbury, North Carolina; epidemics of smallpox were emerging or reemerging at St. Louis, Alton, Camp Douglas, Johnson's Island, Fort Delaware, and Point Lookout in the North, and Danville in the South. In the last three months of the year alone the deaths in the six Federal prisons ravaged by smallpox totaled nearly 1,500 and were on the increase. The Union POW population stood at nearly 41,000, the greatest numbers held at Point Lookout, Rock Island, Camp Douglas, Camp Morton, Fort Delaware, Camp Chase, Old Capitol, Johnson's Island, and Alton. The Confederacy held nearly 21,000, mainly concentrated in Richmond, Charleston, Columbia, Macon, Lynchburg, and Danville. Authorities on both sides now realized the war would not be a temporary affair. For the most part, POWs on both sides had come to the same conclusion.

Chapter 8

THE OVERSEERS

Beyond the "dead-line" fell his head—
The eager sentry drew his mark
and with a crash the bullet sped
into his brain, and all was dark.

First Lieutenant G. H. Hollister,
2nd Ohio Regiment

The men chosen to oversee, run, and guard the prisons were assigned arbitrarily. Prison commandants and guards received no special training and had no special qualifications for their assignments. As a result, POWs often suffered a great deal from their captors' lack of direction, lack of interest, and lack of compassion.

Prison commandants, in both the North and South, fit into four different categories: 1) those who were appointed to the position to use the guard unit as a core to assemble enough men to form a full regiment and then head out with them to the seat of war, 2) those who received their position purely out of political patronage, 3) those who had been captured and been released after taking the Oath of Allegiance, preventing them from serving elsewhere, and 4) those who had been severely wounded or were just plain incompetent elsewhere.

These men seldom held a rank higher than colonel, yet they might oversee a facility holding anywhere from 3,000 to 20,000 prisoners. A colonel out in the field, on the other hand, never oversaw more than 1,000 to 1,500 men.

The practice of rapidly transferring commandants in and out of the facilities did not help matters. Under such circumstances, many tended to ignore the sufferings of the prisoners and rarely bothered to seek improvement of conditions or even to exercise authority over acts of violence by the guards. In fact, some never bothered to visit inside the compounds during their short stays. Those who served longer periods, however, often took steps to improve the prisons, but they found their resources and possibilities limited.

161

A few prison commandants were well-liked and later honored by their prisoners, such as Colonel Dimick of Fort Warren and Colonel Richard D. Owen of Camp Morton in the North, and Lieutenant Colonel Robert C. Smith of Danville and Lieutenant J. T. W. Hairston and Colonel Godwin of Richmond in the South. Most, however, proved to be incompetent, inefficient, or just plain ineffective. Some were downright brutal. The most notorious of these in the Confederacy was probably Lieutenant Todd of Richmond.

David Humphreys Todd, born in Lexington, Kentucky, in 1832, was the second of fourteen children in a semiwealthy, slave-owning family. He was also the half brother of Mary Todd Lincoln. The outbreak of Civil War eventually divided the family. Eight of the children supported the Confederacy along with their father while six, including Mary, supported the Union.

According to his family, even by his midteens, David had become notorious. He was in trouble with the law on several occasions and ran away from home, only to return months later with a tattoo of the Chilean flag on his arm. When the Civil War broke out, Todd was working as a plantation overseer, whose responsibility was to keep slaves in line. He was said to be brutal in that position. After receiving his commission in the Confederate army, he was stationed in Richmond and, at 29 years old, placed in charge of Confederate POWs in that city. He quickly gained a reputation for being cruel and harsh and, according to many prisoners' accounts, he harassed and tortured the prisoners at every opportunity. According to a number of prison memoirs, Todd was intoxicated and belligerent most of the time. In October 1861, he was promoted to captain and transferred out of Richmond to the western front. In July 1863, Captain Todd was severely wounded at Vicksburg and died soon afterward.[1]

The Union's equivalent to Todd was probably Albin Francisco Schoepf, the commandant of the Fort Delaware Prison. Although Schoepf was not personally involved in individual cases of abuse, he allowed subordinate henchmen free rein inside the prison to abuse, mistreat, and torture the captives at will.

Born in Poland in 1822, Schoepf received his military education at an Austrian academy and, after working his way up to major in the Polish Legion during the Hungarian revolution, he was exiled to Turkey. He then became an artillery instructor in the Ottoman service. In 1851 Schoepf came to America and, for a time, worked as a beer vendor in St. Louis. Later he went to Washington and took a job as a porter at the Willard Hotel. His former military career came to the attention of Joseph Holt, patent commissioner, who then made Schoepf a draftsman in the patent office. When Holt became secretary of war under President Buchanan, he transferred Schoepf to the War Department and pushed to get him appointed brigadier general at the opening of the Civil War.[2]

Schoepf made a good impression with a victory at Wild Cat Camp, Kentucky, and was given command of a division at Perryville. Shortly afterward he resigned his command, reportedly because of deafness that resulted from a wound. Within six months of the Battle of Perryville, Schoepf was given command of Fort Delaware.[3]

Second in command under Schoepf at Fort Delaware was Captain George W. Ahl, assistant adjutant and inspecting officer. Ahl arrived at the prison with the first large wave of POWs during the second year of the war and supposedly received his appointment from Secretary Stanton. Ahl exercised more authority over the prisoners than did General Schoepf and was, as a result, more intensely despised by them. Ahl's assistant, Lieutenant Abraham G. Wolfe, from Philadelphia, was equally hated by the prisoners, as were Sergeant Jim O'Neil and "a cussing Yank called 'Hike Out.'"[4]

"Old Hike," as he was referred to in some accounts, got his nickname because he was constantly yelling "Hike out! Hike out! You damned rebel sons of bitches!" at the prisoners as he strutted through the barracks wielding a wooden club, or sometimes a rawhide whip, followed by two armed guards with fixed bayonets. "His real name was Adam or Adams," reported Fort Delaware prisoner Charles W. Rivenbark. "[He was] a Vermont Yank who was first sent to the prison as a convict—his crime being that he was the first man to reach Washington City after the Bull Run battle."[5]

His presence in the barracks meant a trip for all of those prisoners to "Hell's Half Acre," a little triangular area lying between the bay and the prison barracks on the northern tip of the island. "Once a week," Rivenbark continued, "he would 'hike' us [out of the barracks] to search our persons, bunks and clothing for contraband articles, and Whack! would come his heavy stick on the person of some poor sick prisoner who was not able to move promptly."[6]

"Once," Rivenbark reported, "he caused about 500 of us to strip, saying he would furnish new clothes, but as soon as we had been 'hiked out' of all clothing except our shirts, right face, forward, double-quick, march! and through the cold mud and water to our cheerless barracks we went . . . to get more clothes as best we could."[7]

"When a new lot of men were brought in," related prisoner Calvin P. Dearing of Virginia, "the sutler was permitted to sell pocket knives at $1 each. Then the guard, under the direction of 'Hike Out,' would force all the knives to be thrown into a barrel [and] they were given back to the sutler, who would repeat the act with the next new bunch."[8]

The authorities at Fort Delaware practiced all sorts of tricks and swindles on the prisoners under their control. Knives, soap, blankets, overcoats, extra sticks of firewood or lumps of coal were all confiscated.

The prisoners learned to hate these keepers with a vengeance. "Hike" was described in a number of accounts as vengeful, bordering on psychotic. Ahl was described as having been excessively strict and petty. Wolfe was said to have strolled through the barracks wearing a Confederate uniform just so he could catch prisoners breaking the rules. The prisoners nicknamed Wolfe "the spaniel" and "the fox," while they referred to General Schoepf as "General Terror."[9]

A number of subordinates in other Union prisons also acquired personal reputations for cruelty and abuse. A Lieutenant Holmes, whose nickname was "Bullhead," slapped and kicked prisoners, both Union and Confederate, at Old Capitol Prison; Lieutenant Charles O. Wood kicked and beat prisoners at Fort Lafayette; and Major Allen G. Brady swindled and physically abused captives at Point Lookout.

Additional thugs with authority in the southern prisons included Richard "Dick" Turner, who was ill-tempered and quick to resort to physical violence at Libby Prison; George W. Alexander, who was involved in medieval torture at Richmond's Castle Thunder; and Lieutenant George W. Emack, who was nicknamed "Yankee-killer" and "Bowie-knife" by the prisoners he commanded.[10]

A number of prison commandants also profited from their positions at the expense of the prisoners. In an incident at Johnson's Island, a prisoner escaped and was later recaptured at Newark, Ohio. Upon his return to the prison, Major William S. Pierson informed him that the government had incurred an expense of $10 in his recapture and that amount would be deducted from his money being held. In another incident, Major Pierson and the prison sutler arranged for photographs to be taken of the island and prison with the intent of selling copies to the prisoners as mementos of their stay. They set the price at $5, but few photos were sold. Soon afterward, prisoners were prohibited from ordering necessities from the sutler unless they also gave Pierson permission to deduct the cost of a photograph from their money. Out of "kindness," however, Pierson reduced the price of each photo to $3. "So," complained one prisoner, "a man could not buy a plug of tobacco unless he also contributed three dollars for the benefit of the sutler and his master."[11]

Sometimes the commandants or their subordinates worked in collusion with contractors to reduce the quality or quantity of prisoner rations for personal profit. Such cases happened at Camp Chase, Camp Douglas, and Point Lookout. In one incident, a commissary was dismissed from service for his underhanded dealings but, because of political influence, was later reinstated.[12]

Money was automatically confiscated to be credited to the prisoner's account, but in some cases credit was never given. In the South it was often claimed that such packages or envelopes had been chewed up by rats while stored in warehouses. In other instances, perhaps, it was simply a case of poor record-keeping rather than theft. In the North, credit was taken from prisoners' accounts for package delivery charges. At Johnson's Island, for instance, prisoners were charged up to $2 for each package delivery to "defray expenses from Sandusky to the island."[13]

Camp Randall, established at the state fairgrounds near Madison, Wisconsin, was only used as a POW facility for three months during the spring of 1862, yet became well-known for the thefts that occurred there.

In April 1862, a total of 1,156 prisoners from the surrender of Island No. 10 were confined in the stables and cowsheds, and the machinery expo building was used as their mess hall. Governor Alexander Randall, for whom the camp was named, immediately sent the 19th Wisconsin Volunteer Regiment, raw recruits who had just completed training in Racine, for guard duty. The commander of the unit, Colonel Horace T. Sanders, was placed in charge of the POW camp. Within five days the officers and soldiers had diverted the entire stock of supplies intended for the prisoners to their own use, including 168 pint bottles of liquor in the medical stores.[14]

Granted, prison duty was an unpleasant, demoralizing, and disagreeable task. It was seldom, if ever, a duty requested by commanders or troops, so it became necessary for them to be assigned. Except for rotating units who were preparing for, or returning from the front, all of the best commanders, all of the most competent officers, and all of the most physically fit soldiers were sent to the front. The same held true for the guard units. Consequently, those assigned to the POW facilities were the ones left behind. More often than not, they included the ineffective, the incompetent, the undisciplined, the dishonest, the lazy, and those on disability. Some had been POWs themselves. That experience affected men in different ways. Some were more compassionate to their charges because of it and could identify with them, while others became excessively strict, hateful, or violent. According to many prisoners' accounts, the best commandants and the best guards were the seasoned veterans, the ones who had been to the seat of war—those who had "seen the elephant."

Seldom, though, were veterans used. In both the North and the South, such troops were too valuable and needed at the front, especially later in the war. Throughout the conflict, then, a wide variety of troops were tried at various times to fill the duty. In the South, conscripted militia—men eighteen to thirty-five who were drafted for three years' service—were used. The drawback, in this case, was that anyone who was really interested in active service had already joined. In the North, organized companies of the Invalid Corps, made up of veteran troops injured or wounded in combat and unfit for full combat duty but who could perform limited duty, were used. After March 1864, the corps' name was changed to the Veteran Reserve Corps. The Confederacy also had an Invalid Corps, but it was never organized into companies. The Union also used black troops as sentries in a number of prisons after February 1864. At various times, both sides tried using recently trained recruits and men too old for active service. The South even tried those too young for active service, such as cadets from local military schools.[15]

Troops specifically trained for sentry duty were organized for use at Johnson's Island Military Prison when it was first established, but the Union never repeated the procedure for any other facility. These, too, were young, raw recruits. "Some of them are mere children in appearance," observed one Rebel prisoner at the island, "and present a strange contrast to the grim warriors whom they guard."[16]

The 37th Iowa Volunteer Regiment, known as the Graybeards, was another alternative. This three-year regiment was made up of men forty-five years or older and consisted of some of the oldest men in service, including a man of eighty. It was specifically organized to relieve veteran troops from garrison duty and at various times was used to guard prison facilities at St. Louis, Alton, Rock Island, Camp Chase, Camp Morton, and a number of other locations. But Union Surgeon John F. Marsh, during one inspection of a prison where a number of escapes had occurred, referred to the unit as "a regiment of decrepit old men and the most unpromising subjects for soldiers I ever saw."[17]

The Confederacy found that extreme youth wasn't necessarily the answer either. At Salisbury Prison a fourteen-year-old guard shot a POW who had gotten "too close" to the deadline. It had to be explained to the young man that the deadline itself was the actual limit, and if it was crossed and the prisoner refused to go back, then and only then could he shoot the prisoner. Moments later, the young guard was startled upon hearing the gate open, and he quickly turned and fired off a round at the officer of the day as he entered the prison yard. The "jumpy" lad, it was immediately decided, was better suited to duty outside the prison walls.[18]

Such incompetent antics weren't confined to the young or to the South. Many prisoners reported incidents of guards stumbling on the staircases in Gratiot Street and Old Capitol prisons, causing their guns to discharge in the hallways and narrowly missing prisoners in their rooms. Guards also killed themselves accidentally and each other at several prison sites including Richmond, Salisbury, Washington City, St. Louis, Alton, Elmira, and Point Lookout.

"One day two of them was on post in the streets and met up at the end of their lines and commenced fooling with their guns [in] what they called playing bayonets," revealed Point Lookout prisoner Bartlett Yancey Malone, Company H, 6th North Carolina Regiment. "They had their guns cocked [and] presently one of their guns went off and shot the other one through the breast [and] he fell dead; the other one says 'Jim, Jim get up from there, you're not hurt, you're just trying to fool me.'" Within a few days, at this same prison, another guard accidentally (or on purpose) shot himself in the mouth while on sentry duty.[19]

When the guards weren't shooting themselves or each other, they were harassing the prisoners with gunfire. "Our guards represented a rather curious mixture of good-natured indifference and a kind of half-witted cruelty," observed one prisoner. "Without any provocation they fired into one of the blocks," declared another prisoner.[20]

"On [our] first night in that prison," remembered John Robinson, Company B, 12th Louisiana Regiment, regarding his transfer with a large group of captives to Point Lookout Prison, "the guards shot into the prison all around, the fusillade lasting ten minutes. It was like a strong skirmish fight. . . . On the following morning we were told that the firing the night before was simply a custom when a new lot of prisoners were put in."[21]

It is possible what Robinson heard was merely the guards emptying their weapons at the conclusion of their watch, since smoothbore muskets couldn't be unloaded and had to be fired to be cleared, but the possibility also exists that the guards did indeed commence firing into the pen for fun or could have made a practice of clearing their weapons over or into the pens. A number of documented cases do exist of POWs being randomly shot at night. "Their firing into the barracks during the night," declared Rock Island prisoner J. W. Minnich, "became a matter of such common occurrence that men in the outer rows next to the dead line feared to sleep on the upper and middle bunks."[22]

The walls of the Pemberton warehouse in Richmond were said to be scarred by daily or at least weekly shootings inside and outside the building. The same occurred at Richmond's other buildings as well. At Crew's warehouse a prisoner was shot in the head by a sentry from below when the POW stuck his head out the window and taunted the guard.[23]

Shooting at prisoners was said to be a daily activity at many prisons, both day and night. Testimony gathered by the U.S. Sanitary Commission revealed that as many as fourteen shots a day were fired in some prisons—and that was just in the South.

On December 4, 1863, Union guards at the POW Convalescent Barracks in Nashville, Tennessee, were given orders to shoot any prisoners seen in the windows throwing objects down at passersby. That same morning, one prisoner "did throw two pieces of brick out of the window [and] afterward got in the window and was spitting down upon Federal officers." He was shot dead. The next day, another prisoner got up in the window and began "making sport of the sentinel." He, too, was shot dead.[24]

At Camp Chase a guard yelled out from the parapet for the POWs in one of the barracks to extinguish a light and fired into the building, mortally wounding a prisoner. "As sad as this case may be, to wound a perhaps innocent man," equivocated Lieutenant Colonel August H. Poten, 7th Regiment Invalid Corps, in charge of the guard detail, "it has proved to be a most excellent lesson, very much needed in that prison—No. 1—as the rebel officers confined in that prison showed frequently before a disposition to disobey the orders given to them by our men."[25]

At Camp Douglas, a guard saw a prisoner step over the deadline and fired off a round that entered a nearby barracks, wounding two prisoners. In another incident, a guard ordered a prisoner to stop urinating in a street of Prison Square. Before the POW could comply, he was shot. Similar frivolous shootings, having no correlation whatsoever with escape attempts or life-threatening moves against the guard, occurred at Camp Morton, Johnson's Island, Gratiot Street, Point Lookout, and many other POW facilities, both North and South.[26]

Some troops drawing sentry duty weren't just incompetent; they were corrupt. In nearly every prison there were guards who could be bribed for extra food, tobacco, clothing, or to look the other way during an escape. Oftentimes, though, the guards would accept whatever valuable the prisoner had to offer—be it a good pair of boots, a blanket, money, or whatever—only to inform his superiors soon afterward.

"In the dead hours of the night," explained a prisoner at Libby Prison, "men could be seen prowling around the prison, in the hope that some means of escape might [be found]. Often on dark, stormy nights the guards would come up for temporary shelter [against the prison] walls where, unobserved by anyone from the outside, they would enter into conversation with the prisoners, often giving expressions of sympathy. Among them frequently was found a man of Northern birth who had been conscripted into the Confederate army and was at heart a Unionist. Bribes were sometimes offered by the prisoners and taken by the guards; but attempts to escape by that means generally resulted in the prisoner being handed over to the authorities, after he had gotten outside and given up his valuables."[27]

Guards at Danville, Virginia, became notorious for conning POWs out of their blankets. "There was a great deal of stealing of blankets by the guards," observed William W. Wilcox, 124th Ohio Volunteer Regiment. "The men traded their blankets for rice; the guards would bring rice, from 15 to 20 pounds, and offer (an) exchange for our blankets; they would come to the windows and say 'stick your blanket out so I can get hold of the end of it' then two or more of the guards would jerk the blanket away and not [pass up] the rice; the guards would pass in bags of sand in place of the rice and take the blankets." Another prisoner complained, "All sorts of swindles, cheats and tricks were practiced upon us, even to the robbing us of . . . a jacket or pair of pants by specious promises."[28]

If the guards weren't corrupt or mean, they were often inattentive or lax. Two boats were constructed by a group of prisoners at Point Lookout, virtually under the guards' noses, over a period of several days before they were finally discovered and destroyed. Quite often, POWs were able to gather a wide variety of items from around the prisons in preparing their escapes. "Last Sunday," reported one prisoner, "we were all turned out of our blocks by the guard and a general search was made. Some strange articles were brought to light. Among them were ladders, sails, spades and various digging tools."[29]

At Tuscaloosa, Union POWs were able to counterfeit Confederate money for several days before being discovered by the guard. A group of POWs had discovered a printing press and various plates moved off to one corner of their prison building. Teaching themselves its operation, the prisoners began churning out counterfeit money and distributing it through outside sources. "The boys made about $300 in this way," advised one reporter. "The Richmond papers have chronicled with disgust [the counterfeit paper currency's] appearance in that capital."[30]

Another big problem in the prisons was the abuse of alcohol. A number of commandants, guards, and other prison authorities were said to have been intoxicated much of the time. Many eyewitness accounts relating cases of physical abuse or shootings of POWs mentioned that the prison authority involved was drunk when the incident took place. The question also came up in several official boards of inquiry related to the shooting of POWs. Compounding the problem, no doubt, was the fact that during the Civil War, being intoxicated on duty was not a military offense, only any misconduct while in that condition.[31]

Lieutenant William C. Harris of Baker's California Regiment claimed that the entire squad that guarded Ligon's prison during the midnight shift was inebriated much of the time. "It was not until eleven o'clock at night that [we] were again under the protection of the drunken guards," advised Harris. "During the evening a Federal officer who was noted for quaint drollery and waggish humor, approached the sentinel at the door and proposed to stand guard, stating that he desired the soldier to purchase for him a canteen of liquor. To our astonishment, the proposal was accepted; and . . . it must be recorded . . . Federal prisoners of war in Richmond were guarded [for a time] . . . by a United States officer, a prisoner of war." When the guard returned with their full canteen, the POWs generously shared it with him in appreciation.[32]

Relationships between POWs of different battles and guards of various regiments often varied from good to bad. Respect, friendship, or compassion sometimes developed between keepers and those kept at a number of locations at different times. Good rapport formed between Colonel Smith and the prisoners at Danville and Colonel Owen and prisoners at Camp Morton. Captain Chichester and his cadet guards were well-liked by the POWs at Castle Pinckney.

There were also numerous individual cases of renewed relationships or friendships in many prisons. A Private Jack Davis was a guard over his old friend and classmate John Dooley, Company H, 1st Virginia Regiment, at a Baltimore facility and watched out for his friend's best interests while guarding him there. Lieutenant Alonzo Cooper, 12th New York Cavalry, became friends with a guard at Columbia, South Carolina, who later looked the other way as Cooper and a number of his comrades escaped; a POW discovered his brother, who had been living in the South "for a good many years," as one of his guards at Belle Isle Prison; and at Point Lookout one of the U.S. Colored Troops assigned as guards recognized a former master among the prisoners, gave him $10, and befriended him during his stay.[33]

For the most part, though, the lack of trained, competent, qualified, and professional commandants and guards compounded the problems in the prisons. Improper management caused corruption; the unavailability of competent leadership led to chaos; and the lack of training created misunderstanding, frustration, and anger.

As General Winder once observed, "The same difficulty occurs at all the prisons, and if we can get reserves, or any other troops, we must be satisfied and do the best we can with them."[34]

1864

Some of the first Civil War POWs in the west were confined in the barracks of the Alamo, often referred to as the San Antonio barracks (left section of the photo). COURTESY OF THE DAUGHTERS OF THE REPUBLIC OF TEXAS LIBRARY.

Henrico County Jail, reproduced in Harper's. *The jail was one of the first Richmond facilities to come into use for holding prisoners of war in the east.*

The Virginia State Penitentiary on the west side of Richmond.
COURTESY OF THE NATIONAL ARCHIVES.

Richmond's 25th and Main prison buildings, reproduced in Harper's. *The first private building confiscated by the Confederacy for prison use was Ligon's Tobacco Warehouse (center building with step facade). The neighboring buildings soon were pressed into use as well.*

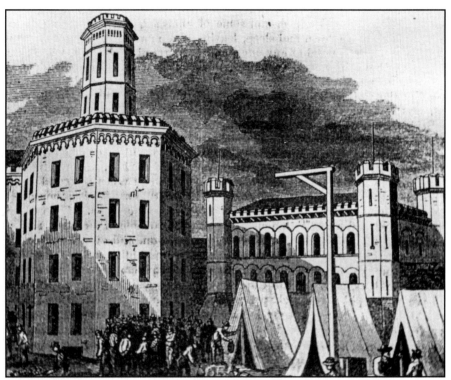

Charleston City Jail, reproduced in Harper's, *was used as a POW facility throughout the war. The first arrivals were held on the first and third floors until their transfer to Castle Pinckney.*

Castle Pinckney, Charleston Harbor. Note the bricked-up casemates, which were used as individual rooms for confining POWs. A great camaraderie developed between the cadet guards (lounging at the top) and the prisoners held below. COURTESY OF THE LIBRARY OF CONGRESS.

Salisbury Prison, North Carolina. By 1864, POWs resorted to climbing the oak trees located throughout the compound for the acorns. Courtesy of the North Carolina Collection, University of North Carolina Library at Chapel Hill.

A detailed view of the main prison building, drawn by Sergeant Fred Will, 20th Massachusetts Volunteer Regiment, a prisoner held at Salisbury. Courtesy of the North Carolina Division of Archives and History.

The infamous Tombs prison in New York City, reproduced for Valentine's Manual of Old New York.

Fort Lafayette was referred to as the American Bastille by prisoners held there. It became the last Union facility to release its POWs, the last one leaving in March 1866. COURTESY OF THE NEW YORK SOUTHERN SOCIETY.

Castle Williams on Governors Island in New York Harbor held Confederate enlisted men; Fort Columbus, on the other end of the island, held Confederate officers. COURTESY OF THE NATIONAL ARCHIVES.

Fort Warren in Boston Harbor. A seldom-seen view of the fort's garrison standing in formation on the interior parade grounds.
COURTESY OF THE BOSTONIAN SOCIETY.

POWs under guard at Fort Warren. Conditions remained fairly stable at this facility until the collapse of the exchange cartel.
COURTESY OF THE U.S. ARMY MILITARY HISTORY INSTITUTE.

Fort McHenry's stockade-enclosed stables. By May and June 1863, more than 1,500 prisoners would be confined in a facility with a capacity of 600. DETAIL FROM AN E. SACHSE & CO. LITHOGRAPH, COURTESY OF ENOCH PRATT FREE LIBRARY.

Fort Delaware, referred to as the Fort Delaware Death Pen by Confederate prisoners. COURTESY OF THE MASSACHUSETTS COMMANDERY MILITARY ORDER OF THE LOYAL LEGION, U.S. ARMY MILITARY HISTORY INSTITUTE.

This sketch of Fort Delaware by D. Auld, 43d Ohio, appeared in Harper's Weekly *in June 1863. Although the first group of prisoners moved into Fort Delaware in April 1862, the prison did not become a full-fledged POW facility until three months later, when 3,000 more were moved in. The prison became well known as a brutal place of confinement under the command of General Schoepf.* COURTESY OF THE HALL OF RECORDS, DELAWARE STATE ARCHIVES.

Gratiot Street Prison, St. Louis. Originally a medical college, it was converted to prison use in December 1861. Among other renovations, the school's dissecting room was used as a mess hall. COURTESY OF THE ST. LOUIS MERCANTILE LIBRARY ASSOCIATION.

This sketch of Camp Douglas, Chicago, appeared in A History of Camp Douglas *in 1866. Originally a training and rendezvous camp established on the south side of the city, twenty acres were later enclosed by a high-board fence to establish "Prison Square."*

Camp Butler in Springfield, Illinois, was a scaled-down version of Camp Douglas. COURTESY OF THE NATIONAL ARCHIVES.

The main entrance of Camp Morton, Indianapolis, displays an example of Victorian architecture. Officials later took the time to carve "Military Prison Camp Morton" in the middle ribbon trim over the gate. COURTESY OF THE HARGRETT LIBRARY, UNIVERSITY OF GEORGIA.

The interior of Camp Morton, which shows the fairground exhibition barns and halls in the background. The capacity of the confinement area was originally estimated at 2,000. COURTESY OF THE HARGRETT LIBRARY, UNIVERSITY OF GEORGIA.

Old Capitol Prison, Washington. Although the facility would become known as the place of confinement for Confederate spies and the Lincoln conspirators, to the majority of the prisoners held there, it was most notable for its strict discipline and its infestation of bedbugs. COURTESY OF THE LIBRARY OF CONGRESS.

A rear view from Canal Street of Libby Prison in Richmond. Within three days of the prison's establishment, it held 700 POWs; within ten months it held nearly 1,500. Eventually, it would hold an average of 4,200. COURTESY OF THE NATIONAL ARCHIVES.

The front entrance of Libby Prison. Note the guardhouse positioned at the corner to provide the guard with a full view of two sides of the buildings. The whitewash, regularly applied after November 1862, helped the prison look cleaner but was used primarily for security reasons. Potential escapees attempting to climb down the walls at night could be spotted easily against the white background. COURTESY OF THE NATIONAL ARCHIVES.

Belle Isle, Richmond. Numerous historical accounts have pre-sented this prison as being in operation throughout the war. In truth, between June 1862 and October 1864, the prison was established and abandoned three different times. The site was used for only eighteen months. COURTESY OF THE LIBRARY OF CONGRESS.

Castle Thunder, Richmond. Inmates, upon finding themselves confined there, often noted that they must have "invoked the thunder of the gods" to deserve such a wretched place. COURTESY OF THE LIBRARY OF CONGRESS.

This sketch appearing in Prison Life in the Old Capitol *is of the Carroll Prison Annex, Washington. Located to the rear on the next block east of the Old Capitol Prison, the area later became known as the Old Capitol Annex.*

This photograph of Camp Chase in Columbus, Ohio, is a rare glimpse of the conditions inside a prison. Note the closely situated living quarters and the deeply sloped streets. COURTESY OF THE NATIONAL ARCHIVES.

Johnson's Island Military Prison in Sandusky, Ohio, sketched by former prisoner James Andrews for Confederate Veteran. *Although Colonel Hoffman considered Johnson's Island the model military prison, POWs recalled only that the place was known for its cold weather and rats.*

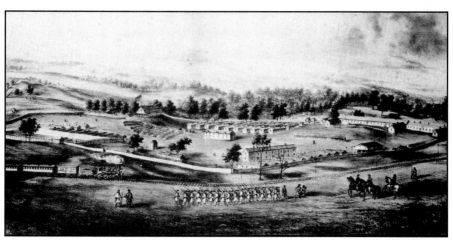

Camp Randall, Madison, Wisconsin. Nearly 1,200 prisoners were moved into this former training camp for a three-month period in early 1862. Within ninety days, 140 POWs died. COURTESY OF THE STATE HISTORICAL SOCIETY OF WISCONSIN.

Danville's Prison No. 6. A smallpox epidemic broke out in this Dibrell Brothers Tobacco Warehouse, and nearly 1,300 prisoners eventually died. COURTESY OF THE MASSACHUSETTS COMMANDERY MILITARY ORDER OF THE LOYAL LEGION, U.S. ARMY MILITARY HISTORY INSTITUTE.

Camp Ford, Texas. Although the prison wasn't established until July 1863, it quickly grew into the largest military prison west of the Mississippi. Courtesy of Archives Division, Texas State Library.

A view of the interior of Rock Island Military Prison in Illinois shows the deadline marked out by white stakes. Although Union authorities denied their use, this clearly shows that deadlines existed. Courtesy of the Department of the Army, Rock Island Arsenal Museum.

Rock Island prisoners standing in line for roll call and rations. POWs on both sides found much of their time consumed by standing in line for everything. COURTESY OF THE DEPARTMENT OF THE ARMY, ROCK ISLAND ARSENAL MUSEUM.

Elmira Prison Camp, New York. The long barracks were originally estimated to be capable of holding up to 4,000 prisoners. More than 9,500 prisoners were confined there by late 1864. COURTESY OF THE LIBRARY OF CONGRESS.

Fort Jefferson, Dry Tortugas Island. The nation's largest fort, construction on the massive structure began in 1846 and remained incomplete in 1861, when it began accepting prisoners. Still, it was ideally isolated for holding POWs. COURTESY OF THE MASSACHUSETTS COMMANDERY MILITARY ORDER OF THE LOYAL LEGION, U.S. ARMY MILITARY HISTORY INSTITUTE.

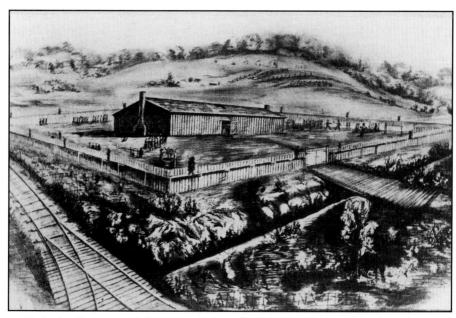

Cahaba Prison, Alabama. Although this sketch implies that the roof was complete, it was only partially finished when the first POWS arrived. COURTESY OF THE LIBRARY OF CONGRESS.

Andersonville, Georgia. Officially known as Camp Sumter, nearly 33,000 POWs were held here during one period; 12,000 died and were buried here. COURTESY OF THE LIBRARY OF CONGRESS.

Castle Reed at Andersonville. A seldom-seen view of the officers' compound used in the beginning days of the prison. Union officer POWs were later transferred to Macon, and the use of Castle Reed reverted to holding Confederates awaiting courts-martial.

Camp Oglethorpe, Macon, Georgia. This compound became most noted among Union prisoners for the number of escape tunnel operations beneath the enclosure.

Camp Sorghum, Columbia, South Carolina, appearing in
Sketches of War History, 1861-1865. *A wide-open field surrounded
by a guard line supported by cannon, the prison site acquired its
name from the large quantity of sorghum molasses provided as
the food ration.*

Camp Asylum, Columbia, South Carolina, sketched by prisoner O. R. Dahl, 15th Wisconsin Infantry. Camp Sorghum prisoners later moved to this location, a portion of the South Carolina State Hospital grounds surrounded by a stockade fence.

Millen Prison, Georgia. Officially named Camp Lawton and constructed with the same plans as Andersonville, this compound was larger, containing forty-two acres, and was somewhat better organized. COURTESY OF THE HARGRETT LIBRARY, UNIVERSITY OF GEORGIA LIBRARIES.

Chapter 9

THE GROWING PRISON CRISIS

*To assemble large numbers of men in crowded quarters . . . keep them
for months deprived of sufficient food . . . is certain to make them hogs,
and very likely to make them devils.*

Anthony M. Keiley, *The Prisoner of War*

A s 1864 began, authorities on both sides privately confided a number of concerns that the previous lack of organization and planning were taking a toll within the military prisons. Overcrowding, which doubled and tripled the original set capacities, was becoming the norm, while smallpox spread through the northern camps and chronic diarrhea and dysentery hit prisons in the south.

"[M]any prisoners are men worn down by disease, fatigue, and hardship," advised William A. Carrington, Confederate medical director, in a January 15 letter to Secretary Seddon, "and these conditions being aggravated by confinement and the hardships inseparable from prison life, cause the death of many, and others to be totally unfit for the duties of a soldier. I respectfully suggest that all such Federal prisoners . . . be paroled and offered to the Federal agent of exchange for return to the North and at the same time that application be made for similar privileges for our own soldiers held as prisoners of war in the United States."[1]

"[T]he ratio of mortality does not exceed that of our own prisoners in the hands of the enemy," General Winder later offered in defense out of his frustration. "[T]he mortality is incident to prison life . . . I do not contend . . . that the quarters, fuel, and rations of the prisoners have been such as were most conducive to their health and comfort. . . . The deficiency in commissary supplies, which has not been confined to this department and for which I am not responsible, has prevented the supply of rations necessary to the health of the prisoners."[2]

Colonel Hoffman advised Secretary Stanton of the problems emerging in the Union's prisons: "[I]t would facilitate the management of the affairs of prisoners of war and lead to a more direct responsibility if the commanders of stations where prisoners are held could be placed under the immediate control of the Commissary-General of Prisoners. . . . [T]hrough frequent change of commanders it is impossible to establish a uniform and permanent system of administration."[3]

"I request that my position in connection with the prisons . . . may be defined," Winder seemed to echo to his secretary of war when similar confusion and lack of control developed in the prisons outside Richmond at about the same time. "I do not wish to be understood as complaining . . . I simply wish to know how I stand in relation to them, for it would be embarrassing for me to issue orders when I had no right to do so, and it would be just as embarrassing for me to neglect to issue orders when I ought to do so."[4]

By midyear Winder was placed in command of all prison facilities in Virginia, Alabama, and Georgia. It wasn't until November 1864, that he was named commissary general of all Confederate prisons. But by then it was practically too late. Both sides reluctantly realized that far-ranging problems had developed beyond their ability to control.

ROCK ISLAND

By the end of January 1864, little more than seven weeks into its existence, 635 of the 8,000 POWs confined at the Rock Island facility were sick, and 325 had died. During the same period, seven of the guards had perished. The POWs, as at nearly all the facilities by this time, no longer cared, or were unable to properly police the grounds or make any substantial effort at any kind of sanitary practices. Rock Island was in the midst of coping with an epidemic and was still without a hospital. When Surgeon and Acting Medical Inspector Augustus M. Clark arrived on February 10, he immediately directed that certain barracks in the southwest section of the compound be designated as hospital facilities and that pesthouses be erected about a half mile outside the prison along the south shore of the island. By the end of February there were still 708 sick and another 346 deaths. The 671 burials took place in a graveyard established about four hundred yards south of the prison. The site was then moved in mid-March, at Clark's suggestion, to a new site one thousand yards southeast of the prison. Union guards, who were succumbing to the smallpox in increased numbers, were buried one hundred yards northwest of the POW cemetery.[5]

The pesthouses were completed that same month and all prisoners suffering from smallpox were moved there. The eleven barracks previously used for them were thoroughly cleaned and whitewashed and, afterward, used as noncontagious disease wards. Meanwhile, as prisoner rations were reduced and the savings placed in a prison fund, a hospital was built from $30,000 that was eventually accumulated in the account.[6]

Rock Island's first commandant was Colonel Richard H. Rush, Invalid Corps, an Englishman from Pennsylvania who, early in the conflict, had commanded the only regiment of Union lancers to see active service in the Civil War. He was relieved in mid-January 1864, by Colonel Andrew J. Johnson of the Invalid Corps, later designated the 4th Regiment, Veteran Reserve Corps, who would remain in command until the war ended.[7]

Unique among the Civil War's prisons, rations at Rock Island were issued in bulk. "Each company of prisoners receives ten days at a time," declared Colonel Johnson, "they having the entire control of the distribution among themselves." One forty-gallon cauldron was placed in each cookhouse and the POWs cooked their own food. Water for the prisoners was supplied by a steam pump which drew it from the river. Whenever the pump malfunctioned, water became scarce, although there was a small artesian well in the compound that supplied some water. Two coal burning stoves in each barracks supplied heat for the prisoners.[8]

By the time Clark left in mid-March the number of sick in the camp had climbed to 1,555, including 420 cases of smallpox, out of the total prison population of 7,260. "Almost all the suffering that has actually occurred," noted Medical Inspector Norton S. Townshend, "has been in consequence of the transportation of prisoners during the extreme cold weather and from the breaking out of the smallpox among them."[9]

As warmer weather arrived, the smallpox declined and cases of pneumonia subsided. Then sanitation became the big concern. "Already the twelve large sinks have been filled and the privies removed three times," advised Captain Reynolds, the assistant quartermaster. "In the spring the camp will unavoidably be muddy and filthy. In the summer the stench caused by excrements will be insufferable."[10]

Reynolds suggested the construction of a reservoir on a small bluff overlooking the prison to help flush out soon-to-be-built open sewers throughout the camp. He also recommended using prison labor to complete the project, paying forty cents a day to be credited to the prisoners' sutler accounts. Hoffman eventually approved the project but insisted that the pay be lowered to only ten cents a day for mechanics and five cents for laborers. Reynolds got the project going, but the system provided little benefit to the POW camp because its completion wasn't until just three months before the war ended.

In the meantime, the antiquated steam pump in the northwest corner of the enclosure, which used a three-inch wooden supply pipe to pump water into four cisterns, stopped working on several occasions, leaving only the artesian well, with a nine-inch bore and 125-foot depth, located just inside the prison's west gate, as the only source of water for more than 8,000 men.

Although the barracks at Rock Island were elevated anywhere from one to three feet off the ground, escape by tunneling was often attempted. On June 14, 1864, ten POWs tunneled out from beneath their barracks and escaped under the south wall. The last two POWs to emerge from the hole were captured by the sentry, who quickly gave the alarm. Guards spread out in all directions and apprehended three more on the island, while a fourth drowned attempting to swim the 400-foot-wide south channel of the Mississippi River. Four more were captured later near the Rock River in Illinois.[11]

In all, forty-one POWs successfully escaped during the prison's existence. Many more would try but fail. In one case, on October 24, 1864, a POW was shot and killed while desperately attempting to escape under the north wall at 1:30 in the afternoon.[12]

Additional security at the prison included a barge fitted with a six-pounder field piece, a twenty-four-pounder howitzer, and a guard crew of thirty-five men anchored in the river with full view of the compound.[13]

By late 1864, conditions at the camp would become even worse. The poor drainage of the island resulted in a small marsh forming in the southwest corner of the enclosure into which the camp sludge would accumulate. Throughout the summer the prison population remained at around eight thousand captives, and by late in the year the total number of deaths reached 1,623.[14]

Northern newspapers, led by the local Rock Island, Illinois, *Argus* and carried by the New York *Daily News*, ran articles comparing the Rock Island Military Prison to some of the worse Southern prisons, later calling it the Andersonville of the North. "Many have taken 'the oath,' any oath," reported one letter published in the newspaper, "to save themselves from actual starvation. All the released ones say that no man can live on the rations given, and there are men who would do anything to get enough to eat. Such is the wretched, ravenous condition of these poor starving creatures that several dogs which have come to the barracks with teams have fallen victims to their hunger, and they are trapping rats and mice for food."[15]

In order to escape these conditions, many POWs did take the oath. In fact, by December, 1864, nearly 1,800 would—more than at any other prison, North or South. These men were placed in quarters separated from the others by a highboard fence and, reportedly, received better rations and care. During this same period a group of POWs attempted to counter the defections by re-enlisting prisoners into the Confederate service. By February 1865, they had signed up and formed ten companies of 130 men each. Apparently the other 5,000 or so POWs no longer cared one way or the other. They were probably too busy just trying to survive until their release.[16]

Colonel Johnson was finally compelled to write a response to critical newspaper editors in defense of his prison administration. "The treatment of them here and all issues to them," declared Johnson in his letter to the *Argus*, "are made strictly in accordance with orders from the War Department . . . instead of placing them in fine, comfortable barracks, with three large stoves in each and as much coal as they can burn both day and night, I would place them in one with no shelter but the heavens, as our poor men were at Andersonville. Instead of giving them the same quality and nearly the same quantity of provisions that the troops on duty receive, I would give them, as near as possible, the same quantity and quality of provisions that the fiendish rebels give our men; and instead of a constant issue of clothing to them, I would let them wear their rags, as our poor men in the hands of the rebel authorities are obliged to do; in other words, had I the power, strict retaliation would be practiced by me. Again, if discretionary power rested with me, I would arrest and confine the known sympathizers with the rebellion residing in Rock Island and Davenport, and quite a large number would be quickly added to our list of prisoners, and those communities would be relieved from a more dangerous element than open rebels in arms."[17]

Whether Johnson meant to lie or just got carried away is uncertain, but the fact was that coal and clothing were never issued so easily, and there were never more than two stoves in a barracks building. By the time of his letter, prisoner rations were far from the quantity issued to regular troops. They had been reduced under orders of the War Department twice by then.[18]

The true conditions at the prison, and, for that matter, at any of the Civil War's prisons, can best be gauged by its death rate. By the end of the war, 1,964 Rock Island POWs had succumbed to smallpox and exposure out of a total of 12,400 confined over its twenty month period of existence. Thus, the facility's death rate ran nearly 16 percent of the total confined.[19]

ALTON PRISON

Farther down the Mississippi River, treatment of smallpox and various other diseases had also become a full-time job. Like Rock Island, Alton Prison lacked a proper hospital facility, and authorities there tried to cope by using a number of makeshift accommodations. A new hospital was authorized and its construction was completed in the autumn of 1864.

It was true that the authorities were finally attempting to improve conditions, but the situation had gotten so far out of hand at Alton that catch-up measures had virtually no effect. Although prison officials failed to file a monthly report in December 1864, according to prisoner Griffin Frost, who worked at the hospital as a trustee, there were 170 deaths that month. Based on the information that was officially reported for the other months, such a number doesn't seem an exaggeration, especially in view of documentation that indicates a smallpox epidemic was still raging within its walls and that 122 deaths were officially reported the following month and a total of 256 reported within the following ninety days. Including Frost's information, then, a total of 1,508 POWs are believed to have died at Alton Penitentiary during the course of the war. Considering that a total of nearly 8,000 prisoners are believed to have been held here during those four years, such a number would indicate that deaths at this prison would eventually run nearly 19 percent of the total confined.[20]

That figure does not reflect the total devastation that resulted from Alton Prison's epidemics. Guards were also incapacitated, and the smallpox spread into the town as well, causing a large number of deaths there.

In addition to the overwhelming problems of death and illness at Alton, the prison continued to be plagued with problems of overcrowding, disorganization, mismanagement, and inadequate security. After Captain Freedley was replaced by Major Thomas Hendrickson, 3rd U.S. Infantry, few months passed in which there wasn't at least one escape. In August 1863, Hendrickson and his regiment were transferred out and Colonel George W. Kincaid of the 37th Iowa Volunteers took over as commandant, while his regiment of "Graybeards" took over guard duty.

The prisoner escapes continued. In fact, they accelerated at the Graybeards' expense. On December 7, 1863, Secretary Stanton received General William Orme's inspection report. "The prison is much too crowded," advised Orme, "[and] the wall surrounding this prison is in some places in bad condition and propped up, much facilitating chances of escape." Before the month ended, a total of twenty-three POWs fled to freedom past the Graybeards and through Alton's dilapidated fence.[21]

This prison also held up to two hundred U.S. military convicts in one of the jailyard buildings. According to Frost they were the most dangerous of those confined at the prison, sometimes attacking and robbing POWs, and were often seen "bucked and gagged" in the yard for misbehavior. There were also at least seven women incarcerated at Alton during the war. Mary Nicholson of Memphis and Mollie Hyde of Nashville were released on parole in July 1863. Clara Judd of Memphis was released in August. By 1864, four others were in custody: Florence Lundy of Memphis, a Miss Goggin, a Mrs. Hanie, and a Mrs. Mitchel. All of these women were confined in a "damp, cold, partitioned-off room in the cellar" of the main prison building away from the other inmates.[22]

In mid-January 1864, the Iowa regiment was transferred out and Colonel William Weer, 10th Kansas Volunteer Infantry, became commandant as his regiment took over guard duties. They would remain for the remainder of the war but deaths and escapes from the prison continued.

GRATIOT STREET

The situation was no better in St. Louis. By March, another terrific influx of new arrivals combined with a dramatic increase in illnesses propelled the Gratiot Street prison hospital population to explode to over 1,100 out of a total of 1,800 confined. Horrified at the rate of death and illness within the prison walls, Union surgeon George Rex reported to his departmental headquarters: "[The] repeated attention of the prison authorities has been called to this grave and prolific cause of disease, [but] the evil [overcrowding] still continues unabated, and consequently no hopes in the decrease of the ratio of deaths."[23]

From the day the prison was established, authorities were in a constant battle to prevent overcrowding at Gratiot Street. Besides using Myrtle Street Prison and Alton for its overflow until the POWs could be transferred elsewhere, prisoners were often placed in the Schofield and Benton Barracks, both being former training camps in St. Louis, as well as the state penitentiary at Jefferson City. Even with these efforts the prison remained overcrowded well into the early months of 1865. By that time, conditions inside had collapsed beyond description. In addition, the prison was often the scene of Union retaliation executions. One of the most controversial occurred on October 29, 1864, when six Confederate prisoners were randomly chosen and led out to be shot by a firing squad.[24]

As at other facilities of this type, commandants were reassigned several times during the prison's existence. The facility's first commandant, Colonel Tuttle, was transferred in May of 1862 and replaced briefly by Captain John Bishop. He served only a few months before being replaced around December by Captain William J. Masterson, a civilian from the provost marshal's department given the rank of captain and paid $100 a month to manage the city's two prisons.

Masterson became one of the most hated commandants in the history of the prison. Sources indicate he was "a small, 'self-important,' intelligent Irishman who weighed 120 pounds," and Frost's book adds that he was "cruel, ungentlemanly, and insulting in a purely personal manner." Masterson held his position only until August 1863, when he was charged with stealing commissary stores that were intended for distribution among the prisoners and was, himself, incarcerated in the prison.[25]

His replacement was Major Herman Schloeter, 9th Wisconsin Infantry, who served for about a month before he was replaced by Captain Charles C. Byrne of the 1st Missouri Volunteer Regiment. By the spring of 1864, Byrne was reassigned and Colonel John P. Sanderson, provost marshal general, Department of the Missouri, took command. The most popular and highly respected of all the prison commandants to reign over the Gratiot-Myrtle Street prison compounds was Captain Robert C. Allen, 40th Missouri Volunteer

Infantry, who took command in the fall of 1864 and remained in that capacity until the end of the war.

CAMP DOUGLAS

Camp Douglas was experiencing escape problems much like Alton and problems of disease and an ever-increasing number of inmate deaths much like Rock Island and St. Louis. Its commandants were rotated in and out of the facility one after another, possibly in a feeble attempt to halt the declining conditions at the camp. However, every commandant experienced the same frustrations as the one who preceded him.

Colonel James A. Mulligan, 23rd Illinois (Irish) Regiment, who had been captured at Lexington, Missouri, and released on parole, was the camp's first commandant who had to deal with it as a POW facility. Within the first few weeks, escapes began. "At first," reported I. N. Haynie, adjutant general of Illinois, "sympathizing friends abusing the liberality of the authorities, passed into the rebel's quarters knives, pistols or money, carefully concealed within loaves of bread, articles of food or clothing . . . Homespun pantaloons and coats were carefully lined with greenbacks, and other devices adopted to furnish the imprisoned recipient with means to break the guard or to bribe the guard."[26]

A succession of commandants followed, including Colonel Daniel Cameron, 65th Illinois (Scottish) Regiment, who had been captured at Harper's Ferry and released on parole, and Colonel Joseph H. Tucker, 69th Illinois Volunteer Infantry, who had been the camp's commandant when it was first established as an instruction facility. Tucker again took command with two regiments of ninety-day volunteers as guards, in June 1862. Even by then, only four months after being established as a POW facility, Camp Douglas was a mess.

"There has been the greatest carelessness and willful neglect in the management of the affairs of the camp," complained Colonel Hoffman, "and everything was left by Colonel Mulligan in a shameful state of confusion. . . . Colonel Cameron knew nothing of the affairs of the prisoners. . . . [T]he police of the camp had been much neglected and was in a most deplorable condition. . . . Much labor and large expenditures will be necessary."[27]

Hoffman went on to reveal what efforts Tucker was making to prevent escapes from the camp. "[T]he commanding officer has two detectives, whom he represents to be very reliable men, employed in the camp under the pretense of being prisoners to find out, if possible, the aiders in the escape of prisoners from the camp, but thus far he has only been able to learn that it was probably a sutler who was discharged some time ago who sold clothing to prisoners."[28]

Escapes continued and more commandants followed, among whom were General Jacob Ammen, U. S. Volunteers, who took over command in January

1863; Colonel DeLand, who took command the following August; and Brigadier General William W. Orme, who assumed personal supervision the following December. In May 1864, Colonel Benjamin J. Sweet, 8th Regiment Veteran Corps, was assigned supervision of the prison camp. With Sweet's command, radical changes were put into effect to prevent escapes, but the declining condition of the health and welfare of the camp continued to be ignored.

To prevent tunneling, flooring was replaced in the prisoners' barracks and the buildings were elevated on posts four feet above the ground. To prevent escapes by fence climbing, an additional twelve-foot-high solid oak barricade was constructed with an elevated walkway for guards around the existing fences to create a triple plank enclosure from which the sentry could look down into the pen.

Colonel Sweet tightened up security within the camp as well. Candles were no longer issued, to prevent their possible use as light for tunneling; prisoners were no longer allowed to walk the cross streets of the enclosure; and at daybreak the prisoners were required to lay in bed until a bugle sounded to signal they were allowed to get up.

"The men were made to retire at sundown," complained prisoner Thomas Head, "and were not allowed to talk to one another after [we] laid down. If the Federals heard any talking at night in the barracks they would shoot into the house through the crowd." R. T. Bean continued, "Many a Minie ball went crashing through our barracks at night at some real or imaginary noise. It was dangerous even to snore."[29]

With security increased, Union authorities and even many of the prisoners were convinced escapes had become a thing of the past at Camp Douglas. "[Y]et," declared Bean, "one night about ten o'clock there was the hurried tramping of feet in my barracks, and about half a dozen men of Company H, 8th Kentucky, with a heavy wooden mall rushed to the fence, pounded a hole in it, and jumped out. . . . A regular volley greeted them." Guard Edwin Greble, Company B, 196th Pennsylvania Volunteers, noted in his diary concerning this escape on Tuesday, September 27, 1864, "There were several wounded, one seriously as the cheek and part of his tongue were taken off. He was the one that had the wooden hammer."[30]

According to Bean, several got away but most were captured and returned to the camp with ball and chains and placed into the lockup. "A lieutenant found two and struck one of them with his sword," Greble noted in his diary. "Two others were caught in a haystack. The captain struck his sword into the stack and one of the Rebs yelled."[31]

"The place of close confinement, or dungeon, in use is utterly unfit," declared Augustus Clark, on another inspection, referring to the lockup where captured escapees were confined. "It is a 'dungeon' indeed. . . . In this place at the time I visited it were confined twenty-four prisoners, the offense of all, I believe, being attempts to escape. The place might do for three or four prisoners, but for the number now confined there it is inhuman. At my visit I remained but a few seconds and was glad to get out, feeling sick and faint."[32]

The lockup was a room eighteen feet square, lit by one closely barred eighteen-by-eight-inch window about six feet above the floor. The only entry into the room was by a hatch about twenty inches square in the ceiling. The floor, according to Clark, was constantly damp, and an intolerable stench radiated from the sink in the corner of the room.

About the time Colonel Sweet took command, a reduction in rations took place by orders from Washington. "The prisoners' ration," declared one captive, "was to each man one half loaf of baker's bread daily, together with about four ounces of meat and a gill of beans or potatoes . . . When retaliatory measures were adopted, the stoves were taken away." Another captive added, "Our sutler was restricted to the sale of tobacco, stamps, and paper. All vegetables were cut off, and tea, coffee, and sugar became things of the past. One-third of our bread was cut off and two-thirds of our meat."[33]

With the elimination of vegetables, scurvy soon occurred in epidemic numbers. "Lips were eaten away, jaws became diseased, and teeth fell out," recalled Bean. "If leprosy is any worse than scurvy, may God have mercy upon the victim."[34] Authorities began to provide onions, potatoes, vinegar, and fresh beef to the prisoners to eliminate the scurvy but not before many had already succumbed to the illness. Then smallpox broke out again and another epidemic raged through the camp, taking lives indiscriminately.

Many people of Chicago offered relief and assistance to the captives held in their city during these times, not as a matter of politics but purely out of compassion. Until the Union government put a stop to the practice, prominent people of wealth in the community often gave both their time and financial aid toward the care of the sick and destitute prisoners. The "Relief Committee of Citizens" gave collections from local churches to the camp to aid the prisoners, and provided medicines and druggists to help the post surgeon.[35]

In late 1864 many political prisoners from the surrounding counties were added upon the discovery of several plots to release prisoners. By then the camp had a population of 12,082. During the next two months, the prison continued to hold over 11,000 captives.[36]

CAMP CHASE

A smallpox epidemic hit Camp Chase in mid- to late 1864. Eventually, 2,260 prisoners would die at Camp Chase. Immediately south of the prison, and across a stream that ran along its edge, was a ten acre site in which the dead were laid to rest.

Even under harsh conditions, the POWs were able to devise forms of entertainment to pass the time more pleasantly. As at many other prisons, Camp Chase prisoners established their own form of government within their compounds, electing a governor, a legislature, courts, running from a superior court on down to a police court, and other appointments necessary to carry on the workings of a governmental body.

"The prisoners were not allowed to collect in large groups," related R. H. Strother, Company E, 4th Kentucky (CSA) Cavalry, "so in order to have public speaking and hold the election, it was necessary to get permission from the officers in charge of the prison, which they readily gave."[37]

To keep the prison population informed, a prison newspaper, called the *Camp Chase Ventilator*, was established. "We communicated between prisons by tying a note around a small stone," reported one prisoner, "and tossing it over the dividing walls when the guard's back was turned to us. In this way we got news from prisons Nos. 2 and 3 and from the outside when 'fresh fish' came in."[38]

Other forms of entertainment within the walls of the camp were louse races, louse fights, and rat hunting. "A 'rat killing' was about the only real amusement we had," reported prisoner George Moffett. "Fresh meat, regardless of the species, was too much of a rarity among these hungry men to be discarded on account of an old prejudice. When properly dressed and fried in pork grease, a rat has the exact flavor of a squirrel. The uninitiated would never know the difference." Another prisoner admitted, "I often paid one dollar each for rats and ate them without bread. . . . One day we got a stray dog in our room but he escaped."[39]

The food situation grew worse as time went on at Camp Chase. In the beginning, under state control, the quality of food supplied to the camp, especially the meat, was very low. Federal authorities discovered that state-arranged suppliers were actually cheating the government by charging for a certain quality of product but providing a greatly inferior one. Amid rumors of kickbacks and payoffs, the commissary officer was dismissed. Rations improved for a while but eventually declined again as the months passed.

"For several weeks," reported prisoner J. Coleman Alderson, "our daily rations consisted of twelve ounces of baker's bread, eight ounces of unsound salted white lake fish, one tablespoonful of navy beans, and a spoonful of vinegar. Sometime in September [1864] these were cut down to a thin slice of bread or a tin cup of cornmeal, spoiled lake fish, and eight or ten navy beans once or twice a week. . . . The guards threw melon rinds, apple cores, and parings into the [compound] and enjoyed our scuffle for them."[40]

Although rat hunting had the added benefits of preventing starvation and making money, the all-time favorite sport at Camp Chase was louse racing. "I have seen a room full of grown men thrown into great excitement over these races," declared prisoner John King. "The race course . . . was on the surface of an inverted tin pan. This would be sufficiently heated to produce a lively movement of the louse without destroying life. . . . [C]arefully selected from their large herd and brought up to the appointed place. . . . they were formally entered for the race under some name such as Phil Sheridan, Sherman, Pope, or Hunter. Our men thought too much of their own chivalrous generals to give their names to a miserable louse . . . at a given signal the racers would be thrown together in the center of the heated tin, and at once away they would go, making every effort to escape the heat. . . . The goal was the periphery of the pan, the one reaching this circle first to be declared the victor in the race. . . . [T]hese insects would invariably run in a constantly extending circle, round and round the center from which they started until the rim or outer edge of the inverted pan had been reached."[41]

Another variation of this form of entertainment was the louse fights, again utilizing the heated pan. "Bringing these insects together," reported King, "only a little encouragement was necessary to excite them into a violent passion and the fight would begin and only end on the death or the retreat of one or the other of the combatants."[42]

JOHNSON'S ISLAND

At Johnson's Island in Ohio, it was the rats that held the prisoners' undivided attention. "[T]he prison swarmed with large wharf rats," declared prisoner J. F. Cross, Company B, 5th North Carolina Regiment.[43]

Within a year of its establishment, Johnson's Island became another of several major Union prisons where the catching and eating of rats became common practice for the POWs in an effort to supplement their diet.

"One thing I notice and cannot help mention," POW R. F. Webb would later observe, "is the morbid appetites of the men here . . . they are like a parcel of famished wolves whose hunger is never satisfied."[44]

"Rats are found to be very good for food," agreed prisoner Horace Carpenter. "This bull pen abounds with them," marveled another prisoner. "They are fat and gentle and easily killed. . . . We have actually taken to eating [them]. . . . I myself saw half a dozen . . . dressed for the pot."[45]

The sinks, or latrines, were excavations eighteen feet long, five feet wide, and five feet deep, covered by sheds, at the rear of the barracks. The island was flat, loamy clay soil, which drained poorly. In addition, a bed of solid rock existed no more than eight feet below the surface.

"Owing to the geological formation," observed Richard H. Coolidge, U.S. army medical inspector, "sinks cannot be dug more than eight feet deep, and blasting to a greater depth is extremely difficult. . . . It follows that in a few weeks' time the sinks become full and new pits have to be opened. This has been so often repeated that the ground north and south of the prison barracks for a distance of fifty feet on either side may now be considered as one continuous sink, very superficially covered, and saturating the whole ground down to the rock. At my inspection these sinks were in the filthiest condition imaginable, the excrementitious matter in some of them rising high above the seat and covering the floor."[46]

The conditions of the sinks bred rats by the score and provided the inmates with a hunting ground for extra food. Prisoner Joseph Ripley of Tennessee became well-known among the inmates as one of the best at catching rats. He would often treat his fellow captives to mighty feasts.

The prisoners at Johnson's Island, and at about seven other Union prisons as well, resorted to eating rats for a variety of reasons. Foremost, of course, was the actual reduction of rations that took place in all the Union prisons combined with the abundance of rats in the enclosures. But an additional cause here, and in several other prisons, was the post's method of distributing rations.

In the beginning, regular rations were issued every day except Sunday. Other items, such as sugar, coffee, beans, and rice or hominy, were given out in quantities to be consumed over a six- to ten-day period. Beef was issued three or four days a week and pickled pork the other two or three days. Bread was baked on the island in large ovens and was distributed each day, one loaf to every four men.

Then came the reduction, followed by another. "We are now beginning to feel to some extent the vengeance of the Government of the United States," complained one prisoner. "They have stopped our rations of sugar, coffee and candles. We get nothing but bread and meat with a few beans."[47]

But the biggest problem with the reductions was that the men were starving and could no longer extend their distributions. It created a vicious cycle of starving, eating, and starving again.

"The rations which were distributed at noon each day," confessed Henry Shepherd, "were expected to sustain life until the noon of the day following. During this interval, many of us became so crazed by hunger that the prescribed allowance of pork and bread was devoured ravenously as soon as received. . . . For six or seven months I subsisted upon one meal [every] 24-hours."[48]

By mid-1864, Johnson's Island, like all the other military prisons had become overcrowded and filthy. For one thing, Mr. Johnson, who used to pick up the garbage to slop his hogs, had sold them all by then and no longer came over to the island to haul it off. The grounds had become trashy and were often mires of mud; the buildings and the stockade were badly in need of whitewashing; problems with the latrines remained the same; and the shallow wells had become over-used and were now often dry.

In June 1864, Colonel Charles W. Hill, 128th Ohio Volunteer Infantry, took over as commandant. Under his command, the enclosure was slightly enlarged, several buildings were repaired, two additional buildings and a wash-house were constructed, and an extra water pump was installed.

In the midst of all the construction, more escape attempts were made. "Several wagons were engaged in hauling sand," reported one prisoner, "and our men procuring blue pants with caps would get in the empty wagons and hop out at the gate. About forty had succeeded in eluding . . . the guards and had gotten out of the bull pen before they were discovered . . . all but two were recaptured."[49]

Prisoner recreation at Johnson's Island was similar to that at the other institutions. Religion played a big part and nearly every denomination was represented. The prison also had its own debating society, a thespian band, and the Young Men's Christian Association of Johnson's Island, which looked after the sick and more needy prisoners.

Gambling had its place, as did the manufacturing of trinkets, which were sold in town with the help of guards. Wood carving became a cottage industry, and the fad among Johnson's Island inmates seems to have been the making and carving of elaborate chairs that often displayed the name, regiment, and state of the craftsman.

Being a major POW facility, Johnson's Island was also the scene of many formal executions. On the grounds of the prison stood two small houses, separated from the rest of the compound, where the condemned were held. Each building was divided into eight small rooms, each about seven feet high, two and a half feet wide—and just long enough to lie down in. A little window, about six inches by one and a half inches, admitted the only light and fresh air. Each prisoner confined there had a ball weighing sixty-four pounds connected to a six-foot chain attached to one leg, with shackles riveted upon the ankle. Handcuffs secured the prisoner's wrists. During the day he was allowed to sling the ball over his shoulder and walk around within a staked off area of about fifteen square feet in front of the building. At sunset, each condemned prisoner was locked up separately in his compartment. One of the last executions there is believed to have been the September 1, 1864, hanging of a prisoner from Kentucky charged with murder.[50]

On September 23, 1864, a tornado ripped through the prison at 8:30 in the evening during a severe thunderstorm. Nearly half of the stockade fence was blown down, carrying away the guards stationed along the top. Three prisoner blocks were destroyed and a wing of the hospital building was carried away. Trees all across the island were blown down as well. A number of prisoners were hurt, but none seriously, and no one tried to escape. "How could we?" one prisoner questioned. "We are on a small island with as many troops to guard us as we have prisoners. And off shore sat a gunboat, able to shell any part of the island at any time."[51]

During Johnson's Island's existence, the health of the prisoners was generally good. The prevalent diseases were typhoid fever, pneumonia, and smallpox. The post physician, Dr. Timothy Woodbridge, is credited for the above-average care that the prisoners received and the professional, sanitary management of the hospital, especially in view of the lack of healthy meals, the lack of heat, and the developing unsanitary conditions of the camp.

OHIO PENITENTIARY

The Ohio Penitentiary experienced some minor problems during early 1864. On February 20, authorities broke up another planned POW escape, again involving the prison's dining utensils. "They had stolen, one by one, a lot of the table knives," reported John Brough, Ohio's new governor, "and . . . had ground them to sharp pointed and dangerous weapons." Brough went on to relate that a surprise search of the cells, conducted by state officials, had turned up nine such knives and two files, evidently kept concealed since General Morgan's escape. All had again gone unnoticed by the Federal guards. "I have cleared the west wing of convicts," Brough continued, "and placed these prisoners there . . . and all eating implements [are] counted out and in to them daily."[52]

By mid-March all POWs, a total of sixty-five at the time (others having been released for various reasons) were transferred to Fort Delaware by order of Secretary Stanton. Those at the Allegheny Penitentiary were transferred to Point Lookout.

POINT LOOKOUT

By mid-1864, Maryland's Point Lookout had come into its own as a major Union prison. By June, more than 15,500 POWs were confined there—more than at any other Union facility.

Although inconvenient during the winter months because of the harsh, cold winds, the location of the rear of the prison pen, which was backed up to the bay, was a blessing at other times of the year. "[G]ates led from the enclosures to a narrow belt of land between the fence and the water," prisoner Anthony Keiley noted, "which was free to the prisoners during the day."[53]

Piles had been driven into the bay to prevent escapes, and a designated area was staked off in the water where prisoners could bathe. The POWs also used this access for washing clothes and finding additional food such as clams, lobsters, fish, and whatever else they could catch. "On one occasion," claimed C. W. Jones, Company H, 24th Virginia Cavalry, "when the tide on the bay was high it brought ashore an old dead sea gull which had been dead a month or more. It was picked up by a hungry rebel and devoured with gusto. . . ."[54]

Point Lookout was another prison where men were driven to supplement their diet. Nearly all contemporary accounts agree that the amount of rations issued there was never enough, especially after the last officially mandated reduction. "It was just sufficient to maintain life, yet leaving every one in a continual state of yearning hunger," declared Randolph Shotwell. "The ration for a day was about sufficient for a well man one meal," declared J. B. Traywick. "It was said by the prison authorities to be one-half ration, allowing three meals per day. I would consider it one-third ration a day."[55]

The Point Lookout rations were supposed to consist of pork two out of three days, with beef on the third. "[O]ccasionally the ribs of the beef were round," explained Traywick, "which showed that it was mule-beef."[56]

Pound loaves of bread were given out to be divided between two prisoners, and a pint of soup went with each loaf. On Saturday, two days' rations were issued to stretch out over Sunday. As in nearly all the prisons by this time, the POWs ate it all in one sitting and got through the Sabbath the best they could.[57]

The manner of serving rations at Point Lookout was unusual. Food rations were placed about twenty inches apart all along the tables of the messhalls and the prisoners were led into the halls by their company or squad sergeants. As they were marched in, they were brought to a halt in position directly opposite a ration. "The meat was usually about four or five ounces," advised Keiley. "These we seized upon, no one being allowed to touch a piece, however, until the whole company entered."[58]

The rations were served in this manner twice a day. Eaten between 8 A.M. and 9 A.M., breakfast consisted of soup and two to three crackers or hardtack. Before the government-sanctioned ration reduction, breakfast had included five crackers and a cup of coffee with sugar or molasses, and sometimes meat. Dinner was served between 3 P.M. and 4 P.M. and consisted of fresh or pickled meat, soup and bread, more hardtack, and three potatoes or some other vegetable. The soup provided was usually rice or bean soup, but most prisoners argued that it was closer to rice or bean water.

With such lean rations, prisoners resorted to catching seafood, purchasing or bartering for others' food, or as at several other facilities, catching and eating the abundant, large wharf rats that scurried around the enclosure.

Finding enough fresh water was a constant problem at Point Lookout. Wells supplied water for the camp, but they proved to be too shallow and were strongly impregnated with iron and alkaline salts. "[There were] eight wells," advised James C. Elliott, Company F, 56th North Carolina Regiment, "no two of which contained the same kind of water." The well water at Point Lookout smelled bad, looked bad, and induced chronic diarrhea in many captives. "It colors everything black in which it is allowed to rest," declared Keiley, "and a scum rises on the top if it is left standing during the night."[59]

A boat was later arranged to transport fresh water to the camp but its trips were quite irregular.

General Marston had been relieved of command of the Point Lookout prison in December 1863, by Brigadier General Edward W. Hinks. On April 20, 1864, Colonel Alonzo G. Draper, 36th U.S. Colored Troops, took command. By that time there were nearly twenty hospital tents set up south of the prisoner compound to handle the sick, which were averaging one hundred a day, while the seriously ill, averaging twenty to thirty per day, were being taken to the nearby Union hospital. Besides chronic diarrhea, dysentery and typhoid fever had become epidemic at this camp while smallpox, scurvy, and the itch had become quite common.[60]

Within a month, two hundred were sick in the camp and thirteen hundred more were confined in the hospital when James H. Thompson, surgeon in charge of the Point Lookout POWs, began to complain about the water. "[It is] to this state of water I attribute largely the increased amount of fatality of disease during the past month," he declared.[61]

There were still nearly 1,200 sick in July, and more than 200 had died the previous month. Between June and October 1864, more than 740 POWs died out of an average of 13,042 held.[62]

The prisoners were not completely innocent in the situation. An inspection revealed that the prison grounds and quarters had become exceedingly unhealthy. "[T]he sinks are not at all thought of, requiring a little extra exertion to walk to them," remarked W. F. Swalm of the U.S. Sanitary Commission. "They void their excrement in the most convenient place to them, regardless of the comfort of others."[63]

The latrines at Point Lookout were built out over the bay on the east side of the camp for use in the daytime. With up to fifteen thousand POWs crowded into the pen, the prisoners on the far ends of the camp apparently found it easier to relieve themselves where they were rather than to elbow through the crowd to get to the sinks—a trip that might take as long as half an hour or more. However, large boxes or tubs were provided in the camp for nighttime use.

By July, Brigadier General James Barnes, U.S. Volunteers, took command of the prison, and he turned the internal operations of the prison over to Major Allen G. Brady, the provost marshal. It is difficult to determine if Major Brady was a scoundrel or a saint. Some prisoners praised him while others despised him. However, there is no doubt he was a strict disciplinarian, with questionable ethics.

"He brands us 'Rebels' and treats us as if we were criminals of the lowest type," complained Captain Robert E. Park, 12th Alabama Regiment. Prisoner

C. W. Jones thought he was kind, and "an excellent, brave and good soldier." Others said he was "cruel and heartless" and that he was hated by all the captives. There were also claims that he sometimes galloped his horse through the crowded pen, trampling prisoners who couldn't move out of the way fast enough.[64]

According to his official reports, he was professional in carrying out his duties and was attentive to the prisoners' needs. He argued long and hard for additional clothing supplies for the POWs, but his requests seem to have gone ignored by the Quartermaster Department. It was later determined, however, that there had been discrepancies in some of his acquisitions. For instance, nearly $2,000 of the prison fund was spent on "blankets" when the government furnished surplus army blankets at no charge to the prisoners. In another case, $500 worth of mackerel was purchased and charged to the prison fund as "vegetables" during a time when the prisoners were suffering from scurvy and needed vegetables badly. It was later found that the mackerel was sold to the prisoners by the sutler, which, of course, was illegal. Some prisoners were under the impression that the sutler was Major Brady's brother-in-law and that they made thousands of dollars manipulating records and siphoning off cash from purchases of rations, clothing, and medicines intended for the prisoners.[65]

"Major Brady, of New York State," reported J. B. Traywick, "was a shrewd man of powerful administrative abilities. . . . [H]is whole conduct toward the prisoners impressed me that he enjoyed two things immensely—first, the suffering and humiliation of the prisoners; secondly, the fact he was their despot."[66]

It was under Brady's direction that thirty-two thinly clad prisoners were ushered out of their quarters in the middle of the night and placed in the blockhouse in subzero weather without food, water or heat for two days after a guard was found dead near their quarters. "Major Brady, with the audacity of the wolf before eating the lamb," related Traywick, "proceeded to ask each man if he knew who killed the guard." Each claimed ignorance. Brady threatened them with being confined in the cold blockhouse until the guilty one was discovered. He later threatened to shoot all thirty-two. Still, no one confessed.[67]

Other authorities then located the person responsible on the other side of the camp and discovered that he had tossed a brick at the guard. It was never determined if it was a malicious act or if the guard, reportedly intoxicated at the time, might have fallen and suffered an accidental death. Whatever the cause, the guilty POW was never punished, but three of the prisoners held in the blockhouse died from exposure soon after returning to their quarters.[68]

The guards at Point Lookout were just as controversial. The 5th New Hampshire joined the original detail in early 1863. By November, guards had shot four POWs, killing two and wounding two, in escape attempts. A total of sixteen different shootings are recorded in various prisoner diaries, with one reporting seven killed and fourteen wounded over a fifteen-month period, while another told of four killed and seven wounded during the year 1864. There were probably more that weren't witnessed but, at the same time, official records mention only four during the course of the prison's existence that had cause for investigation.[69]

Various other regiments took over the guard detail when the New Hampshire troops were transferred out. Some included the 4th Rhode Island Volunteer Regiment; the 10th Regiment U.S. Veteran Reserve Corps; the 166th Company, 2nd Battalion; the 1st U.S. Volunteers; and the 139th Ohio Infantry Regiment. On February 25, 1864, the guard detail included, for the first time, the 36th U.S. Colored Infantry Regiment.

"For the first time in my life," reported prisoner Hutt, "I have seen a Regt. of Negro troops in full uniform and with arms." The wall detail was armed with muskets and the inside detail carried revolvers. "Negro troops guarded the outside walls," reported prisoner James Elliott, "and white men patrolled inside after night." Later, black troops guarded both inside and outside the prison.[70]

The Point Lookout guards, both black and white, were extremely strict and easily provoked. In March 1864, Sergeant Edwin Young, Company A, 2nd New Hampshire Volunteer Regiment, while patrolling the interior of the pen, shot and killed a prisoner after a brief argument. "I turned to go away," testified Young, "but he followed me, and shaking his fist at me telling me I did not dare shoot, and was a coward. I immediately drew my revolver and told him I would, immediately upon which he threw open his coat, and placing himself in a defiant position dared me to shoot, upon which I cocked my revolver and fired." After a board of inquiry, no further action was taken.[71]

On the night of April 18, a guard in the 36th U.S. Colored Troops shot a prisoner who continued to defecate on the ground near his tent after being ordered to stop. On the night of April 21, a prisoner talking in his tent was overheard by a guard of the 36th U.S. Colored Troops. He was ordered out of his tent and made to "doublequick" across the camp and back. That same night, another prisoner was heard talking in his tent by a guard who ordered the prisoner out and fired into the tent when he refused, mortally wounding one of the other POWs in the tent who was asleep. "The shooting of a prisoner," warned Colonel Hoffman, "except when compelled by a grave necessity can-not be excused, and such an act for a slight offense . . . can be considered little less than wanton murder." No further action was taken. After several more complaints, Hoffman issued a similar reprimand in August 1864, and again let the matter drop.[72]

Various other black regiments having guard duty at Point Lookout included the 5th Massachusetts Colored Cavalry, the 3rd and 4th Maryland Colored regiments, and the 24th and 28th Colored Infantry regiments. For all the cruelty and brutality blamed on the black regiments who guarded there, they were also praised as being instrumental in breaking up a prison theft ring. "There was some men in camp," remembered prisoner B. Y. Malone, "who had been going about [at night] cutting tents and slipping men's Knapsacks, Hats, Boots, and sometimes, would get some money." The thieves were later found to be Virginians when they were caught by the black guards on duty one night. "They were then placed under guard," reported Malone, "and made to wear a Barrel Shirt [and marched] up and down the Streets with large letters [tent Cutters] on them."[73]

Assisting the guard units in their duties was the *Roanoke*, an ironclad with three in-line turrets. Its fore and aft turrets housed both a 15-inch smoothbore Dahlgren and a 150-pound Parrott rifle. Its center turret possessed a 15-inch and an 11-inch smoothbore Dahlgren. All of this awesome firepower covered every approach to the site as well as the prison pen itself.

Meanwhile, daily activities in the prison continued. Between dawn and sunrise reveille sounded and the prisoners gathered into line for roll call. After breakfast, the men busied themselves with a wide variety of occupations and pastimes along "Pennsylvania Avenue," along the beach, and throughout the camp.

"My strong forte," declared C. W. Jones, "was molasses taffy and corn mush, with black strap syrup. Whenever I could collect enough of the material together I could fry flap jacks so thin you could read through them, and dilute the molasses so that it would run on a board. My price for a platable dish was five hardtacks and a chew of tobacco. By pushing my trade I would soon collect enough hardtack and tobacco to last me a week, with careful economy." Anthony Keiley added, "[Y]ou would find gingerbread and molasses-candy of domestic manufacture for sale, and, strangely enough, one or two regular eating-houses, where a very respectable dinner could be obtained for fifty cents!"[74]

According to other prisoners, there were always one or two shoemakers or repairmen, and just as many tailors and barbers. Another source of profits was the "washerwomen" detail conducted on the beach at low tide. These men collected clothing from other prisoners and spent the day washing them in the saltwater as the waves came in against the bank along the beach.[75]

Every form of value was used at Point Lookout, from hardtack to a chew of tobacco. "In truth," offered Keiley, "the 'hard-tack' may be considered the unit of value in prison. One of them would purchase a single chew of tobacco anywhere in camp; eight would buy a United States postage stamp; ten, a loaf of bread."[76]

The number of successful escapes from Point Lookout was low compared to the number of prisoners held. During the prison's twenty-four-month existence, more than 52,000 prisoners passed through its gates but only fifty succeeded in escaping. None of the successful escapes occurred in winter. They were all in the warmer months. One method used was to swim beneath some of the floating debris, such as a box or barrel, while in the designated bathing area and drift with it until out of the guards' sight. The POW would then climb out of the water and take to the woods. Others occasionally concealed themselves, while on work details, on the barges or other government boats that landed at Point Lookout with supplies.[77]

FORT DELAWARE

By mid-1864, Fort Delaware had fully evolved into the proverbial Union hellhole. It held more than nine thousand prisoners, with an average of eighty-eight deaths a month. The barracks hurriedly thrown up on the parade grounds in early 1862 and the stockade-enclosed barracks later erected northeast of the fort had become thoroughly dilapidated. General Schoepf finally requested to have all of the fort-enclosed barracks removed.

As at all the other prisons, a number of major problems had developed by this time. "The last monthly report shows miasmatic disease largely predominating and most fatal," declared one official during a mid-year inspection. "The number of deaths has been proportionately large. . . . Since the deprivation of tea and coffee, disease seems to have increased and the sick [have] not prospered as well. . . . The privies here are a nuisance and source of complaint. They are not set far back enough for the excrescence to be removed by the tide, consequently the odor from it is most foul. . . . A large number of cases of itch are reported, [and] some tendency to scurvy exists . . ."[78]

The food rations provided at Fort Delaware were as poor as its water supply. Two meals were served each day. According to one prisoner, breakfast was "about one square inch of boiled bacon, or an inch and a quarter of boiled beef, very slimy; and a slice of baker's bread," while dinner "consisted of precisely the same quantity of bread and meat, with the addition of half a tin cup full of slop." Other accounts agree. "Breakfast consisted solely of one slice of bread and one small slice of meat," wrote George Moffett, "without any liquid to wash it down except the green, brackish water we drew from the old tank in the prison yard."[79]

The method of serving these meals was originally similar to Point Lookout's method. Prisoners were marched into a large mess hall by division, entering the hall on one end and exiting on the opposite. Without dishes, the men's rations were placed about eighteen inches apart along a narrow table, where the procession was brought to a halt. Each prisoner turned to the table, picked up the ration in front of him, turned toward the exit, and marched out in procession. Division after division was served in this manner, occupying about two hours.

By the summer of 1864, the distribution of rations took place on "Hell's Half Acre" and consisted of two hardtacks and a square inch of pickled meat set out on the ground, with the addition of weak bean soup for the day's second meal.

By fall, catching and eating the rats that infested the island became common practice. Still, with the lack of vegetables in their diet, prisoners continued to suffer. Between November 1863 and February 1864 alone, at least one of every eight Confederate prisoners had scurvy. The rate continued unabated as the year progressed. By this time over $17,000 had accumulated in the Fort Delaware prison fund, but authorities refused to use any of it to purchase vegetables.[80]

Even the general public wasn't allowed to help. On July 28, the local community held a benefit picnic six miles from Fort Delaware in McCrone's Woods near New Castle, with the intent to raise money to buy vegetables and other antiscorbutics for the scurvy-ridden prisoners. Before the benefit ended, however, the district's provost marshal showed up with sixty men of the 114th Ohio Regiment, broke up the affair, and arrested some of "the highest of social standing" in the community. They were later taken to Fort McHenry, where they were imprisoned for nearly a month for their efforts.[81]

From the time barracks were built outside the fort, the prison population had fluctuated anywhere from around 3,000 to more than 9,000 until July 1863, when it jumped to 12,595. From then on it continued to fluctuate from 3,000 to 8,000 until May 1864, when the population began to average around 9,000, where it remained until the end of the war. As at other prisons, when the population increased the number of sick grew out of proportion, and within a short time so did the mortality rate.

Smallpox took the most lives there, although scurvy, dysentery, measles, and chronic diarrhea were also prevalent. According to Dr. C. C. Herrington, Company E, 8th Confederate Cavalry, when he was there, "unwholesome bread and water produced diarrhea in numberless cases." Still, from the day the prison was established up to July 1863, only 132 POWs had died. Then, in July alone there were 111 deaths, and 700 more died in September and October from a smallpox epidemic. From then on, sickness continued to take a high toll among the captives. An eight-hundred-bed hospital was established on the island, but usually more than 1,000 were sick at one time.[82]

"The prisoners," observed Medical Inspector General Barnes, "have no bedding and so little clothing that it is impossible to enforce cleanliness." Surgeon Charles Crane, who inspected the prison shortly thereafter, noted that "they have been much crowded together, sick and well, in the same barracks, which it has been impossible to keep clean. . . . There have been many deaths at this place. . . . The result of their being crowded together in large numbers in a confined space." As conditions continued to worsen, one physician wryly observed there was more life *on* the POWs of Fort Delaware than there was *in* them.[83]

By November 1863, nearly eighty bodies a month were being hauled out and buried. At other periods, there were as many as twenty-five a day. The ground surrounding the facility was entirely too marshy, so bodies had to be taken to the New Jersey shore by tug for burial at Fort Mott, on Finn's Point.

"The manner of burial," recalled prisoner W. H. Moon, "was to dig a ditch six feet wide and six feet deep, put in three boxes containing corpses one on top of the other, then extend the ditch, using the dirt to cover the boxes." The burials were done by prisoner details sent out under guard. Other prisoners recalled that on some days so many had to be buried that corpses were stacked into the graves completely nude and without boxes. "We placed as many as possible," reported prisoner Chris J. Conradt, who went on several burial details, "usually about 12 (in each grave)."[84]

To this day, Fort Delaware's burial ground is the only cemetery in the North in which Confederate graves cannot be individually identified. "The number of deaths rendered it impossible to dig a grave for each body separately," General Schoepf later claimed in his own defense. "I had, therefore, three buried in each grave . . . there is secured to each coffin a card, on which is the name, company, and regiment, and this card is covered with leather so as to enable parties to find the remains easily."[85]

"Some who lost loved ones there have gone there since the war looking for their dead but could not find them," one former prisoner reported after the war. "They were told of burial in this or that ditch but they could not tell where." As a result, today instead of individual headstones, one large monument stands on the site to mark the area of their interment.[86]

Prisoners at Fort Delaware formed a religious-social group called the Christian Association of Fort Delaware, sometimes called the Confederate States Christian Association for the Relief of Prisoners. Between 1864 and 1865, it worked as a social agency in an attempt to uplift prisoners' moral and religious spirit. It distributed Bibles and prayer books among the prison population and solicited contributions from the outside. The president of the association was Dr. Isaac W. K. Handy, a Presbyterian minister from Portsmouth, Virginia, who was arrested while visiting his former home in Delaware and confined at the prison for fifteen months. When the association attempted to organize chapters in other Union prisons, Fort Delaware authorities quickly imposed restrictions on the group to end any such efforts.[87]

A form of recreation unique to Fort Delaware was the making of beer to sell among the prisoners. Several inmates developed a fermentation process from a concoction of molasses, ginger, and cornmeal, which yielded a beerlike drink that easily sold among the captive population. "[It was] villainous at best," recalled one prisoner, "but extra-villainous when heated to a lukewarm temperature by hours under a vertical sun. Unfortunately the scarcity and putridity of the drinking water, and the predisposition to scurvy created by a diet of dry crackers and rusty salt meat, gives us all a craving for acid drinks, and many men sell their clothes to get funds to buy this 'small beer.'"[88]

In April 1865, the first issue of the prison newspaper, the *Fort Delaware Prison Times*, appeared. Completely handwritten and marked off into columns, the four page journal was published by J. W. Hibbs, 13th Virginia Infantry Regiment, with a number of other Confederate POWs.

FORT WARREN

Conditions continued to decline in the Union's other fort prisons. Fort Warren in Boston was reestablished as a prison facility in July 1863 when 120 POWs were moved back into it. Later, a few more were moved in and the population remained around 150 for a long time afterward. It slowly began to climb to 180, then 290, and then to 346. Throughout 1864 the number in the prison remained around 300. Finally the population hit an all-time high of 394 captives in February, 1865—the maximum capacity of the institution still being only 175.[89]

As this intense overcrowding developed, many other changes took place at Fort Warren. Colonel Dimick continued to protest the number of prisoners transferred to the facility and in December 1863, was transferred "for reasons of health." He soon retired officially.[90]

Dimick's successor, Major Stephen Cabot, 1st Battalion Heavy Artillery, Massachusetts Volunteers, tightened up on the rules as soon as he took command. Newspapers, trade with the sutler, and alcoholic beverages were quickly prohibited. Officers were no longer allowed to roam the island and were restricted to the interior of the fort. The prison population was allowed to steadily increase and the prisoners began to complain.

Under Cabot, the prisoners' food rations were reduced to eight ounces of cooked meat, a half pint of soup, and two potatoes on three days, with beans or hominy on the other days, and fourteen ounces of bread. "It was difficult to make our scanty fare hold out," groused one prisoner, "and two-thirds of the time I went to bed hungry."[91]

Still, they seem to have been better fed than at the other prisons. "They have been informed over and over again," insisted Cabot, "that the ration allowed them was the old ration of the army, with the exception of two or three articles . . . I find that the bread is so good that some eat more than their allowance . . . and thus many deprive others of their full share."[92]

Although a total of only twelve prisoners died at this prison, the lowest number of deaths in any military prison of this size, many apparently suffered from illnesses at various periods. One prisoner noted that there were from thirty to forty POWs in the hospital much of the time.[93]

Many attributed the low mortality rate to the efforts of the prison physician, Dr. DeWitt C. Peters, and his well-equipped ward, which was funded by private contributions from Boston residents.

Peters was a surgeon in the Union army who had been taken prisoner in Texas and later released on parole. After his exchange he devoted himself to the care of the sick prisoners at Fort Warren's hospital. He also occasionally volunteered his services at the hospital facilities on Governors Island in New York and in Baltimore.[94]

The small number who did die at Fort Warren were buried on Deer Island in Boston Harbor, along with those brought in from New York's Fort Lafayette and Governors Island.

As became a common practice in all the prisons, a succession of commandants followed Dimick's transfer. By mid-1864, Major Cabot was transferred and replaced by Major Augustus A. Gibson of the 3rd U.S. Artillery. Major Gibson served until mid-January 1865, when Major Harvey A. Allen, 2nd U.S. Artillery was assigned to the post. Major Allen served until all the POWs were finally released.

FORT McHENRY

In September 1863 Colonel Peter A. Porter, 8th New York Volunteer Artillery, replaced Commandant Morris at Baltimore's Fort McHenry. Porter served in this position for several months before being transferred out to the seat of war. He was later killed at the Second Battle of Cold Harbor in June 1864. Morris was then reassigned as commandant and served in that capacity until the war ended.

Throughout the period of Fort McHenry's use as a prison facility, there were thirty-seven reported escapes. Most of these were individual efforts, though as many as fourteen escaped in October 1863, and another twelve escaped in January 1864.[95]

Although there was severe overcrowding at times and there were the usual complaints regarding the quality and quantity of food and medical care, only thirty-three Fort McHenry POWs died. The majority of these took place after February 1865, when the war was nearly over.[96]

CAMP MORTON

Conditions at Camp Morton had deteriorated much earlier and a lot more drastically than those at Forts Warren and McHenry. By early 1864, life at

Camp Morton had become as harsh as the Fort Delaware experience, minus the physical brutality.

Prisoners were doing all they could to escape the confines of the camp. A small rail fence was erected along the inside of the prison barricade to serve as the deadline and keep POWs off the fence. In April 1864, a trench about ten feet wide and six feet deep was dug around the camp, just inside the fence, to help discourage tunneling attempts, but the tunneling efforts continued.

One method used by the men at Camp Morton to dispose of or hide the dirt that resulted from such efforts was to tuck their trouser cuffs into the tops of their socks and fill their pants with the dirt. Each prisoner would then wander over to the board plank over the latrine and casually tug on his trousers as he stood there, causing the cuffs to come up out of his socks and allowing the dirt to flow out into the basin.[97]

In another effort to stop escapes, Colonel Stevens recommended adding flooring to the prisoner barracks and raising them off the ground as was done at Camp Douglas. "[S]uitable to prevent tunneling," requested Colonel Stevens, "there having been over one hundred attempts during the past year."[98]

By early 1864, there were thirty-eight hospital tents arranged in pairs along both sides of a street at right angles to the hospital buildings, which contained nearly 400 sick and another 175 in their quarters. The prevailing diseases at Camp Morton at that time were pneumonia, scurvy, erysipelas, and intermittent fevers.[99]

Burials took place at the city cemetery under contract with a local undertaker. "There were about twenty deaths a week," claimed prisoner G. M. Brosheer. "An old house on the grounds [served] as a deadhouse until a new building [was built]."[100]

"The asthenic character of the prevailing diseases," explained Surgeon Charles J. Kipp, U.S. Volunteers, in July 1864, "is undoubtedly caused by overcrowding in the barracks and by the exhalations from the ground, which has served as a receptacle for the excreta of thousands of men who have been stationed here since the beginning of this war. Most of the prisoners occupy poorly ventilated buildings and have an average allowance of about eighty cubic feet of air space to a man. . . . The camp covers an area of nearly four and a half square acres and contains 4,964 men.[101]

By August 1864, there were 224 tents adjacent to the hospital containing 1,340 sick and dying prisoners, while the hospital and barracks, also containing sick, were still overcrowded. Anywhere from 436 to 484 POWs were crammed into the barracks, while 554 occupied one of the old cattle sheds. More than 1,000 were housed in hot, sweltering tents pitched side by side between the buildings. The population was 5,000 POWs and political prisoners, of which a total of 172 had died during this and the previous month.[102]

Prison authorities finally realized that the dilapidated tents were unfit for winter use. Commandant Ambrose Stevens requisitioned a shipment of old Union uniforms, stripped off the military buttons, and had them distributed among the prisoners. He had the cattle shed extended and moved 585 POWs from some of the worn-out tents to the new addition. Many of the other tents were then moved to higher ground. His request for additional barracks and hospital space was turned down.

As the winter of 1864–65 hit Camp Morton, more than three hundred more POWs died. In January 1865, Federal authorities finally approved plans to build another three hospital buildings for the prisoners at the camp, but it proved to be too little, too late. By the time the war ended, 1,763 prisoners had perished.[103]

The total number of prisoners held at Camp Morton during its twenty-five months of operation is unknown. Several months passed without a report being filed by the commandant, but other sources show that at least 9,000 POWs passed through the prison gates. If that is the case, then nearly 20 percent died while incarcerated there. It is also estimated that at least 150 successfully escaped, although there were times when as many as 35 were able to get beyond its walls, only to be recaptured. Of the total number of deaths, at least seven were prisoners shot and killed while attempting to escape.[104]

FORT MASSACHUSETTS (SHIP ISLAND)

By the end of 1864 the Union had established three additional prisons along the coast of the Gulf of Mexico: Fort Pickens, Fort Massachusetts, and Fort Jefferson. Fort Pickens, two miles off the Florida coast, southwest of Pensacola, actually held POWs as early as September of 1862, but never more than eighty-five prisoners at one time, and for several months held as few as two. The fort was a small star-shaped, stone and masonry structure built on the western tip of Santa Rosa Island. Eventually, 280 POWs and political prisoners passed through its gates during the course of its three-year existence.

Fort Massachusetts had been built as a defense fortification in 1859 on Ship Island, a long, narrow barrier island about ten miles off the coast of Mississippi, between Biloxi and Gulfport. Having regained and occupied the fort since early 1862, Union authorities transferred 1,229 POWs into the facility for confinement in October 1864.

Many of these POWs had been captured in Confederate hospitals in recently captured southern cities and towns. Their ages ranged from some of the youngest soldiers, eleven to fifteen years of age, to some of the oldest, men of fifty to seventy-five.[105]

The POWs were held on the parade grounds of the fort with, typically, little planning. "[T]hey arrived here destitute of tents," complained Colonel

Ernest W. Holmstedt, the prison commandant, "and none could be furnished on the island. The cooking of the rations were prepared in the open air, as not a board of lumber, not even for coffins, could be procured at this place."[106]

"[They] came unannounced," explained John H. Gihon, the post surgeon, "and for whose reception and proper care no previous provision had been made. We are without houses, tents, blankets, bedding, or any of the necessary means for furnishing a hospital. The men themselves are in a most filthy condition. . . . Out of nearly 1,500 there were not 300 who did not report themselves to the surgeon in charge here as being afflicted with disease. The prevailing complaints are measles, scurvy, smallpox, diarrhea, dysentery, typhoid and intermittent fevers, rheumatism, and almost every variety of contagious, cutaneous disease that results from the neglect of personal cleanliness."[107]

In that first month, five died. Over the next three months, eighty-five more died. "Most of the deaths that have taken place," insisted Gihon, "were cases of chronic diarrhea and dysentery, pneumonia, consumption, typhoid and other fevers. All of these were sick, and most of them helpless at the time of their arrival at this post."[108]

Colonel Holmstedt's regiment, the 74th U.S. Colored Infantry, assisted by the 77th Illinois Volunteers, pulled the guard duty at the fort. In the first two months of operation, a POW was shot by a guard. "The cooks for the prisoners of war have repeatedly complained about being unable to attend to their duties if not protected from the annoyances of other prisoners of war who crowd around the cook-houses," explained Colonel Holmstedt. "[Prisoner] J. C. Dunclin persisted in cooking some victuals for himself at the cook's stove in spite of repeated warnings from the sentinel. . . . Sentinel Private George Rice left his post and told them he would 'waste no more time in telling them to leave' and returned to his post, from where he again ordered them to leave but Private J. C. Dunclin, of Lockhart's battalion, obstinately persisted to disobey, when Private George Rice, of Company K, [74th Colored Infantry], raised his gun and shot him dead. As much as I regret the occurrence of this affair . . . the shooting of Private J. C. Dunclin, prisoner of war, has had a good effect on the surviving, undisciplined crew."[109]

Used, dilapidated tents finally arrived for the prisoners along with five hundred sets of clothing. The tents were immediately put to use but not the clothing. "The clothing received from the military authorities at New Orleans should not be issued to prisoners," ordered Major George Blagden, assistant to the commissary general of prisoners, "as arrangements have been made between the United States Government and the rebel authorities by which each is to furnish its own prisoners with necessary supplies."[110]

As a result, the prisoners continued to suffer from exposure, and the tents furnished as shelter provided very little. "The tents now occupied by the prisoners," admitted Holmstedt, "are so rotten that a norther tears them down by the dozen."[111]

The construction of cheap barracks for the Ship Island prison had been proposed as early as November 1864, but was never approved. Since that time, Colonel Holmstedt had made repeated requests. In March 1865, he made yet another appeal.

"If prisoners of war are to be kept at this station," pleaded Holmstedt, "barracks must be erected, as tents last no time here. The tents wherein the prisoners are at present are nearly worthless, and if allowed to rot away without providing other means to house them the prisoners will be forced to lie on the bare sand beach." The barracks, of course, never came into existence, while the prison reached its all-time population high in April 1865, with 4,356 POWs.[112]

FORT JEFFERSON (DRY TORTUGAS ISLANDS)

The third facility the Union utilized in the Gulf was probably its most interesting. Fort Jefferson, sixty-eight nautical miles west of Key West, Florida, at Tortugas Harbor in Garden Key, was the largest nineteenth-century coastal fort in the United States. The massive six-sided brick structure had a half-mile perimeter and nearly covered the twenty-five acres of Garden Key, one of seven small islands that extend westward out into the Gulf from the lower tip of Florida. The fortress walls were eight feet thick and fifty feet high, and were surrounded by a shark-infested backwater moat seventy feet wide and thirty feet deep.[113]

Construction on the fort began in 1846, and was originally designed to support three gun tiers for 450 cannon and garrison quarters for fifteen hundred men. Fifteen years later, at the outbreak of the Civil War, the project still had not been completed. Within the sixteen-acre court area were huge foundations for the unfinished three-story officers' and enlisted men's quarters, unfinished powder magazines, and two other buildings.

To prevent Florida's seizure of the half-completed unarmed fort as a defensive post, Federal troops quickly occupied Fort Jefferson at the beginning of the war. Except for a few warning shots fired at passing Confederate privateers, the fort saw no other action during the conflict, but because of its isolated position it served well as a Federal prison, holding Union soldiers convicted of criminal offenses and those under court-martial by late 1861.[114]

Some of the first prisoners were sent by George B. McClellan, who became upset when members of the 2nd Maine Infantry refused to turn out because their three-month enlistment had expired. By September, sixty-three of them found themselves incarcerated at Fort Jefferson. Others continued to be sent there as President Lincoln commuted many army deserters' death sentences to long terms of confinement at the isolated facility.[115]

When additional space was needed for POWs in mid-1864, Union officials decided to utilize Fort Jefferson. Up to that time, few civilians knew that such a place existed, but it had already acquired nicknames such as the "Gibraltar of the Gulf," and "America's Devil's Island" among Union military men. In fact, many of them considered it one of the most desolate spots on earth and some, who had spent time there on garrison duty or as prisoners, later claimed it wasn't really a prison after all—it was a tomb.[116]

The first shipment of POWs arriving at Fort Jefferson in December 1864 were completely taken aback by the view. Before them was a mammoth structure of unparalleled proportions. Its ocher-colored walls and the brilliant white shale beach of the island glared blindingly under the scorching tropical sun. Its climate proved to be extremely humid, stiflingly hot, and intensely oppressive.[117]

The ship dropped anchor in deeper water and took the prisoners to shore, a few at a time, in dories. They were marched to the fort and across the drawbridge, lowered over the moat, and turned over to the prison commandant, Colonel Charles Hamilton, 110th New York Volunteers, and his four companies of guards.

Once inside the prison, the POWs found that it harbored murderers, rapists, robbers, army deserters, and spies. Many, dressed in gray flannel overalls, moved around the yard carrying iron balls attached to their ankles by chains. The Confederates were assigned to quarters in dank cells of the casemates. Each contained a plank bed and a wooden bench. The only light came from three slits, or loopholes, four inches wide on the inside spreading to two feet wide on the outside, that were located seven feet above the stone floor. The walls were cracked from the settling, shifting, and sinking of the foundation and were covered with mold and mildew. Moisture also collected on the walls and floor, making them continually damp and slimy. In the yard, the cracked walls were covered with lichen and draped with Spanish moss. The only available fresh water in the compound came from an elaborate system of storage tanks and ducts built into the fort's foundation, which collected rainwater along the fort's battlements. Bedbugs, graybacks, roaches, scorpions, and mosquitoes liberally inhabited the place.

Wooden barracks had been built for the garrison, but living conditions were so harsh and the site was so isolated that previous guard regiments were often rotated through Fort Jefferson rather quickly to prevent rebellion among the troops. The authorities had already experienced one such mutiny.[118]

"[O]ur duty is pretty hard here," said Eli Emigh, 110th New York Volunteer Regiment. The 110th proved to be a well-disciplined unit and would go on to perform the garrison duty at Fort Jefferson through the end of the war.[119]

Rations at the fort consisted of salt pork or salt beef, potatoes, bread, and coffee. Fish was sometimes provided, as were large turtles that were caught and put into the moat with the sharks until they could be butchered. Supply ships that arrived once a week from New Orleans or twice a week from Key West sold vegetables and fruit to the POWs and the garrison when such items were available. Because vegetables weren't available often enough, or the POWs couldn't afford the high prices, scurvy became the prevailing disease. POWs also suffered and died of dysentery and chronic diarrhea. Burials took place on nearby Bird Key.

The Dry Tortugas prison population ranged anywhere from five hundred to nine hundred men. Successful escapes were very rare. Some methods included stowing away on one of the delivery vessels or stealing small boats, or anything that would float, and heading out to sea. One of the most famous escapes was made by George St. Leger Grenfell, transferred from Camp Douglas in November 1864. He and four others succeeded in getting out of the prison and off the island in a small boat, and they were never seen or heard from again.[120]

Many escapes were probably prevented by the fort's infamous moat. One particularly large shark that roamed its waters was named Provost Marshal by the guards, and they often fed it by throwing some of the fort's stray cats into the channel.[121]

If a failed escape attempt didn't result in death, it was often followed by a thumb-hanging, a beating, being fitted with a thirty-pound ball and chain, or confinement in the fort's underground magazine.

The actual number of successful escapes from this prison is unknown. Some sources estimate from thirty to forty but those figures may simply reflect the number who disappeared and were never captured. On several occasions, guards remained at their post as they watched the shark named Provost Marshal "capture" a prisoner who attempted a moat crossing. Sometimes they even helped get the shark's attention by shooting the escapee to put the scent of blood in the water.[122]

The total number of Confederate POWs confined there with the Union military convicts is unknown. Colonel Hamilton never filed a monthly report for the prison. As a prison for Union soldiers, it wasn't required. Some estimates indicate that around three hundred POWs might have been confined there.

Conditions in Confederate prisons deteriorated as quickly as those in the North during 1864. By midyear Richmond held over 15,000 POWs, the majority being concentrated at the six-acre site on Belle Isle. The year had opened with over 6,000 POWs on the island but within months the population had increased to somewhere between 8,000 and 10,000.[123]

BELLE ISLE

As at the Union prisons, Belle Isle POWs were not allowed to use the latrines during the night for security reasons. Consequently, each new day revealed excrement in the streets and in the vacant areas between the tents. "The whole surface of the camp has thus been saturated with putrid animal matter," reported William A. Carrington, surgeon in charge of U.S. prisoners at Belle Isle.[124]

By March, medical inspectors reported that one-fourth of the prisoners were ill. The prevailing diseases were typhoid fever, diarrhea, dysentery, and catarrh, in addition to diseases of the respiratory system.

Sick prisoners were treated in a hospital tent, which had no floors or beds. The prisoners were placed on the straw-covered ground, with logs for pillows. The more severe cases were transported to hospitals in Richmond. According to Carrington, there was an average 1,200 sick confined in the city hospitals.

"The majority of cases die of chronic diarrhea," reported John Wilkins, surgeon in charge of Richmond's General Hospital No. 21. "It is so common . . . for the patients from Belle Isle to be speechless or delirious and unable to give their names, etc. . . . During the past month, 337 cases were admitted and 265 died.[125]

The lack of a wholesome diet only added to the prisoners' health problems. Originally the rations consisted of a two-inch-thick by four-inch-long "half-brick" of cornbread, a small slab of bacon, and a cup of pea soup. Bacon was soon eliminated because it became difficult to obtain.

"Our bread," reported one prisoner, "was baked in sheet iron pans, 12 by 18 inches and two inches deep. These would be filled with batter made of unsifted corn meal, without salt or other seasoning, then put in these pans and baked in a brick oven."[126]

Although these small loaves of cornbread were called "half-bricks" by the prisoners, they were referred to as "cards" by the Confederates. When baked, they would then be stacked up in front of the cook house on the sand, with no covering, until the next ration call.

The soup was made of water from the James River in large potash or "scalding" kettles over an open fire and was later served to the POWs from wooden buckets. "[It] contained a considerable amount of pods, leaves, stems, and dirt," insisted one prisoner, "with multitudes of weavil or black bugs which would rise to the top to the thickness of an inch and formed the principal ingredient of our soup . . . [I] at first tried to strain them out but after a few days, simply broke up bread into the soup and ate it bugs and all."[127]

Belle Isle prisoners were often caught stealing food and were, consequently, punished. On January 3, 1864, nine men were bucked and gagged for stealing soured beans from a slop barrel near the cookhouse. The men had devised a plan in which they obtained permission to pass through the gate area to see the commandant. Once outside, they instead walked to the cook-house to the barrels containing swill, scooped up hatfuls of the stuff, and ran back into the camp, where they were immediately taken up by the guards.

The next day, a chicken belonging to the commandant was grabbed by a prisoner when it flew up onto the bank that surrounded the camp. It was eaten in short order and the eight thousand prisoners confined at the prison at the time were informed they would go without rations that day because of that one unknown chicken thief.[128]

On January 15, the commandant lost his dog. It wandered into the camp and was immediately seized by several prisoners who killed it, skinned it, and ate it. Commandant Virginius Bossieux was infuriated over the loss and sus-pended rations for another day.[129]

"After this occurrence and once [the prisoners got] a taste of fresh meat," revealed prisoner Charles Fosdick, "the boys contrived all manners of projects to decoy an unwary dog across the line. . . . They were so persistent in their efforts that in short time there was not a live dog left on Belle Isle!" Guards lost several pets and mascots in this manner. "I saw a man kill a dog and eat part of it," confessed prisoner Daniel McMann, "and he sold the rest of it— I got some."[130]

Besides having an intense desire for food, there were a number of prisoners who suffered from the lack of tobacco. "Their craving for this article became so great," reported one prisoner, "they would give their last morsel of food for a few crumbs of a small twist, that would last but a day. They would chew this till the last particle of strength of the tobacco was gone, then dry the old quid and smoke it."[131]

In February 1864, the Belle Isle prisoners were moved to a newly estab-lished prison in Georgia. On February 7, the captives began departing in groups of four hundred. "We were roused from our gentle slumbers during the night," quipped John Ransom, "counted off and marched to the cars, loaded into them, which had evidently just had some cattle as occupants, [and] started southward."[132]

They were a ragged group by this time, dirty beyond description. Many had only one item of clothing left and, as one surgeon estimated, nearly 90 percent weighed less than 100 pounds. They were nothing more than "skele-tons of men in rags," said one prisoner. In addition, "many had lost their rea-son," as another doctor later testified, "and were in all stages of idiocy and imbecility."[133]

By March 24, 1864, the last of this group left Belle Isle. The following June, six thousand more were confined here but they were all transferred out to Danville and Salisbury by late October.

Finally, the Belle Isle C.S. Military Prison was closed for good.

In its eighteen months of periodic operation between 1862 and 1864, more than 20,000 prisoners were received at various times. It is estimated that nearly 1,000 died; however, only 125 marked graves exist in the island's cemetery. Lieutenant Bossieux maintained that only 164 died at the prison and while it is known that many died in the hospitals of Richmond, former prisoners all claim a higher figure because they saw hundreds carried out of the camp while there. What's more, it was a Confederate official, Dr. William A. Carrington, medical director at Richmond, who reported that the death rate on Belle Isle had reached 10 per day by November and December of 1863 and had, at times, reached 15 to 25 per day.[134]

But as bad as conditions were at Belle Isle, there were few attempts to escape. "The Lieutenant [Bossieux] has spies who are on the watch," one prisoner confided. "The authorities know all about any conspiracy almost as soon as it is known among ourselves." The few prisoners who did attempt to escape are believed to have drowned.[135]

LIBBY PRISON

The concentration of POWs in the city, the resulting rumors, and actual escape attempts caused the civilian population to be often placed on alert. Workers there, the arsenal, and government departments were organized into regiments to be called to the field in the absence of the regular militia whenever a raid was imminent. These men literally worked with their muskets at their sides.[136]

In an effort to prevent inmates from helping invading forces if a raid became successful, Thomas and Dick Turner arranged for Libby Prison to be mined. "We were informed one morning by the negroes who labor around the prison," recalled Lieutenant Colonel Charles Farnsworth, 1st Connecticut Cavalry, "that during the night they had been engaged in excavating a large hole under the center of the building and that a quantity of powder had been placed therein." More than two hundred pounds of black powder, to be exact. That next morning, Dick Turner entered the prison to announce that any attempt to break out or to help an invading force would result in the prison being blown up.[137]

By the winter of 1864, the prison was well protected against escape. "The cellar floor through which [Colonel Thomas] Rose and his associates had dug their tunnel . . . had been masoned over," reported one prisoner, "and under the later arrangement of the guards it would have been impracticable . . . to secure admission to this floor without observation."[138]

In response to citizen demands for tighter security, a system of ropes and pulleys were installed at prison staircases, which could then be raised or lowered at the discretion of prison officials. The prisoners were now confined to their upstairs rooms. Nero, Captain Alexander's infamous guard dog, was brought over from Castle Thunder to patrol the Libby grounds.[139]

By winter the interior of the prison was still damp and the walls were spotted with lichen. Half of the prison's seventy-six windows were without glass. Wood rations were limited to only two or three armloads for each room, which had two stoves to accommodate up to four hundred men.

Eventually the overcrowded conditions along with the lack of sufficient sleep, food, and heat led to an increase in illnesses. Scurvy, chronic diarrhea, dysentery, and typhoid pneumonia became the most prevalent diseases and, before long, two to three deaths per day were not uncommon.

Bodies were placed in the west cellar and allowed to accumulate until a full wagon-load was obtained. Prison blacks were then given the detail of removing the bodies in their various stages of decay and transporting them to Oakwood Cemetery for burial. Like the middle cellar, used for storing cooking implements and carpentry tools, and the east cellar, used for holding straw, the west cellar was completely accessible from the street. Rats, breeding profusely in the straw of the east cellar, had complete access to the morgue.

"I have known of bodies being partially devoured by dogs [and] hogs . . . during the night," insisted Lieutenant Colonel Farnsworth. There was even one instance when heavy rains caused the James River to flood the cellars. The rats headed for high ground while the accumulation of bodies floated down the river.[140]

DANVILLE

Illness and death also became problematic at the Danville Prison in Virginia. Before the facility became a prison center, several of Danville's warehouses had been converted into military hospitals and placed under the direction of Doctor Fauntleroy, a local physician. The main hospital, for Confederate soldiers, was on the corner of Jefferson and Loyal streets. Another structure used as a hospital was built during the war on a hill overlooking the prisons and railroad shops of the Danville and Western Railway, while a third facility was established after the prisoners arrived for use as a smallpox ward. This was located nearby on what was referred to as Poor House Hill in the town's black neighborhood. By January 1864, all three hospitals were overcrowded and treating an average of four hundred to five hundred POWs.[141]

"[T]he mayor and common council of Danville," wrote Mayor Thomas P. Atkinson in a letter to Confederate Secretary of War Seddon, "petition for the removal of the Yankee prisoners located among us to some other place, or at least outside the limits of the corporation of Danville. . . . The hospitals of the prisoners and sick are located in the very heart of the town, and are not all in one place, but scattered in the most public and business places, so as to infect the whole atmosphere of the town with smallpox and fever now raging within the limits of the corporation."[142]

There is no record of any response by the War Department and although additional petitions were filed, the Confederate government continued to confine the prisoners where they were. By the end of January there were still four thousand POWs confined in the city; smallpox raged through the facilities, through the business district, and through the town. Danville undertaker John J. Hill found himself busier than ever before.[143]

Parasites were another big problem in the Danville prison buildings. "The beasts crawled over the ground from body to body," exclaimed prisoner George Putnam. "By daylight, they could be picked off and the first occupation of the morning was usually to free oneself from their immediate presence."[144]

Several escape attempts caused prison security to be tightened. Prisoners were no longer allowed access to the ground levels or yards of the buildings. When latrine use was necessary, prisoners were escorted out six at a time under heavy guard, and they were not allowed within six feet of the guard. Any violation of this rule resulted in the POW being shot or bayoneted. At the same time, POWs were no longer allowed at the windows of their buildings for any reason. Several violations of this latter rule subsequently occurred, and the violators were immediately shot. "They shot seven men for looking out," claimed prisoner Joseph Grider. "[O]ne was shot on my floor."[145]

Prisoner John Carroll, 5th Maryland (U.S.) Infantry, had his arm shattered during one such incident and hadn't even been at the window. "A man standing near me was washing his tin plate out of the window and some drops of water fell on the head of the guard below," explained Putnam. "Without a word of caution, the guard turned, put up his piece, and fired. The ball, missing the man at whom it was directed, went through the floor a little farther along and shattered the arm of a fellow who was entirely innocent in the matter."[146]

By late summer, the smallpox subsided and chronic diarrhea became the prevalent cause of death at Danville. Of 51 deaths in September, 40 were the result of diarrhea. It continued killing the POWs through the winter. During the three month period of November 1864, through January 1865, there were 416 deaths, 267 of which were from chronic diarrhea. Burials were conducted on land about a mile and a half outside of town.[147]

By October 1864, Major Mason Morfit was transferred out and Captain A. M. Braxton took over command of the Danville complex. He only served a couple of months before he was replaced by Lieutenant Colonel Robert C. Smith.

Colonel Smith, once a line officer, had suffered a wound to the shoulder, and was no longer fit for field duty. He also had POW experience, having been captured and imprisoned in the North for some time. The captives at Danville described him as a "kind, sympathetic man who would not voluntarily inflict any unnecessary hardships upon those under his charge." He quickly decided that he disliked the position of prison commandant and requested transfer several times.[148]

"He must do as other commanders of prisons have done and are still doing," responded Brigadier General John H. Winder to one of Smith's transfer requests, "that is, to make the best use he can of the means of his command. Relieving him would not remedy the evil; it would only throw it on somebody else." Stuck where he was, Smith began to drink heavily in order to isolate himself from the rapidly declining conditions of the prison.[149]

By January 1865, rations were down to nothing but cornbread. Prisoners had very little in the way of clothing, many lacked shoes, and, according to one prisoner, of 350 men who occupied one floor of a building, no more than 70 had even a scrap of a blanket.[150]

The guards, Colonel P. M. Henry's regiment of Virginia Reserves, living on the same rations as the POWs, were overworked and exhausted.[151]

"The prisons at this post," advised Arthur S. Cunningham, during an official inspection of the prison, "are in a very bad condition, dirty, filled with vermin, little or no ventilation, and there is an insufficiency of fireplaces for the proper warmth of the Federal prisoners therein confined. . . . It is a matter of surprise that the prisoners can exist in the close and crowded rooms. . . . The mortality at the prison, about five per day, is caused, no doubt, by the insufficiency of food . . . and for the reasons in addition, as stated above."[152]

SALISBURY

If conditions seemed bad at Danville, then the state of Salisbury Prison was utterly deplorable. The Salisbury pen had remained fairly stable up into 1864 despite a continuing number of changes in command. Captain Swift Galloway, Company H, 3rd North Carolina Regiment, had taken over as commandant back in 1863 and held the post for several months. He was succeeded around July 1864, by Colonel John A. Gilmore of the 27th North Carolina. Both of these men were considered good administrators. Gilmore had been severely wounded in battle and was unable to perform any further active service. His prison guard was composed of three companies of men known as Freeman's Battalion, with Captain C. D. Freeman in charge. At this time the prison population consisted of 310 Confederates under sentence of court-martial, 96 deserters, and 164 political prisoners.[153]

Colonel Gilmore resigned in September because of deteriorating health and was replaced by Major John H. Gee of the 11th Florida Regiment. Gee was a physician in Quincy, Florida, before the war, but General Braxton Bragg later remarked that he had been appointed to the position of commandant at Salisbury because of his "prudence and discretion" in being able to properly handle a number of "hard cases" at the prison.[154]

Within weeks of assuming his new duties, Gee received orders from Richmond to prepare the prison for "a very large number of prisoners." Since the only well was one located beneath some oak trees near the center of the stockade, Gee began preparing for arrivals by having more wells dug. In order to be done in time, his men dug throughout the next several days and by candlelight at night. At the same time, carpenters began work to enlarge the stockade.[155]

Before these improvements could be completed, a train rolled into Salisbury on October 5, 1864, with 5,000 prisoners on board. Major Gee was devastated. In the following weeks more trains arrived. Gee immediately complained to Richmond authorities but was ignored. By the end of October, 10,321 POWs were incarcerated at the Salisbury Prison.[156]

The officers and privates were corralled into separate portions of the prison. Officers were kept on the eastern side, where most of the buildings were, and the privates were cordoned off into the western portion, where trees were the only shelter. The two groups were kept apart by nothing more than a line of guards, but there weren't enough guards to control the population.

Confederate convicts and Federal POWs were in a continuing feud that often led to violent gang fights. Several killings occurred during this time, and muggings increased dramatically. Quite often guards could hear the cries of "help!" and "murder!" as they walked the parapets at night, but couldn't do anything about it. "One night," reported Reverend A. W. Mangun, the prison chaplain, "a [prisoner] was thrown from the upper window [of the main factory building] and taken up dead."[157]

Numerous attempts were made to escape. The most successful scheme developed was "the smallpox ruse," in which the prisoners would use red-hot needles to burn small holes all over their faces and bodies, then present themselves to the surgeon of the post. He would immediately order them to the prison hospital, located outside the stockade after October 1864. From there, prisoners were able to escape easily.[158]

Conditions became so chaotic at the prison that, finally, by order of the War Department, fifteen hundred additional guards were sent to assist in its daily operations. More than a thousand of these were senior reserves and the rest were mostly junior reserves, boys seventeen and eighteen years old but some as young as twelve. Except for Freeman's three hundred men, the guards turned out to be too old or too young to do an adequate job.

It wasn't long before the Salisbury POWs began to suffer intensely from hunger. Adequate supplies became unattainable in the area for the number confined. Prisoners resorted to climbing the oak trees for acorns and fishing crusts and bones from the sewage ditches and slop barrels. Within a short time, the wells became contaminated and typhoid broke out. The prisoners began dying at an alarming rate, sometimes as many as 75 a day. The average number of deaths dropped to 37 a day for a three-month period, but then jumped back up. In one eight-day period, 526 POWs had to be buried.[159]

The bodies were piled up each morning in the deadhouse. At 2:00 P.M. the prison's front gates were opened and a wagon drove into the yard. A work detail made up of prisoners piled the bodies onto the wagon and accompanied them out of the stockade, under heavy guard, to a nearby cornfield west of the prison. There, the prisoners were instructed to throw the bodies into pits measuring six feet wide, four feet deep, and sixty yards long. "The bodies were laid in them without covering," Reverend Mangum reported. "They were laid side by side, as closely as they would lie, and when the number was too large for the space that was dug, one would be placed on top between every two." By February 1865, there would be eighteen rows of these pits. The former physician in charge of the camp had no death records kept and no markers were used.[160]

Bodies were buried without clothing so that it could be given to the living. Most of the new arrivals were already in poor physical and mental condition when they arrived from Richmond. Many lacked clothing and shoes, and those who did have them were often mugged and stripped of everything by groups of other prisoners. Conditions became so bad at one point that prisoners petitioned the prison authorities for help, and the offending inmates were later transferred to a newly established prison at Andersonville, Georgia. These offenders eventually became the infamous "raiders" that would become so well-known in Andersonville's history.[161]

A lack of medical supplies and shelter added to the pandemonium inside the Salisbury stockade. The old buildings on the east side were overflowing with officers, while the privates had no shelters on the west. Tents were provided, but not enough were available. After Gee made several requests to Richmond, two hundred tents in various conditions finally arrived, but the number remained entirely inadequate. Nearly 50 percent of the inmates were still without shelter. Prisoners began burrowing into the ground for protection against the elements. Before long, the entire enclosure was honey-combed with holes.

"They were square or round holes dug some three feet deep, with a mud-thatched roof," explained Reverend Mangum. "[With] a hole being punched through to the surface at one end and a little chimney further built up out of baked earth. Over the entrance there was a little porch or projection that, as long as it withstood the rain itself, kept the water from the main part of the burrow. . . . The tenant had either to sit or lie down in them; they were too shallow for him to stand erect. . . . [T]hey not infrequently died there alone, and were not discovered for days."[162]

To make matters worse, the unusually severe winter of 1864–65 brought snow to a depth of three inches across Salisbury on several different occasions between November and March. The red clay soil held rainwater or melting snow until the surface became a boggy mire. Ditching was attempted several times but failed to sufficiently drain the grounds.

Wood was a long distance away and thirty-nine wagons impressed for its delivery still couldn't provide an adequate supply. "There were but two stoves," reported prisoner Junius Browne, "both old and broken, in the room; and they gave out no heat, but any quantity of smoke, which filled the apartment with bitter blueness."[163]

At the end of November, the prison quartermaster arranged for a chimney to be built for the factory building to provide better ventilation for the old stoves. On December 1, when construction of the chimney had reached the third floor, unsound brick at the bottom gave way and the entire structure collapsed, killing one prisoner and injuring several more. Guards were immediately ordered to clear the structure and in the process several prisoners broke away and ran back to the building to obtain their only remaining possessions. They were immediately shot down by the guards.[164]

Major Gee was finally able to transfer the Union officers to Danville, thus providing more room and shelter for the remaining 6,500 POWs. It was also decided that six buildings would be constructed for additional shelter. Before the frames were completed, however, General Winder arrived to inspect the prison and declared the place entirely unfit. He advised that he would transfer the prisoners to a new site in South Carolina and ordered the construction stopped. The move, though, never took place.

"I feel a touch of sorrow," guard David McRaven wrote, "when I look off my stand on the garrison and see the amount of suffering and wretchedness." But the conditions for the sentries were no better. McRaven wrote that he needed shoes and another blanket. "Many of us," he continued, "[are] nearly barefoot and we get no shoes or clothes of any kind." In other letters he complained that straw for bedding had become scarce around Salisbury and that food was even harder to obtain. "An onion goes here for a dollar," he reported, "[and] apples four dollars per dozen." McRaven wrote home requesting that food be sent, stating: "I have had but little to eat . . . the colonel sent for rations for us and the prisoners but the train broke down on the track and we could get none."[165]

Food became almost nonexistent during several different periods at Salisbury. Rations were issued irregularly and usually consisted of Indian cornbread and weak cowpea soup. Mills for miles around were in use but couldn't meet the daily needs of the prison. Supplies were even impressed from passing trains.[166]

Cleanliness had become as impossible to attain as sufficient food and comfort. Water was scarce. Nearly all the wells had become muddy from overuse and were highly contaminated from the overcrowded grounds. The captives had become covered with the red North Carolina clay and had little left to wear but ragged uniforms, which were covered with vermin.

CHARLESTON

The POW population in Charleston continued to increase from the first of the year. By midyear, rations at the Charleston Jail consisted of no more than a quart of oatmeal and three pints of water a day. According to one prisoner, the USCT prisoners received only "a small piece of cornbread for each man." As the city jail became more crowded, the overflow was moved into the enclosed jailyard at the back of the building. Tents were erected for shelter.[167]

The enclosure around the yard was formed by a high masonry wall connected to the jail building and the city workhouse next door. Groups of prisoners gathered from time to time around an old wooden pump that served as a speaker's platform, while others often sat under an old fig tree that stood in one corner. Several outbuildings that served as privies were situated in the yard.

On July 27, 1864, five hundred additional POWs arrived in the city, transferred from the pen in Macon, Georgia, which was being evacuated as a result of Stoneman's raids in that area. By September, Charleston became the scene of the so-called "retaliation camps." During this time two additional locations in the city held POWs, the O'Connor House at 180 Broad Street and Roper Hospital on the west side of town near Calhoun and Courtenay streets.

The O'Connor House was a large, white, three-story clapboard structure with a two-story extension to the rear. Four Greek Corinthian columns, two stories high, supported a large porch roof across the front of the home. To the prisoners, their luxurious surroundings were a welcome change. According to prisoner Edmund E. Ryan, Company A, 17th Illinois, the Charleston jailyard had become "a dirty, filthy place unfit for human beings to live in."

"Eighty-six of us were taken from the jailyard to the private residence of Colonel O'Connor," recalled one prisoner. "We were treated exactly as well as the Confederates," reported Major Orlando J. Smith of the 6th Indiana Cavalry. "We were hungry sometimes [but] so were they."[168]

Those taken to Roper Hospital, a massive masonry structure with three stories of covered porches across the front, were even more thrilled. "We feel free," one prisoner reported, "although the rebel bayonets still surround us. . . .

[We] passed through the gateway of 'Roper' into the beautiful garden of the hospital. On our right is a palmetto, on our left an orange tree, while around us bloom flowers of every hue, whose very fragrance inspires us with new life. How great the change. Here we are comparatively free. Here all seem better contented. We are assigned quarters on the third floor *piazza;* the hard floor seeming a luxury, and the place itself a paradise."[169]

Within days Union officials came to believe that Federal prisoners were being held in the various sections of Charleston to prevent further bombardment. They soon retaliated by taking six hundred Confederate officer prisoners from Fort Delaware and putting them into an open stockade on Morris Island within range of Confederate shore batteries.

For weeks the bombardment of the city continued over the prisoners' heads and all around them.

"Five hundred officers were already under fire of our own guns at Charleston when [five hundred more] from Savannah were sent there on September 13," reported one prisoner.[170]

"The prisoners constantly wear a forlorn and haggard look," reported Lieutenant Willard W. Glazier, "owing in a great measure to starvation and exposure to danger. . . . Constantly under fire by day and night . . . many have become hopelessly insane while others have been incapacitated for all the duties of life hereafter, nothing but strong nerves and an inflexible will can save one under such circumstances."[171]

To make matters worse, September 1864 was an unusually rainy period in Charleston. It seemed to rain day and night. "We were without shelter, or wood to build fires," reported Glazier, "and were obliged to exercise constantly to keep from chilling . . . the [jail]yard became flooded with water some four or five inches deep, and, with our garments drenched and our limbs benumbed with cold, we were compelled to walk through this flood, in order to keep up circulation of the blood."[172]

"Our rations here [have become] very small," complained prisoner Edmund Ryan, "and, small as they are, we can scarcely get wood enough to cook them. The health of our officers is failing very fast, but the officer in charge of the prison says they cannot be taken to the hospital as there is no room. . . . Our poor privates who are confined here have the scurvy so bad and are so weak from sickness and disease that they are not able to walk."[173]

Before long, yellow fever broke out in the Charleston facilities to add to the calamity. "This is the king of terrors to the Southern people," wrote prisoner John V. Hadley, 2nd Brigade, Wadsworth's Division, 5th Corps, "and as [it] took hold of us with determined fatality, our guards became much alarmed."[174]

"The rebel captain commanding this prison, and also his adjutant, died last night of yellow fever," wrote Glazier on October 5. "We heard from our enlisted men at Charleston Race Course to-day. Starvation, exposure and the frightful ravages of yellow fever, are sweeping them off by the score." Hadley continued, "It was among us five days in [this] city, and it was reported that out of thirty cases among the prisoners, not one recovered."[175]

CAMP FORD

In early spring 1864, many of the POWs at Camp Ford had begun cultivating individual garden plots near their shelters for additional food. By May, however, the POWs who had wintered-over at Shreveport had returned and 340 more from the 36th Iowa Regiment, captured at Marks' Mill, Arkansas, near Moro Creek, had arrived.

"We passed in at the big gate near the [sulphur] spring and found some 6,000 prisoners," exclaimed J. E. Houghland, Company E, 19th Iowa, one of the POWs forcibly marched back from Shreveport. "Our old cabins were occupied and so were the holes in the ground . . . [t]here was no place for us except the bare ground, and such ground [was] filth."[176]

Conditions continued to worsen as the compound became more and more crowded. Over the following weeks an additional 1,186 Union soldiers, captured at Mansfield, Louisiana, during the Red River campaign, arrived. The sudden arrival of nearly 2,000 more captives created pandemonium inside the pen. Gardens were trampled long before they could be harvested. Trees that had provided shade inside the enclosure were immediately hacked down to provide shelter.

"Many have been without a change of underclothing upward of half a year," complained one group of prisoners, "[and] a large part are without shoes, numbers are naked from the waist, and some have nothing but their ragged blankets girt about them in the place of trousers."[177]

"The enclosed ground is entirely too small for the number of men," reported Confederate post surgeon F. W. Meagher. "The filth and offal have been deposited in the streets between the quarters from which arises a horrible stench. A great number of the enlisted men have no quarter or shelter and have to sleep out on the ground with not even a blanket to cover them."[178]

A detail of prison labor was assigned the task of building a prison hospital. A one-story structure forty-eight feet long and eighteen feet wide, with an addition of an eight-foot by thirty-six-foot ward, was built outside the prison walls. It was completed by the end of June 1864. At the same time, the compound was enlarged by about an acre.[179]

Almost immediately, thirty-five to forty patients were moved into the new hospital. The prevailing illness and cause of death of Camp Ford was scurvy, although some deaths also occurred that were peculiar to Camp Ford.

It wasn't at all unusual for the POWs confined there to be confronted with rattle-snakes and copperheads as well as scorpions and tarantulas.[180]

Death from scurvy was caused by a lack of fresh meat and vegetables. The camp's rations originally consisted of a half pint of cornmeal and three fourths of a pound of beef per day. Up until mid-1864, POWs could supplement their meals by purchasing milk and vegetables from local farmers allowed in camp. With the arrival of so many additional prisoners, though, it became a security risk to allow the locals in. At the same time, rations were reduced to provide enough to go around. Supplies were difficult to obtain as well. Eventually, only cornmeal could be provided.[181]

As the weeks passed, conditions in the camp continued to deteriorate. "In the latter part of the summer and the fore part of the fall our prison became extremely filthy," related I. A. Packard, Company A, 32nd Iowa Infantry. "The ground was full of graybacks and maggots. After lying on our blankets over night, you could take them up and scrape up a double handful of maggots under them."[182]

A small dump cart, driven by a local black farmer and escorted by a Confederate guard, previously entered the camp each day to remove trash and rubbish. POWs often enticed the guard off to one side to trade articles or talk him into taking items into town to trade or sell for the inmates while others climbed into the cart and concealed themselves in the debris. Then the guard accompanied the cart and driver to the gate, after which the farmer drove to an isolated hollow a quarter mile away, freed the escapees, dumped the trash, and returned to the stockade for more. One prisoner estimated that nearly 150 POWs escaped in this manner, but most were later run down and recaptured by guards with hounds. As a result of the attempts, however, the practice of having the trash hauled out was terminated.[183]

In nearby Tyler, a small community of several hundred residents with a distillery for making whiskey and medicine for the Confederate military, an armory, a harness shop, and a blacksmithing establishment, the town newspaper referred to the prison site as the "Camp Ford Borough." The prisoners, themselves, however, referred to it as "Ford City."[184]

"Shebangs were arranged in 'streets,' at right angles with a central thoroughfare that prisoners referred to as 'Fifth Avenue,'" declared prisoner A. J. H. Duganne. "Midway down Fifth Avenue, a platform, covered with a canopy of pine boughs, served as the market place." Here, everything that the prisoners made was sold, including additional food items. "I have corn-meal pancakes with a treacle syrup made of melted sugar," advised one prisoner. "I have a slice of bacon . . . [and] coffee made of burnt rye."

Another prisoner proclaimed, "[By winter, we] had built seven turning lathes within the prison, and made combs, rings, chessmen, and other articles to be bartered with rebels for additional items to eat."[185]

Camp Ford was another Civil War prison that had its own newspaper. Named *The Old Flag*, it was established and edited by Captain William H. May of the 23rd Connecticut Regiment. Individual articles were written by some of the prisoners, put together by May, and distributed among the inmates during the frequent concerts given by one of the Iowa regiments' bands.

Conditions remained bad at Camp Ford throughout the winter of 1864–65. "Colonel [Robert A.] Alston [CSA] reports great suffering amongst sick Federal prisoners for want of proper care and medical attention," Major General John G. Walker, commander of the District of Texas, New Mexico, and Arizona during the fall of 1864, wrote to the new prison commandant, Colonel George H. Sweet. "Let me know how this is and do everything in your power to make them comfortable."[186]

Colonel Sweet was just one in a long line of commandants assigned to the camp and then transferred out within a few months. None of these men were stationed there long enough to improve its condition, nor were they ever able to secure the necessary quantities of food, medical supplies, clothing, or other needs. They ranged from some of the best commanders to some of the worst and included, in addition to Major Thomas Tucker, a Colonel Allen, a West Point graduate who had resigned his U.S. service to join the Confederacy and was regarded by the prisoners as a kind and educated gentleman who treated the prisoners fairly; a Colonel Anderson, who seems to have had no impact on the POWs one way or another; Lieutenant Colonel J. P. Borders, who was despised by the prisoners and is said to have issued arbitrary orders. Under Borders, numerous unwarranted shootings of prisoners occurred. In fact, documentation supports that at least four POWs were killed by guards during his command.[187]

There were more than fifty documented tunneling attempts at Camp Ford with only a handful successful. "Tunneling began in March, 1864," admitted one prisoner. "The shaft was sunk some eight feet deep, and it was proposed to tunnel out below the northern stockade to a small enclosure just beyond the line of sentinels. . . . We disposed of all the excavated earth by dragging it in a box to the shaft opening, thence transporting it in water buckets to the different cabins and depositing it in fire places to raise the hearths. Fifteen men escaped but were recaptured within days, ran down by the Rebel guard cavalry and bloodhounds."[188]

Of four planned mass escapes, only one, involving more than fifty men, came close to success. Once out, they often found the territory between them and the Union lines extremely rugged and hostile. One group of three, in late 1864, fought the elements and evaded Confederate patrols and search parties for nearly three months, only to be recaptured and returned to the camp.[189]

Quite similar to other prisons, to fail in such attempts meant certain punishment. Many escapees were returned and hung by their thumbs in full view of the other prisoners. Some were forced to promenade around camp wearing only a barrel, while still others were held in solitary confinement.

Even without accurate, detailed records, it can be estimated that as many as 6,000 POWs passed through the gates of Camp Ford during its twenty-one month existence. The average monthly population of the enclosure during 1864 was around 4,700. The number of deaths is uncertain as well. Estimates range from 232 to 286, so it might be safe to say that at least 232 perished at the prison camp.[190]

The year of 1864 turned out to be the watershed period for the military prison systems on both sides. By that year, the facilities had become filled beyond capacity, and were plagued by uncontrollable filth, epidemics, and hundreds of deaths each month. The prisons were no longer simply holding facilities for POWs; they had become much worse. Several generations would pass before the proper words to describe these compounds would be coined.

The South sought to remedy the situation by opening a new facility in south-central Georgia, while the North opted to enclose a New York recruiting camp they had once considered as early as June 1862. With the establishment of Andersonville in the South and Elmira in the North, the era of the Civil War's concentration camps was about to begin.

Chapter 10

ESCAPE

Patriotism tends to fade with long imprisonment and suffering; As in all prisons, loyalty can become negotiable.

Author Unknown

After prolonged periods of incarceration, prisoners understandably became eager to leave the confines of their enclosures by whatever means available. Some obtained paroles for special details working as clerks, cooks or kitchen help, hospital stewards, or grave diggers; gathering or chopping wood; serving on water details; or even working in shops or factories that they knew produced war goods for the enemy. In Huntsville, Texas, many prisoners eagerly volunteered to work in the prison shops that produced uniforms and blankets for the Confederacy; in Richmond many willingly worked in the Tredegar Iron Works, which made Confederate cannon; and in Danville many worked at the Heck, Brodie & Company factory in nearby Deep River, North Carolina, which manufactured bayonets. At the same time, POWs held at Fort Delaware and Point Lookout eagerly volunteered to unload Union supply ships as they came in at the nearby docks.[1]

The two governments often sent military officials and even religious leaders into the prisons to persuade the inmates to take an Oath of Allegiance. Most refused and preferred to suffer in the pens, but there were those who did take an oath to join the opposing army. At Salisbury Prison, eighteen hundred Union captives took the oath administered by a Catholic priest. Later in the war, Confederate military officials would recruit large numbers at Andersonville, Florence, and Columbia, mainly because the prisoners there were convinced, by that time, that they had been abandoned by their own government.[2]

"For more than a week during the middle of February," one of the POWs lamented, "every waking hour was spent in anxious expectancy of Sherman, listening for the far-off rattle of his guns, straining our ears to catch the sullen boom of his artillery . . . [but] Sherman came not."[3]

Confederate authorities had begun enlisting some imprisoned Federals as early as March 1863, but serious recruitment didn't begin until September 1864, when more than eight hundred took the oath at the Florence pen, and at least that many accepted it at Andersonville. Eventually, the Confederate government would form two units, the 1st and 2nd Foreign Battalions, out of their recruited prisoners.[4]

Some of these prison recruits would serve remarkably well in their "galvanized" status. In December 1864, Union forces ran up against the 10th Tennessee (CSA) Regiment, containing 254 former POWs, at Egypt Station, Mississippi. "[T]he greater part of these men were on the rebel skirmish line," reported Major Addison A. Hosmer, "and when our forces came within range they opened a heavy fire, killing 3 officers and 20 men and wounding 74 others; [we] then made a charge, [and] they threw down their arms and surrendered. Immediately after their capture they alleged that they had been prisoners of war at Andersonville and joined the rebel service to escape death from starvation and disease." Major Hosmer failed to mention, however, that the "galvanized Rebels" were responsible for three-fourths of his casualties that day and that they had thrown down their weapons under the charge only because they were completely out of ammunition.[5]

Not many of those who took the oath became that dedicated, however. Most took it under the condition that they would not be required to fight their former comrades. They were often placed in internment camps outside the prison walls, where they received preferential treatment, including additional rations when possible.

"There were many among us," admitted prisoner John McElroy, held at a number of different Confederate prisons, "who, feeling certain that they could not survive imprisonment much longer, were disposed to look favorably upon the Non-Combatant's Oath, thinking that the circumstances of the case would justify their apparent dereliction from duty." Fort Delaware prisoner David A. Deaderick of Tennessee wrote, "When the men here lose all hope in the success of our cause, and their grit gives out, they apply for the oath and are put in separate barracks, and fed and treated better than the rest of us. We [too] call them 'Galvanized.'"[6]

The Federal government solicited its prisoners to take the oath almost from the war's beginning. The Union secretary of war finally ordered the cessation of these efforts in September 1864, but by that time, according to the New York *Times*, a total of 3,800 had taken the oath and donned the Union uniform to avoid further incarceration. Of that number, nearly 1,500 had been enlisted at Point Lookout and sent to the Department of the Northwest, 450 had been enlisted at Fort Delaware into the 3rd Maryland Cavalry and sent to the Department of the Gulf, and 1,750 had been enlisted among the Rock Island inmates and had been sent to different locations in Pennsylvania and, later, assigned to service on the Plains for use on the Overland route.

As the war dragged on, the number of prisoners continued to accumulate, and the conditions of the prison camps worsened; the Federal government found itself burdened by several thousand more POWs who wanted to take the oath. "These men have applied to enlist in our army," declared Major Grenville M. Dodge in a letter to the assistant adjutant general. "I respectfully submit if we had not better organize a regiment of these men and put them on the plains, where they can be made of use to our Government, relieve our prisons . . . [and not be such] a burden and expense to us." Eventually, nearly 6,000 of these "galvanized Yankees" were organized into six regiments and assigned to the western frontier.[7]

Throughout the war, however, escape became the most popular method to avoid confinement in either side's prisons. The first known successful escape from a Civil War POW camp is believed to be the one completed by Sergeants T. D. Parker, Franklin Cook, and R. E. Ellenwood of Companies I and E of the 8th U.S. Infantry, in August 1861, while held in Texas.

Surrendered as part of Lieutenant Colonel Isaac V. D. Reeve's command in May, these men were some of the first POWs paroled to the limits of Bexar County and then later moved under guard to Camp Van Dorn for confinement. "The enemy violated the obligations of the local parole," they later advised, "by placing them under guard and so reducing their issues of clothing and rations as to render [them] in a state of suffering." The three escaped in August while paroled out on a pass and made their way on foot across south Texas, over the Rio Grande into Mexico, and down to Tampico. Unable to get help from the U.S. consul at Tampico, they sought help from the British consul and got passage on an English ship to Havana. From there they were able to secure transportation on board a steamer bound for New York Harbor and arrived there on October 19.[8]

The first documented escape of a Confederate from a Federal prison may very well be that of First Lieutenant George W. Alexander, who later became commandant of Castle Thunder. Alexander, on a Confederate naval expedition that captured the U.S. steamboat *Saint Nicholas* in June 1861, by boarding her disguised as a laborer or mechanic, was apprehended by Governor Thomas H. Hicks and the Dorchester Guards at Cambridge, Maryland, on July 12, 1861. He was confined at Fort McHenry and charged with treason in committing piracy and for being a spy. After securing a Federal uniform from his wife during one of her visits, Alexander made his successful escape on September 7, sustaining a badly sprained ankle from his leap from the fort's ramparts. He finally arrived in Richmond sometime around October 2.[9]

As the war progressed, escapes continued, but official tabulations were not kept until July 1862. The number of escapes up until that time are unknown, but between July 1862, and April 1865, exactly 1,200 POWs successfully escaped from Union prisons. By 1864, with the dramatic increase in prison populations, the number of escapes increased as well. During a four-month period, 150 of about 1,900 confined at the Federally controlled prison at New Orleans escaped.[10]

During the existence of the Confederacy's Salisbury Prison, perhaps as many as five hundred to six hundred men escaped. For example, one morning a ladder was found propped up against the inside of the stockade fence, and the Confederate authorities had no idea how many prisoners might have escaped during the night.[11]

In many prisons, both North and South, POWs were able to deceive the sentinels and simply walk out the front gates. It happened on numerous occasions in Richmond and St. Louis, especially early in the war when prisoners darkened their hands and faces with charcoal or some other substance and walked out with the black servants or work details. In both locations, the ploy was tried so many times that the use of blacks as prison laborers had to be abolished completely. For a time the ploy was also used at Camp Douglas, along with a variety of other maneuvers.

"We have been building, fencing, laying sewers, water pipes, etc.," mused the commandant, Colonel Charles V. DeLand, in late 1863. "This has left large holes in the fence, openings in the ground, and during the days there have been large numbers of workmen passing to and fro among the prisoners. Of course all this has produced confusion. Prisoners have slid out the holes in the dark, have passed out as workmen, and in a variety of ways have eluded the vigilance of the guards."[12]

The most desperate form of escape was to rush or scale the prison walls, and it occurred at a number of locations. Alton Prison authorities were plagued by such occurrences. After more than fifty escapes from that institution, Stanton and Hoffman sent Brigadier General William Orme of the U.S. Volunteers, to inspect the facility.

Among other problems, Orme found the prison fence in bad need of repair, and he recommended that it be rebuilt immediately. "It could be cheaply rebuilt by the labor of prisoners," he suggested. By the time Stanton received Orme's report, more than twenty more Alton POWs had fled.[13]

On September 27, 1864, at least twenty Confederate prisoners at Camp Morton had assembled a half dozen ladders from their bunks over the previous few weeks and put a plan of escape into motion. "The plan on the part of the prisoners," advised commandant Ambrose Stevens, "seems to have been to commence throwing stones at the sentry on the walk, draw the fire, and then rush on the fence and escape."[14]

"I was on duty on the night of [the twenty-seventh]," reported James E. Pierson, Company H, 43rd Kentucky [Indiana] Volunteers, assigned as a guard. "Shortly after 8 o'clock I saw a number of rebels run from the barracks toward the end of my beat. They had ladders which they set against the fence and began to climb up . . . there were about fifteen or twenty [with] four or five ladders. [When] one of them [straddled] the fence . . . I shot at him, he exclaimed, 'O Lord,' and fell back inside the fence."[15]

Other sentries on other posts also opened fire. Altogether, eight weapons were discharged, two prisoners were killed, and several others were wounded, as evidenced by trails of blood from those who got away, and a number were driven back into the barracks.[16]

On November 14, as the bugler sounded curfew, sending the POWs to their quarters, and the oncoming shift guard detail marched toward the enclosure, the prisoners began a general disturbance, throwing rocks and water-filled bottles, and sixty POWs stormed the wall. A barrage of shots rang out, but thirty-one POWs got away.[17]

Attempts were also made to scale the walls surrounding Camp Chase in Ohio. "Preparations were made by constructing ladders from planks taken from our bunks and hidden conveniently under the barracks," related prisoner J. Coleman Alderson. "We armed ourselves with stones, knives, and forks. At the appointed time, Sunday afternoon, religious services were held in the streets. . . . Just before the close of the services we noticed that the guards were being doubled. We had been betrayed, and the attempt was therefore abandoned."[18]

"Many attempts were made to escape, but we were always betrayed by some Judas, whom we called 'razorbacks,' or a spy from the outside pretending to be a 'fresh fish,'" Alderson professed. "(F)requent reports were received from the prison stewards and from detectives employed inside the prison," acknowledged Lieutenant Colonel August H. Poten, assistant commandant of Camp Chase, "that a conspiracy existed among the prisoners [to escape]."[19]

Even more daring and desperate was the escape method of attacking the armed guards in an attempt to get out of prison. Still, it happened on a number of occasions at several locations. On November 5, 1863, one such group rushed a guard unit entering the front gate of Camp Chase. The sentries stationed along the parapet commenced shooting into the crowd. One prisoner was killed and several wounded before the escape attempt was broken up. At Camp Morton, on August 17, 1864, eight POWs on a work detail outside the camp overpowered the guard, enabling six of the prisoners to escape.[20]

Similar attempts were made at Salisbury and Danville but both were unsuccessful. At Salisbury, on November 25, 1864, prisoners became desperate after they had gone forty-eight hours without rations and were suffering from the bitter cold. Moments after the afternoon relief guard entered the prison, a crowd of prisoners rushed and disarmed them. "(After) overpowering the relief guard of nine men and a sergeant," the commandant wrote in his official report, "they succeeded in getting possession of most of the guns and commenced an attack on the sentinels on the parapet." One guard on post was shot and killed as a ball passed through the board plank beneath him. "At the same time, a rush of about 1,000 [prisoners] was made for the water gate and that part of the fence near the sinks where there was no troops [stationed]."[21]

As the mob crashed into the gates, outside guards turned their cannons and opened fire with grape and cannister. Several shots missed the compound and struck a hotel at the edge of town, just beyond the prison. Additional guards and a number of armed citizens of Salisbury arrived and began firing into the stockade. By that time, prisoners were throwing brickbats and baked earth-balls, an indication that the uprising had been planned in advance. Guards, some as young as fourteen and fifteen, stood their post, dodging and firing. As the cannoners found their range, prisoners began to scatter, running to take cover and diving into burrows, buildings, and tents for shelter. The riot lasted only ten minutes. "The result of the whole affair," reported the commandant, "was 2 of the guard killed, 1 mortally wounded and some 8 or 10 slightly wounded. The prisoners had 13 killed, 3 mortally wounded, and 60 others wounded."[22]

The prisoners at Danville made their bid for freedom on December 10, 1864. Led by Brigadier General Alfred N. A. Duffie, 1st U.S. Cavalry, and Colonel William C. Raulston, 24th New York Cavalry, the prisoners rushed two sentries who had entered Prison No. 3 to escort a group out for the evening water detail. Their plan was to overpower the guard, evacuate the building, capture the other guards, seize their weapons, and release all the prisoners in the other buildings. The initial scuffle inside the doorway, however, aroused the sergeant of the guard as he arrived with three additional sentries. Immediately he slammed and bolted the door as other guards sounded the alarm. Amid the confusion inside the building, the prisoners abandoned their attempts and tried to flee back upstairs. A guard standing outside fired a shot at Raulston as he ran by a window. He stumbled, but found his way back to the building's third floor. As the commandant and a detail of guards, with muskets loaded and bayonets fixed, stormed into the building, they found the POWs calmly sitting around playing checkers, reading, talking, or feigning sleep. Colonel Raulston was found bleeding profusely from a gut shot. Guards took him to the hospital for treatment, but he died five days later.[23]

A handful of individual soldiers became well-known in their day for the daring escapes they made from military prisons. In addition to John Hunt Morgan's escape from the highly secure Ohio Penitentiary and John Winston's across the thick ice at Johnson's Island, there were several others who received their share of publicity and basked briefly in the light of fame.

Probably one of the most successful escapees was Absalom C. Grimes of Hannibal, Missouri. Grimes was captured a total of five times during the war and escaped each time, twice while under sentence of death. His first capture came in December 1861, near Springfield, Missouri, as a member of Company K,

1st Missouri Cavalry (CSA). He later escaped and rejoined his troops at the Battle of Pea Ridge. Wounded there, he was captured again and taken back to Springfield for incarceration. This time, he devised an escape hatch, helped others to escape, and went into Springfield himself on numerous occasions to socialize but returned to the prison each night. Grimes was seen in town by off-duty military officials, and the shed where he was confined was searched several times, but the secret exit could never be located. Finally, the prison commandant challenged Grimes to visit him at his house sometime. Grimes showed up that night and was quickly arrested and transferred to St. Louis' Gratiot Street Prison. Not long afterward, while being transferred to the Alton prison, he escaped again. Captured and incarcerated a third time, he escaped within two weeks. Finally he was captured and incarcerated a fourth time, tried, and given a death sentence.[24]

"I was sent to Gratiot Street Prison," recalled Grimes, "on September 2, 1862, on the charge of being a rebel mail-carrier and spy. They brought me in guilty and I was sentenced to death; the day of execution being fixed for the second Friday in October, 1862. I was placed in solitary confinement, with handcuffs, ball and chain."[25]

"During the day," Grimes continued, "[I] would lay on my mattress in one corner of the room and cut a narrow groove across three of the floor planks. This I did in two places and split the tongues of the grooves with a dirk-knife. By inserting thin strips of wood in the cut places, the floor looked perfectly sound and was not observed by the prison officials." At night Grimes removed the boards and crawled beneath the floor to work on a foundation wall leading to an alleyway. "It took me two nights to cut through the wall, which was of brick 18-inches thick, and the foundation of stone two feet thick," Grimes later revealed. "On the night of October 2, a few days before my execution, I disengaged myself from my shackles and a 32-pound shell [and made my] escape."[26]

Grimes wasn't seen again until he was captured in June 1864. Again he was incarcerated at Gratiot Street and sentenced to be hanged. This time, all of his attempts at freedom failed, including one on June 20, just a couple weeks after his recapture. "There were in our room five prisoners, four of us being condemned men," Grimes recounted. "We scrubbed out our room and were sent with three guards to a lower yard while the floor dried. Previous to going there we had formed a plan to attack the guards and try to escape."[27]

The result was that the sentries on post began firing upon the prisoners as soon as they jumped the guard escort. "Two guards standing on each side of the gate outside the yard fired upon me," related Grimes. "One shot passed through my right leg to which I had a 32-pound shell attached. [Prisoner James H.] Colclaisair, on getting outside of the fence, was shot by a guard through the head, killing him instantly. When the yell was given that we had made the attack and the gate open, [prisoners] John Carlin, Jasper Hill, Alfred Yates, and several others, made a break for our yard. [Prisoner] William McElhany had his knee-cap shot off, and several others were shot. By this time, reinforcements of the guards had arrived and the game was blocked." In all, five men escaped, two were killed; two, including Grimes, were wounded; and the rest were recaptured.[28]

After this thwarted escape attempt, Grimes was transferred to the Missouri State Penitentiary in Jefferson City for safekeeping. While awaiting execution, he was inexplicably given an unconditional pardon by President Lincoln. On December 10, 1864, Grimes was released and sent home.[29]

While there were eventually more than one hundred successful escapes from Gratiot Street Prison, there were only four documented escapes from the Fort Warren Military Prison. Undoubtedly the fort's distance, the swift cold waters of the harbor, and the tolerable living conditions inside the facility all had some influence. In addition, not only were guards posted in and around the fort, sentinels also patrolled along the seawall and were positioned all along the shore. Still, four POWs managed to escape, and they did so by squeezing themselves through the seven-inch-wide loopholes on the ground level of the fort in August 1863.

"In the basement under the room which we were confined was a pump where we obtained water," confided Joseph W. Alexander, a North Carolinian in the Confederate States navy who was captured in Savannah on the ironclad *Atlanta* on June 17, 1863. "[I]n the outer wall of this basement were two holes called musketry loopholes." According to Alexander, the loopholes were over six feet high and two to three feet wide on the inside of the wall, which gradually narrowed to a little more than a six-foot-high, seven-inch-wide opening on the outside of the wall.[30]

After making several attempts to squeeze through the opening, Alexander discovered that by removing his clothes he could crawl out, although with great difficulty. Three other prisoners with him, Lieutenant C. W. Reed, Lieutenant James Thurston, and Reed Sanders, a political prisoner from Kentucky, also tried and, because they were thinner than Alexander, easily maneuvered through the opening once they took their clothes off. Realizing escape was possible, they returned to their room to plot their getaway.

"Waiting for a dark night," related Alexander, "we one by one squeezed through the loophole, and lowered ourselves down into the dry ditch between the main and water batteries. We made our way cautiously over the water battery and then through the grass towards the sea-wall."[31]

The prisoners, carrying their clothing, immediately saw the sentries patrolling the seawall and crouched down in the grass. They noticed that the guards' patrol consisted of walking toward each other at left-shoulder-arms along the top of the wall, meeting, and then turning and walking away from each other to a certain distance where they met another guard patrolling in the same manner. As the two guards closest to the prisoners met, then turned and walked away from each other, the prisoners quietly ran up and scaled the wall where the guards, with their backs to one another, were farthest apart.

After resting momentarily, Reed and Sanders hid along the shore as Alexander and Thurston quietly slipped into the water. "I determined that we would swim over [to that part of] the island on which the lighthouse stood," wrote Alexander, "get a boat and return for Reed and Sanders, neither of whom, being poor swimmers, were willing to run the risk."[32]

The two swimmers had noticed a large wood target at the water's edge that the fort's garrison sometimes used for practice. Removing it, they placed their clothes on top and pushed the target out in front of them as they swam. "Though it was August," Alexander later recalled, "the water seemed as cold as ice." After what seemed like hours, the men, exhausted and nearly numb with cold, finally neared their destination.

"[W]e stopped for a moment, letting our feet sink under us," related Alexander. "We both touched bottom at the same time, and, straightening up, we waded ashore, pulling the target after us."[33]

The men set out along the shore and eventually found a small sailboat dragged up on the beach. Shoving the craft into the water, they set off to pick up their comrades. Upon nearing the fort, the men lowered the sail to avoid detection by the sentinels. They waited and watched, but there was no sign of the other two. As the night sky crept toward dawn, fearing their position would soon be revealed to the guards, the two men reluctantly hoisted the sail and turned the boat toward the open sea.

"[A]fter getting outside to what we considered a sufficient distance from the land," revealed Alexander, "we headed up the coast, intending to land in New Brunswick [Canada]." The two men alternately slept and sailed for some distance. By the next evening they ran close to shore at Rye Beach, New Hampshire, where they obtained food and more clothing, and sailed off expecting to reach Canada by morning. Before reaching that destination, however, a U.S. revenue cutter bore down on them and after coming up alongside, took them into custody.

Taken into the Portland, Maine, harbor, the escapees were incarcerated in the city jail for a month before they were transferred back to Fort Warren in shackles. There they learned that their two comrades had been captured by the sentries along the shore the night of the escape and had been returned to the fort to be held in irons. Although it was only a brief reprieve, their remarkable feat is considered the only successful escape from Fort Warren. It generated a lot of publicity and made these POWs a legend.

A number of POWs found escape from Fort Delaware a possibility too. "Expert swimmers could take advantage of the tide at certain hours," reported one prisoner, "[but] if they were wrong, they were swept out to sea and drowned."[34]

According to the official records, no escapes took place prior to General Schoepf becoming commandant. The longer he was there, the more willing the prisoners became to take their chances with the sea. The first escape occurred two months after Schoepf took command, in June 1863. By the end of the war, fifty-one more would be reported. Probably the most notable, however, occurred in August 1864.

At about nine o'clock one night, prisoners Joe Deupree, William B. Rodgers, and Benjamin Kelly successfully eluded guards and entered the bay with canteens tied to their waists as floats. Guided by the lights of nearby Delaware City, they drifted with the waves for six hours. As the tide rose and the waves became larger, the lights were no longer visible and the men became separated. Deupree, exhausted and half frozen, came alongside a vessel and was taken aboard only to discover that he was within fifty yards of shore. By daylight he was back in Fort Delaware Prison receiving his punishment. Rodgers and Kelly reached shore at separate locations and eventually found their way back to Confederate lines to rejoin their regiments.[35]

Sometime later, Deupree did successfully escape Fort Delaware by assuming the name, company, and regiment of a sick prisoner scheduled for exchange who had died shortly before his scheduled departure.[36]

Another escape that became famous and propelled the participants into nineteenth-century stardom occurred on December 18, 1864, at Salisbury Prison. Often referred to as "The Walk of the Journalists," four prisoners— Albert D. Richardson and Junius H. Browne, both reporters for the New York *Tribune*, William E. Davis of the Cincinnati *Gazette*, and sixteen-year-old merchant marine Henry Mann—bluffed their way past guards and successfully completed a 340-mile journey back to Union lines. They later provided newspaper accounts of the daring getaway.

Browne and Davis were prison trustees who worked at the hospital dispensary outside the prison walls. Having to go out and return each day through the gates, they were given passes and soon became well-known to the inner prison guards as well as the sentry surrounding the outside. After a while, they were no longer required to show their passes. On December 18, Browne gave his pass to his good friend Richardson, and the three passed through the prison gate along with Mann, who had been given Davis's pass and was carrying a box of medicine bottles. They passed through the second line of sentinels and walked about the hospital enclosure for a time to alleviate suspicion, then quickly slipped away to hide in a nearby barn. After twenty-four hours passed and no unusual activity was noticed, the men emerged, split up for better odds, and began their trek to Union-held territory. After nearly a month, Browne walked into Knoxville, Tennessee, and two days later Richardson rode in on horseback.

In time, many prisoners devised a wide variety of methods to flee the confines of their facilities. They feigned sickness or particular diseases in order to get to the prison hospitals located outside the prison walls. Then too, inmates pretended to be dead at a number of different prisons in order to be carried outside, or they would attempt to scale the wall under cover of darkness if the bodies were left stacked inside the gate.

At one prison, a POW pretended to be dead and allowed himself to be loaded onto a wagon and hauled off toward the burial ground. Once the wagon got a good distance from the prison, he slipped away.[37]

At Salisbury one of the POWs sent out under heavy guard on a burial detail was a ventriloquist. With the first shovelful of dirt thrown down on the body, it began protesting loudly, or so thought the guards, who ran away. The men of the burial detail then escaped in the opposite direction.[38]

POWs in other prisons devised methods unique to the facilities in which they were held. At Gratiot Street, and later at Alton, inmates often set fires to create diversions for the guards. The method is believed to have been developed or at least greatly encouraged by prisoner Ebenezer Magoffin, who was held at both locations. The first time it was used was two months after he arrived at Gratiot Street for incarceration.

On February 24, 1862, the roof of the prison caught fire. The flames were quickly extinguished by prison authorities. Within a half hour a pile of mattresses at the entrance to the second floor of the south wing burst into flames. That, too, was extinguished, just as the bed of Magoffin, in the southwest corner of the wing, flared up. It also was extinguished, and all 177 Confederate officers were prevented from escaping that day. In the months that followed, fires erupted several more times, but all were unsuccessful in aiding an escape. Once Magoffin was transferred to Alton, suspicious fires began to break out there, which did aid a number of escapes. Inmates continued to use this method long after Magoffin got out of the facility.[39]

At Danville, Union POWs developed what they called "the old furnace road to freedom." It was along the hundred-yard path traveled by the water party. At one point, the route passed the back of a foundry and there, when the furnace was "out of blast," it was possible to tumble into the cavity of the furnace when the guard was inattentive and lay there until nightfall to make way through the backcountry to North Carolina. This ploy was only successful three to four times, but it went unnoticed for over five weeks.[40]

Daily roll calls failed to reveal the continuing escapes because a hole had been sawed in the floor, in the corner farthest from the stairway, between the second and third levels of the prison and covered with a blanket. The usual habit of the Sergeant of the Guards was to enter the second floor and stand in the doorway as he counted the prisoners. He would then proceed up the stairs to the upper floor, preventing any prisoners to pass him, and count the number of POWs on the third floor. As escapes continued for more than a month, prisoners on the second floor would hoist the same number of POWs that corresponded to the number of escapees through the hole onto the third floor as the sergeant proceeded up to that level to count heads. This worked until an escapee was captured and it was learned he had absconded from Danville, where no report of an escape had been filed. When a second escapee was captured, a detailed search of the Danville buildings revealed the method used, and the hole was quickly sealed.[41]

At Point Lookout, hardtack crates often served as building material for Confederate prisoner housing. The hardtack came in fifty-pound boxes made of white pine or some other light and easily worked wood, about thirty-two inches long by twenty inches wide and twelve inches deep. The prison commissary or sutler sold the empty containers to the prisoners for anywhere from ten to fifteen cents each, depending on the demand.

"These were knocked to pieces carefully," revealed one prisoner, "the nails all saved, and the boards put away, until longer pieces of wood in sufficient numbers to make a frame were procured from outside. This accomplished, and the boards nailed on carefully, the 'A tent' was slit up the back, and stretched across the ridge pole of the new domicile to form the roof."[42]

One group of prisoners eventually came up with the idea of using the boxes to make parts of two canoes that they could quickly connect on the day of their planned escape. Guards, however, discovered the carefully concealed parts of the craft and burned them along with the prisoners' cracker box house and belongings, leaving them totally destitute for their efforts.[43]

There were also spur-of-the-moment plans that sometimes worked. At Rock Island, three POWs were taken out of the compound on a work detail to repair the roof of a nearby building. As they were returning, one of the prisoners remembered he had left his tools behind at the job site and asked the guard to return with him while the other two POWs waited where they stood. Unbelievably, the Union guard complied and returned with the prisoner. The other two ran off, undoubtedly owing a great debt to their comrade.[44]

Of all escape methods, tunneling was no doubt the most popular. Contemporary accounts often mentioned anywhere from three to ten tunnel excavations going on at the same time in some prisons, including Camp Morton, Camp Douglas, Rock Island, Macon, Salisbury (where as many as sixteen tunnels were in progress during one period), and Danville.

Within two months of the establishment of Danville Prison, where POWs were allowed some access to the ground floors and backyards of the warehouses for exercise, excavations were in progress at Prisons 3, 4, and 5. At No. 5, an informer alerted the authorities before the project was completed. The cavity was refilled and the men were bucked and gagged for punishment.

Those in No. 3 inadvertently burrowed too close to the surface of the prison yard, and during the night a sentry on patrol fell through and broke his arm.

"[H]e yelled murder," remembered prisoner George Putnam, "and the guard next to him fired off his piece. Then followed a general firing of pieces into the darkness and the turning out of the entire prison guard. . . . Nothing more serious happened, however, than the spoiling of our sleep for the early morning hours." Once the guard was pulled from the hole, the tunnel was traced back to the building's cellar, where it was sealed off from further use.[45]

Meanwhile, the efforts in No. 4 led to success. When it was completed, after nearly four weeks' work, the tunnel extended 147 feet, opening out into the back yard of a black family's shanty. More than seventy Danville POWs made their escape before the tunnel was discovered.[46]

Sixty prisoners escaped through an eighty-foot-long tunnel from Gratiot Street Prison on December 12, 1862, after one man at a time dug in the hole and hoisted dirt out by means of a tin pan connected to a cord over a period of several weeks. However, a number of the men were recaptured before they got out of the city.[47]

The most famous escape of this type during the war was the Hamilton-Rose tunnel at Richmond's Libby Prison in February 1864. It was a tunneling effort led by prisoner Thomas E. Rose, a colonel at the time in the 77th Pennsylvania Volunteers. Though Rose received all the publicity for the incident and wrote about it after the war, he was not the mastermind of the plan. It was actually Major Andrew G. Hamilton of the 12th Kentucky Cavalry who first conceived of the idea.

Hamilton suggested they begin the tunnel behind the stoves in one of the fireplaces. Then a partition wall was followed downward for three or four feet. This placed them below the floor of the cook and hospital rooms. From there they worked their way through another wall, gaining access to "Rat Hell," a room in the east cellar used for the storage of straw to an average depth of two feet across the floor, which subsequently attracted large colonies of rats. From there they were able to escape detection as they began tunneling outward from the prison.[48]

"The work was all accomplished secretly and at night," explained prisoner James Wells, 8th Michigan Cavalry, "after 'lights out' or nine o'clock, [when] everybody in the prison was supposed to be laying down, two men, having first quietly removed the bricks, would go down and take turns digging throughout the night. In the meantime two or three others would remain on watch in different parts of the prison, ready to give the signal or help the two workmen up on the first approach of day. The night's work done, the bricks were carefully replaced, covered over with soot and dirt which was always plentiful behind the stove, and in this condition the place was left secure from observation until night came on again."[49]

A selected group of prisoners took turns digging the tunnel over the next several weeks using clam shells and case knives. The tunnel was eight to nine feet below the surface of the ground and, upon completion, measured sixteen inches in diameter and fifty to sixty feet long. Dirt was removed by means of a cord connected to a wood box, which was originally used as a spittoon in one of the prison rooms. As the box filled, it was drawn out of the hole by another prisoner and emptied in the cellar, where it was spread evenly across the floor and covered with straw.

"One night," remembered one of the diggers, Lieutenant Frank E. Moran, 21st Wisconsin Regiment, "when [Major B. B.] McDonald was the digger, so confident was he that the desired distance had been made, that he turned his direction upward, and soon broke through to the surface. A glance showed him his nearly fatal blunder. . . . McDonald saw that he had broken through in the open lot which was all in full view of a sentinel who was dangerously close. Appalled by what he had done, he retreated to the cellar and reported the disaster to his companions." [50]

Someone went and woke Colonel Rose, who came down to inspect the hole, which was just big enough to poke a man's head out. He then stuffed one of the men's shirts into it, and the excavation continued with the hope that the guard wouldn't notice the shirt or bother to inspect it. Four days later, on the evening of February 9, after forty-seven continuous days of digging, 109 prisoners made their escape through what would become known as the "Great Yankee Tunnel." Colonel Abel D. Streight, 51st Indiana, being the highest ranking officer confined in the prison, was the first to go out. [51]

"About twenty-five of the prisoners are said to have been in on the secret," reported Lieutenant Colonel Frederic F. Cavada, 114th Pennsylvania, "these were to make their escape early in the evening, and were to have two hours start; after that, the rest of the prisoners were to be informed, and all who were strong enough to make the attempt were to be allowed to go out." [52]

The following morning, Libby's remaining prisoners, about twelve hundred, took their usual positions for roll call. Dick Turner and clerk Ross began counting and immediately noticed the absence of a number of prisoners. Thinking there must have been a mistake, they recounted and arrived at the same result.

The authorities were completely exasperated as to how the escape could have occurred. At first they thought 115 prisoners were missing but later revised the figure to 109. The authorities, thinking bribed guards were responsible, arrested a number and placed them in irons. By evening, however, a prison adjutant, Lieutenant John LaTouche, discovered the tunnel and immediately notified other prison officials. [53]

In the subsequent search throughout Richmond and the surrounding countryside, two prisoners were found to have drowned trying to swim across the James River. As the days passed, forty-eight more, including Rose, were recaptured. They were punished by being placed in irons, in the dark recesses of the prison cellars, and put on a diet of cornbread and water. In all, fifty-nine escaped Libby Prison through the tunnel and reached their lines.[54]

Nearly all prisons, in both the North and South, had some form of punishment for attempting to get away. "[A] failure to escape," recalled one prisoner, "meant a suspension by the thumbs until the anguish of pain would drive some into insanity, or ordered to hard labor on the grounds with a ball and chain fastened to one's feet and legs, or to be 'bucked and gagged' daily, for hours at a time and left to lie in this wretched condition on the frozen ground or to be maimed for life by being shot . . . yet, with all these tortures witnessed by us daily, in the desperation of suffering and starvation, men would often run the risk."[55]

Unfortunately, there were many more failures than successes. According to prisoner Wells, "plan after plan was devised for escape, only to be proved impractical." Individual, group, and general escapes were devised time after time, only to be discovered by the authorities, revealed by a traitor among the prisoners, or accidentally foiled by a miscalculation of some type.

One group dug a tunnel beyond their prison stockade and broke through the surface right in the middle of the guard detail's campfire. Stunned, the guards jumped to their feet, and when a POW sprang to the surface among the embers, they ran off, completely startled. At another prison, a tunnel was dug over a period of several weeks, but before it was completed a cow grazing on the outside of the prison fell through, alerting the guards, who traced the tunnel back to its source.[56]

Tunneling became so prolific at some northern prisons that Federal officials later removed the barracks' floors or elevated the buildings on posts to prevent concealment of the work. By mid-1864, most prisons had a deep ditch excavated along the fence within the compound, or several yards distant around the outside, in an effort to prevent or reveal such efforts. Still, the tunneling continued.[57]

When Union prisoners did escape from Southern prisons, they were often helped along their escape route by friendly blacks. Prisoner John Ransom jumped from a railroad car while being transferred to Savannah and was later fed and assisted through enemy lines by them all along his route until he reached the front. Willard Glazier and another POW conned their way out of the temporary stockade at Columbia and later ran across some blacks who led them to safety, and one, later, guided them out of enemy territory.

"The country outside of cities and villages in the south is always so sparsely settled that, once on the road, and no hounds upon the track, one can readily find places of concealment," explained Glazier. "Of course it was our policy at the first to keep comparatively scarce for a time; but soon after dark we struck the road, and directly came upon a company of negroes returning from work upon government fortifications. . . . After assuring ourselves of their color, we agreed to make their acquaintance. This was readily done after convincing them we were not rebels in disguise . . . as it would have been death to them to have been found in our society. One of the party, Ben Stedman by name, was soon secured as a guide; and, to avoid unpleasant surprises, we agreed upon keeping in his rear, as he would be always safe, while a recognition of ourselves would be neither safe nor pleasant."[58]

Escapees in Texas usually fled toward the Mississippi River and then headed north. In Virginia, they usually moved toward the northeast or to the nearest front, except POWs who had escaped Danville, where they, along with those from Salisbury, often headed toward the nearby North Carolina mountains to hide out or seek a safe route. "These mountains meant to us more than a bit of scenery," advised one prisoner. "We associated with them the possibilities of freedom. It was the general talk that if a man could make his way to the recesses of the mountains, and that if he did not starve or freeze in the wilderness, and if he struck the right kind of darkies or the right kind of Southern deserters, he might possibly finally get through to our lines."[59]

Confederate soldiers who escaped confinement in the far north usually fled to the Canadian border. Various means of transportation were utilized to get there. The usual crossing was at Rouses Point, New York, which led on to Montreal.[60]

Upon reaching Montreal, escapees made contact with one of several leading citizens who sympathized with the Confederate government. Most of these contacts were former citizens of the South willing to render assistance to escaped Confederates and to help raise money for their journey back to the South. One of these was a Mr. Parsons, editor of the Montreal *Evening Telegraph.* Assistance was usually obtained for passage on the Grand Trunk Railway to Quebec, and on into Halifax, Nova Scotia.[61]

"So bitter is the feeling in this place against the Yankees," declared one Confederate escaped prisoner regarding Halifax, "that a Federal officer cannot walk the streets, with uniform on, without being subject to insult even from the little boys in the city."[62]

One Halifax resident who aided Rebel escapees was Alexander Keith, Jr. Among other things, Keith acted as a relay agent for messages between Confederate agents in Canada and Richmond. He also was one of several prominent men in the city who provided money, time, and influence on behalf of the Confederacy.[63]

Because there were usually a number of blockade runners undergoing repairs in the port at Halifax, passage was usually arranged on one of them for the return of escaped POWs to the South. "After three weeks delay in Halifax," wrote escaped Confederate prisoner D. U. Barziza, "I shipped aboard the royal mail steamship *Alpha,* in company with some half dozen Confederates, and after a passage of about four days arrived at St. Georges, in the Bermuda Islands."[64]

St. George's Harbor was often crowded with blockade runners. Large, deep-drafted European freighters arrived at this neutral way station almost daily to off-load their cargo onto the sleek, fast, low-profiled ships whose captains were willing to attempt the run past Union vessels into the southern harbors. "The British have a garrison at St. Georges," Barziza continued. "I saw the Confederate flag flying from six or seven steamers in this port, and saw the stars and stripes, 'alone in its glory,' floating from an insignificant looking brig."[65]

In the Bermuda Islands, contact was made with an agent who also had charge of a large amount of stores and munitions belonging to the Confederate government. From there the escapees were usually placed on a blockade runner that was heading for the coast of North Carolina.

"Blockade runners keep a man at the mast-head during the day, who reports every vessel in sight," explained a former POW. "If a steamer is discovered, without waiting to find what she is, the ship is hauled off, and runs her out of sight. So it happens that, sometimes, two blockade runners are running from each other. All of these ships are built very light, carry powerful machinery, and are very fast. They are painted white from stem to stern, so as not to be so easily discovered at sea."[66]

After outrunning or outmaneuvering Union blockaders, the blockade runner often arrived at the North Carolina coast under the protection of Fort Fisher at Confederate Point. There, supplies and former POWs were unloaded. Other ports were sometimes used as the process continued over and over throughout the war.

A number of major plots to release all the prisoners at several facilities also developed during the war. Johnson's Island became the main target of most of these, but Camp Douglas, Camp Butler, and Rock Island were involved in some Confederate plans. There was also a failed Union attempt, the Kilpatrick-Dahlgren Raid on Richmond's prisons.

One of the earliest plots was an unsubstantiated rumor involving Johnson's Island only six months after it was established. "A scheme is reported to be on foot in Canada by Southern sympathizers to release the prisoners on the island," warned Adjutant General Lorenzo Thomas in a dispatch to Commandant Pierson dated June 18, 1862. "Be on your guard." Additional Union troops were rushed to the island from Camp Chase but nothing more materialized.[67]

Then, in November 1863, Lord Richard B. P. Lyons, British consul at Baltimore, advised Federal officials in Washington that his staff had uncovered a plot to attack Johnson's Island to release the POWs with plans to proceed with them on an attack of Buffalo, New York. Union authorities immediately notified

Governor Tod of Ohio and placed two artillery batteries on Cedar Point, a peninsula that commanded the entrance to Sandusky Bay, and moved the steamer *Michigan*, with its fourteen guns, into its waters. Tod rushed six companies of the 12th Ohio cavalry to the scene.

By all indications, Lyons' tip was well-founded. According to some sources Confederate Secretary of War James Seddon and Navy Secretary Stephen R. Mallory had contacted Major Robert D. Minor of the "Naval Battalion," actually the 4th Virginia Battalion, and suggested a covert plan to free Confederate prisoners on the island. Reportedly, the Confederate government furnished $110,000 and twenty-two naval officers for the effort. Minor and B. P. Loyall reached Montreal on October 21 and established communication with the prisoners through the personal columns of the New York *Herald*. In one final ad it was announced that a "carriage will be at the door a few nights after the 4th of November."[68]

A flurry of Union activity began. The sutler was ordered off the island. The mail was stopped. Rifle pits were dug at lakeside. Artillery was rolled into place. Those on Cedar Point were put on constant alert. More reinforcements arrived until the number of Union troops in the area swelled to several thousand. They sat throughout the following days and nights and waited, closely watching the horizon.[69]

"I remember an amusing incident connected with this excitement," recalled one prisoner. "One still, calm, dark night, about twelve o'clock or after, a mischievous fellow stepped out on the steps of his block and crowed three times like a shanghai; scarcely had the echo died away, when it was answered in the same manner from the other end of the yard. Immediately the long roll beat to arms, and the Yankees were formed, waiting for the attack, whilst those of the rebels, who were awake, laughed at their scare, and quietly kept between their blankets."[70]

November 4 came and went. Perhaps the additional fortification of the island frustrated all of the clandestine efforts. Whatever the cause, nothing ever materialized from this plot.

The fear of an attack on the facility out of Canada continued throughout the following months. In January 1864, additional troops—five regiments of the 3rd Division, VI Army Corps—were assigned to build up and reinforce fortifications and to help guard the prisoners. Months were spent maintaining these fortifications until September, when island authorities were alerted to yet another serious threat.

"[P]arties will embark today at Malden [on the Canadian side of the Detroit River] on board the *Philo Parsons*," advised Benjamin H. Hill, Detroit's assistant provost marshal in an urgent dispatch to Captain John C. Carter, commander of the *Michigan*, on September 19, "and will seize either that steamer or another running from Kelley's Island . . . am again assured that officers and men have been brought by a man named Cole. A few men to be introduced on board under guise of friends of officers. An officer named Eddy to be drugged. [We] look upon the matter as serious."[71]

Hill's tip, too, was well-founded and based on fact. In 1864, Confederate Captain Charles H. Cole, Nathan B. Forrest's Cavalry Corps, escaped from Johnson's Island and fled into Canada. There, he contacted Confederate agents and, with information he supplied about the prison and its security, a plot to free the nearly twenty-five hundred Johnson's Island POWs developed. Confederate authorities chose their acting naval master, Captain John Yates Beall, to lead what turned out to be an elaborate rescue scheme.[72]

The plan involved commandeering a couple of passenger boats, including the *Philo Parsons,* waiting for Cole to send up a flare signal from the *Michigan,* where he, under the guise of a Philadelphia banker, would attend a dinner party on board, seize control of the ship, and have its big guns turned on prison headquarters with the demand to surrender the island.[73]

"I think it was about 2 o'clock on the afternoon of the 19th when Captain Carter came to my office and submitted two telegrams which he received from Lt. Col. B. H. Hill," the prison commandant, Colonel Charles W. Hill, later reported. "He proposed to at once arrest Cole. I concurred in the proposition and he departed for his ship." Cole was arrested in his Sandusky hotel room that afternoon while getting ready for the dinner party, and taken aboard the *Michigan* for interrogation. Commandant Hill was notified of the arrest around 4 P.M. and proceeded out to the ship at once to participate in the questioning.[74]

"He [Cole] represented that there was to be a land expedition to come into Sandusky that evening on the different railroads," advised Colonel Hill, "that there had been some talk among the conspirators to charter a propeller and get up ostensibly a mere boat ride, the men to be attended a part of the way from Detroit River by lewd women to keep up appearances; stated that the 'thirty shares' mentioned in the telegram of Norris to him meant thirty men, and that that number would come into Sandusky on the different trains to arrive that evening."[75]

Actually, the party of men, mostly Copperheads out of Ohio posing as mechanics and laborers bound for Chicago, had increased to fifty-four with the addition of escaped prisoners found in Canada. Their responsibility was, among other things, to seize the National Guard Armory in Sandusky and cut the telegraph wires to isolate the town. Under interrogation, Cole revealed a number of surprising names involved in the plot. Among them were Jacob Thompson, a Mississippian who had been President James Buchanan's secretary of the interior; James C. Robinson, the Democratic candidate for governor of Illinois, who was also involved in a plot to liberate POWs at Camp Douglas and Camp Butler; and several leading citizens and businessmen of Sandusky.[76]

Once Cole implicated these men and revealed the size of the plot, Federal authorities scrambled to make arrests. A number of the conspirators eventually did jail time for their participation. Charles Cole, incarcerated as a spy at Fort Lafayette, would later testify against a number of others and continue his imprisonment until February 10, 1866. John Y. Beall, however, was doomed to be hanged as a spy at Fort Columbus on Governors Island toward the end of the war.[77]

All the major attempts to liberate prisoners during the Civil War failed miserably. The Union, too, lost a leader in its attempt to free the POWs held in Richmond's prisons in March 1864.

In the now-famous incident, General Hugh Judson Kilpatrick persuaded President Lincoln and Secretary Stanton to authorize a raid on the Confederate capital to liberate all the prisoners of Libby and the other facilities. Under the plan, Kilpatrick was to ride into the city with 3,584 handpicked cavalry troops, six guns, eight caissons, three supply wagons, and four ambulances, with Colonel Ulric Dahlgren and 500 supporting troops riding in from another direction, and Brigadier General George A. Custer creating a diversionary raid in Albemarle County. Upon reaching the outskirts of Richmond, however, Kilpatrick realized he had lost the element of surprise and found the city more heavily fortified than he had anticipated. He quickly turned back, but Colonel Dahlgren continued from his position and rode into a trap. Dahlgren was killed and his command was captured.[78]

Unfortunately, the POWs in both the North and South seemed destined to suffer where they were, without rescue or relief, until war's end, which seemed nowhere in sight.

1864–1865

Chapter 11

PRISON COMPOUNDS

His legs were so bowed dat he couldn't lie still,
An' he had no nails on his toes;
His neck was so crooked dat he couldn't take a pill,
So he had to take a pill through his nose.

Lyrics of a popular song from the 1850s

The tragic period of Civil War concentration camps was inaugurated with Elmira Prison in the North and Andersonville in the South.

ELMIRA

The most remarkable aspect about Elmira Prison is that, unlike the other POW facilities around the country up to that time, it didn't start out as a fairly acceptable place of confinement and then slowly degenerate into a concentration camp; Elmira Prison was one from the very day it began.

"Elmira was nearer Hades than I thought any place could be," declared G. T. Taylor, Company C, 1st Alabama Battalion of Heavy Artillery. "If there was ever a hell on earth, Elmira was [it]," added prisoner F. S. Wade. No one ever confined at Elmira Prison disagreed. One prisoner summed it up later by saying when he arrived he found it not only to be a hellhole, but a hellhole under siege.[1]

The site—one mile west of Elmira, west-central New York, about six miles north of the Pennsylvania border—was originally established in 1861 as a rendezvous and training camp for new recruits. In 1862, Union authorities considered enclosing its barracks at the same time that Camp Chase, Camp Douglas, Camp Morton, and a number of other locations were utilized as prisons.

What later became Elmira Prison was originally known as Post Barracks, one of four recruit camps around Elmira, and known as Camp No. 3 to the Federal authorities. Of the four camps situated in different parts of the town, as well as other camps at Albany, Utica, Rochester, and Buffalo considered for prison use back in 1862, the one later utilized was the one described as the worst of all.[2]

"[It is on] a plot of ground quite level, not easily drained and considerably lower than the surrounding country," reported Captain Henry Lazelle. "In consequence . . . [it] becomes at wet seasons quite soft and muddy. . . . The water from the wells on the grounds and from the junction canal south of it is unfit for use and must be hauled." The other posts originally considered were on higher ground with better water supplies. Still, due to the severe overcrowding of their existing prisons and the constant accumulation of additional POWs, authorities proceeded to convert Camp No. 3 in May 1864.[3]

"You will receive instructions from the Adjutant-General," Colonel Hoffman advised Lieutenant Colonel Seth Eastman, commander of the "Draft Rendezvous camp" at Elmira, "to set apart the barracks on the Chemung River."

Eastman answered, "There are two sets of barracks at this post, situated about two miles apart. They are designated as Nos. 1 and 3. The latter is on the Chemung River. . . . These barracks were built to comfortably accommodate 3,000 troops without crowding. The bunks are double. The buildings are in excellent condition and well ventilated. Four thousand prisoners of war could be quartered in them, and there is plenty of ground room in which tents could be pitched to accommodate 1,000 more. . . . There is no hospital at these barracks, hence hospital tents will have to be used for the sick. A new hospital for 200 patients is being erected about one mile from the barracks."[4]

"Barracks No. 3 has been placed in complete condition for the accommodation of 10,000 prisoners," Quartermaster General Meigs declared when he notified the office of the assistant quartermaster nearly five weeks later, ignoring Eastman's recommendation that no more than five thousand could be accommodated. "Eight acres of land have been inclosed with a substantial board fence, twelve feet high, with sentry boxes and elevated platforms have been constructed. Wells have been sunk, and all the necessary arrangements made for immediate occupation."[5]

Nothing was done to increase the capacity of the thirty-five barracks that sat in compound No. 3. Similar to the training camp barracks of Camp Butler and Camp Douglas, the one-story wood structures measured sixteen by one hundred feet and accommodated ninety-five to one hundred troops comfortably in each. The ceilings were just high enough to allow two rows of crudely built double bunks, forty-five to fifty in each building. Short of expanding each building or constructing more, neither of which was attempted, funded, or authorized by the Federal government, the maximum capacity remained at 4,000 with an additional 1,000 to be housed in tents. Meanwhile, Hoffman and Meigs continued to refer to a capacity of 8,000 to 10,000.[6]

On July 6, 1864, the first POWs arrived at the Elmira Prison Camp. They consisted of 399 of the 400 originally transferred from Point Lookout to help relieve the overcrowding there. One escaped on the way. On July 11, 249 more arrived from Point Lookout, and on July 12, 502 more.[7]

"We were escorted to the 'pen' by a large concourse of admiring citizens," reported Anthony Keiley, a member of one of the first three groups transferred from Point Lookout. "A march of about a mile [from the train depot] brought us to our prison. We filed in, were counted, divided into companies of a hundred, the roll called, and we were led off to our quarters."[8]

"Back of the thirty-four or thirty-five barracks," reported Keiley, "is a row of wooden buildings containing the adjutant's office, dispensary, various rooms of Yankee sergeants, store-rooms, and the like, and back, again of these, the mess-rooms and cook-houses, which extend to the lagoon."[9]

In immediate command of the prison, under Lieutenant Colonel Eastman, was Major Henry V. Colt of the 104th New York Volunteer Regiment. "[A] gentleman, fair and fat, of not quite forty, five and a half feet high, with a florid complexion," according to Keiley, "[with] a very prepossessing appearance and manner, a jaunty way of cocking his hat on the side of his head, and a chronic attack of smoking cigars, which he invariably holds in his mouth at about the angle at which mortars are ordinarily fired."[10]

"There was [also]," continued Keiley, "a long-nosed, long-faced, long-jawed, long-bearded, long-bodied, long-legged, endless-footed, and long-skirted curiosity Captain [William] Peck, ostensibly engaged in taking charge of certain companies of 'Rebs,' but really employed in turning a penny by huckstering the various products of prisoners' skill—an occupation very profitable to Peck, but generally unsatisfactory, in a pecuniary way, to the 'rebs.'"[11]

On July 15, a fourth trainload of POWs en route to the prison collided head-on with an eastbound coal train outside of Shohola, Pennsylvania, along the Delaware River in Pike County. Forty-eight prisoners and seventeen guards were killed, and ninety-three POWs and sixteen guards were injured. In the confusion, five POWs escaped. "[W]e were roused about midnight," related Keiley, "with a request that we would come and help the wounded in, a train having arrived with the surviving victims of the catastrophe. Many of them were in a horrible condition, and when I went to the hospital the following Monday I found the wounds of many still undressed, even the blood not washed from their limbs, to which, in many instances, the clothing adhered, glued by the clotted gore."[12]

Throughout the following days, POWs continued to arrive from all directions. By the end of the month, 4,424 were confined there, two had managed to escape, and eleven had died. "You are authorized to lease a half-acre lot in the Woodlawn Cemetery in Elmira as a burying ground for deceased prisoners of war," Hoffman advised Colonel Eastman at the end of the month, "and you are also authorized to employ a laborer at $40 per month to dig the graves." Eastman obtained the services of the Woodlawn Cemetery sexton, John W. Jones, a former slave from Leesburg, Virginia, who lived near the prison, to take charge of the Confederate burials. Jones would go on to do a meticulous job and keep accurate death records throughout the existence of the prison.[13]

By the end of August, there were more than 9,600 POWs confined at Elmira. The initial arrivals had filled the barracks and A-tents were now in use. "The barrack accommodations did not suffice for quite half of them," observed one prisoner. "Thinly clad as they came from a summer's campaign, many of them without blankets, and without even a handful of straw between them and the earth, it will surprise no one that the suffering, even at that early day, was considerable."[14]

By August 7, the tent supply was exhausted. Tents arriving the following week still were insufficient. Many men, poorly clad, with some wearing nothing but dirty underwear and having no blanket, found themselves sleeping out in the open air with no shelter whatsoever. By the end of August there were 115 more deaths. In September, another 385 perished.[15]

A majority of the deaths during this period were from diarrhea and dysentery. Exposure was, no doubt, a contributing factor, and scurvy also broke out in epidemic proportions during the month. By September 11, there were 1,870 reported cases. Before long, Elmira led all the northern prisons in its death rate—ten per day.[16]

Colonel Eastman soon complained to Washington authorities that the camp was overcrowded and requested them to stop sending prisoners. Besides the housing problems, he pointed out, it required three hours to feed nearly 10,000 POWs in shifts of 1,800 at a time. "[I]f they can get through their breakfast by 11 A.M. and their dinner by 6 P.M.," Colonel Hoffman curtly reported, "[then] nothing more is necessary."[17]

Eastman also complained that the pond inside the camp had become a cesspool, that it was causing illness, and that something had to be done to remedy the situation immediately. "The drainage of the camp is into this pond or pool of standing water," agreed Post Surgeon E. F. Sanger during his inspection, "and one large sink used by the prisoners stands directly over the pond which receives its fecal matter hourly. . . . Seven thousand men will pass 2,600 gallons of urine daily, which is highly loaded with nitrogenous material. A portion is absorbed by the earth, still a large amount decomposes on the top of the earth or runs into the pond to purify."[18]

In spite of Eastman's and Sanger's concerns, they received the full impact of responsibility for the unsanitary, chaotic, and wretched conditions of the camp. "[O]n the 21st of September," noted prisoner Keiley, who was assigned as clerk of death records, "I carried my report up to the major's tent, with the ghastly record of twenty-nine deaths yesterday." The subsequent recriminations led to Eastman's removal shortly thereafter.[19]

Colonel Benjamin F. Tracy took over as prison commandant, with his regiment, the 127th U.S. Colored Troops, taking over guard duty. In September, construction of additional hospital wards and barracks began. Hoffman advised that the buildings, 100 feet by 22 feet to accommodate 120 POWs with a 20 by 22-foot kitchen on the end of each, be "erected upon the cheapest plan and to be neither plastered nor ceiled." In addition, three-tiered bunks would be crammed into the facilities. All labor would be done by the prisoners.[20]

In October the death rate was an average of nine a day. At the end of November, a total of 483 POWs had died in the previous sixty-one-day period. No doubt, the sexton at Woodlawn found himself overworked and underpaid. At the rate the prisoners were dying, he was barely averaging more than sixteen cents per burial for all his work and record keeping.[21]

"Since August, the date of my assignment to this station, there have been 2,011 patients admitted to the hospital [and] 775 deaths out of a mean strength of 8,347 prisoners of war, or 24 per-cent admitted and 9 per-cent died," explained the post's medical officer in a formal letter to the surgeon general. "[We] have averaged daily 451 in hospital and 601 in quarters. . . . At this rate the entire command will be admitted to the hospital in less than a year and 36 per-cent [will] die."[22]

The medical staff went on to emphasize the problems with the lagoon at the camp. "The soil is a gravel deposit sloping at two-thirds of its distance from the front toward the river to a stagnant pond of water 12 by 580 yards, between which and the river is a low sandy bottom subject to overflow when the river is high. This pond received the contents of the sinks and garbage of the camp until it became so offensive that vaults were dug on the banks of the pond for sinks and the whole left a festering mass of corruption, impregnating the entire atmosphere of the camp with its pestilential odors, night and day. . . . The pond remains green with putrescence, filling the air with its messengers of disease and death, the vaults give out their sickly odors, and the hospitals are crowded with victims for the grave."[23]

One benefit Foster's Pond provided in its deplorable, wretched, condition, however, was that it became a haven for an alternative food source. "We invented all kinds of traps and deadfalls to catch rats," admitted prisoner F. S. Wade. "Many found an acceptable substitute in rat, with which the place abounded," agreed another prisoner, "and these Chinese delicacies commanded an average price of about four cents apiece." Rats quickly became part of the prison's complex bartering system. One rat could be traded for five chaws of tobacco, one haircut, or a number of other items.[24]

As at several other prisons, the POWs also resorted to eating dogs and cats that strayed into the compound. "Every day Northern ladies came in the prison, some of them followed by dogs or cats," continued Wade, "which the boys would slip aside and choke to death. The ribs of a stewed dog were delicious, [but] a broiled rat was superb."[25]

Clearly the daily rations provided by the Elmira authorities were inadequate or, as one prisoner later put it, "seemed to be only enough to feed disease." Another prisoner remembered, "About eight or nine in the morning we were furnished a small piece of loaf bread and a small piece of salt pork or pickled beef each, and in the afternoon a small piece of bread and a tin plate of soup, with sometimes a little rice or Irish potato in the soup where the pork or beef had been broiled."[26]

With no more to eat than that, an atmosphere of starvation constantly existed at Elmira. It wasn't uncommon to see prisoners going through the refuse barrels or garbage heaps behind the cookhouses, or to see them pick up apple peelings and other "edibles" that had been trampled down into the mud of the pathways, wipe them off, and eat them with hardly any hesitation.

"I have seen a mob of hungry 'rebs' besiege the bone-cart," admitted one prisoner, "and beg from the driver fragments on which an August sun had been burning for several days."[27]

By December, their miserable existence and fight for survival intensified. The frigid cold weather swept in and, with it, smallpox arrived from Governors Island. Within weeks, smallpox became epidemic, which led to a smallpox camp established away from the prison at nearby South Creek. "The camp was several wall tents," advised prisoner Miles O. Sherrill, "with cots having two Confederates laying on each in reverse order—heads on opposite ends of the cot."[28]

As winter pounded the area, the southern POWs found this part of New York state intolerable. "[F]or at least four months of every year," complained Keiley, "anything [here] short of a polar-bear would find locomotion impracticable."[29]

Most of the additional barracks and wards authorized by Colonel Hoffman had been completed by mid-October; however, many tents were still in use, and the new buildings, without insulation, interior walls, or ceilings, didn't provide much additional comfort.

"The winters are exceedingly cold and bleak at Elmira," admitted U.S. Surgeon William J. Sloan, "and the buildings were hastily erected of green lumber, which is cracking, splitting, and warping in every direction."[30]

Each barracks had one stove to serve two hundred or more occupants. "Around each stove was a chalk mark, five feet from the stove, marking the distance we should keep, so that all could be warm," explained one prisoner.[31]

It wasn't unusual to see Elmira's prisoners standing ankle-deep in snow for roll calls during this time of year. "Snow and ice several feet thick covered the place from December 6 to March 15," complained one prisoner. The temperature dropped to eighteen degrees below zero on at least two different occasions. "My health is not good in this cold climate," complained prisoner Sitgreaves Attmore in a letter written to his cousins back home, "every thing now being covered with ice and my clothing thin and scarce . . . I sometimes fear I shall never see you all again."[32]

It was no wonder then, that in addition to smallpox, pneumonia struck down Elmira's POWs as well. From December 1864, through March 1865, 1,471 prisoners of war succumbed to the ravages of the camp. Nearly 500 died in the month of March, alone, averaging more than 15 per day.[33]

It was also in March that the inevitable finally happened. With the spring thaw, and the heavy runoff of melted snow, the Chemung River nearby began to run fast and furious.

"The rapid rise of the stream on the night of the 16th," reported Colonel Tracy, "made it clear that the low flat upon which the smallpox ward was located would be whelmed and the fence swept away." Nearly three hundred sick POWs were left stranded and isolated at the smallpox camp by the quickly rising water.[34]

"Rafts were accordingly built to convey this number," continued Tracy, "and the removal was accomplished without any casualty. They were placed in six old barracks on the highest ground of the camp. These barracks are very old and nearly useless, having been kept standing through the winter only by means of props and braces outside. . . . The river continued to rise until the entire camp, except about an acre, was flooded . . . I immediately took measures to rebuild the fence . . . About 2,700 feet were carried away."[35]

As early as July 1864, a number of Elmira citizens had erected an observation tower, similar to the one at Camp Douglas, outside the compound. For the nominal fee of fifteen cents each, spectators were allowed to climb up to the platform to observe the POWs in their daily activities. In August, W. and W. Mears went into direct competition with that tower by building a similar observatory nearby that was twenty feet taller, charged a reduced admission of only ten cents, and sold refreshments at its base.

"A clearer view across the different avenues of the enclosure can be seen from this Observatory," claimed its local newspaper ads, "than from any other position." Although the observatory was built at "considerable expense," apparently such ventures were profitable. According to one prisoner, "one of the proprietors, who was part of the management of our pen, assured me that the concern paid for itself in two weeks."[36]

While the towers might have brought profit to some prison officials, they seem to have inspired humanitarian efforts from the town's citizens. As at Fort Delaware, however, such efforts were often hampered by the Federal authorities. Several women from town established a school at the prison and entered daily, bringing books for the prisoners. At the same time, townsfolk gathered clothing for them, but prison officials refused to distribute it. Religious services for the POWs were also conducted several times by Thomas Beecher, brother to famed abolitionist Henry Ward Beecher and author Harriet Beecher Stowe, but they ceased with the arrival of the harsh winter months because prison officials refused to provide an enclosed shelter.[37]

FORT DELAWARE/MORRIS ISLAND

In August 1864, a rumor spread through the prison compound of Fort Delaware that six hundred of their number were to be sent off and placed under fire of the Confederate batteries in South Carolina's Charleston Harbor in retaliation for alleged cruelties Union soldiers were suffering. This came just a few weeks after fifty prisoners had been sent away under a similar threat but later exchanged under special circumstances.

"We were so certain that this . . . was a bluff," advised Captain Walter MacRae, Company G, 7th North Carolina Regiment, "that everyone was anxious to go. Many, whose names were not on the list, gathered up their poor belongings— watches, rings, a little money—anything and everything of value which had escaped confiscation, and came and laid them down at the feet of [those who had been chosen by lottery] if haply they might persuade some one to exchange places."[38]

Few of these prisoners realized that this move was being contemplated as a result of the Confederate authorities having placed POW Union officers in the various locations scattered throughout Charleston since the 13th of June. "The Federal batteries on Morris Island," according to Charles M. Busbee of the 5th North Carolina Regiment, "were shelling the City of Charleston, imperiling the lives of non-combatants, consisting of women, children, and old men."[39]

On August 20, the six hundred chosen prisoners were gathered together at Fort Delaware. Destined to become known in Civil War history as the "Immortal Six Hundred," the POW group was made up of 186 prisoners from Virginia, 111 from North Carolina, 60 from Georgia, 49 from Tennessee, 35 from Kentucky, 31 from Louisiana, 27 from Arkansas, 26 from Alabama, 24 from South Carolina, 22 from Mississippi, 10 from Florida, 8 from Missouri, 6 from Maryland, and 5 from Texas, representing all of the states having regiments in the Confederate army.

The group was marched aboard the steamer *Crescent City* and crammed into its hold, where rough bunks, four tiers high, were lined up from stem to stern. Only one hatch was open, making the hold fairly dark, crowded, and stiflingly hot. A battalion of infantry patrolled the deck and guarded the open hatch. The POWs were required to remain in the hold and endure such conditions for the entire eighteen day journey to South Carolina. Two gunboats remained alongside the ship as escort, while the naval supply steamer *Admiral* brought up the rear of the convoy.

Along the way the convoy stopped over at Fortress Monroe, Virginia, for a day or two, leaving the POWs confined in the ship's hold. When the convoy resumed its southbound journey, it was announced to the prisoners that they were being taken on to Charleston for exchange.

Prisoners soon found conditions from the extreme August heat and poor ventilation of the hold unbearable. A lack of rations and decent drinking water added to their misery. As many began to suffer from scurvy and seasickness, the filth and stench in the hold worsened. A lack of latrines and the refusal to allow captives on deck added vomit and excrement to the increasingly intolerable conditions.

"The heat of the ship's boilers, the heat of the weather, and the seasickness made our condition a veritable orthodox hell," insisted Major John Murray, "a regular sheol in miniature form . . . much worse than those English soldiers in the Black Hole of Calcutta."[40]

Several days out, as the steamer neared Cape Romain, South Carolina, William Baxter, the second mate left in charge of the vessel while the ship's captain went down to his berth, noticed that the two gunboats had drifted back, out of sight. Immediately, Baxter steered the *Crescent City* toward shore, apparently, it was later alleged, with the intent to allow the POWs to escape.

When the crew of the *Admiral* noticed the steamer making toward shore, they lit lights and sent up rockets. According to Captain Prentiss, in command of the guard on board the *Crescent City*, Baxter ignored the lights and rockets and continued in a direct line toward Cape Romain. Within moments, the vessel ran aground. In the confusion, prisoner George W. Woolford of South Carolina made a dash for freedom. Others started but were held back by the 157th Ohio, the sentry regiment on board. A standoff ensued as one of the gunboats, coming up from the rear, located the *Crescent City* and fired a warning shot as it steamed at full speed ahead toward the stranded craft. The reappearance of the gunboats enabled the crew and guards to regain control of the vessel, and the POWs were forced back down into the hold. The captain and the second mate were immediately arrested, but Baxter was the only one placed in irons. Meanwhile, the escort craft remained at the side of the foundering vessel to guard against onshore Confederate attacks until high tide took the *Crescent City* back out into deeper water and the trip to Morris Island continued.

The next day, August 25, the *Crescent City* anchored at Hilton Head Island, South Carolina. "The officers of the ship allowed the drinking water to give out," complained prisoner Busbee, "and while off Hilton Head it was announced that the drinking water was out. We went without water from the morning of one day to the afternoon of the next, about thirty hours. I, with many others, tried the experiment of letting down a bottle through a little porthole into the sea and endeavored to slake our thirst with water from the ocean, but we found it impossible to do so."[41]

That night, another prisoner slipped overboard and escaped. Exactly how it was accomplished has never been revealed, but prisoner G. H. Ellerson, captain, 3rd Alabama Regiment, somehow made good his escape.[42]

After various stops, the convoy arrived at Morris Island on September 5. The prisoners, however, remained confined in the ship's hold for another two days while the onshore stockade pen was completed. "On 7 September, we disembarked at Morris Island," related MacRae, "and when we finally came out into the light of day, and had a look at each other, we were astonished to note the ravages made by the terrible heat and the nauseous confinement. One could scarcely recognize his best friends."[43]

"We were ordered," added Murray, "to turn out and form in line on the beach. After forming and the counting of our number was finished the order was given to march. . . . We had not gone over half-mile before some of our men, weakened from the eighteen days on the filthy prison ship, fell, from prostration, in the sand." Those who had fallen were ordered up at the point of a bayonet and force-marched to the pen by soldiers of the 54th Massachusetts Colored Regiment, who had been detailed to Morris Island as guards.

"[T]he stockade was erected on the beach about forty or fifty feet from the water," observed Busbee. "When we reached the stockade prison-pen gate," advised Murray, "we were again halted, counted off by fours and sent inside the inclosure, where a negro sergeant assigned us to tents, putting four men in each small A-tent which would not comfortably hold more than two men."[44]

The stockade, consisting of two acres, was square and built of fifteen- to twenty-foot pine poles driven into the sand and cleated together with pine boards. Like many of these types of pens, a parapet for the guards ran along the top of the compound giving a full view of the interior. About ten feet from the inside of the stockade fence, a rope, supported on pickets driven into the sand, served as the prison deadline. Tents were arranged in parallel rows, forming streets or pathways between every two rows. "At the head of the middle street," advised Murray, "was placed a Mitrailleuse Requa gun, loaded and ready to open upon our camp at a moment's notice."[45]

Colonel William Gurney, 127th New York Volunteer Regiment, was the prison's commandant. Colonel Edward N. Hallowell, of Philadelphia, and brother to the prominent abolitionist Richard Price Hallowell, was in charge of the guard unit, the 54th Massachusetts. (Colonel Robert Shaw, the regiment's original commander, was killed during the assault on Battery Wagner the year before.)

"Colonel Hallowell," declared Murray, "was about the meanest fellow our misfortunes brought us in connection with. . . . He treated us like animals . . . there was nothing this fellow left undone to make us uncomfortable and annoy us; he never let one opportunity pass to show his hatred for the South and her soldiers."[46]

Morris Island was a seemingly worthless expanse of sand that jutted into the ocean in a long narrow strip, four miles south of Charleston. Running nearly north and south, it was about four miles long and varied in width anywhere from one hundred yards at its narrowest point to half a mile at its broadest. The island was separated from nearby James Island on the west by Vincent's Creek and by a number of broad marshes that were intersected by numerous saltwater creeks. The Atlantic Ocean washed up along its eastern shore. The island's entire surface was barely above sea level and consisted of glaring stretches of white sandy hillocks, sparsely dotted with coarse grasses, that constantly changed contours with every high wind.

Yet this island, as worthless as it seemed, had become a vital strategic location at the entrance to the harbor in the concentrated bombardment of Charleston. Along with its other siege guns, the Union had erected an eight-inch Parrott rifle, dubbed the "Swamp Angel," in the marshes adjacent to Morris Island. At fifteen-minute intervals, the big gun pumped out 150-pound incendiaries into the city. Later, seacoast mortars were moved in and, still later, a thirty-pounder Parrott rifle.

The prison stockade had been built in front of what had been Battery Wagner, with the Star of the West Battery a little farther northeast down the beach toward the end of the Morris Island peninsula, and Battery Gregg even farther down the beach at the point. "Our position," explained MacRae, "was such that every shot or shell from the guns on Sumter and Moultrie and other Confederate batteries, must either pass close over our heads, or right through the pen."

"[T]he stockade was placed in the line of fire of the Confederate batteries on Sullivan's Island which were shelling Battery Wagner," added Busbee. "The Confederate gunners would cut their fuses so as to endeavor to prevent any shell from exploding in our neighborhood, but on more than one occasion a shell exploded prematurely and on one occasion that I well remember, a shell burst directly over the stockade and threw several of its fragments among us."[47]

For the first two days of the prisoners' confinement, the shelling activity remained somewhat subdued. Perhaps gunners of both sides were simply testing and checking their range. The Confederate artillerymen were well aware that POWs had been placed in a stockade on the island, and Union artillerymen knew that Federal prisoners were confined at strategic locations throughout the city.

On September 9, however, all hell broke loose in one of the most spectacular aerial displays that any of these men would ever witness. "At early noon," reported one prisoner, "the Federal batteries on Morris Island, and all the guns of the Yankee fleet [around the harbor] opened on the Confederate forts and Charleston city." Another prisoner exclaimed, "They opened fire right over our heads. [Then] we saw a puff of smoke blow out from Fort Moultrie, and almost immediately, heard the rush of a fine, large shell. It passed howling over our heads and smashed into the nearest embrasure, where it exploded with much havoc."[48]

"Our batteries all replied," proclaimed Murray rather proudly, "and for two or three hours the duel lasted. The shells from Sumter and our other batteries fell thick and fast upon the island, most of them uncomfortably close to our stockade." The duel continued off and on for several days but was never as intense as the shelling that occurred on September 9. The POWs soon grew accustomed to the constant shelling above and around them.[49]

Rations at the Morris Island Prison consisted of sour cornmeal, "which would stand alone when the barrel was knocked from it," as one prisoner put it, and occasionally a one-inch-square piece of "hog-meat" and a few pickles. Once the supply of these items was depleted, only hardtack was issued. "Our rations," complained Murray, "was a menu for wooden gods. It consisted of four hardtack army crackers, often rotten and green with mold, and one ounce of fat meat, issued to us at morning roll call . . . for dinner, we received one-half pint of bean or rice soup . . . for supper, we were allowed all the wind we could inhale." Their drinking water was obtained by digging holes in the sand, "and then waiting until sufficient very insipid water would ooze out of the sand to quench thirst."[50]

After six and a half weeks, both sides realized that their plan to halt the shelling hadn't worked and agreed to move their prisoners elsewhere. Although several shells had burst over the POWs and showered the pen with shrapnel, no serious injuries were inflicted and no shells actually fell into the stockade. Likewise, the Union POWs held throughout Charleston witnessed some close calls, but no serious injuries occurred. On October 23, the Morris Island prisoners were loaded onto schooners and transferred to Fort Pulaski for confinement.

In all, only 558 of the original 600 removed from Fort Delaware were actually confined in the Morris Island pen. Thirty-nine had been removed from the ship at Hilton Head Island and held in jail there before being transferred to Beaufort, South Carolina. Two escaped on the way and one died. Three more died while confined in the pen. Two POWs were shot and wounded by guards while confined at the pen.[51]

The remaining POWs arrived at Fort Pulaski on Cockspur Island in the Savannah, Georgia, harbor on October 22. The fort, a massive, irregular pentagon structure with thick brick walls surrounded by a moat, had been taken over by the Union in April 1862.

"Our quarters at Fort Pulaski," explained Busbee, "were in the casements of the fort. We slept in double wooden bunks of two stories, three men in the upper bunk and three in the lower. Our rations were very meagre, but we got four crackers per day instead of mush. After I left Fort Pulaski I understood that the prisoners who remained ate all the cats in the fort, of which there was quite a number, stewing them on the stove in tin cans. Fort Pulaski is not a pleasant habitation at any time. . . . It was particularly exasperating to be encased within a dungeon-like hole and gaze while almost starving through the grated casement window at oysters in abundance clinging to the sides of the moat."[52]

Because of severe overcrowding at Fort Pulaski, 222 POWs were transferred to Hilton Head the following November. They were initially kept in tents until a large log structure in town was converted for their use. Prisoners at both locations continued to suffer from inadequate rations and from the cold winter weather. Few, if any, had blankets. "All the blankets given us at Fort Delaware," reported a prisoner, "were taken from us before we left the prison ship *Crescent City.*"[53]

On March 3, 1865, the POWs were told again that they would be exchanged but had to be transferred to another location. The following day they were marched on board a small steamer and began a voyage north, stopping off at Hilton Head for the remaining prisoners. They were soon transferred to a larger vessel, the *Illinois,* and on March 7, arrived at Fortress Monroe, where they learned they were being returned to Fort Delaware. Before arriving at that destination, however, a total of seventy-five prisoners had to be dropped off at various hospitals along the route while two died in the hold of the ship and were buried at sea. Those remaining were eventually held at Fort Delaware until the end of the war.[54]

HART'S ISLAND

The final prison established by the Union was on Hart's Island in New York City and it quickly evolved into the city's most horrible site. Located in Long Island Sound about twenty miles north of the city and just a few miles south of David's Island, Hart's Island wasn't even used until April 1865, the month the Civil War came to an end, yet 235 POWs perished there.[55]

It, too, was nothing more than a concentration camp. The first POWs arrived on April 7 and were immediately placed into a stockade enclosure of about four acres. "Two thousand and twenty-nine prisoners of war were received," noted Henry W. Wessells, the prison commandant. "They seem to be healthy with few exceptions, and tolerably well clothed . . . The guard is entirely insufficient consisting of a small detachment sent with them from City Point. Three hundred and fifty effective men are required."[56]

General Wessells had originally served in the 8th Kansas along the trouble-some Missouri-Kansas border early in the conflict, but had most recently been captured at Plymouth, North Carolina, as part of the Union force surrendered there in April 1864. As a POW he was one of the Union officer hostages placed under Union guns firing on Charleston. He became one of the lucky ones to be involved in a special exchange months later.

Hart's Island originally served as a draft rendezvous camp for this area of New York. Colonel Hoffman suggested using the site to confine POWs as early as August 1864, and added that "the guard and prisoners . . . be placed in old tents until it becomes absolutely necessary to put them in quarters, when sheds may [then] be erected by the labor of prisoners."[57]

Although tents were used for the overflow, for the most part a portion of the rendezvous barracks were used for both guards and prisoners from the day the prison began its operation. Within three weeks, a total of 3,413 POWs were crammed into the post's tiny enclosed area. "We were placed in wards of a hundred to each ward, with three rows of bunks and two men to a bunk," advised J. S. Kimbrough, Company K, 14th Georgia. "The first ward was composed mostly of jail birds, blacklegs, and toughs from Petersburg, and their nocturnal rounds of robbery and thieving were a terror to the camp."[58]

"Our rations," Kimbrough continued, "consisted of four hard tacks, a small piece of pickled beef or mule, and a cup of soup per day. Often have I eaten my two day's rations at one meal and subsisted upon water and wind until the next drawing. Many men would peddle their crackers for tobacco, giving a cracker for a chew. . . . A game of Keno, with a cracker or a chew for a stake, was played with as much excitement, interest, and science as though hundreds of dollars were at stake."[59]

Hart's Island wasn't completely cleared of prisoners until July 1865. Within those four months, nearly 7 percent of all those "healthy and tolerably well clothed" prisoners had died. "The largest portion of deaths," declared U.S. Medical Inspector George Lyman, "occurred from chronic diarrhea, brought with them, and pneumonia, which began to appear a few days after their arrival. . . . The men being poorly clad, the weather wet and cold, and the barracks provided with no other bedding than such as the prisoners brought with them, the pneumonia cases developed rapidly . . . increased, probably, to some extent by the crowded and unventilated condition of the barracks."[60]

Nearby Fort Schuyler, having a capacity of five hundred prisoners, also came into use as a POW facility in 1864. This fort, named for the Revolutionary War general Philip J. Schuyler, had been acquired by the Federal government in 1833 and was located on a Bronx peninsula where Long Island Sound joined the East River. Although briefly manned as a defensive post during the Civil War, when it came into use as a prison, the POWs were held within several large rooms of the fort's interior.

About the same time, Riker's Island, in the East River south of Fort Schuyler, was also pressed into use. There were only about two or three storage buildings on the site and fresh water was scarce, yet authorities estimated the island was capable of holding up to one thousand prisoners. Within a short time barracks were built for the guard, and Confederate prisoners were moved onto the island. Water was eventually supplied by cisterns filled with runoff water from the roofs.

Another New York City location used for confining POWs for various periods before the war ended included Ward's Island in the East River just west of Riker's Island.

The Confederate government, too, was having a difficult time finding enough space or establishing enough prisons for their accumulation of POWs.

CAHABA

In January 1864, authorities had decided to establish a permanent prison facility at the unfinished red-brick cotton warehouse at Cahaba, Alabama, which had been used as a gathering point for the military district's political and Union prisoners for several months. "A brick wall inclosing an area of 15,000 square feet, covered by a leaky roof with 1,600 feet of open space in its center," complained R. H. Whitfield, the surgeon assigned to the post, upon inspecting the site, "[with] four open windows, and the earth for the floor."[61]

The structure was merely a shell. The building was owned by Samuel M. Hill, a wealthy local merchant and planter who had arranged for the construction of the building in 1861 but, once the walls and a portion of the roof were finished, work on the project stopped when the war broke out. The Confederate government later seized the partially completed structure for its own use and began erecting a twelve-foot-high wide-plank fence around the one-third-acre site. Inside the roofless building, "sleeping roosts" five tiers high were erected along the walls. By the end of March 1864, there were already 660 prisoners held at the site.[62]

"The sleeping arrangements," continued Whitfield, "consist of rough lumber, without straw or bedding of any kind . . . not forty to the hundred men. These bunks, but recently constructed, accommodate but 432 men, so that 228 men are forced to sleep upon the ground."[63]

Water for the prisoners was supplied by an open trench that ran from an artesian well located two hundred yards away, outside the prison wall. "In its course," observed one official, "it has been subjected to the washings of the hands, feet, faces, and heads of soldiers, citizens, and negroes, buckets, tubs, and spittoons of groceries, offices and hospital, hogs, dogs, cows, and horses, and filth of all kinds from the streets and other sources."[64]

The prison yard enclosed by the fence measured about thirty-five feet by forty-six feet and could be used by the prisoners only during the daytime. It also served as the cook yard. Guards patrolled an elevated walkway around the outside of the fence, and two small cannons protruded out of two portholes in the north end of the stockade wall.

"Looking into these muzzles," declared prisoner John L. Walker, 50th Ohio Volunteer Regiment, "I could see the tin can which contained a charge of canister ready for any outbreak which might occur in the prison."[65]

Rations were the standard issue of raw meat and cornmeal. Originally a quart of meal and a quarter pound of meat were issued to each prisoner but as the compound became more crowded and supplies had to be dispersed among a larger group, rations were reduced to a pint of meal, perhaps an eighth-ounce piece of meat, sometimes with a small portion of beans or cowpeas. The prisoners were required to do their own cooking, usually in messes of up to ten. As in nearly all the prisons, morning roll call and rations were at 7:30 A.M. and evening roll call and rations was at 5:00 P.M. All lights were required to be out by 9:00 P.M.

The thick walls of the warehouse were about 14 feet high and measured 193 feet by 116 feet on the outside. There was no way to heat the partially finished building, so open fires were allowed on the dirt, or sandy, floor. As a result, prisoners often suffered from the high concentration of lingering smoke on cold nights but weren't allowed to go outside the building after dark.[66]

The warehouse prison was located on the central east end of the city, at the end of Capital Street, on the bank of the Alabama River. About a block north of this location, the Alabama was joined by the Cahaba River. These two rivers had caused the city problems from its very beginning. The town had once been the state's capital, from 1819 to 1826, but the capital was moved to Tuscaloosa because of the constant flooding at Cahaba. The town remained the seat of Dallas County government, but its population, which had once been more than 5,000, had dwindled to only 680 whites and 2,000 slaves by the beginning of the Civil War.[67]

Assigned as commandant to the prison was Captain Howard A. M. Henderson, Company E, 28th Alabama Regiment, who also served as assistant commissioner of prisoner exchange. Because of those duties, he often left the facility to the charge of Lieutenant Colonel Samuel S. Jones, 22nd Louisiana Regiment, who was intensely disliked by the prisoners. "By what strange and malignant destiny," wondered prisoner Jesse Hawes, 9th Illinois Cavalry, "were cowards and cruel men so often placed in charge of the prisons."[68]

Jones reportedly had been a bookkeeper for a large New Orleans whole-sale house before the war. He had joined the Confederate service shortly after hostilities broke out but had been captured as a prisoner of war twice, each time being paroled and exchanged, before his assignment at Cahaba. By many accounts, his previous POW experiences had left him quite bitter. "Colonel Samuel Jones was guilty of many, many inhuman acts," recalled Walker. "He would frequently walk along the dead line, and finding a poor comrade sitting so close to it that an inch or two of his body happened to extend over, the only notice he would give this unfortunate fellow was a kick from his boot."[69]

Henderson, on the other hand, was well-liked by the POWs. "It was often in [his] power," advised Hawes, "to extend kindnesses and courtesies to prisoners, and we are glad to note that the opportunity was not infrequently embraced."[70]

The Cahaba prisoners, numbering over 1,500 by May 1864, were guarded by 161 local troops along with a special detail of eighteen men with field pieces. Although the Confederate prison was officially known as the "Cahaba Federal Prison," because it held Federal POWs, it was unofficially known by the locals as "Castle Morgan," in honor of Colonel John Hunt Morgan, who successfully escaped from the Ohio Penitentiary about the time the Cahaba pen was established.[71]

By May 1864, officials ordered the prison closed, and between May 16 and May 29, moved its inhabitants to Andersonville. The sick, unable to travel, remained at Cahaba. Within a month, the Georgia pen was so severely over-crowded that the Cahaba prison was officially reopened and the sick prisoners still there became the nucleus of a new, growing population. By September, a total of 2,500 were incarcerated in the small pen built for 500; by October the population thankfully dropped to 2,151. Eventually, though, the population gradually climbed to the staggering number of 3,000 captives, providing less space per man than what was eventually endured by the Andersonville prisoners.[72]

As the prison population grew out of control, the Cahaba facility became plagued by rats, lice, and muggers. "Hardly would I get to sleep," reported a prisoner regarding the rats, "when one or more would be snuffing about some portion of my body." Waking up throughout the night to kick rats away was a small annoyance compared to the lice, that worked on the prisoners constantly. "[T]hey crawled upon our clothing by day," complained Hawes, "crawled over our bodies, into the ears, even into the nostrils and mouths by night."[73]

As in all the crowded prisons during this period, the POWs at Cahaba were forced to contend with a few desperate prisoners who turned predatory and began to plunder their fellow captives. They attacked without warning to take food, clothing, blankets, fire-stick rations, or anything that had become valuable to survival in the camp.

Sickness, too, began to take a toll. A hospital was established at the Bell Tavern Hotel two blocks away on Vine Street. The prevailing diseases became scurvy, dysentery, and chronic diarrhea. Relatively few prisoners, however, are believed to have died at Cahaba. Some sources have claimed as many as 750 to 800 deaths, but local researchers, who studied Confederate, Union, and the Cahaba hospital records, have accepted the number of 225 total deaths until further documentation is discovered. That figure, however, still represents over 7 percent of the total confined.[74]

Not all of Cahaba's POWs were confined to the penned-in warehouse. By October 1864, at least ten captured Federal officers had been assigned government-furnished quarters in town, limited to a daytime parole within the city limits. Such liberal practices had been eliminated at all the other prisons, in both the North and South, by late 1862.[75]

Prisoners at Cahaba had access to a wide variety of reading material. A Mrs. Amanda Gardner, who lived in a house across the street, northwest from the prison, opened her extensive private library to the POWs and provided them, through the guards, with books on any subject, including poetry, science, philosophy, religion, travel, or history.[76]

Not all were interested in simply reading, however. As in all the prisons, many attempts were made to escape, but records fail to indicate how many might have been successful. Several crawled out under the flooring of a latrine and down its drainage ditch, only to be apprehended later and returned; at least twelve tunneled their way out from the dirt floor of the warehouse to the nearby riverbank, beyond the stockade, but were later recaptured; and a number of others cut and carved their way out through the brick of the warehouse or through the stockade fence.

"On the morning of Friday, January 20 [1865], there was a mutiny in the Federal prison under my command," reported Captain Henderson. "The prisoners simultaneously rushed upon the interior guards, disarmed and captured them. They then placed them under guard in the water-closets." In the meantime, two guards stationed outside the main gate gave the alarm and alerted the reserve guard in town. The battalion was ordered out under arms and, with the artillery rolled into position, the uprising was quelled. The ringleaders were quickly rounded up and placed into irons.[77]

In the first week of March 1865, the Alabama and Cahaba rivers unexpectedly overflowed their banks and flooded the entire area. The prison was inundated, and several prisoners drowned. Many were left standing in cold, waist-deep water while others climbed to the rafters of the warehouse and remained there for several days until help arrived. During that time, it was reported, Colonel Jones even came to the prison in a boat to check on the captives, but refused to help them.[78]

After three days, boats arrived and moved up to seven hundred POWs to Selma. The remaining 2,300 floundered in the water, mud, and mire of the prison for another ten days before conditions returned to normal.

ANDERSONVILLE

The second facility to be established by the Confederacy in 1864 was the infamous Andersonville Prison, which became nothing more than a concentration camp. Like Elmira in the North, Andersonville Prison was, from day one, one of the most wretched places of confinement that words could describe. Within months of the prison's establishment, prisoners reported entering the front gates and literally doubling over and vomiting upon their first sight and smell of the interior.[79]

The prison's location had been selected by Captain W. Sidney Winder, General John Winder's son. Back on November 24, 1863, Captain Winder was directed to find a location deep in the Confederacy that was safe from attack and where food was abundant for a new prison facility to help relieve overcrowding in Richmond and several other locations. Confederate officials originally intended to build a prison of barracks to hold 8,000 to 10,000 POWs.[80]

Captain Winder found what he thought was a perfect location in southwest central Georgia, at Station Number 8 along the Georgia Southwestern Railroad. The site was easily accessible by train, the area was abundant in grain and produce, and it was a long distance from the seat of war. A local resident, Benjamin Dykes, who also owned and operated the area's sawmill and gristmill, offered a beautiful site for the prison, just a mile and a half east of the railroad line, that was heavily wooded with pine and oak, with the ground sloping down on both sides to a wide stream, a branch of Sweet Water Creek. Orders were given to begin construction, but because of local opposition to the prison, labor was difficult to obtain and work was delayed. Slaves were finally impressed from surrounding plantations, but construction was delayed again because a road into the area had to be cleared by axmen before work could proceed.[81]

Meanwhile, conditions in the South made it impossible to build barracks. Rail lines and food processing and distribution centers were crippled throughout the Upper South. In desperation, the Confederate government ordered that a simple stockade—in effect just a corral, the cheapest, most economical form of confinement—be completed as soon as possible. Beginning in January, and in the ensuing weeks, the site was cleared. Then the felled trees were limbed, round-hewed, trimmed off at twenty-foot lengths, and dropped endwise into five-foot deep trenches to build a double stockade wall fifteen feet high in the form of a parallelogram, enclosing sixteen and a half acres. In their haste, the builders left only two trees standing inside the enclosed area. Without further delay, the first prisoners were moved into the facility on February 25, 1864, before the stockade walls were completed.

Southwestern's Station No. 8 was the only one along this end of the line that had a name. It was called Anderson Station, as was the little village of six buildings on the west side of the tracks. Several contemporary sources claimed that the town was named for Union General Robert Anderson and even the *New York Times* gave that account in November 1865. The confusion might have started because the prison was officially known in the Confederacy as "Camp Sumter," in honor of that Confederate victory at the opening of hostilities in Charleston Harbor where General Anderson surrendered. The possibility of the prison, where nearly 13,000 Union soldiers died, being named in honor of a Union general would indeed be ironic, but the truth is, the railroad station by which the POW facility became known was actually named in honor of John W. Anderson, superintendent of the railroad company.[82]

It is not generally known that Captain Henry Wirz, the Andersonville commandant who was hanged at the end of the war, was not the prison's first or only commandant. Colonel Alexander W. Persons, 55th Georgia Infantry, was assigned that post on February 17, 1864, and was in charge of organizing a guard unit for the facility. Colonel Persons served in that capacity until he was replaced by General Winder on June 17. By the time General Winder was in charge there were nearly 22,300 prisoners in the pen that was built for only half as many, and already more than 2,600 had died.[83]

"These prisoners had been confined on Belle's Island and were in a most pitiable condition—half starved, half naked [when they arrived at Andersonville]," admitted James C. Elliott, Company F, 56th North Carolina Regiment, who was a guard on a prisoner train that arrived from Richmond in March. "Most of them had been in prison for months and very few had a change of garments. They were ragged, lousy, filthy and infested with smallpox, and most of them had diarrhea and scurvy and were so weak that when they would swing down out of the box-cars their legs would give away when their feet struck the ground, and they would fall in a heap on the ground."[84]

With a majority of the POWs arriving there in such deplorable, sickly conditions, the reason for Andersonville Prison's high death rate was quite clear. These opprobrious circumstances had already been established when Captain Wirz arrived on March 25, 1864, and he never had supreme command over the compound; that authority was held by Colonel Persons and, later, by General Winder.[85]

From the very first day there had been no organized arrangement of the compound's interior, and by the time Wirz arrived it was too late to try to establish some order. Prisoners had simply been turned into the stockade and left to themselves.

The first arrivals built huts scattered throughout the compound from scrap wood left within the stockade. Later arrivals lived in tents, lean-tos, or out in the open under scraps of blankets or rags. Sometimes the POWs simply dug holes, covered the bottoms with pine needles, and erected blankets on sticks over the depressions to serve as shelters. These, too, were scattered throughout the compound with no semblance of order.

As contingents of POWs continued to arrive, it quickly became apparent that additional space would be needed. Before Persons was relieved of command, he took it upon himself to have the stockade enlarged by ten more acres. A prisoner detail of 130 men was put to work to enlarge the stockade on the north side. It was completed on June 30, after Winder had assumed command. On July 1, a ten-foot-wide hole was knocked into the existing stockade wall, and 13,000 of the compound's 25,000 POWs were ordered to relocate within two hours or lose all their possessions. A stampede to relocate began, and by the morning of July 2, even the remaining portions of the old north wall were gone, having been used during the night by the prisoners for fuel and shelter.[86]

The Confederate authorities originally had Andersonville prison constructed as both an offensive and defensive fortification. The main stockade wall was surrounded by a second row of pine logs that was sixteen feet high. A third row, twelve feet high, was begun but never completed. These additional walls were intended to secure the facility against attack from either side. If the inner stockade was rushed or stampeded by the great mass of prisoners inside, the second wall provided an additional barrier. On the other hand, if there was an attempt to charge the stockade from the outside in an effort to release the prisoners, the other wall provided additional protection and presented a formidable obstacle to an attacking cavalry or infantry unit. At the same time, the four angles of the outer line were further strengthened by earthworks, which gave a commanding position where cannon were mounted for an unobstructed sweep of the entire enclosure.

Although officer prisoners were not held in the Andersonville stockade, the prison did have a smaller, second stockade one half mile west of the main facility, toward Anderson Station, to hold officers. Called Castle Reed, it was a pen of hewn logs 15 feet high and 195 feet by 108 feet that surrounded open-sided shed barracks. Up to sixty-five Union officers were held there until May 1864, when they were transferred to Camp Oglethorpe in Macon. Afterward, the pen was used only to confine Confederate soldiers who had committed various offenses.

When the new July addition expanded Andersonville to a total of twenty-six and a half acres, it raised the estimated capacity of the stockade to 10,000 POWs. At that number, though, there were an average of 377 POWs per acre. Within a few weeks of the addition's completion, the population was up to 29,000, or an average of nearly 1,100 POWs crowded onto every acre.[87]

The transferring of POWs from Richmond, Danville, Cahaba, and other locations continued throughout the following weeks. The Southwestern Railroad, which originally had only two daily scheduled stops at Anderson Station, began scheduling special trains to handle the extra traffic. When the all-time population high of nearly 33,000 was reached in August 1864, Andersonville became, in effect, the fifth largest "city" in the Confederate States of America.[88]

As the stockade became more and more crowded, the amount of rations continued to diminish. First the salt went, then the sweet potato. In time, the amount of cornmeal was reduced, and finally meat was totally eliminated. Rations continued to decrease in size and the number of days they were issued. The POWs became desperate. One day when the bread wagon was rolled into the pen to issue rations, it was rushed by a mob and all the bread was stolen. Captain Wirz responded by cancelling any further rations for that day. On some occasions, guards on the parapet would drop a chunk of cornbread into the pen just to watch the frenzy it created. According to some prisoners, guards would also drop food inside the deadline so they could take shots at the prisoners scrambling for it.[89]

"We had a craving desire for onions, potatoes, pickles, meat and salt," advised one prisoner, "none of which we had had for months; any green substance would be eagerly devoured. Our mess had one stalk of green corn, about knee high, growing by our sleeping ground, and guarded it as though it were gold. A crazy fellow came along one day, snatched the stalk, and ran away into the crowd, eating it as fast as he could, destroying our entire summer's crop."[90]

It was also partly out of desperation, and partly for amusement, that many of these prisoners developed methods for catching the low-flying swallows that often swarmed over the stockade in the evenings. According to one witness, the birds were often eaten raw when they were barely dead.[91]

Another form of amusement was a game called Odd or Even. Several POWs would sit in a circle and each would take a turn placing his hand inside some part of his clothing. Upon pulling his hand out, he would call out "odd or even?" Each player in the circle would declare one or the other and then they would proceed to count the number of vermin which came out on the player's hand to see who won. The object was to have the most vermin and be correct in declaring the total as odd or even.[92]

Two regiments guarded the prisoners at Andersonville: the 55th Georgia and the 26th Alabama. "The Alabamians were intelligent and kind hearted," declared one prisoner, "[and] the Georgians were ignorant and brutal. The Alabamians would talk to us from their posts, while the Georgians were liable to shoot if we spoke to them."[93]

"There was also a battalion or two of cavalry," added another prisoner, "and what was still more formidable, a large pack of bloodhounds, which consisted of two enormous Cuban bloodhounds and about forty half-bloods. These were used before the war for hunting down runaway slaves and now they were kept to scent out and bring back runaway Yankee prisoners."[94]

Despite the number and size of those hounds, there were still 329 successful escapes from Andersonville during its fifteen months of existence. Most occurred during the work details.[95]

The first escape attempt at the prison occurred within a week of the first arrivals. Fifteen men scaled the east wall, using a rope made of strips of cloth. All were recaptured within twenty-four hours with the aid of the dogs, but the incident caused the establishment of a deadline around the inside of the stockade. "A few days [after the escape attempt]," explained prisoner John McElroy, Company L, 16th Illinois Cavalry, "a gang of Negroes came in and drove a line of stakes down at a distance of twenty feet from the stockade. They nailed upon this a strip of stuff four inches wide, and then an order was issued that if this was crossed or even touched, the guards would fire upon the offender without warning."[96]

No doubt the dogs foiled a great many more escape attempts, but after the deadline was established, tunneling became the method of escape and with it, of course, came the informers. Every prison had them. In a typical situation, in May 1864, the commandant walked through the camp surrounded by a squad of guards looking for tunnels. One POW, thinking he might get special consideration for doing so, ran toward the commandant and told him about a tunnel under construction. The authorities made the participants refill the discovered tunnel and then arranged for their punishment. That night the informer was nearly beaten to death, and by the next morning he was being chased around the stockade by inmates intending to punish him some more. The informer ran inside the deadline, claiming protection of the guard. The guards, however, shot the informer to death for being inside the line. "A general hurrahing took place," advised prisoner John L. Ransom, 9th Michigan Cavalry, "as the rebel had only saved our men the trouble of killing him."[97]

That wasn't the first man killed on the wrong side of Andersonville's deadline. The first came the very morning after the boundary was established. Although history has lost his name, he was a German nicknamed "Sigel," wearing the white crescent of the 2nd Division of the 11th Corps. "[H]e spied an old piece of cloth lying on the ground inside the Dead Line," explained McElroy. "He stooped down and reached under for it. At that instant the guard fired. The charge of ball-and-buck entered the poor fellow's shoulder and tore through his body. He fell dead, still clutching the dirty rag that had cost him his life."[98]

When word got back to the North about Andersonville's deadline, it became infamous. It was written about time and again by the northern press, and, at the war's end, Union government officials publicly condemned its use. Prior to all this publicity, few people knew what a deadline was or that such a thing even existed. The problem was, of course, that all the hoopla was purely government propaganda. All the stockade-type prisons had deadlines for security purposes, and Union prisons were no exception. That fact was kept hidden from the American public until well after the war, with the return of Confederate prisoners, yet while the northern press and the public were whipped into a rage over Andersonville's deadline, Union guards were shooting POWs in the "deadruns" of Rock Island, Johnson's Island, Camp Douglas, and similar places.

The guards at Andersonville occasionally performed escape drills, for their own benefit as well as that of the prisoners. "Blank cartridges were . . . fired over the camp by the artillery," revealed one prisoner, "and immediately the greatest commotion [began] outside. It seems that the signal in case a break is made is cannon firing and this was to show us how quick they could rally and get into shape."[99]

As time went on, Andersonville became one of the prisons where escapes became more innovative. The dead became so plentiful that not much attention was paid to them. When a prisoner died, he was simply placed in the path in front of his tent until removed by a detail of USCT prisoners. Several POWs were able to escape by pretending to be dead. They would be carried out and left with the stack of bodies outside the gate awaiting burial. As soon as darkness came, they jumped up and ran off. This ruse was successful a number of times before Captain Wirz changed the policy and had all dead bodies stacked inside the gate to await examination by a surgeon before being taken out of the compound for burial.

The prevailing diseases and main causes of death at the prison were scurvy, diarrhea, dysentery, typhoid, smallpox, and hospital gangrene. Diarrhea and dysentery, by themselves, were responsible for 4,529 deaths between March 1 and August 31, 1864.[100]

Death not only became commonplace, but murder, either by guards or by raiders among the prisoners, became an everyday occurrence as well. The largest and most vicious of these raider groups was led by William "Mosby" Collins, Company D, 88th Pennsylvania Regiment. They called themselves the "Mosby Rangers" and dominated life within the prison for some time. They looted and murdered at will until, finally, out of desperation, other prisoners banded together. With permission from the commandant, the majority of POWs took matters into their own hands. They arrested the raiders, held a trial, and proceeded to meet out punishment to twenty-four of its members, including the hanging of six of them. Three of the other eighteen later died from beatings.[101]

In the midst of all this death, some POWs and prison officials have insisted, one life came into existence. Captain Harry Hunt of Buffalo, New York, and his new wife, Janie Scadden Hunt, were captured on their ship along the coast of North Carolina in mid- to late 1863. Mrs. Hunt quickly disguised herself as a male to prevent being separated from her husband. After a brief incarceration in North Carolina, they were transferred to Andersonville.[102]

"I heard a very small infant crying," related Dr. W. J. W. Kerr, regarding passing by the southwest corner of the stockade one day in July, 1864. "On investigating I found it was the three-day old son of Captain and Mrs. Hunt, and that the baby had been born in the prison." Upon the discovery that a woman and a baby were confined in the stockade, Kerr managed to get Captain Hunt a work detail in the prison hospital, and Janie Hunt and the baby moved out to a private home outside the stockade. Later, Dr. Kerr circulated a petition among other post surgeons and prison authorities to secure a release for the Hunts. After some difficulty, they were eventually discharged on parole.[103]

Little documentation exists to prove or disprove the original rumors of this prison birth or Kerr's later explanation in an attempt to confirm them. The Hunt family seems to have faded into history, and never came forward to confirm or deny Kerr's story. Coincidentally and suspiciously, however, the Rock Island *Argus* of March 30, 1864, reported a similar incident rumored to have occurred in the Rock Island pen, which, was being referred to as the "Andersonville of the North" at that time. Years later, research revealed that these rumors, magnified and spread across Rock Island and eventually into the local newspaper, came about as a result of the birth of a puppy to a dog being kept by one of the POWs.[104]

By September 1864, the majority of prisoners were transferred out of Andersonville because Union forces had recently moved into the area and had occupied Atlanta. In the weeks that followed, as many as 3,000 to 6,000 POWs were dispersed among the other southern facilities.

"At about midnight, September 7, 1864, our detachment was ordered outside at Andersonville [to be loaded onto trains]," advised one prisoner. "The men were being let outside in ranks of four, and counted as they went out. They were very strict about letting none go but the well ones, or those who could walk. The rebel adjutant stood upon a box by the gate, watching very close. Pitch pine knots were burning in the near vicinity to give light."

"We were induced by the rebel authorities to believe that this unexpected movement was for a general exchange," added Ira E. Forbes, 16th Connecticut Volunteer Regiment, "[and] with this belief our men could be sent away with only a small force guarding them."[105]

Those too weak or too sick to travel remained, leaving 8,218 POWs in Andersonville at the end of September. A large number of those died in October and November, leaving a total population of 1,359 in December.[106]

General Winder moved on to take command of another prison as Colonel George C. Gibbs arrived in October to assume command of the Andersonville pen. From then on, the facility took the role of a convalescent camp. Those who gained enough strength to travel were transferred to other facilities. Colonel Gibbs would eventually go on to parole the remaining Andersonville prisoners at Baldwin, Florida, on May 4, 1865.

MACON

The facility at Macon, Georgia—officially named Camp Oglethorpe in honor of the founder of the state, James Oglethorpe—was located about a quarter mile southeast of town in the old fairgrounds. The camp consisted of fifteen to twenty acres containing a large building used as a hospital and a number of sheds and stalls, all surrounded by a highboard fence.

The enclosure, situated between a triple set of railroad tracks and the Ocmulgee River, stood twelve feet high and was constructed of close-fitting, heavy upright boards. A sentry walkway around the top was occupied by heavily armed guards at twenty-pace intervals.

"[T]he gate," reported one prisoner, "(was) spanned from post to post by a broad, towering arch, showing on its curve, in huge black letters 'Camp Oglethorpe'. . . . We were conducted first to the office of the prison, which stood but a few feet from the gate, and there halted and detained until preparation could be made within for another examination."[107]

The prisoners were thoroughly searched, which even included unraveling their clothing linings to locate hidden money, and were led up to the stockade gate one at a time. "The guard pounded the boards with the butt of his gun," remembered prisoner John Hadley, "the bolt glided back, the hinges creaked, the big gate swung open and then there appeared before us a sea of ghostly, grizzly, dirty, haggard faces, staring and swaying this way and that."[108]

All around the inside of the enclosure, an ordinary picket fence three and a half feet high, sixteen feet out from the wall, served as the prison deadline. At the northwest corner of the stockade was a large grove of pine trees. A small stream ran through the west end. The large one-story frame building, once the floral hall for the fair, stood at the center of the enclosure and was often occupied by two hundred POWs. The remainder slept in the sheds and stalls or created their own shelter in the yard. The Macon pen held anywhere from 600 prisoners in 1862 to 1,900 in 1864. Captain W. Kemp Tabb served as the prison commandant for some time until he was relieved by Captain George C. Gibbs in June 1864. Gibbs served in this capacity until transferred to Andersonville in October.[109]

Rations at Macon, consisting of one pint of unsifted cornmeal per day, four ounces of bacon twice a week, and enough peas for two soup dinners per week, were issued in five- or seven-day allotments and left to the POWs to manage the rations through that period. "The only fights I saw in prison," noted one Macon prisoner, "grew out of the dividing of rations, and they were not infrequent."[110]

Roll call at Macon was conducted in a sort of herding process. "The Officer of the Day would come in each morning with twenty guards and deploy them across the north end of the pen," explained one of the prisoners, "then all began whooping and holloring and swearing to drive us to the south end. This being accomplished, an interval between the guards was designated as the place for the count, which was effected by our returning, one by one, through that interval, into the body of the inclosure."[111]

Prisoner accounts indicate that the guards at Macon ranged from the very young to the old, and were possibly Georgia Reserves. A fourteen-year-old guard shot at H. P. Barker, 1st Rhode Island Cavalry, in May 1864, for touching the deadline fence and on June 11, Lieutenant Otto Grierson, 95th New York Volunteers, was shot and mortally wounded by a guard who thought the POW was in the creek preparing to escape. Grierson, reportedly was simply bathing at the time.[112]

The sentry detail at the prison included five cannon outside the stockade, aimed at the interior. At night, guards built fires at short intervals between the deadline and the stockade fence to provide light for added security.

As in nearly all prisons of this type, in the North as well as the South, the guards were required to call out their post and report the hour throughout the night. "Thus," recalled one prisoner, "at ten o'clock the cry would begin 'Post number one—ten o'clock and a-l-l's well.' 'Post number two—ten o'clock and a-l-l's well,' and so on down the line."[113]

Some guards weren't without humor. A number of prisoners, both Confederate and Union, recalled hearing sentries call out the popular 1860's saying "And h-e-r-e's your mule" after calling out the post and the time. On a particular stormy night in July 1864, when General Sherman was known to be conducting operations around Atlanta, and guards at Macon had endured a heavy downpour for over an hour, the POWs heard post number one announce the hour of eleven. "The cry was followed through the line," recalled Hadley, "until it got to Post number five who sang out—'Post number five—eleven o'clock,—Sherman's got Atlanta,—and I'm w-e-t as hell!'" The laughter resounded throughout the camp and along the parapet before the cry continued around the posts and the prisoners began discussing the possibility of the news.[114]

The Macon pen also became well-known for the constant tunneling operations throughout the compound. "There were three tunnels under way at one time," reported one prisoner, "and all came near being successful . . . the three had capacity to let every prisoner out by midnight . . . but the treachery of an Illinois Captain revealed the whole scheme and our guards came in . . . without a guide and deliberately took possession of the holes."[115]

"The manner of making the subterranean avenues was simple but slow," admitted Hadley. "The beginning of each, at Macon, was under a bunk built a few inches from the ground. As soon as dark came, the boards composing the bunk were laid aside, and the work began." Prisoner Willard Glazier added, "Our plan of operation was as follows. [S]elect a bunk in some shed near the 'dead line;' sink a hole or 'well' as we termed it, straight down to the depth of five or six feet, then start the tunnel proper towards the stockade, under which it passed."[116]

The number of successful escapes from Macon is unknown, as is the number of deaths. Disease and illness began taking a toll during the summer months, with dropsy, scurvy, and chronic diarrhea being the most prevalent, but by July 1864, authorities began shipping the prisoners out of Macon, sending six hundred to Charleston and the remaining six hundred to Savannah, because of the approach of George Stoneman's troops.

SAVANNAH

The POWs began arriving in Savannah, Georgia's largest city and one of the South's major ports, on July 29 and continued to arrive over the next several days. "As we were the first Yankees ever in the city," declared one prisoner, "the citizens manifested a great curiosity to see us."[117]

The POWs were escorted off the trains by their guards, the 5th Georgia Reserves, and conducted to the U.S. Marine Hospital grounds on the eastern edge of the city. There they were enclosed in a stockade that had been erected around the orchard adjacent to the hospital. A number of large old oak trees were also enclosed within the structure to provide additional shade. Thirty to forty tents had been pitched with bunks inside, awaiting their arrival and all ill prisoners were given medicine mixed with vinegar and water and a half tablespoon of whiskey mixed with water.[118]

The Savannah stockade was officially known in the Confederacy as Camp Davidson. The prisoners were guarded by the 1st Georgia Volunteers, who had once been POWs themselves. Colonel Richard A. Wayne, a local resident, served as commandant of the camp, while a Major Hill served as commandant of the interior. "I am pleased to say," advised one Union prisoner, in regard to Hill, "that he and his officers and men, generally, treated us humanely and in marked contrast with the authorities at Macon." Another prisoner agreed, "So great is the contrast between our treatment here and at other places, that we cannot but feel that fortune has certainly smiled kindly upon us for once."[119]

The prisoners received better rations at Savannah. They were divided into groups of twenty, and one skillet was issued to each group. Rations, consisting of one pint of cornmeal, one pound of fresh beef, and one gill of rice, were issued daily and one ounce of salt was issued every fourth day. In addition, sutlers were allowed to sell in the camp.

"The authorities have been kind enough to make an issue of brick, with which to build ovens," noted prisoner Williard Glazier. "We raise them about two feet from the ground. The brick are arranged in an oval form, and strongly cemented together with mortar made of clay, which is very adhesive, and serves as a good substitute for lime and mortar. We use the ovens principally for baking our corn bread, which is prepared by stirring the meal and cold water together."[120]

By September, Savannah became crowded with POWs as more and more were transferred in from the general abandonment of Andersonville. Another stockade was hastily constructed on the grounds of the nearby city jail to take the overflow from the Marine Hospital stockade, which was mainly for officer POWs. The new stockade began taking prisoners on September 7.

"It was another pen," recalled a prisoner who had recently arrived from Andersonville, "with high walls of thick pine plank." The compound's interior was bare common ground. Spaces between the boards allowed the prisoners a view of the outside until a twenty-foot deadline was established around the inside of the stockade on the second day. The guards were mostly sailors from the Confederate fleet sitting in Savannah's harbor, although a few were drawn from the town's infantry garrison. For additional security, four artillery batteries of twenty-four pieces were stationed around three sides of the pen.[121]

Lieutenant Samuel B. Davis, who had also served at Andersonville, was appointed commandant of this second pen as its original population of three thousand grew, within days, to more than six thousand. Some estimates put the total combined population of both Savannah stockades around this time at ten thousand POWs.[122]

The extremely ill prisoners who arrived from Andersonville were placed in wall tents outside the jail's stockade on open ground that was simply surrounded by a guard line as security against escapes. Days later the ill were moved into new wall tents inside the Marine Hospital pen.

When Union forces began threatening the city by mid-September 1864, the movement of prisoners began again. By September 12, officers from the Marine Hospital compound were being transferred to Charleston and Columbia, South Carolina. By the end of October, the remaining prisoners from this stockade and the ones at the city jail were being transferred to Columbia and a newer pen recently completed at Millen, Georgia.

Prisoners put the number of deaths at Savannah anywhere from two to several hundred. The discrepancy seems to be because the city served as a POW facility for Union officers for a total of six weeks, overlapped with another six weeks as a confinement facility for Union enlisted men. The officer accounts agree that only two died in the Marine Hospital compound during the six weeks they were there. Many more among the enlisted men in the jail stockade, or at least among the severely sick in the hospital tents, probably did die. All accounts agree, however, there were no escapes from the Savannah facilities.

COLUMBIA

When the first wave of Savannah POWs arrived at Columbia, South Carolina, they were confined in the Richland County Jail with about 230 other prisoners. The jail, an old structure located near the center of town, contained 132 officers and 99 privates by September 1864. It also housed 27 Confederate deserters, several political prisoners, and a number of civilians held on criminal charges.[123]

"Most of the privates are confined in the yard of the jail, which is formed by a rotten wood fence," reported one Confederate official. "Three or four tunnels have been discovered and several prisoners escaped, but [were] recaptured; one prisoner [was] wounded while attempting to escape through a tunnel."[124]

The POWs in the county jail were guarded by local militia, with Major A. J. Green in command of the post and Captain R. D. Senn in command of the guard. Sentinels patroled inside the fence and twelve were positioned around the outside. They worked in two reliefs, three hours at a time.

Rations were issued by the post commissary, and the POWs were allowed to make additional food purchases and to receive the local newspapers. The officers were allowed into the yard for exercise after signing an oath not to escape. The new arrivals, however, severely taxed the already overcrowded jail.

As larger contingents arrived from Savannah and a number of other locations, including those who had been sent to Charleston in October, the county jail was deemed impractical. Arriving prisoners were immediately herded onto a four-acre field, south of the Congaree River, about two miles west of downtown Columbia. The field consisted of a gentle sloping hill covered by scrub pine, with a small brook running along its base. Small pine branches, about eighteen inches long, were placed at intervals of fifty to sixty feet apart to serve as a deadline.

"There was no stockade, no fence, no water but from a brook, no shelter not even for the sick," complained one Union soldier. Another prisoner recalled, "[A] guard and dead line was established and in the open field, with no covering save the broad canopy of heaven, our band, numbering upwards of fifteen hundred men, was obliged to remain."[125]

Unprepared for their arrival, local Confederate officials contacted a military school at Hillsborough and requested a company of cadets as guards. That afternoon, forty "arrogant little guards" arrived to relieve the Charleston troops that had been pulling the duty. "They came down in their suits of fine gray cloth," one prisoner bitterly complained, "their paper collars, blackened boots, and white gloves, not only to guard the Yankee prisoners but to teach the common soldiers a touch of science in the profession."[126]

As the days passed, a thirty-foot clearing was cut through the brush around the prison camp, and a line of guards, ten paces apart, was established along this area. Along the inner edge of this clearing, pins or stakes, fifteen inches high and thirty feet apart, were pounded into the ground to serve as the deadline. Packs of bloodhounds and several pieces of artillery were also moved in and situated at strategic locations around the camp.

Within a short time, this prison camp became known among the POWs as Camp Sorghum because of the abundance of the sorghum-molasses rations issued there on a weekly basis. Whether due to shortages or an inability to obtain it, no meat of any kind was issued. POWs were simply provided with five to seven pints of unsifted cornmeal and a heaping quantity of sorghum-molasses at five- to seven-day intervals. "They did not give us enough of anything here but air, water and room," lamented one of the prisoners.[127]

As the nights grew colder, the prison commandant, Lieutenant Colonel Robert S. Means, a disabled officer of the Invalid Corps, allowed the POWs to go out beyond the deadline to gather firewood under heavy guard and after giving their oath not to escape. Later, in preparation for winter, the prisoners were furnished with axes and shovels to build their own quarters. Additional axes were available, for fifty dollars each, from a sutler allowed to operate around the camp.[128]

The more familiar the POWs became with the surrounding countryside on wood details, the more frequently they tried to escape. The young cadets were supplemented by additional troops in an effort to prevent what soon became nightly escapes. "Our camp was thrown into a state of wild excitement, owing to the escape of three prisoners who ran the guard," reported a Union soldier. "Several shots were fired at them as they passed the outer line, but without doing them any injury."[129]

Before long, the mayor of Columbia, along with a number of leading citizens, and eventually the Columbia *Advertiser,* began complaining about the large population of POWs in the area, their perceived preferential treatment, and the constant escapes.

General Winder responded, "It must be manifest to all that it is vain to guard a large, or even small, body of reserves in an open plain. There is no soldier who can not flank pickets and elude guards in dark and foggy nights; add to this, the guards are raw reserves and without drill, and so small a force that drill is impossible, they being constantly on guard duty. It is for these reasons that I have so earnestly asked for temporary use of the male asylum in this city."[130]

While the state hospital board of regents considered Winder's request, the prisoners of Camp Sorghum found novel ways to amuse themselves. They began cooking down a portion of the sorghum-molasses given to them in such large quantities and finding all kinds of new uses for it. "They made it into balls and threw it at the guards after dark," admitted one prisoner. "Men would reduce great kettles full of it to wax, and from the wax make figures of every conceivable shape [and] made and hung effigies of Confederate celebrities."[131]

Camp Sorghum also became well-known for a silly game, called "Buzz," that was developed by the prisoners. "As many as a hundred men would gather themselves into a circle," explained a prisoner, "set a 'dunce-block' in the center, a referee at one side, and then commence counting rapidly around to the right. Instead of calling out numbers divisible by seven, or multiples of seven, you should say "buzz;" as in 1, 2, 3, 4, 5, 6, buzz; 8, 9, 10, 11, 12, 13, buzz, etc., each man calling but one number. When a man called a number when he should say "buzz" he was caught, and as a penalty had to go to the dunce-block in the center and sing a song or tell a story. . . . This game, foolish as it may seem, produced many roars of laughter at Camp Sorghum.[132]

The numerous escapes continued. As soon as night came, escapees sprinted past the guards at any opportunity. When shots failed to bring them down, packs of dogs usually did. A number of prisoners were mauled, and at least one documented case exists of a Camp Sorghum POW being killed by a pack of sentry dogs.[133]

By the first week of December, there had been 373 successful escapes, a number of POWs wounded by gunshots, and several suffering from dog bites. Reluctantly, the hospital board gave permission to move the POWs to a more secure facility owned by the state. "The board of regents," advised Mr. M. La Borde, its president, "in view of the great necessity of receiving the prisoners and protecting our defenseless women and children from any injury which may occur from their going at large, deem it expedient to allow General Winder the use of the grounds of the State asylum east of the buildings, under such restrictions as the board may adopt."[134]

By the third week of December 1864, the open field that had become known as Camp Sorghum was abandoned, and the approximately 1,200 remaining POWs were moved to a temporary stockade enclosure on the east side of the hospital.

The South Carolina State Hospital stood at Elmwood and Bull streets on the north side of Columbia. The facility had been the state's asylum for the mentally ill since 1822, and as soon as the prisoners arrived at their new surroundings, they began to refer to it as Camp Asylum, a name that eventually became recognized officially by Confederate government authorities. Within a few weeks, Major Elias Griswold relieved Colonel Means of command.

Meanwhile, General Winder was arranging for a new prison site to be established somewhere in the area. "I have selected a site at the fourteen-mile post from Columbia on the Charlotte railroad," he later advised. "I propose . . . to purchase the tract spoken of, and to erect an officers' stockade and a stockade for the [enlisted] prisoners."[135]

The site was at Killian's Mill, fourteen miles northeast of Columbia. His proposal included a stockade large enough to hold fifteen thousand POWs, comprised of those currently held at Columbia; at a newly established and already overcrowded pen at Florence, South Carolina; and at all of the area's county jails, which were holding a number of overflow prisoners from all of these places. Winder also proposed naming the site Camp Maxey Gregg, in honor of the Confederate general from Columbia who had helped draft the state's Ordinance of Secession and had been killed in the first battle of Fredericksburg.[136]

As at Andersonville, the local carpenters and laborers in the neighborhood of Killian's Mill refused to work on the project because they didn't want a prison in the area. Finally, the Confederate secretary of war authorized the impressment of black Union POWs to begin the work and to complete it as quickly as possible.[137]

By mid-January 1865, the safety of the Columbia area was being threatened by the enemy. On January 15, five hundred Camp Asylum POWs were quickly transferred to Charlotte, North Carolina, for confinement in an open field. Most of the remaining seven hundred POWs were shipped out to Millen, Georgia, by mid-February.

"[T]he site recently purchased by the Government at Killian's Mill," complained Colonel Henry Forno, in command of prisoners in the Columbia area, "I had been ordered to erect a prison at that place; had all the timber cut, trenches dug, and ready to begin raising, when the evacuation of Columbia obliged me to discontinue work."[138]

FLORENCE

Florence, South Carolina, was a point eighty miles east of Columbia where three sets of railroad tracks intersected, with a machine shop, a hotel, a church, two small stores, three taverns, and several homes, located nearby. The most prominent feature at the site was an immense pine forest.[139]

The Florence stockade was hastily established when Andersonville's position was threatened in mid-September 1864. By mid-October nearly thirteen thousand POWs occupied the site, but it wasn't completed until sometime around October 19.[140]

Located in the pine forest, one and a half miles east of the settlement, the stockade prison enclosed twenty-three and a half acres. A creek, six feet wide and five inches deep, ran from north to south through the center. The interior of the stockade sloped off from both sides toward the stream, causing nearly six acres to be low, swampy marshland unsuitable for encampment. In effect, the Florence pen was nothing but a smaller Andersonville. Until Andersonville was developed, the Salisbury pen was regarded as the Confederacy's worst prison, but with the establishment of Florence, according to many prisoners who spent time in both or all three, the stockade at Florence was considered, by far, the most wretched place of all.[141]

The first prisoners from Andersonville arrived on September 14, 1864, and were marched through the settlement to the site east of town. Known locally as "the old field," the tract consisted of nearly five hundred acres of rolling, sandy, tillable land in the center of the pine forest that was once part of several plantations in the business of producing turpentine and rosin. The POWs were ushered to the center of the clearing and surrounded by a guardline while a stockade was erected around them by local slaves impressed into service during the following weeks.[142]

"We gathered leaves, grass and pine boughs," remembered Charles Fosdick, one of the original five thousand prisoners transferred there from Andersonville, "and spread them under the scrubby pines." Sam Boggs recalled that "the tops and refuse of trees from which the stockade timbers were cut were left on the ground, and prisoners used them to construct huts and dugouts. Some were too sick or weak to make anything but a hole [and] frequently some of these mud dens would cave in on the occupants and they would be smothered."[143]

"The great majority of [the prisoners] look emaciated and sickly," admitted Lieutenant Colonel W. D. Pickett, Confederate inspector general, "and are without blankets and almost without clothing. As a consequence, there is a great deal of suffering these cool nights and much additional sickness must follow. . . . The principal diseases are scurvy and diarrhea, which carry off from twenty to fifty per day. The present sick-list is 785. The hospitals are made of the boughs of trees, are of temporary character, and will afford very little protection from rain."[144]

The prison commandant was Colonel George P. Harrison, Jr., who became well-known for his fair treatment of the prisoners, and the guard consisted of the 5th Georgia Regiment along with five battalions of reserve troops and several detachments of artillery. Lieutenant Thomas G. Barrett commanded the prison's interior and became intensely hated by all the prisoners.

"Barrett was the most brutal fool I ever met," declared one prisoner. "On the least provocation he would become so enraged that he would stamp and swear at everyone near him." Another prisoner noted, "All who were in the different prisons in the South will agree, that Barrett was the most cruel man we ever came in contact with. He had a little more brains than some of the rest, and this extra intellect was entirely given to cruelty. He would shoot into squads of men [and] knock down and kick the life out of [others]."[145]

According to several accounts, Lieutenant Barrett caught one prisoner flanking for rations and had him stripped of his remaining clothes and beat with a leather "cattails" whip. "[H]e cut the miserable man's back into shreds," remembered one prisoner who witnessed the incident, "and he died before they got him untied."[146]

More POWs transferred from Andersonville and other locations continued to stream into Florence through the end of October and into the first half of November. Before long, the population had topped fifteen thousand and the stockade became more crowded than any of the others, including Andersonville.[147]

The Florence stockade was built somewhat differently than previous ones. Its sixteen-foot walls, consisting of unhewn sturdy logs of oak and pine, had earth thrown up against the outside, which provided an earthen walkway around the enclosure, except at the front and rear gate openings, for the sentry to patrol along, while artillery pieces, directed toward the compound's interior, sat at the top of each corner. The additional dirt was provided by digging a deep, wide trench around the outside, several yards out from the enclosure, to expose any tunneling. Inside the compound, trenching around the interior, fifteen to twenty feet from the wall, served as the deadline. Later, a deadline was established by laying thin poles in wooden crotches along the edge of the trench.

Rations, at first, consisted of a little flour, a pint of cornmeal, two to three sweet potatoes, and a little meat once a day. Sometimes a few beans, peas, or a gill of rice was substituted for the potatoes. By December, only cornmeal was provided. Lieutenant Colonel John F. Iverson arrived later that same month to relieve Colonel Harrison of command. By that time the prison population had been reduced to nearly eleven thousand, through specially arranged exchanges of the sick and the deaths of others, and nearly sixteen hundred of those were confined to the prison hospital.[148]

The hospital was established in the northwest corner of the pen after it was cleared of prisoner dugouts and the construction of crude sheds was completed. The sick were carried in and laid on beds of pine needles in two double rows under each shed. Each double row was referred to as a ward, and a path was left between the feet of the row on either side so the prisoner-attendants could get around to each patient.

"But," observed one prisoner, "nothing was done to bathe or cleanse the bedridden or to exchange their lice-infested garments for others. The long-tangled hair and whiskers were not cut, nor indeed, were any of the commonest suggestions for the improvement of the condition of the sick put into execution. Men who had lain in their mud hovels until they had become helpless and hopeless were admitted to the hospital usually only to die."[149]

At Florence, death came easily, and insanity, too, seemed almost epidemic. "We had many insane men at Andersonville," said prisoner John McElroy, "but the type of the derangement was different. . . . [T]he insane of Florence were of a different class; they were the boys who had laughed at such a yielding to adversity in Andersonville, and felt a lofty pity for the misfortunes of those who succumbed so. But now the long strain of hardship, privation and exposure had done for them what discouragement had done for those of less fortitude in Andersonville. The faculties shrank under disuse and misfortune, until they forgot their regiments, companies, places and date of capture, and finally, even their names. I should think that by the middle of January, at least one in every ten had sunk to this imbecile condition. It was not insanity so much as mental atrophy—not so much aberration of the mind as a paralysis of mental action. The sufferers became apathetic idiots, with no desire or wish to do or be anything."[150]

By January 1865, apathy had indeed swept the camp. It became a general belief among many POWs that those who preferred to live in "manholes," shelters two feet deep and just large enough to lie in that were sometimes covered with sticks and earth, had unconsciously prepared their own graves and were just waiting to die. Each morning many were, in fact, found dead in those holes. Between the end of September 1864 and the end of January 1865, at least 2,802 POWs died at Florence. Contemporary accounts place the number of deaths even higher, claiming as many as 4,000 to 6,000. It probably seemed to those who were there that up to one-third of their comrades were sick or dying. Even Colonel Iverson admitted deaths averaged thirty-five to forty per day before he took command of the prison. The dead bodies often lay in the camp for a day or two before they were taken out for burial. The interments were made trench-fashion at the edge of the woods, a quarter-mile north of the main gate. No official record was kept of the deaths.[151]

A number of POWs, however, maintained their fortitude and refused to give up, no matter what adversities they faced. Scurvy swept over the Florence prison, and it became infamous for the number of cases that occurred there. Hundreds of men were reduced to a crippled state, and a number cut off their own toes or feet in order to survive.

One of the most famous, fully documented cases was that of John W. January of Company B, 14th Illinois Cavalry. By early 1865, he suffered from scurvy and gangrene, and came down with a severe fever. He remained delirious for three weeks before the fever broke and his reasoning returned. "My feet and ankles five inches above the joints presented a livid, lifeless appearance and soon the flesh began to slough off," explained January. "[B]elieving that my life depended upon the removal of my feet, I secured an old pocket knife and cut through the decaying flesh and severed the tendons. The feet were unjointed, leaving the bones protruding without a covering of flesh for five inches."[152]

During the four and a half months of the prison's existence, fifty-eight POWs escaped, mostly by rushing the guard line before the stockade was erected.

The frequency of those first escapes apparently became a great novelty to the local citizenry. "I suppose you have heard how our part of the country is overrun by the Yankee prisoners," wrote Louisa Jane Harllee, wife of General William C. Harllee, to her cousin on September 25, 1864, "as they are not confined at all, and with a very poor guard, of course they are making their escape in great numbers. There was considerable excitement when they first commenced escaping, and they were being caught on almost everybody's plantation but they were being very humble, and have attempted no violence, their object alone seems to be to get something to eat and to escape to the coast . . . in fact so many are taken every day that they have ceased to be a novelty in passing by. A stockade is being made in which to confine them, and it will be sufficiently completed to receive them Tuesday [September 27]."[153]

Once the walls were erected, any further escapes were limited to the work details. Another 326 POWs went on to enlist in the Confederate service to avoid further suffering in the prison.

MILLEN

General Winder had anticipated establishing the pen at Millen, Georgia, as early as mid-1864, when Andersonville had reached capacity and another prison was badly needed to handle the overflow. Millen, however, remained unable to receive POWs until the second week of October. By then it was nearly too late. It came into use for only a month and a half before it had to be abandoned.

Millen is located in the heart of Jenkins County, east Georgia, nearly forty-five miles south of Augusta. In August 1864, a site five miles north of the town was leased from Mrs. C. M. Jones for the establishment of a new stockade prison. Again, locals refused to work on the project, and authority had to be obtained to impress slave labor, teams and wagons, and the lumber and sawmills.[154]

This stockade, too, resembled Andersonville, but it was much larger and better organized inside. The pen, hastily constructed of rough logs, measured nearly fourteen hundred feet square and enclosed forty-two acres. Winder later declared that it was the largest prison in the world. The interior of Millen was high and grassy instead of the low and sandy fields at Andersonville. A good stream ran through the compound without a marsh on either side. At Millen the creek was bordered by firm banks, and a ditch carried water from the stream down through the sinks. To help prevent disorder and to aid in policing the grounds, the interior was divided by sixteen-foot-wide streets into thirty-two sections. Each section was further divided into ten segments. Limbs from the stockade logs and additional felled trees were left on the ground in the compound's interior for the prisoners' use in constructing shelters.

Prisoners began arriving, mostly from Savannah and Andersonville, in mid-October. POWs continued to arrive in the following days until the Millen population climbed to 6,000, then to 7,000. Within a few more days the population topped out at 10,299.[155]

The Millen stockade prison was officially named Camp Lawton, in honor of the current Confederate quartermaster general, Alexander R. Lawton, who had served as colonel of the 1st Georgia Regiment early in the war and had been severely wounded at Antietam. Captain D. W. Vowles served as the prison's commandant.

"(He) was the best of his class it was my fortune to meet," remembered one prisoner, referring to Captain Vowles. "Compared with the senseless brutality of Wirz, the reckless deviltry of Davis, or the stupid malignance of Barrett, at Florence, his administration was mildness and wisdom itself. He enforced discipline better than any of those named, but had what they all lacked—executive ability—and he secured results that they could not possibly attain, and without anything like the friction that attended their efforts."[156]

A majority of the POWs agreed that the rations issued at Millen were better too. They were issued a cupful of good-quality, finely ground cornmeal and received fresh beef on several occasions. That issue caused great excitement among the inmates. "On the first occasion," admitted a prisoner, "the meat was simply the heads of the cattle killed for the use of the guards. Several wagon loads of these were brought in and distributed. We broke them up so that every man got a piece of the bone, which was boiled and reboiled, as long as a single bubble of grease would rise to the surface of the water, every vestige of meat was gnawed and scraped from the surface, and then the bone was charred until it crumbled, when it was eaten." Sorghum was issued in lieu of beef at other times. Barrels of it were often rolled into the stockade and issued out in allotments of one-fourth pint per man.

On the evening of November 7, additional excitement erupted among the prisoners when a small alligator was discovered in a reservoir near the creek. A portion of the stream's lower end had been planked and the sides boarded up for sanitary use. Water was also damned near this point to be used to forcibly carry off the sludge. It was in this pool that the gator was discovered, captured, killed, and eaten by a number of POWs, making such an experience, not to mention the alternative meat source, unique among the Civil War's prisons.[157]

Millen was no different than the other prisons, however, when it came to suffering, sickness, and death. After long confinement at other prisons, the Millen POWs continued to be weak and sickly. Hospital tents were set up in the southeast corner of the stockade but, as at Florence, few recovered. Some were so severely ill that they were exchanged at Wilmington under special arrangements, but even with those gone, 486 POWs died in the prison's first month of operation.[158]

According to various contemporary accounts, there might have been as many as seven hundred deaths during Millen's six weeks' of operation. Due to a lack of official records, however, the exact number will never be known.

The criminal element among the prisoners surfaced again at Millen. After several fights, the prison commandant sent troops into the compound to arrest the raiders, who were then put in stocks and held.[159]

On November 14, two contingents of POWs were moved out of Millen, six hundred at a time. The following day, another twelve hundred were moved out. The transfers continued as the days passed. By the end of the month, Millen was completely abandoned. The movement of Sherman's Union forces toward the sea had threatened the safety of the site.

Although Captain Vowles had seemed well-liked by all the prisoners, he was later accused of exploiting them. He apparently used his "executive ability" to develop a scheme for personal profit. When the opportunity arose to exchange sick POWs, he charged eager prisoners $60 each to switch their names for those scheduled to be exchanged, sending out a number of well prisoners in place of the severely sick and dying. There were so many accusations, in fact, that General Winder later declared that Vowles should never be allowed to receive a similar command.[160]

The Millen POWs, loaded onto flatcars, had been trained toward Savannah. According to the prisoners, the night trips were cold, and it rained most of the time. A bitter, cold wind threatened to freeze the wet, tattered rags that they wore, and a number of the captives died during the trips. At Savannah they were given hardtack, transferred from the Georgia Central Railroad line to the Atlanta and Gulf, and steamed southbound out of town. After some delay and confusion among Confederate officials, the POWs finally arrived at the Blackshear Camp.

BLACKSHEAR

The Confederates began evacuating a number of prisons and moving the POWs to Blackshear, deep in southeast Georgia, in Pierce County. The strain on the Confederacy, though, was becoming apparent. "I experienced great trouble with prisoners by having, at one time, three trains broken down between Savannah and this place," complained Colonel Henry Forno (CSA), commanding the post, "and [have had] great difficulty in obtaining supplies."[161]

The first contingent of six hundred prisoners from Millen arrived on November 16. Blackshear Prison was nothing more than an open camp in an out-of-the-way place, surrounded by a guardline, including some heavy artillery pieces.

The 2nd Georgia Reserve Regiment and three companies of the 4th Georgia Reserves pulled the duty. Still, each night a number of POWs escaped.

Prisoner trains continued to arrive until the camp held more than five thousand POWs. Because of problems with supplies, rations consisted of whatever was available, given out once a day. Sweet potatoes were given out one day, rice on another, and a small ration of beef on yet another day. The beef issue was the result of guards visiting surrounding plantations and driving several cattle back to the camp, where they were killed, butchered, and the meat dispersed among the Confederates and the POWs.

Within a week, the prisoners who had arrived on the first trains were informed that they would be transferred back to Savannah for exchange. They were given two days' rations of cornmeal and fresh beef and sent on their way. Upon reaching Savannah, however, the POWs found themselves exiting the train between two heavy lines of guards with fixed bayonets. They immediately realized that they weren't to be exchanged. Upon boarding a second train, they were transported to Charleston, South Carolina, for confinement.[162]

At the same time, Colonel Forno shipped out additional prisoners to other points, leaving only twenty-five hundred POWs at Blackshear by December 7, 1864. "I have been in a state of uncertainty ever since I came here," complained Forno. "I had orders from general headquarters, Savannah, to parole the prisoners and send them to Savannah. I sent under that order 1,042 and before I could send more the trains were taken off for troops from Thomasville [Georgia]. On the 5th instant, orders were forwarded to me to ship prisoners to Thomasville without delay . . . I sent 400 . . . I also sent Captain Moreno with orders to impress slave labor and put up an inclosure. . . . I had another train sent, on which I put 1,200 prisoners and the guard."[163]

The Confederates were in a quandary. By mid- to late December they had POWs going in every direction and were never certain where they were at any one time. The POWs moved from Blackshear to Charleston were sent back for confinement at Florence, while some were sent to different locations, and still others seemed to be traveling in circles, surrounded by guardlines along the railroad tracks during the night and heading out to some other destination each morning.

"[T]he Rebels were terribly puzzled what to do with us," observed one prisoner. "We were brought to Savannah, but that did not solve the problem; and we were sent down the Atlantic & Gulf road as a temporary expedient."[164]

Meanwhile, the threat of Sherman's approach continued to worsen. On December 10 and 11 the remaining Blackshear POWs were loaded onto open platform cars with guards sitting around or standing on the sides—six guards to a car, about sixty prisoners per car, and thirty to forty such cars to a train—and moved slowly out of Blackshear.[165]

On the first night, the trains stopped and prisoners camped along the tracks. The next morning they climbed upon the cars and moved out again, en route to Charleston via Savannah. Guards did double duty during the entire trip and soon became tired and worn out. Many of the prisoners took advantage of the situation and jumped from the slow-moving train to run off into the nearby woods.[166]

The number of successful escapes from Blackshear or the train ride away from there remains unknown, but it was said to be a lot. Contemporary accounts also fail to mention the number of gravesites left behind when the area was evacuated.

As Sherman's forces approached Florence in mid-February, Confederate officials experienced greater stress and confusion. Again, they frantically looked for some area of safety for their POW accumulation. Some officials argued that they should be sent to Wilmington for exchange. Others wanted them sent to Salisbury, which was extremely overcrowded by that time, and still others insisted that they be split up and confined at Charlotte and Raleigh. In the process, General Winder collapsed and died at Florence. Within days, Colonel Forno assumed overall command of the POW situation and immediately sent twelve hundred of Florence's captives to Charlotte, with the hopes of sending seven thousand more to Raleigh.[167]

"Seven-thousand prisoners—about 3,000 sick—very destitute of clothing; rations very short; no meat at all," Colonel Iverson reported in a hasty dispatch to the adjutant general's office from Florence, "ought to be removed to a safer point immediately but cannot be done unless more troops are sent me." As Confederate officials nervously awaited the arrival of additional troops, daily dispatches kept them abreast of Sherman's movements through the countryside.[168]

"One day all of us who were able to walk," recalled Florence prisoner John McElroy, "were made to fall in and march over to the railroad where we were loaded into box cars. The sick, except those who were dying, were loaded into wagons and hauled over. The dying were left to their fate without any companions or nurses."[169]

Upon abandonment of the Florence pen, even with the sick still lying around, Confederate officials attempted to destroy the structure, possibly to prevent it from gaining the notoriety that Andersonville had already obtained in the northern press. "Rebels attempted to burn the stockade wall by firing piles of wood thrown against it on the inside," one correspondent reported later, "but the fire refused its work and only scorched the logs at seventy-five or a hundred points of the long line."[170]

Ignoring the Andersonville, Millen, and Blackshear sites, each of which had a few remaining sick or dying inmates left behind by the evacuations, Sherman's Union forces entered Savannah on December 21, concluding his March to the

Sea. Florence, too, was virtually ignored by Union forces maneuvering in and around the South Carolina area. Meanwhile, Sheridan was aggressively moving through Virginia to cut off Lee's retreat from Appomattox, and Grant maintained a strong hold on other vital areas. It was becoming clear to many that the day of "checkmate" was approaching, and many Confederate officials realized, too, that the POW situation was destined to become a political albatross around their necks.

Chapter 12

RELEASE AND REVENGE

> *At last men came to set me free.*
> *I asked not why, and recked not where;*
> *It was at length the same to me. . . .*
> *I had learned to love despair.*
>
> Francois de Bonnivard

By mid- to late 1864, the prisons of both sides had become so crowded that it often took several hours to get through the mass of people to the other side. By that time the prisons had become concentration camps, or death camps. As survival became more difficult, many diversionary activities declined. Prisoners no longer played ball, chess, checkers, or card games, and the little commercial enterprises were gone. Inmates, their clothing by now reduced to rags, were left to wander. Increasingly there became a lack of space, a lack of privacy, and no place to withdraw. The monotony of existence gnawed upon the men. Gradually they lost all sense of time; they became edgy and tempers grew short.

Violent regional conflicts sometimes occurred. A fight broke out between prisoners from New York and Kentucky in a Richmond prison, and at Salisbury, where Confederate deserters were held with Union POWs for a time, a fight broke out between the two sides that rivaled any battle.[1]

Personal disputes often resulted in death. In Richmond, one prisoner killed another over a blanket. At Andersonville, a prisoner killed his own brother for food, buried him beneath his tattered tent, and slept over him for some time. At Camp Chase, one prisoner killed another by stabbing him repeatedly with a pocketknife during an argument. At Johnson's Island, a political prisoner killed a Confederate POW in a confrontation. At Camp Douglas, in March 1865, a POW stabbed and killed a fellow prisoner; it was the third time since his incarceration that he had knifed a fellow prisoner during an argument.[2]

283

Fistfights over food became common. At least twenty fights among the prisoners were noted in just one day by John Ransom at Andersonville. "It beats all what a snarling crowd we are getting to be," he noted in his journal. "The men are perfectly reckless and had just as soon have their necks broken by fighting as anything else."[3]

No matter what food they received, POWs learned to eat it quickly for fear it would be seized by others around them. Vicious and sometimes deadly fights broke out over a few pieces of spoiled meat. "The worst side of human nature becomes visible," observed prisoner George Bailey. "[S]carcity of food often pitted prisoner against prisoner; desperate soldiers fought one another." Ransom agreed, "The animal dominates."[4]

Besides violent fights over food, the sight of prisoners diving to the ground and licking it when a bucket of soup was spilled was not at all unusual. "A man shows exactly what he is in [the pens]," observed one prisoner. "No occasion to be any different from what you really are. Very often [we] see a great big fellow in size, in reality a baby in action, actually sniveling and crying, and then again you will see some little runt, 'not bigger than a pint of cider,' tell the big fellow to 'brace up' and be a man."[5]

Constant pestering by vermin flared already short tempers. By late in the war, nearly all the prisons were crawling with bedbugs, lice, cockroaches, rats, and mice. Prisoner James Williamson, while incarcerated at Old Capitol Prison, was tormented by mice all through the night. "They appear to think it funny chasing one another under the board pillow at my head," he protested, "and their running over my back and crawling about the folds of my blanket. When I shake them off they scamper away only to return when they see I am quiet again."[6]

During the warmer months, flies and mosquitoes swarmed over the open-pen facilities in unprecedented numbers. "Millions and millions of flies swarmed," remarked prisoner Sam Boggs, "and . . . they lit into our mush, bedding-places, and on the faces of the sick and dying."[7]

"A dead man, one of the prisoners, was the other day carried out to the dead yard," commented another prisoner, "the hair on his head stiff with lice and nits—the lice creeping into his eyes in great numbers, and, as he lay with his mouth open, the lice were thick crawling in and out of his open mouth."[8] "Millions upon millions of mosquitoes came to feast on our emaciated bodies," remembered Sam Boggs, "[and] their buzzing hum added to the bedlam."[9]

"Today [I] saw a man with a bullet hole in his head over an inch deep," reported John Ransom about another POW roaming the prison facility, "and you could look down in it and see maggots squirming around at the bottom."[10] "I had much rather engage in a dozen battles than remain a dozen months in prison," said Johnson's Island prisoner James B. Mitchell, Company B, 34th Alabama, in February 1865.[11]

By the last year of the war, conditions in nearly all the prison compounds were beyond imagination. Death was a daily occurrence, and the prisoners had grown oblivious to it.

"(T)he dead are being gathered up," observed a prisoner, "(t)he bodies are stripped of their clothing in most cases as soon as the breath leaves, and in some cases before, the row of dead presents a sickening appearance. Legs drawn up and in all shapes. They are black from pitch pine smoke and laying in the sun. Some of them lay there for twenty hours or more, and by that time are in a horrible condition."[12]

At Elmira, nearly 3,000 fell victim to the hopeless conditions there; at Andersonville, nearly 13,000. At Alton, Camp Douglas, Camp Butler, Camp Randall, and Rock Island, a combined total of nearly 9,000 succumbed. Untold numbers fell victim at Richmond, including Belle Isle, and nearly 1,300 died at Danville. At Camp Chase, Camp Morton, and Gratiot Street, a total of more than 5,000 suffered and died. At Florence and a number of other South Carolina locations, more than 2,800 perished. At New York City, Old Capitol Prison, Point Lookout, and Fort Delaware, a combined total of nearly 8,000 died, and at Salisbury Prison another 3,700 perished.

"[S]o many of my comrades had fallen by the wayside," one POW sadly reflected about life in the Civil War's prisons, "or were broken and maimed for life."[13]

In illustration of what was to come, one of the first major POW groups to gain its freedom after the cartel collapse emerged from confinement at Salisbury Prison as a conglomeration of frail, wilted, run-down human beings. Similar scenes would follow in the coming months, in the North as well as the South.

In January, 1865, Major Gee was replaced by General Bradley Johnson as commandant of Salisbury Prison. On February 16, Richmond authorities notified Johnson that a general exchange would soon take place and that it was permissible to notify the prisoners. Five days later the announcement was made and, according to one prisoner, "[T]he commotion began. Such shouting and singing! No tongue nor pen can describe the joy and happiness this welcome message brought to the prisoners."[14]

But transportation proved impossible to secure. Finally, on February 22, those who were not too weak, crippled, or ill were escorted out of Salisbury on foot. "About half past 12 o'clock," one prisoner recalled, "the men were formed into columns and marched out at the north gate protected on each side by a heavy guard of rebel soldiers."[15]

Thin, tattered, and haggard, the former soldiers slowly plodded along the road toward Greensboro, North Carolina. The column, numbering more than twenty-eight hundred men, stretched nearly three miles long. Some walked in twos, supporting one another; some in threes, supporting or dragging the middle person along the route between them; and some were even carried on the backs of others.[16]

Of the 2,800 men who began the fifty-one-mile trip from Salisbury, only 1,800 made it to Greensboro. Two hundred were left in Lexington and another 500 were abandoned along the road the following day. All together, nearly 1,000 fell by the wayside, too weak to continue, or died along the route.[17]

In the following days, groups of prisoners continued to be escorted out of Salisbury in this manner until 5,149 captives had been evacuated. Upon reaching Greensboro, prisoners were shipped out by train to Wilmington, where they were allowed to enter their own lines on March 2, 1865. By the end of March only 500 prisoners, unable to begin the trip, remained in Salisbury. They were, however, quickly moved to Charlotte, North Carolina, when word was received that Stoneman's Union forces were nearing the site.

As Federal troops rode into Salisbury on April 12, they found the prison being used as a storage depot by the Confederate army. Stoneman remained in the area for a few days, rounded up a number of Confederate officials and soldiers, and confined them at the prison. At the same time, he had his troops fill the numerous shelter holes that remained within the compound. Upon his departure, Stoneman had the 12th Ohio Regiment set fire to the prison.

Similar procedures were followed as Federal troops rode into Camp Ford out west and a number of other prison locations, including Columbia, South Carolina. There, Union troops released sixty Federal officers and a number of political prisoners still imprisoned in the Richland County Jail. Then, mysteriously, the whole city was set afire. Controversy raged for many years after the war over who was responsible for burning the capital of the first state that had seceded from the Union. The town's citizens blamed Union occupation troops, while the troops maintained that the citizens must have done it.

There was no question who burned down the capital city of the Confederacy. When Grant took Petersburg, he opened the road to Richmond. The night of April 2, Confederate officials, defense troops, and many civilians fled the capital as prison commandants all around the city arranged for the evacuation of their captives. By the early morning hours of April 3, Captain Alexander had successfully evacuated Castle Thunder, sending most of the inmates to Danville, and Libby had been mostly evacuated except for a few sick and wounded POWs still held in the prison hospitals. Major Thomas Turner was the last to leave. He remained in his office to the end, burning as many prison records as possible.[18]

By 3 A.M., Richmond was abandoned, and in flames. Buildings on Main, Cary, and Canal Streets between 8th and 18th, fell as the fire consumed one structure after another. Nearly all of the tobacco factories and warehouses once used to confine prisoners of war were destroyed.

When the advance party of the 4th Massachusetts Cavalry galloped into the ruins nearly five hours later, they found that the city's two most infamous buildings, the Libby warehouse and Castle Thunder, had survived the destruction and still stood, almost defiantly, in the midst of the rubble.[19]

Later that day, additional Federal forces rode into the city and confiscated the remaining prison buildings, including the Pemberton warehouse. "The dirt [on the floors] was three inches thick and alive with vermin," reported L. L. Crounse, a correspondent for the New York Times, who was accompanying the invading forces into Richmond. "A strong force of men have been engaged two days in carrying out the accumulation of the past three years. . . . and yet on this floor, in this condition, prisoners were obliged to sleep either upon the dirt itself or upon piles of decaying straw."[20]

Union authorities used Castle Thunder as a guardhouse to confine those arrested for looting and other misdemeanors. Nero, the ferocious guard dog for which Alexander once refused $700 in gold but then abandoned upon his evacuation to Danville, was confiscated by Union military officials and later taken to New York City. The key to Castle Thunder's front door was also later taken to New York and eventually auctioned off on the steps of the Astor House to help raise funds for the orphans of Union soldiers.[21]

After Richmond passed into Federal hands, up to seven hundred Confederates were gathered from around the city and confined in Libby Prison. Union Lieutenant John Bishop, a former commandant of the Gratiot Street Military Prison in St. Louis, was placed in charge of the facility during the occupation of the city. Most of these new Libby prisoners were city officials and minor Confederate authorities, much like those who were later held in Salisbury Prison. The notorious commandants that the Union officials wanted had all successfully fled the city and eluded capture. Alexander had fled to Danville, Thomas Turner to Canada. Dick Turner got out of the city as well but would later be apprehended.[22]

Then it was the Union's turn. Not to be cheated by the Confederates who fled Richmond, Union authorities burned many of the remaining Richmond buildings containing cotton, tobacco, or supplies that had survived the original conflagration. They had originally intended to spare the Pemberton building from the torch, but when they set fire to a warehouse full of tobacco next door, Pemberton went up in flames as well.[23]

When the war officially came to an end on April 9, 1865, arrangements were made to formally release the remaining POWs of both sides. It is said that at Camp Ford in Texas, the guards, upon learning Lee had surrendered, just pulled out and headed for home, leaving the remaining prisoners to simply walk off on their own to find transportation out of the area. At nearly every other location, however, the POWs were held anywhere from several more weeks to several more months.

"Totally unprepared for the series in which the war terminated," reported prisoner Harry Gilmore, "we remained under a sort of bewilderment as from time to time we learned of the evacuation of Richmond, then of General Lee's surrender, and, finally, of that of General J. E. Johnston. . . . The war was over, and there was no alternative left us but to accept defeat, and obtain our release on such terms as the United States government felt inclined to grant."[24]

The United States felt inclined to grant no release immediately and temporarily ignored the plight of the prisoners they held. Instead, U.S. authorities moved quickly to locate, run down, and arrest many of the Confederate prison commandants and officers, including Major John H. Gee of Salisbury; Lieutenant Colonel John F. Iverson and Captain Thomas G. Barrett of the Florence pen; Major Thomas P. Turner and Captain George W. Alexander of Richmond; Richard Turner of Libby; Captain D. W. Vowles of Millen; Captain Henry Wirz, Captain W. Sidney Winder, and Captain Richard B. Winder of Andersonville; and many others. The publicity and propaganda associated with Andersonville made it inevitable that the victors would seek retaliation for what happened in the Confederate prisons, and with the recent death of General John Winder, full responsibility for Andersonville fell on Wirz. What had happened in the North would be ignored for the time being.[25]

During the days that followed Appomattox, the U.S. government arranged for train and boat transportation for the POWs liberated from southern prisons. Meanwhile, more than sixty-four thousand Confederate prisoners remained in twenty-two different northern facilities across the United States. Waiting to be released, these prisoners were required to take and officially sign, the Oath of Allegiance in a long, drawn-out process that would take several months. The various prisons conducted the releases differently. Some released POWs in alphabetical order after they had taken the oath; some released them by state, even including in reverse order of how their respective states seceded from the Union,—with those from South Carolina given last consideration; and some prisons simply released their POWs in disorganized, small groups.[26]

When President Lincoln was assassinated on April 14, a ripple of shock, panic, and anger rolled across the nation and entangled the southern POWs still confined. "A few days after Lincoln was assassinated," noted H. C. Murphy, held at Hart's Island in New York, "there was talk of retaliating on us and I thought we would be shot. . . . We were [no longer] allowed to collect in groups and the guards had orders to shoot if they found as many as three talking together." Prisoner J. S. Kimbrough also recalled that Hart's Island guards were instructed to fire into the crowd if there was any "demonstration of approval or rejoicing" shown among the POWs over Lincoln's death.[27]

"Some people wanted to kill the prisoners and the whole Southern people," remarked Thomas Head, confined at Camp Douglas at the time. "The prison was threatened with a mob [of Chicago citizens], but [the] excitement soon abated."[28]

Two weeks later, the *Sultana,* arranged by the government to transport 2,000 recently liberated POWs north, exploded, killing a number of former prisoners. Nearly 1,000 of those on board the *Sultana* were from the Cahaba prison. Although the exact number of Cahaba POWs that perished in the disaster is unknown, total loss of life was estimated at 1,500 to 1,700. The following day, April 28, 1865, the remaining 700 prisoners confined at the facility were released.[29]

By the end of May there were still 48,400 southern POWs in custody, with nearly 19,000 at Point Lookout alone. The discharge of southern POWs had been halted from mid- to late April with Lincoln's death, but gradually releases from Rock Island, Camp Douglas, and a number of other facilities resumed. On May 27, the first Union prisoners from Camp Ford began arriving at Fort Smith, Arkansas, after having covered a distance of nearly three hundred miles. They arrived with stories of being allowed to "escape" in large numbers by the guards.

By May, Union authorities had resumed the releases at nearly all the Federal facilities. Throughout May and June, releases continued, several hundred at a time. By the end of July, only 2,500 POWs, including the 1,000 at Elmira, remained incarcerated. Only 200 were being held in nine other Union facilities by the end of the month.[30]

Some released prisoners, such as some of those from Point Lookout and those incarcerated in New York's military prisons, including Elmira and the Governors Island facilities, were furnished train transportation to Richmond or other major southern points. Many others, especially in the midwest, were simply released and left on their own. Being without money and with no way to contact friends or relatives, they had no choice but to walk home.

S. John Dyer and Noah Francis of Haywood County, North Carolina, began walking after they had endured months of misery incarcerated at Camp Douglas. After nearly six hundred miles, Noah collapsed and died in Virginia. After burying his long-time friend there, Dyer sadly continued his journey home, alone.[31]

Sam Hardinge, released from Fort Delaware, also found himself very weak. He could hardly move, yet he was simply escorted out of the prison and left to make it on his own to the nearest town, sixteen miles away. Unable to secure transportation, he trudged on swollen, rag-encased feet for four painful hours until he reached Wilmington, Delaware, where he obtained help from friends.[32]

J. H. Tomb, once a chief engineer in the Confederate States navy and released with a number of others from Fort Warren, never realized that his prison was one of the better places of confinement until months after the war. "When we reached Fortress Monroe," remembered Tomb, "we found out how fortunate we were in being sent to Fort Warren in place of Fort Delaware. There were several thousand Confederates on the steamer. . . . There were hundreds of our men who had been in Fort Delaware and other prisons that would never recover. It was so on all the other transports. When we arrived at Aiken's Landing and had begun to make a line for shore, I assisted over the gang plank some of our poor fellows that I felt would never see their homes again. One poor fellow from Tennessee was a mere skeleton."[33]

Many emaciated individuals were emerging from the prisons by this time, getting along the best they could in their efforts to get home. "I weighed 170 pounds when I went there," declared James Carson Elliott upon his release from Point Lookout, "and got away with 145 pounds." James Mitchell, who was released from Johnson's Island on June 13, 1865, noted, "I am exceedingly thin weighing only 121 pounds."[34]

Of course, the situation was the same in the South. E. W. McIntosh, Company E, 14th Illinois Infantry, weighed 175 pounds when captured and confined at Andersonville. Upon his release he weighed 65 pounds.[35]

John King, released from Camp Chase, noted another consequence of life in prison that was often experienced by many on both sides. "Ten months had passed since I had barely eaten enough to keep me alive," he advised. "Brought now into the presence of food in abundance, I ate more than my stomach could digest. As soon as this was ejected, the pangs of hunger would return, and [knowing] what the result would be, I could not refrain from eating more [again]."[36]

Thousands of former POWs found similar and additional problems upon their release. "When I was captured," recalled Abner Small of Maine, who was held nearly seven months in Libby, Danville, and, finally, in Salisbury, "I was the proud possessor of a new staff uniform ornamented with gold lace. Five months later, my most intimate friends would have failed to recognize me. . . . It was not until after I was paroled that I took those trousers off; I couldn't have done so before, because after sewing up the legs while I had them on, I couldn't get my feet through."[37]

Thomas J. Stokes arrived home in Texas wearing exactly what he had been wearing the day he was released from Camp Chase. "In war-worn pants and faded grey coat," his sister commented, "[he] presented a spectacle never to be forgotten."[38]

R. Eldridge Medford, known as R. E. to friends and family, also made the long walk to Haywood County. Finding himself constantly bothered by body lice from his long stay at Camp Douglas, he finally stripped down near Cosby, Tennessee, just before crossing into North Carolina, and bathed in the Pigeon River. Afterward, he donned a blue shirt and a pair of pants he had made from a blanket he had saved for the occasion, and proudly arrived home in North Carolina in style.[39]

Most of the releases from northern prisons took place in June and July of 1865, but several hundred remained in such places as Fort Lafayette, Fort McHenry, Johnson's Island, Old Capitol, and Nashville through August and September. Other POWs, such as some of the Confederate officials gathered up at the war's end, continued to be held into October and November. Fort Lafayette became the last Union prison to hold POWs, releasing the last ones in November. However, political prisoners would continue to be held there as late as March 1866.[40]

Meanwhile, the publicity and propaganda associated with the prisons continued. As in all wars, before and since, the POW situation created bitterness among the families of those who survived the incarceration as well as those who died, on both sides. Many accused one government or the other of being incompetent, callous, or deceitful. In an effort to end the controversy and bring the war to a close, the U.S. government brought charges against southern prison commandants.

Captain Henry Wirz was brought to trial on war crimes before a special military commission in Washington on August 23, 1865. He was charged with conspiring with others to impair and injure the health and destroy the lives of soldiers held under his authority and in the deaths of thirteen specific prisoners of war. After a two-month trial, he was found guilty and sentenced to death.

"[H]e and his co-conspirators must be held responsible," declared Judge Joseph Holt, in a review of the case. "The Andersonville prison records contain a roster of over 13,000 dead, buried naked, maimed, and putrid, in one vast sepulcher. . . . Under this proof, which has not been assailed, nearly 10,000, if not more, of these deaths must be charged directly to the account of Wirz and his associates. This widespread sacrifice of life was not made suddenly or under the influence of ungovernable passion, but was accomplished slowly and deliberately, by packing upward of 30,000 men like cattle in a fetid pen—a mere cesspool—there to die for need of air to breathe, for want of ground on which to lie, for lack of shelter from sun and rain, and from the slow, agonizing processes of starvation, when air and space and shelter and food were all within the ready gift of their tormentors."[41]

Unwittingly, Judge Holt had summed up the situation in nearly every large military prison, both North and South. But the real facts went ignored. Never mind that the Union pens were just as unsanitary. Never mind that death rates in Union compounds were comparable. Never mind that the Union had been more capable of feeding its POWs but deliberately reduced the amount of rations a number of times. Never mind that when northern newspapers described the dirty, encrusted floors of the Richmond prisons for their readers back home, their descriptions could have fit the condition of the floors for Gratiot Street, Alton, and nearly every other northern prison building at the time. Never mind that the crops, mills, and railroad lines throughout the South had been destroyed as quickly as possible by Union troops or that it became officially sanctioned to do so in order to paralyze the South, or, as one official put it, to bring the South to its knees. Never mind that certain medicines had been declared contraband— the first time in any war—and blockaded to prevent them from reaching the South.

And never mind that when former POWs returned north and told of seeing Union prisoners walking around southern prisons with maggot-infested wounds there was a logical, scientific reason for it, which the northern press never bothered to explain to the public. In fact, such eye-witness testimony, in and of itself, was successfully used as further propaganda against the Confederacy. In truth, since medical supplies were often in short supply, it was an alert Confederate doctor who, having run out of chloroform, recalled that maggots could be used to aid in the prevention and treatment of gangrene. Such a discovery had originally been made by Napoleon's medics. It turned out that maggots release a chemical called *allantoin,* which aids them in the digestion of necrotic material; as a result, new tissue growth is promoted. Although repulsive, this cleaning technique would go on to be used as late as World War I and continues to be taught in present-day military survival schools.[42]

Throughout October 1865, a number of people undoubtedly tried to point out some of these facts to explain what had happened in the southern prisons, and many former POWs insisted that northern prisons had been no different, in most cases. None of it mattered, however. The victorious government and its public were still angry and insisted on revenge. Since Andersonville was like a hell on earth, they must have reasoned, then Wirz must be the devil.

On November 10, 1865, Henry Wirz was led to the same scaffold where the Lincoln co-conspirators were hanged four months before and escorted up the steps. He had reportedly been advised his life would be spared if he would simply implicate Jefferson Davis, but Wirz refused. Moments later the trap door fell out from beneath him and Wirz was left dangling in history, held fully responsible for what had happened in the Civil War's military prisons.[43]

Since that time, historians have often written that Captain Wirz remains the only Confederate tried and executed for war crimes at the end of the Civil War, which is not quite true. He was actually the third. And all three were POW related.

The first was Captain John Beall for the part he played in the elaborate *Philo Parsons* scheme to release the prisoners of Johnson's Island. In the waning days of the war, when many POWs such as those at Salisbury and a few other locations were being transferred out for release, Beall was led to the gallows and hanged on February 24, 1865.[44]

Next to be tried and convicted, and without accompaniment of political motivation evidenced in the other two, was Captain Champ Ferguson for his participation in the executions of blacks on the Saltville battlefield the morning following the battle. Tried and convicted by the Federal government after the war, he was hanged on October 25, 1865, in front of a detachment of U.S. Colored Troops.[45]

John Gee was tried by a military commission in February 1866 on the charge of cruelty and conspiracy regarding his management of Salisbury. By then the wrath of the victors had begun to subside. After a five-month trial, Gee was acquitted on all charges and released. Likewise, Iverson, Barrett, Vowles, Sidney and Richard Winder, and a number of others spent some time in prison but were never brought to trial. Most of these men, too, were released by mid-1866.[46]

Richard Turner had been arrested and was held in Libby for a short time, but escaped. He was later apprehended and held in the state penitentiary in Richmond. He also was paroled in June 1866. Somehow the former commandant of Belle Isle, Virginius Bossieux, escaped the attention of Union authorities altogether. He continued to live in Richmond, unmolested by the government, after the war. George Alexander and Thomas Turner succeeded in eluding capture and would go on to live in Canada a number of years. Once the political climate cooled, however, they moved back to the United States—Alexander to his beloved Baltimore, and Turner to Memphis.

The names of Jefferson Davis, James Seddon, and Howell Cobb had been originally included as co-conspirators in Wirz's original charge but were later dropped. They were never brought to trial, either. Cobb and Seddon were released from prison after several months, as was the former Confederate vice president, Alexander Stephens, who had been held in Fort Warren. Stephens was paroled in October 1865. Davis was not released until May 1867.

There was no substantial excuse for what happened at Andersonville, that is certain. If there was an ability to put up stockade walls two rows thick (and in some places three rows were used); if areas could be expanded from sixteen and a half acres to twenty-six and a half when the authorities decided to do so; and when more than ten thousand men could be quickly evacuated—the same being true at Salisbury, Florence, Millen, and other prisons—then it would seem that adequate food and shelter could have been provided as well, had there been a sincere effort. After all, authorities experienced few problems getting the POWs to those locations, and they had few problems pulling them out when it became absolutely essential.

The problem with hanging Wirz, however, is that there was no substantial excuse for what happened at Elmira, Fort Delaware, Rock Island, Alton, Gratiot Street, or a number of other Union facilities, but such knowledge was withheld from the public until well after the trapdoor lever was pulled, and the men who authorized the pulling of that lever were well aware of the truth.

The apathy of both sides cannot and should not have been blamed on any one individual, although both sides had abusive men in positions of authority. The responsibility of care for POWs rested with military or wartime government policy—and POWs clearly were not their first priority. Personal stress and prejudices, the press's bias and propaganda, the actual abilities of both sides, and the main objective of victory sought by both sides—and the lengths they were willing to go to achieve that goal—and you have what happened in the Civil War's prisons.

For many who survived the prisons, the experience continued to be a shattering experience. Some who had spent long periods in the pens were bitter, some were humiliated, and some were apathetic or pensive. Many arrived home with long-term illnesses or afflictions. Others simply choked back the tears and tried to go on with their lives. For all prisoners, life would never be the same.

Former prisoner George Washington Smith was one of many who continued to suffer from his confinement. While incarcerated at Alton Prison his feet were frozen. For the rest of his life he could only wear soft carpet slippers; stiff shoes were out of the question. He also suffered periodically from dysentery and other prison-contracted afflictions long after his release.[47]

George J. Codori of Pennsylvania, who suffered in the Salisbury pen for twenty months, died only three days after returning home to his wife and children.[48]

"My oldest brother, John D. Cleveland, was taken prisoner and sent to Gratiot Street Prison," recalled Charles B. Cleveland, himself a prisoner confined at Ship Island, "and kept [there] three months, and then [sent] to Alton Prison in Illinois and kept there a long time. His health was so impaired that he never rallied [and] died soon after the war."[49]

Sidney Lanier, formerly of Company I, 4th Georgia Regiment, who became a famous poet after the war, died prematurely at the age of thirty-nine from the tuberculosis he contracted while confined at Point Lookout prison camp.[50]

Like so many others, when Thomas Stokes was released from his long confinement at Camp Chase, he returned home, according to his sisters, a completely different man. "He was lean to emaciation," said his sister, Mary. "A constant cough, which he tried in vain to repress, betrayed the deep inroads which prison life had made upon his system."[51]

Many prisoners had come back as walking, talking skeletons. Some, after a number of months or years, had to be placed in insane asylums. Some, according to relatives, turned to the bottle for comfort or in an effort to forget. Still others became residents of disabled soldiers' homes established by their individual states. A great number of these men spent many years after the war trying to normalize their lives or trying to get a pension for disabilities created by their imprisonment.

Although a number of books and magazine articles were published by the survivors of prison camps after the war, especially at the turn of the century, no study of these men was ever done. Survivors as a whole were never thoroughly interviewed or studied.

Recent studies and research on survivors of prison camps from World War II and the Korean and Vietnam conflicts do, however, provide some insight into what the soldiers' condition might have been as they returned home from the Civil War. Those who spend long periods in confinement often develop what was known after World War II as "survivor's syndrome" or after Vietnam as "post-tramatic stress syndrome"—the inability to concentrate; ghastly memories triggered by familiar sights, sounds, smells, or events; medical problems; and suppressed memories of their own conduct during confinement of which they are ashamed, sometimes referred to as survivors' guilt. Many of these survivors also suffer from disabilities such as blindness and paraplegia as a result of long term starvation. Memory loss is often serious, sometimes a result of minor or severe brain damage, and reactive psychotic neuroses occur in many survivors, with paranoia and depression being the most prominent. Others experience problems with postwar adjustment, finding themselves unable to adapt to accepted behavior or to deal with everyday problems and concerns.[52]

Flora Mae Fulbright Ward, at age 87, recalled stories passed down through her family about her uncle, T. Jefferson Rogers, who served in Company E, 29th Regiment, North Carolina Troops, and was later captured and confined for nearly two years at Johnson's Island. Upon his return home he was in extremely poor health, went blind, and died at an early age within two years of the war's conclusion. "They say he was never the same after he returned," said Flora Mae.[53]

Although the death rates in the prison camps are shocking enough, statistics fail to show the number who died as a result of their confinement soon after returning home. If it was possible to provide such numbers, the result would surely be staggering.

"I weigh only 117 pounds," one prisoner commented upon his release from Andersonville, "at one point I was down to around 95 pounds. . . . My cheeks are sunken, eyes sunken, sores and blotches both outside and inside my mouth . . . my teeth are loose and I lost four from the effects of scurvy . . . and my right leg the whole length of it, red, black and blue and tender of

touch. My eyes, too, are very weak, and in a bright sun I have to draw the
slouch hat away down over them. . . . When taken prisoner [I] was fleshy,
weighing about one hundred and seventy-five, round faced, in fact an overgrown,
ordinary, green-looking chap of twenty. [I] had never endured any hardships
at all and was a spring chicken. As has been proven, however, I had an iron
constitution that has carried me through, and above all a disposition to make
the best of everything no matter how bad, and considerable will power with the
rest. When I think of the thousands and thousands of thorough-bred soldiers,
tough and hearty and capable of marching thirty, forty, and even fifty miles in
twenty-four hours and think nothing of it [who died in the prisons], I wonder
and [keep] wondering that it can be so—that I am alive."[54]

Nearly 56,000 soldiers were unable to make that claim. For those who did
survive, their time in those hellholes no doubt remained the most harrowing
experience they would ever live, and relive, to the end of their days.

PAST AND PRESENT

I n the months following abandonment of the Andersonville pen, local residents broke into the prison warehouses and made off with the remaining supplies. Relic hunters later arrived and ransacked the stockade.

"In the days when it was packed with from thirty to thirty-five thousand men," reported Sidney Andrews, who visited the site in November 1865, "the whole surface was covered with tents and mud-and-stick cabins. Of these not more than fifty remain . . . complete as is the general destruction, the ruins are of wonderful suggestiveness. You find half a stool, a broken knife, the handle of a huge wooden spoon, a split checkerboard, an old pipe, a bit of cunning carving on a beam."[1]

The weather, roaming livestock, and additional waves of souvenir hunters continued to destroy the Andersonville stockade for years after the war. Mr. Dykes, owner of the land, advertised in out-of-state newspapers and sold bottled water from Providence Spring, made famous by so many inmate accounts about the prison.[2]

In December 1890, the Georgia Department of the Grand Army of the Republic purchased the site. It was later turned over to the Women's Relief Corps, and still later, in 1910, it was donated to the people of the United States. In 1970, Andersonville Prison became a national historic site.

The north gate, which was a double-gate system with a small courtyard in between, has been reconstructed. The original hinges, lock, and key from the prison were used in making the present hand-forged replicas. Reconstruction continues and when complete will include three hundred feet of the stockade wall and four guard towers.[3]

Nearby, the Andersonville National Cemetery, about a quarter mile northwest of the original prison site, contains the graves of the 12,919 Union soldiers who died while confined there. Ironically, the cemetery, which contains 25 percent of the total number of POWs that were held at the prison, includes more acreage than the original prison stockade.[4]

Andrews also visited the Florence pen on his tour through the South after the war. There he found nearly one hundred prisoner huts still standing in the stockade and more than a thousand holes that had once been used as shelter, but the prison flagpole, which once stood fifty feet out in front of the center of the stockade's west wall, was nearly gone by that time. "Its stump only remains," he recalled, "[because] loyal and disloyal alike [have] cut chips of memento therefrom."[5]

As time went on, this stockade, too, slowly succumbed to the weather, vandals, and souvenir hunters. Today, the only reminder of the Florence prison's existence is the National Military Cemetery along present-day National Cemetery Road, off U.S. Highway 76, one mile east of town.

Likewise, the Camp Lawton stockade, abandoned deep in the long-leaf pine forests near Millen, Georgia, eventually fell victim to the elements, and the Blackshear location grew over and disappeared too. Camp Oglethorpe, in Macon, went on to serve as a parole site at the end of war but was torn down sometime later, and both Savannah stockades were dismantled in October 1864 as soon as they were emptied of POWs.

In the months that followed the end of the Civil War, not only did Alabama's Cahaba prison fade into memory, the town did as well. An 1865 flood submerged the prison and devastated the community. The following year the county seat was moved to Selma, which is situated high on a bluff above the Alabama River, ten miles north of Cahaba. What was left of the town slowly deteriorated.

The prison warehouse site was sold for back taxes in 1869 and was resold to another owner in 1871. The building is believed to have been dismantled and the bricks carted off to Selma. By 1885 the town had been virtually abandoned and the prison site obliterated by overgrowth.[6]

The total number of POWs confined at Cahaba during its existence was estimated at around five thousand. Shortly after the war, 162 bodies of those who had died were removed from the little prison cemetery and reburied at the Marietta National Cemetery near Atlanta, Georgia. Today, however, 224 depressions can still be seen in the ground at the prison cemetery, and another grave was recently discovered between the river and the prison. What happened to those other bodies is unknown. Perhaps, as some local researchers speculate, some were reclaimed by relatives. Some sources indicate that conditions at Cahaba were just as bad as those at Andersonville and, because it was more crowded and just as unsanitary, more POWs actually died there than were officially reported. In fact, many of those same sources claim that in June 1865, the steamer *Autauga* sank in the river near Prattville, in Elmore County, Alabama. On board, it is said, were 750 to 800 exhumed remains of Cahaba POWs being shipped to Marietta for reburial.[7]

Farther west, all that exists today of Camp Ford are a few graves some distance from the original prison site and a Texas state historical marker erected near the spot. Camp Groce, on the other hand, has a much more prominent marker. For the most part, Camp Groce was no longer a POW facility by January 1864. It remained abandoned for some time but served as a Confederate army separation center at the end of the war. The buildings were later dismantled. The Liendo Plantation, on Wyatt Chapel Road, with its sixteen-room Greek Revival mansion built in 1853, still stands outside Hempstead and currently serves as a well-run, well-maintained bed and breakfast. Today, nothing remains as a reminder of the old prison camp except for nearly twenty graves near the original site.

The Texas State Penitentiary at Huntsville was used as a POW facility for only six months. However, a small number of black prisoners captured from U.S. forces and political prisoners were held there and used as additional prison labor through June 1865. The facility was replaced years later by a more modern one.[8]

In South Carolina, what had once been Camp Sorghum is now part of West Columbia, rebuilt years ago. The original Richland County Jail has likewise been replaced. However, the state hospital still exists, and what is known as the Mills Building is the original structure, although it has been extensively renovated since the Camp Asylum days. Killian's Mill eventually evolved into Killian, South Carolina, along present-day Interstate 77.

Several hundred Federals perished in Charleston's prisons during the war. Years afterward, some Federal authorities admitted that the Confederate's claim that there had been no intention to deliberately place prisoners under bombard-ment might be true. After all, the guards were in just as much danger as the prisoners, and the city remained occupied by civilians the entire time. Such later revelations, though, were of no comfort to the more than two thousand POWs, both Union and Confederate, who had endured the perpetual barrage of shelling for anywhere from thirty to sixty-plus days.

Charleston's makeshift prisons survived the war. By 1876, the portico of the old Guard House became the scene of a sniping incident during riots in the city. In 1886 an earthquake damaged the building to such an extent that it had to be torn down. The wrought-iron grill containing the sword design that once covered its windows is now at The Citadel, while the sword gate is at a private residence at 32 Legare Street.[9]

The old city jail suffered a similar fate during the Quake of '86 and was later replaced, while the racecourse and the O'Connor House have ceased to exist. An expanded and more modern Roper Hospital still stands.

Castle Pinckney's appearance changed dramatically after it was no longer used as a POW facility. When it was garrisoned by Confederate troops, tons of sand and turf were added to the interior and exterior walls to increase protection against bombardment. Additional guns were mounted in the facility as Union forces began an operation of sinking stone-laden ships in the harbor in an attempt to disrupt blockade running. But the fort never fired a shot and soon fell into a secondary role again. Some of the fort's guns were later removed to strengthen other fortifications around the harbor, and the fort took little or no part in the heavy fighting around the harbor entrance during 1863–64. At the evacuation of Charleston on February 17, 1865, the fort was abandoned by its Confederate garrison and was occupied by the 21st U.S. Colored Troops the next day. It was turned over to the Federal government at the end of the war.[10]

Over the years, the old two-story fort became filled with sand and debris. The seawall was torn down in 1890, and a station for the lighthouse service was established sometime later. This was abandoned in 1916, but the facility was later used as a supply base for the Army Corps of Engineers.

The five-acre site was declared a national monument in the 1920s but remained abandoned and ignored. In the 1950s it was declassified, declared surplus government property, and sold to the South Carolina Port Authority. Plans to make it a museum failed several times over the following years, and in 1967 a fire destroyed the fort's wooden buildings. Today, the crumbling, sand-filled walls of the fort are still visible, albeit overgrown with weeds and brush, as it sits idle in Charleston Harbor. The gunports and main entrance have since been sealed with brick, and no entrance remains to the casemates that once held Union prisoners.

The deterioration of the Salisbury pen in North Carolina was much faster. Within six months after the war it, too, was visited by travel writer Sidney Andrews. "The walls of the old factory building stand intact," he later wrote, "but roof and floors and windows are all gone. The small brick buildings exist only as half a dozen irregular piles of rubbish. Some of the hundred great oak-trees within the stockade are already dead or dying. The fence shows only a line of post-stumps and post-holes. The ditch has been partially filled. . . . Three-fourths of the great pen is covered with a sprawling fireweed . . . yet signs remain. You find, in strolling about, the broken bowl of an earthen pipe, the well-worn blade of a belt knife, even the regulation button of a soldier's coat."[11]

By 1936 one dilapidated cottage still remained on the site, but all that is left of the prison today is a small national cemetery, located a short distance away in what was once the cornfield outside the pen. Of the cemetery's 11,700 Civil War graves, the names of less than two hundred POWs are known. Today Salisbury pen is completely built over, but a visit to the local library yields a cassette tape player with a walking tour of the original prison site.

Danville, Virginia, still offers tangible evidence of its Civil War history. Of the three hospitals and six prison buildings used there during the war, two of the prison buildings still exist, though privately owned. Prison No. 5 is at 514 High Street, and the portentous and ornate Prison No. 6 sits at 300 Lynn Street.

There is also much present-day interest in Richmond, but one must know where to look. In spite of the heavy death toll of Union prisoners in the city, very few marked graves exist. Oakwood Cemetery and the small National Cemetery outside the city on Williamsburg Road contain a few, as do several other small graveyards throughout the area, but the final resting places for hundreds of POWs are unknown. It's possible that many bodies were reclaimed by relatives after the war but highly unlikely that so few would be left in the city, especially given the claims of those who witnessed so many reported deaths at Belle Isle. Although many of Belle Isle's ill were taken to hospitals in the downtown area prior to their deaths, some contemporary accounts claim to have seen bodies buried on the north side of the island. Today there are no such indications, but some sources indicate that the National Cemetery east of town was established with the reinterred bodies that were originally buried at Belle Isle.

The Confederacy officially returned the island to its owners on February 10, 1865. After Belle Isle went back into private hands it was sold, around the turn of the century, to the Virginia Power Company. Portions of that company's operations remained on the island for some time. The land was acquired by the City of Richmond years later and became a focal point of interest in the Civil War during the 1960s. The Old Dominion Steel and Iron Company conducted operations on the island, which became extensively damaged by hurricanes during the 1960s and 1970s. Finally, the island was identified by the city and national governments as a potential park site, and considerations for placing historical markers there were discussed. Today, a footbridge connects Oregon Hill Park along the mainland to Belle Isle, now known as the James River Park, which contains jogging and walking paths and an environmental education center. The city apparently is still somewhat sensitive about the accusations of the past—a large historical display map just east of the footbridge explains the history of nearby Brown Island but fails to expound on the history of Belle Isle and the part it played in the city's history.

The Castle Thunder facility in Richmond was also returned to its previous owners, the heirs of John Enders, after the war. In 1879 the structure that had originally escaped the burning of Richmond was finally set on fire and burned to the ground, bringing an end to Castle Thunder's strange existence within the city. Today the site is a paved parking lot for the Phillip Morris Tobacco Company.[12]

In retrospect, Libby Prison was no worse than any other Civil War prison, North or South. Many historians believe today that one reason this Richmond prison became so infamous was that it held only officers, who were generally better educated than enlisted men, and they wrote a disproportionate share of the postwar books about prison life. Nearly all Union prisoners remembered seeing "the

Libby" because it was a depot prison where most were taken before being transferred to another location.[13]

A large bronze plaque has been prominently positioned along the concrete
flood wall near the original site of the prison, but the disposition of the original
building has a more bizarre history.

Ownership of the Libby building eventually reverted to Mrs. George S.
Palmer. The structure was used by the Southern Fertilizer Company for some
time afterward, but by the late 1880s William H. Gray of the Knights Templar
Assurance Association of Chicago became interested in the building as a museum.
He, along with partners Josiah Cratty, John A. Crawford, Charles Miller, and
the architectural firm of Burnham and Root, paid $23,000 for the building,
intending to move the structure to Chicago. Dismantling of the old prison began
in December 1888.[14]

Once the dismantling was completed, the parts were loaded onto 132 cars
of the Chesapeake and Ohio Railroad and transported toward the midwest, but
outside Ashtabula, Ohio, the train derailed and scattered the parts over a wide
area. After several weeks of salvage operations, the prison's timbers were recovered
and, except for several hundred bricks that were left along the railroad right-of-
way, the shipment continued its trip to Chicago. In December 1889, after an
expense of $200,000, the Libby Prison War Museum on Chicago's Wabash
Avenue between 14th and 16th streets was opened to the public. Among its most
popular attractions were an interior doorway of the prison, a chisel said to
have been used by escaping prisoners during excavation of the "Great Yankee
Tunnel," and a collection of POW relics and Civil War portraits and papers
from both the North and the South, owned by Charles F. Gunther. The biggest
attraction, however, was the collection of perfectly preserved names and regiments carved into the prison timbers by individual prisoners during their long,
boring hours of confinement.[15]

The prison museum remained popular for nearly four years, but interest
had nearly died out by the beginning of the Chicago World's Fair in May 1893.
By 1895 the museum was out of business, and negotiations began in an attempt
to have the building moved to Washington, D.C. These attempts failed and
in 1899 museum directors voted to tear down the building. Souvenir hunters
converged upon the site during its demolition and carried off many bricks.[16]

Building contractors also hauled off truckloads of the bricks to use in new
constructions. The Chicago Historical Society salvaged a portion of these, and
a number of the bricks were later used to build the north wall of the society's
Civil War Room exhibit. The beams and timbers of the old prison were purchased
by a farmer from LaPorte, Indiana, who used them to build a new barn near
Hamlet, Indiana. The barn stood for nearly sixty years. On October 20, 1962,
with renewed interest in the Civil War during its centennial, a marker was erected

near the barn, causing tourists to trespass over the property for a number of years. Frustrated by the destruction that it caused, the owners sold the barn to realtor Charles K. Mercer, who planned to tear it down and reassemble the barn on his property in Spencer, Indiana. However, as of 1990, the two truckloads of timbers remained somewhere in storage with the names of many former Libby prisoners carved into its wood.[17]

In late June and early July 1865, thirty-nine remaining prisoners at Alton, Illinois, were moved to Gratiot Street Prison in St. Louis to await release. By mid-July all government property at Alton was turned over to the department divisions or sold off. The prison building later was returned to the state.[18]

For many years historians believed that the prison building was sold sometime afterward and then completely razed, but in the early 1970s a cleanup program on the Alton riverfront uncovered an old stone wall of the original building. By 1985, debris and overgrowth had been cleared away and a state historical marker was placed at the site. Today that portion of the prison, on Williams Street between Broadway and Fourth, is all that is left of the notorious facility on the limestone bluffs overlooking the Mississippi River. McPike's (or Smallpox) Island is no longer visible in the river due to the higher water level created by the present-day Alton Dam.

At the close of the war, Joseph McDowell returned to St. Louis and reestablished his medical school at a different location. His original building was condemned due to disrepair and filth. In June 1878, the south wing of the old prison building was declared unsafe and was demolished by order of the fire department. The octagonal tower, with its odd-looking dome, and the north wing remained until well after 1883. Today, nothing remains of Gratiot Street Prison, or of Myrtle Street Prison for that matter, as both became victims of urban renewal long ago. The Ralston-Purina World Headquarters building now stands on the original site of the city's old medical college prison.[19]

Farther up the Mississippi, more than one thousand Rock Island POWs were exchanged in February 1865, with another two thousand more in March. The remaining POWs were released on parole throughout May, June, and July.

The prison's 214 wood buildings, 116,589 pounds of cast-iron pipe and 1,400 feet of wrought-iron pipe, having a total value of $89,113, were turned over to the Ordnance Department the following August. Several barracks, officers' quarters, and the hospital continued in government use until 1909.[20]

Today, nothing is left of the prison. Where it once stood, the Rock Island Arsenal Golf Course now exists. Arsenal shop buildings stand where the pesthouses and hospital once stood, and the home of the commanding general of the Ordnance Weapons Command sits where the prison headquarters once existed. Now all that remains are the Confederate and National Cemeteries; the national burial ground contains 171 graves of Union soldiers who died doing guard duty at the post. Both cemeteries are on the Illinois side of the island, which is officially called Rock Island Arsenal today. It remains the government's largest manufacturing arsenal. A blockhouse of old Fort Armstrong has since been reconstructed near its original site, and there is also a small museum and Corps of Engineers Clock Tower Building and visitors' center on the island. The Arsenal's library and museum present an excellent display of the island's past, and its staff has conducted extensive research into the installation's role as a Civil War prison.[21]

Camp Butler, Illinois, continued as an instruction and demobilization camp throughout the war, even after it ceased to be a POW facility. Its main hospital also received Union soldiers released from southern prisons for months after hostilities ended. Today, nothing remains. By 1874 most of the land had already been returned to cropland and has remained so except for a few added residences. Sometimes, in a newly plowed field, after one of the area's heavy rains, an artifact or two can still be found. Otherwise, the only indication that the prison ever existed is the nearby Camp Butler National Cemetery.

By July 1865, the last POWs had left Camp Douglas in Chicago. In November the government property was sold off. A number of barracks and fences were pulled down and the lumber sold. Other buildings were sold to the highest bidder. One purchaser obtained a single row of barracks and moved them to the 700 block of East 37th Street in Chicago. Renovated, they served as apartment residences until 1940, when they were razed. Nothing remains of Camp Douglas today. Originally bounded by Cottage Grove Avenue on the east, Forest Avenue on the west, 31st Street on the north, and 33rd Street on the south, a modern high-rise development, a shopping center, and a school now cover the area.[22]

A total of 30,000 POWs are believed to have been held at Camp Douglas during the course of the war. Of that number, it was originally believed that as many as 3,500 had died. The U.S. government now concedes that perhaps as many as 4,454 perished at the prison. Burials for the camp were done by contract at the city cemetery. There, on Confederate Mound in the Oakwoods Cemetery, Solomon F. Cook and many of his comrades have rested in peace since their agonizing stay in Chicago's Camp Douglas Military Prison.[23]

The remaining POWs at Camp Chase, Ohio, were also released in June and July of 1865. Today, the cemetery here is the only reminder that Camp Chase ever existed. Often referred to by the inmates as "the City of the Dead," the burial ground is located south of the compound's original site. Shortly after the war, the buildings and fences were dismantled and the planks were used to build a fence around the cemetery. After years of neglect, various southern organizations persuaded the Federal government to take care of the site. In the late 1890s a stone wall was constructed around the cemetery, a memorial arch was erected at its entrance, and a rock monument was dedicated. Since that time, the city of Columbus has extended beyond the site where Camp Chase once stood. By the turn of the century, the original grounds had already become part of a housing subdivision.[24]

The POWs at Johnson's Island, Ohio, were paroled out in alphabetical order. The last six prisoners were transferred out to Forts Lafayette and Delaware in September 1865. The prison buildings were later dismantled, the lumber and other items sold off, and the land turned back over to Mr. Johnson for farming. By the early 1900s, much of Johnson's Island was devoted to grape culture.[25]

Since then, development has threatened the site several times. As a result, twenty-two acres have been set aside. Walking paths and possible rebuilding of Fort Hill and part of the prison block and stockade wall have been proposed. At this time the only reminders are a few redoubts and, three hundred yards from where the prison once stood, the white marble markers of the graveyard. In 1910 a monument was placed here in memory of the Confederate dead.

Controversy over the number of dead in this cemetery has continued for many years. The number most commonly given is 206, and most historians agree. But prisoners' memoirs often claim to have seen more, and there is evidence that seems to support them. A number of human bones have been uncovered outside the marked cemetery boundary that are believed to be bodies buried during the winter of 1862–63. In 1866, eleven additional bodies were found in another area outside the cemetery. In June 1910, quarry workers found more remains near Fort Hill, near the original location of the prison's pest-house. In 1990, additional remains were uncovered near the site of Fort Hill.[26]

Not only does evidence seem to suggest that the accepted figure of 206 deaths at Johnson's Island is erroneous, but that figure was never supported by the official records to begin with. A close examination of those records plainly shows that the reported number of deaths at Johnson's Island between July 1862 and September 1865 is a total of 235, but that does not include any deaths that might have occurred in the period between February 24 and June 30, 1862, when the reporting of such information was not required of the commandants. Therefore, to set the record straight, at least 235 POWs perished at Johnson's Island Military Prison during the course of its operation.[27]

Local authorities confounded the situation in Indianapolis concerning the Camp Morton dead. The Confederate prisoners were originally buried in marked trench graves in the city's old Greenlawn Cemetery. After the war, a number of bodies were claimed and returned to relatives in the South, but no official records were kept. By the 1870s, the Vandalia Railroad had taken part of the cemetery grounds for an expansion. Bodies were exhumed and reburied in two parallel unmarked trenches nearby. During further urbanization of Indianapolis, the cemetery was emptied and the bodies dispersed among several different burial locations across the city. Controversy later erupted over whether or not all of the bodies had been found and moved from the railroad relocation site. Then a number were moved a second and third time from the smaller cemeteries, causing further confusion. Finally, in 1931, the War Department moved all known Confederate graves to Crown Hill Cemetery, where they were placed in a common gravesite along the north side of Section 32. They remain there to this day.[28]

The original site of Camp Morton went on to serve as the Indiana State Fairgrounds, with the addition of a new exhibition hall where the prison camp once existed, for another thirty years. In the 1890s, as the city expanded and crowded the location, the property was sold, and a new fairgrounds was established elsewhere. Today, a boulder bearing an inscription about Camp Morton sits near the location of the original site at 19th Street and Alabama Avenue, and nearby is a residential subdivision known as Morton Place.[29]

The Union's stockade prisons suffered similar fates. Upon hearing of Lee's surrender, the POWs at Elmira had hoped that conditions would improve at their prison. Some claimed that nothing changed, while others believed that they were no longer guarded as closely. Finally, in May 1865, POWs were paroled out, a few at a time, by state. Men from the states of Missouri, Kentucky, West Virginia, and Louisiana were some of the first to leave.[30]

The last remaining POWs left Elmira by mid-July 1865. Today, nothing remains of Elmira Prison. After the war the tents were burned, and the buildings were dismantled and sold off. Even Foster's Pond was eventually filled in and covered over. Except for an inconspicuous little bronze plaque embedded in the curb of the street near the site, the tombstones marking the Southern soldiers' graves in Woodlawn Cemetery are all that is left of the facility. Even those call into question the accuracy of the official records, which indicate a total of 2,933 deaths. A casual walk through the grounds today reveals 3,022 Confederate graves, which doesn't take into account any that might have been shipped back home at the families' request after the war.[31]

At Point Lookout, Maryland, there were still 22,000 POWs being held at the end of April 1865. Eventually they were released in a combination of alphabetical order and reverse order of states that seceded from the Union. By June 30 all the prisoners had been released, but a large number of their comrades had been left behind in the numerous burial grounds around the central and northwest portions of the peninsula. Today it is known that at least 3,584 POWs died at Point Lookout.[32]

After the war and dismantling of the camp, a number of graves were moved to the Tanner Creek area of the point. The resort hotel was later reopened and operated until it burned down around 1878. That same year, a Coast Guard station was established on land adjoining the old lighthouse. In the late 1920s, another summer hotel was built but met with little success. By 1937, the Coast Guard Station became inactive and the point, for the most part, became deserted.[33]

Since the Civil War, nearly half of the Point's original land area has been reduced through storm and wave erosion. In 1962, the state of Maryland purchased 495 acres there and established a state park for camping, fishing, boating, and swimming. Since then, present-day park rangers and guides have claimed seeing apparitions while on nightly patrol of the park of raggedly clad Confederate soldiers running from one side of the road to the other. Others have seen similar figures standing along the road from a distance, only to have them disappear as the park security approached. The nearby lighthouse, built in 1830, is also said to be haunted by former inmates of the camp. According to the park guides, the spirits there are believed to be some of those who were killed during attempts to escape.

The Union's Morris Island stockade in Charleston Harbor remained standing for a long time after it was abandoned but eventually succumbed to relic hunters and the elements. Of the other facilities used for the "Immortal Six Hundred," Fort Pulaski is the only one that still stands. Located east of downtown Savannah, at the estuary of the Atlantic Ocean and the Savannah River, the fort, having two drawbridges, has since been designated as a national monument offering tours, exhibits, and demonstrations of Civil War garrison life.

Nearly all of the Union's fort prisons still exist today. When the war ended, Fort Jefferson continued to be used as a military prison. Six hundred Union soldiers were confined there when some of the accused Lincoln conspirators—Michael O'Laughlin, Samuel Arnold, Edward Spangler, and later, Dr. Samuel A. Mudd—arrived in July 1865. O'Laughlin later died at the prison during a yellow fever epidemic, while Arnold, Spangler, and Dr. Mudd were pardoned in 1869. The fort remained in use until a hurricane swept over the Florida island in 1873. A year later the decaying fort, still uncompleted, was abandoned and remained so until the Spanish-American War. It was from this fort that the ill-fated last voyage of the U.S.S. *Maine* began in 1898. The fort was abandoned again by 1906 but served as a seaplane base during World War I. Afterward, the fort was abandoned for good. Hurricanes and fires continued to destroy some of its buildings over the following years until it was declared a national monument and protected in 1935. Since then, the fort has been partially rehabilitated, and private excursions can be arranged. Some of the fort's original fifteen-inch smoothbore and ten-inch rifled guns are still in place.[34]

The Union's other Gulf Coast prisons also still exist. Fort Massachusetts on Ship Island and Fort Pickens on Santa Rosa Island are now part of the Gulf Islands National Seashore. Tours of the Fort Pickens ruins, just west of Pensacola Beach, and of Fort Massachusetts are available through the National Park Service. The long, narrow Ship Island is constantly moving westward each year, as the forces of the wind and wave action that created it continually transfer sand from its eastern tip to its western side. Today, both islands are still covered with dunes dotted with sea oats, salt grass, and other prime examples of coastal island vegetation and wildlife. There is no indication, however, that Confederate prisoners of war were once confined here—deep within the South.

Farther north, Fort McHenry, which had held POWs until September 1865, served as an infantry post from 1865 until it was abandoned in 1900. In 1915 the fort and grounds were leased to the city of Baltimore as a park but were reclaimed and used as a military hospital during World War I. In 1925 the site was designated a national park.[35]

Today, Fort McHenry has been restored to its pre-Civil War appearance. Several of the interior buildings now contain displays of the fort's history, concentrating on its 1814 bombardment and the writing of the "Star Spangled Banner." Little is mentioned of its role as a Civil War prison, how it was sometimes crammed with up to three times its estimated capacity, or that the newspaper-editor grandson of the man who wrote the "Star Spangled Banner" was held here as a political prisoner at the outbreak of the war.[36]

Fort Warren's last six POWs were released in October 1865, but these were mostly Confederate officials arrested at the end of the war. Besides Confederate Vice President Stephens, the group included the Confederate postmaster general, John H. Reagan. The majority of POWs confined there had been released the previous June and July. These Confederate soldiers knew that the fort's commandant, Major Allen, was a North Carolinian who had remained loyal to the Union. For that they were unforgiving and refused to shake his hand upon their departure.[37]

Following the Civil War, new and bigger guns were added to the fort. Garrisons were stationed there during the Spanish-American War and World War I. During World War II, the fort was part of the area's antisubmarine defenses and served as the control center for mines placed in Boston Harbor.

In the 1960s, the island was cleaned up and underbrush and dead trees cleared away in anticipation of transforming the island into a recreation area, to include a swimming pool, a picnic area, and a refurbished fort. In 1963 a memorial was dedicated to the Confederate POWs who died there. Today the site is listed in the National Register of Historic Places and is part of the Boston Harbor Islands State Park system. The fort is partially restored, and further efforts continue. The island contains a visitors' center, a large dock, picnic grounds, and a gravel beach with tours of the fort available throughout the summer.

Like Point Lookout, Fort Warren is rumored to be haunted. Supposedly, a ghost, referred to as the "lady in black," roams through certain portions of the fort, weeping softly, even today. Reports exist of soldiers from the end of the Civil War through World War II who have claimed to have seen the appariton at one time or another. According to the legend, she was the wife of a Confederate soldier held there during the Civil War who secretly got onto the island and entered the fort by a hidden tunnel. Dressed as a sentry, she gained access to the casemate cells, located her husband, and was in the process of helping him escape when they were confronted by guards. The woman raised a pistol to fire at the intruders, but the gun exploded upon discharge and a fragment fatally wounded her husband. The lady was then captured and placed under military arrest as a spy and held at the fort. Unable to locate any feminine attire anywhere on the island, the military authorities provided her with a flowing black gown or robe. After being tried and sentenced, she was later hanged at the fort.[38]

Research into whether such an incident, or any similar occurrence, might have taken place at Fort Warren has eluded documentation. However, according to the *New York Times,* a shattered pistol was found in a long-abandoned casemate of the fort in 1936 and, during later renovations of the structure, a tunnel leading to this area from the outside was discovered.[39]

At Fort Delaware, officials seemed reluctant to release their POWs at the conclusion of the war. On April 10, 1865, they announced Lee's surrender to their prisoners by firing the fort's 131 guns in celebration. In May there were still eight thousand captives held at the site. As the prisoners were gradually being released from other locations in the North, General U. S. Grant found it necessary to write Secretary Stanton on June 27, 1865, "I would respectfully recommend that all of the officers now at Fort Delaware be discharged on taking the oath of allegiance."[40]

All but 110 prisoners were released by the end of July. Two of the last POWs were Dick and Charlton Morgan, brothers of John Hunt Morgan of Kentucky. By the end of August, sixty prisoners remained, including two political prisoners, Burton Harrison, private secretary to Jefferson Davis, and Francis Lubbock, governor of Texas. These prisoners were moved back into the fort and held in rooms over the sally port and in casemates on the north side behind the officers' quarters as authorities prepared to dismantle the prison pens.

As the last of the prisoners were released, Burton Harrison continued to refuse to take the allegiance oath and became the last prisoner to leave Fort Delaware, on January 16, 1866.[41]

Eventually the officers' houses, hospital, and other buildings outside the fort were razed. With these gone, Fort Delaware continued to be part of the eastern coast defense system. In 1896, money was appropriated to update the fort's guns. They were in place as the Spanish-American War began. Small garrisons were briefly stationed on the island during World Wars I and II. In 1943 all of the fort's guns were removed to be used for badly needed scrap metal. In 1944 the fort was closed, and by 1945 it was declared surplus property.

Today the fortress is part of Fort Delaware State Park and is operated as a Civil War museum. Its present-day condition, however, is best summed up by former prisoner George Moffett. "[T]he old prison buildings have all been removed and the grounds since adorned and beautified," he observed years after the war. "The visitor could hardly realize that upon this fair spot of land could have been enacted [such] horrible cruelties."[42]

In our nation's capital, the remains of Civil War prisons have been eliminated altogether. According to the official records, a total of 5,761 POWs had been held at Old Capitol Prison, of which 457 died. Unofficially the death rate was probably higher. More than 1,000 were held at various times, and half that number were often transferred out during the month while an additional 500 or more were received. In November 1863 alone, more than 2,760 prisoners were held and 1,870 of them were transferred out that same month. In addition, prison officials failed to file reports for this prison during its first year and a half of operation, finally sending their first report in May 1863, having been required to do so since July 7 of the previous year.[43]

After the end of hostilities, the secretary of war directed that Old Capitol Prison be dismantled as early as November 29, 1865, little more than two weeks after Henry Wirz was hanged. The U.S. Supreme Court now occupies that location.

The Carroll Prison Annex was also torn down. Its original site is now occupied by the Folger Shakespeare Library. The county jail, too, was later razed, as was the penitentiary on Arsenal Hill. The penitentiary had been taken over by the Ordnance Department as early as September 1862, and was used as a munitions storehouse for the remainder of the war. Its convicts were transferred to the state penitentiary in Albany, New York, while the court-martialed soldiers were sent to Old Capitol Prison. The body of John Wilkes Booth was originally buried under the stone floor of the old Arsenal Penitentiary, but the family later had it moved to a plot in Maryland.

Inmates who died while incarcerated in the Old Capitol Prison complex were buried on the Washington area property owned by Robert E. Lee. Called Arlington, the estate was abandoned when Lee left for Virginia in April of 1861 to accept command of that state's defenses. Union authorities quickly confiscated the property and later began burying the dead as close as possible to Lee's mansion. Before long, a number of graves dotted the grounds. George L. Rhinehart, a Confederate soldier of the 23rd (or 26th) North Carolina Infantry, was the first to be buried there. By the end of the war there were 377 Confederate graves. In May 1864, Arlington Cemetery was officially established. These graves remained until the 1870s, when 241 were removed by the states of Virginia, North Carolina, and South Carolina for burial in their home states.[44]

George Washington Curtis Lee, eldest son of General Lee, later sued for the return of the estate. The U.S. Supreme Court ruled in his favor in 1882, but, by then, thousands of graves covered the property. Agreement was finally reached to pay Lee $150,000 for the land and the house, thereby creating the Arlington National Cemetery.[45]

In 1898, a number of Confederate veterans began an investigation into the whereabouts of additional Confederate dead from the Civil War prisons in Washington, D.C. The monthly returns originally filed by prison officials only admitted to fifty, but the number of graves in Arlington had already proved that false. Official records later indicated more than four hundred tabulated deaths.[46]

Additional graves were found at Woodside, Maryland, and Wirz's grave was located in the Mount Olivet Cemetery on the east side of Washington. After much research, 128 additional Confederate graves were discovered in the old Soldiers' Home Cemetery of the city, bringing the total number of deaths in Old Capitol Prison and its annexes to approximately five hundred. This figure did not include those who were immediately claimed by family members and shipped home during the war. So, if we are to accept the Federal government's figures of the total number confined there as being 5,761 POWs, then the death-rate at this facility ran nearly 9 percent—a far cry from what officials, back then, were willing to admit.[47]

New York City became not only the first northern location to receive POWs in the Civil War, but also the last to give them up. There were still forty prisoners at Fort Lafayette as late as October 1865. By November most of the POWs were released, but a number of political prisoners continued to be held. The last four were released in the ensuing months, one in January 1866, two the following February, and the last one in March, making this facility the last major Union prison to hold prisoners of war.[48]

Today nothing remains of the fort. After the war, the facility, with its towering walls of stone eight feet thick and thirty feet high, stood idle in the bay for many years. It served as a munitions magazine through both world wars and was leased to the city in 1948. For a while there was talk of making it into a nightclub or saving it as a historic site, but neither plan ever materialized. Finally, in February 1960, it was torn down so the island could be utilized to support the east tower of the Verrazano-Narrows Bridge, then under construction. The rubble that was once Fort Lafayette was dumped off the Staten Island shore to help support the west tower of the bridge.[49]

The original Tombs prison no longer exists, either. It was razed in October 1898, and replaced by a newer facility on the opposite side of the street. After its completion in 1902, it was said to resemble a "gloomy medieval fortress" and continued to be known as the Tombs.[50]

After the Civil War, several changes took place on Governors Island. By the turn of the century, the land area of this site had dwindled from 170 acres to about 70 as a result of wave erosion. Its original size was regained, however, by using fill from subway excavations and dredged channels. In 1904 the original name of Fort Jay was restored to Fort Columbus, and Castle Williams was used as a disciplinary barracks of the U.S. Army for many years. In addition, the island served as headquarters for the Second Corps Area. In the 1930s, additional structures were built to house the 16th U.S. Infantry, including barracks, officers' housing, a polo ground, stables, and target ranges. The Works Progress Administration also had facilities on the island. Today, Fort Jay still survives, and Governors Island is still used for military purposes.

Riker's Island has continued to grow since the Civil War. While confining POWs, the island consisted of eighty-seven acres. By 1884 it had increased to four hundred acres, from the dumping of old metal, cinders, dirt from subway excavations, and refuse. Today, appropriately enough, the entire island is used as a penitentiary for the city of New York.

Hart's Island still confines prisoners. Over the years it developed into the city's reformatory prison, and a portion of the island serves as the city cemetery.

Fort Schuyler still survives, but not as a military installation. It was used for military purposes up until 1911, and then the garrison was moved to new facilities on nearby Fisher's Island. The site remained idle until it was leased to the state of New York in 1937 to house the New York State Merchant Marine Academy. That school still uses those facilities today.

Ward's Island now houses the Manhattan Psychiatric Center, and although the Ludlow Street Jail no longer exists, it lasted well into the 1890s. David's Island was ignored over the ensuing years and gradually returned to a natural state.

Since the Civil War, Bedloe's Island has been renamed. After the prisoners were transferred from the island's fort in October of 1861, it remained idle until reactivated as a POW facility in October of 1863. The fort then continued in this role until December 1864, after which it served as a POW hospital facility. Today, Bedloe's Island is referred to as Liberty Island. Fort Wood, named in honor of Eleazar Wood, a hero of the War of 1812, was renovated to serve as the base for the Statue of Liberty erected on the site in 1886. Ironically, what has become one of the nation's most prominent landmarks—one that symbolizes freedom to the world—is supported by a fort that once held Americans prisoner.

Appendix A

THE LANGUAGE OF
THE PRISON CAMPS

In nearly all prison environments the inmates develop a prison language or slang of their own, and those held in the Civil War's military prisons were no exception. The following is a list of slang terms often used by the prisoners, along with their meanings.

bakehouse: Usually a small building just outside the prison walls where wheat or corn bread was baked for the prisoners as well as for the garrison stationed there for guard duty. At some facilities this was done by a detail of POWs and, at others, by prison officials or by those in their employ.

barrel shirt: A form of punishment consisting of a large flour barrel, with top and bottom knocked out and armholes cut into the sides, placed over the prisoner to be worn as a shirt, held in place by shoulder straps. The nature of the prisoner's crime was often painted on the sides of the barrel in large letters. Often, the prisoner was then paraded through the compound under heavy guard and followed by a drummer to call attention to his crime.

blue backs: Confederate paper currency.

bone butter: The hardened fat residue obtained after boiling down bits of bone in water and filtering the result through cloth; formed into cube shape, it was used as a valuable commodity in some prisons.

boneyard: A callous reference to the prison cemetery and perhaps a (subconscious) attempt to distance themselves from the horror of all the

313

deaths. After seeing numerous deaths in the prisons, which often included friends and comrades, it wasn't uncommon for the POWs to become insensitive to such matters.

bowie (knife): A stout single-edged, fixed blade hunting knife with part of the back edge curved concavely to a point, carried in a sheath. It was always confiscated from a prisoner upon capture.

brick: A small loaf of cornbread about the size of a normal brick.

buck (knife): Short for buckhorn; a stag-handled knife, usually referring to those used in hunting having one large fixed blade, often carried in a sheath. These, too, were immediately confiscated upon capture.

bucked and gagged: A form of punishment inflicted on prisoners. It consisted of placing the prisoner in a sitting position, tying a stick or rag across his open mouth, tying his wrists together and slipping them over his drawn-up knees, and then wedging a longer stick beneath his knees and across his forearms. Prisoners were often made to sit in this position in the hot sun, cold, or rain for hours.

bull pen: The enclosed portion of a stockade prison; the area where prisoners were actually held or confined.

buttons with hens on: A term used by Union soldiers, referring to Confederate uniform buttons; highly sought after by Union guards as souvenirs.

Buzz: A game played by Union soldiers to help pass the time while held at Camp Sorghum prison.

cards: As slang: half brick size loaves of cornbread, about the size of playing cards.

case knife: A fixed-blade knife carried in a sheath. Depending on size, it was sometimes left with the prisoner when discovered during a search.

chaw: A one-inch-square cut of chewing tobacco; became a unit of currency within the confines of prison.

chinches: Bedbugs.

chum: A close friend, mess mate, or bunkmate. One with whom possessions or rations were usually shared.

corn dodger: A small, cake-size serving of cornbread.

deadhouse: The prison morgue, often just a shed or similar structure; location where dead POWs were kept until taken to burial grounds.

deadline: A line established within the prison, designated either by a trench or stakes on which slats were nailed to mark the limit to which prisoners were allowed to roam within the prison compound. The violation of crossing this line resulted in instant death, as the guards were instructed to shoot to kill. This line was usually drawn several feet from the wall but its distance from the wall varied from prison to prison. Although the Union denied that such lines existed in their prisons, they were common in both northern and southern facilities.

deadrun: The prohibited area between the deadline and the stockade wall.

depot prison: Established locations used to hold a number of POWs until transportation could be arranged or enough prisoners could be gathered for transportation to a major facility. Some of these sites were used over and over throughout the war, especially in the east and depending on where the action was at the time. Length of stay in a depot prison ranged anywhere from a few days to weeks or even months, depending on the circumstances. The Baltimore city jail and the Columbia, South Carolina, city jail were two prime examples. Columbia later evolved into a major facility as did Cahaba Prison, which was also originally established as a depot prison facility. Also called stop-over prisons.

dirk (knife): A straight-bladed dagger, often carried concealed on the inside of the boot. These sometimes escaped notice by the captors and were valued by the prisoners. These weapons made it into several different prison compounds and were also used in several escapes.

dry cod: A prisoner who had endured incarceration for several months.

eagles: A term used by Confederate prisoners referring to Union guard uniform buttons; occasionally used as a reference to Union guards.

faro: The most popular gambling game with cards in the United States during the nineteenth century; played with a permanent banker who dealt the cards from a dealing box.

folding bowie (knife): Another popular nineteenth-century single-bladed knife that had a four-and-one-half-inch-long blade that folded back into its nearly six-inch handle. If carried in the belt it was almost always confiscated, but it sometimes escaped notice if carried in the pocket.

flanking (for rations): Maneuvering around in order to be counted in two different groups, enabling the prisoner to receive a double amount of rations. If caught, it usually resulted in severe punishment.

fresh fish: Brand-new prisoners; new arrivals to the prison facility.

galvanized: The term applied to Confederate prisoners who took the Oath of Allegiance to the Federal government and also to those prisoners who enlisted in the Union army and wore its uniform. However, in many cases they were not allowed to leave the prison but were kept in separate quarters and treated better than the Confederate prisoners in the remainder of the prison camp.

grape: Short for grapevine; referred to false or baseless rumors and reports heard in prison; often introduced with: "The latest grape circulation . . ."

grapevine telegram: A note attached to a stone, thrown over the wall. Used most often in prisons where a wall separated officer prisoners from enlisted-men prisoners so the two different groups could communicate or pass on information.

graybacks: Body lice.

greenbacks: Federal or U.S. paper currency.

greenhorn: Used in some facilities as a reference to a new prisoner, but also used in many facilities as a reference to a new guard or a guard who lacked battlefield experience—the worst type, according to many POWs.

jackknife: The type commonly referred to today as a pocketknife. These were easily concealed and often went unnoticed by the captors. In addition, men of the nineteenth century considered such a knife a necessity; so even when they were noticed, they were often examined by the captors and handed back to the prisoner. Jackknives were used extensively inside the prison. Prisoners used them for food preparation, as eating utensils, for whittling, for cutting hair, and in a wide variety of other uses.

jewelry attached: Referring to an iron ball and chain attached to one's leg.

Lincoln hirelings: What Union soldiers (or POWs) were often called by southerners.

Lincoln coffee: What any coffee made from substitutes was called. The boiling of parched corn, rye, and even wood splinters were several methods resorted to. A derogatory term referring to the belief that President Lincoln was responsible for the current state of affairs and what the prisoners were reduced to doing in order to have some simulation of coffee.

manholes: Pits dug by prisoners as shelter against the elements when no other form of shelter was available.

mess: A group of three to twenty POWs who cooked rations, ate, and/or sheltered together.

muggers: Came into general use during the Civil War, meaning the same then as it does today; prisoners who jumped upon other prisoners and robbed them of valuables such as blankets, clothing, tradable items, or food. Often occurred as a "fresh fish" first entered the compound—if done anytime later, it was referred to as a raid.

nineteenth-century expressions: The most popular humorous catchphrases in use during the Civil War included "Here's your mule!" "Well, here we are again!" and "I've seen the elephant." Slang terms or expressions that came into general use included "let 'er rip," "snug as a bug in a rug," "scarce as hen's teeth," and "between shit and sweat" (meaning the same as today's "between a rock and a hard place").

nostalgia: Used in the context of prison life in the 1860s to mean homesickness.

on the chines: A form of punishment in which a prisoner was forced to stand and balance himself on the top edges of a flour barrel, which had the head knocked out, for long periods of time. While straddled in this position, the prisoner was often handed a heavy log to cradle in his arms. If he refused to take the log or later dropped it, he was immediately shot by the guards.

paroled: Became a slang term used by POWs referring to any prisoner who was shot dead by prison guards; an ironic reference to the fact that the man's body would now be allowed to leave the prison.

pesthouse: A small building separate from the hospital where those with highly contagious diseases were kept for care; often located a short distance outside the prison walls.

pickled sardines: Veteran prisoners; those who had been incarcerated for a very long period. They had the respect of their fellow prisoners and were often looked up to by virtue of their survival and the fact that they had learned the ways of the camp.

pigeon roosts: The prisoners' reference to sentry boxes located at intervals along the top of prison stockade walls.

prison fund: Established by Federal officials in the Union prison system; all savings in the budget from the reduction of rations went into a slush fund account along with the unclaimed money of POWs who died, money mailed to them, or money otherwise confiscated. This account was supposed to be used for the benefit and relief of prisoners, such as building additional barracks, improving sanitation systems, or purchasing vegetables to prevent scurvy. Instead, at many institutions the accounts became almost sacred and never used, while at others they were embezzled, pilfered, or badly mishandled. At the end of the war Colonel Hoffman proudly turned over more than $1,845,000 in prison fund monies, including nearly $545,000 from Point Lookout, nearly $317,000 from Fort Delaware, nearly $182,000 from Camp Douglas, nearly $121,000 from Camp Chase, and nearly $108,000 from Johnson's Island.[1]

raid: This originally referred to the jostling, pushing, or shoving toward newly arrived prisoners as they entered the compound in order to ask about the progress of the war or to make other inquiries. By 1863, however, the term was being used in reference to groups of prisoners who converged upon other inmates or their shelters with the intent to steal their valuables such as blankets, clothing, tradable items, or food.

raiders: Those who committed a raid.

razorback: A Judas; one who informed on fellow POWs for special privileges or treatment; a spy in the prison population who would inform the authorities of any plans or rumors of escapes.

riding Morgan's mule: A form of punishment in which the prisoner was forced to sit on, or straddle, a large sawhorse for hours at a time. The rail on which the prisoner sat was sometimes 15 feet above the ground and accessible only by a ladder. If the prisoner joked about needing spurs, bricks were hung from his feet.

salt fish: Another term sometimes used for a veteran or experienced POW in the camp.

scrip: A reference to sutler's tickets; used in place of money.

seeing the elephant: An 1840s gold rush expression meaning an experience eagerly looked forward to but resulting in woeful hardship, danger, and disappointment when the opportunity finally arose; an experience that cost you more than you had bargained for. The expression is derived from the story of a farmer who had heard of elephants but had never seen one. Upon learning the circus was coming to town, he loaded up his wagon with eggs and vegetables and headed out in that direction. Along the route he came across the circus parade led by the elephant. It terrified the horse, which reared, bucked, pitched and overturned the wagon, and ran away, leaving the farmer stranded with a destroyed wagon and his produce and eggs scattered, broken, ruined, and worthless. When he finally completed his long walk back home, he walked in the door and told his wife, "Well, I've seen the elephant."

semi-Yankee: A person who lived in the south and was pro-Union; a Union sympathizer in the south having strong abolitionist tendencies; Castle Thunder Prison in Richmond was said to be full of "semi-Yankees."

shebang: A hut or shelter that was personally erected by a prisoner. By the end of the war the term "the whole shebang" would come into use to mean "the complete works" or the whole thing created.

sink: The military term for latrine or toilet.

speculators: Prisoners who hoarded cash, food, or trinkets of value with the intent to sell or trade them later at a greater profit.

spit-whiskey: A term derived after prisoners began holding their whiskey rations in their mouths, which they would then spit into a tin cup once deep inside the prison population, thus allowing it to be sold or traded to others. Whiskey rations were often used as payment to inmates who had volunteered for work details inside or outside the prison and were commonly dispensed at or near the front gate of some prisons during the first year or so of the war. The practice, along with the whiskey ration itself, was abolished as the war progressed.

sporting: A term used by guards; watching or looking for opportunities to shoot prisoners; synonymous with the word "hunting."

spring-back (knife): A popular nineteenth-century knife having a three-and-one-half-inch blade that folded back into its handle with a loud "click" because of a strong back-spring. The knife originated among the woodsmen, trappers, and mountain men, and the blade had a needle-sharp spear point for piercing and a wide "belly curve" for slicing. These knives were sometimes successfully concealed and smuggled into the prisons because they were not much larger than a jackknife.

stand off the wolf: A term used by prisoners meaning "to prevent hunger."

stick carry: A form of punishment in which a prisoner was forced to stand for long periods with a heavy limb or log positioned across his shoulders and behind his head, with his arms extended straight out from his sides and lashed to it.

stove rats: Prisoners who continually crowded around the few stoves in the prison camp on cold days.

swallow the yellow dog: To take the Oath of Allegiance to the U.S. government.

sweatbox: A coffin-size box about eighteen inches wide and six feet tall in which a prisoner was forced to stand for long periods as a form of punishment. A lid or cover was placed over the opening to add to the discomfort.

Tennessee high step: A term used by Union prisoners referring to having diarrhea; also referred to as the Virginia high step, Georgia high step, or wherever the soldier happened to be confined.

thumb hanging: Another form of punishment used in the prisons. Captives were suspended with cords by their thumbs from an overhead horizontal pole with their toes barely touching the ground. They were left, slowly swinging, in this position for hours. (Some postwar POW drawings show the prisoner suspended by the thumbs with his hands tied behind his back. Such a procedure is questionable, at least with any expectation of later releasing the prisoner, as such a position would not only be agonizingly painful, but the shoulders would dislocate almost immediately.)

trading, trucking, & tracking: A term used by prisoners meaning to live by one's wits; wheeling and dealing to survive.

turncoats: Traitors; prisoners who would inform on their fellow prisoners for special privileges or extra rations in return; would often involve informing prison authorities of tunnel operations or other plans to escape.

"Well, here we are again!": A nineteenth-century expression that came to be used humorously, meaning "seems like I've been here or done this before." A POW transferred to another prison camp would stop just inside the prison gate, look around curiously at the overcrowded conditions, the ragged occupants, and the filth and use this expression, to the delight and laughter of all those around him. The expression originated with the very popular nineteenth-century circus ringmaster and political humorist Dan Rice, who opened every show with those words as he traveled from one small town to another all across the country, both north and south, before the war.

wooden overcoat: A form of punishment similar to the barrel shirt but different in that there were no armholes cut into the sides, thereby confining the prisoner's arms within the barrel, and instead of knocking the barrelhead out, a hole was cut in it just large enough to allow the prisoner's head to poke through.

Yankee well: A hole or tunnel dug by Union prisoners in an attempt to escape from a Confederate prison.

yuunk: Someone with whom there is displeasure. POWs often referred to a relative or girlfriend who didn't write very many letters to them, or only wrote them very short letters, as a "yuunk." The origin of the word is unknown, but it might be that the POWs just couldn't bear to call them a "skunk" when they wrote letters of complaint home about the situation. Used at a number of locations, the term was most common among POWs at Camp Chase and Johnson's Island.

MEDICAL GLOSSARY

The POWs suffered from a variety of illnesses and diseases, many of which were referred to in terms seldom used today. The following is a list of the medical terms often heard in the Civil War's military prisons or seen in contemporary sources, along with what they mean.

ague: A frequent nineteenth-century term for malarial fevers or chills.

alvine flux: Diarrhea; loose bowels.

acute diarrhea: Differed from regular diarrhea in that it was uncontrollable. Often referred to as "projectile" diarrhea today.

catarrh: An inflammatory infection of the mucous membranes, especially in the nose and throat.

cholera: Caused by unsanitary conditions; symptoms include diarrhea, vomiting, muscle cramps, and dehydration, which often leads to death if untreated. Often found in human feces, the bacteria is spread by flies, unsanitary handling of food, and contamination of the water supply.

chronic: Constant or of long duration; a classification used by Civil War physicians regarding both diarrhea and dysentery, which became the leading causes of death during the Civil War.

consumption: Known today as tuberculosis.

continued fevers: A classification of diseases used in the Civil War that included typhoid fever, malaria, and the like.

diarrhea: As referred to in the Civil War, all cases of flux in which frequent stools were not accompanied by straining.

diseases of indulgence: A reference used for the venereal diseases of gonor-
   rhea, syphilis, etc.

dysentery: As used in the Civil War, all cases of flux in which frequent stools
   were accompanied by straining; bloody diarrhea.

dyspepsia: Indigestion; sometimes called a bilious attack; includes heartburn.

eruptive fevers: A classification of diseases during the Civil War that included
   smallpox, measles, scarlet fever, and erysipelas.

erysipelas: An infection of the skin and tissues beneath the skin; accompanied
   by a high fever and a marked toxic reaction.

flux: Excessive abnormal discharge from the bowels.

inflammation of the lung: A term used during the Civil War in reference to
   what is known today as pneumonia.

malaria: A disease spread by mosquitoes that causes debilitating fevers, chills,
   and weakness.

miasma: Noxious atmosphere; the bad air or poisonous effluvium, once thought
   to emanate from putrescent matter, swamps, etc. and float in the air, especially
   in night mists, responsible for or causing diseases.

nostalgia: Used as a Civil War medical term referring to homesickness or deep
   depression; was even listed as a cause of death in some cases.

paroxysmal fever: Known today as malaria.

pesthouse: A shelter used to isolate those infected with a contagious disease,
   such as smallpox, eruptive fevers, etc.; separate buildings, sheds, or tents were
   used at the various prisons.

scorbutic diathesis: A Civil War medical term for scurvy or malnutrition.

scurvy: A disease caused by the lack of ascorbic acid in the body. Advanced
   symptoms include spongy gums, loosening of the teeth, and bleeding under
   the skin and in the mucous membranes.

typhoid: An intestinal infection caused by bacteria.

yellow fever: Sometimes called "the black vomit"; a disease spread by mosquitoes
   that destroys the liver and kidneys. Among other symptoms, the skin turns
   yellow or jaundiced.

Appendix C

PRISON QUICK–REFERENCE GUIDE

UNITED STATES MILITARY PRISONS

Prison Name	State	Facility Type	Years in Existence				Maximum Capacity	Most Held	Escapes	Deaths
			'61	'62	'63	'64	'65				
Atheneum Prison	WV	3	see Wheeling								
Albany Penitentiary	NY	1	—	X	X	?	?	?	?	?	?
Allegheny City	PA	1	—	—	X	X	—	?	118	0	0
Alton	IL	1	—	X	X	X	X	800	1,891	120	1,508
Arsenal Penitentiary	DC	1	X	?	—	—	—	?	?	?	?

323

UNITED STATES MILITARY PRISONS (continued)

Prison Name	State	Facility Type	Years in Existence					Maximum Capacity	Most Held	Escapes	Deaths
			'61	'62	'63	'64	'65				
Baltimore City Jail	MD	1	X	X	X	?	?	?	700?	?	?
Bedloe's Island	NY	2	see Fort Wood								
Benton Barracks	MO	3	X	X	?	?	?	?	?	?	?
Bingham Building	MO	3	see Guerrilla Prison								
Camp Butler	IL	4	—	X	X	—	—	2,100	2,186	203	866
Camp Chase	OH	4	X	X	X	X	X	4,000	9,423	37	2,260
Camp Dennison	OH	3	—	X	?	?	?	?	?	?	?
Camp Douglas	IL	4	—	X	X	X	X	6,000	12,082	317+	4,454
Camp Hoffman	MD	5	see Point Lookout								
Camp Morton	IN	3 (FG)	—	X	X	X	X	2,000	5,000	150+	1,763
Camp Randall	WI	4 (FG)	—	X	—	—	—	3,000?	1,260	?	142
Carroll Prison	DC	3	—	X	X	X	X	1,000	2,763*	16*	457*
Castle Thunder	MD	3	—	X	?	?	?	?	?	?	?
Castle Williams	NY	2	X	X	X	X	X	250?	713	?	?
Charleston	WV	1	—	X	X	?	?	?	?	?	?

UNITED STATES MILITARY PRISONS (continued)

Prison Name	State	Facility Type	Years in Existence '61	'62	'63	'64	'65	Maximum Capacity	Most Held	Escapes	Deaths
Chester	PA	3	—	—	X	?	?	?	?	?	?
Chicago	IL	4	see Camp Douglas								
Cincinnati	OH	3	see McLean Barracks								
Columbus	KY	1	—	X	—	—	—	?	?	?	?
Columbus	OH	4	see Camp Chase								
David's Island	NY	4 & 5	—	—	X	X	X	1,800	3,000	?	?
Dry Tortugas Islands	FL	2	—	—	—	X	X	900+?	300?(POWs)	?	?
Duff Green's Row	DC	3	see Carroll Prison (combined with Old Capitol)								
Edward's Island	NY	5	—	—	X	X	?	?	?	?	?
Elmira	NY	4	—	—	—	X	X	5,000	9,441	17	2,933
Evansville	IN	3	—	X	?	—	—	?	500	?	?
Forest Hall	DC	3	X	X	?	?	?	?	?	?	?
Fort Columbus	NY	2	X	X	X	X	X	250?	?	?	?
Fort Craig	NM	3	X	?	—	—	—	?	?	?	0
Fort Delaware	DE	2	X	X	X	X	X	?	12,600	52	2,460

UNITED STATES MILITARY PRISONS (continued)

Prison Name	State	Facility Type	Years in Existence '61	'62	'63	'64	'65	Maximum Capacity	Most Held	Escapes	Deaths
Fort Jefferson	FL	2	see Dry Tortugas Islands								
Fort Lafayette	NY	2	X	X	X	X	X	50	163	2	2+
Fort Massachusetts	MS	2	see Ship Island								
Fort McHenry	MD	2	X	X	X	X	X	600	6,957	37	33
Fort Mifflin	PA	2	—	—	X	X	—	200	215	42	3
Fort Monroe	VA	2	X	X	X	X	X	?	50?	?	?
Fort Norfolk	VA	2	—	—	—	X	?	?	?	?	?
Fort Pickens	FL	2	—	X	X	X	X	?	146	11	2
Fort Pulaski	GA	2	—	—	—	X	X	336?	558	0	0?
Fort Riley	KS	2	—	X	—	—	—	?	17?	?	8
Fort Schuyler	NY	2	—	—	—	X	X	500	500?	?	?
Fort Wayne	IN	3	—	X	?	—	—	?	500	?	?
Fort Warren	MA	2	X	X	X	X	X	175	394	4	12
Fort Wood	NY	2	X	—	X	X	—	?	108	0	3
Georgetown	DC	3	see Forest Hall								

UNITED STATES MILITARY PRISONS (continued)

Prison Name	State	Facility Type	'61	'62	'63	'64	'65	Maximum Capacity	Most Held	Escapes	Deaths
					Years in Existence						
Governors Island	NY	2	X	X	X	X	X	500		1	47
Gratiot Street	MO	3	X	X	X	X	X	500	1,800	109+	1,140
Guerrilla Prison	MO	3	—	—	X	—	—	?	15	?	5
Hart's Island	NY	4 & 5	—	—	—	—	X	?	3,446	4	235
Hilton Head	SC	1, 3 & 5	—	—	—	X	X	800?	800	?	?
Hope Slater	MD	1	X	X	X	?	?	?	?	?	?
Indianapolis	IN	3 (FG)	see Camp Morton								
Irving Block	TN	3	see Memphis								
Jefferson City	MO	1	see Missouri Penitentiary								
Johnson's Island	OH	4	—	X	X	X	X	1,000	3,256	12	235
Kansas City	MO	3	—	—	X	—	—	?	15	?	5
Knoxville	TN	1	—	—	X?	X?	?	?	?	?	4?
Lafayette	IN	3	—	X	?	—	—	?	500	?	28
Lexington	KY	1	—	X	X	X?	?	?	?	?	?
Little Rock	AR	3	—	—	—	X	X	?	718	3	217

UNITED STATES MILITARY PRISONS (continued)

Prison Name	State	Facility Type	Years in Existence '61	'62	'63	'64	'65	Maximum Capacity	Most Held	Escapes	Deaths
Louisiana State House	LA	3	—	X	X	—	—	?	?	?	?
Louisville	KY	1 & 4	—	—	X	X	X	?	6,737	25	343
Ludlow Street Jail	NY	1	X	—	—	—	—	?	?	?	?
Lynch's Slave Pen	MO	3	see Myrtle Street Prison								
Madison	WI	4 (FG)	see Camp Randall								
Mare's Island	CA	4	—	—	X	?	—	?	20?	?	?
Maxwell House	TN	3	see Nashville								
McLean Barracks	OH	3	—	—	X	X	—	?	179	10	4
Memphis	TN	3	—	—	—	X	X	?	582	1	3
Missouri Penitentiary	MO	1	—	—	—	X	—	?	15?	0	0
Morris Island	SC	5	—	—	—	X	—	558?	558	0	3
Moyamensing Penitentiary	PA	1	—	—	X	?	?	?	?	?	?
Myrtle Street	MO	3	X	X	X	X	X	100	150	?	?
Nashville	TN	3	—	—	X	X	X	?	7,460	36	359
New Albany	IN	3	—	X	?	—	—	?	500	?	?

UNITED STATES MILITARY PRISONS (continued)

Prison Name	State	Facility Type	Years in Existence '61	'62	'63	'64	'65	Maximum Capacity	Most Held	Escapes	Deaths
New Orleans	LA	1	see Parish Prison								
Newport News	VA	5	—	—	—	—	X	10,000	3,490	17	168
New York City	NY	1–5	thirteen different prisons								
Ohio Penitentiary	OH	1	—	—	X	X	—	?	68	5	0
Old Capitol	DC	3	X	X	X	X	X	500	2,763*	16*	457+*
Paducah	KY	3	—	X	X?	?	?	?	?	?	?
Parish Prison	LA	1	—	—	X	X	X	?	1,856	226	213
Pittsburgh Penitentiary	PA	1	see Allegheny Penitentiary								
Point Lookout	MD	5	—	—	X	X	X	10,000	22,000	50	3,584
Richmond	IN	3	—	X	X?	?	?	500	500?	?	?
Riker's Island	NY	4	—	—	—	X	X	1,000	1,000?	?	?
Rock Island	IL	4	—	—	X	X	X	10,080	8,607	41	1,960
St. Charles	MO	1	X	?	—	—	—	?	?	?	?
St. Louis	MO	3	four different prisons								
Schofield Barracks	MO	3	X	?	?	?	—	?	?	?	?

UNITED STATES MILITARY PRISONS (continued)

Prison Name	State	Facility Type	Years in Existence					Maximum Capacity	Most Held	Escapes	Deaths
			'61	'62	'63	'64	'65				
Ship Island	MS	2	—	—	—	X	X	?	4,430	5	103
Springfield	IL	4	see Camp Butler								
Springfield	MO	3	X	?	—	—	—	?	?	?	?
Tennessee State Penitentiary	TN	1	see Nashville								
Terre Haute	IN	3	—	X	?	—	—	?	500	?	?
Tombs Prison	NY	1	X	X	—	—	—	300	40(POW)	0	0
Ward's Island	NY	4	—	—	X?	X	?	?	?	?	?
Washington County Jail	DC	1	X	?	—	—	—	100	240(?POW)	?	?
Washington DC	DC	1 & 3	see Old Capitol & Forest Hall								
Western Penitentiary	PA	1	see Allegheny Penitentiary								
Wheeling	WV	1 & 3	—	—	X	X	X	?	497	12	2

Maximum Capacity: estimated maximum capacity when built
Most Held: the maximum number of prisoners held at any one time
Facility Types:
    1 – existing jail or prison
    2 – coastal fortification
    3 – converted building
    4 – barracks enclosed by high fence
    5 – clusters of tents enclosed by high fence
    6 – barren stockades
    FG – converted fairgrounds
    OA – open area or field surrounded by guard detail
?: unknown or best available figure, but not absolute
+: plus; some sources indicate a possibility of more
*: combined totals of both Old Capitol and Carroll Prisons

Note: The above are the major or better known locations, although many others exist. Additional locations were used anywhere from several weeks to several months, while some were used throughout the war as depot prisons or gathering places before shipping POWs out to larger, major facilities.

CONFEDERATE STATES MILITARY PRISONS

Prison Name	State	Facility Type	Years in Existence '61	'62	'63	'64	'65	Maximum Capacity	Most Held	Escapes	Deaths
Alexandria	VA	1	X	—	—	—	—	?	?	?	0
Americus	GA	1	X?	—	X	X?	?	?	?	?	?
Andersonville	GA	6	—	—	—	X	X	10,000	32,899	329	12,919
Atkinson's Factory	VA	3	X	X	X?	X?	X?	?	?	?	?
Atlanta	GA	1 & OA	X	X	X?	X	—	?	?	?	?
Augusta	GA	1	X?	—	X	X?	?	?	?	?	?
Barrett's Factory	VA	3	—	X	X	X?	X?	?	1,200	?	?
Baton Rouge	LA	3	X	X	—	—	—	?	?	?	?
Belle Isle	VA	6	—	X	X	X	—	3,000	10,000	0?	300+?
Blackshear	GA	6	—	—	—	X	—	5,000	5,000+	?	?
Botanico-Medical	TN	3	see Memphis								
Boerne	TX	6	—	X	—	—	—	?	350	0	0
Bridge Prison	MS	3	see Jackson; converted covered bridge								
Cahaba	AL	3	—	—	X?	X	X	500	3,000?	?	225?
Camp Asylum	SC	3	see Columbia								

CONFEDERATE STATES MILITARY PRISONS

Prison Name	State	Facility Type	Years in Existence					Maximum Capacity	Most Held	Escapes	Deaths
			'61	'62	'63	'64	'65				
Camp Davidson	GA	5	see Savannah								
Camp Ford	TX	6	—	—	X	X	X	?	4,900	4+	232+
Camp Groce	TX	3	—	—	X	—	—	?	500+	?	20?
Camp Lawton	GA	6	see Millen								
Camp Maxey Gregg	SC	4	see Killian's Mill								
Camp Oglethorpe	GA	3 & 6 (FG)	see Macon								
Camp Sorghum	SC	OA	see Columbia								
Camp Sumter	GA	6	see Andersonville								
Camp VanDorn	TX	OA	X	—	—	—	—	?	?	?	?
Camp Verde	TX	OA	X	X	—	—	—	?	350?	?	?
Castle Godwin	VA	3	X	X	X	—	—	75?	600	?	?
Castle Lightning	VA	3	—	X	?	?	?	?	?	?	?
Castle Morgan	AL	3	see Cahaba								
Castle Pinckney	SC	2	X	X	—	—	—	150	300	0	0
Castle Reed	GA	4	see Andersonville (officers' stockade)								

CONFEDERATE STATES MILITARY PRISONS (continued)

Prison Name	State	Facility Type	Years in Existence					Maximum Capacity	Most Held	Escapes	Deaths
			'61	'62	'63	'64	'65				
Castle San Marcos	FL	2	see St. Augustine								
Castle Thunder (2*)	VA	3	—	X	X	X	X	1,400	3,000+	?	?
Charleston (6)	SC	1, 2 & 3	—	X	X	X	X	1,100	1,100	?	?
Charleston City Jail	SC	1 & 5	X	X	X	X	X	300	900	?	?
Charleston Guard House	SC	1	X	X	X	X	X	300	300 ?	?	?
Charleston Race Track	SC	(FG)	see Charleston								
Charlotte	NC	OA	—	—	—	—	X	1,800	1,200	30+	?
Chattanooga	TN	1	see Swim's Jail								
Columbia	TN	1	see Fort Misner								
Columbia (4)	SC	1, 3, 5, 6 & OA	—	—	—	X	X	?	2,000	373	?
Crew's	VA	3	see Pemberton Warehouse (Crew & Pemberton Warehouse)								
Dalton	GA	OA?	—	—	—	X	—	?	?	?	?
Danville	VA	3	—	—	X	X	X	3,700	4,000	70+?	1,297
East Point	GA	OA	see Atlanta								
E.D.M. Prison	VA	3	—	X	X	X?	X?	?	?	?	?

CONFEDERATE STATES MILITARY PRISONS (continued)

Prison Name	State	Facility Type	'61	'62	'63	'64	'65	Maximum Capacity	Most Held	Escapes	Deaths
				Years in Existence							
Edward's Prison	VA	3	—	X	X	X?	X?	?	?	?	?
Florence	SC	6	—	—	—	X	X	?	1,500+	?	?
Fort Misner	TN	1	?	?	?	X	?	?	?	?	?
Frederick County Jail	VA	1	see Winchester								
Fulton County Jail	GA	1	see Atlanta								
Galveston	TX	3	—	—	X	—	—	?	100?	?	?
Gleanor's Factory	VA	3	see Castle Thunder					650	?	?	?
Goldsboro	NC	3 & OA	—	—	—	X	X	?	500+	?	?
Gordonsville	VA	3	—	X?	?	?	?	?	?	?	?
Grant's Factory	VA	3	—	—	X	X	X	?	?	?	?
Greensboro	NC	OA	—	—	—	—	X	1,800	1,800	?	?
Gwathmey Warehouse	VA	3	X	X?	?	?	?	?	?	?	?
Harwood's Factory	VA	3	X	X	X	X?	X?	?	?	?	?
Hempstead	TX	3	see Camp Groce								
Henrico County Jail	VA	1	X	X	X	X?	X?	?	?	?	?

CONFEDERATE STATES MILITARY PRISONS (continued)

Prison Name	State	Facility Type	Years in Existence					Maximum Capacity	Most Held	Escapes	Deaths
			'61	'62	'63	'64	'65				
Houston	TX	3	—	—	X	—	—	?	100?	?	?
Howard's Factory	VA	3	X	X	X	X?	X?	?	?	?	?
Huntsville	TX	1	—	—	X	—	—	?	232?	?	?
Jackson	MS	3	—	—	X	—	—	?	?	?	?
Killian's Mill	SC	4	see Columbia; planned facility, never completed								
Knoxville	TN	1	X	X?	—	—	—	?	?	?	?
Libby Warehouse	VA	3	—	X	X	X	X	1,000	4,221	60+	20+?
Ligon's Warehouse	VA	3	X	X	—	—	—	500?	600	?	?
Lumpkin's Jail	VA	1	see Castle Godwin								
Lynchburg	VA	1 & 3 (FG)	—	X	X	X?	?	500?	500+	?	?
Macon	GA	3 & 6 (FG)	X	X	X	X	—	600?	1,900	?	?
Marietta	GA	?	?	?	X	?	?	?	?	?	?
Maxwell House	TN	3	see Nashville								
Mayo's Factory	VA	3	X	X	X?	—	—	500?	500	?	?
McCurdy's Warehouse	VA	3	—	X	X?	?	?	?	?	?	?

CONFEDERATE STATES MILITARY PRISONS (continued)

Prison Name	State	Facility Type	Years in Existence					Maximum Capacity	Most Held	Escapes	Deaths
			'61	'62	'63	'64	'65				
McDaniel's Jail	VA	1	see Castle Godwin								
Memphis	TN	1 & 3	X	X	X?	—	—	?	?	?	?
Meridian	MS	4	—	—	X?	X	X	?	700	?	?
Millen	GA	6	—	—	—	X	—	?	10,299	?	488+
Mobile	AL	?	—	—	X	X	X	?	?	?	?
Montgomery	AL	?	X	—	—	X?	X?	?	?	?	?
New Orleans	LA	1	see Parish Prison								
O'Connor House	SC	3	—	—	—	X	—	?	86	0	0
Palmer's Factory	VA	3	see Castle Thunder; served as part of complex; cap: 400								
Parish Prison	LA	1	X	X	—	—	—	?	?	?	?
Pemberton Warehouse	VA	3	X	X	—	—	—	?	?	?	?
Petersburg	VA	3 & (FG)	—	—	X?	X	X	?	?	?	?
Prince Street Jail	VA	1	see Alexandria								
Prison Town	TX	6	see Boerne								
Raleigh	NC	3, 4 & (FG)	X	X	X	X?	X?	?	500?	600+	?

CONFEDERATE STATES MILITARY PRISONS (continued)

Prison Name	State	Facility Type	Years in Existence					Maximum Capacity	Most Held	Escapes	Deaths
			'61	'62	'63	'64	'65				
Richland County Jail	SC	1	?	?	?	X	X	?	500?	?	?
Richmond City Jail	VA	1	X	X	—	—	—	?	?	?	?
Richmond (15)	VA	1 & 3	X	X	X	X	X	?	13,500	?	200+
Roper Hospital	SC	3	—	—	—	X	—	?	200+?	0	0
Ross's Factory	VA	3	—	X	X?	X?	X?	?	200?	?	?
St. Augustine	FL	2	X	—	—	—	—	?	?	?	?
Salado Camp	TX	OA	see Camp VanDorn								
Salisbury	NC	3 & 5	X	X	X	X	X	2,000	10,321	500+	3,700
San Antonio	TX	3	X	—	—	—	—	?	360+	?	?
San Antonio Springs	TX	OA	—	X	—	—	—	?	350+	?	?
San Pedro Springs	TX	OA	—	X	—	—	—	?	350	12	?
Savannah (3)	GA	1, 5 & OA	—	—	—	X	—	?	6,000?	0	2+?
Selma	AL	3	—	—	—	X	X?	?	?	?	?
Scott's Factory	VA	3	—	X	X	X?	X?	?	?	?	?
Shreveport	LA	3	—	—	X	?	?	?	?	?	?

CONFEDERATE STATES MILITARY PRISONS (continued)

Prison Name	State	Facility Type	Years in Existence					Maximum Capacity	Most Held	Escapes	Deaths
			'61	'62	'63	'64	'65				
Smith's Factory	VA	3	—	—	X	X	X	?	?	?	?
Smith Slave Mart	GA	3	see Macon (officially: Davis Smith Negro Mart)								
Swim's Jail	TN	1	—	X	X?	—	—	?	?	?	?
Talladega	AL	3	?	?	?	X?	?	?	?	?	?
Taylor's Factory	VA	3	X	X	—	—	—	?	?	?	?
Texas State Penitentiary	TX	1	see Huntsville								
Thomasville	GA	?	?	?	?	X?	X	?	?	?	?
Tuscaloosa	AL	3	X	X	X	—	—	?	?	?	?
Virginia State Penitentiary	VA	1	see Richmond								
Warwick & Barksdale Mill	VA	3	—	X	X	?	?	4,000	?	?	?
Whitlock's Warehouse	VA	3	see Castle Thunder; served as part of complex; cap: 350								
Winchester	VA	1 & 3	—	X	X	X	?	?	?	?	?

Maximum Capacity: estimated maximum capacity when built or confiscated
Most Held: the maximum number of prisoners held at any one time
Facility Types:
1 – existing jail or prison
2 – coastal fortification
3 – converted buildings
4 – barracks enclosed by high fence
5 – clusters of tents enclosed by high fence
6 – barren stockades
FG – converted fairgrounds
OA – open area or field surrounded by guard detail
?: unknown or best available figure, but not absolute
+: plus; some sources indicate a possibility of more
*: another "Castle Thunder" was located in Petersburg, Va., so named because of the constant cannon fire heard in the distance.

Note: The above are the major locations, although many others existed. Unfortunately, very little information is known about many of the southern prisons. In some instances, only the fact that a certain location was used is all that is known. Not unlike the Union, the Confederate government used additional locations anywhere from several weeks to several months, while some were used throughout the war as depot prisons or gathering places before shipping POWs out to larger, major facilities.

NOTES

INTRODUCTION

1. Private letter, Solomon F. Cook to Martha Cook, dated August 23, 1863. Sybil Frazier Ball Family Papers. Copy on file with author.

2. Sybil Frazier Ball Family Papers.

3. Ibid.; National Archives, R G 109, M598, roll 53, vol. 188; "POWs at Camp Douglas," muster roll 300, sheet 1.

4. Ibid.; National Archives, R G 109, M598, roll 58, vol. 200; "POWs Who Died at Camp Douglas," Register No. 1, p. 172.

5. Francis T. Miller, ed., *The Photographic History of the Civil War* (New York: The Review of Reviews Co., 1911) 7:43, 50, hereafter referred to as Miller, *Photographic History.* Figures are based on those of General F. C. Ainsworth, U.S. Record and Pension Office: Total of 462, 634 Confederates (which includes those who surrendered at war's end) and 211,411 Union captured during the war; Stewart Brooks, *Civil War Medicine* (Springfield: Charles C. Thomas, 1966), p. 126. Total enlistments: Union—2,893,304, Confederate—between 1,227,890 and 1,406,180; figures based on Livermore and Adjutant General's Office (1885). Therefore, combined total of enlistments of both sides would be between 4,299,484 and 4,121,194. See also Thomas L. Livermore, *Numbers and Losses in the Civil War* (Boston: Houghton Mifflin, 1901), pp. 6–7.

6. Miller, *Photographic History,* 7:43, 50. A total of 247,769 Confederates were paroled on the field, leaving 214,865 who were incarcerated, while 16,668 Union were paroled on the field, leaving 194,743 incarcerated.

7. Ibid. These are probably the best figures, based on Ainsworth, but even the statistics are cause for argument. According to the *World Almanac* for 1890 (American Publishing Co.), p. 95, the Adjutant General's Office lists the total number of prisoners who died in Confederate prisons as 30,156 and in Federal prisons as 30,152. Soon after the war, even Secretary Stanton came up with different (and ridiculously lower) figures. Simply reviewing the death totals in Appendix C of this book reveals a total of 30,205 deaths in Confederate prisons and 25,531 in Union prisons, and these are merely partial figures with many Confederate prison totals listed as "unknown" (and, therefore, omitted in the total) and the many minor depot prisons, such as the Union's Camp Nelson, Kentucky, with sixty graves, and Cairo, Illinois, with sixty-three graves, not included. No doubt, the exact number of deaths in the prisons will never be known.

8. Based on figures in Brooks, *Civil War Medicine,* p. 126; Union battle deaths of 110,070 and estimated at 94,000 for Confederates, compared to total enlistments.

9. William B. Hesseltine, *Civil War Prisons: A Study in War Psychology,* (Columbus: Ohio State University Press, 1930), p. 55, hereafter referred to as Hesseltine, *Prisons: A Study.*

10. Bruce Catton and Richard M. Ketchum, *The American Heritage Picture History of the Civil War* (New York: American Heritage/Bonanza Books, 1982), p. 10; Paul M. Angle, *A Pictorial History of the Civil War Years* (Garden City, NY: Doubleday, 1967), p. 11; Keith Ellis, *The American Civil War* (New York: Putnam's Sons, 1971), p. 23; John S. Tilley, *Facts The Historians Leave Out* (Montgomery: Paragon Press, 1951), pp. 36–39; William C. Davis, *Jefferson Davis* (New York: Harper Collins, 1991), pp. 304 and 306. On February 8, 1861, the secession convention adopted a constitution for a provisional Confederate government. Within thirty days (on March 6) the Confederacy called for 100,000 volunteers for a provisional army. That same month, the U.S. government ordered its military to secure the coastal fortifications. See also *War of the Rebellion: A Compilation of the Official Records of the Union and Confederate Armies,* Series I, Vol. I, pp. 9, 82–83, and 352.

11. Cynthia Owen Philip, ed., *Imprisoned in America* (New York: Harper & Row, 1973), pp. 5–6; W.P.A., *Connecticut* (New York: Oxford University Press, 1938), p. 499; W. Storrs Lee, "Stone Walls Do Not a Prison Make," *American Heritage* (February, 1967), pp. 40–43; Eric Williams, ed., *Famous Escapes* (New York: W. W. Norton, 1953), pp. 16, 22, 38, 49, 91, and 114.

12. Ibid.

13. U.S. War Department, *War of the Rebellion: A Compilation of the Official Records of the Union and Confederate Armies* (Washington: Government Printing Office, 1894–1899), Series II, Vol. III, pp. 681–82, hereafter referred to as O.R., with all references to Series II unless otherwise noted.

14. O.R. Vol. III, p. 8.

15. Private letter, Matthew M. Rogers to T. J. Rogers, dated October 29, 1861. Robert Fulbright Family Papers. Copy on file with author.

16. W. Storrs Lee, "Stone Walls Do Not a Prison Make," *American Heritage* (February, 1967), pp. 43 and 92.

17. See O.R., Vol. I, pp. 92 and 104; D. U. Barziza, *Decimus et Ultimus Barziza, The Adventures of a Prisoner of War, 1863–1864,* ed. R. Henderson Shuffler, (Austin: University of Texas Press, 1964), p. 91, hereafter referred to as Barziza, *Adventures of a POW.*

18. New York *Times,* 3 Feb 1864, p. 4:4.

19. Richmond *Daily Dispatch,* 28 Sept 1863, p. 1:5.

20. O.R., Vol. VII, p. 607.

21. John Ransom, *Andersonville* (Philadelphia: Douglas Brothers, 1883), p. 24; John Dooley, *John Dooley, Confederate Soldier, His War Journal,* ed. Joseph T. Durkin, (Washington: Georgetown University Press, 1945), pp. 28–29, hereafter referred to as Dooley, *His War Journal;* New York *Herald,* 6 May 1864, p. 1:6; Clifford Dowdey, *Experiment in Rebellion* (Garden City, NY: Doubleday), p. 90; Jean H. Baker, *Mary Todd Lincoln* (New York: W. W. Norton, 1987), pp. 32, 41, 48, 222–23.

CHAPTER 1

1. O.R. Vol. I, p. 10; J. J. Bowden, *The Exodus of Federal Forces From Texas 1861* (Austin: Eakin Press, 1986), pp. 54 and 56, hereafter referred to as Bowden, *Exodus.*

2. O.R., Series I, Vol. I, p. 623; Series II, Vol. I, p. 56; Bowden, *Exodus,* pp. 99–100.

3. O.R., Series I, Vol. I, pp. 550–53; Bowden, *Exodus,* pp. 90–91, 100–101.

4. Arthur M. Wilcox and Warren Ripley, *The Civil War At Charleston* (Charleston: The News and Courier and the Evening Post, 1989), pp. 19–20, hereafter referred to as Wilcox/Ripley, *C. W. at Charleston.*

5. Bowden, *Exodus,* p. 89.

6. Miller, *Photographic History*, p. 30; Stephen Schwartz, *22 Months A Prisoner of War* (St. Louis: A. F. Nelson, 1891), p. 27, hereafter referred to as Schwartz, *22 Months a POW.*
7. O.R., Vol. 1, pp. 8, 58–60.
8. Bowden, *Exodus,* p. 105; Schwartz, *22 Months a POW,* pp. 27, 66, 68.
9. Ibid., p. 69.
10. Ibid., pp. 74–75. Graham had taken a fifteen-day leave and never returned.
11. Ibid., pp. 77–78.
12. Ibid., pp. 78–80.
13. Ibid., pp. 80 and 92.
14. Ibid., pp. 88, 91, 137.
15. Ibid., pp. 94 and 137.
16. Ibid., pp. 99, 101–2.
17. Ibid., pp. 109–11.
18. Ibid., p. 126.
19. Ibid., p. 145.
20. Ibid., pp. 146–47. The site is known today as Boerne, Texas.
21. O.R., Vol. I, p. 104.
22. Private letters and papers, Charles C. and Henry W. Spencer, and Larose A. Wynne Family Papers; Senate Report, 42nd Congress, 2nd Session, Report No. 45 (Feb. 21, 1872); National Archives, RG 107, M421, roll 3, frame 120. Copies provided to author, courtesy of Larose Wynne.
23. Miller, *Photographic History,* vol. 7, pp. 208 and 210.
24. Charleston (SC) *Daily Courier,* 13 Dec 1861, p. 4:1; *New York Times,* 16 Mar 1862, p. 3:5; Williard W. Glazier, *The Capture, The Prison Pen, And The Escape* (Albany: J. Munsell, 1866), p. 143, hereafter referred to as Glazier, *The Capture.*
25. O.R., Vol. III, p. 8.
26. O.R., Vol. VI, pp. 503–4.
27. Miller, *Photographic History,* vol. 7, p. 40.
28. O.R., Vol. IV, p. 375.
29. Stanley Kimmel, *Mr. Davis' Richmond* (New York: Coward-McCann, 1958), p. 33.
30. Patricia L. Faust, ed., *Historical Times Illustrated Encyclopedia of The Civil War* (New York: Harper & Row, 1986), p. 836, hereafter referred to as Faust, *Encyclopedia;* Stewart Sifakis, *Who Was Who in the Civil War* (New York: Facts on File Publications, 1988), p. 723, hereafter referred to as Sifakis, *Who Was Who.*
31. National Historical Society, *The Image of War: 1861–1865, End of an Era,* Vol. IV, p. 402, hereafter referred to as NHS, *Image of War.*
32. O.R., Vol. VIII, p. 997 for total U.S.; southern totals derived from the total sum of the individual Confederate prison populations cited in a number of prison accounts, including inspections cited in O.R., Vol. VII.
33. O.R., Vol. VIII, p. 768.
34. NHS, *Image of War,* p. 409.
35. Miller, *Photographic History,* pp. 42–43; William C. Davis, *Fighting Men Of The Civil War* (New York: Gallery Books, 1989), p. 183.
36. James I. Robertson, Jr., *Soldiers Blue and Gray* (Columbia: University of South Carolina Press, 1988), p. 194; Sam S. Boggs, *Eighteen Months a Prisoner under the Rebel Flag* (Lovington: Boggs Publishing, 1887), p. 35, hereafter referred to as Boggs, *Eighteen Months.*

CHAPTER 2

1. Emory M. Thomas, *The Confederate State of Richmond* (Austin: University of Texas Press, 1971), p. 24, hereafter referred to as Thomas, *State of Richmond.*
2. Ibid., p. 106. Also known as McDaniel's Negro Jail, it was bounded by Franklin, Lumpkin, and Union streets.

3. Sandra V. Parker, *Richmond's Civil War Prisons* (Lynchburg: H. E. Howard, 1990), p. 3, hereafter referred to as Parker, *Richmond's Prisons; New York Times,* 20 Nov 1861, p. 2:4, which gave a final total of 1,500 captured.

4. Kimmel, *Mr. Davis' Richmond,* p. 79; Parker, *Richmond's Prisons,* p. 4; William C. Harris, *Prison-Life in the Tobacco Warehouse at Richmond by a Ball's Bluff Prisoner* (Philadelphia: George W. Childs, 1862), p. 129, hereafter referred to as Harris, *Prison Life; New York Times,* 27 Feb 1862, p. 8:4.

5. Harris, *Prison Life,* p. 129.

6. Parker, *Richmond's Prisons,* p. 6; Harris, *Prison Life,* p. 32. Harris advised 2,838 were brought in.

7. Harris, *Prison Life,* p. 31.

8. Ibid., pp. 23–24; Thomas, *State of Richmond,* p. 62.

9. Harris, *Prison Life,* p. 31.

10. *Charleston Daily Courier,* 14 Sept 1861, p. 1:4.

11. O.R., Vol. III, p. 718.

12. Harris, *Prison Life,* p. 9. Harris was a first lieutenant in Baker's 1st California Regiment (71st Pennsylvania Regiment), captured in October 1861. William Howard Merrell, *Five Months in Rebeldom* was published by Adams and Dabney.

13. O.R., Vol. III, p. 756; Parker, *Richmond's Prisons,* p. 3, 6–7, 14, 50; Thomas, *State of Richmond,* pp. 21–22.

14. *New York Times,* 27 Feb 1862, p. 8:3.

15. Harris, *Prison Life,* p. 32.

16. Faust, *Encyclopedia,* pp. 165–66; Sifakis, *Who Was Who,* pp. 143–44; Harris, *Prison Life,* pp. 101–2, 105, 169–71.

17. Glazier, *The Capture,* p. 41; Thomas, *State of Richmond,* p. 60.

18. Dowdey, *Experiment In Rebellion,* p. 90; *New York Times,* 14 Aug 1861, p. 1:1.

19. Bela Estavan, *War Pictures from the South* (London: Routledge, Warne, and Routledge, 1863), p. 298.

20. *New York Times,* 21 Dec 1861, p. 5:1.

21. Ibid., 18 Jan 1862, p. 2:6.

22. Paul M. Angle and Earl Schenck Miers, *Tragic Years 1860–1865* (New York: Simon and Schuster, 1960), pp. 740–41, hereafter referred to as Angle/Miers, *Tragic Years;* Robert H. Kellogg, *Life and Death in Rebel Prisons* (Hartford: L. Stebbins, 1866), pp. 364–65, hereafter referred to as Kellogg, *Rebel Prisons.*

23. *New York Times,* 21 Dec 1861, p. 5:1.

24. Ibid., 27 Feb 1862, p. 8:3; Harris, *Prison Life,* pp. 24, 72–75; Thomas, *State of Richmond,* p. 62.

25. O.R., Vol. III, pp. 681–82.

26. Charleston *Mercury,* 14 Sep 1861, p. 2:1.

27. Ibid.

28. Ibid., 18 Sep 1861, p. 2:2; 19 Sep 1861, p. 2:1.

29. *New York Times,* 4 Jan 1861, p. 1:6; *Philadelphia Inquirer,* 13 Apr 1861, p. 1:4; Charleston *News and Courier,* 9 Mar 1958, p. 6C:1; Charleston *Evening Post,* 28 Jun 1983, p. 16B:1.

30. Wilcox/Ripley, *C.W. at Charleston,* p. 3.

31. NHS, *Image of War,* p. 405; Miller, *Photographic History,* pp. 25, 27, 127.

32. Ibid.; Hesseltine, *Prisons: A Study,* p. 62.

33. Faust, *Encyclopedia,* pp. 119–20. Many of those photos exist today as the only remaining evidence of prison life inside Castle Pinckney. Published accounts of daily life inside are rare. Hesseltine, *Prisons: A Study,* pp. 62–63; Wilcox/Ripley, *C.W. at Charleston,* pp. 27–28.

34. *Charleston Mercury,* 14 Sep 1861, p. 2:1.

35. Charleston *Daily Courier,* 13 Dec 1861, p. 4:1.

36. Ibid.

37. Charleston *News and Courier,* 6 May 1946, p. 10:1; *New York Times,* 16 Dec 1861, p. 8:1; 24 Dec 1861, p. 4:6.

38. Ibid., 15 Dec 1861, p. 1:1.

39. Ibid., 24 Dec 1861, p. 4:6; *Charleston Mercury,* 12 Dec 1861, p. 2:1.

40. Ibid.

41. Ibid.

42. *New York Times,* 24 Dec 1861, p. 4:6.

43. Ibid.

44. Ibid.

45. Wilcox/Ripley, *C. W. at Charleston,* p. 4.

46. O.R., Vol. III, pp. 723, 730–31, 733.

47. Greensboro (NC) *Daily News,* 8 Nov 1936 (library clipping, no page number); A. W. Mangum, "Salisbury Prison," *Histories of the Several Regiments and Battalions from North Carolina in the Great War 1861–'65,* ed. Walter Clark (Goldsboro: Nash Brothers, 1901), vol. IV, pp. 745–46, hereafter cited as Mangum, "Salisbury Prison."

48. *Greensboro Daily News,* 8 Nov 1936.

49. O.R., Vol. III, pp. 682 and 693.

50. Mangum, "Salisbury Prison," pp. 745–46. Trinity College of Durham, N.C., is known today as Duke University.

51. Ibid., p. 746.

52. Ibid., p. 748.

53. The famous lithograph showing POWs playing baseball at the prison was first published in 1863 by Sarony, Major & Knapp of New York (*Civil War Times Illustrated,* vol. XIV, no. 6 [October 1975] p. 3).

54. *New York Times,* 1 Feb 1865, p. 8:2.

55. Ibid., 16 Jun 1861, p. 1:4.

56. James F. Richardson, *The New York Police,* (New York: Oxford University Press, 1970), pp. 60–61.

57. O.R., Vol. III, p. 37.

58. Ibid., p. 36.

59. Ibid.

60. *New York Times,* 16 Mar 1862, p. 3:5.

61. Henry Collins Brown, ed., *Valentine's Manual of Old New York* (New York: Gracie Mansion Publishers, 1924), pp. 188–89.

62. *New York Times,* 16 Oct 1898, p. I.M.6:1.

63. Ibid.

64. Ibid.

65. Ibid., 16 Mar 1862, p. 3:5.

66. Ibid.

67. O.R., Vol. III, p. 10; Vol. II, p. 228; *New York Times,* 24 Sep 1861, p. 1:5.

68. Francis K. Howard, *Fourteen Months in American Bastiles* (Baltimore: Kelly, Hedian & Piet, 1863), p. 18, hereafter referred to as Howard, *Fourteen Months; New York Times,* 18 Jan 1862, p. 2:5.

69. Howard, *Fourteen Months,* p. 18.

70. Ibid.

71. Ibid., pp. 18, 22, 29.

72. Miller, *Photographic History,* p. 56.

73. *New York Times,* 18 Jan 1862, p. 2:5; Howard, *Fourteen Months,* p. 36.

74. O.R., Vol. VI, p. 690; Howard, *Fourteen Months,* pp. 18–19; ["An Eye-Witness," *The Bastile in America* (London: Robert Hardwicke Publishers, 1861), pp. 10 and 16]; Lawrence Sangston, *Bastiles of the North, by A Member of the Maryland Legislature* (Baltimore: Kelly, Hedian & Piet, 1863), pp. 23, 26–27, hereafter referred to as Sangston, *Bastiles.* Although there are memoirs that claim a population as high as 190 during periods of 1861, there are no accurate records.

According to government reports, which don't reflect that period, highs of 135 were reached in February and again in November, during 1864. Buried deep in the O.R., however, one can find that in February 1862, 163 prisoners, 112 POWs and 50 political prisoners were unmercifully crammed into the facility, so 190 might not be an exaggeration.

75. "Right Flank," *Fort-LA-Fayette Life,* (London: Simpkin, Marshall & Co., 1865), p. 43.

76. *New York Times,* 24 Sep 1861, p. 1:5.

77. "Right Flank," *Fort-LA-Fayette Life,* p. 39; Howard, *Fourteen Months,* pp. 17–30.

78. Howard, *Fourteen Months,* p. 28.

79. *New York Times,* 18 Jan 1862, p. 2:5.

80. O.R., Vol. III, p. 45.

81. Ibid., pp. 47–50.

82. *New York Times,* 31 Oct 1861, p. 1:4.

83. W.P.A. *New York City Guide* (New York: Oxford University Press, 1939), pp. 413–15.

84. O.R., Vol. VI, p. 688; Vol. VIII, p. 999.

85. Ibid., Vol. VIII, p. 190.

86. Ibid., Vol. VI, p. 688.

87. Constance McLaughlin Green, *Washington: Village and Capital 1800–1878* (Princeton: Princeton University Press, 1962), p. 252.

88. *Charleston Mercury,* 8 Aug 1861, p. 3:4.

89. Minor H. McLain, "The Military Prison At Fort Warren," *Civil War Prisons,* ed. William B. Hesseltine (Kent: Kent State University Press, 1962) p. 33, hereafter referred to as McLain, "Fort Warren"; O.R., Vol. III, pp. 661–62; Vol. VII, p. 409.

90. Howard, *Fourteen Months,* p. 55; Sangston, *Bastiles,* p. 78.

91. Sangston, *Bastiles,* pp. 65–66.

92. Ibid., p. 79.

93. Ibid., p. 84.

94. Ibid., p. 70.

95. Ibid., pp. 67–68.

96. Ibid., p. 85.

97. Ibid., pp. 71 and 78.

98. McLain, "Fort Warren," p. 37.

99. O.R., Vol. I, pp. 571 and 587.

100. Ibid., Vol. VI, p. 240.

101. Ibid., pp. 255 and 721.

102. Miller, *Photographic History,* p. 44; Faust, *Encyclopedia,* p. 272.

103. W.P.A. *New Jersey* (New York: Viking Press, 1939), p. 632.

104. Ann L. B. Brown, "Fort Delaware: The Most Dreaded Northern Prison," *Civil War Quarterly,* vol. X (September 1987), p. 36, hereafter referred to as Brown, "Fort Delaware."

105. John H. King, *Three Hundred Days In A Yankee Prison* (Atlanta: Jas. P. Davis, 1904), p. 72, hereafter King, *Three Hundred Days;* O.R., Vol. IV, p. 207.

106. J. Thomas Scharf, *History of St. Louis City & County* (Philadelphia: Louis H. Everts, 1883), p. 418, hereafter referred to as Scharf, *History of St. Louis.*

107. Ibid.

108. Ibid., pp. 404 and 418.

109. William Hyde and Howard L. Conard, *Encyclopedia of the History of St. Louis* (St. Louis: Southern History Co., 1899), vol. 3, p. 1333; William B. Hesseltine, "Military Prisons of St. Louis, 1861–1865," *Missouri Historical Review,* (April 1929) pp. 381–82, hereafter referred to as Hesseltine, "Prisons of St. Louis."

110. O.R., Vol. VI, p. 48; William Parrish, *A History of Missouri,* (Columbia: University of Missouri Press, 1971), p. 66; *Daily Missouri Democrat,* 23 Dec 1861, p. 3:4; 24 Dec 1861, p. 2:3; 25 Dec 1861, p. 3:5.

111. Ibid.

112. Ibid.

113. O.R., Vol. III, pp. 185–86; Hesseltine, "Prisons of St. Louis," p. 384.

114. Ibid.; Absalom Grimes, *Absalom Grimes, Confederate Mail Runner*, ed. M. M. Quaife (New Haven, CT: Yale University Press, 1926), pp. 88–89, hereafter referred to as Grimes, *Confederate Mail Runner.*

115. Hesseltine, "Prisons of St. Louis," p. 389.

116. Griffin Frost, *Camp & Prison Journal* (Quincy, IL: Quincy Herald Book and Job Office, 1867), p. 32, hereafter referred to as Frost, *Prison Journal.*

117. Henry M. Cheavens, "A Missouri Confederate in the Civil War: The Journal of Henry Martyn Cheavens, 1862–1863," ed. James E. Moss, *Missouri Historical Review* (October 1962), p. 33, hereafter referred to as Cheavens, "A Missouri Confederate."

118. *Daily Missouri Democrat*, 31 Dec 1861, p. 2:6.

119. Ibid., 27 Dec 1861, p. 3:5; Scharf, *History of St. Louis*, p. 418.

120. Frost, *Prison Journal*, p. 29; Hesseltine, "Prison of St. Louis," pp. 387 and 390; Cheavens, "A Missouri Confederate," p. 29.

121. Ibid., p. 391.

122. Frost, *Prison Journal*, p. 30.

123. *Daily Missouri Democrat*, 18 Jan 1862, p. 2:3, 30 Jan 1862, p. 3:4; review of daily "Military Prison Reports" between 31 Dec 1861 and 10 Mar 1865.

124. *New York Times*, 20 Nov 1861, p. 4:4.

CHAPTER 3

1. Ramsdell Papers, entry #4403 in the Southern Historical Collection, Manuscripts Department, Wilson Library, University of North Carolina at Chapel Hill, Julius F. Ransdell Diary, p. 47.

2. George Haven Putnam, *A Prisoner of War in Virginia 1864–5* (New York: G. P. Putnam's Sons, 1912), pp. 10–11, hereafter referred to as Putnam, *Prisoner of War.*

3. O.R., Vol. V, p. 477.

4. Boggs, *Eighteen Months*, p. 12.

5. Grimes, *Confederate Mail Runner*, pp. 37 and 40; Cheavens, "A Missouri Confederate," pp. 26–27; Miller, *Photographic History*, p. 33; John Scott, *Story of the Thirty-Second Iowa Infantry Volunteers* (Nevada, IA: Private publisher, 1896), p. 361.

6. Cheavens, "A Missouri Confederate," pp. 28–29; Charles W. Rivenbark, "Two Years At Fort Delaware," *Histories of the Several Regiments And Battalions from North Carolina in the Great War 1861–'65*, ed. Walter Clark (Goldsboro: Nash Brothers, 1901), vol. IV, pp. 725–26, hereafter referred to as Rivenbark, "Fort Delaware."

7. R. F. Webb, "Prison Life At Johnson's Island," *Histories of the Several Regiments And Battalions from North Carolina in the Great War 1861–'65*, ed. Walter Clark (Goldsboro: Nash Brothers, 1901), vol. IV, p. 662, hereafter referred to as Webb, "Johnson's Island;" U.S. Sanitary Commission, *Narrative of Privations and Sufferings of United States Officers and Soldiers While Prisoners of War in the Hands of Rebel Authorities* (Philadelphia: King and Baird Press, 1864), p. 151, hereafter referred to as U.S. Sanitary Comm., *Narratives*. Although considered war propaganda by historians today, the contents of the commission's report should be considered in any thorough study of the Civil War's prisons because some of the claims can be verified by other independent sources. One also should consider the tremendous impact these individual claims and various testimonies had on the general public in their day and for many years after the war. No doubt there were political reasons for the book's publication in 1864; however, the only quotes about prison conditions used in this text are the ones verified by additional independent sources. See also U.S. House of Representatives, *Report on the Treatment of Prisoners of War by the Rebel Authorities During the War of the Rebellion*, Report No. 45, (Washington: GPO, 1870).

8. Henry E. Shepherd, *Narrative of Prison Life at Baltimore and Johnson's Island, Ohio* (Baltimore: Commercial Printing & Stationery Co., 1917), pp. 7–9.

9. Boggs, *Eighteen Months,* p. 17.

10. Glazier, *The Capture,* p. 102; Alonzo Cooper, *In and Out of Rebel Prisons* (Oswego, NY: R. J. Oliphant, 1888), pp. 39–40.

11. Putnam, *Prisoner of War,* pp. 16–19; Ransom, *Andersonville,* p. 204.

12. Walter G. MacRae, "Confederate Prisoners at Morris Island," *Histories of the Several Regiments And Battalions from North Carolina in the Great War 1861–'65,* Walter Clark (Goldsboro: Nash Brothers, 1901), p. 714, hereafter referred to as MacRae, "Morris Island;" John Ogden Murray, *The Immortal Six Hundred* (Winchester, VA: Eddy Press, 1905), pp. 69–70, 72; John Dunkle, *Prison Life During The Rebellion* (Singer's Glen, VA: Joseph Funk's Sons Printers, 1869), p. 20.

13. Ransom, *Andersonville,* p. 53; Putnam, *Prisoner of War,* p. 32; Glazier, *The Capture,* p. 90; Samuel C. Foster, "We are Prisoners of War," *Civil War Times Illustrated,* vol. XVI, no. 2 (May 1977), p. 31.

14. John V. Hadley, *Seven Months A Prisoner* (Indianapolis: Meikel & Co., 1868), p. 59.

15. Ramsdell Diary, p. 51.

16. Ibid., p. 49; Rivenbark, "Fort Delaware," pp. 725–26.

17. Ibid.

18. Hadley, *Seven Months A Prisoner,* p. 48.

19. Ibid.; Ransom, *Andersonville,* p. 76; John McElroy, *Andersonville: A Story of Rebel Military Prisons* (Toledo: D. R. Locke, 1879), pp. 220–21; Miles O. Sherrill, *A Soldier's Story* (Raleigh: n.p., 1911), p. 11.

20. Ransom, *Andersonville,* p. 66; Kellogg, *Rebel Prisons,* p. 56.

21. U.S. Sanitary Comm., *Narratives,* p. 173.

22. Ibid., pp. 51, 147, 164.

23. Putnam, *Prisoner of War,* pp. 25–26.

24. Kellogg, *Rebel Prisons,* pp. 364–65; Hadley, *Seven Months A Prisoner,* p. 42.

25. Ibid.

26. Webb, "Johnson's Island," p. 666.

27. Boggs, *Eighteen Months,* p. 35.

28. Frost, *Prison Journal,* pp. 144–45.

29. U.S. Sanitary Comm., *Narratives,* p. 58.

30. Duganne, *Twenty Months,* p. 382.

31. Ibid., p. 383.

32. O.R., Vol. VII, p. 1284; Randolph Shotwell, "The Prison Experiences of Randolph Shotwell," ed. J. G. DeRoulhac Hamilton, *The North Carolina Review,* vol. II, no. 2 (April 1925), p. 343, hereafter referred to as Shotwell, "Prison Experiences;" Francis Atherton Boyle, "The Prison Diary of Adjutant Francis Atherton Boyle, C.S.A.," ed. Mary Lindsay Thornton, *The North Carolina Review,* vol. XXXIX, no. 1 (Winter 1962), p. 80, hereafter referred to as Boyle, "Prison Diary;" *Confederate Veteran,* vol. VIII (1900), p. 122.

33. O.R., Vol. III, pp. 498–500; Vol. IV, pp. 204–5; Charles Fosdick, *Five Hundred Days in Rebel Prisons,* (Bethany, MO: Clipper and Job Office, 1887), pp. 19–20; A. J. H. Duganne, *Twenty Months in the Department of the Gulf* (New York: n.p., 1865), p. 246; Hesseltine, "Prisons of St. Louis," pp. 384, 387, 390; Faust, *Encyclopedia,* p. 109.

34. Duganne, *Twenty Months,* p. 380.

35. Abner R. Small, *The Road to Richmond,* edited by Harold A. Small (Berkeley: University of California Press, 1939), p. 167; Frost, *Prison Journal,* p. 116.

36. Brooks, *Civil War Medicine,* p. 128.

37. Francis Amasa Walker, *A Life of Francis Amasa Walker,* ed. James P. Munroe (New York: H. Holt & Co., 1923), pp. 93–94.

38. Boggs, *Eighteen Months,* pp. 32–33. Although historians today doubt some of Boggs's claims, many of them are heavily supported by other POW diary entries. As one example, see William Marvel's *Andersonville: The Last Depot* (Chapel Hill: University of North Carolina Press, 1994), pp. 190 and 292.

39. Putnam, *Prisoner of War,* p. 44.
40. James J. Williamson, *Prison Life in the Old Capitol* (West Orange, NJ: Williamson Pub., 1911), p. 31, hereafter referred to as Williamson, *Prison Life.*
41. O.R., Vol. VII, pp. 809–10.
42. Boggs, *Eighteen Months,* p. 29.
43. Ransom, *Andersonville,* p. 63.
44. Ibid.; O.R., Vol. VI, pp. 584–85, 650.

CHAPTER 4

1. O.R., Vol. III, pp. 169, 216, 247, 257; Hugh P. Williamson, "Military Prisons in the Civil War," *The Bulletin,* (July 1960), p. 330; Hesseltine, *Prisons: A Study,* p. 37.
2. W.P.A., *Illinois* (Chicago: A. C. McClurg & Co., 1939), p. 153.
3. O.R., Vol. VI, p. 392.
4. Ibid., p. 970.
5. Ibid., Vol. VI, p. 393; Vol. VIII, pp. 986–1000.
6. Ibid. Vol. III, p. 237; Vol. IV, p. 489.
7. Frost, *Prison Journal,* p. 108.
8. *Confederate Veteran,* Vol. XIV (1906), pp. 60–61.
9. O.R., Vol. VI, p. 393.
10. Ibid., Vol. IV, p. 317.
11. Ibid., p. 318.
12. Ibid., pp. 488–89.
13. Ibid., p. 763.
14. Ibid., p. 740.
15. Ibid., pp. 740–41.
16. Ibid., p. 761.
17. Ibid., pp. 763–64.
18. Ibid., p. 765.
19. *Daily Missouri Democrat,* 20 Feb 1862, p. 4:2.
20. Haynie, *History of Camp Douglas,* p. 8.
21. Ibid., p. 4; *Site of Camp Douglas* pamphlet (Chicago Historical Society, n.p., n.d.), pp. 1–2.
22. Haynie, *History of Camp Douglas,* p. 4.
23. Thomas A. Head, *Campaigns and Battles of the Sixteenth Regiment Tennessee Volunteers* (Nashville: Cumberland Presbyterian Pub. House, 1885), p. 486, hereafter referred to as Head, *Sixteenth Regiment;* R. T. Bean, "Seventeen Months in Camp Douglas," *Civil War Quarterly,* September 1987), p. 13.
24. Frost, *Prison Journal,* p. 276.
25. Haynie, *History of Camp Douglas,* p. 14.
26. Ibid., p. 10; O.R., Vol. IV, p. 106.
27. *Site of Camp Douglas,* pamphlet, p. 5.
28. O.R., Vol. IV, pp. 106–7, 155, 253–54.
29. Ibid., p. 238.
30. William S. Peterson, "A History of Camp Butler, 1861–1866," *Illinois Historical Journal* (Summer 1989), pp. 75–79, hereafter referred to as Peterson, "Camp Butler;" O.R., Vol. V, pp. 379–81; Vol. VI, p. 377.
31. Peterson, "Camp Butler," p. 79; *Illinois State Register,* 24 Feb 1862, p. 3:3.
32. Peterson, "Camp Butler," p. 79.
33. *Illinois State Journal,* 26 Feb 1862, p. 3:4.
34. Peterson, "Camp Butler," p. 79.
35. *Illinois State Register,* 10 Mar 1862, p. 3:5; 11 Mar 1862, p. 3:4.
36. *Illinois State Journal,* 21 Apr 1862, p. 3:2; 24 Apr 1862, p. 3:2.

37. Camilla A. Corlas Quinn, "Forgotten Soldiers: The Confederate Prisoners at Camp Butler 1862–3," *Illinois Historical Journal* (spring 1985), p. 38, hereafter referred to as Quinn, "Forgotten Soldiers;" *Confederate Veteran*, vol. XXXVI (1928), p. 173.

38. Quinn, "Forgotten Soldiers," p. 38.

39. O.R., Vol. IV, pp. 245–46.

40. *Illinois State Journal*, 24 Mar 1862, p. 3:1.

41. Peterson, "Camp Butler," p. 80.

42. O.R., Vol. III, pp. 270, 274, 277, 333.

43. W.P.A., *Indiana* (New York: Oxford University Press, 1941), pp. 210 and 221.

44. A. B. Feuer, "John McGrady and the Confederate Prisoners at Camp Morton," *Civil War Quarterly* (September 1987), p. 43, hereafter referred to as Feuer, "Camp Morton;" Frost, *Prison Journal*, p. 255.

45. O.R., Vol. III, pp. 277 and 333; Frost, *Prison Journal*, p. 250.

46. O.R., Vol. III, p. 517.

47. Ibid.

48. Ibid., pp. 515 and 518.

49. Ibid., pp. 517–18.

50. Ibid., p. 517.

51. Ibid., pp. 516–17.

52. O.R., Vol. III, pp. 54–58, 122–24, 129, 135–36; Hesseltine, *Prisons: A Study*, pp. 39–40; Faust, *Encyclopedia*, p. 398.

53. Ibid., pp. 163 and 171; Vol. VI, pp. 365 and 851; Miller, *Photographic History*, p. 64; Edward T. Downer, "Johnson's Island," *Civil War Prisons*, ed. William B. Hesseltine (Kent, OH: Kent State University Press, 1962) pp. 105–6, hereafter referred to as Downer, "Johnson's Island."

54. O.R., Vol. III, pp. 135–6.

55. Ibid., p. 510; Vol. VI, pp. 759–60.

56. O.R., Vol. IV, pp. 206–7.

57. Ibid.

58. Ibid., p. 205.

59. O.R., Vol. III, pp. 498–99.

60. Ibid., Vol. IV, p. 197.

61. Ibid., pp. 206–7.

62. *Confederate Veteran*, Vol. XX (1912), pp. 295–96. See a possible verification of this (two Virginia Camp Chase POWs shot while being ordered to put lights out; one was killed and one was wounded), O.R., Vol. V, pp. 139 and 143.

63. Ibid., Vol. XIII (1905), p. 106.

64. O.R., Vol. VI, pp. 1069–70.

65. Ibid., p. 868.

66. Ibid., p. 1063.

67. King, *Three Hundred Days*, p. 80.

68. Williamson, *Prison Life*, p. 50; Sigaud, *Belle Boyd*, p. 54; Faust, *Encyclopedia*, p. 544; Miller, *Photographic History*, p. 289.

69. Miller, *Photographic History*, p. 289; Williamson, *Prison Life*, pp. 33–34.

70. Sherrill, *A Soldier's Story*, p. 9.

71. James N. Bosang, "Chinch Harbor," *A Civil War Treasury of Tales, Legends and Folklore* ed. Benjamin A. Botkin (New York: Promontory Press, 1960), pp. 445–47.

72. Williamson, *Prison Life*, pp. 4, 26–27, 35.

73. Williamson, *Prison Life*, p. 36; Mahony, *Prisoner of State*, pp. 202–3; O.R., Vol. III, p. 471.

74. Ibid., pp. 36–37, 303–4.

75. Williamson, *Prison Life*, p. 76.

76. Ibid., pp. 26–27.

77. Williamson, *Prison Life*, pp. 60 and 79.

78. Ibid., p. 25.

79. Mahony, *Prisoner of State*, p. 316.

80. Ibid.; O.R., Vol. V, pp, 118, 316–17.

81. Ibid., p. 317.

82. Mahony, *Prisoner of State*, p. 292; Williamson, *Prison Life*, p. 54.

83. Ibid., p. 53.

84. Ibid., pp. 29–30.

85. Ibid., p. 55.

86. Ibid., p. 22.

87. Ibid.

88. Ibid., p. 26.

89. Ibid., p. 28; Faust, *Encyclopedia*, p. 544.

90. Brown, "Fort Delaware," pp. 36–37; Shotwell, "Prison Experiences," p. 346; O.R., Vol. VIII, pp. 986–88.

91. McLain, "Fort Warren," p. 42; O.R., Vol. III, pp. 45–46; O.R., Vol. V, p. 512; Vol. VIII, pp. 986–87.

92. Ibid., Vol. VIII, p. 987; Faust, *Encyclopedia*, p. 110.

93. Hesseltine, *Prisons: A Study*, p. 112.

94. *Confederate Veteran*, Vol. XXI (1913), p. 109.

95. O.R., Vol. IV, pp. 15–66; Vol. VIII, pp. 986–87.

96. Ibid., Vol. IV, p. 255; Vol. VI, p. 377; Peterson, "Camp Butler," p. 81.

97. O.R., Vol. VIII, p. 986–87; Peterson, "Camp Butler," p. 81; Quinn, "Forgotten Soldiers," pp. 41–42.

98. Parrish, *A History of Missouri*, p. 66; Hesseltine, "Prisons of St. Louis," pp. 387–88.

99. Ibid.

100. Frost, *Prison Journal*, p. 103.

101. Parrish, *A History of Missouri*, p. 66; Hesseltine, "Prisons of St. Louis," p. 388.

102. Parker, *Richmond's Prisons*, p. 7; *New York Times*, 27 Feb 1862, p. 8:4.

103. Previous sources have indicated various first names for the original owners of the Libby warehouse. "William" was used in many published at the turn of the century (Putnam, p. 27 and W.P.A., *Virginia*, p. 288, for example) and "Luther" appeared in various sources published in the 1950's, but his background was often confused with Luther, Jr. (born 1874 and died April 1944). In Junior's obituary, however, we find: "He was the son of George W. Libby, ship chandler, whose warehouse was converted into Libby Prison during the Civil War." Luther Libby (Sr.) was the "father" portion of the Civil War era business. George W. Libby was the "son portion." (See also *Confederate Veteran*, XXXVIII (1930) p. 138, and Parker, *Richmond's Prisons*, p. 9.)

104. *New York Times*, 6 Nov 1863, p. 1:2.

105. Ibid.; U.S. Sanitary Comm., *Narratives*, p. 164; Glazier, *The Capture*, p. 46; Parker, *Richmond's Prisons*, p. 11. Turner entered VMI in 1860 as part of the graduating class of 1862, but joined the military in 1861.

106. *New York Times*, 6 Nov 1863, p. 1:2; Cavada, *Libby Life*, pp. 138–39; Parker, *Richmond's Prisons*, p. 11. Thomas and Richard Turner were often confused in prisoners' memoirs and were occasionally described as a composite figure. Adding to the confusion (according to Parker, p. 11), Dick Turner did have a brother named Thomas Provall Turner. The descriptions used in the text of this book are believed to be the most accurate descriptions available after being sorted out from the various sources.

107. *New York Times*, 6 Nov 1863, p. 1:2; O.R., Vol. VIII, pp. 764 and 783.

108. Century Co., *Famous Adventures And Prison Escapes Of The Civil War* (New York: The Century Co., 1915) pp. 213–14, hereafter referred to as Century Co., *Prison Escapes;* Parker, *Richmond's Prisons*, p. 11.

109. Parker, *Richmond's Prisons*, pp. 9–10.

110. James M. Wells, "The American Civil War, 1861–1865: James M. Wells," *Famous Escapes*, ed. Eric Williams (New York: W. W. Norton & Co., 1953), p. 146, hereafter referred to as Wells, *Famous Escapes*.

111. U.S. Sanitary Comm., *Narratives*, pp. 32–34.
112. Parker, *Richmond's Prisons*, pp. 14–15.
113. U.S. Sanitary Comm., *Narratives*, p. 158.
114. Miller, *Photographic History*, p. 72; Parker, *Richmond's Prisons*, pp. 15, 40, 52.
115. Fosdick, *Five Hundred Days*, p. 15.
116. O.R., Vol. III, p. 711; Parker, *Richmond's Prisons*, p. 17.
117. Parker, *Richmond's Prisons*, p. 14.
118. Ibid., p. 19.
119. Ibid., p. 18.
120. *Richmond Daily Enquirer*, 12 Aug 1862, p. 1:6. Across the street from Castle Thunder was a building similar in appearance to Libby called Castle Lightning, which mostly held criminally accused Confederate soldiers and civilians but sometimes included the overflow from Castle Thunder. Late in the war, a complex of converted tobacco factory warehouses in Petersburg, VA, also became known as "Castle Thunder." That name was derived from the constant thunder of cannon fire that the POW inmates heard off in the distance.
121. O.R., Vol. VIII, p. 765.
122. Parker, *Richmond's Prisons*, p. 18; O.R., Vol. III, pp. 724–25.
123. Parker, *Richmond's Prisons*, pp. 18–19.
124. *New York Times*, 24 May 1865, p. 4:6; Putnam, *Prisoner of War*, p. 28.
125. *Daily Missouri Democrat*, 21 Aug 1863, p. 1:4; *New York Times*, 27 Feb 1862, p. 8:4; Thomas, *State of Richmond*, p. 157.
126. Angle/Miers, *Tragic Years*, pp. 1023–24; Parker, *Richmond's Prisons*, p. 16.
127. Parker, *Richmond's Prisons*, pp. 14 and 22.
128. Mangum, "Salisbury Prison," p. 747.
129. Ibid., p. 748; Hesseltine, *Prisons: A Study*, p. 169.

CHAPTER 5

1. *New York Times*, 11 Dec 1861, p. 6:1.
2. Ibid.
3. Ibid.
4. Ibid.
5. O.R., Vol. III, pp. 5–6.
6. Ibid., Vol. I, p. 511.
7. Ibid., p. 523.
8. Ibid.
9. Ibid., p. 505.
10. Ibid., p. 507.
11. Ibid., p. 509; Miller, *Photographic History*, Vol. 7, p. 98.
12. O.R., Vol. I, p. 511.
13. Ibid., p. 512.
14. Ibid., p. 513.
15. Ibid., Vol. III, p. 8.
16. *New York Times*, 20 Nov 1861, p. 4:4.
17. *New York Times*, 11 Dec 1861, p. 8:4.
18. Ibid., 3 Sep 1861, p. 2:4.
19. Ibid.
20. O.R., Vol. II, pp. 54–55, 125.
21. *New York Times*, 8 Sep 1861, p. 4:2.
22. O.R., Vol. I, pp. 526–27.
23. *New York Times*, 5 Jan 1862, p. 1:5; 13 Dec 1861, p. 3:2; O.R., Vol. III, pp. 812–13.
24. Ibid., Vol. IV, pp. 13, 19, 39.

25. Ibid., pp. 45 and 169.

26. O.R., Vol. I, pp. 166–67.

27. *New York Times,* 24 Jul 1862, p. 4:3.

28. Ibid.; O.R., Vol. IV, p. 821; Vol. VIII, p. 987; Miller, *Photographic History,* pp. 102 and 109.

29. Ibid., p. 106; O.R., Vol. IV, pp. 329–30; Jefferson Davis, *The Rise and Fall of the Confederate Government,* (New York: D. Appleton & Co., 1881), p. 588.

30. O.R., Vol. IV, pp. 237 and 271; see also pp. 329–30 for Confederate response.

31. Ibid., Vol. I, pp. 77–78.

32. Miller, *Photographic History,* p. 108.

33. Ibid., p. 110.

34. Ibid.

CHAPTER 6

1. George W. Williams, *A History Of The Negro Troops in The War Of The Rebellion* (New York: Harper & Brothers, 1888), p. 86, hereafter referred to as Williams, *Negro Troops;* Ervin L. Jordan, Jr., *Black Confederates And Afro-Yankees In Civil War Virginia;* (Charlottesville: University Press of Virginia, 1995), pp. 218, 220–22, 264, hereafter referred to as Jordan, *Black Confederates And Afro-Yankees.*

2. Ibid., pp. 99, 218–19; William A. Gladstone, *United States Colored Troops,* (Gettysburg: Thomas Publications, 1990), p. 104. Although regarded today as the first, there were actually earlier organized regiments. In May 1862, what was known as the "Black Regiment" was organized in Cincinnati to aide in building fortifications around the city. The unit was never armed or provided with uniforms, and it served only as a military work regiment. It was disbanded after three weeks. At about the same time, what was referred to as the "Hunter Regiment" was organized by General David Hunter, commander of Union forces in the Department of the South. Armed and equipped, the unit became known as the 1st South Carolina Colored Infantry but was never sanctioned by the Federal government. The regiment was later disbanded, except for one company that became the core of a reorganized 1st South Carolina in January 1863. This unit was eventually mustered into Federal service as the 33rd U.S. Colored Troops.

3. Joseph T. Wilson, *The Black Phalanx; A History Of The Negro Soldiers Of The United States* (Hartford: American Publishing Co., 1890), pp. 228 and 231, hereafter cited as Wilson, *The Black Phalanx.*

4. Ibid., p. 239.

5. Gladstone, *U.S. Colored Troops,* p. 121; Williams, *Negro Troops,* pp. 140 and 324; Walter L. Williams, "Again In Chains," *Civil War Times Illustrated* (May 1981), pp. 38 and 41; O.R., Vol. VIII, p. 109.

6. Williams, *Negro Troops,* p. 315: *Richmond Enquirer* 17 Dec 1863; O.R., Series I, Vol. XXXIII, p. 867.

7. O.R., Vol. IV, p. 954.

8. Wilson, *The Black Phalanx,* p. 315.

9. Jordan, *Black Confederates And Afro-Yankees,* pp. 277–78.

10. O.R., Vol. VI, pp. 21–22.

11. Walter L. Williams, "Again In Chains," p. 39.

12. Warren Lee Goss, *The Soldier's Story* (Boston: Lee and Shepard Pub., 1868), p. 61; O.R., Vol. VI, pp. 924–25, 960–61; O.R., Series I, Vol. XXXIX, Pt. 1, p. 557; Wilson, *The Black Phalanx,* pp. 328–29.

13. Faust, *Encyclopedia,* pp. 277–78; Williams, *Negro Troops,* pp. 257–72; O.R., Vol. VII, pp. 64–65, 155–56; Wilson, *The Black Phalanx,* pp. 349–53.

14. Ibid.

15. Ibid.

16. Robertson, *Tenting Tonight,* p. 35; Faust, *Encyclopedia,* p. 654; Williams, *Negro Troops,* pp. 228–30, 235–40; Faust, *Encyclopedia,* p. 654; Sifakis, *Who Was Who,* p. 215. General Robertson was never prosecuted for his involvement. He returned to his home state of Texas after the war and became a practicing attorney. He went on to become the last surviving Confederate general, dying on April 20, 1928.

17. O.R., Vol. VII, pp. 459–60. Such atrocities were witnessed by Goss, who also mentioned seeing some black soldiers escaping death by quickly changing clothes, *The Soldier's Story,* pp. 61–62.

18. O.R., Vol. V, p. 797; VII, pp. 33 and 78; Series I, Vol. XXXIV, Pt. III, p. 562.

19. O.R., Vol. VI, p. 705. The POW's name was Amos Bares, of Pennsylvania.

20. Ibid., Vol. V, pp. 966–67; Vol. IV, pp. 945–46; Vol. VI, pp. 54, 73, 1022–23; Vol. VIII, pp. 586–87, 633–34.

21. Ibid., Series I, Vol. XXXIX, Pt. 1, pp. 720–21; see also Vol. VIII, pp. 175–76.

22. Ibid., Vol. VI, pp. 139–40.

23. Asa B. Isham, *Prisoners of War and Military Prisons with General Account of Prison Life and Prisons in the South during the War of the Rebellion* (Cincinnati: Lyman and Cushing, 1890), pp. 209–10, hereafter referred to as Isham, *Prisoners of War.* For verification of this account see Wilson, *Black Troops,* p. 281.

24. B. F. Booth, *Dark Days of the Rebellion* (Indianola, IA: Booth Pub. Co., 1897), p. 115; Homer B. Sprague, *Lights and Shadows in Confederate Prisons* (New York: G. P. Putnam's Sons, 1915), p. 54.

25. Boggs, *Eighteen Months,* p. 33. For verification that doctors ignored wounded black POWs at Andersonville, see Marvel, *Andersonville: The Last Depot,* pp. 42–43.

26. O.R., Vol. VI, p. 1053; Vol. VIII, pp. 26, 109, 355, 362–63; Walter L. Williams, "Again In Chains," pp. 40 and 43. At the same time, blacks were used as labor by Union officials for the construction of various military projects, O.R., Vol. VI, pp. 253–54; Boggs, *Eighteen Months,* pp. 33–34. For verification of this from independent sources, see Marvel, *Andersonville: The Last Depot,* pp. 155–56. The sergeant's name was Otis Knight, killed July 22, 1864.

27. O.R., Vol. VIII, p. 153.

28. Alva C. Roach, *The Prisoner of War and How Treated* (Indianapolis: The Railroad Pub. Co., 1865), p. 45.

29. Williams, *Negro Troops,* pp. 140 and 324; Walter L. Williams, "Again In Chains," pp. 38 and 41; O.R., Vol. VIII, p. 109.

30. Walter L. Williams, "Again In Chains," p. 38.

31. O.R., Vol. VII, pp. 606–7.

CHAPTER 7

1. U.S. Sanitary Comm., *Narratives,* pp. 132–33; Ransom, *Andersonville,* p. 9; U.S. Sanitary Comm., *Narratives,* p. 150; Fosdick, *Five Hundred Days,* p. 12.

2. U.S. Sanitary Comm., *Narratives,* p. 134.

3. Parker, *Richmond's Prisons,* p. 34; Ransom, *Andersonville,* p. 6; Fosdick, *Five Hundred Days,* p. 13.

4. Ransom, *Andersonville,* p. 9.

5. Ibid. Various sources spell Hyatt's name as "Hiatt" or "Hight"; Fosdick, *Five Hundred Days,* p. 21.

6. Ransom, *Andersonville,* p. 32.

7. Ibid., p. 6.

8. Ibid., p. 8; U.S. Sanitary Comm., *Narratives,* p. 158; Fosdick, *Five Hundred Days,* p. 12.

9. O.R., Vol. VI, p. 482.

10. Ransom, *Andersonville,* p. 20.

11. U.S. Sanitary Comm., *Narratives*, p. 148.

12. Parker, *Richmond's Prisons*, pp. 40, 50–53, 59; O.R., Vol. VI, pp. 1087–88.

13. *Army and Navy Journal*, 5 Dec 1863, p. 230:2.

14. Parker, *Richmond's Prisons*, pp. 12, 22–23, 40, 50; Kellogg, *Rebel Prisons*, p. 365.

15. U.S. Sanitary Comm., *Narratives*, p. 151; Wells, "Escape," p. 138; Putnam, *Prisoner of War*, pp. 25–26.

16. Kellogg, *Rebel Prisons*, p. 365; Century Co., *Prison Escapes*, p. 187.

17. Glazier, *The Capture*, p. 64; Cavada, *Libby Life*, pp. 34, 36, 41; Parker, *Richmond's Prisons*, pp. 21, 38, 46–47.

18. Putnam, *Prisoner of War*, pp. 20–21.

19. Parker, *Richmond's Prisons*, pp. 20, 34–35.

20. Cavada, *Libby Life*, p. 36; Henry Steele Commager, ed., *The Blue and the Gray*, (New York: Bobbs-Merrill Co., 1973), Vol. 2, p. 106.

21. Parker, *Richmond's Prisons*, p. 21; Faust, *Encyclopedia*, p. 120.

22. Parker, *Richmond's Prisons*, pp. 28–31.

23. Ibid.; O.R., Vol. V, pp. 894 and 901. The POWs hated Alexander so much that they had plotted his assassination (Parker, *Richmond's Prisons*, p. 30).

24. Parker, *Richmond's Prisons*, pp. 31 and 33.

25. Ibid., p. 26.

26. *Daily Missouri Democrat*, 21 Aug 1863, p. 1:4.

27. Parker, *Richmond's Prisons*, pp. 20–21.

28. *Daily Missouri Democrat*, 21 Aug 1863, p. 1:4.

29. O.R., Vol. VI, pp. 455–56, 439.

30. Ibid., Vol. VIII, pp. 475–76; Hadley, *Seven Months A Prisoner*, p. 43; James I. Robertson, Jr., "Houses Of Horror," *Virginia Magazine of History and Biography* (January 1961), pp. 330–31.

31. Putnam, *Prisoner of War*, p. 34.

32. Robertson, "Houses of Horror," p. 331; Glazier, *The Capture*, p. 93; O.R., Vol. VII, p. 974.

33. Putnam, *Prisoner of War*, p. 35; Small, *Road to Richmond*, p. 177.

34. Putnam, *Prisoner of War*, p. 36.

35. Ibid.

36. U.S. Sanitary Comm., *Narratives*, p. 146; Asa B. Isham, "Care of Prisoners of War, North and South," *Sketches of War History 1861–1865* (Cincinnati: Robert Clark & Co., 1888), Vol. II, p. 221, hereafter referred to as Isham, "Care of Prisoners."

37. Putnam, *Prisoner of War*, pp. 39 and 40.

38. U.S. Sanitary Comm., *Narratives*, pp. 130–34.

39. Ibid.; Putnam, *Prisoner of War*, p. 36; O.R., Series I, Vol. XLVI, Pt. II, p. 1151.

40. Putnam, *Prisoner of War*, p. 43.

41. O.R., Vol. VI, pp. 658–59; U.S. Christian Commission, *Record of Federal Dead* (Philadelphia: James B. Rodgers Printer, 1866), pp. 16–21; Boggs, *Eighteen Months*, p. 14.

42. Duganne, *Twenty Months*, pp. 246 and 249.

43. Ibid.; Clement A. Evans, ed., *Confederate Military History* (Atlanta: Confederate Publishing Co., 1899), Vol. XI, p. 115.

44. Duganne, *Twenty Months*, pp. 249–50; Works Progress Administration, *Texas* (New York: Hastings House, 1940), p. 632; Patricia Sharpe and Robert S. Weddle, *Texas* (Austin: Texas Monthly Press, 1982), p. 321; "The Liendo Plantation" pamphlet (n.p., n.d.), p. 2.

45. Duganne, *Twenty Months*, pp. 255 and 271; O.R., Vol. VI, pp. 53–54.

46. William P. Coe Papers, Library of Congress, Manuscripts Division, Entry 179, letter from Charles C. Nott, POW at Camp Groce, to William P. Coe, dated September 21, 1863.

47. Duganne, *Twenty Months*, p. 243.

48. Ibid., pp. 243 and 254.

49. Ibid., p. 272.

50. Ibid., pp. 254, 256, 275.

51. O.R., Vol. VI, pp. 54 and 383. Dispatch dated 16 Oct 1863; Dispatch dated 2 Nov 1863.

52. Ibid., p. 493. Letter dated 10 Nov 1863.

53. Duganne, *Twenty Months,* pp. 255 and 273.

54. Ibid., pp. 255–56, 382.

55. Ibid., p. 271.

56. Ibid., pp. 277 and 286.

57. William P. Coe Papers, Library of Congress, Manuscripts Division, entry 179, letter from William P. Coe, POW at Camp Ford, to wife, dated December 24, 1863.

58. A. A. Stuart, *Iowa Colonels and Regiments* (Des Moines: Mills & Co., 1865), p. 356.

59. Duganne, *Twenty Months,* pp. 335–36.

60. James B. Tucker and Norma Tucker, "Great Escape From Rebel Prison," *America's Civil War* (March 1995), p. 37; Stuart, *Iowa's Colonels and Regiments,* p. 356.

61. Duganne, *Twenty Months,* p. 334.

62. Frost, *Prison Journal,* p. 42.

63. O.R., Vol. V, pp. 588–89.

64. *Daily Missouri Democrat:* review of daily "Military Prison Reports" between January 2, 1863 and December 31, 1864; O.R., Vol. VIII, pp. 991–95.

65. *Daily Missouri Democrat,* 1 Aug 1863, p. 2:4; 4 Aug 1863, p. 4:3; 5 Aug 1863, p. 4:2.

66. O.R., Vol. VI, pp. 61, 96, 392–93; Vol. VIII, pp. 988–1000.

67. O.R., Vol. VI, pp. 968–69.

68. *Confederate Veteran,* Vol. XIV (1906), pp. 60–61.

69. Hesseltine, *Prisons: A Study,* p. 181; NHS, *Image of War,* Vol. IV, p. 399; O.R., Vol. V, p. 588.

70. Haynie, *History of Camp Douglas,* p. 12.

71. O.R., Vol. VI, p. 372.

72. Ibid., p. 373.

73. Ibid.

74. Ibid., p. 374.

75. Ibid., pp. 848–49.

76. Ibid., Vol. V, p. 379.

77. Ibid., p. 380.

78. Ibid., pp. 380 and 382.

79. Ibid., pp. 250–51.

80. Ibid., p. 381; Peterson, "Camp Butler," p. 83.

81. Peterson, "Camp Butler," p. 83.

82. Ibid.; Quinn, "Forgotten Soldiers," p. 44; O.R., Vol. VIII, pp. 986–93.

83. Faust, *Encyclopedia,* pp. 109–10.

84. O.R., Vol. IV, pp. 198–99; Vol. VIII, p. 1000.

85. King, *Three Hundred Days,* p. 80.

86. Ibid.; O.R., Vol. IV, p. 198.

87. O.R., Vol. IV, p. 198.

88. Ibid.

89. *Confederate Veteran,* Vol. XX (1912), p. 294; King, *Three Hundred Days,* pp. 74–75.

90. Henry Kyd Douglas, *I Rode With Stonewall* (Chapel Hill: University of North Carolina Press, 1940), p. 260.

91. Shepherd, *Narrative of Prison Life,* p. 16.

92. Webb, "Johnson's Island," pp. 667–68.

93. Shepherd, *Narrative of Prison Life,* p. 10.

94. Ibid.

95. Thomas S. Kenan, "Johnson's Island," *Histories of the Several Regiments And Battalions from North Carolina in the Great War 1861–'65,* ed. Walter Clark (Goldsboro: Nash Brothers, 1901), Vol. IV, p. 690; J. F. Cross, "N. C. Officers In Prison At Johnson's Island, 1864," *Histories of the Several Regiments And Battalions from North Carolina in the Great War 1861–'65,* ed. Walter Clark (Goldsboro: Nash Brothers, 1901), Vol. IV, p. 704.

96. *Raleigh News & Observer,* 21 Sep 1958, p. 4:5.

97. Kenan, "Johnson's Island," p. 691.

98. Ibid.

99. Barziza, *Adventures of a POW,* p. 101.

100. O.R., Vol. VI, pp. 878–80; Vol. VIII, pp. 993–94.

101. Ibid., Vol. V, pp. 227–28, 258.

102. Ibid., Vol. VII, p. 555.

103. Ibid., Vol. V, p. 259.

104. Ibid., pp. 227–28, 391.

105. Ibid., Vol. VI, p. 3.

106. Ibid., p. 424.

107. Ibid., pp. 424–27.

108. Ibid., p. 493.

109. Ibid., pp. 878–80; Vol. VIII, pp. 993–94.

110. Ibid., pp. 986–1003.

111. Ibid., Vol. V, p. 290.

112. Webb, "Johnson's Island," p. 665.

113. *Confederate Veteran,* Vol. VIII (1900), p. 489.

114. O.R., Vol. VI, p. 135.

115. Barziza, *Adventures of a POW,* p. 88.

116. Randolph Abbott Shotwell, *The Papers of Randolph Abbott Shotwell,* North Carolina Historical Comm., Raleigh, 1931), p. 160, hereafter referred to as Shotwell, *Papers;* Miller, *Photographic History,* p. 65; Hesseltine, *Prisons: A Study,* p. 193; *Confederate Veteran,* Vol. I (1893), p. 153; Vol. III (1895), p. 172; Vol. IV (1896) p. 71.

117. Sifakis, *Who Was Who,* pp. 572–73; Miller, *Photographic History,* p. 58; Barziza, *Adventures of a POW,* p. 88; O.R., Vol. VI, p. 525; Vol. VII, pp. 810–11, 1256.

118. *Confederate Veteran,* Vol. XIII (1905), p. 107.

119. Ibid., Vol. XX (1912), p. 114; Vol. XIII (1905), p. 107.

120. Ibid., Vol. XXI (1913), pp. 592–93.

121. O.R., Vol. VIII, p. 347. See also Vol. VI, pp. 893–94.

122. Robertson, *Tenting Tonight,* p. 119.

123. *Confederate Veteran,* Vol. XIII (1905), p. 106.

124. Boyle, *Prison Diary,* p. 65; Shotwell, "Prison Experiences," pp. 344–45.

125. Barziza, *Adventures of a POW,* p. 89.

126. O.R., Vol. VIII, p. 347.

127. Brown, "Fort Delaware," p. 37; W. Emerson Wilson, *Fort Delaware,* (Newark: University of Delaware Press, 1957), p. 11. Shed barracks were built on three different occasions. A number were built inside the fort's walls on the parade grounds between April and June 1862 for the first arrivals. Additional sheds to house 2,000 more were built outside the walls shortly thereafter. When Hoffman visited the site, barracks to accommodate an additional 5,000 were ordered.

128. Shotwell, "Prison Experiences," p. 333.

129. *Confederate Veteran,* Vol. XIII (1905), p. 107.

130. Shotwell, "Prison Experiences," p. 333.

131. Ibid., Vol. XX (1912), p. 11; Vol. XV (1907), p. 213; Shotwell, "Prison Experiences," p. 336.

132. Shotwell, "Prison Experiences," p. 338.

133. *Confederate Veteran,* Vol. XXI (1913), p. 227.

134. Ibid.; O.R., Vol. VI, p. 275; *Frank Leslie's Illustrated Newspaper,* No. 411, Vol. XVI (15 Aug. 1863), p. 326.

135. *Confederate Veteran,* Vol. XXXIV (1926), p. 390.

136. O.R., Vol. VI, pp. 115 and 132.

137. Works Progress Administration, *The Ohio Guide* (New York: Oxford University Press, 1940), pp. 252, 256–57.

138. O.R., Vol. VI, p. 664.

139. *Daily Missouri Democrat,* 21 Aug 1863, p. 3:3.

140. O.R., Vol. VI, p. 479.

141. Faust, *Encyclopedia,* p. 543.

142. O.R., Vol. VI, pp. 669 and 775.

143. Ibid., pp. 665, 723–29.

144. Ibid., pp. 606, 626, 632, 644, 662; Faust, *Encyclopedia,* p. 543.

145. *New York Times,* 16 Oct 1864, p. 2:5.

146. Anthony M. Keiley, *In Vinculis: or The Prisoner of War, by a Virginia Confederate* (Petersburg, VA: "Daily Index" Office, 1866), p. 67, hereafter referred to as Keiley, *In Vinculis;* O.R., Vol. VI, pp. 132, 183, 214; O.R., Vol. VII, p. 859; Works Progress Administration, *Maryland* (New York: Oxford University Press, 1940), p. 482.

147. Beitzell, *Point Lookout,* p. 21.

148. Keiley, *In Vinculis,* p. 59.

149. Ibid.

150. Ibid.

151. O.R., Vol. VI, p. 577.

152. Ibid., pp. 368 and 390; Barziza, *Adventures of a POW,* p. 89.

153. J. B. Traywick, "Prison Life at Point Lookout," *Southern Historical Society Papers,* Vol. 18, p. 432; O.R., Vol. VI, p. 718.

154. Keiley, *In Vinculis,* p. 68; Traywick, "Point Lookout," p. 433.

155. Beitzell, *Point Lookout,* pp. 88 and 195.

156. Charles Warren Hutt, "The Diary Of Charles Warren Hutt," *Chronicles of St. Mary's* (May 1970), p. 8; Keiley, *In Vinculis,* p. 68.

157. O.R., Vol. VI, pp. 281, 634, 663.

158. Ibid., p. 196; Clifford W. Stephens, comp., *Rock Island Confederate Prison Deaths,* (Rock Island: Blackhawk Genealogical Society, 1973) p. 39, hereafter referred to as Stephens, *Rock Island Deaths.*

159. Stephens, *Rock Island Deaths,* p. 40; Otis Bryan England, *A Short History Of The Rock Island Prison Barracks* (Rock Island: Historical Office U.S. Army, 1985), p. 7, hereafter cited as England, *Rock Island;* O.R., Vol. VIII, pp. 993–95.

160. *Western Journal of Commerce,* 22 Aug 1863, p. 3:5.

161. Ibid.

162. O.R., Vol. VI, p. 245.

163. Ibid., p. 381.

164. *Western Journal of Commerce,* 3 Apr 1863, p. 3:5; 7 Apr 1863, p. 3:4; *Daily Journal of Commerce,* 29 Jul 1863, p. 3:1; Richard S. Brownlee, *Gray Ghosts of the Confederacy* (Baton Rouge: Louisiana State University Press, 1958), pp. 115–16; A. Theodore Brown, *Frontier Community: Kansas City to 1870* (Columbia, MO: University of Missouri Press, 1963), pp. 181–83.

165. *Daily Journal of Commerce,* 29 Jul 1863, p. 3:1.

166. Ibid., 11 Aug 1863, p. 3:1.

167. John McCorkle, *Three Years with Quantrell* (Armstrong, MO: Armstrong Herald Printing, 1914), p. 102. (The first editions of McCorkle's book had the name Quantrill misspelled.)

168. Ibid., pp. 89–90.

169. Ibid., p. 91.

170. *Western Journal of Commerce,* 15 Aug 1863, p. 3:4; E. M. McGee would go on to become mayor of Kansas City in 1870. Mrs. George C. Bingham (the former Eliza Thomas) was the second wife of General George Caleb Bingham, who would go on to become a noted American artist after the war. Eliza Bingham inherited the building from her father, Dr. Robert S. Thomas, who died in 1859.

171. Elmer L. Pigg, "Bloody Bill, Noted Guerrilla of the Civil War," *The Trail Guide,* (December 1956), p. 21, hereafter referred to as Pigg, "Bloody Bill;" McCorkle, *Three Years with Quantrell,* p. 91.

172. Ibid.

173. Ibid.; Pigg, "Bloody Bill," pp. 20–21.

174. *Daily Journal of Commerce,* 15 Aug 1863, p. 3:1; McCorkle, *Three Years with Quantrell,* pp. 90–91; Pigg, "Bloody Bill," pp. 20–21. The exact first names, ages, and injuries are as varied as the number of sources. Some claimed Josephine was the oldest, others that it was Mary, also referred to as Mollie by her family, further complicating the issue. Some claimed Jenny, referred to as Janie or Jennie in some sources, was paralyzed for life, others that it was Mollie. The contemporary newspaper accounts misspelled or apparently misunderstood some names that were given for the victims while at the scene of the disaster. The facts and descriptions finally settled on for this book relied heavily on the sources closest to the families involved (such as those who rode with and knew the brothers, husbands, cousins, etc., of the victims, or the authors who had actually interviewed descendants) and are believed to be the most accurate possible.

175. *Western Journal of Commerce,* 15 Aug 1863, p. 3:4.

176. Pigg, "Bloody Bill," pp. 19–22; Theodore Brown, *Frontier Community,* p. 183. Some historians have since claimed Quantrill led the savage 21 Aug 1863 raid on Lawrence, Kansas, in retaliation for the deaths of the women. In truth, the sacking of Lawrence was planned a week before the Kansas City disaster (Pigg, "Bloody Bill," p. 22), but no doubt Quantrill's men rode into that town seething with vengeance. Ewing was a brother-in-law to General William T. Sherman, who would adopt a similar scorched-earth policy of destruction later in the war. Although twin sisters Susan Vandiver and Armenia Gilvey were released to relatives for burial soon after their deaths, the bodies of Charity and Josephine were taken by Federal authorities and buried in an undisclosed location. The whereabouts of those graves was not revealed to family members until 1913.

CHAPTER 8

1. Harris, *Prison Life,* pp. 129–30; Baker, *Mary Todd Lincoln,* pp. 32, 41, 48, 222–23.

2. Barziza, *Adventures of a POW,* p. 88; Miller, *Photographic History,* p. 65; Sifakis, *Who Was Who,* pp. 572–73.

3. Ibid.

4. Brown, "Fort Delaware," p. 38; Rivenbark, "Fort Delaware," p. 727; *Confederate Veteran,* Vol. XXI (1913), p. 481; Faust, *Encyclopedia,* p. 272.

5. Rivenbark, "Fort Delaware," pp. 727–28; *Confederate Veteran,* Vol. IV (1896), p. 435.

6. Ibid.

7. Ibid., p. 728.

8. *Confederate Veteran,* Vol. XXI (1913), p. 592–93.

9. Rivenbark, "Fort Delaware," pp. 727–29; Shotwell, "Prison Experiences," pp. 346 and 350; Faust, *Encyclopedia,* p. 272; Brown, "Fort Delaware," p. 38.

10. Louis A. Sigaud, *Belle Boyd: Confederate Spy* (Richmond: Dietz Press, 1944), p. 89, hereafter referred to as Sigaud, *Belle Boyd;* Williamson, *Prison Life,* p. 60; Edwin W. Beitzell, *Point Lookout Prison Camp for Confederates* (Leonardtown, MD: St. Mary's Historical Society, 1983), p. 182, hereafter referred to as Beitzell, *Point Lookout;* James I. Robertson, Jr., *Tenting Tonight: The Soldier's Life* (Alexandria, VA: Time-Life, 1984), p. 119; Harris, *Prison Life,* pp. 124, 133–34.

11. Barziza, *Adventures of a POW,* pp. 99–100; Webb, "Johnson's Island," p. 669.

12. O.R., Vol. IV, pp. 677–80; Vol. VI, pp. 803, 811–12, 824, 1116–17; Miller, *Photographic History,* p. 48.

13. O.R., Vol. VI, pp. 61, 489, 686; Beitzell, *Point Lookout,* p. 99; I. N. Haynie, *A History of Camp Douglas* (Little Rock: Eagle Press, 1991), p. 13; Parker, *Richmond's Prisons,* pp. 45, 56–57; Webb, "Johnson's Island," p. 669; Glazier, *The Capture,* p. 56; Frederic F. Cavada, *Libby Life* (Philadelphia: King and Baird, 1864), pp. 192–93; R. Randolph Stevenson, *The Southern Side* (Baltimore: Turnbull Brothers, 1876), p. 251.

14. Robert W. Wells, *Wisconsin in the Civil War* (Milwaukee: Milwaukee Journal, 1962), pp. 15–16; Richard N. Current, *The History of Wisconsin* (Madison: State Historical Society of Wisconsin, 1976), Vol. II, p. 342.

15. Faust, *Encyclopedia,* pp. 160–61, 383, 780; Mark M. Boatner III, *The Civil War Dictionary* (New York: David McKay Co., 1959), pp. 172 and 870, hereafter referred to as Boatner, *C. W. Dictionary.*

16. Webb, "Johnson's Island," p. 680.

17. O.R., Vol. VII, p. 65.

18. O. Edward Cunningham, "Strike for Liberty," *Civil War Times Illustrated,* Vol. XIV, No. 6 (October 1975).

19. Bartlett Yancy Malone, *The Diary of Bartlett Yancy Malone,* ed. William Whatly Pierson, Jr. (Chapel Hill: University of North Carolina Press, 1919), p. 48, hereafter referred to as Malone, *Diary.*

20. Putnam, *A Prisoner of War,* p. 66; Webb, "Johnson's Island," p. 684; See also O.R., Vol. VI, pp. 901–2.

21. *Confederate Veteran,* Vol. XIV (1906), p. 514.

22. Ibid., Vol. XVI (1908), p. 34.

23. O.R., Vol. VI, p. 1111.

24. Ibid., pp. 650–51.

25. Ibid., p. 854.

26. Ibid., pp. 892, 1110–11; Vol. VIII, pp. 66–68, 115–16, 291.

27. Wells, *Famous Escapes,* p. 149.

28. U.S. Sanitary Comm., *Narratives,* p. 146; Rivenbark, "Fort Delaware," p. 727.

29. Rivenbark, "Fort Delaware," p. 681.

30. *New York Times,* 15 Jun 1861, p. 4:4.

31. Robertson, *Soldiers Blue and Gray,* p. 98.

32. Harris, *Prison Life,* p. 98.

33. Cooper, *In and Out of Rebel Prisons,* p. 108; Ransom, *Andersonville,* p. 24; New York *Herald,* 6 May 1864, p. 1:5.

34. O.R., Vol. VIII, p. 33.

CHAPTER 9

1. O.R., Vol. VI, pp. 843–44.

2. Ibid., p. 1051.

3. Ibid., p. 313.

4. Ibid., p. 1042.

5. Ibid., pp. 1001–2; Vol. VIII, pp. 993–94.

6. Stephens, *Rock Island Deaths,* pp. 42–43.

7. O.R., Vol. VI, pp. 584, 635, 663; Sifakis, *Who Was Who,* p. 561. Colonel Johnson is listed throughout the O.R. index, Vol. VI through Vol. VIII, as Andrew J. Johnson; however, he only signed his reports "A. J. Johnson." According to more recent, detailed, local research, it is believed his first name was actually Adolphus (see: England, *Rock Island Prison Barracks,* pp. 26–27).

8. O.R., Vol. VIII, p. 17.

9. Ibid., Vol. VI, pp. 848, 1001–2.

10. Ibid., p. 1003.

11. Ibid., Vol. VII, p. 415.

12. Ibid., p. 1037.

13. Ibid., p. 537.

14. Ibid., Vol. VI, p. 948; Vol, VIII, pp. 993–99.

15. Ibid., Vol. VIII, pp. 15–18, 37; Vol. VII, p. 1284. The letter was dated 27 Dec 1864.

16. Vol. VIII, pp. 201–2.

17. Ibid., pp. 17–18.
18. Based on numerous contemporary accounts regarding a lack of bedding, worn-out clothing, etc. For example, see O.R., Vol. VI, p. 948; war diary of Lafayette Rogan as quoted in Stephens, *Rock Island Deaths*, p. 49, and other researched sources including the numerous accounts in *Confederate Veteran*, most notably Vol. VIII (1900), p. 122, among many others.
19. O.R, Vol. VIII, pp. 993–1003; Stephens, *Rock Island Deaths*, pp. 41, 51–52.
20. Frost, *Prison Journal*, p. 210; O.R., Vol. VIII, pp. 986–1003.
21. O.R., Vol. VI, pp. 662–63; Vol. VIII, p. 993.
22. Frost, *Prison Journal*, pp. 109, 185, 187; O.R., Vol. VI, pp. 123, 149, 153, 282, 967.
23. *Daily Missouri Democrat*, 14 Mar 1864, p.4:2; O.R., Vol. VII, p. 1103.
24. Ibid., pp. 1061, 1118–19; *Daily Missouri Democrat*, 31 Oct 1864, p. 1:4.
25. Frost, *Prison Journal*, pp. 114 and 119; Grimes, *Confederate Mail Runner*, pp. 168–69.
26. Haynie, *History of Camp Douglas*, p. 6 and 13.
27. O.R., Vol. IV, p. 111.
28. Ibid.
29. Head, *Sixteenth Regiment*, p. 476; Bean, "Seventeen Months in Camp Douglas," p. 16.
30. Ibid., p. 15; Edwin Greble Papers, Library of Congress, Manuscripts Division, entry 368. Daily diary of Edwin Greble, August 10 to October 29, 1864, while stationed at Camp Douglas, Illinois, on sentry duty, p. 32.
31. Ibid., pp. 33–34.
32. O.R., Vol. VI, p. 374.
33. Head, *Sixteenth Regiment*, pp. 477 and 486; Bean, "Seventeen Months in Camp Douglas," p. 15.
34. Ibid., p. 16.
35. *Site of Camp Douglas*, pp. 4–5; Head, *Sixteenth Regiment*, pp. 478–86.
36. Haynie, *History of Camp Douglas*, p. 11; O.R., Vol. VIII, pp. 523–25, 644–46, 684–89, 999–1000.
37. *Confederate Veteran*, Vol. VIII (1900), p. 430.
38. Ibid., Vol. XX (1912), p. 295.
39. Ibid., Vol. XIII (1905), p. 106; Vol. XX (1912), p. 296.
40. Ibid.
41. King, *Three Hundred Days*, p. 93.
42. Ibid., p. 94.
43. Cross, "N.C. Officers In Prison At Johnson's Island, 1864," p. 704.
44. Webb, "Johnson's Island," p. 669.
45. Horace Carpenter, "Plain Living at Johnson's Island," *Century Magazine* (March 1891), p. 715; Cross, "N.C. Officers In Prison At Johnson's Island," p. 704; Webb, "Johnson's Island," pp. 685–86.
46. O.R., Vol. VIII, p. 330.
47. Webb, "Johnson's Island," p. 669.
48. Shepherd, *Narrative of Prison Life*, p. 15.
49. Webb, "Johnson's Island," p. 685.
50. Ibid., 685–86.
51. O.R., Vol. VII, pp. 876–77; Webb, "Johnson's Island," p. 687; Cross, "N.C. Officers In Prison At Johnson's Island," p. 704.
52. O.R., Vol. VI, p. 986.
53. Keiley, *In Vinculis*, p. 58.
54. C. W. Jones, "In Prison at Point Lookout," *Chronicles Of St. Mary's* (December 1963), p. 6.
55. Shotwell, *Papers*, p. 155; Traywick, "Prison Life at Point Lookout," p. 434.
56. Ibid.
57. Keiley, *In Vinculis*, p. 64.
58. Ibid.

59. James Carson Elliott, *The Southern Soldier Boy* (Raleigh: Edwards & Broughton Printing, 1907), p. 32; Keiley, *In Vinculis,* p. 67.

60. Beitzell, *Point Lookout,* p. 21.

61. O.R., Vol. VII, p. 399.

62. Ibid., p. 488; Vol. VIII, pp. 996–98. This average also includes the number of political prisoners being held during this period.

63. O.R., Vol. VI, p. 576.

64. Robert Emory Park, "Diary, June 6, 1864–June 15, 1865," *Southern Historical Society Papers,* Vol. 2, p. 237; Jones, "In Prison at Point Lookout," p. 5; Traywick, "Prison Life at Point Lookout," p. 435; Robertson, *Tenting Tonight,* p. 119.

65. O.R., Vol. VI, pp. 1116–17; Traywick, "Prison Life at Point Lookout," pp. 431–35; Beitzell, *Point Lookout,* pp. 40, 99, 101.

66. Traywick, "Prison Life at Point Lookout," p. 435.

67. Ibid.

68. Ibid.

69. O.R., Vol. VI, pp. 1097–1106; Vol. VII, pp. 163–65, 383–85; Hutt, "Diary," pp. 7–8, 13, 21; Malone, *Diary,* pp. 44, 47–48, 52; Beitzell, *Point Lookout,* p. 26.

70. Hutt, "Diary," p. 6; see also Malone, *Diary,* p. 46, for date verification; Elliott, *The Southern Soldier Boy,* p. 32.

71. O.R., Vol. VI, p. 1103.

72. Ibid., Vol. VII, pp. 163–65, 177, 182.

73. Malone, *Diary,* p. 47. See also Hutt, "Diary," p. 4 and 9. He, along with his mess mates, became a victim of the tent cutters.

74. Jones, "In Prison at Point Lookout," p. 5; Keiley, *In Vinculis,* p. 75.

75. Ibid., p. 77.

76. Ibid., p. 78.

77. O.R., Vol. VIII, pp. 991–1002; Beitzell, *Point Lookout,* p. 41.

78. O.R., Vol. VII, p. 421.

79. Shotwell, "Prison Experiences," p. 340; *Confederate Veteran,* Vol. XIII (1905), p. 107.

80. Robertson, *Tenting Tonight,* pp. 118–19; O.R., Vol. VII, p. 421 (amount of fund in May 1864).

81. W.P.A., *Delaware* (New York: Hastings House, 1955), pp. 330–31.

82. O.R., Vol. VIII, p. 347, 986–1003; Brown, "Fort Delaware," p. 40.

83. O.R., Vol. VI, p. 235 and 281; W. Emerson Wilson, *Fort Delaware,* p. 16.

84. *Confederate Veteran,* Vol. XV (1907), p. 213; Vol. VI (1898), p. 266.

85. Ibid., Vol. XX (1912), p. 114; Vol. XXII (1914), p. 125; O.R., Vol. VI, p. 525.

86. *Confederate Veteran,* Vol. XX (1912), p. 114.

87. Dr. Handy gives a full account of his experiences at Fort Delaware and with the association in his book, *United States Bonds; or, Duress by Federal Authority,* (Baltimore: Turnbull Bros., 1874).

88. Shotwell, "Prison Experiences," p. 347.

89. O.R., Vol.. VIII, pp. 991–1003.

90. McLain, "Fort Warren," p. 44.

91. Harry Gilmore, *Four Years In The Saddle* (New York: Harper & Bros. Pub., 1866), p. 289.

92. O.R., Vol. VI, p. 1024; Gilmore, *Four Years In The Saddle,* p. 289.

93. Sangston, *Bastiles,* p. 84.

94. Ibid.; O.R., Vol. I, pp. 62 and 703.

95. O.R., Vol. VIII, pp. 986–1003.

96. Ibid.

97. Feuer, "Camp Morton," p. 47.

98. O.R., Vol. VII, p. 917.

99. Ibid., Vol. VII, pp. 96–98.

100. Frost, *Prison Journal,* pp. 253–54.

101. O.R., Vol. VII, p. 513.

102. Ibid., pp. 554–55.

103. Ibid., Vol. VIII, pp. 134, 999–1000.

104. Ibid., Vol. VIII, pp. 986–1003; Faust, *Encyclopedia,* pp. 110–11. Although the exact figures are unknown, the estimate that more than 9,000 were held here is based on the fact that more than 4,000 POWs were held prior to the prison being emptied and another 5,000 were held during its second stage of operation.

105. Ibid., Vol. VII, pp. 1258–59.

106. Ibid., Vol. VII, p. 1259.

107. Ibid., VIII, pp. 998–1000; Vol. VII, p. 1260.

108. Ibid.

109. Ibid., p. 1246; Charles C. Enslow papers, Library of Congress, Manuscripts Division, entry 279, letter dated December 14, 1864, the day before the shooting of the POW. Apparently, the turmoil between white POWs and black guards was plain to see and had been building for some time.

110. O.R., Vol. VIII, pp. 201 and 323.

111. Ibid., p. 323.

112. Ibid., pp. 323, 416–7; 1001–02.

113. Del Marth and Martha J. Marth, ed., *The Florida Almanac* (Gretna, FL: Pelican Publishing, 1983), p. 52; W.P.A., *A Guide to Key West* (New York: Hastings House, 1941), pp. 100–01; Samuel Carter III, *The Riddle of Dr. Mudd* (New York: G. P. Putnam's Sons, 1974), pp. 42–43; 224–29, hereafter referred to as Carter, *Dr. Mudd.*

114. Ibid.

115. Ronald H. Bailey, *Forward To Richmond* (Alexandria: Time-Life, 1983), p. 16; Carter, *Dr. Mudd,* p. 227.

116. Carter, *Dr. Mudd,* pp. 42–43, 224–29; W.P.A., *Guide to Key West,* p. 99.

117. Carter, *Dr. Mudd,* pp. 83, 221, 224, 226, 306.

118. Ibid., pp. 228 and 274.

119. Private letter, Eli Emigh to Maryreth A. Fowler, dated December 25, 1864. Civil War collection of Niles Schuh, Florida. Copy on file with author courtesy of Mr. Schuh; Carter, *Dr. Mudd,* p. 228. Although the O.R..fails to reflect one way or the other, we know that the 110th New York was there in December 1864, based on Emigh's letter, and was still there as late as 1867 when Dr. Mudd was incarcerated at the fort.

120. Carter, *Dr. Mudd,* p. 336; Sifakis, *Who Was Who,* pp. 266–67. It is believed that all five died at sea. No trace was ever found, and all five failed to return home after the war.

121. Carter, *Dr. Mudd,* pp. 227 and 244.

122. Ibid., pp. 243–44.

123. Parker, *Richmond's Prisons,* p. 59; Faust, *Encyclopedia,* p. 54; Miller, *Photographic History,* p. 72; O.R., Vol. VI, p. 1087; Ransom, *Andersonville,* p. 33. The exact numbers are unknown. At the time there were nearly 4,000 at Libby, 3,000 in the Castle Thunder complex, and according to Parker, "a record" 8,000 at Belle Isle, although other sources, including a Confederate physician who inspected the site, advised there had already been up to 10,000 confined on the island by March 1864 (O.R., Vol. VI, p. 1087). In addition, Richmond newspapers had announced as early as October 1863, the intention to build permanent shelter to house up to 20,000 POWs on the island (Parker, p. 52). That, of course, never took place, nor did the population ever reach that number.

124. O.R., Vol. VI, p. 1087.

125. Ibid., p. 1089. According to William A. Carrington, Confederate medical director, of the 2,200 Belle Isle POWs admitted to Richmond's hospitals in that month, February 1864, 590 died (O.R., Vol. VI, p. 1080).

126. Fosdick, *Five Hundred Days,* p. 13.

127. Ibid. Although some of Fosdick's assertions have been questioned by a number of historians, it is a documented fact that river water was pumped into Libby and Alton prisons and brought in directly at Danville and a number of other locations. For an unrelated source containing

corroborating testimony, see the Julius F. Ramsdell papers, entry 4403 in the Southern Historical Collection, Manuscripts Department, Wilson Library, University of North Carolina at Chapel Hill. Julius Ramsdell diary, August to October 1864 while held at Belle Isle. He complains of the black beans rations being boiled in dirty river water (p. 53) as well as the bread smelling strongly of spruce (p. 58). He later learned from a guard that the bread was made with "a preparation of spruce for rising" (p. 59).

128. Ransom, *Andersonville*, pp. 27–28.

129. Ibid., p. 30.

130. Fosdick, *Five Hundred Days*, p. 14; U.S. Sanitary Comm., *Narratives*, p. 143.

131. Fosdick, *Five Hundred Days*, p. 19.

132. Ransom, *Andersonville*, p. 50.

133. Robertson, *Tenting Tonight*, p. 135; Geoffrey C. Ward, *The Civil War: An Illustrated History* (New York: Alfred A. Knopf, 1991), p. 336; U.S. Sanitary Comm., *Narratives*, p. 58.

134. O.R., Vol. VI, pp. 588, 1084–89.

135. Ransom, *Andersonville*, p. 20.

136. *Confederate Veteran*, Vol. XII (1904), p. 23.

137. U.S. Sanitary Comm., *Narrative*, p. 160. For corroborating details see Cavada, *Libby Life*, pp. 195–97; Glazier, *The Capture*, pp. 81–82; Hesseltine, *Prisons: A Study*, p. 132; O.R., Vol. VIII, p. 344.

138. Putnam, *Prisoner of War*, pp. 27–28.

139. Ibid.; Cavada, *Libby Life*, p. 194.

140. Parker, *Richmond's Prisons*, pp. 49–50; Century Co., *Prison Escapes*, p. 191; Putnam, *Prisoner of War*, p. 41; U.S. Sanitary Comm., *Narratives*, p. 159.

141. O.R., Vol. VIII, p. 476; Robertson, "Houses of Horror," p. 329.

142. O.R., Vol. VI, pp. 888–90.

143. Ibid.; U.S. Christian Comm., *Record of the Federal Dead*, p 16.

144. Putnam, *Prisoner of War*, pp. 41–43.

145. U.S. Sanitary Comm., *Narratives*, p. 131.

146. Putnam, *Prisoner of War*, p. 67.

147. U.S. Christian Comm., *Record of the Federal Dead*, pp. 16, 27–38.

148. Sprague, *Lights and Shadows*, pp. 81–82; Cooper, *In and Out of Rebel Prisons*, p. 218; O.R., Vol. VIII, p. 33.

149. O.R., Vol. VIII, p. 33; Sprague, *Lights and Shadows*, p. 83.

150. O.R. Series I, Vol. XLVI, Pt. II, p. 1151; Vol. VIII, p. 139; Putnam, *Prisoner of War*, p. 40.

151. O.R., Series I, Vol. XLVI, Pt. II, p. 1151.

152. Ibid.

153. Mangum, "Salisbury Prison," pp. 752–54.

154. Ibid., p. 754.

155. Ibid., pp. 754–55.

156. Ibid., p. 756; Miller, *Photographic History*, p. 88.

157. Mangum, "Salisbury Prison," pp. 755–56.

158. Ibid., p. 753.

159. Ibid., p. 761; David Olando McRaven, "The Correspondence of David Olando McRaven and Amanda Nantz McRaven," ed. Louis A. Brown, *The North Carolina Review* (January 1949), p. 57, hereafter referred to as McRaven, "Correspondence"; Sidney Andrews, *The South Since the War* (Boston: Ticknor and Fields, 1866), p. 104.

160. Mangum, "Salisbury Prison," p. 766.

161. Ibid., pp. 753, 755–56.

162. Ibid., p. 758.

163. Junius H. Browne, *Four Years in Secessia* (Hartford: O. D. Case, 1865), pp. 315–18.

164. Mangum, "Salisbury Prison," pp. 758–59; Booth, *Dark Days of the Rebellion*, pp. 216–17; McRaven, "Correspondence," p. 67. Sources vary with anywhere from two to ten listed as killed in this mishap and the shooting that resulted, and an undetermined number injured.

165. McRaven, "Correspondence," pp. 57, 61, 86, 88, 93.

166. Ina W. VanNoppen, "The Significance of Stoneman's Last Raid," *The North Carolina Historical Review* (July 1961), p. 347.

167. Edmund Ryan, "Cahaba To Charleston: The Prison Odyssey of Lt. Edmund E. Ryan," ed. William M. Armstrong, comp. William B. Hesseltine, *Civil War Prisons* (Kent, OH: Kent State University Press, 1962), pp. 119–20, hereafter referred to as Ryan, "Cahaba to Charleston."

168. Hadley, *Seven Months A Prisoner,* p. 83; Miller, *Photographic History,* p. 161.

169. Glazier, *The Capture,* p. 158.

170. Hadley, *Seven Months A Prisoner,* p. 81.

171. Glazier, *The Capture,* p. 142.

172. Ibid., pp. 152–53.

173. Edmund Ryan, "Cahaba To Charleston," p. 120.

174. Hadley, *Seven Months A Prisoner,* p. 84.

175. Glazier, *The Capture,* pp. 160–61; Hadley, *Seven Months A Prisoner,* p. 84.

176. J. E. Houghland, "The 19th Iowa in Battle and in Prison," *The National Tribune Scrap Book No. 1* (Washington DC: The National Tribune, 1909), pp. 76–77, hereafter cited as Houghland, "The 19th Iowa."

177. O.R., Vol. VII, pp. 208–9.

178. Duganne, *Twenty Months,* p. 415; Houghland, "The 19th Iowa," p. 77.

179. Duganne, *Twenty Months,* p. 414.

180. Ibid., p. 382.

181. Scott, *Thirty-Second Iowa Infantry,* p. 363; Miller, *Photographic History,* p. 96.

182. Scott, *Thirty-Second Iowa Infantry,* p. 364.

183. Ibid., pp. 363-64.

184. Faust, *Encyclopedia,* p. 110; Evans, *Confederate Military History,* Vol. XI, pp. 115–16; Duganne, *Twenty Months,* pp. 333 and 338.

185. Duganne, *Twenty Months,* p. 377 and 381; Scott, *Thirty-Second Iowa Infantry,* p. 364.

186. O.R. Vol. VII, p. 913; Lurton D. Ingersoll, *Iowa and the Rebellion* (Philadelphia: J. B. Lippincott, 1866), p. 737.

187. Duganne, *Twenty Months,* p. 408; Evans, *Confederate Military History,* Vol. XI, p. 117; Faust, *Encyclopedia,* p. 110.

188. Duganne, *Twenty Months,* pp. 346–53.

189. Tucker/Tucker, "Great Escape," p. 37; Faust, *Encyclopedia,* p. 110.

190. Faust, *Encyclopedia,* p. 110; Tucker/Tucker, "Great Escape," p. 37; Scott, *Thirty-Second Iowa Infantry,* p. 364; Duganne, *Twenty Months,* pp. 346–53.

CHAPTER 10

1. Parker, *Richmond's Prisons,* p. 24; Steven A. Channing, *Confederate Ordeal* (Alexandria: Time–Life, 1984), p. 20; O.R., Vol. VII, pp. 1057–58. According to a number of contemporary accounts, Fort Delaware POWs apparently were forced to labor in the beginning, but after months in captivity, especially by mid-1864, they eagerly volunteered for the duty.

2. Mangum, "Salisbury Prison," p. 767; Ransom, *Andersonville,* p. 81.

3. McElroy, *Andersonville: A Story of Rebel Military Prisons,* p. 585. Emphasis added by author; Ranson, *Andersonville,* pp. 81 and 166.

4. Walter Brian Cisco, "Galvanized Rebels," *Civil War* (September to October, 1990) p. 50; O.R., Vol. VIII, p. 544.

5. O.R., Vol. VIII, pp. 554–55; Cisco, "Galvanized Rebels," p. 53.

6. McElroy, *Andersonville: A Story of Rebel Military Prisons,* p. 498; David Anderson Deaderick papers, Library of Congress, Manuscripts Division, entry 239, letter written home to family in Tennessee from Fort Delaware Prison, dated February 4, 1865. (Soldiers of both armies referred to those who switched sides as being galvanized.)

7. *New York Times,* 2 Mar 1865, p. 1:4; O.R., Vol. VIII, pp. 358–59; Cisco, "Galvanized Rebels," p. 49.

8. O.R., Vol. I, p. 65.
9. Ibid., Vol. II, pp. 226, 379–80; Vol. III, pp. 724–25.
10. Ibid., Vol. VIII, pp. 986–1001.
11. Mangum, "Salisbury Prison," p. 767.
12. O.R., Vol. VI, pp. 434–35.
13. O.R., Vol. VI, p. 663; Vol. VIII, p. 993.
14. Ibid., Vol. VII, p. 916–17.
15. Ibid.
16. Ibid.
17. Feuer, "Camp Morton," p. 47.
18. *Confederate Veteran,* Vol. XX (1912) pp. 296–97.
19. Ibid.; O.R., Vol. VI, p. 855.
20. Ibid.
21. Ibid., Vol. VII, p. 1230.
22. Ibid.
23. Putnam, *Prisoner of War,* pp. 50–55; Small, *Road to Richmond,* pp. 176–77; Cooper, *In and Out of Rebel Prisons,* pp. 227–28; Sprague, *Lights and Shadows,* pp. 113–19.
24. Grimes, *Confederate Mail Runner,* pp. 39–43, 87–93; Scharf, *History of St. Louis,* pp. 419–21; *Missouri Democrat,* 2 Sep 1862, p. 1:2.
25. Scharf, *History of St. Louis,* p. 420.
26. Ibid.; Grimes, *Confederate Mail Runner,* pp. 90–91, 93–96.
27. Ibid., p. 420, 180–85.
28. Ibid., p. 421, 166–70; O.R., Vol. VII, pp. 398–99.
29. Grimes, *Confederate Mail Runner,* p. 203. See also O.R., Vol. VIII, pp. 347 and 395, for verifying source.
30. J. W. Alexander, "An Escape From Fort Warren," *Histories of the Several Regiments and Battalions from North Carolina in the Great War 1861–'65,* ed. Walter Clark (Goldsboro: Nash Brothers, 1901), Vol. IV, p. 735.
31. Ibid., p. 736.
32. Ibid., p. 737.
33. Ibid., p. 738.
34. Ibid.; Rivenbark, "Fort Delaware," p. 729.
35. *Confederate Veteran,* Vol. III (1895), p. 172; Vol. XXII (1914), pp. 227, 279; Vol. XXV (1917), pp. 512–13.
36. Ibid., Vol. III, p. 172.
37. Ransom, *Andersonville,* p. 79.
38. Mangum, "Salisbury Prison," p. 752; Miller, *Photographic History,* pp. 144–46.
39. Scharf, *History of St. Louis,* pp. 419, 428–30.
40. Putnam, *Prisoner of War,* pp. 56, 60–65.
41. Ibid.
42. Keiley, *In Vinculis,* p. 78.
43. Keiley, *In Vinculis,* pp. 73–74.
44. England, *Rock Island,* pp. 17–18.
45. Robertson, "Houses of Horror," p. 333; Putnam, *Prisoner of War,* p. 59.
46. Isham, *Prisoners of War,* p. 206; Boggs, *Eighteen Months,* pp. 12–13. Various other accounts place the number who escaped anywhere from seventy-five to eighty-six.
47. Scharf, *History of St. Louis,* p. 420.
48. I. N. Johnson, *Four Months in Libby, and the Campaign Against Atlanta* (Cincinnati: R. P. Thompson, 1864) p. 55. The third longest documented tunnel (sixty-six feet) was excavated over a two-month period by Berry Benson, Company H, 1st South Carolina Infantry, and nine other POWs at Elmira Prison in the fall of 1864.
49. Wells, *Famous Escapes,* p. 150.
50. Century Co., *Prison Escapes,* p. 218.

51. Ibid., pp. 218–19; Johnson, *Four Months in Libby,* pp. 95–96; Cavada, *Libby Life,* p. 172.

52. Cavada, *Libby Life,* p. 172.

53. Glazier, *The Capture,* pp. 75–76.

54. Ibid., pp. 71–72; Cavada, *Libby Life,* p. 173; Century Co., *Famous Escapes,* p. 234. See also O.R., Vol. VI, pp. 953, 966, 980.

55. King, *Three Hundred Days,* p. 85.

56. Wells, *Famous Escapes,* p. 149; Miller, *Photographic History,* p. 148; Glazier, *The Capture,* pp. 132–33.

57. Robert H. Moore II, "Breakout!" *Civil War Times Illustrated* (November to December 1991): 56. According to prisoner Washington B. Traweek, of the "Jeff Davis" Artillery Co. of Alabama, who was one of the ten POWs involved in the Benson tunnel (see n. 48), twenty-eight tunnels were under construction at one time at Elmira during the fall of 1864.

58. Glazier, *The Escape,* pp. 195–96.

59. Putnam, *Prisoner of War,* pp. 33–34.

60. Barziza, *Adventures of a POW,* p.110.

61. Ibid., p. 112.

62. Ibid., p. 115.

63. Ibid., p. 116. Another Halifax operative was James P. Holcombe.

64. Ibid., p. 117.

65. Ibid.

66. Ibid., p. 118. Additional Bermuda contacts were Norman S. Walker and John T. Bourne, Confederate agents stationed there.

67. O.R., Vol. IV, p. 37.

68. Barziza, *Adventures of a POW,* pp. 80–81. Based on "Johnson's Island Plot, An Historical Narrative of the Conspiracy of the Confederates, in 1864, To Capture the U. S. Steamship Michigan on Lake Erie, and Release the Prisoners of War in Sandusky Bay," by Frederick J. Shepard, *Publications of the Buffalo Historical Society,* Vol. IX (1906), pp. 1–51; *New York Times,* 9 Nov 1864, p. 5:3.

69. Ibid.

70. Barziza, *Adventures of a POW,* p. 81.

71. O.R., Vol. VII, p. 842.

72. Ibid., pp. 901–6; Barziza, *Adventures of a POW,* pp. 80–81, based on "Johnson's Island Plot," by Shepard.

73. Ibid.; *The New York Times,* 9 Nov 1864, p. 5:3; Hesseltine, *Prisons: A Study,* pp. 108–9; Alan Axelrod, *The War Between The Spies* (New York: Atlantic Monthly Press, 1992), pp. 240–43.

74. O.R., Vol. VII, p. 901.

75. Ibid.

76. Barziza, *Adventures of a POW,* p. 80; O.R., Vol. VII, pp. 904–5.

77. O.R., Vol. VII, pp. 901–6; Vol. VIII, p. 881.

78. Boatner, C. W. Dictionary, pp. 460–61.

CHAPTER 11

1. *Confederate Veteran,* Vol. XX (1912), p. 327; Vol. XXXIV (1926), p. 379; Sherrill, *A Soldier's Story,* p. 15.

2. O.R., Vol. IV, pp. 67–74.

3. Ibid., p. 70.

4. Ibid., Vol. VII, p. 152 and 157.

5. Ibid., p. 425.

6. O.R., Vol. VII, pp. 152, 157, 425; Keiley, *In Vinculis,* pp. 129–30; Matthew S. Walls, "Northern Hell On Earth," *America's Civil War* (March 1991), p. 25.

7. Keiley, *In Vinculis,* p. 129; James I. Robertson, Jr., "The Scourge of Elmira," *Civil War Prisons,* ed. William B. Hesseltine (Kent, OH: Kent State University Press, 1962), p. 83.

8. Keiley, *In Vinculis*, p. 129.

9. Ibid., pp. 130–31.

10. Ibid., pp. 131–32.

11. Ibid., p. 133.

12. Ibid., p. 155; O.R., Vol. VII, pp. 488–89; Keiley, *In Vinculis*, p. 155.

13. O.R., Vol. VII, p. 505.

14. Robertson, "The Scourge of Elmira," p. 84; Walls, "Northern Hell On Earth," p. 25; O.R., Vol. VII, pp. 505, 997–98; *The Civil War News*, April 1991, p. 37:1; Robertson, "The Scourge of Elmira," p. 92.

15. Keiley, *In Vinculis*, p. 136.

16. O.R., Vol. VII, pp. 560, 584, 918–19, 1136; Vol. VIII, pp. 997–98; Robertson, *Soldiers Blue and Gray*, p. 205; Robertson, *Tenting Tonight*, p. 129.

17. O.R., Vol. VII, p. 786.

18. Ibid., p. 604.

19. Keiley, *In Vinculis*, p. 145. Although Keiley is referring to Sanger, Eastman was ousted that same month, several weeks before Sanger (O.R., Vol. VII, pp. 786 and 919).

20. O.R., Vol. VII, pp. 918–19, 1173.

21. Ibid., Vol. VIII, pp. 998–99.

22. Ibid., Vol. VII, p. 1092.

23. Ibid., pp. 1092–93.

24. *Confederate Veteran*, Vol. XXXIV (1926), p. 379; Keiley, *In Vinculis*, p. 146; Walls, "Northern Hell On Earth," p. 26.

25. *Confederate Veteran*, Vol. XXXIV, (1926), p. 379. A number of Elmira women established a prison school and entered the compound almost daily to conduct classes.

26. Sherrill, *A Soldier's Story*, pp. 10–11; *Confederate Veteran*, Vol. XX (1912), p. 327.

27. Keiley, *In Vinculis*, p.146; Walls, "Northern Hell On Earth," p. 26.

28. *Confederate Veteran*, Vol. XX (1912), p. 327; Sherrill, *A Soldier's Story*, p.12.

29. Keiley, *In Vinculis*, p. 129.

30. O.R., Vol. VII, p. 1136.

31. *Confederate Veteran*, Vol. XXXIV (1926), p. 379.

32. Ibid., Vol. XX (1912), p. 327; Walls, "Northern Hell On Earth," p. 27; William Attmore Papers, entry 3607 in the Southern Historical Collection, Manuscripts Department, Wilson Library, University of North Carolina at Chapel Hill. Letter from Sitgreaves Attmore dated February 8, 1865, while confined at Elmira Prison, "3rd Barracks, Ward 44."

33. O.R., Vol. VIII, pp. 999–1001.

34. O.R., Vol. VIII, pp. 419–20.

35. Ibid.

36. John Kaufhold, "The Elmira Observatory," *Civil War Times Illustrated* (July, 1977), p. 35; Keiley, *In Vinculis*, pp. 156–57.

37. Ibid.; King, *Three Hundred Days*, pp. 37–38; *Confederate Veteran*, Vol. XXXIV (1926), p. 379; Walls, "Northern Hell On Earth," p. 27; Robertson, "The Scourge Of Elmira," p. 94.

38. MacRae, "Morris Island," p. 713.

39. Busbee, "Under Fire At Morris Island," p. 620.

40. Murray, *The Immortal Six Hundred*, pp. 70 and 72.

41. Busbee, "Under Fire At Morris Island," p. 621.

42. Murray, *The Immortal Six Hundred*, p. 272; MacRae, "Morris Island," p. 715. In all the memoirs and books, no one seems to know how Ellerson was able to slip away unnoticed. Some sources have since wrongly indicated the name to be J. H. Ellison of the 2nd Alabama. Regarding Woolford's escape, some sources indicate that name to be Woodford, and even Murray used the two different spellings on two different pages referring to the same incident; however, the official roll of the POWs on board at the trip's beginnings show no other name but Woolford.

43. MacRae, "Morris Island, pp. 715–16.

44. Murray, *The Immortal Six Hundred*, p. 92–93; Busbee, "Under Fire At Morris Island," p. 621.

45. Murray, *The Immortal Six Hundred*, p. 95.
46. Ibid. Busbee and MacRae's memoirs agree that Hallowell was immensely disliked by the POWs.
47. MacRae, "Morris Island," p. 715; Busbee, "Under Fire At Morris Island," p. 622.
48. Murray, *The Immortal Six Hundred*, p. 101; MacRae, "Morris Island," p. 716.
49. Murray, *The Immortal Six Hundred*, p. 101.
50. Ibid., p. 100.
51. Ibid., p. 268.
52. Busbee, "Under Fire At Morris Island," pp. 623–24.
53. Murray, *The Immortal Six Hundred*, p. 97.
54. Ibid., p. 186.
55. O.R., Vol. VIII, pp. 1001–3.
56. Ibid., p. 481.
57. Ibid., Vol. VII, p. 595.
58. Ibid., Vol. VIII, p. 1001; *Confederate Veteran*, Vol. XXII (1914), p. 500.
59. Ibid.
60. O.R., Vol. VIII, pp. 665, 1001–3.
61. Ibid., Vol. VI, p. 1124.
62. William O. Bryant, *Cahaba Prison and the Sultana Disaster* (Tuscaloosa: University of Alabama Press, 1990), pp. 17 and 19, hereafter referred to as Bryant, *Cahaba Prison;* O.R., Vol. VI, p. 1124.
63. O.R., Vol. VI, p. 1124.
64. Ibid.
65. John L. Walker, *Cahaba Prison and the Sultana Disaster* (Hamilton, OH: Brown & Whitaker, 1910), pp. 5–6, hereafter referred to as Walker, *Cahaba.*
66. Bryant, *Cahaba Prison*, p. 20.
67. Ibid., pp. 28–29. The spelling of the town's name fluctuated between Cahawba and Cahaba from its beginning, as did the name of the river nearby. Cahaba was eventually settled upon in later years. (Bryant, *Cahaba Prison*, pp. 25–26).
68. Peter A. Brannon, "The Cahawba Military Prison, 1863–1865," *The Alabama Review* (July 1950), p. 172, hereafter referred to as Brannon, "Cahawba;" Bryant, *Cahaba Prison*, p. 42; Jesse Hawes, *Cahaba: A Story of Captive Boys in Blue* (New York: Burr Printing House, 1888), p. 250, hereafter referred to as Hawes, *Cahaba.*
69. Walker, *Cahaba*, p. 13.
70. Hawes, *Cahaba*, pp. 253–54.
71. Brannon, "Cahawba," p. 165; Bryant, *Cahaba Prison*, p. 24.
72. Ibid., pp. 32, 167–68, 171; Hawes, *Cahaba*, p. 446; James W. Elliott, *Transport To Disaster* (New York: Holt, Rinehart and Winston, 1962), p. 58; Hesseltine, *Prisons: A Study*, p. 116.
73. Hawes, *Cahaba*, p. 210 and 212.
74. Brannon, "Cahawba," pp. 169 and 173; Bryant, *Cahaba Prison*, pp. 65–69.
75. O.R., Vol. VII, pp. 1001–2. Elsewhere such practices occurred only during the less crowded first phase of military prison incarcerations, before the collapse of the cartel.
76. Bryant, *Cahaba Prison*, pp. 79–89.
77. O.R., Vol. VIII, p. 117.
78. *New York Times*, 8 Apr 1865, p. 3:3; Hawes, *Cahaba*, p. 448.
79. Ransom, *Andersonville*, pp. 65–67.
80. Miller, *Photographic History*, p. 74; O.R., Vol. VI, p. 558.
81. Miller, *Photographic History*, pp. 74 and 76; Andrews, *The South Since the War*, pp. 300 and 302; Peggy Sheppard, *Andersonville Georgia U.S.A.* (Andersonville: Sheppard Publications, 1973), p. 43; David E. Roth, ed., *Blue & Gray Magazine*, Vol. III, Issue 3 (1985), p. 11, hereafter cited as Roth, *Blue & Gray; New York Times*, 26 Nov 1865, p. 1:1.
82. The Andersonville Guild, *Welcome To Andersonville* pamphlet (n.p., n.d.), p. 1. Distributed by the local historical preservation society. Copy on file with author. Additional research has uncovered other contemporary sources that insist the town was named after General Robert

Anderson's father. Genealogical research into this aspect might prove interesting, especially if he worked for the railroad.

83. O.R., Vol. VI, pp. 965–66, 993; Vol. VII, p. 438; Ransom, *Andersonville*, pp. 53 and 89; McElroy, *Andersonville: A Story of Rebel Military Prisons*, p. 315. Since then some sources have indicated W. Sidney Winder was the first commandant and Persons was the second; however, since the first POWs didn't arrive until February 25, and Persons was assigned to the post on the 17th and officially assigned commandant on the 26th, Sidney was never commandant over anything but a work detail and an empty stockade. Thus Persons was the first commandant of the prison as a POW facility.

84. Elliott, *The Southern Soldier Boy,* p. 40.

85. Sheppard, *Andersonville Georgia U.S.A.,* p. 17; Roth, *Blue & Gray,* p. 9.

86. Roth, *Blue & Gray,* p. 11.

87. The original estimate of 8,000 to 10,000 was actually with barracks. The sixteen-and-one-half-acre pen, without barracks, had a capacity of only 6,000.

88. Roth, *Blue & Gray,* p. 9; McElroy, *Andersonville: A Story of Rebel Military Prisons,* p. 19.

89. Ransom, *Andersonville,* pp. 27, 71, 83; Marvel, *Andersonville: The Last Depot,* p. 56.

90. Boggs, *Eighteen Months,* p. 32.

91. Ibid.

92. Ransom, *Andersonville,* p. 92.

93. Boggs, *Eighteen Months,* p. 32.

94. Fosdick, *Five Hundred Days,* p. 37.

95. Ovid L. Futch, *History of Andersonville Prison* (Gainesville: University of Florida Press, 1968), p. 49.

96. McElroy, *Andersonville: A Story of Rebel Military Prisons,* pp. 106–8.

97. Ransom, *Andersonville,* pp. 69, 77–78; Marvel, *Andersonville: The Last Depot,* pp. 65–67.

98. McElroy, *Andersonville: A Story of Rebel Military Prisons,* p. 141; Marvel, *Andersonville: The Last Depot,* p. 50. Marvel's research recovered the POW's name for history. It was Caleb Coplan, an Ohioan captured at Chickamauga. According to Marvel, the incident occurred on April 9, 1864.

99. Ransom, *Andersonville,* p. 122.

100. Ibid.; Brooks, *Civil War Medicine,* pp. 6 and 127.

101. Ransom, *Andersonville,* p. 83; McElroy, *Andersonville: A Story of Rebel Military Prisons,* p. 206; Robertson, *Soldiers Blue and Gray,* p. 203; Marvel, *Andersonville: The Last Depot,* pp. 97–100, 141–44.

102. Sheppard, *Andersonville Georgia U.S.A.,* pp. 38–39; *Confederate Veteran,* Vol. XXIII (1915), p. 318; O.R., Vol. VIII, pp. 789 and 791. According to one source, Captain Hunt's first name might have been Herbert instead of Harry.

103. *Confederate Veteran,* Vol. XXIII (1915), p. 318.

104. England, *Rock Island Prison Barracks,* p. 37. Local newspapers were referring to Rock Island Prison as the Andersonville of the North by this time, mid-1864, which might be further basis for the Andersonville legend.

105. Ransom, *Andersonville,* p. 132; Glazier, *The Capture,* pp. 323–24.

106. McElroy, *Andersonville: A Story of Rebel Military Prisons,* p. 321; O.R., Vol. VIII, p. 532.

107. Hadley, *Seven Months A Prisoner,* p. 59.

108. Ibid., p. 62.

109. Ibid., pp. 67–68; Glazier, *The Capture,* pp. 103, 106, 111; O.R., Vol. VIII, p. 765.

110. Hadley, *Seven Months A Prisoner,* p. 52.

111. Ibid., p. 70.

112. Glazier, *The Capture,* pp. 104 and 111; O.R., Vol. VIII, p. 765. The guards were possibly the 5th Georgia Reserves at this time.

113. Hadley, *Seven Months A Prisoner,* p. 65.

114. Ibid., pp. 65–66.

115. Ibid., p. 70.

116. Ibid., p. 71; Glazier, *The Capture,* p. 106.

117. Hadley, *Seven Months A Prisoner*, p. 78.
118. Ransom, *Andersonville*, pp. 135–37.
119. Hadley, *Seven Months A Prisoner*, p. 78; Glazier, *The Capture*, p. 128.
120. Glazier, *The Capture*, p. 131.
121. McElroy, *Andersonville: A Story of Rebel Military Prisons*, p. 401.
122. Ibid., pp. 402 and 409; Ransom, *Andersonville*, pp. 145 and 152.
123. O.R., Vol. VII, p. 611.
124. Ibid.
125. Hadley, *Seven Months A Prisoner*, p. 88; Glazier, *The Capture*, p. 169.
126. Hadley, *Seven Months A Prisoner*, p. 87.
127. Ibid., p. 89.
128. O.R., Vol. VII, p. 1046; Hesseltine, *Prisons: A Study*, pp. 165–66.
129. Glazier, *The Capture*, p. 174.
130. O.R., Vol. VII, p. 1184.
131. Hadley, *Seven Months A Prisoner*, p. 91.
132. Ibid., pp. 91–92.
133. Ibid., pp. 93–94; Glazier, *The Capture*, p. 184.
134. Ibid., p. 94; O.R., Vol. VII, pp. 1196 and 1179.
135. O.R., Vol. VII, pp. 1196–97.
136. Ibid., Vol. VIII, p. 213; Columbia Chamber of Commerce, *Greater Columbia* pamphlet (n.p., n.d.), p. 12; Sifakis, *Who Was Who*, p. 266; Rawley W. Martin Papers, entry 3401 in the Southern Historical Collection, Manuscripts Department, Wilson Library, University of North Carolina at Chapel Hill. Various letters from engineer John A. Hayden to Rawley Martin, "Commanding prisons of South Carolina" regarding a number of strategic locations examined within the state for establishing a new prison.
137. O.R., Vol. VIII, p. 213.
138. Ibid., p. 463.
139. Andrews, *The South Since The War*, p. 191.
140. O.R., Vol. VII, pp. 817 and 972.
141. Andrews, *The South Since The War*, p. 192; O.R., Vol. VII, p. 972; Fosdick, *Five Hundred Days*, pp. 80–100; Boggs, *Eighteen Months*, pp. 57–62; McElroy, *Andersonville: A Story of Rebel Military Prisons*, pp. 524–33, 262–3.
142. *New York Times*, 17 Dec 1864, p. 4:6; Andrews, *The South Since The War*, p. 192.
143. Fosdick, *Five Hundred Days*, p. 89; Boggs, *Eighteen Months*, p. 57.
144. O.R., Vol. VII, p. 973.
145. Boggs, *Eighteen Months*, p. 60; Fosdick, *Five Hundred Days*, pp. 87–8.
146. Boggs, *Eighteen Months*, p. 62.
147. McElroy, *Andersonville: A Story of Rebel Military Prisons*, pp. 558–59; Fosdick, *Five Hundred Days*, p. 85.
148. Kellogg, *Life and Death in Rebel Prisons*, p. 320; Fosdick, *Five Hundred Days*, p. 98; O.R., Vol. VII, p. 1197; McElroy, *Andersonville: A Story of Rebel Military Prisons*, p. 579.
149. McElroy, *Andersonville: A Story of Rebel Military Prisons*, p. 544.
150. Ibid., pp. 576–77.
151. Fosdick, *Five Hundred Days*, p. 131; Andrews, *The South Since The War*, p. 195; *New York Times*, 17 Dec 1864, p. 1:6; U.S. Department of the Interior, *Andersonville* pamphlet (GPO, 1991) p. 1; O.R., Vol. VII, p. 979.
152. McElroy, *Andersonville: A Story of Rebel Military Prisons*, pp. 535–36, 544–45; Boggs, *Eighteen Months*, p. 64; Fosdick, *Five Hundred Days*, p. 100; *Minonk News-Dispatch*, 22 June 1933, p. 1:1, 11 Aug 1949, 21 Feb 1974 (clippings, n. pn.)
153. William C. Harllee Papers, entry 1550 in the Southern Historical Collection, Manuscripts Department, Wilson Library, University of North Carolina at Chapel Hill. Letter from Louisa Jane Harllee to her cousin Ann Eliza Harllee; McElroy, *Andersonville: A Story of Rebel Military Prisons*, pp. 546–47, based on a March 1, 1869, U.S. Government report.
154. O.R., Vol. VII, pp. 509 and 565.

155. Ransom, *Andersonville*, p. 154; McElroy, *Andersonville: A Story of Rebel Military Prisons*, p. 456; Hesseltine, *Prisons: A Study*, p. 157. According to Ransom, the prison still wasn't completed when he arrived on October 25.

156. McElroy, *Andersonville: A Story of Rebel Military Prisons*, pp. 456–57.

157. Ibid., pp. 458–59.

158. Ransom, *Andersonville*, p. 164.

159. Ibid., p. 163; Hesseltine, *Prisons: A Study*, p. 157; McElroy, *Andersonville: A Story of Rebel Military Prisons*, p. 460.

160. Ransom, *Andersonville*, p. 163; O.R., Vol. VIII, pp. 754 and 765.

161. O.R., Vol. VII, p. 1204.

162. Ransom, *Andersonville*, pp. 203–5.

163. O.R., Vol. VII, p. 1204.

164. McElroy, *Andersonville: A Story of Rebel Military Prisons*, p. 493.

165. Ransom, *Andersonville*, p. 204.

166. Ibid.

167. O.R., Vol. VIII, pp. 209–13, 218, 224–25, 234, 238–39, 244–45, 249–57. Winder died from a heart attack on February 7, 1865.

168. Ibid., p. 218.

169. McElroy, *Andersonville: A Story of Rebel Military Prisons*, p. 587.

170. Andrews, *The South Since The War*, p. 194.

CHAPTER 12

1. Robertson, *Tenting Tonight*, p. 122; Mangum, "Salisbury Prison," p. 756.

2. Ibid., pp. 122 and 753; O.R., Vol. VIII, pp. 258, 401, 403, 405, 637.

3. Ransom, *Andersonville*, p. 67.

4. Bailey, *Private Chapter of the War* (St. Louis: G. I. Jones & Co., 1880), p. 21; Ransom, *Andersonville*, p. 39.

5. Ransom, *Andersonville*, p. 39.

6. Williamson, *Prison Life*, p. 67.

7. Boggs, *Eighteen Months*, p. 34.

8. Fosdick, *Five Hundred Days*, p. 102.

9. Boggs, *Eighteen Months*, p. 41.

10. Ransom, *Andersonville*, p. 91.

11. James B. Mitchell papers, Library of Congress, Manuscripts Division, entry 637, letter written home to parents from Johnson's Island, dated February 9, 1865.

12. Ransom, *Andersonville*, p. 117.

13. Elliott, *The Southern Soldier Boy*, p. 52.

14. Booth, *Dark Days of the Rebellion*, p. 285.

15. Ibid.

16. Mangum, "Salisbury Prison," p. 769.

17. Ibid., p. 770.

18. Parker, *Richmond's Prisons*, p. 67.

19. *Philadelphia Inquirer*, 10 Apr 1865, p. 1:3–4.

20. *New York Times*, 10 Apr 1865, p. 1:6.

21. Putnam, *A Prisoner of War*, p. 29; *New York Times*, 24 May 1865, p. 4:6; Parker, *Richmond's Prisons*, p. 68. Nero was last known to be in the possession of Sidney Munn in New York City.

22. *New York Times*, 10 Apr 1865, p. 1:6, 21 May 1865, p. 3:1; *Philadelphia Inquirer*, 12 Apr 1865, p. 1:4; *Evening Star* (Washington, D.C.), 15 Apr 1865, p. 1:6; Hesseltine, *Prisons: A Study*, pp. 258–59.

23. *New York Times*, 10 Apr 1865, p. 1:5; *Philadelphia Inquirer*, 10 Apr 1865, p. 1:3; *Daily Picayune* (New Orleans, LA), 5 May 1865, p. 1:6; Miller, *Photographic History*, p. 180.

24. Gilmore, *Four Years In The Saddle*, p. 291.

25. *New York Times*, 10 Apr 1865, p. 1:5; *Philadelphia Inquirer*, 10 Apr 1865, p. 1:3; O.R., Vol. VIII, p. 782–83.

26. O.R., Vol. VIII, p. 1002.

27. *Confederate Veteran*, Vol. XIX (1911), p. 219; Vol. XXII (1914), p. 500.

28. Head, *Sixteenth Regiment*, p. 478; Elliott, *The Southern Soldier Boy*, p. 49.

29. *Daily Picayune*, 5 May 1865, p. 1:6; Bryant, *Cahaba Prison*, pp. 127–28.

30. O.R., Vol. VIII, p. 1003.

31. Milner family papers and interview with descendants, June 15, 1995.

32. Sigaud, *Belle Boyd*, p. 182.

33. *Confederate Veteran*, Vol. XXI (1913), p. 110.

34. Elliott, *The Southern Soldier Boy*, p. 50; James B. Mitchell papers, Library of Congress, Manuscripts Division, entry 637, letter written home to his parents. Mitchell was twenty years old upon his release.

35. E. W. McIntosh, "Patronize An Old 'Vet,'" *Civil War Times Illustrated*, (February 1976), p. 45.

36. King, *Three Hundred Days*, pp. 98–99.

37. Small, *Road to Richmond*, p. 185.

38. Mary A. H. Gay, *Life in Dixie During the War* (Atlanta: Charles P. Byrd, 1897), p. 60.

39. Medford-McCracken family papers.

40. O.R., Vol. VIII, pp. 1003–4.

41. Ibid., p. 781.

42. Brooks, *Civil War Medicine*, p. 85. Chloroform, when available, was the accepted contemporary remedy for cleaning wounds to prevent gangrene. The use of maggots for such purposes is referred to as "chemical debridement." See also Cunniungham, *Doctors in Gray*, p. 234.

43. O.R., Vol. VIII, pp. 537–38, 773–74, 792–93, 783–94; Sheppard, *Andersonville Georgia U.S.A.*, p. 31.

44. O.R., Vol. VIII, pp. 83–84, 279–82, 398–400, 416. Beall's trial began on January 17; within five weeks he was found guilty and hanged.

45. Clement Eaton, *A History of the Southern Confederacy* (New York: McMillan, 1954), p. 104; Vernon H. Crow, *Storm In The Mountains* (Cherokee, NC: Press of the Museum of the Cherokee Indian, 1982), pp. 98–99; Sifakis, *Who Was Who*, p. 215.

46. O.R., Vol. VIII, pp. 782–83, 819, 881–82, 956–60; J. G. DeRoulhac, *Reconstruction in North Carolina* (Gloucester, MA: Peter Smith, 1964), pp. 163–65.

47. Williamson, "Military Prisons in the Civil War," p. 330.

48. *Civil War Times*, February/March, 1995, p. 85:1.

49. *Confederate Veteran*, Vol. XXXI (1923), p. 18.

50. Miller, *Photographic History*, p. 124; Sifakis, *Who Was Who*, p. 374.

51. Gay, *Life in Dixie During the War*, p. 60.

52. Anton Gill, *The Journey Back From Hell* (New York: William Morrow, 1988) pp. 6, 62–64, 99, 472. During the Civil War, of course, post-tramatic stress syndrome went untreated and unrecognized, but today we know that POWs suffered long after they emerged from the prison pens.

53. Fulbright family papers and interview, May 26, 1990.

54. Ransom, *Andersonville*, pp. 158–59.

EPILOGUE

1. Andrews, *The South Since the War*, pp. 304–5.

2. *New York Times*, 26 Nov 1865, p. 1:1; Sheppard, *Andersonville Georgia U.S.A.*, p. 43.

3. U.S. Department of the Interior, *Andersonville* pamphlet (GPO, 1991), p. 2, and author's personal visit to the site, May 2, 1992.

4. *New York Times,* 26 Nov 1865, p. 1:1; Dorance Atwater, *Prisoners Who Died At Andersonville Prison, Compiled by Private Dorance Atwater* (Andersonville: National Society of Andersonville, 1865), more commonly referred to as "the Atwater Report," p. VI; W.P.A. *Georgia* (Athens: University of Georgia Press, 1940), p. 330. Though the prison stockade contained only twenty-six-and-one-half acres, the cemetery contains twenty-eight. Today, the Andersonville Prison Historical Park contains a total of eighty acres.

5. Andrews, *The South Since the War,* p. 193.

6. Bryant, *Cahaba Prison,* p. 25.

7. Ibid., p. 67; *The Civil War News,* January/February 1991, p. 22:4.

8. O.R., Vol. VIII, p. 659.

9. Miller, *Photographic History,* pp. 163 and 165.

10. *Charleston News and Courier,* 6 May 1946, p. 10:1.

11. Andrews, The South Since the War, p. 105.

12. Parker, *Richmond's Prisons,* p. 68.

13. National Historical Society, *Image of War,* pp. 396–97.

14. Parker, *Richmond's Prisons,* p. 69.

15. Ibid.; *St. Louis Globe-Democrat,* 7 May 1889, p. 4:6; *New York Times,* 8 May 1889, p. 5:5; Putnam, *Prisoner of War,* p. 24; Parker, *Richmond's Prisons,* p. 69; *New York Times,* 28 Jan 1892, p. 5:5; Hesseltine, *Prisons: A Study,* pp. 257–58.

16. Parker, *Richmond's Prisons,* p. 70.

17. Ibid.

18. O.R., Vol. VIII, pp. 661, 700–701, 1003.

19. Ibid.; Scharf, *History of St. Louis,* p. 421.

20. T. R. Walker, "Rock Island Prison Barracks," *Civil War Prisons,* ed. William B. Hesseltine (Kent, OH: Kent State University Press, 1962), p. 59.

21. Stephens, *Rock Island Deaths,* pp. 51–52.

22. O.R., Vol. VIII, p. 714; *Site of Camp Douglas,* pp. 7–8.

23. O.R., Vol. VIII, pp. 986–1003; U.S. Department of Interior, *Andersonville,* pamphlet, p. 1.

24. *Confederate Veteran,* Vol. IV (1896), pp. 246–47; Vol. V (1897), p. 455; Vol. XX (1912), p. 297.

25. O.R., Vol. VIII, pp. 701 and 739; Shepherd, *Narrative of Prison Life,* p. 10.

26. *Civil War News,* January/February 1991, p. 3:1; Oct 1991, p. 2:1.

27. O.R., Vol. VIII, p. 986–1003.

28. Feuer, "Camp Morton," pp. 48–49; *Civil War News,* November/December 1991, p. 34:1.

29. Ibid.

30. *Confederate Veteran* Vol. XX (1912), p. 327; Vol. XXXIV (1926), p. 379; Robertson, "The Scourge Of Elmira," p. 86.

31. *Civil War News,* January/February 1992, p. 52:5.

32. Beitzell, *Point Lookout,* p. 120. This is, without a doubt, the most accurate figure. Mr. Beitzell extensively researched the prison's history and has documented that the O.R. totals concerning deaths are wrong. Later, increased, figures placed on monuments erected at the site were also incorrect. See pages 115–75 and 198–99 of his book for details.

33. W.P.A., *Maryland* (New York: Oxford University Press, 1940), p. 482; Beitzell, *Point Lookout,* p. 103.

34. W.P.A., *Guide to Key West,* pp. 102–3; Marth/Marth, *The Florida Almanac,* p. 53.

35. W.P.A., *Maryland,* p. 256.

36. Francis K. Howard, editor of the *Baltimore Daily Exchange,* was the grandson of Francis Scott Key. Howard was arrested by Federal authorities in the early morning hours of September 14, 1861, and his house was ransacked during an extensive search in front of his wife and children; afterward he was hustled off for incarceration in the fort.

37. McLain, "Fort Warren," p. 46.

38. W.P.A., *Massachusetts* (Boston: Houghton Mifflin, 1937), pp. 141–42; *New York Times,* 14 Aug 1960, p. II 23:2.

39. *New York Times,* 14 Aug 1960, p. II 23:2.

40. Ann Brown, "Fort Delaware," p. 40; O.R., Vol. VIII, p. 673.

41. Ann Brown, "Fort Delaware," p. 40.

42. *Confederate Veteran,* Vol. XIII (1905), pp. 108–9.

43. O.R., Vol. VIII, pp. 990–1004; Although monthly returns reflect only 50 deaths at the prison (combined with Carroll Prison), other sources verify 457 during the existence of the facility. By the end of the war, 377 had been buried nearby. In later years additional graves were discovered in the vicinity.

44. *Confederate Veteran,* Vol. XII (1904), p. 201.

45. W.P.A. *Washington City and Capital* (Washington, DC: GPO, 1937), pp. 438–39, 605–6.

46. *Confederate Veteran,* Vol. XII (1904), p. 201.

47. Ibid.

48. O.R., Vol. VIII, p. 1004.

49. *New York Times,* 2 Apr 1949, p. 17:1; 3 Feb 1960, p. 35:6; W.P.A. *New York City Guide* (New York: Oxford University Press, 1939), pp. 413–15.

50. *New York Times,* 16 Oct 1898, p. I.M. 6:1; 22 July 1948, pp. 25:3; Henry Collins Brown, ed., *Valentine's Manual of Old New York* (New York: Gracie Mansion Pub., 1924), pp. 188–89; W.P.A., *New York City Guide,* pp. 413–15.

APPENDIX A

1. O.R., Vol. VIII, pp. 62–63, 767–68.

BIBLIOGRAPHY

PRIMARY SOURCES

Published Material

Alexander, J. W. "An Escape From Fort Warren." *Histories of the Several Regiments and Battalions from North Carolina in the Great War 1861–'65.* Edited by Walter Clark. Vol. 4. Goldsboro, NC: Nash Brothers, 1901.

Andrews, Sidney. *The South Since the War.* Boston: Ticknor and Fields, 1866.

Atwater, Dorance. *Prisoners Who Died At Andersonville Prison, Compiled by Private Dorance Atwater.* Andersonville: National Society of Andersonville, 1865.

Bailey, George W. *Private Chapter of the War.* St. Louis: G. I. Jones, 1880.

Barber, Lucius W. *Army Memories of Lucius W. Barber, Company "D," 15th Illinois Volunteer Infantry.* Chicago: J. M. W. Jones, 1894.

Barziza, D. U. *Decimus et Ultimus Barziza, The Adventures of a Prisoner of War, 1863–1864.* Edited by R. Henderson Shuffler. Austin: University of Texas Press, 1964. Originally published anonymously in 1865.

Barton, D. S. *Three Years with Quantrell: A true story told by his scout John McCorkle.* Armstrong, MO: Armstrong Herald Printing, 1914.

Bean, R. T. "Seventeen Months in Camp Douglas." *Civil War Quarterly* 10 (September 1987).

Boggs, Sam S. *Eighteen Months A Prisoner Under The Rebel Flag, A Condensed Pen-Picture of Belle Isle, Danville, Andersonville, Charleston, Florence and Libby Prisons.* Lovington, IL: Boggs Pub., 1887.

Booth, B. F. *Dark Days of the Rebellion, or Life in Southern Military Prisons.* Indianola, IA: Booth Publishing, 1897.

Bosang, James N. "Chinch Harbor." *A Civil War Treasury of Tales, Legends And Folklore.* Edited by B. A. Botkin. New York: Promontory Press, 1960.

Boyle, Francis Atherton. "The Prison Diary of Adjutant Francis Atherton Boyle, C.S.A." Edited by Mary Lindsay Thornton. *The North Carolina Historical Review* 39:1 (Winter 1962).

Browne, Junius H. *Four Years in Secessia.* Hartford: O. D. Case, 1865.

Busbee, Charles M. "Experience Of Prisoners Under Fire At Morris Island." *Histories of the Several Regiments And Battalions from North Carolina in the Great War 1861–'65.* Edited by Walter Clark. Vol. 5. Raleigh: E. M. Uzzell, 1901.

Cavada, Frederic F. *Libby Life: Experiences of a Prisoner of War in Richmond, Va., 1863–64.* Philadelphia: King and Baird, 1864.

Carpenter, Horace. "Plain Living at Johnson's Island." *Century Magazine* (March 1891).

Cheavens, Henry Martyn. "A Missouri Confederate in the Civil War: The Journal of Henry Martyn Cheavens, 1862–1863." Edited by James E. Moss. *Missouri Historical Review.* 57:1 (October 1962).

Confederate Veteran. Nashville, Tennessee. 40 vols., 1893–1932. Reprint, Wilmington, NC: Broadfoot Publishing, 1987.

Connelley, William E. *Quantrill and the Border Wars.* Cedar Rapids, IA: Torch Press, 1910.

Cooper, Alonzo. *In and Out of Rebel Prisons.* Oswego, NY: R. J. Oliphant, 1888.

Corcoran, Michael, *The Captivity of General Corcoran. The Only Authentic and Reliable Narrative of the Trials and Sufferings Endured, During His Twelve Months' Imprisonment In Richmond and Other Southern Cities.* Philadelphia: Barclay, 1864.

Cross, J. F. "N.C. Officers In Prison At Johnson's Island, 1864." *Histories of the Several Regiments And Battalions from North Carolina in the Great War 1861–'65.* Edited by Walter Clark. Vol. 4. Goldsboro, NC: Nash Brothers, 1901.

Davis, Jefferson. *The Rise and Fall of the Confederate Government.* Vol. 2. New York: D. Appleton, 1881.

Dooley, John. *John Dooley, Confederate Soldier, His War Journal.* Edited by Joseph T. Durkin. Washington: Georgetown University Press, 1945.

Douglas, Henry Kyd. *I Rode With Stonewall.* Chapel Hill: University of North Carolina Press, 1940.

Duganne, A. J. H. *Twenty Months in the Department of the Gulf.* New York: n.p., 1865.

Dunkle, John [Fritz Fuzzlebug, pseud.] *Prison Life During the Rebellion.* Singer's Glen, VA: Joseph Funk's Sons Printers, 1869.

Elliott, James Carson. *The Southern Soldier Boy.* Raleigh: Edwards & Broughton, 1907.

Estavan, Bela. *War Pictures from the South.* 2 vols. London: Routledge, Warne, and Routledge, 1863.

Evans, Clement A. Ed., *Confederate Military History.* Vols. 1, 11 and 12. Atlanta: Confederate Publishing Co., 1899.

Eye-Witness. *The Bastile in America.* London: Robert Hardwicke Pub., 1861.

Foote, Morris C. "Narrative of an Escape from a Rebel Prison Camp." *American Heritage Civil War Chronicles* 3:1. (Summer 1993).

Fosdick, Charles. *Five Hundred Days in Rebel Prisons.* Bethany, MO: Clipper Book and Job Office, 1887.

Foster, Samuel C. "We are Prisoners of War." *Civil War Times Illustrated* 16:2 (May 1977).

Fraser, John. *A Petition Regarding The Conditions in the C.S.M. Prison at Columbia, S.C., by Col. John Fraser.* Edited by George L. Anderson. Lawrence: University of Kansas Libraries, 1962.

Frost, Griffin. *Camp & Prison Journal.* Quincy, IL: Quincy Herald Book and Job Office, 1867.

Gay, Mary A. H. *Life in Dixie During the War.* Atlanta: Charles P. Byrd, 1897.

Gilmore, Harry. *Four Years In The Saddle.* New York: Harper & Bros., 1866.

Glazier, Willard W. *The Capture, The Prison Pen, and the Escape, Giving an Account of Prison Life In The South.* Albany: J. Munsell, 1866.

———. *Down the Great River.* Philadelphia: Hubbard Bros., 1887.

Goss, Warren Lee. *The Soldier's Story.* Boston: Lee and Shepard, 1868.

Grant, Ulysses S. *Personal Memoirs of U. S. Grant.* Vol. 2. New York: Charles L. Webster & Co., 1885.

Grigsby, Melvin. *The Smoked Yank.* N.p.: Sam T. Clover Pub., 1888.

Grimes, Absalom. *Absalom Grimes, Confederate Mail Runner.* Edited by M. M. Quaife. New Haven, CT: Yale University Press, 1926.

Hadley, John V. *Seven Months A Prisoner, by "An Indiana Soldier."* Indianapolis: Meikel & Co., 1868.

Handy, Isaac W. K. *United States Bonds; or Duress by Federal Authority: A Journal of Current Events during an Imprisonment of Fifteen Months at Fort Delaware.* Baltimore: Turnbull Brothers, 1874.

Harris, William C. *Prison-Life in the Tobacco Warehouse at Richmond by a Ball's Bluff Prisoner.* Philadelphia: George W. Childs, 1862.

Hawes, Jesse. *Cahaba: A Story of Captive Boys in Blue.* New York: Burr Printing House, 1888.

Haynie, I. N. *A History of Camp Douglas, A Prisoner Of War Camp At Chicago, Illinois, 1861–1865.* Little Rock: Eagle Press, 1991. Originally published in 1866.

Hazelton, George C., Jr. *The National Capitol.* New York: n.p., 1897.

Head, Thomas A. *Campaigns and Battles of the Sixteenth Regiment Tennessee Volunteers.* Nashville: Cumberland Presbyterian Publishing, 1885.

Headley, J. T. *The Great Rebellion.* Vol. 2. Washington: National Tribune Publishers, 1898.

Holmes, Anne Middleton. *Algernon Sydney Sullivan.* New York: New York Southern Society, 1929.

Houghland, J. E. "The 19th Iowa in Battle and in Prison." In *The National Tribune Scrap Book.* Washington: National Tribune Pub., 1909.

Howard, Francis K. *Fourteen Months in American Bastiles.* Baltimore: Kelly, Hedian & Piet, 1863.

Howard, McHenry J. *Recollections of a Maryland Confederate Soldier and Staff Officer under Johnston, Jackson, and Lee.* Baltimore: Williams & Wilkins, 1914.

Hutt, Charles Warren. "The Diary of Charles Warren Hutt." Edited by Edwin W. Beitzell. *Chronicles of St. Mary's,* 18:5, 18:6 (May & June 1970).

Ingersoll, Lurton D. *Iowa and the Rebellion.* Philadelphia: J. B. Lippincott, 1866.

Isham, Asa B. "Care of Prisoners of War, North and South." *Sketches of War History 1861–1865.* Edited by Robert Hunter, Ohio Commandery of the Military Order of the Loyal Legion of the United States. Vol. 2. Cincinnati: Robert Clark, 1888.

———. *Prisoners of War and Military Prisons with General Account of Prison Life and Prisons in the South during the War of the Rebellion, including statistical information pertaining to Prisoners of War.* Cincinnati: Lyman and Cushing, 1890.

James, Frederic Augustus. *Frederic Augustus James' Civil War Diary.* Edited by Jefferson Hammer. Madison, NJ: Fairleigh-Dickinson University Press, 1973.

Jeffrey, William H. *Richmond Prisons, 1861–1862.* St. Johnsbury, VT: Republican Press, 1893.

Johnston, David E. *Four Years A Soldier.* Princeton, WV: n.p., 1887.

Johnston, Isaac N. *Four Months in Libby, and the Campaign Against Atlanta.* Cincinnati: R. P. Thompson, Methodist Book Concern, 1864.

Jones, C. W. "In Prison at Point Lookout." Edited by Edwin W. Beitzell. *Chronicles of St. Mary's,* 11:12 (December 1963).

Jones, John B. *A Rebel War Clerk's Diary at the Confederate States Capitol.* 2 vols. New York: Old Hickory Bookshop, 1935.

Keady, William G. "Incidents of prison life at Camp Douglas." *Southern Historical Society Papers* 12. (July to December 1881).

Keiley, Anthony M. *In Vindulis: or The Prisoner of War, by a Virginia Confederate*. Petersburg, VA: Daily Index office, 1866.

———. "Prison-pens, North." *Southern Historical Society Papers* 18 (July to December 1884).

Kellogg, Robert H. *Life and Death in Rebel Prisons*. Hartford, CT: L. Stebbins, 1866.

Kenan, Thomas S. "Johnson's Island." *Histories of the Several Regiments And Battalions from North Carolina in the Great War 1861–'65*. Edited by Walter Clark. Vol. 4. Goldsboro, NC: Nash Brothers, 1901.

King, John H. *Three Hundred Days in a Yankee Prison*. Atlanta: Jas. P. Davis, 1904.

Lavender, John W. *The War Memories of Captain John W. Lavender, C.S.A.* Edited by Ted R. Worley. Pine Bluff, AR: W. M. Hackett and D. R. Perdue, 1956.

Lawrence, George A. [Guy Livingston, pseud.] *Border and Bastille*. New York: W. I. Pooley & Co., 1863.

Ludwig, M. S. "My Escape From a Rebel Prison." In *The National Tribune Scrap Book*. Washington: National Tribune Pub., 1909.

MacRae, Walter G. "Confederate Prisoners At Morris Island." *Histories of the Several Regiments And Battalions from North Carolina in the Great War 1861–'65*. Edited by Walter Clark. Vol. 4. Goldsboro, NC: 1901.

Mahony, D. A. *The Prisoner of State*. New York: Carleton Pub., 1863.

Malone, Bartlett Yancy. *The Diary of Bartlett Yancy Malone*. Edited by William Whatley Pierson, Jr. Chapel Hill: University of North Carolina Press, 1919.

Mangum, A. W. "Salisbury Prison." *Histories of the Several Regiments And Battalions from North Carolina in the Great War 1861–'65*. Edited by Walter Clark. Vol. 4. Goldsboro, NC: Nash Brothers, 1901.

McElroy, John. *Andersonville: A Story of Rebel Military Prisons*. Toledo: D. R. Locke, 1879.

McIntosh, E. W. "Patronize An Old 'Vet.'" *Civil War Times Illustrated* 14:10, (February 1976).

McRaven, David Olando, and Amanda Nantz McRaven. "The Correspondence of David Olando McRaven and Amanda Nantz McRaven." Edited by Louis A. Brown. *The North Carolina Historical Review*, 31:1 (January 1949).

Merrell, William H. *Five Months in Rebeldom; or Notes from the Diary of a Bull Run Prisoner, at Richmond*. Rochester, NY: Adams and Dabney, 1862.

Mines, John F. "Life in a Richmond Prison." *Southern Historical Society Papers* 10 (July to December 1880).

Moran, Frank E. "Colonel Rose's Tunnel At Libby Prison." In *Famous Adventures And Prison Escapes Of The Civil War.* New York: The Century Co., 1915.

Murray, John Ogden. *The Immortal Six Hundred: A Story of Cruelty to Confederate Prisoners of War.* Winchester, VA: Eddy Press, 1905.

Nichols, Annie M. "A Rebel 'Victory' on Lake Erie." *The National Tribune Scrap Book.* Washington: National Tribune Pub., 1909.

Page, James Madison. *The True Story of Andersonville Prison, A Defense of Major Henry Wirz.* New York & Washington: Neale Publishing, 1908.

Putnam, George Haven. *A Prisoner of War in Virginia 1864–5.* New York: G. P. Putnam's Sons, 1912.

Ransom, John L. *Andersonville.* Philadelphia: Douglas Brothers, 1883.

Reid, Warren D. "Escaped from Fort Delaware." *Southern Historical Society Papers* 36 (July to December 1893).

Richardson, Albert D. *The Secret Service, the Field, the Dungeon, and the Escape.* Philadelphia: Jones Brothers, 1865.

"Right Flank." *Fort-LA-Fayette Life.* "Extracts" from the prison publication. London: Simpkin, Marshall & Co., 1865.

Rivenbark, Charles W. "Two Years At Fort Delaware." *Histories of the Several Regiments And Battalions from North Carolina in the Great War 1861–'65.* Edited by Walter Clark. Vol. 4. Goldsboro, NC: Nash Brothers, 1901.

Roach, Alva C. *The Prisoner of War, and How Treated.* Indianapolis: The Railroad Publishing House, 1865.

Ryan, Edmund E. "Cahaba To Charleston: The Prison Odyssey Of Lt. Edmund E. Ryan." Edited by William M. Armstrong. *Civil War Prisons.* Compiled by William B. Hesseltine. Kent, OH: Kent State University Press, 1962.

Sangston, Lawrence. *Bastiles of the North, by A Member of the Maryland Legislature.* Baltimore: Kelly, Hedian & Piet, 1863.

Schwartz, Stephan. *22 Months a Prisoner of War.* St. Louis: A. F. Nelson Publishing Co., 1891.

Scott, John. *Story of the Thirty-Second Iowa Infantry Volunteers.* Nevada, IA: pvt. pub., 1896.

Shepherd, Henry E. *Narrative of Prison Life At Baltimore and Johnson's Island, Ohio.* Baltimore: Commercial Ptg. & Sta. Co., 1917.

Sherrill, Miles O. *A Soldier's Story, Prison Life and Other Incidents In The War of 1861–'65.* Raleigh: n.p., 1911.

Shotwell, Randolph Abbott. "The Prison Experiences of Randolph Shotwell." Edited by J. G. DeRoulhac Hamilton. *The North Carolina Historical Review* 2:2 (April 1925).

———. *The Papers of Randolph Abbott Shotwell.* Edited by J. G. DeRoulhac Hamilton. 3 vols. Raleigh: The North Carolina Historical Commission, 1931.

Small, Abner R. *The Road to Richmond; The Civil War Memoirs of Major Abner R. Small of the Sixteenth Maine Volunteers. Together with the Diary which he kept when he was a Prisoner of War.* Edited by Harold A. Small. Berkeley: University of California Press, 1939.

Spotswood, Thomas E. "Horrors of Camp Morton." *Southern Historical Society Papers* 18 (July to December 1884).

Sprague, Homer B. *Lights and Shadows in Confederate Prisons: A Personal Experience, 1864–5.* New York: G. P. Putnam's Sons, 1915.

Stephens, Alexander H. *The War Between the States.* Vol. 2. Philadelphia: National Publishing Co., 1870.

Stevenson, R. Randolph. *The Southern Side: or Andersonville Prison.* Baltimore: Turnbull Brothers, 1876.

Stille, Charles J. *History of the U.S. Sanitary Commission.* New York: Hurd Houghton, 1869.

Stuart, A. A. *Iowa Colonels and Regiments.* Des Moines: Mills & Co., 1865.

Toney, Marcus B. "Our dead at Elmira." *Southern Historical Society Papers* 29 (January to June 1890).

Traywick, J. B. "Prison life at Point Lookout." *Southern Historical Society Papers* 18 (July to December 1884).

Trow, Harrison. *A True Story of Chas. W. Quantrell and his Guerrilla Band As Told by Captain Harrison Trow.* Edited by John P. Burch. Vega, TX: pvt. pub., 1923.

Union Soldier. *Incidents in Dixie, by a Union Soldier.* Baltimore: James Young Printer, 1864.

U.S. Christian Commission. *Record of the Federal Dead Buried from Libby, Belle Isle, Danville and Camp Lawton Prisons and at City Point, and in the Field before Petersburg and Richmond.* Philadelphia: James B. Rodgers Printer, 1866.

U.S. Sanitary Commission. *Narrative of Privations and Sufferings of United States Officers and Soldiers While Prisoners of War in the Hands of Rebel Authorities.* Philadelphia: King and Baird Press, 1864.

U.S. War Department. *War of the Rebellion: A Compilation of the Official Records of the Union and Confederate Armies.* 128 vols. Washington: GPO, 1880–1901.

Urban, John W. *Battle Field and Prison Pen, or Through the War, and Thrice A Prisoner in Rebel Dungeons.* Philadelphia: Edgewood Publishing, 1882.

Walker, Francis Amasa. *A Life of Francis Amasa Walker.* Edited by James P. Munroe. New York: H. Holt & Company, 1923.

Walker, John L. *Cahaba Prison and the Sultana Disaster.* Hamilton, OH: Brown & Whitaker, 1910.

Webb, R. F. "Prison Life At Johnson's Island." *Histories of the Several Regiments And Battalions from North Carolina in the Great War 1861–'65.* Edited by Walter Clark. Vol. 4. Goldsboro, NC: Nash Brothers, 1901.

Wells, James M. "The American Civil War, 1861–1865: James M. Wells." *Famous Escapes.* Edited by Eric Williams. New York: W. W. Norton, 1953.

Whitman, George Washington. *Civil War Letters of George Washington Whitman.* Edited by Jerome M. Loving. Durham, NC: Duke University Press, 1975.

Williams, George W. *A History Of The Negro Troops in The War of The Rebellion 1861–1865.* New York: Harper & Brothers, 1888.

Williamson, James J. *Prison Life in the Old Capitol.* West Orange, NJ: Williamson Publishing, 1911.

Wilson, Joseph T. *The Black Phalanx; A History Of The Negro Soldiers Of The United States.* Hartford, CT: American Publishing Company, 1890.

Newsapers
Alton *Telegraph* (IL)
Army and Navy Journal
Asheville *Times* (NC)
Charlotte *Observer* (NC)
Charleston Daily Courier (SC)
Charleston Evening Post (SC)
Charleston *News and Courier* (SC)
Charleston Mercury (SC)
Civil War News
Daily Journal of Commerce (Kansas City, MO)
Daily Missouri Democrat (St. Louis, MO)
Daily Picayune (New Orleans, LA)
Evening Star (Washington, DC)
Frank Leslies' Illustrated Newspaper
Goldsboro *Daily News* (NC)
Harper's Monthly
Harper's Weekly
Illinois State Journal (Springfield, IL)
Illinois State Register (Springfield, IL)
Minonk *News-Dispatch* (IL)
Mountaineer (Waynesville, NC)
New York Herald
New York Times
Philadelphia Inquirer
Raleigh *News & Observer*
Richmond *Daily Dispatch*
Richmond *Daily Examiner*

St. Louis *Globe*
St. Louis *Post-Dispatch*
Salisbury *Post* (NC)
Western Journal of Commerce (Kansas City, MO)

Documents, Diaries, Manuscripts, and Letters
National Archives, Washington, D.C.
RG 109, Entries 236–39, 313–16. Miscellaneous records and correspondence
for Gratiot Street and Myrtle Street prisons in St. Louis and Alton prison
in Illinois.
RG 109, Chapt. IX, Vol. 199½, E 313–16, E 109. Prison orders and letters
for Fort Warren, Fort McHenry, and Johnson's Island.
RG 109, Chapt. IX, Vol. 243. A sutler account containing POW names and
purchases at Columbia, S.C., Military Prison, November 1, 1864 to February 19, 1865.
RG 249, Misc. Records, Vol. 12, pp. 374–96, pp. 398–403, pp. 407–20.
Cahaba prison hospital morning reports, patients returned to prison, and
register of deaths.
RG 249, E 7, Vols. 1–5. Commutation for POW rations and miscellaneous
correspondence from the U.S. Adjutant and Inspector General's Office
regarding prisoners of war held by the C.S.A.
RG 249, Chapt. IX, Vol. 232, E 45, E 53; Roll 957, Roll 962. Miscellaneous
letters and orders regarding Richmond prisons. Miscellaneous correspon-
dence from Quartermaster's department March 7, 1863 to April 1, 1865,
regarding Richmond's prisons.
RG 249, E 45, Vol. 12, pp. 272–357. Register of POW deaths and miscellaneous records at Danville prison hospital, November 1863 to April 1865.
RG 249, E 45, Vol. 12, pp. 430–57. Miscellaneous records and register of
POWs at Florence, S.C., Prison.
RG 249, E 53, Vol. 18. Register of POWs admitted to various Danville hospitals and miscellaneous records, November 1863 to March 27, 1865.
RG 249, Vols. 69, 93, 94, 96, 97, 98, 99, 101–6. Register of black and civilian
POWs received at Richmond; "Nominal Lists of Prisoners" received, July 23,
1861 to April 2, 1865, showing name, rank, company, regiment, date and
place of capture, date received at Richmond, prison location transferred,
paroled, exchanged, or died.
RG 249, Roll 962 and 957. John Adams C.S.A. Federal prisons April 13,
1862.
RG 393. Miscellaneous letters received at Johnson's Island.

RG 393. Miscellaneous letters received at POW prison in Raleigh, N.C.

RG 109, Microfilm 598, Roll 47, Vols. 167–68. Fort Delaware register of POWs admitted to prison hospital, deaths, and morning reports.

RG 109, M598, Roll 53, Vol. 188. Camp Douglas general register of prisoners.

RG 109, M598, Roll 58, Vol. 200. Camp Douglas register of POWs confined, exchanged, released, and deceased.

RG 109, M598, Roll 67, Vols. 222–23. Elmira register of POWs confined and deceased.

RG 109, M598, Roll 79, Vols. 267–68. Hart Island POW register and miscellaneous records.

RG 109, M598, Roll 111, Vol. 352. Point Lookout, letters sent.

RG 109, M598, Roll 136, Vol. 406. Ship Island miscellaneous records.

RG 109, M598, Roll 137, Vol. 409. Fort Warren, letters sent.

Library of Congress, Washington, D.C.

Babcock, John C. Papers.

Barstow, Wilson. Papers.

Buford, Charles. Papers.

Bulloch, Irvine S. Papers.

Coe, William P. Papers.

Conley, Isaiah. Papers.

Crossly, Sylvanus. Papers and Diary.

Davis, Jefferson. Papers.

Deaderick, David Anderson. Papers.

Enslow, Charles C. Papers.

Fritsch, Friedrich Otto. Papers.

Fuller, Joseph Pryor. Papers and Diary.

Greble, Edwin. Papers.

Habersham Family. Papers.

Hall, George Washington. Papers.

Hammond, James Henry. Papers.

Hill, Sara Jane Full. Papers.

Hills, William G. Diary.

Hitchcock, Ethan Allen. Papers.

Homsher, Charles Wesley. Papers and Diary.

Hotchkiss, Jedediah–McCullough, Samuel. Papers.

Long, Brekinridge. Papers.

Lurton, Horace Harmon. Papers.

Manigault, Louis. Papers.

McLennan, Roderick. Papers.

Mitchell, Benjamin. Papers.
Mitchell, James B. Papers.
Phillips, Phillip. Papers.
Remey, George Collier. Papers.
Remey Family. Papers.
Reed, Charles Wellington. Papers and Sketch Books.
Scott, John White. Papers.
Steiner, Walter Ralph. Papers.
Swann, John S. Papers.
Walker, James. Papers.
Westervelt, H. C. Papers.
Willis, Edward. Papers.

Southern Historical Collection, Wilson Library, University of North Carolina at Chapel Hill.
Attmore Family. Papers.
Barnard, S. G. Papers.
Barringer, Rufus C. Diary.
Basinger Family. Papers.
Battle Family. Papers.
Bigham Family. Papers.
Blanchard Family. Papers.
Bruin Family. Papers.
Cabarrus & Slade Family. Papers.
Civil War, misc., Papers.
Colston, Raleigh E. Papers.
Fairchild, George N. Papers.
Fortescue, Louis. Papers, including Diary.
Gray, Charles C. Papers, including Diary.
Harllee, William C. Papers.
Martin, Rawley W. Papers.
McGimsey Family. Papers.
McMichael, James R. Papers.
Miller, George K. Papers.
Olmstead, Charles H. Papers.
Ramsdell, Julius F. Papers, including Diary.
Richardson, Henry B. Papers.
Sampson, Ira B. Papers.
Street, John K. Diary.
Wallace, James T. Diary.
Willis, Charles A. Diary.

Privately held letters, diaries, and manuscripts

Blankenship, David, Company D, 64th North Carolina. Private papers, letters, accumulated war record, and POW experiences. Twenty-two months in Louisville Military Prison and Camp Douglas. Danny R. Slagle Family Papers, Buncombe County, NC.

Byrd, William Arrington, Sergeant, Company B, 50th Georgia. Private papers and accumulated experiences and war record. Byrd-Rainey Family Papers, Haywood County, NC.

Cook, Solomon Floyd, Company G, 62nd North Carolina. Accumulated war and POW records. Fifteen months at Louisville Military Prison and Camp Douglas. Died at Camp Douglas, December 11, 1864. Frazier-Ball Family Papers, Haywood County, NC.

Craig, James Edward, Company C, 6th South Carolina Cavalry (Partisan Rangers). Private papers and accumulated war record. Dr. Edward Hay Family Papers. Buncombe County, NC.

Dyer, Stamey John, Company C, 62nd North Carolina. Captured at Cumberland Gap. POW letters from Camp Douglas and accumulated war record and POW experiences. Milner Family Papers, Haywood County, NC.

Emigh, Eli, Company F, 110th New York Volunteers. Letter, while stationed as guard at Fort Jefferson, Dry Tortugas Island. Private collection. Niles Schuh, Washington County, FL.

Fender, Allen, Company B, 29th North Carolina. Later transferred to Company K. Private papers and accumulated war record. Danny R. Slagle Family Papers. Buncombe County, NC.

Henderson, Lewis J., Forrest's Cavalry Corps (Rangers), Army of Tennessee (CSA). Private letters. Byrd-Rainey Family Papers. Haywood County, NC.

Jackson, James Holden, 31st Tennessee Infantry Battalion. Captured and held at Gratiot Street Military Prison. Private papers, accumulated war experiences, and POW records. Joel Jackson Family Papers, Jackson, Madison County, Tennessee.

Jenkins, Charles "Doc," Sergeant, Company F, 29th North Carolina. Private papers, accumulated service records, and photo. Burchfield Family Papers, Buncombe County, NC.

McKamy, James A., Colonel, Walker's Battalion, Thomas's Legion, (69th North Carolina). Private family papers and accumulated service and war record. D. M. Tedford Family Papers, Huntingdon County, Pennsylvania.

Medford, R. Eldridge, Company C, 70th North Carolina. Letters, papers, accumulated war record, and POW experiences. Held twenty-two months at Camp Douglas. Medford-McCracken Family Papers, Haywood County, NC.

Peek, Garrett, Company A, 2nd North Carolina Mounted Infantry (Union). Accumulated war and service record. Danny R. Slagle Family Papers. Buncombe County, NC.

Price, William Thomas, 9th North Carolina (1st Cavalry). Accumulated letters, personal papers, and service record. Price-Cole Family Papers, Haywood County, NC.

Richards, John Gardiner, Chaplain, Company G, 10th South Carolina Volunteers. Pocket diary, September 29, 1864 to January 24, 1865. Dr. Edward Hay Family Papers. Buncombe County, NC.

Rogers, Thomas Jefferson, Company E, 29th North Carolina. Fifty-two letters from twenty-four different Confederate soldiers addressed to T. J. Rogers during the course of the war and accumulated war and service record. Robert Fulbright Family Papers, Haywood County, NC and St. Louis, Missouri.

Shaw, Lewis, Company D, 8th Tennessee Cavalry (Union). Captured at Morristown, Tennessee, and confined at Danville Prison fifteen months. Died at Danville, February 26, 1865. Accumulated war, service, and POW records. Danny R. Slagle Family Papers, Buncombe County, NC.

Shenkle, William J., Company C, 116th New York. Taken prisoner near Port Hudson, Louisiana, June 8, 1863, and believed confined at the Mansfield Court House until transferred to City Point the following month on parole. As part of some of the very last to be exchanged, as well as being part of the original Port Hudson-Vicksburg POW controversy in the collapse of the cartel, he quickly rejoined his regiment. Letters, private papers, and accumulated war and POW records. David R. Watson Family Papers, Buncombe County, NC.

Spencer, Charles Clozen, Memphis, Tennessee, civilian arrested along with son, Henry Spencer, and incarcerated at Gratiot Street Prison as political prisoners. Accumulated private and public papers, official documents, and private letters. Larose Adams Wynn Family Papers, Memphis, Shelby County, Tennessee.

Stringfield, William Williams, Captain, Company E, 31st Tennessee Infantry, later, Major in Thomas's Legion (69th North Carolina). Personal letters and accumulated war and service records. Stringfield-Love Family Papers, Haywood County, NC.

Tedford, George Washington, Company F, 7th Arkansas Cavalry, later attached to Company F, Jackman's Regiment, Missouri Cavalry. Captured Newton County, Arkansas, and incarcerated, first, at Springfield, Missouri, depot prison, then Gratiot Street and, later, Alton Military Prison. Died at Alton Prison on February 2, 1865. Private papers and letters, including those of other family members who served, and accumulated war and POW records. D. M. Tedford Family Papers, Huntingdon County, Pennsylvania.

Thompson, John Harley, enlisted at Greene County, Tennessee. Accumulated service records. Bertha Thompson Gamble Family Papers, Wilkesboro, NC.

SECONDARY SOURCES

America's Civil War. Vol. 1 to Vol. 9. (May 1988 to September 1996).

Angle, Paul M. and Earl Schenck Miers. *Tragic Years 1860–1865.* 2 vols. New York: Simon and Schuster, 1960.

———. *A Pictorial History of The Civil War Years.* New York: Doubleday & Co., 1967.

Axelrod, Alan. *The War Between The Spies.* New York: Atlantic Monthly Press, 1987.

Bailey, Ronald H. *Forward To Richmond.* Alexandria, VA: Time-Life Books, 1983.

Baker, Jean H. *Mary Todd Lincoln.* New York: W. W. Norton & Co., 1987.

Barnes, Joseph K., ed. *The Medical and Surgical History of the War of the Rebellion.* 3 vols. in 5 parts. Washington: GPO, 1876.

Beitzell, Edwin W. *Point Lookout Prison Camp For Confederates.* Leonardtown, MD: St. Mary's County Historical Society, 1983.

Bill, Alfred Hoyt. *The Beleaguered City.* New York: Alfred A. Knopf, 1946.

Boatner, Mark M. III. *The Civil War Dictionary.* New York: David McKay Co., 1959.

Botkin, Benjamin A., ed. *A Civil War Treasury Of Tales, Legends And FolkLore.* New York: Promontory Press, 1960.

Bowden, J. J. *The Exodus of Federal Forces from Texas 1861.* Austin: Eakin Press, 1986.

Bowman, John S., ed. *The Civil War Almanac.* New York: World Almanac Publications, 1983.

Brannon, Peter A. "The Cahawba Military Prison, 1863–1865." *The Alabama Review* 3:3 (July 1950).

Brooks, Stewart. *Civil War Medicine.* Springfield, IL: Charles C. Thomas, 1966.

Brown, A. Theodore. *Frontier Community: Kansas City to 1870.* Columbia: University of Missouri Press, 1963.

——— and Lyle W. Dorsett. *K.C.—A History of Kansas City, Missouri.* Boulder, CO: Pruett Publishing Co., 1978.

Brown, Ann L. B. "Fort Delaware: The Most Dreaded Northern Prison." *Civil War Quarterly* 10 (September 1987).

Brown, Dee. *The Galvanized Yankees.* Champaign: University of Illinois Press, 1963.

Brown, Henry Collins, ed. *Valentine's Manual of Old New York.* New York: Gracie Mansion Publishing, 1924.

Brown, Louis A. *The Salisbury Prison: A Case Study of Confederate Military Prisons, 1861–1865.* Wendell, NC: Broadfoot's Bookmark, 1980.

Brownlee, Richard S. *Gray Ghosts of the Confederacy: Guerilla Warfare in the West, 1861–1865.* Baton Rouge: Louisiana State University Press, 1958.

Bryant, William O. *Cahaba Prison and the Sultana Disaster.* Tuscaloosa: University of Alabama Press, 1990.

Buenger, Walter L. *Texas History.* Boston: American Press, 1983.

Burnham, T. O. H. P., ed. *Stars and Stripes in Rebeldom.* Boston: H. O. Houghton, 1862.

Carter, Samuel, III. *The Riddle of Dr. Mudd.* New York: G. P. Putnam's Sons, 1974.

Casy, Robert J. *The Texas Border.* New York: Bobbs-Merrill, 1950.

Catton, Bruce and Richard M. Ketchum. *The American Heritage Picture History of The Civil War.* New York: American Heritage/Bonanza Books, 1982.

———. *Reflections on the Civil War.* New York: Berkley Books, 1984.

Century Company, comp. *Battles And Leaders Of The Civil War.* Vols. 3 and 4. New York: The Century Company, 1888.

———, comp. *Famous Adventures and Prison Escapes of the Civil War.* New York: The Century Company, 1915.

Channing, Steven A. *Confederate Ordeal.* Alexandria, VA: Time-Life Books, 1984.

Cisco, Walter Brian. "Galvanized Rebels." *Civil War* 8:5 (September to October 1990).

Civil War Times Illustrated. 1:1 to 35:5 No. 5 (April 1962 to October 1996).

Clark, Walter, ed. *Histories of the Several Regiments And Battalions from North Carolina in the Great War 1861–'65.* 5 vols. Goldsboro and Raleigh: Nash Brothers and E. M. Uzzell, 1901.

Clarke, H. C., comp. *The Confederate States Almanac, and Repository of Useful Knowledge, For 1862.* Vicksburg, MS: 1862. Reprint. Summerville, GA: Brannon Publishing, n.d.

Commager, Henry Steele, ed. *The Blue and the Gray.* 2 vols. New York: Bobbs-Merrill, 1973.

Crow, Vernon H. *Storm In The Mountains.* Cherokee, NC: Press of the Cherokee Indian, 1982.

Cunningham, H. H., *Doctors in Gray.* Baton Rouge: Louisiana State University Press, 1958.

Cunningham, O. Edward. "Strike for Liberty." *Civil War Times Illustrated* 14:6 (October 1975).

Current, Richard N. *The History of Wisconsin.* 3 vols. Madison: State Historical Society of Wisconsin, 1976.

Day, Lewis W. *The Story of the One Hundred and First Ohio Infantry.* Cleveland: W. M. Bayne, 1894.

Davis, Burke. *Our Incredible Civil War.* New York: Ballantine Books, 1960.

Davis, William C. *The Fighting Men Of The Civil War.* New York: Gallery Books, 1989.

———. *Commanders Of The Civil War.* New York: Gallery Books, 1990.

———. *Jefferson Davis, The Man And His Hour.* New York: Harper-Collins, 1991.

Dowdey, Clifford. *Experiment In Rebellion.* Garden City, NY: Doubleday, 1946.

———. *Lee.* Boston: Little, Brown and Co., 1965.

Downer, Edward T. "Johnson's Island." *Civil War Prisons.* Edited by William B. Hesseltine. Kent, OH: Kent State University Press, 1962.

Duke, Basil W. *History of Morgan's Cavalry.* Cincinnati: Miami Printing and Publishing, 1867.

Dyer, John Will. *Reminiscences: or Four Years in the Confederate Army.* Evansville, IN: Keller Printing & Publishing Co., 1898.

Eaton, Clement. *A History of the Southern Confederacy.* New York: Macmillan, 1954.

Elliott, James W. *Transport To Disaster.* New York: Holt, Rinehart and Winston, 1962.

Ellis, Keith. *The American Civil War.* New York: G. P. Putnam's Sons, 1971.

England, Otis Bryan. *A Short History Of The Rock Island Prison Barracks.* Rock Island: Historical Office, U.S. Army Armament, Munitions, and Chemical Command, 1985.

Faust, Patricia L., ed. *Historical Times Illustrated Encyclopedia Of The Civil War.* New York: Harper & Row, 1986.

Fehrenbach, T. R. *Lone Star.* New York: Collier Books, 1985.

Fellman, Michael. *Inside War: The Guerrilla Conflict in Missouri during the American Civil War.* New York: Oxford University Press, 1989.

Feuer, A. B. "John McGrady and the Confederate Prisoners at Camp Morton," *Civil War Quarterly* 10 (September 1987).

Freeman, Douglas Southall. *R. E. Lee.* 4 vols. New York: Charles Scribner's Sons, 1947.

Futch, Ovid L. *History of Andersonville Prison.* Gainesville: University of Florida Press, 1968.

Garrison, Webb. *Civil War Tales.* Nashville: Rutledge Hill Press, 1988.

———. *The Lincoln No One Knows.* Nashville: Rutledge Hill Press, 1993.

Garwood, Darrell. *Crossroads Of America.* New York: W. W. Norton, 1948.

Gibbons, Tony. *Warships And Naval Battles Of The Civil War.* New York: Gallery Books, 1989.

Gill, Anton. *The Journey Back From Hell.* New York: William Morrow, 1988.

Gladstone, William A. *United States Colored Troops 1863–1867.* Gettysburg: Thomas Publications, 1990.

Graham, Martin F. "The Immortal 600: Their Long Journey to Freedom." *Civil War Quarterly* 10 (September 1987).

Green, Constance McLaughlin. *Washington: Village and Capital 1800–1878.* Princeton, NJ: Princeton University Press, 1962.

Hagen, Harry M. *This is Our Saint Louis.* St. Louis: Knight Publishing, 1970.

Haley, James L. *Texas.* New York: St. Martin's Press, 1985.

Hamilton, J. G. DeRoulhac. *Reconstruction in North Carolina.* Gloucester, MA: Peter Smith, 1964.

Harwell, Richard B., ed. *The Confederate Reader.* New York: Longmans, Green and Co., 1957.

———, ed. *The Union Reader.* New York: Longmans, Green and Co., 1958.

Hassler, William. "Vignettes: Point Lookout." *Civil War Quarterly* 10 (September 1987).

Hemmerlein, Richard F. *Prisons and Prisoners of the Civil War.* Boston: Christopher Publishing House, 1934.

Hesseltine, William B. *Civil War Prisons: A Study in War Psychology,* Columbus: Ohio State University Press, 1930.

———, ed. *Civil War Prisons.* Kent, OH: Kent State University Press, 1962.

———. "Military Prisons of St. Louis, 1861–1865." *Missouri Historical Review* 23:3 (April 1929).

Horan, James D. *Confederate Agent.* New York: Crown Publishers, 1954.

Hyde, William and Howard L. Conrad, eds. *Encyclopedia of the History of St. Louis.* St. Louis: The Southern History Company, 1899.

Ingmire, Frances & Carolyn Ericson, comps. *Soldiers & Sailors Who Died In Federal Prisons & Military Hospitals in the North.* Washington: National Archives, 1984.

Johnson, Rossiter. *Campfires And Battlefields.* New York: Gallant Books, 1960.

Jordan, Ervin L., Jr. *Black Confederates and Afro-Yankees in Civil War Virginia.* Charlottesville: University Press of Virginia, 1995.

Kimmel, Stanley. *Mr. Davis' Richmond.* New York: Coward-McCann, 1958.

Kaufhold, John. "The Elmira Observatory." *Civil War Times Illustrated* 15:4 (July 1977).

Lattimore, Ralston B. *Fort Pulaski.* Washington: GPO, 1954.

Leech, Margaret. *Reveille In Washington 1860–1865.* New York: Harper Brothers, 1941.

Lee, W. Storrs. "Stone Walls Do Not a Prison Make." *American Heritage.* 18:2 (February 1967).

Livermore, Thomas L. *Numbers and Losses in the Civil War in America 1861–65.* Boston: Houghton Mifflin and Co., 1901.

Logue, Larry M. *To Appomattox and Beyond, The Civil War Soldier in War and Peace.* Chicago: Ivan R. Dee, 1996.

Lonn, Ella. *Desertion During the Civil War.* New York: The Century Press Co., 1928.

Marsh, David D. *The History of Missouri.* 3 vols. N.p.: Lewis Historical Publishing Co., 1967.

Marth, Del and Martha J. Marth. *The Florida Almanac.* Gretna, FL: Pelican Publishing Co., 1983.

Marvel, William. *Andersonville: The Last Depot.* Chapel Hill: University of North Carolina Press, 1994.

McLain, Minor H. "The Military Prison At Fort Warren." *Civil War Prisons.* Edited by William B. Hesseltine. Kent, OH: Kent State University Press, 1962.

Meketa, Jacqueline Dorgan. "A Poetic Plea From Prison." *Civil War Times Illustrated* 30:1 (March to April 1991).

Miller, Francis Trevelyan, ed. *The Photographic History of the Civil War.* 10 vols. New York: The Review of Reviews Co., 1911.

Mitchell, Patricia B. *Yanks, Rebels, Rats, & Rations.* New York: Dover Publications, 1993.

Mitchell, Reid. *Civil War Soldiers.* New York: Viking Press, 1988.

Moore, Robert H., II. "Break Out!" *Civil War Times Illustrated.* 30:5 (November to December 1991).

Moore, Samuel J. T., Jr. *Moore's Complete Civil War Guide To Richmond.* Richmond: n.p., 1978.

National Historical Society, ed. *The Image of War: 1861–1865, End of An Era.* Vol. 4. Garden City, NY: Doubleday, 1983.

National Tribune. *The National Tribune Scrap Book No. 1, Stories Of The Camp, March, Battle, Hospital And Prison Told By Comrades.* Washington: National Tribune Publishing, 1909.

Nevins, Allan. *The War For The Union.* New York: Charles Scribner's Sons, 1971.

Parker, Sandra V. *Richmond's Civil War Prisons.* Lynchburg, VA: H. E. Howard, 1990.

Parrish, William E. *A History Of Missouri.* Columbia: University of Missouri Press, 1971.

Peterson, William S. "A History of Camp Butler, 1861–1866." *Illinois Historical Journal* (Summer 1989).

Philip, Cynthia Owen, ed. *Imprisoned In America.* New York: Harper & Row, 1973.

Pigg, Elmer L. "Bloody Bill, Noted Guerrilla of the Civil War." *The Trail Guide* 1:4 (December 1956).

Pluskat, Ken J. "On To Prison, By A Soldier Of The 9th Massachusetts." *Civil War Times Illustrated.* 29:2 (May to June 1990).

Pollard, Edward A. *Observations in the North: Eight Months in Prison and on Parole.* Richmond: E. W. Ayres, 1865.

———. *The Lost Cause; A Southern History of the War of the Confederates.* New York: E. B. Treat, 1866.

Prichard, James M. "General Orders No. 59: Kentucky's Reign of Terror." *Civil War Quarterly.* 10 (September 1987).

Quinn, Camilla A. Corlas. "Forgotten Soldiers: The Confederate Prisoners at Camp Butler 1862–3." *Illinois Historical Journal* (Spring 1985).

Ramage, James A. "John Hunt Morgan's Escape from the Ohio State Penitentiary." *Civil War Quarterly* 10 (September 1987).

Reid, Major Pat and Maurice Michael. *Prisoner of War.* New York: Beaufort Books, 1984.

Richardson, James F. *The New York Police.* New York: Oxford University Press, 1970. (Contains background and history of original Tombs prison.)

Robertson, James I., Jr. "Houses of Horror: Danville's Civil War Prisons." *Virginia Magazine of History and Biography* 69:1 (January 1961).

———. *Civil War Sites in Virginia, A Tour Guide.* Charlottesville: University Press of Virginia, 1982.

———. "The Scourge of Elmira." *Civil War Prisons.* Edited by William B. Hesseltine. Kent, OH: Kent State University Press, 1962.

———. *Soldiers Blue and Gray.* Columbia: University of South Carolina Press, 1988.

———. *Tenting Tonight: The Soldier's Life.* Alexandria, VA: Time-Life Books, 1984.

Roth, David E., ed. "The General's Tour—Andersonville: The Story of an American Tragedy . . ." *Blue & Gray Magazine* 3:3 (1985).

Scharf, J. Thomas. *History of St. Louis City and County.* Philadelphia: Louis H. Everts & Co., 1883.

Sharpe, Patricia and Robert S. Weddle. *Texas.* Austin: Texas Monthly Press, 1982.

Shenkman, Richard. *Legends, Lies & Cherished Myths of American History.* New York: Harper & Row, 1988.

Sheppard, Peggy. *Andersonville Georgia U.S.A.* Andersonville: Sheppard Publications, 1973.

Shomette, Donald G. *Shipwrecks of the Civil War, The Encyclopedia of Union and Confederate Naval Losses.* Washington: Donic Ltd., 1973.

Sifakis, Stewart. *Who Was Who in the Civil War.* New York: Facts on File Publications, 1988.

Sigaud, Louis A. *Belle Boyd: Confederate Spy.* Richmond: Dietz Press, 1944.

Site Of Camp Douglas. 8-page pamphlet with photos. Courtesy of Chicago Historical Society.

Southern Historical Society Papers. 52 vols. Richmond: Southern Historical Society, 1876–1952.

Speer, Lonnie R. "A Hell On Earth." *Civil War Times Illustrated* 34:3 (July to August 1995).

Stephens, Clifford W., comp. *Rock Island Confederate Prison Deaths.* Rock Island: Blackhawk Genealogical Society, 1973.

Stepp, John W., ed. *Mirror of War: The Washington Star Reports the Civil War.* Englewood Cliffs, NJ: Prentice-Hall, 1961.

Swint, Henry L., ed. *Dear Ones at Home, Letters from Contraband Camps.* Nashville: Vanderbilt University Press, 1966.

Taylor, Frank H. *Philadelphia in the Civil War 1861–1865.* Philadelphia: Dunlap Printing, 1913.

Thomas, Emory M. *The Confederate State of Richmond.* Austin: University of Texas Press, 1971.

Tidwell, William A. *April '65, Confederate Covert Action in the American Civil War.* Kent, OH: Kent State University Press, 1995.

Tilley, John S. *Facts The Historians Leave Out.* Montgomery, AL: Paragon Press, 1951.

Time-Life, ed. *The Civil War.* 28 vols. Alexandria, VA: Time-Life Books, 1983–85.

Towner, Ausburn. *Our County and Its People, A History of the Valley and County of Chemung.* Syracuse, NY: D. Mason, 1892.

Tucker, James B. and Norma Tucker. "Great Escape From Rebel Prison." *America's Civil War* 8:1 (March 1995).

U.S. Department of the Interior. *Andersonville.* Pamphlet. Washington: GPO, 1991.

U.S. House of Representatives. *Report on the Treatment of Prisoners of War by the Rebel Authorities During the War of the Rebellion.* Report 45. Washington: GPO, 1870.

Vandiver, Frank E. *Their Tattered Flags.* New York: Harper's Magazine Press, 1970.

Van Noppen, Ina W. "The Significance of Stoneman's Last Raid." *The North Carolina Historical Review.* 38:3 (July 1961).

Walker, T. R. "Rock Island Prison Barracks." *Civil War Prisons.* Edited by William B. Hesseltine. Kent, OH: Kent State University Press, 1962.

Walls, Matthew S. "Northern Hell On Earth." *America's Civil War* 3:6 (March 1991).

Ward, Geoffrey C. with Rick Burns and Ken Burns. *The Civil War, An Illustrated History.* New York: Alfred A. Knopf, 1991.

Wells, Robert W. *Wisconsin in the Civil War.* Milwaukee: Milwaukee Journal, 1962.

Whitman, George Washington. *Civil War Letters of George Washington Whitman.* Edited by Jerome M. Loving. Durham, NC: Duke University Press, 1975.

Wilcox, Arthur M. and Warren Ripley. *The Civil War At Charleston.* Charleston: The News And Courier and The Evening Post, 1989.

Wiley, Bell I. *The Life of Johnny Reb, The Common Soldier of the Confederacy.* Indianapolis: Bobbs-Merrill, 1943.

———. *The Life of Billy Yank, The Common Soldier of the Union.* Indianapolis: Bobbs-Merrill, 1952.

———. *The Common Soldier Of The Civil War.* Harrisburg, PA: Eastern Acorn Press, 1989.

Williams, Eric, ed. *Famous Escapes.* New York: W. W. Norton, 1953.

Williams, Walter L. "Again In Chains." *Civil War Times Illustrated.* 20:2 (May 1981).

Williamson, Hugh P. "Military Prisons in the Civil War." *The Bulletin* 16:4 (July 1960).

Wilson, James Grant, ed. *The Memorial History of the City of New York.* 4 vols. New York: New York History Co., 1893.

Wilson, W. Emerson. *Fort Delaware.* Newark: University of Delaware, 1957.

Wooten, Dudley G., ed. *A Comprehensive History of Texas 1685 to 1897.* Dallas: William G. Scarff, 1898.

Works Progress Administration. *Alabama.* American Guide Series. New York: Richard R. Smith, 1941.

———. *Connecticut.* American Guide Series. New York: Oxford University Press. 1938.

———. *Delaware.* American Guide Series. New York: Hastings House, 1955.

———. *Florida.* American Guide Series. New York: Oxford University Press, 1939.

———. *Georgia.* American Guide Series. Athens: University of Georgia Press, 1940.

———. *Illinois.* American Guide Series. Chicago: A.C. McClurg, 1939.

———. *Indiana.* American Guide Series. New York: Oxford University Press, 1941.

———. *Key West, A Guide to.* American Guide Series. New York: Hastings House, 1941.

———. *Maryland.* American Guide Series. New York: Oxford University Press, 1940.

———. *Massachusetts.* American Guide Series. Boston: Houghton Mifflin, 1937.

———. *Mississippi.* American Guide Series. New York: Oxford University Press, 1938.

———. *New Jersey.* American Guide Series. New York: Viking Press, 1939.

———. *New York City Guide.* American Guide Series. New York: Oxford University Press,1939.

———. *North Carolina.* American Guide Series. Chapel Hill: University of North Carolina Press, 1939.

———. *Ohio Guide.* American Guide Series. New York: Oxford University Press, 1940.

———. *South Carolina*. American Guide Series. New York: Oxford University Press, 1941.

———. *Tennessee*. American Guide Series. New York: Viking Press, 1939.

———. *Texas*. American Guide Series. New York: Hastings House, 1940.

———. *Virginia*. American Guide Series. New York: Oxford University Press, 1940.

———. *Washington City and Capital*. American Guide Series. Washington: GPO, 1937.

———. *West Virginia*. American Guide Series. New York: Oxford University Press, 1940.

Yanak, Ted and Pam Cornelison. *The Great American History Fact-Finder*. Boston: Houghton Mifflin, 1993.

INDEX

399